AF361363

The collected works of Ruqaiya Hasan

Volume 4 Context in the System and
Process of Language

Edited by Jonathan J. Webster

Social order is not part of the 'nature of things', and it cannot be derived from 'the laws of nature'. Social order exists *only* as a product of human activity. No other ontological status may be ascribed to it without hopelessly obfuscating its empirical manifestations. Both in its genesis (social order is the result of part of human activity) and its existence in any instance of time (social order exists only and in so far as human activity continues to produce it) it is a human product.

P. L. Berger and T. Luckmann, *The Social Construction of Reality.* (1966: 70)

The Collected Works of Ruqaiya Hasan

Volume 4

Context in the System and Process of Language

Edited by Jonathan J. Webster

SHEFFIELD UK   BRISTOL CT

Published by Equinox Publishing Ltd.

UK: Office 415, The Workstation, 15 Paternoster Row, Sheffield, South Yorkshire
       S1 2BX
USA: ISD, 70 Enterprise Drive, Bristol, CT 06010

www.equinoxpub.com

First published 2016

British Library Cataloguing-in-Publication Data

A catalogue record for this book is available from the British Library.

ISBN-13   978 1 904768 39 5 (hardback)
           978 1 904768 40 1 (paperback)

Library of Congress Cataloging-in-Publication Data
Landmarks in CALL research: looking back to prepare for the future, 1995–2015 / Edited by Greg Kessler.
    pages cm. – (Advances in CALL Research and Practice)
Includes bibliographical references and index.
ISBN 978-1-78179-360-2 (pb)
1. Language and languages–Computer-assisted instruction–Research. 2. Language and languages–Study and teaching–Research. I. Kessler, Greg (Linguist) editor. II. CALICO Journal.
P53.28.L33 2016
418.00285–dc23
                          2015033344

Typeset by S.J.I. Services, New Delhi
Printed and bound by Lightning Source Inc. (La Vergne, TN), Lightning Source UK Ltd. (Milton Keynes), Lightning Source AU Pty. (Scoresby, Victoria).

For Michael who created the context of enquiry

Contents

Acknowledgements

'Language and society in a systemic functional perspective'. In *Continuing Discourse on Language: A Functional Perspective Volume 1*, edited by R. Hasan, C.M.I.M. Matthiessen and J. Webster, 2005, 55–80. Reprinted by permission of Equinox.

'Meaning, context and text – fifty years after Malinowski'. In *Systemic Perspectives on Discourse*, edited by James D. Benson and Williams S. Greaves, 1985, 16–50. Reprinted by permission of Ablex Publishing.

'What's going on?: A dynamic view of context in language'. In *The Seventh LACUS Forum*, edited by J.E. Copeland and P.W. Davis, 1980, 37–50. Reprinted by permission of Cassell & Co.

'Wherefore context: language in social life'. In *Grammar and Discourse: Proceedings of the International Conference on Discourse Analysis*, edited by Ren Shaozeng, William Guthrie and I.W. Ronald Fong, 2001. Reprinted by permission of University of Macau Publication Centre.

'The conception of context in text'. In *Discourse in Society: Systemic Functional Perspectives*, edited by Peter H. Fries and Michael Gregory, 1995, 183–283. Reprinted by permission of Ablex Publishing.

'Speaking with reference to context'. In *Text and Context in Functional Linguistics*, edited by Mohsen Ghadessy, 1999, 219–328. Reprinted by permission of John Benjamins Publishing Company.

'The place of context in a systemic functional model'. In *Continuum Companion to Systemic Functional Linguistics*, 2008, 166–189. Reprinted by permission of Continuum International Publishing Group.

Editor's preface

As I write this preface to Professor Ruqaiya Hasan's fourth volume in this series of her Collected Works, I think back to an interview a few years back with both Professor Hasan and Professor Halliday in their home in Sydney. During that interview, Professor Hasan spoke eloquently of our need as human beings to be part of a community. And out of that need to belong in community comes our sense of humanity. But without meaning there can be no community, no sense of shared humanity. Need for community makes meaning, and in turn meaning shapes human communities. As Hasan writes in the concluding lines of this volume, 'I have always felt that it is the meaning potential of language that makes the world go round ...'

Because the social and the semiotic are interdependent, as Hasan explains, 'inequality arising from the distribution of social power and control raises issues that linguistics might help us understand but bringing about change simply by languaging without social action appears rather problematic.' As demonstrated by her contribution to SFL-inspired pedagogy, Hasan is not one to just talk about making social change. She shares with Professor M. A. K. Halliday the expectation that (here quoting Halliday from the same interview) 'the clear and honest and objective thinking' being done in the present should 'in the long run' have 'some sort of effect' – some impact on humanity.

The papers in this volume range over a period of three decades, one as recent as 2014 and another dating back to 1981 (which I recall reading back then with great interest as a recent PhD graduate in sociolinguistics). Her writings have contributed much to the development of SFL theory, particularly on the topic of the relation between context and text. It is a testimony to the 'truth' (not used lightly) in her scholarship that what was published three decades ago still remains relevant today. At the same time, one also observes how her ideas have developed over the years, as evidenced, for example, in her discussion about how system networks can help achieve a paradigmatic description of context.

Through her scholarship, Professor Hasan makes meaning – changing the way we think about, describe and explain what's going on when people use language in the context of a situation. It is her recognition of the semo-genic power of language and her commitment to 'making social change' which continues to inspire new generations of scholars in the 'struggle to understand how and why language works'.

I

Language in the Context of Life in Society

Editor's introduction

Appropriately, the first chapter in this volume – 'Language and society: a systemic functional perspective', a paper originally appearing in *Continuing Discourse on Language: A Functional Perspective* (Equinox 2005) – clearly establishes the author's ideological position, namely, that 'the social and the semiotic are inseparable: their co-evolution is the history of humanity'. As Professor Ruqaiya Hasan explains, it is an ideological position which is rooted in the writings of Malinowski, Firth, Bernstein and Halliday, and fundamental to SFL's 'struggle to understand how and why language works'. This 'interdependence of the social and the semiotic' becomes apparent in the ways 'we use language to do things in social life', prompting exploration into 'situationally appropriate discourse' (register) describable in terms of 'the nature of the activity (field)', 'interactant relations (tenor)', and 'changing modes of contact'.

In 'Meaning, Context and Text – Fifty Years after Malinowski' (1985), Hasan takes issue with 'unscholarly reading' of Malinowski, which seems more intent on 'keeping alive legends' than critically acknowledging his 'failure to recognize the full implications of the systemicity of language.' Systemicists, on the other hand, recognizing the dialectic between text, meaning and context, have responded to Malinowski's 'underestimation of systemicity' by attempting to answer such crucial questions as:

- What aspects of the context can always be reconstituted by the language of a narrative utterance, more generally, any displaced text?
- Why is it that the language of a displaced text invariably permits the reconstitution of these and no other contextual phenomena?

Coded messages, passed between us, turn the subjective into the intersubjective, the private into the public. As Hasan explains in *What's Going On?: A dynamic view of context in language* (1981), there are multiple semiotic codes at work in both text creation and interpretation. Formed out of systems of social convention, these codes not only convey but also shape our perception. The individual, writes Hasan, 'can be seen as a being who has been actively shaped by the sum of his own interactions and hence by the nature of the multiple semiotic codes prevalent in his community.' The blurring of artificially imposed dichotomies between the individual and the social, the unique and the conventional follows from an appreciation of the inherently social nature of interaction, 'no matter how personal the ends it is made to achieve.'

'Wherefore context? The ontogenesis of meaning exchange' (2001), the concluding chapter in this first section on *Language in the context of life in society* was first presented at the International Conference on Discourse Analysis at the University of Macau in October 1997. Unapologetically, Hasan begins by acknowledging that the paper 'offers neither any technicalities that can be readily borrowed and quickly applied to the analysis of another text of one's choosing, nor does it make an appeal to our moral sense of responsibility.' Hoping instead to 'enhance our understanding of the place of context in the system and process of language', she puts forward a way of conceptualizing the category of context which rests on the principle that society, semiosis and the brain form 'a trinity no one member of which can exist without the other two.'

1 Language and society in a systemic functional perspective [2005]

No linguist or phonetician thinks that the last word [on the theory or description of language, *RH*] has been said; no doubt by 1980 our theories will have been extended, and in part replaced, by newer ideas ... it is a commonplace of science that the more complex the theory, the simpler the description: the simpler, that is, the explanation of the events which the theory is devised to account for. (Halliday, McIntosh and Strevens 1964: 140)

1.1 Introduction

In SFL, the recognition of a relationship between language and society has existed from the very beginning.[1] As early as 1964, Halliday, McIntosh and Strevens described language as 'a form of activity of human beings in societies' (page 4): they devoted an entire chapter to 'Users and Uses of Language' (1964: 75–110), and alongside the familiar concept of DIALECT VARIATION, they introduced the concept of REGISTER VARIATION. Today, with the rise of interest in sociolinguistics, text-linguistics and pragmatics, the authors' characterization of language as a form of human activity appears so obvious that it seems nothing out of the ordinary; but the 1960s were different as any unbiased history of linguistics will concede. Besides, it is not so much the characterization of language itself that is important; what really makes the difference is whether that observation is actually used to probe the object of study. I see the ordinary sounding statement in Halliday *et al.* as indicative of the orientation that informed the development of SFL's unique programme of research on language:[2] it voiced a productive principle, the pursuit of which enabled SFL to offer a 'scientific' description of 'how language works' taking into account the 'internal organization' of language as well as its 'external relations' to phenomena crucial to its evolution.

What I am calling SFL was not then known as SFL: the two stories, one about how Halliday's linguistics got called 'systemic functional linguistics' and the other about how SFL used this simply formulated principle in its search for an understanding of the nature of human language, are deeply intertwined. Seeing language as process, 'activity', rather than *only* as a system enclosed within itself, viewing it as part of human 'behaviour potential', and relating that behaviour potential to the cultural frame: all this and much else, was implicit in that simple statement.[3] Here, if you like, is an actual instance of the development of 'objective knowledge' (Popper 1972). The history of SFL's evolution suggests that the seeds of SFL understandings are embedded within the deep semantics of some proposition which when explored with understanding leads to further knowledge.[4] From this point of view, Popper's 'knowledge without a knowing subject' is *only* 'the potential of knowledge', and it is illogical to suggest, as Popper does, that objective knowledge can be actually brought into being without the intervention of a 'knowing subject': knowing subjects are needed who have a sense of how to explore semiotic structures, and who possess the requisite semantic orientation for engaging in such activities.

In this chapter I attempt to provide a brief account of SFL's continuing struggle to understand how and why language works. Since the work of language is *always* and *only* done in society, the struggle to understand why and how language works is also the struggle to understand the nature of the relationship between language and society, hence the importance of asking where, why, and how people use language and what is indicated from these facts about the nature of language. My account of how Halliday proceeded from the initial observation will not be organized chronologically: instead, it will be concept based for two reasons. First, it is not an exaggeration to say that Firth had already presented us with many acute observations on this topic (Butt 2001; Hasan 1987a, 1995, 1999a): what remained was further exploration of these and a theorization whereby their relationship to other concepts could be established so as to produce a comprehensive account of how and why language actually works (see Butt 2005; Butt and Wegener 2007).[5] Second, as a sub-text of this chapter, I hope to show how concepts in use become the basis for the exploration of other ideas regarding which one might have had no inkling whatsoever at the start of the intellectual journey. From this perspective, the chapter is an implicit rebuttal of Popper's approach to the way theoretical knowledge develops.

In my view, his claim is flawed because he misses the crucial point that knowledge is a semiotic construal (Kappagoda 2005); as such it can only originate in discursive social activities (Hasan and Butt 2011). The obvious implication is that the growth of knowledge from whatever starting point requires the semiotic activity of human beings in societies.

1.2   Register: the context-language connection

Halliday *et al.* (1964: 87) introduce their category of register as follows:

> A dialect is a variety of language distinguished according to the user … It is possible also to recognize varieties of a language along *another* dimension, distinguished according to use. Language varies as its function varies; it differs in different situations. The name given to *a variety of language distinguished according to use is 'register'*. [italics added].

Like all varieties of language, register is a variety that reveals itself through an examination of the process of language. Unlike the analysis of social practice in the ethnomethodological approaches, the category of register is not based on a hermeneutic analysis of *instance by instance* language use; it relies on the recognition of regularities in *types* of language use. So the validity of a postulated category must depend on the establishment of the principle(s) underlying these regularities. The formulation by Halliday *et al.* suggests two directions for such validation: (i) the distinctive character of the social situation in which language is functioning, and (ii) the demands a category of register such as, say, 'consultation between doctor and patient' would make on the system of language, i.e., the description of registers under focus 'on the basis of their formal properties' (Halliday *et al.* 1964: 90).[6]

1.2.1 Conceptualizing context for register analysis

Situation is a large word. If it is to be of use as a theoretical term in the description of the linguistic category of register, then it must be theorized and the theorization must treat language as the central point of reference.[7] SFL had already inherited the concept of context of situation from Malinowski via Firth (Butt 2001; Butt 2005; and also Butt and Wegener 2007). R. Firth (1964) had explicitly distanced himself from what he saw as Malinowski's overly 'material' view of the situation, where it was taken to refer to anything and everything surrounding the language event.[8] Interpreting context in this way implies that describing a situation becomes as improbable a feat as 'transcribing infinity' (Cook 1990). Firth's view (1957: 182) had been

> that 'context of situation' is best used as a schematic construct to apply to language events and that it is a group of related categories at a different level from grammatical categories but rather of the same abstract nature. A *context of situation for linguistic work* brings into relation the following categories:
>
> A. The relevant features of PARTICIPANTS: person, personalities.
>   (i) The VERBAL ACTION of the participants.
>   (ii) The NON-VERBAL ACTION of the participants.
> B. The RELEVANT OBJECTS.
> C. The EFFECT of the verbal action.

Halliday *et al.* (1964: 90) adopt these views but with some modification, recognizing 'three dimensions' of social environment for discourse:

- FIELD OF DISCOURSE, referring to what is going on, i.e., the social activity;
- MODE OF DISCOURSE, referring to the 'medium or mode', e.g., written or spoken; and
- STYLE OF DISCOURSE, referring to 'the relations among participants', which following Gregory (1967) was re-named 'TENOR OF DISCOURSE'.

This conceptualization of context of situation has stood the test of time: the three dimensions of field, tenor and mode have invariably proved 'relevant' in the description of register, and no need has been felt for others. Over the years, the concept of context has changed significantly (see section 1.3); but even with variant frameworks of linguistics (e.g. Martin 1992) the three dimensions have been retained.

1.2.2 Language in the analysis of register

Halliday *et al.* point out that by contrast with dialects which largely differ in EXPRESSION SUBSTANCE, registers differ primarily in FORM: 'the crucial criteria [for the recognition, *RH*] of any register are to be found in its grammar and its lexis' (p. 88).

> Probably lexical features are the most obvious. Some lexical items suffice almost by themselves to identify a certain register: 'cleanse' puts us in the language of advertising, 'probe' of newspapers, especially headlines, 'tablespoons' of recipes or prescription, 'neckline' of fashion reporting or dress making instructions. ...
>
> Purely grammatical distinctions between different registers are less striking, yet there can be considerable variation in grammar also. Extreme cases are newspaper headlines and church services; but many other registers such as sports commentaries and popular songs, exhibit specific grammatical characteristics. Sometimes, for example, in the language of advertising, it is the combination of grammatical and lexical features that is distinctive.

This tradition of going directly to form (today's lexicogrammar) in the analysis of register has largely maintained itself in SFL. Halliday *et al.* are careful to emphasize that the identity of registers is not determined by reference to situation; thus (1964: 89):

> It is by their formal properties that registers are defined. If two samples of language activity from what on non-linguistic [i.e., situational, *RH*] grounds, could be considered different situation-types show no differences in grammar or lexis, they are assigned to one and the same register: for the purposes of the description of the language there is only one situation-type here, not two.[9]

1.3   Register and context: relations of language and society

The relationship between the language of a register and the situation type in which its use would be communally seen as appropriate was described as one of correlation or correspondence. Thus lamenting the absence of corpus-based 'hard' linguistic criteria for register identification, the authors comment that 'There is enough evidence for us to be able to recognize the major *situation types to which formally distinct registers correspond*' (1964: 90; italics introduced). Unlike Firth's 'restricted varieties' registers are not 'marginal or special'.

> Between them, they cover the total range of our language activity. ...
> *language is not realized in the abstract: it is realized as the activity
> of people in situations, as linguistic events which are manifested in a
> particular dialect and register.* (1964: 89; emphasis added)

If on the basis of these statements, we take register as a category of language, then by the same token situation type can be treated as a category of culture: in fact, in introducing CONTEXT OF SITUATION, Malinowski had talked of CONTEXT OF CULTURE as well; for him, the two were in an inalienable relation. It is reasonable to suppose that if the relationship between register and situation is one of correspondence, then the same would be true of language and culture. There is obviously some problem in reconciling this view of the relations of language and society with those that were current then, such as that of language as an autonomous system.

Firth was convinced, however, that integrating context of situation into his linguistics framework would enable 'statements of meaning', making 'sure of the sociological component' (Firth 1957: 182). From his writings on how language functions in the living of life, one might derive three main claims:

(a) language use reflects social situation: given a naturally occurring piece of language, the nature of the corresponding context of situation can be predicted;
(b) conversely, given a context of situation, speakers can be expected to successfully predict the likely utterances; in the implied regularities of behaviour lies the measure of our originality; and
(c) language is a critical tool for creating, maintaining, and changing not only persons and personalities but also social institutions and values.

Thus to quote Firth (1957: 185):

> The bonds of family, neighbourhood, class, occupation, country
> and religion are knit by speech and language. We take eagerly to
> the magic of language because only by apprenticeship to it can we
> be admitted to association, fellowship, and community in our social
> organizations which ministers to our needs and gives us what we
> want or what we deserve. The emphasis is on society and fellowship,
> in which a man may find his personality.
>
> The various forms of local and familiar speech may be stated by
> means of constructs, so called cultural systems, the elements of which
> we may regard as values to the people, who *by continuing to give*

utterance to them maintain them or modify them by their activity.
[italics introduced]

What Firth describes above is the web of social relations which all normal members of society experience; his statements also concern the role of language in the construal of culture. Given our own experience of living in society, the claims he is making can hardly be denied. And from Firth onwards, this claim had been frequently repeated.[10] But this is not to say that they were explicitly supported by the existing linguistic theory to which SFL is historically related; and here is one reason why not. Correlation or correspondence is a 'weak' relation to postulate. It is tangential and raises an important question: is the co-occurrence guided by some underlying principle? The frequently repeated claims of its sure and easy verifiability could clearly not be treated as an answer: arguments for a stronger relation were needed. The insight gained by Halliday's linguistics was that SITUATION TYPE, later referred to as RELEVANT CONTEXT (Hasan 1973c), can be reconstituted on the basis of a text's language precisely because what crucially settles its *identity* is language use: *relevant context is linguistically construed.*[11]

This does not imply that relevant context is internal to language: it is after all an abstraction from context of situation and so must contain parts of extra-linguistic phenomena.[12] But, in this sense, all situation would be EXTRA-LINGUISTIC. What distinguishes the theoretical category 'situation type' or 'relevant context' are its two characteristics. (a) Relevant context is that part of the MATERIAL SITUATIONAL SETTING which is *illuminated by the human acts of speaking* whereby the elements of the extra-linguistic situation become 'encapsulated' in the language used with reference to it.[13] (b) It is thus not only extra-linguistic but also *social*, i.e., it necessarily implicates 'an other' since it arises as a manifestation of a ways of being, doing and saying: the possibility of an other is always already there in every linguistic act whether in the act's initiation, or its continuation or response to it as a semiotic object: I take this, in fact, as the true meaning of Bakhtin's notion of DIALOGISM.

The crucial identity of situation type/relevant context, thus, does not reside in the situation's material content *per se*; it resides in the time-binding effect of language use, which makes this relevant context free of time and space, i.e., from the here and now of language in use. The 'situation' surrounding the production of a text is never fully encapsulated in the language of that particular text, since on any one occasion the participants' own interpretation of it is refracted through their perception of what they are engaged in doing.

Their interpretations are conditioned by their experiences of participation in various other language events: they thus have a 'selective relation' to what is 'really there'. This is what makes them decide what to do, what to say: a text is simply the manifestation of the activity of speaking with reference to context as that context is perceived by the interactants in that specific location. The time-binding effects of encapsulation in language implies that the relevant context is freed from spatio-temporal restrictions: context may be *actual* – referring to some aspects of the here and now of the discourse; or, *imaginary* as for example in a novel, where it needs not refer to the here and now of discourse production; or, it may be *virtual* as in certain register types which involve generalizations, and hypothetical or conditional statements, and so on (Cloran 1994; Hasan 2001b).

As pointed out, the prediction about language and situation works in both directions, which implies that the relationship between the two orders of abstraction, namely, language and society, is not that of correspondence or determination: if this were the case, one would predate the other. Instead of this sequential ordering of the two phenomena, *the relation between language and society is dialectical*. Language creates, maintains, and changes human society while this stable *and* yet forever changing society puts pressure on linguistic resources for making a specific range of meanings, with consequences that are far-reaching indeed for both language and society (see sections 1.4–1.6). While Firth's discourse and that of Halliday *et al.* (1964) had created the interest in exploring the relations of language and society, it is the effort to understand how 'real' language works in social life that has helped systemic linguists to recognize the problems inherent in early approaches. The effort to resolve those problems led to the re-conceptualization of 'situation type': *situation type – or relevant context – is not simply an abstraction from material situation, it is also crucially a construct based on linguistic meaning.*

1.4   Situation type, meaning and discourse

As I see it, there were at least two important reasons for the emphasis Halliday *et al.* placed on formal patterns in the definition of register, which appears to by-pass the stratum of semantics: first, they were establishing points of contrast and similarity between register and dialect variation. Dialect, or more precisely 'accent' (Abercrombie 1965), is variation realized primarily at the expression plane, i.e., it concerned the phonological/phonetic patterns. In the context of language teaching, which was a major concern of the 1964 publication, it was important to point out that register variation is, in principle, independent of accent variation, that speaking the cockney 'dialect' is no impediment to teaching or learning the language of, say, physics. The second reason lay in the conceptualization of meaning inherited from Malinowski and Firth.

Malinowski's context of situation has been so regularly enlisted in the analysis of register variation that the main impetus for his introduction of the concept is often forgotten. Having encountered severe problems in translating widely divergent cultures (see Steiner 2005), one of Malinowski's main concerns was how to get the Kiriwinian meanings across to his readers to whom both the culture and the language were entirely unknown: translating from Kiriwinian into English was not quite like translating from English into French or German, for in the latter cases the cultures converged much more closely, and the languages had been in spatial and historical contact. His solution to this problem took him to an exploration of how anyone learns their meanings in the first place. It was to resolve this problem that Malinowski initially introduced the concept of context of situation and context of culture: for him, these concepts are as much capable of explaining how meanings become accessible as they are of explaining how language functions in the living of life (Hasan 1985c; Butt and Wegener 2007): the deep fact is of course that meaning is central to the living of life (Hasan 1999a).

Malinowski identified certain environments, for example 'the infantile uses of words' or the use of language in everyday practical activities, where language functions more as a mode of action than of reflection.[14] In such practical environments the relation between saying and meaning is relatively transparent as compared to occasions where language is used to 'reflect': '… words are uttered within the situation to which they belong and *uttered so that they achieve an immediate practical effect. For it is in such situations that words acquire their meaning*' (Malinowski 1935: 52; my emphasis). Malinowski saw such contexts as furnishing the best environment for the mediation of meaning to the infant, a novice. A small child does not learn meaning through dictionaries, nor through reflection on the nature of the universe nor even by analysing the internal organization of her/his language: Instead the child learning how to mean makes his first encounters with linguistic meaning precisely in environments where the meaning of the utterances is in comparatively direct contact with the context. As can be readily appreciated, Malinowski was accounting here for the ontogenesis of what Saussure had called 'signification', i.e., 'reference'.[15] Saussure was certainly right in pointing out that 'valeur' determines the scope of 'signification', but 'valeur' is not where the baby's mind initially makes contact with meaning.[16] Speaking with reference to the context of situation is, thus, Malinowski's solution to the problem of the internalization of referential meaning: this removes the closure caused by Saussure's insistence that the relation between the signified and signifier was arbitrary, while restricting the scope of linguistic investigation of 'the arbitrary' becoming 'the habitual' by banishing *parole*, and focusing solely on the study of *langue* (Hasan 1985c, 1987a; Thibault 1997).

The Malinowskian association between context and meaning was adopted by Firth, and those views form the foundation of SFL. Rejecting the main trends of contemporary linguistics, Firth declared that 'the main concern of descriptive linguistics is to make statements of meaning' (Firth 1957: 190): and as for meaning, it rested between language and context. Although his concept of meaning has been shortsightedly described as 'mischievous' (Lyons 1966), there is another, more interesting interpretation. What Firth really wanted from his theory of meaning was to account for both Saussure's VALEUR and SIGNIFICATION, i.e., both SENSE and REFERENCE. Firth recommended that:

> To make statements of meaning in terms of linguistics, we may accept the language event as a whole and then deal with it at *various levels, … beginning with social context and proceeding through syntax and vocabulary to phonology and even phonetics.* (Firth 1957: 192; emphasis mine).

According to Firth, this inter-subjectively objective description of linguistic meaning calls for the abolition of appeals to inaccessible phenomena such as mental states of intending and believing, desire and decision, and so on. Instead according to Firth, linguistic meaning had to be described by examining how language 'comes to mean', i.e., by discovering a *language's various modes of meaning.* Insight into these modes of meaning is provided by the schematic constructs recognized at the various levels as set up in a viable framework for linguistic description. For Firth, the levels essential for the description of language are: (a) the environment in which language works – its SOCIAL CONTEXT; (b) the formal patterns of language – its SYNTAX AND VOCABULARY; and (c) the sound patterns of language – its PHONOLOGY AND PHONETICS.

Absent from this conception is a specific component/stratum in the linguistic theory called 'semantics' i.e., the level of linguistic meaning, although occasionally, there is mention of semantics as something demanding attention within the structure of language. This, at first sight, might appear logical since for Firth the job of making meaning was 'dispersed' across the strata; in his view, the three levels were sufficient to account for the production of linguistic meaning. More specifically, in his scheme 'reference' (signification), echoing Malinowski, is achieved by level (a), i.e., by reference to the social environment; 'sense' (valeur) is achieved via patterns of collocation and colligation on level (b), i.e., by syntax and vocabulary; *and* their manifestation, impinging on and making contact with the sensing human body is achieved by the patterns of level (c), i.e., phonology and phonetics: the analysis of meaning production is 'dispersed' over the three levels of linguistic description.[17] Thus in the theoretical framework that SFL inherited from Firth, there was no place for a separate component called 'semantics' whose categories would 'describe' the reservoir of linguistic meaning, accessible at least in theory to all speakers of a given language in the same way that the lexicogrammar of a language is normally assumed to be. In this scheme, to say that 'the crucial criteria of any given register are to be found in its grammar and its lexis' is to affirm also the 'valeur' of linguistic patterns (Halliday *et al.* 1964: 88). So far as meaning as a whole was concerned it would be the joint contribution of 'context' and 'formal and phonological patterns'.

Lack of space does not permit a detailed discussion of the pressures that led to the recognition of semantics as one of the indispensable strata in SFL. All of these pressures came from the actual use of the 'schematic constructs' in the analysis of 'real' data for some research program or other. Main amongst these was the participation of Halliday's linguistics in Bernstein's research projects (Halliday 1973b; Turner 1973; Hasan 1973a, 1973b, 1973c, 1984c; Hasan, Cloran, Williams and Lukin 2007). But equally important were two other developments: (1) interest in children's language learning as an off-shoot of the Nuffield Project (for a record, J. Pearce, G. Thornton and D. Mackay 1989; Christie and Unsworth 2005), soon followed by the case study of an infant learning how to mean (Halliday 1975a; see section 5);[18] and (2) the development of system networks (for details, Matthiessen 2007) representing substantial fragments of the grammar and phonology of English (e.g. Halliday 1967a, 1967b, 1967c, 1968, 1969) which provided a clearer sense of how linguistic form construes meanings. This at once revealed both the power and the weakness in Firth's contextual approach to linguistic meaning. Its strength was demonstrated by showing conclusively the 'non-arbitrary' relationship between meaning and wording: linguistic meanings are the artifact of the formal resources of language. But at the same time, researchers were hampered by the lack of any mechanism for actually representing the semantic potential of language in the way that the formal potential is represented by the lexicogrammatical system networks. This, in turn, means that there are no terms for talking about meaning. Let me elaborate on the drawbacks of this position.

Following Firth, the orientation of description in SFL has been paradigmatic: in fact, this is what explains the term 'systemic' in its name. A SYSTEM NETWORK is a device for representing the analysis of units at the various strata in terms of a calibrated set of OPTIONS whose value is determined through their 'systemic relations', while the REALIZATION STATEMENTS attached to the systemic options help establish recognition criteria (Halliday 1992a; Hasan 1995; Matthiessen 2007): so ideally, the definition and recognition criteria for categories under analysis are maximally explicit and their accuracy is open to being tested and debated. *In the Firthian approach this possibility is denied to the categories of linguistic meaning.* It is true that there are no linguistic meanings that are not construed lexicogrammatically;[19] but it is also equally true that in a functional model, there is no place for form without meaning; nor is it possible to postulate the principle of a one to one relationship between a lexicogrammatical unit and a unit of meaning. Firth has himself declared (1957: 190) that '… each word … used in a new context is a new word'.[20] For example, it is a common place of linguistics, that the lexicogrammatical category 'declarative' does not *always and only* construe a category of meaning called 'statement'/'assertion'. And when it comes to categories of meaning such as, say, 'statement' or 'question' or 'offer', we need to be clear about what each category is capable of meaning, before we say something about its realization. Whether the concern is with lexicogrammatical or with the semantic analysis, the definition and recognition criteria for the categories need to be explicit and precise (which does not necessarily mean a one to one calibration of the two). Perhaps in ordinary language, a word may have a new meaning depending on its company; but the introduction of this protean property of words, occurring in theoretical discourse and referring as technical terminology to descriptive categories of linguistics, would wreak havoc – this was pointed out none other than Firth who described 'linguistics as language turned back upon itself'. So far as meanings are concerned, their definition as a descriptive category needs to be seen in relation to context, while their recognition criteria are lexicogrammatical: these principles are accepted in the Firthian framework. However, the categories need to be seen also in relation to each other: to use Firth's own reasoning, the value of the category 'declarative' is partly due to its systemic relation to the category 'interrogative'. Ideally the set of three-way relations just described is built into a system network.[21]

The system networks, which attempt to represent such meaning relations in explicit and precise terms, describe the MEANING POTENTIAL of a language at the semantic stratum as well (Hasan, Cloran, Williams and Lukin 2007). In other words, the statement of potential is system based, which is what permits it to describe instances as well; by contrast, Firth's approach to meaning is entirely process-based. A comprehensive account of language, such as SFL aspires to be, cannot choose between process *or* system: it must attend to *both*. To resolve this problem, what the theory had to develop at this point was a *paradigmatic description of meaning potential calling for explicit realization statements.*

When it came to presenting a systemic statement of what mothers might say in the social context of control (Halliday 1973b), it was quite obvious that the best way to proceed was through a paradigmatic description of the meaning potential relevant to that environment with the lexicogrammar featuring as the construer of those semantic categories. Figure 1.1 presents the categories as postulated by Halliday.

Figure 1.1: Options in warning and threat: a fragment from Halliday (1973b: 89)

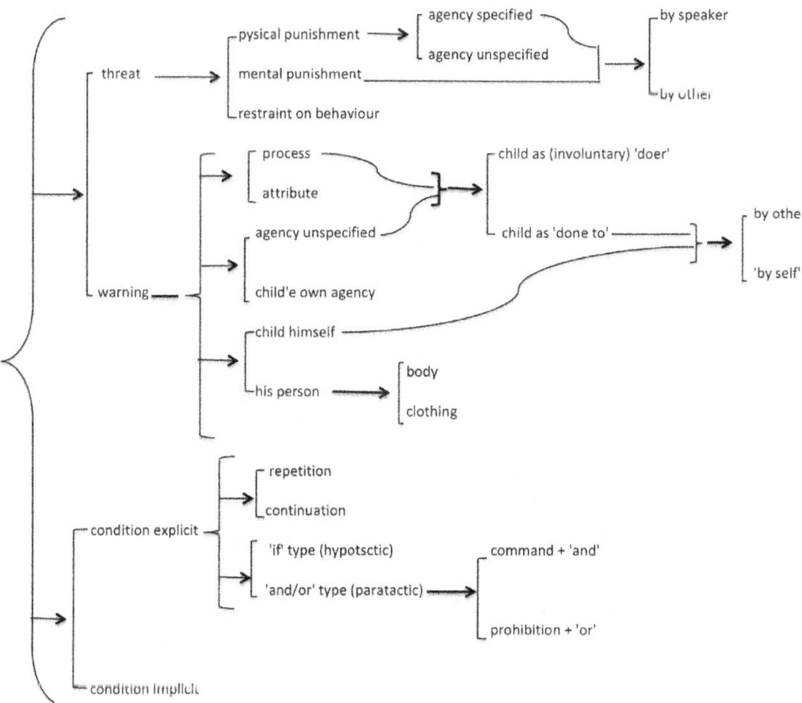

It would have been almost impossible to make the 'statements of meaning' pertinent to the context of maternal control purely through Firth's levels (b) and (c), i.e., lexicogrammar and phonology/phonetics. Anyway, even if feasible, the Firthian description would have failed to provide a systematic LANGUAGE OF DESCRIPTION for discourse about meaning, in the way that discussions are possible today concerning 'declarative', 'transitive', 'marked theme', etc. as categories at the stratum of lexicogrammar. In drawing his semantic network of threats and warnings, what Halliday (1973b) initiated was the invention of a language for semantic description, without which discourse and debate on meaning in a context under focus would have been almost impossible. In view of these developments, Halliday's SFL now recognizes four language internal strata (see Figure 1.2): (a) **semantics**, which introduces the systemic potential of meaning, (b) **lexicogrammar**, comparable to Firth's levels of grammar and lexicology, (c) **phonology**, and (d) **phonetics**, the two together comparable to Firth's level (c).

Figure 1.2: The stratal organization of language as a semiotic system

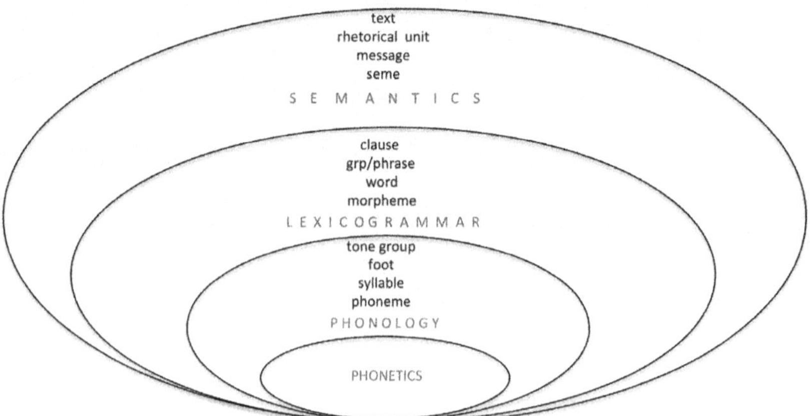

In Figure 1.2, the Firthian level (a), i.e., the social environment is not included. Figure 1.3 (Hasan 2012: 255) builds social context into the picture, thus representing language as a social semiotic system. The social context, functioning as an environment for the system and process of language, is naturally external to it; the recognition of the environment as integral to the theory is one indication that language is a semiotic system working in the social life of its speakers: the stratum is necessary in a theory that professes to be a social semiotic. Without the insertion of 'context'

Figure 1.3: Language as a social semiotic: strata in a functional theory (Hasan 2012: 255)

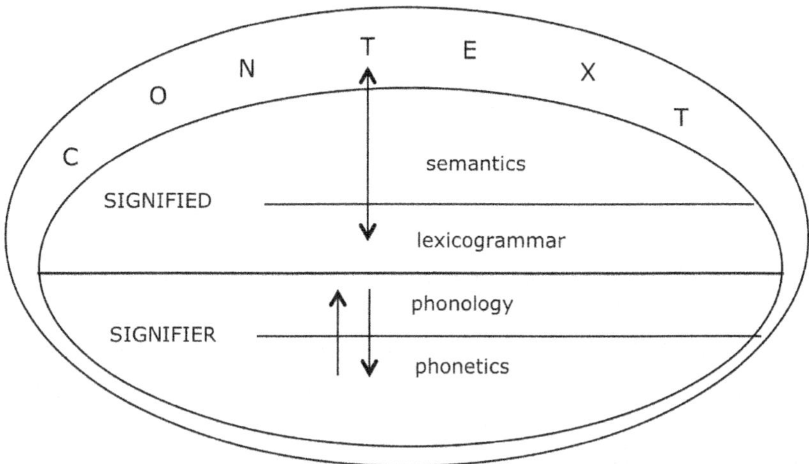

as an integral part of the theory, it is difficult to ground the systemic nature of discourse.[22]

These developments in the conceptualization of meaning and, particularly, the recognition of semantics as a stratum of the system of language have been highly significant for SFL over the last three decades; as I attempt to show briefly in the following sections, its effects have penetrated the entire 'syntax' of SFL theory.

1.4.1   Meaning, register, and text

One such area was closely related to the concept of register, namely the study of text. SFL had focused on the concept of text from the early 1960s: it was not the 'infinity of sentences' that fascinated it; rather, it was the infinite variety in the midst of stable patterns of continuity in texts that SFL found significant. Initial studies of cohesion (Halliday 1964; Hasan 1964, 1968, 1973b) were already suggesting the relevance of semantic categories. Cohesion was found to be 'essentially a semantic concept' with formal realizations. More specific semantic concepts relevant to cohesion such as 'co-reference, co-interpretation' and 'presupposition' were to arrive later in Cohesion in English (Halliday and Hasan 1976) where text was defined as 'a unit of meaning', realized as clauses. (Hasan's concept of COHESIVE HARMONY, though first published in 1984, was developed by 1973b.[23])

Clearly, every text pertains to some register, which suggests that meaning must be at least as crucial to the description of register as it is to that of text. It was my view (Hasan 1973b, 1973c) that the crucial register identification criteria were more efficiently and economically provided in terms of meanings: the very idea of register as 'situationally appropriate discourse' calls for a meaning-based characterization of register. If 'each word when used in a new context is a new word' as claimed by Firth, its newness is not in how it looks or sounds, but in what it means, and this can be attributed to the newness of its social and linguistic environments. The analysis of register was further extended by postulating a GENERALIZED STRUCTURE POTENTIAL (GSP) for register types (Hasan 1978; see also the last chapter of this volume): the GSP specifies both the similarities and the variations that could be expected to occur within one register family. Any text instantiating a register variety within the scope of that register family would draw upon one and the same GSP. The realization of the elements of textual structure was stated in semantic terms, and these are realized as lexicogrammatical patterns capable of construing that meaning in that environment (Hasan 1984c, 1985b). On the basis of an informal survey of the realization of text, Hasan (1973c) had postulated two categories of meaning; TEXT-WIDE, which resonated across the text as a whole and LOCALIZED, which had bearing only to some specific location in the text. The development of the GSP further elaborated the notion of 'localized meaning', suggesting that the 'location' was identifiable by reference to the elements of the GSP. Despite these beginnings, it still remains true that the majority of systemic linguists seldom move to the semantic aspects of register-specific patterns in their register analysis perhaps because lexicogrammatical analysis is already systemized and so readily available for most units. However, recently a new beginning has been made (Matthiessen, Lukin, Butt, Cleirigh and Nesbitt 2005), which 'disperses' the register characterization to the four linguistic strata.

The idea of the SCHEMATIC STRUCTURE of a text was developed by Martin (1985a, 1992; Ventola 1987) and other colleagues; along the way, the relation between the schematic text structure and the textual parameters became much weaker; certain major changes to the stratal design of the (genre based) linguistic theory were also introduced by Martin (1985a, 1992), which still leave many questions unanswered and call for scholarly discussion and debate.[24] The main applications of Martin's genre-based approach have been in the educational context where it has made significant contribution (e.g., Christie and Unsworth 2005; Martin and Rose 2005).

1.4.2   Meaning in the description of society and language

So far as the relationship of society and language is concerned, the recognition of language as a meaning potential had significant outcomes. Malinowski and Firth had both seen context of situation as related to the process of language: social practice was the frame within which meanings became tangible to the participants. The recognition of meaning potential pertaining to specific contexts led to the realization that the cultural reservoir of linguistic meaning, in its genesis and its maintenance, was inalienably related to social practices: the nature of the activity (field) and the interactant relations (tenor) exercise pressure on the semantic evolution of language as do changing modes of contact, thus contributing to the creation of new linguistic resources, while renewing and/or changing the old patterns. The case study of a child learning how to mean was indicative of the role of linguistic interaction in the child's cognitive development (Painter 1984, 1999; Thibault 2004a, 2005). As neuroscience was to establish a decade later, it is the semiotic systems of meaning whose use in the experience of living personalizes human brain turning it into 'mind'. The claims that had been made about the inter-organism nature of language (Bernstein 1971; Halliday 1974a; Thibault 2004b) and its role in the formation, maintenance and change of society received theoretical support (Hasan 1999c, 2009a). Developments in the shape of the theory have now enabled it to support the claim that human relationship to social life and to language is primarily and actually their relation to meanings. If human beings have intuition, which is perhaps a word for referring to inferences based on experience and not yet externalized, its foundation lies in the meaning of experiences, which is not to deny that form is part of the same story, but to be used in interaction, form as such has to be 'translated' by the mind as meaning (Halliday and Matthiessen 1999). The solidary relation between meaning and form should deter the practitioners of SFL from prioritizing one or the other.

It was around this stage of the development of SFL that expressions such as 'social semiotic', 'socio-semiotic', 'social semantics', began to appear in its literature.[25] SFL was on its way to grappling with the concept of functionalism.

1.5   Registers, contexts and the concept of metafunction

An advantage of the Firth-Halliday approach to understanding language has been that one's legitimate area of enquiry is not artificially limited in the name of what Bourdieu somewhat sneeringly called 'linguistic scienti-ficity'. Seeing language as a form of human social action does not preclude attempts to understand the SEMIOTIC LOGIC of language as a sign system, and *vice versa*. Thus as indicated above, the logic of linguistic form was investigated with reference to language use in social context, so that, given the systemic linguists' paradigmatic orientation, a substantial part of the grammar of English was represented in system networks. The formal orga-nization of language as revealed by the disposition of the system networks formed the basis of Halliday's (1970a) METAFUNCTIONAL HYPOTHESIS.[26] The representation of form as the system networks of 'choice in context' is immensely powerful for indicating the set of relations between the vari-ous options, some configuration of which describes a unit under focus at a linguistic stratum. Halliday noticed that the lexicogrammatical patterns, represented by the system networks, were naturally falling into specific groups, each with its own denser relations of dependence and/or simul-taneity: the density of such relations between the various options was an intra-system feature; across the systems, i.e., inter-systemically the density appeared to be remarkably low (Halliday 1970a). Seen as the linguistic resource for the construal of meaning, each of these relatively indepen-dent system networks appeared to 'correspond to certain basic functions of language', i.e., they construed meanings that served specific general func-tions in the life of the community. On the basis of this pattern of meaning construal, Halliday identified three such 'general' functions, namely, (a) the ideational, (b) the interpersonal, and (c) the textual (Halliday 1973b; Matthiessen 1995, 2007; Butt and Wegener 2007).

These functions form the organizing principle for context, semantics and lexicogrammar (Halliday 1970a, 1973a, 1979b). It was in describing the meaning potential of maternal threats/warnings that Halliday (1973b: 72–102) first clearly enunciated his hypothesis of metafunctional resonance across the three strata.[27] The discussion of metafunctions was explicitly in terms of language as 'a form of activity of human beings in societies' as evident from Figure 1.4 (Halliday 1973b: 101).[28]

The argument went thus: it is undeniable that people use language as 'a form of activity in social contexts of situation' (Halliday *et al.* 1964); the relevant context of such activity is linguistically defined: relevant context is that which is encapsulated in the language as it is being used to partici-pate in the activity. On the basis of this language three relevant parameters can be can identified: speakers' social action, i.e., the *field of discourse*, their social relations, i.e., the *tenor of discourse*, and their modes of con-tact, i.e., the *mode of discourse*. Since the parameters have been deduced

Figure 1.4: The functional resonance of context, semantics and lexicogrammar

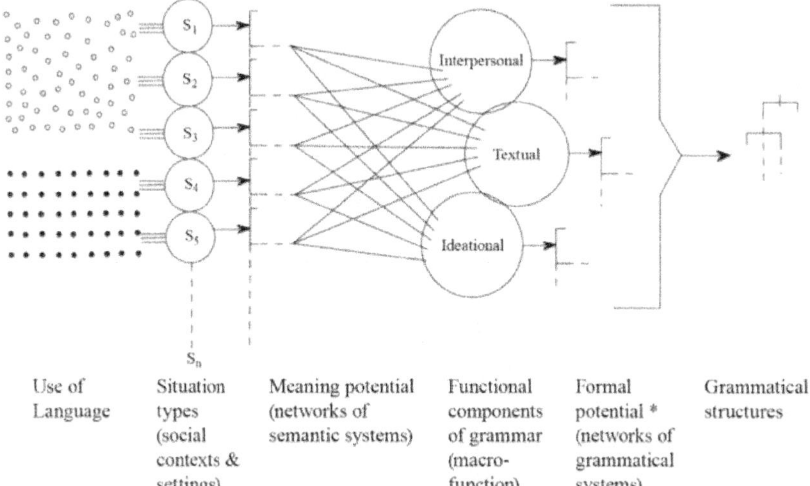

Use of Language	Situation types (social contexts & settings)	Meaning potential (networks of semantic systems)	Functional components of grammar (macrofunction)	Formal potential * (networks of grammatical systems)	Grammatical structures

from the language used for doing things with words, it stands to reason that language must have resources for construing these parameters: these resources are furnished by what might be called the 'powerhouse of langue' i.e., its lexicogrammar. Wrapping up the argument, Halliday suggested (1973a: 65–66):

> Language is as it is because of its functions in the social structure, and the organization of behavioural meanings should give some insight into its social foundations.
>
> This is the significance of functional theories of language. *The essential feature of a functional theory is not that it enables us to enumerate and classify the functions of speech acts, but that it provides a basis for explaining the nature of the language system*, since the system itself reflects the functions that it has evolved to serve. The organization of options in the grammar of a natural language seem to rest very clearly on a functional basis, as has emerged from the work of those linguists, particularly of the Prague school, who have been aware that the notion 'functions of language' is not to be equated merely with a theory of language use but expresses the principle behind the organization of the linguistic system.[29]

The SFL conception of FUNCTIONALITY IN LANGUAGE differs from the conception of functionalism in almost all other linguistic theories. The nearest to SFL conception is Prague school's functionalism, though the impressive linguistic evidence for the recognition of the postulated metafunctions provided in SFL (Halliday 1979b) is absent even from the Prague School's account; this is, however, not the place to elaborate on this theme (Hasan, forthcoming). The systemic and metafunctional orientation to which the systemic paradigmatic description led Halliday's linguistics are built into the name of his theory of linguistics. Understanding language as a resource for social action in society is what SFL is really about.

I close this section with a theme which was to re-emerge in SFL years later but which was first introduced in this very context of studying language as meaningful behaviour in society (Halliday 1973a: 67):

> The image of language as having a 'pure' form (*langue*) that becomes contaminated in the process of being translated into speech (*parole*) is of little value … We do not want a boundary between language and speech at all, or between pairs such as langue and parole, competence and performance – unless these are reduced to 'can do' and 'does'.

1.6   Context and language system: society at work

Ever since Saussure, the relationship of *parole* and *langue* has haunted linguistics. Over the years, they have been polarized, and considered mutually irreconcilable. The extreme manifestation of this polarization occurred with the arrival of early Chomskyan TG, which is represented today in many formalistic models of language based on Chomsky's view of language. Although the concepts 'competence' and 'performance' differ considerably from 'langue' and 'parole' (Hasan 1987a, 1999a; Thibault 1997), in one respect Saussure's linguistics is similar to the more recent formalistic models: for doing 'linguistics proper', all of them treat any consideration of language use and therefore of the social context as unnecessary, if not reprehensible: the only exception to this might be pragmatics. The premise was that to be scientific, linguistics as the discipline that reveals the nature of language must exclude investigation of both language data and language environment. In Chomsky's model, since language is a mental organ, performance has no part to play in explaining the nature of that organ; consideration of society is logically cut off at its very base. In Saussure, *langue* is seen as rooted in the community; so the exclusion of *parole* from the scope of linguistics is clearly illogical, since the community comes in contact with language only through its use. The dominance of formalistic models has, not surprisingly, meant that concepts such as context of situation have had a 'bad press' (Hasan 1985c, 2001a). And when thanks to such scholars as Searle, Grice, and the ethno-methodologists, context of situation came to acquire academic legitimacy, it still remained a commonsense concept, referring largely to intra-organism states. In short, context like real language data, had, at worst, no place in linguistics, and at best, it tended to be seen as a sello-tape for sealing the cracks in the felicitous working of speech acts or for holding on to syntactic/semantic hypotheses: it was employed for 'making sense of' ambiguities, contradictions, and the taken-for-granted nature of shared experience, that bastion of relevance. Largely rooted in instances of practice, or parole, performance, speech act, call it what you will, context had no place in the discourse of language system. However, in SFL, the continued research on the place of context in the linguistic theory has produced a different situation.

The 1970s saw Halliday engaged in the case study of a child learning his mother tongue (Halliday 1973a, 1975a, 1979a), producing research which, though highly labour intensive, has been replicated (Painter 1984, 1999; Oldenburg-Torr 1997).[30] These studies charted out the important stages in the process that all children have to go through from infancy onwards in learning how to mean. Firth (1957) had argued for the centrality of SPEECH FELLOWSHIP for the development of personality and language in society; Halliday (e.g., 1975a) in his turn drew attention to what he called the child's MEANING GROUP which played the most central role in the processes of children learning how to mean. In this view of learning the mother tongue, the emphasis was not on counting the number of phonemes, words and/or structures which the child might be able to produce at some stage of his/her young life; rather, the emphasis was on what forms of socially recognizable activities children could engage in with their developing 'language'. Halliday (1980) identified 'three aspects of children's language development: learning language, learning through language and learning about language'. Painter, Derewianka and Torr (2005) present a brief account of all three aspects. These studies have documented the ontogenesis of language system; they have demonstrated that language development begins much earlier than at 18 months and goes on beyond the magic age of four; they demonstrated also that the initial navigational lines in the growing child's cognitive map are drawn through shared talk (Painter 1999; Hasan 1984e, 1989, 1992b, 2004b, 2008; Cloran 1994, 1999b; Williams 1995, 2001). These are valuable findings, but the most relevant here: the growing child's developing language showed very clearly that under the pressure of being put to use in the living of life in society, a system's given state alters, but without any evidence of jarring discontinuity in its original design. In other words, change is an endemic condition of all systems whose origin is in social life, language not excepted.

Over the years these studies have augmented the understanding of the far-reaching effects of examining language in its social context without ignoring the form of language: an outstanding characteristic of SFL is its respect for both socio-logic and for semo-logic (Hasan 1999a). Here I want to draw attention especially to insights that sharpened SFL's approach to two persistent themes in linguistics: (a) the relationship of process and system; and (b) the relationship of language and cognition.

1.6.1   Parole and langue: the dialectic of process and system

As the extract at the close of section 1.5 shows Halliday, like Firth, has always rejected the need to choose between system and process. What really put the relation between the two in its proper perspective in SFL were three further developments: (a) the EVIDENCE OF SYSTEMATIC CHANGE from child language development; (b) the clarification of the role of INSTANTIA-TION; and (c) the incorporation of PROBABILITY into linguistic description (on instantiation and probability see Matthiessen 2007). To put it in a nutshell, Halliday's position is that process is continuously becoming system albeit so gradually that it seldom draws attention to itself. Halliday (1996: 30, 1999) suggests that there is no dichotomy between system and process – langue and parole; they are the same phenomenon seen from different time-depths:

> Saussure problematized the nature of the linguistic fact; but he con-fused the issue of instantiation by setting up language and parole as if they had been two distinct classes of phenomena. But they are not. There is only one set of phenomena here, not two: langue (the lin-guistic system) differs from parole (the linguistic instance), only in the position taken up by the observer. Langue is parole seen from a distance, and hence on the way to being theorized about.

This is, in fact, a more sophisticated and better theorized version of what Halliday *et al.* (1964: 89) had said in beginning their research on language: '... language is not realized in the abstract: it is realized as the activity of people in situations, as linguistic events which are manifested in a par-ticular dialect and register.' In this view instance and system are simply two faces of the same phenomenon. Halliday uses the powerful analogy of weather and climate to clarify this relation: it is instances of climate acting as day-by-day weather, that from a particular time depth, are seen as the climate. It is the instances of language in use text by text, that at a certain time depth appear as language system. Systems are not created instantaneously; they evolve over time and are encountered only as actual instances of some category.

Because the process of language in fact instantiates the system of language, linguistics cannot choose between system and process: it must attend to both, because predictability, a gift of system, and novelty, an inevitable element of instance, together play an important part in maintaining and changing the system: between the certainty of system and the uncertainty of instance lies probability. Linguistics had banished the instance; critical studies shuns the system. Halliday suggests (1993: 8–9):

> if you put the two together, the text is revealed for what it is, an act that has meaning because it is not *sui generis*; it is the actualizing of a potential, by means of processes that are patterned, in an important sense predictable. So there is an emotional gradient here as well as an intellectual one. We resist being told how much of what we 'choose' to say is programmed, either as ready-made pieces of wording, as Pawley (1985) made clear, or in the probability profiles revealed by large scale quantitative studies (Nesbitt and Plum 1988; Halliday and James 1993). Yet no child could ever learn a mother tongue if it was not characterized by massive regularities of these two complementary kinds.

So while it is true that behind each instance – each text – lies the system, i.e., the structure of a language's meaning construing resources – it is equally true that this system itself acquires the properties it has because each instance causes some perturbation in the system of language: this principle is at the heart of the metafunctional hypothesis. Very often in sociolinguistic studies, we tend to focus on language as an active force in social life – creating, maintaining and changing society; the perspective just described suggests a complementary focus on society as an active force in language, developing, maintaining and changing our semiotic 'capital'.

1.6.2 Language, society and mind

The three aspects of children's language development identified by Halliday included the contribution of semiotic (and I mean semiotic, not just linguistic) interaction in children's cognitive development. Recent research on the formation of cognition in neurological science supports this perspective. It has, as Thibault (2005) remarks, made it possible to open a long needed dialogue between SFL and research in neuroscience (Williams and Lukin 2004). Instead of treating 'cognition' as something given entirely by nature, the expert opinion in neuroscience now suggests that 'mind' is 'personalized brain', a personalization that results from the experience of living. Since for the majority of us, the experience of living in society is also the experience of living with semiosis, especially linguistic semiosis, it follows that in the making of human mind language in social life plays a massive part.

The contribution of the habitual exchange of meanings to mental development is typically presented as if children's mental life is a 'monochromatic' universe in which a certain range of concepts were the only important consideration for measuring growth: evidence for this view floods in by focusing on one single aspect of the modern complex societies, namely, concepts valued by the educational institutions. This aspect of mental development in children is socio-economically desirable, and such work (Donaldson 1992; Painter 1999) provides valuable insight into the crucial part played by linguistic interaction in the formation of a particular kind of consciousness; nonetheless, it only tells half the story, particularly since the successful development story of that genre normally told about children belong to a particular social group. Human societies have always been complex and we do not know of any society where the dominating and dominated groups have not co-existed; the idea that all children anywhere in a society could internalize those concepts if those in their meaning group conversed in a particular way is, to say the least rather simplistic. The scope of this chapter does not allow an elaboration of this theme here, but the long interest of some SFL linguists in Bernstein's code theory (Hasan 1999c; Hasan *et al.* 2007; Cloran 1994, 1999a; Williams 2005) has added another dimension to this research in the relationship of linguistic interaction and the making of the human mind. Sociolinguistic research using the SFL model has found that, as Bernstein predicted, subjects with different social positioning tend to have a significantly different pattern of linguistic interaction (Hasan 1989, 1992b; Cloran 1994, 1999a; Williams 1995, 2001, 2005). In other words, linguistic interaction never achieves anything that ignores the context of its speakers; its achievements respond to what both the interactants consider relevant.

In general terms, the variation these scholars have discovered, can be described as a difference in the subjects' ways of meaning, which itself arises from the internalization of a different sense of what is relevant. Playing on a well-known formulation in a different context by Whorf (1956), relevance is not something that stares us in the face from the environment out there, presenting the same face to all perceivers: its identity is given by the form of consciousness that has developed through the experience of living; if the experience of living is different between sub-communities then their consciousness will be different, and so too will be their linguistic interactions, with attention to different details. The social is as significant as the semiotic: the problem lies in the fact that the two act and re-act with consciousness as it continues to develop through life. Here lies the secret of the 're-production' of major social institutions and beliefs; here is where 'truths' are created which to the believer appear indisputably universal: meaning only that the believers' experience has given overwhelming evidence to that effect. With this research we have come close to establishing the linguistic realization of ideology whose etiology is in social structure. What we as yet lack is any study of how ideologies are modified, how already socialized persons and personalities change, how orders of relevance are altered. The need to understand this is urgent; it is this issue that the educational institutions should focus on. In the absence of this understanding, most talk of social change is vacuous. Human beings do not run out of the capacity to learn: but learning is by necessity selective, and selection is governed by the perception of relevance which itself develops in the living of life.

1.7　Concluding remarks

So recalling the beginning of this chapter, the story of SFL's name is also the story of its struggle to understand the relationship between language and society. It is also a story that suggests there is no substitute for using the tools in hand in order to find out how they can be improved to do a better job, no matter the tools are material or semiotic. SFL's struggle to understand began with an ordinary observation: we use language to do things in social life. In attempting to explore the implications of this observation, the framework moved step by step from Firth's 'system and structure' to Halliday's 'scale and category' to 'systemics' to 'systemic functional linguistics', with signs of a definite shift to meaning reclaiming its place in semiosis. On the way, this linguistic theory established the dialectic of: (a) language and society; (b) process and system; (c) language form and language function; and (d) language and cognition. These achievements have not solved all problems, but they have gone a long way in justifying its description as a social semiotic theory of language.

This is not to say, though, that it has yet realized its full potential in showing what its description of the area that concerns sociolinguistics would look like. Certainly SFL's description of language's semo-logic is powerful enough to bring to light new findings in the realm of language variation; also there are some indicative studies in a wide range of areas. But the majority of work in language variation in SFL remains concerned with register, where the description is often skewed to human action with human relation, a second. Work in the area of ideology and power, particularly in today's politico-economic climate, is urgently needed. Equally important is the issue of social change: while SFL inspired pedagogy has been concerned with 'making social change', and in action it is a powerful pedagogy, the theorization of social change has remained conspicuous by its absence, as is also the study of the course of actual change either in personalities or in practices. One is tempted to say: SFL has indicated the intimate interdependence of the social and the semiotic; inequality arising from the distribution of social power and control raises issues that linguistics might help us understand but to bring change simply by languaging without social action appears rather problematic. We know linguistic inter-action 'makes mind', but it only makes minds suited to the social environment of the speech fellowships. For making social change we need to understand and activate both simultaneously.

Finally, it is necessary to add that the actual process of struggle is seldom captured in the history that attempts to write it down: the recount is only a representation; it irons out the wrinkles in the telling. This said, I would not go so far as the sentiment Punch attributed to Anon (Williams 1956: 170): 'History is something that never happened, written by a man (*sic!*) who wasn't there.' The woman writing this history *was* there; but she, like all speakers, is subject to the rule that relevance is ideologically refracted. In my ideology the social and the semiotic are inseparable: their co-evolution is the history of humanity. By 2050, theories will have moved; I venture to hope, that despite that change, the social semiotic *orientation* will still survive.

Notes

1   In fact, this interest in the social was part of the inheritance from Firth, who had an acute sense of the crucial role language plays in the formation of individuals and societies. Hasan (1995) and Butt (2001) on the influence of Firth on Halliday's linguistics; see also Butt (2005).

2   There is no implication that they, themselves, viewed the statement this way, or that they singled it out as anything momentous; it is precisely because they take this view of language for granted that I here treat it as revealing a fundamental orientation in Halliday's linguistics.

3   Those familiar with ACTIVITY THEORY introduced by Vygotsky's and developed by Leont'ev would understand the claim I am making.

4   See Matthiessen (2007), Butt (2005), Butt and Wegener (2007), Christie and Unsworth (2005), which record aspects of the development of SFL.

5   Firth had rejected the possibility, and indeed the desirability, of comprehensive accounts of language, which, according to him, was so deeply variegated that no single framework could succeed in accounting for it.

6   At this stage the term 'lexicogrammar' had not been introduced, though the seminal statement about 'lexis as delicate grammar' was already on the floor (Halliday 1961/2002: 54).

7   Bowcher (2007) has argued in favour of extending the concept of context to account for all types of semiotic activities, not just the linguistic type. Clearly this is desirable since naturally occurring language use always involves extra-linguistic modes of meaning. However, I have not followed my own recommendation (e.g., in Hasan 1973c) in my own studies of context because of the un-even-ness of the understanding of other, extra-linguistic systems for meaning: unlike linguistics, they have not had a long tradition of descriptive language that would enable me to show how they act in cooperation with language.

8   In this sense, Malinowski's context of situation could probably be more easily applied to the analysis of 'multimodal' texts than Halliday's as developed in Hasan (1999b), etc., but with the drawback that the analysis would be lacking theoretical perspective on the relations of the various semiotic systems, as well as the un-even development in the descriptive frameworks for the various specific systems. In my opinion, such development is a necessary step if the burgeoning field of 'inter-semiotic' studies is to flourish (Martinec 2005).

9   The observation in the last clause is precisely where the need for the distinction between 'material situation setting' and 'situation type' (Hasan 1973c, 1981) may be appreciated; the latter in time became 'relevant context'. The distinction reconciles the essentially wide reach of the term 'situation' and the need to define the basis for considering some segment of it as 'relevant'. What is 'relevant' can be established beyond doubt only as the activity progresses in the sense that the relevant is that which is identified, in some way, by the language as it comes during the course of the SPEECH EVENT.

10   There is no suggestion that Firth was alone in these views. Mead (1934) presents views that are remarkably similar to those of Firth's though set in the context of the fashioning of the human mind.

11   Ellis (1966) had also suggested a similar distinction under the term 'immediate situation', contrasting with wider situation, which bore less direct relevance to text. For details regarding the evolution of the notion of context (see Hasan 1973c, 1978, 1981, 1995; Matthiessen 2007; Butt 2005; and Butt and Wegener 2007).

12   As the following chapters show, the distinction between material situational setting, material elements of situation and relevant context has required constant re-thinking. My latest views are presented in the last chapter of the present volume [notes added 2012, RH].

13   There are degrees of 'encapsulation'; it is seldom an all or none affair. Whatever was there in the situation surrounding the language act, but did not get encapsulated, simply remains 'the material situational setting'; it had the potential of relevance but that potential did not get actualized (Cloran 1994; Hasan *et al.* 2005).

14   With hindsight it is perhaps possible to appreciate that Malinowski was making a distinction between ancillary and constitutive uses of language, which are so closely related to 'local' and 'disembedded/decontextualized knowledge' (Cloran 1994; Hasan 1973c, 2001b).

15   Malinowski also attempted to account for valeur, but this account was less impressive (Hasan 1985a).

16   The data of child language learning, whether studied in a functional perspective or formal, supports this position. One might add also that this is where the foundation of the 'conventional' relationship between the signified and signifier is located. The baby acts as an ideal learner: she/he 'listens' to grasp the meaning; her/his primary contact is with the signifier; the signified is mediated contextually, hence the insistence on 'practical' use of language.

17   See Greaves (2007) on the role of phonology in meaning construal.

18   The case study had begun in early 1970. See Halliday (2003) for substantial discussions.

19   For the role of phonology in the construal of meaning see Greaves (2007).

20   I take 'word' here to stand for 'linguistic pattern'.

21   Later Halliday (1996) used the term 'trinocular perspective' to describe this 'above', 'below' and 'around' context to ensure the viability of description.

22   This paragraph has been introduced here in order to clarify my understanding of how Halliday's SFL may be represented faithfully, without the exclusion of all essential relations. No figures were actually inserted in the chapter originally since most of this information was available from Hasan, Matthiessen and Webster (eds) (2005, 2007).

23   I refer to Chapter 2 entitled Cohesive Categories of an unpublished document (1973b, mimeo), which circulated widely amongst colleagues both in UK and in Australia in the 1970s.

24 For some discussion of his 'discourse semantics' see Matthiessen (2007); for objections to the over-all framework see Hasan (1995) presented in this volume as Chapter 5.

25 Halliday's first use of 'social semiotic' to describe his approach to language occurred in an address to the Eleventh International Congress of Linguists, August 1972, Bologna (Halliday 1975b); he attributed the origin of the term to Greimas (1969).

26 It was the focus on systemic representation of grammar that earned Halliday's model the name of 'systemic linguistics' ('systemics' for short). See Matthiessen (2007) on system networks and the paradigmatic axis.

27 At this stage, the term *meta*-functions was not in use; instead *macro*-function was used to distinguish this sense of 'function' from both the formal function (e.g., Subject, Actor, etc.) and the discursive function such as persuasion, threat, warning, explaining, etc.

28 This figure has been discussed by Butt (2001); Butt and Wegener (2007); Hasan (1995); Halliday (1977a).

29 In the original version, I had elided a few sentences. I have restored all those elisions since some SF colleagues, such as Fawcett, seem to have forgotten the details; they maintain that originally Halliday's metafunctional organization pertained only to the semantic stratum; it did not include 'syntax and lexicon'. Halliday has not altered his position in this respect; in my view these colleagues have just misinterpreted his arguments: their reading has been selective. This is not to claim that Halliday is necessarily right; simply that the argument used to support the invention of a 'systemic syntax' is without a systemic functional basis.

30 Malinowski (1923) had already argued that it was in the experience of participation in early communication in social context that the young child first encountered his mother tongue, and that such early experience of meaning and context working together acted as the mediator of early linguistic meaning for the child.

2 Meaning, context and text – fifty years after Malinowski [1985]

2.1 Introduction

Perhaps a more accurate title for this chapter[1] would have been *Malinowski Forty Years after Himself*, since I am not concerned with reviewing developments in the study of meaning, context and text since Malinowski began writing; rather I would like to review the traditional reviews of Malinowski. Any comparison of his position with that of some of the famous modern authorities in these areas is largely incidental upon this primary concern. The time seems ripe – both historically and academically – for such an enterprise. Historically, we are close to the first centenary of Malinowski's birth, and we are some six decades away from his last writings. But more important is the change in the academic scene: the recent revolution against the so-called Chomskyan revolution in linguistics cannot but draw attention to Malinowski. There has grown a practice, in the past decades, among linguists, anthropologists, AI specialists – in fact just about anyone interested in language – to begin their own discussion of some linguistic problem by first drawing attention to the inadequacies of the present day dominant linguistic models. As an example let me quote Schank and Abelson, AI specialists, who claim that 'linguistics has managed to miss the central problems', because linguists have concerned themselves with '… considerations of semantics at the level of "can one say this string? Will it mean something?". People already know what they want to say and that it is meaningful' (Schank and Abelson 1977: 7): the authors go on to criticize linguists for failing to understand understanding. For this failure they offer the following reasons (Schank and Abelson 1977: 9) [emphasis added, RH]:

semantic features are considerably more important than linguists had generally been willing to acknowledge ... there has been *increasing recognition that context is of overwhelming importance in the interpretation of text*. Implicit real world knowledge is very often applied by the understander [*sic!* RH], and this knowledge can be very highly structured. The appropriate ingredients for extracting the meaning of a sentence, therefore, are often nowhere to be found within the sentence.

To Malinowski, writing in 1923, approximately half a century before Schank and Abelson produced their famous book, none of this would have sounded even original, leave aside revolutionary. In this first essay concerning context, Malinowski claimed (1923: 307) that:

utterance and situation are bound up inextricably with each other and the context of situation is indispensable for the understanding of the words. Exactly as in the reality of spoken or written language, a word without *linguistic context* is a mere figment and stands for nothing by itself, so in the reality of a spoken living tongue, the utterance has no meaning except in the *context of situation*.

I must admit I find Malinowski's formulation preferable to that of Schank and Abelson's, for, in him, there is not the hidden assumption that one's knowledge of the world is sharply distinct from one's knowledge of language. For Malinowski there was a continuity between words and action, between social knowledge and the social semiotic system of language, the recognition of which is only just beginning to become fashionable amongst those dealing with language. But perhaps in making these comments I am anticipating myself, so let me begin by saying what has led me into this topic.

2.1.1 Malinowski among the world of scholars

A few months ago, I was asked if I could name a small book on Malinowski, such as perhaps Culler's *Saussure* (Culler 1976). True to the Malinowski-Firth prediction, my text was affected by the properties of its linguistic context; so I asked: 'How about Fontana Modern Masters?'. I was told they do not have one. I have checked since, and sure enough, Malinowski is no modern master. This state of affairs seems to me quite typical; and it is typical both of Malinowski and of intellectual fashions in the academic world. Let me develop this comment.

2.1.2 High calibre, low visibility

First, it is typical of Malinowski to miss the Modern Masters series. After all, Raymond Firth's *Man and Culture: An Evaluation of the Work of Bronislaw Malinowski* opens as follows (R. Firth 1964: 1. *Emphasis added*, RH.): 'This book has been written because some of us have *thought for a long while that too little attention has been paid to the work of Bronislaw Malinowski.*' With very minor adjustments, I too could have begun with these same words without violating any truth conditions! Of course, Raymond Firth was concerned mainly with Malinowski the anthropologist, about whom Edmund Leach (1964: 119) comments: '… Malinowski transformed ethnography from the museum study of items of custom into the sociological study of systems of action.' Coming from Edmund Leach, this is high praise indeed: he is by no means entirely uncritical of Malinowski's contributions to his chosen field as most anthropologists would agree. Insofar as boundaries in the realm of knowledge have any reality, I shall, however, not be concerned in this paper with Malinowski, the anthropologist. By taking this position, I am claiming a neutral stance about his hypotheses regarding the origins of cultural institutions. Though quite obviously the possibility exists that the same teleological stance could have been carried over into his thinking about language; but, in fact, the situation appears somewhat different, as I hope will emerge later.

An early appraisal of Malinowski's contribution to linguistics comes from one of his close contemporaries, J. R. Firth (1964: 150): 'The most outstanding anthropological contribution to linguistics in recent years is Malinowski's *Supplement* to Ogden and Richards' *Meaning of Meaning.*' And, again writing in *Man and Culture*, R. Firth (1964: 94) declared: 'We can be proud to include him as one of the makers of linguistics as we now understand it in this country.' Though not as caustic in his criticism as Edmund Leach, J. R. Firth could hardly be described as an unquestioning admirer of Malinowski's views on language in relation to context. I mention this to emphasize the fact that the appraisals presented above are taken from discerning readers. The positive endorsements are, thus, doubly interesting as they highlight the fact that despite being seen as a scholar of appreciable stature by some discerning scholars, Malinowski typically did not attract as much attention as might have been expected. The question naturally arises: why has his work been so undervalued? Malinowski's main contribution to linguistics – as J. R. Firth was quick to recognize – was his elaboration of the relationship between language and the context of situation. Today most literature in linguistics, whether concerned with models for the description of language as system, or for text production, text comprehension, for translation, or any other form of application, recognizes the centrality of similar ideas under such impressive labels as 'knowledge of the world', 'belief system', 'logic of conversation', and so on. I doubt if these high-sounding concepts of today are better reasoned out, made more objective, theoretically more viable or even more explicit than Malinowski's own description of context of situation and of culture – which is not to claim perfection. Why has the modern terminology caught on, bringing such prestige to the 'creators' of great ideas, and why is reference to Malinowski still an occasion for his denigration?

2.2   The company Malinowski keeps

I suggest that the questions raised above can bear serious investigation; it might actually provide useful insight into the convention-bound behaviour of the academic community. I shall make a modest beginning in this direction by saying a few words about intellectual fashions, which, at their zenith, are treated by the pundits as totally self-evident, logically sound truths. How the fashions begin is not obvious; sometimes though there are over-arching themes that underlie the categorization of scholars.

2.2.1   The low value of social explanations

Malinowski's categorization in the intellectual field is a case in point: note the good company he keeps in being ignored by Fontana Modern Masters. The series includes neither Boas, nor Sapir, nor Firth – and of course, to think of Whorf in this connection would be total anathema. Turning Bolinger's (1968) phrase around, one might say that our minds are so in the grip of scholarly misrepresentations (Alford 1980; Hasan 1984a, 1985a) that one despairs of Whorf ever getting a fair hearing. But one might wonder: what have Boas, Sapir, Firth and Whorf in common with Malinowski? I would suggest that the obvious thing they have in common is their commitment to the essentially social foundation for a human being's ability to function as an individual. Despite important differences, each of these scholars thought of language as inextricably bound up with culture, of culture as a force essential to the shaping of the individual, while for each the essence of linguistics is, to use Whorf's expression, 'the quest of meaning' (Whorf 1956: 73). In other words, these linguists can be grouped together by virtue of the fact that they attach importance to precisely the two factors for the neglect of which Schank and Abelson upbraid today's linguists – namely, commitment to statements of meaning (Firth 1957) and an acceptance of the centrality of social context in the creation and the interpretation of discourse, linking thus to the shaping of consciousness, which is the centre of individuality.

2.2.2   Rejection of social perspective in linguistics

I suggest that in the consistent neglect of a group of the above type lies the second aspect of what is typical in Malinowski missing the Modern Masters series. By tacit consent it is typical of our time to either ignore such scholars of language, or if they are noticed, it is equally typical for them to be misrepresented. Note for example that when Schank and Abelson criticize modern linguistics for underplaying semantics and for ignoring context, they do not seem to be at all aware of the existence of any of these scholars – and it would be too much to expect that they would look out for distant linguistic traditions such as those popular in Europe. For Schank and Abelson, as for many scholars, linguistics is largely synonymous with the Chomskyan revolution, one of whose main contributions to the field of linguistics is precisely to accentuate this questionable dissociation of language from the life of the speech community.[2] It is hard to choose between this neglect and such misrepresentation of, for example, Malinowski's position as can be found in the writings of linguists such as Palmer or Leech, to mention but two. Needless to say, Whorf probably remains the most misrepresented of all. At the mention of Whorf's name, a galaxy of impressive names immediately springs to mind, such as, Black (1959), Bolinger (1968), Brown (1976), Cole and Scribner (1974), Greenberg (1954), Hockett (1954), Berlin and Kay (1969), Lenneberg (1971) and so on – all claim to have proved that the Whorfian hypothesis 'in its present form' is untenable; some recommending the dubious distinction between a 'weak' and 'strong' Whorfian hypothesis. Ironically, it remains to be demonstrated that what they have refuted is, in fact, *the* Whorfian hypothesis!

There is a danger that these comments might be read as an effort to politicize academic evaluation – worse still, they may be attributed to paranoia. So let me add at once that in drawing attention to the neglect and the misrepresentation of sociologically oriented linguistics, I do not imply any conscious academic conspiracy. However, there remains the fact that *all ideology, including academic ideology, thrives by keeping the other point of view out of view*. One may not set out consciously to achieve this aim, but large differences in ideology inevitably lead to a failure in sharing the assumptions and motivation underlying an enterprise. Notwithstanding the popularity of Gricean maxims (Grice 1975), at least in academic pronouncements it is not automatically and unquestionably evident what constitutes sufficient evidence for saying what is being said – much less, what it means to be truthful, or relevant. Inevitably, if the structure of beliefs, aims and attitudes is at variance, failures in textual interpretations will occur. Instead of interpreting metaphors, such readers arrive at a metamorphosis of the message. The five scholars I have named have all – except perhaps Boas – suffered in this respect. Views have been assigned to them, which the analysis of their own writing would reject as not theirs; their position is exaggerated beyond recognition, rendering their views so untenable as to be suitable only for merciful oblivion.

2.2.3 Nature, culture and individuality

So far I have emphasized that culture as the main driving force in the life of the individual is not a theme that is readily favoured, least of all in linguistics. We insist on seeing the individual as a free agent in a free society, the sole architect of his own destiny, himself the shaper of his own personality. And more relevant to the discussion here, we see him as the most significant element in the production of his parole, if not in the creation of his langue. To be sure, in an important sense, the onset of linguistic behaviour in any instance lies with the individual, and I do not mean by this only what Saussure called the 'executive side' of parole (de Saussure 1966: 13) but also the *motivational and intentional elements of behaviour*: these too must be traced, at least in the first instance, to the individual. But this does not seem to me to be the end of the enquiry into behaviour. If 'individual-ness' is at the core of behaviour, it also seems important to point out that the belief in the autonomy of the human organism turning itself into an individual is neither intuitively obvious nor empirically substantiated. Individuality and inter-subjectivity are mutually dependent; and this argues for a social, i.e., interactive base as essential to the creation of individuality. If we dissociate the individual from his cultural context, insisting that most of what is significant to the shaping of individuality is by definition a-social, then, logically the final mainsprings of intention, motivation and execution have to be sought not so much in the social environment as within the organism.[3] And this, in the last resort, leads to a biologism whose popular name in linguistics is the 'innateness hypothesis'. This popular stance on the individual has the appearance of being entirely reasonable, because in the relevant literature nothing comes to the surface which might throw any doubt on it, such as for example, the obvious fact of cultural differences, such as ideas about beauty, bravery and even gods and morality. The evidence for such cultural differences is so very strong that linguists do have to recognize them; but the segregation of disciplines helps to render the evidence harmless by relegating it to surface phenomena which are said to have only secondary importance in human affairs. It is argued that the deepest stratum consists of the species-specific innate attributes which are by definition universal; by contrast, culture-specific phenomena simply lie on the surface. These attitudes are implicit in the ways in which we talk about meanings, understanding, perception and cognition. So we claim that the semantic space for mankind is the same; or we insist on the centrality of 'the knowledge of the world' rather than of 'acculturation' to understanding; and so far as perception and cognition are concerned, they are thought of as basically the same across the human race. In this view, the physical and material is far more 'real', far more central than the social: metaphorically, we overplay Freud and underplay Durkheim, ignoring that our worst conflicts do not arise from being identical, but from an intolerance of the different.

This preoccupation of modern linguistics with innateness, this insistence on the primacy of intra-organic approach to language (Halliday 1974a, 1977b), is not a breakaway, revolutionary movement. Chomsky (1965) has rightly implied, by referring to distant authorities, that this is a long-standing and popular stance on the Western intellectual scene, which manifests itself in different ways to suit the current dominant ideology of the time. Today's rigid distinction between deep and surface linguistic phenomena is simply a new version of an old academic fashion. Since one assumes the correctness of the tradition which glorifies the innate properties of the human brain, it naturally appears superfluous to ask: what are the factors, if any, which affect the actual development of the potential of this marvellous instrument, the human brain? Those who suggest, as Mead (1934) did, that unlike the human brain, the human mind is a social phenomenon, remain on the periphery of our deliberations about language.[4] This is not because there is a necessary conflict between accepting the species-specific, therefore universal, properties native to the human brain and also acknowledging that the actualization of this potential is subject to social environment (Halliday 1974a, 1975a): the myth of the self-created individuality continues simply because the cultural conventions of academia dictate it; the individual has to be seen as the fulcrum of the social universe. We see then that there is a considerable ideological gulf between those committed to upholding individuality as a divine gift and those for whom the foundation of individuality is essentially in the social experience. Failure in communication between these two groups is not surprising once we see clearly the differences between their basic assumptions. Malinowski, without doubt, belonged to the sociologically oriented group of scholars – as did Mead, Boas, Sapir, Whorf and Firth. The misrepresentation and obscurity from which they have suffered might be described as *an ideologically induced low academic visibility*. However, as I have pointed out there are good reasons for maintaining that individuality is not a meaningful concept without respect for cultural processes.

2.2.4 Breaking away from a-cultural humanity

Be that as it may, in the remainder of this paper, I will focus only on Malinowski the linguist. I intend to argue that his contribution to the study of linguistics deserves less perfunctory, less pejorative and a more serious treatment by the discipline of linguistics. In order to make this case, I will focus mainly on issues relating to context, meaning, and text, since it is in these domains that Malinowski made his main contributions to the study of language. I will first enquire into his views on the relationship between meaning and context; here it seems important to describe the nature of the central problem that Malinowski was attempting to solve. This will take us into a consideration of the Saussurean notion of sign. I will argue that to see the relationship between meaning and context the way that Malinowski saw it implies a recognition of the centrality of human interaction: language without a social community of users is an anomaly.

2.3 Meaning in linguistics

Most semanticists would agree with Palmer (1981: 29) that: 'The problem of semantics is not the search for an elusive entity called "meaning". It is rather an attempt to understand how it is that words and sentences can mean at all ...'. Despite the risk of some oversimplification, it would be correct to claim that the pre-occupations in modern semantics fall under two distinct areas. First there is the concern with questions relating to how a linguistic unit of whatever size comes to have the meaning that it does. To quote Searle (1969: 3): 'How does it happen that when people say, "Jones went home" they almost always mean Jones went home and not, say, Brown went to the party or Green got drunk?' Second, there is the concern with devising techniques following which an explicit representation can be made of the meanings that the linguistic units are perceived to have. It seems to me that important as the second concern is, the first constitutes the substance of our theory of linguistic meaning. And, notwithstanding linguists' disdainful attitude to Malinowski, my claim is that he made his major contribution in this central area of semantics.

2.3.1 Linguistic sign and 'arbitrariness': (i) meaning and sound

It is a commonplace of linguistics that the basic problem – namely, 'how it is that words and sentences can mean at all' – arises from the principle which Saussure (1966: 67) described as 'the arbitrariness of the sign'. This principle according to Saussure (1966: 68) lies at the centre of language; it '... dominates all linguistics ... its consequences are numberless ... (and) not all of them are equally obvious at first glance ...'. Speaking briefly, let me outline what Saussure meant by arbitrariness of the linguistic sign and what he considered as some of its immediate implications. This would help to clarify the problem which, I believe, Malinowski set out, consciously or unconsciously, to resolve. There seems to be sufficient evidence to support the view that Saussure thought of the sign's arbitrariness from two points of view, only one of which is invariably recognized by modern linguists of all persuasions. This popularly recognized aspect of the sign's arbitrariness is described by Culler in the following words (Culler 1976: 19): 'There is no natural or inevitable link between the signifier and the signified ... There is no intrinsic reason why one signifier rather than another should be linked with the concept *dog*.' The *Course* explains that the signifier is un-motivated by meaning in the sense that it 'actually has no natural connection with the signified' (Saussure 1966: 69). Seen from this point of view, the line of arbitrariness between the signifier and the signified coincides with the line which separates the two levels of phonology and phonetics from those of meaning and lexicogrammar (Halliday 1977c).

By contrast, the second aspect of the sign's arbitrariness is not so well publicized: it identifies an issue equally important if not more so. If the first aspect of the sign's arbitrariness concerns the relation between the signified, something as abstract as meaning/idea/concept, and the signifier, a material phenomenon capable of being sensed as an 'acoustic image', the second is concerned with the relation between meaning, that aspect of the sign we call the signified, and those extra-linguistic phenomena, whether concrete or abstract, outside the sign-user or inside, which we treat as (an element of) 'reality': here we are talking about what the 'saying' means, i.e., what it refers to.

2.3.2   Linguistic sign and arbitrariness: (ii) meaning and reality

In the *Course* the term 'signified' is often used as inter-changeable with 'idea', 'concept', and/or 'thought'. In doing this, Saussure's concern had been to argue that 'reality' (i.e., what the sign refers to) does not pre-date the sign, or that language is not a simple naming system. To quote Saussure (1966: 111–112; emphasis added, RH):

> Psychologically our thought – apart from its expression in words – is only a shapeless and indistinct mass. Philosophers and linguists have always agreed in recognizing that without the help of signs we would be unable to make a clear-cut, consistent distinction between two ideas. *Without language, thought is a vague, uncharted nebula. There are no pre-existing ideas, and nothing is distinct before the appearance of language.* … The characteristic role of language with respect to thought is not to create a material phonic means for expressing ideas but to serve as a link between thought and sound, under conditions that of necessity bring about the reciprocal delimitation of units.

The contexts of his discussions, the repeated assertions and the nature of the examples Saussure offered (1966: 111–122) strongly support the interpretation that in his view the relationship of the signified to the extra-linguistic universe was not based on any discernable logical necessity, whether material or intellectual. Concepts, sometimes equated with the 'signifieds', are not delimited by extra-linguistic 'reality' to which sign-units of language 'correspond': rather, concepts relate to reality through signification. Had this not been the case then one could have argued, quite reasonably, for the pre-existence of that which is signified. And had it been possible to hold this latter claim, then it would have been reasonable to think of the signifier simply as a means of expressing/naming a bit of material/abstract reality.

Thus Saussure (1966: 116) points out: 'If words stood for the pre-existing concepts, they would all have exact equivalents in meaning from one language to the next ...'. The physical properties of the phenomena around us do not contain within them any principle whereby they 'themselves' might be segmented into 'referent' units. The fact that a certain domain of physical experience is referred to by *mutton* and *sheep*, in one language, while in another, the same sense data is referred to only by *mouton*, could not possibly be governed by a principle that relies on a material or logical basis. Thus the relationship between the signified and the bits of the extra-linguistic reality to which it relates (by signification) is itself arbitrary – and this is the second, less widely recognized, aspect of the arbitrariness of the linguistic sign to which the *Course* draws the reader's attention. To accept these views about the arbitrariness of the linguistic sign is tantamount to the rejection of the existence of any rational principle(s)[5] for predicting what aspect of extra-linguistic reality any sign might be applicable to: this remains true even if the principle is called 'correspondence theory'. These claims about meaning and reality, original though they might sound, are no more than just a conservative interpretation of Saussure's foundational thinking. Hjelmslev (1961) presents the same view in claiming that reality is kaleidoscopic; it is given a shape, i.e., aspects of it are imbued with reality for the speakers of a language, largely because of the operation of the linguistic signs themselves.

These two aspects of the sign's arbitrariness give rise to most of the productive problems in the study of language. Of these the more relevant to my topic is the second, because it raises the question of the identity, the value and the signification of the linguistic sign.

2.3.3 Linguistic meaning: identity, value and signification of the sign

According to my reading of Saussure (1966), he was able to provide a clearer indication of how he saw a sign's identity and value to be established, but he had relatively less to say about how signification might be established.[6] It is at least a theoretical commonplace of linguistics today that the identity and the value of a sign are determined by treating both the signifier and the signified as 'purely relational entities'.[7] Thus the value of the plural in a three-term system, e.g., in Sanskrit, is different from its value in a two-term system, as in French (Saussure 1966: 116). Firth (1957) maintained that the nature of language is systemic; I would suggest that this systemic quality has evolved in the semiotic system of language in all likelihood as a counterweight to the arbitrary nature of the linguistic sign. In the last resort, the value and identity of the linguistic sign is the defining property of language as a semiotic system: it forms the basis of what I have called (1999a) the 'semo-logic' of language.

2.3.4   Signification and value: one Saussurean paradox

Saussure maintained a clear distinction between value and signification. 'Value' is the function of relations between entities of the same order, e.g., between the dime and the dollar; the value of a dime resides in its relation to a quarter, a nickel, a penny, etc. Its signification, by contrast, resides in 'what it can be exchanged for' (Saussure 1966: 115); i.e., in its relation to entities of a different order. In the case of the dime, for example, one might ask what fixed quantity of bread or milk one might be able to buy with it. The contrast between value and signification is quite clear from this Saussurean example. Value is system-internal, being defined by the relation of one sign to another in the system. As is well recognized in linguistics, this way of conceptualizing value brings it closest to the concept of the 'sense' of a sign (Lyons 1968, 1977). Signification, on the other hand, is not a system-internal relation; it is concerned with the relation between the sign and what the sign is a sign for. This brings the term 'signification' quite close to at least one interpretation of the term 'reference'.

Clear as the distinction is, I believe, it would go against Saussure's intentions to give the impression that the two concepts are completely independent of each other. Let me elaborate this point. As indicated above, Saussure made signification subservient to value. He claimed that without the relations (which determine the value of the sign), 'signification would not exist' (Saussure 1966: 117); if the signification of French *mouton* and English *mutton* is not entirely identical, this is because their value is not identical; indeed it could not be, given that two systems of relations in which they participate are distinct – not simply because the systems belong to two distinct languages but because the systems are not identical. When the relationship is expressed this way, it would appear logical to suppose that so long as the value of the sign can be established without dependence upon its signification, one should be home and dry; the theory would be free of problems and both aspects of the meaning of a sign would have a clear status. Unfortunately, in the *Course*, this does not happen, and before long we find ourselves knee-deep in muddy waters.

If we ask: what kind of relations are essential to the determination of the value of a sign, the standard answer will invoke the concepts of 'syntagm' and 'paradigm'. But I am not convinced that Saussure's 'associative bonds' are entirely interchangeable with 'paradigm', especially if by paradigm is meant a set of items capable of acting as fillers in a slot. This conception of paradigm is more in tune with, for example, Zellig Harris' 'distributional sets' and carries the implication that paradigms can be constructed without awareness of the signification of signs (Harris 1951). It seems obvious that Saussure did not intend his associative bonds to be based entirely on structural relations at the level of grammar. Consider, for example, his treatment of the French word *enseignement* (teaching). I would draw attention, here, particularly to the bond that, according to Saussure, holds between *enseignement* and *apprentissage, education.* It is quite obvious that the quality of the bond between the items here is such that neither, say, *finissage* nor *imploration* could be included in the set. If *enseignement, apprentissage* and *education* constitute members of a paradigm, then this paradigm can be characterized only as a set 'belonging to the same general area of signification' – what we would describe today, perhaps, as 'the same semantic field'.

If this reading is accepted, there is an unavoidable, and, I suspect, perhaps an un-intentional circularity in Saussure's treatment of value and signification. To the question: How is signification of a sign determined?, we have the answer: By its value. To the question: How is the value of a sign determined?, we have the answer: By its associative bonds, one of which is the bond of significative domain. We arrive, then, at an impasse; no signification without value, but equally, *value is unknowable without signification.* This provokes the observation that despite a long and resolute tradition, the ultimate basis for sense relation does not, indeed, could not, lie entirely in the value of the signs; the various conventionally recognized sense relations must rely equally strongly on the referential potential, i.e., the signification of the signs. Seen from this point of view, what began apparently as the subservience of signification to value, resolves itself into a *mutually defining relation.* At the same time, on the basis of other examples in the *Course*, it could be maintained that on other occasions Saussure saw signification as primary – after all, the *raison d'être* of the language sign is not so that it can enter into system(s) of relations; if there is any reason for its existence it is so that it can signify something. Despite this, the *Course* fails to solve this puzzle: how is the relation of signification to be thought of? The question hangs in the air: given that linguistic sign is arbitrary, how do we know that a sign, say, *dog* applies to this or that class of entity, how do we know that people mean *Jones went home* when they produce the sentence 'Jones went home'?

Of course, I am not suggesting that there are no answers in the *Course* at all; only that all answers themselves are problematic. Thus the answer discussed above at some length, is: 'by knowing the value of the signs'. Another answer to be located in the discussions of the *Course* is: 'by knowing the conventions of the speech community'. I have drawn attention to a serious problem in the first answer: it gives with one hand what it takes away with the other. Let me now point to another problem which is inherent in both these answers: this is the problem of the novice trying to learn the language. How, for example, would an infant break into a system of this kind? Obviously not by first constructing the total network of relations into which the signs enter.[8] This would be impossible, both theoretically, because of the interdependence of value and signification, and biologically, in view of the baby's cognitive capacities at this stage. And, if we say that the child learns both value and signification concurrently by being exposed to the conventions of his speech community, the question still remains: how are the conventions of a language made accessible to an immature novice? Quite apart from: how did the conventions begin?

2.4   Malinowski and the intractable problem of signification

It is my belief that Malinowski's main contributions to semantics lay in his attempts to provide an answer to this basic dilemma. Interpreted thus, his work does not run counter to Saussure's; rather, it complements it – it develops suggestions that were no more than hints in Saussure's own writing. It was thus for a good reason that Malinowski raised the question of the infant learning how to mean. Palmer has recently rejected the relevance of this question to the study of meaning, maintaining with certainty: 'We shall not solve problems of semantics by looking at a child learning language, for an understanding of what he does raises precisely the same problems as those of understanding what adults do in their normal speech' (Palmer 1981: 23).

Obviously not all problems in semantics are solved by looking at the child's learning of language. However, Palmer seems to have overstated his case, for there are undeniable differences between the adult and the child. It is only in the case of the adult that the question of an appeal to the notion of semantic competence can be at all entertained, as, for example, by Geoffrey Leech when he concludes his discussion of the ambiguous

phrasal verb *put on* as follows (Leech 1974: 80): 'It is part of our COM-
PETENCE (the rules, categories and so on, that we know by virtue of being
speakers of the English language) to know that *put ... on* has at least the
three dictionary meanings.' And, a few lines later, he goes on to add (Leech
1974: 80): 'We have a justification for ignoring as far as possible the study
of context where it interferes with the study of competence. At least we
see that the study of meaning-in-context is logically subsequent to the
study of semantic competence ...'. Whatever the position for the adult, the
claims[9] Leech makes here cannot be applied to the infant; even an extreme
'nativist' approach would baulk at the idea of innate semantic competence
in infants whereby the value and signification of each linguistic sign is
already located within the folds of the baby's brain. This debate is central
to a clarification of Malinowski's position.

2.4.1   Malinowski's project: the ontogenesis of 'meaning'

Malinowski was not primarily searching for a methodology for the description of the contents of an adult's already existing semantic competence;
rather, the question he sought to answer was: how is such semantic competence created? Two important things follow from this point of departure. First, unlike Leech, for Malinowski, assigning some meaning to a
linguistic unit, i.e., perceiving the value and the signification of the sign,
is not a 'natural' act. The question of how meaning should be described
is logically subsequent to the question: how is the semantic content of a
sign established in the first place? In Palmer's words 'how it is that words
and sentences mean at all'. Second, this preoccupation of Malinowski's
provided him a coherent principle for putting together certain varieties of
language, groupings that at first sight might appear ill-assorted. What can
be in common to 'the infantile uses of words, of primitive forms of significance and of prescientific language among ourselves' (Malinowski 1923:
318) is the fact that in each of these cases, language has 'an essentially
pragmatic character; ... it is a mode of behaviour, an indispensable element
of concerted human action' (Malinowski 1923: 316).

I am tempted to suggest that Malinowski saw the pragmatic function
of language as the primary one, precisely because of its centrality to the
problem of signification. If a sign system is as pervasively arbitrary as
the system of language is, then the only way the signification of signs
can begin to be learnt, i.e., semantic competence begin to be created, is
through the regularity of the correspondence between the sign and what

the sign can establish contact with in the reality of life. From this point of view, those contexts are more important in which such correspondence is immediately observable. And, not surprisingly, these contexts happen to be the ones where language has a 'pragmatic function' in the sense in which Malinowski used the terms; thus, according to Malinowski (1935: 52; emphasis added RH): 'The pragmatic relevance of words is greatest when these words are uttered within the situation to which they belong and uttered so that they achieve an immediate practical effect. *For it is in such situations that words acquire their meaning.*' It is in the environment of such a discussion that Malinowski (1923: 312) makes a claim for the '… dependence of the meaning of each word upon practical experience, and of the structure of each utterance upon the momentary situation in which it is spoken.' Interestingly, it is also in this type of textual environment that the widely misrepresented, and by now infamous, sentences by Malinowski occur. Consider, for example, (Malinowski 1923: 312; emphasis added RH): 'In *its primitive uses, language functions as a link in concerted human activity*, as a piece of human behaviour. It is a *mode of action, not an instrument of reflection.*'

2.4.2 Malinowski, the crude contextualist

Much has been written about these views of Malinowski's. Often a reader might come across comments which leave the impression that Malinowski *only* discussed 'primitive' situations, or that Malinowski's view on the relationship of context to language were made only with reference to 'primitive' languages; often, through a juxtaposition of their names, a reader might be led to believe that there is no appreciable difference between Bloomfield's and Malinowski's so far as their views on meaning are concerned; often the impression will be given that language as 'a mode of action, not an instrument of reflection' is a characterization Malinowski applied indiscriminately to all uses of language. Not one scholar appears to have noticed that there is something peculiar about Malinowski's use of the words 'pragmatic' and 'action', that the domain of their signification in his writings is much wider than it is in our normal usage. I will discuss some of these issues below, beginning with the following citations as proof that Malinowski's position has been misrepresented. First, take Geoffrey Leech who tells us:

> It is noticeable that the situations to which Malinowski, Bloomfield
> and Morris naturally turn when they want to illustrate the contextual-
> ist thesis are all 'primitive' in one sense or another. In fact, contextu-
> alism in its crudest form … is incapable of dealing with any but the
> most unsophisticated circumstances in which linguistic communica-
> tion occurs (say, telling a story, giving a lecture, gossiping about the
> neighbours, reading a news bulletin) observing the situation in which
> speaker and listener find themselves will tell little, if anything, about
> the meaning of the message. (Leech 1974: 74)

The 'contextualist thesis' of Malinowski is about as different from that of
Bloomfield's as Saussure's structuralism is different from that of Harris' or
Chomsky's; and without doubt all of these cases differ appreciably from
Morris' views. Granting the limitations of a short introductory book where
Leech's comment occurs, the fact should still not be overlooked that these
are the ways in which academic profiles are constructed: the view that
Malinowski's 'situation' is the same as Bloomfield's situation (1935) is
widespread. No matter how practical the reasons for juxtaposing the two
names, the result in my opinion is misinformation. Further, even if we were
willing to grant that the only sophisticated uses are those involving displaced language and/or abstract notions as implied by Leech, not all situations which Malinowski discusses could possibly be said to be 'primitive'.
The situations he discussed in some detail included displaced language as
in the telling of story, gossip, boast, magical and religious rituals and decision making. Although Malinowski's account of how context of situation
operated in the interpretation of, say, a story is far from comprehensive, it
is incorrect to suggest that he avoided all but the most simplistic situations
such as perhaps those for the use of direct directives.

Finally, the reason Malinowski insisted on the primacy of 'pragmatic'
contexts, in the sense in which he used that word, is well stated in Leech's
words. It brings home the point that the relationship between words and
context of situation is variable. In their exchanges of meaning, very
young children certainly do not go in for reflection and abstraction. As
commenting on children's use of language, Malinowski points out 'the
pragmatic relevance of words is greatest when these words are uttered
within the situation in which they belong …' (Malinowski 1935: 52).
This, however, did not preclude on his part the recognition of other ways
of using language; rather it implied that there exist contexts of situation
with a qualitatively different relationship to language (see for example his
discussion of stories and rituals in *Coral Gardens and Their Magic* 1935).

To give the impression, even if inadvertently, that there is any disagreement on this point between Leech's position and that of Malinowski's is simply erroneous. Let me add also, that to Malinowski we owe the insight which, incidentally, will always elude atomistic theories of meaning: that the actual environment in which one encounters a text is never irrelevant to its full interpretation; this is quite evident if we compare the interpretations of Shakespeare across the centuries and across distinct cultures (Bohannan 1971).

2.4.3 Malinowski on 'primitive' language as a mode of action

Consider now another opinion, this time by Palmer, another notable scholar in the field of semantics:

> Malinowski's remarks about language as a mode of action are useful in reminding us that language is not simply a matter of stating information. But there are two reasons why we cannot wholly accept his arguments. First, he believed that the 'mode of action' aspect of language was most clearly seen in the 'basic' needs of man as illustrated in the languages of the child or of primitive man. He assumed that the language he was considering was more primitive than our own and thus more closely associated with the practical needs of the primitive society. (Palmer 1981: 52)

It is true that in his earlier work Malinowski (1923) expressed the belief that word and action were so closely related only in primitive languages, i.e., languages of the technologically primitive communities. But in his later publications, he revised this view quite explicitly as shown below:

> I want to make it quite clear that I am not speaking here only of the Trobriand language, still less of native speech in agriculture. I am trying to indicate the character of human speech in general and the necessary methodological approach to it. Every one of us could convince himself from his own experience that language in our own culture often returns to its profoundly pragmatic character. Whether engaged in a technical manipulation, pursuing some sporting activity, or conducting a scientific experiment in a laboratory or assisting each other by word and deed in a simple manual task – words which cross from one actor to another do not serve primarily to communicate

> thought: they connect word and correlate manual and bodily move-
> ments. Words are part of action and they are equivalents to action.
> (Malinowski 1935: 8–9)

Now, on reading this extract, one may react violently against Malinowski's
views on language and thought; however, so far as Palmer's criticism is
concerned it loses a good deal of its force. As we see, the mode of action
aspect applies universally to human languages, not simply to infantile and
primitive ones, though in the latter, it is more marked as also in 'unscien-
tific language among ourselves' (Malinowski 1923: 318), which on reflection does not seem an unreasonable comment. Leaving the infant language
learning aside for the moment, I would read this as a claim about register.
That the register repertoire of non-literate communities does differ from
that of the literate ones is now a recognized fact[10] (Goody 1968, 1977);
that the role of language as instrument, as a mode of action, is variable
across context types is also undeniable. Although Malinowski remarked
on the structural peculiarities of primitive languages, in his writings, it is
the diatypic aspect of their 'primitiveness' to which he drew attention most
frequently; here is a lengthy extract:

> written statements are set down with the purpose of being self-
> contained and self-explanatory. A mortuary inscription … a chapter
> or statement in a sacred book … a passage from a Greek or Latin phi-
> losopher … one and all of these were composed with the purpose of
> bringing their message to posterity unaided, and they had to contain
> this message within their own bounds.
>
> To take … a modern scientific book, the writer of it sets out to
> address every individual reader who will peruse the book and has
> the necessary scientific training … we might be tempted to say met-
> aphorically that the meaning is wholly contained in or carried by the
> book.
>
> But when we pass from a modern civilized language, … to a prim-
> itive tongue, never used in writing ... there it should be clear at once
> that the conception of meaning as contained in an utterance is false
> and futile. (Malinowski 1923: 306–307)

It appears, then, that although Palmer is right in criticizing Malinowski for
thinking in terms of primitive and civilized languages, he is wrong in attrib-
uting to Malinowski the view that the action mode of language is applicable
only to infantile and primitive languages; obviously, Malinowski thought

of these simply as two of the environments which function as the domain, *par excellence*, for the operation of language in its action mode. That words as 'equivalents to action' are more likely to be found in extempore spoken use of language in the course of 'concerted human activities' seems to me quite undeniable; and that 'primitive' communities characteristically lack a written mode of expression also appears obvious.[11]

2.4.4 Infants learning how to mean

But what about the infant? Is Malinowski justified in thinking that language as a mode of action is necessarily a primary stage in the ontogenesis of language? Does a consideration of the child learning language help us to solve any problems in semantics, or is it a fruitless pursuit as Palmer suggests?

Recent studies, not only the functionally oriented ones (Halliday 1975a, 1979a; Bullowa 1979a, Wells 1981), but any others which consider meaning as central to human language (Brown 1973; Bruner 1972; Clark 1973; Dore 1974; Greenfield and Smith 1976; Karmiloff-Smith 1979 and others) provide more than just a sufficient hint that Malinowski's views on the development of language in the young child were surprisingly near the mark. Definitely the action mode of language comes to the fore in the earliest proto linguistic and linguistic systems of communication employed by the child. Malinowski's claim (1923: 319) is that 'The child acts by sound at this stage and acts in a manner which is both adapted to the outer situations, to the child's mental state and which is also intelligible to the surrounding adults.' For the young child, the vocal symbols he produces are 'equivalents of action', and they are of value because of their ability to produce relevant action on the part of others. If it is true that in learning language, the child is learning how to mean (Halliday 1975a), then certainly the child's earliest experiences in (proto-)linguistic communication are of interest. At birth the baby has no access to the verbal signs of the mother tongue; he recognizes neither the signifier nor the signified; but in a few years' time he has 'worked out' a system of relations whereby most of the signs he uses will be imbued with the meanings conventional to his speech community. To study this process cannot but increase our understanding of how a linguistic unit comes to have a meaning in the life of an individual; and this is certainly an important question in semantics.

In his discussion of language development, Malinowski argued that: 'In all the child's experience, words mean in so far as they act and not in so far as they make the child understand and apperceive (1923: 321).' According to Malinowski, the function of language as an instrument of reflection arises at a later stage; he seems to argue that both in the history of the human race and of the individual, the use of language as a mode of action is primary; its use as a mode of reflection is historically later. Hence it is often described as 'secondary' or 'derived'. The suggestion that ontogeny is a replication of phylogeny is beyond the possibilities of proof, but so far as the individual infants of today are concerned, recent research supports the hypothesis of the primacy of the pragmatic function in the young child's development. But what does this tell us about the learning of meaning?

2.4.5   The problem of meaning in learning the mother tongue

It would be misleading to imply that Malinowski provided a detailed answer to this question, but certainly his argument is coherent and clear. In the first place one has to remember the characteristic quality of the pragmatic environment; it is here that there is 'the dependence of the meaning of each word upon practical experience'; language for Malinowski acts upon the environment:

> a small child acts upon its surroundings by the emission of sound which is the expression of its bodily needs and is, at the same time, significant to the surrounding adult. The meaning of this utterance consists in the fact that it defines the child's wants and sets going a series of actions in his social environment. … As inarticulate sounds pass into simple articulations, these at first refer to significant people, or else are vague indications of surrounding objects, above all of food, water, and favoured toys or animals. … As soon as words form … they are also used for the expression of pleasure or excitement … (but) it is when they are used in earnest that they mobilize the child's surroundings. Then the uttered word becomes a significant reaction adjusted to the situation, expressive of the inner state and intelligible to the human milieu. (Malinowski 1935: 6)

The child learns the meanings of the signs of his mother tongue because for the most part the words he is concerned with occur in conjunction with the surrounding socially recognized material reality. His case then runs parallel to the so-called savage; as Malinowski would claim:

The meaning of a word arises out of familiarity, out of ability to use, out of the faculty of direct clamouring as with the infant, or practically directing as with primitive man. *A word is used always in direct active conjunction with the reality it means.* (1923: 322–323; emphasis added. RH)

This must mean also that the determination of the domain of signification is not a sudden thing; it occurs largely because of the regularity of correlation between the sign and what the sign is a sign for. Equally, for the infant, the value of a sign is not determined in one fell swoop; the regular patterns of use in the child's social milieu must play a role in this process and this could be effective only where there is a good deal of 'referential transparency'. This *referential transparency is ensured for the greater portion of the signs in those environments where language acts as instrument.* Recent studies – especially those in the child's learning of the lexicon – have drawn attention to the phenomena of 'overextension' and/or 'narrowing'. The evidence appears strong that the approximate mastery of the acoustic shape of the sign, i.e., the signifier, cannot be confused with the mastery of the signified. The child appears to go through a stage where both the value and the signification of the mother tongue signs are in the process of being defined. Both the sense and reference, the value and the signification, relations have to grow side by side, before the child can reach the stage of approximation to the adult system. In the interim, the child's use as well as understanding of a mother-tongue-like-sign is not the same as in the adult's usage: the signs do not have the meaning for the child which the adult's dictionary credits the sign with; this is a far cry from the acquisition of semantic competence. To study the processes whereby the child's meaning of a sign approximates the adult's meaning of that sign is to study, at least partially, how a linguistic unit comes to have meaning at all. Malinowski was well aware of these implications of the study of 'infantile' utterances:

I believe this problem will have to be studied in infantile speech if we are to arrive at the most important foundations for the science of semantics: I mean the problem of how far and through what mechanisms speech becomes to the child an active and effective force which leads him inevitably to the belief that words have a mystical hold on reality. (Malinowski 1935: 65)

I am suggesting that Malinowski's answer to Saussure's problem of signification was to introduce the concept of context of situation and of culture.

This latter, he sometimes described as the 'context of reference' (1935: 51). The question how a linguistic sign such as *dog* comes to signify an extra-linguistic entity belonging to the class DOG is answered by saying that the process involves an active experience of the word in conjunction with reality within a culturally recognizable context of situation. This is the primary means of entry into the language system. Note that ultimately, the appeal is to convention; but, unlike Saussure, Malinowski provides a clearer indication of what is essential – or at least one aspect of what is essential – to the learning of conventions. The view that the pragmatic context provides the most hospitable environment for the learning of conventions is interestingly in agreement with Lewis' view that conventions arise and are ratified in co-operative problem solving (Lewis 1968). Essentially, then, for Malinowski, meaning is a social semiotic process. He rejected the strong Western tradition of treating meaning as mental entities – concepts, thoughts and ideas having an existence independent of language.

There is indeed a danger in thinking of meaning as a concept. Austin, for example, complains (Austin 1979: 41) of the tendency to treat concept, perhaps because the word is a noun, as 'an article of property, a pretty straightforward piece of goods', which can be part of the 'furniture' of man's mind. Once this step is taken, we may find ourselves recognizing a simple 'commonsense reality' with Leech, namely that, 'meaning is a mental phenomenon and it is useless to pretend otherwise' (Leech 1974). But claims about the 'mental-ness' of phenomena can mean such different things; one needs to be clear how the expression is used. There is a very obvious sense in which every piece of knowledge, practical or created by intellectual activity, is mental. Whatever the child's or adult's understanding of the linguistic sign *dog*, this understanding is surely 'in the brain'; further, it is only because of the structure of the brain that it is possible for humans to arrive at understandings of this sort. But in a rather important sense it does not make the meaning of the sign *dog* a mental phenomenon; *the dictionary may be located in the brain but the specific details relating to each entry in the mental dictionary originate not in the brain but in the social human milieu.*[12] Meaning and mind are created in a social environment (Greenfield 1997; Deacon 1997), through social agencies as Luria (1976) has argued on a basis stronger than that of sheer speculation as is done in today's linguistics. By placing emphasis on the role of cultural contexts in the learning of meaning, Malinowski provides support for Saussure's claim that the discipline of linguistics is an important part of the science of semiology, which is by necessity social.

2.5 Malinowski's concept of language

The comment seems justified, then, that Malinowski is not in opposition to Saussure: not only does he agree with Saussure in believing that, as a sign system, language is embedded in the social life of a community, but also he seems to take into account the existence of the language internal relations, which were emphasized by Saussure as essential for the operation of the linguistic sign. Whatever his reservations might have been against the Durkheimian principle of 'conscience collective', he does not deny the most crucial characteristic of language, namely its coherent inner structure, and the centrality of this to the 'meaningfulness' of a sign. This is obvious from his treatment of a part of the semantic field of 'garden site' in Kiriwinian. In dealing with the relations between such signs of the language as *buyagu, odila, yosewo, baleko, bagula* and others, he shows that he has a fairly sophisticated notion of the linguistic sign. That discussion is concluded as follows (Malinowski 1935: 16): 'The definition of the word consists partly in placing it within its cultural context, partly in illustrating its usage in the context of opposites and of cognate expressions.'

Nor is it possible to maintain the view that Malinowski was so simpleminded about language as to advocate the naming theory of meaning. Consider Malinowski (1935: 21): 'It is obvious that words do not live as labels attached to pieces of cultural reality. Our Trobriand garden is not a sort of botanical show with tags tied on to every bush, implement or activity.' His terminology surely differs from that of professional linguists, but I doubt if his understanding of the relations into which signs enter is less advanced than many practising linguists. Here is Malinowski:

> words do not exist in isolation ... words are always used in utterances. ... A one-word sentence, such as a command ... may ... be significant through its context of situation only. Usually a one-word sentence will have to be explained by connecting it with utterances which preceded it or which follow. To start with single words ... is the wrong procedure. But this I do not need to elaborate; for it is now a commonplace of linguistics that the lowest unit in language is the sentence not the word ... *even the sentence is not a self-contained, self-sufficient unit of speech. Exactly as a single word is ... meaningless and receives its significance through the context of other words, so a sentence usually appears in the context of other sentences and has meaning only as a part of a larger significant whole.* (Malinowski (1935: 22; emphasis added, RH)

In these words of Malinowski, we have the precursor to J. R. Firth's view of meaning as a 'complex of contextual relations' (Firth 1957: 19).

Malinowski was ahead of his time in drawing attention to the relevance of context of situation to the study of language as he was also in predicting the importance of functional approaches to developmental linguistics. At the same time he was, without doubt, one of the few scholars first to point out the need for treating the text as central to the interpretation of the linguistic units of all sizes. For him, unlike Lyons, the language system was not a set of sentences (Lyons 1977: 585); it was a resource for the living of communal life in culturally created contexts, which implies, from the very beginning, the recognition of text as a significant unit of linguistic analysis. That these intuitive insights were not developed by him into a well-articulated coherent linguistic theory is certainly true (Palmer 1981: 53); but this does not throw into doubt the acuteness of his insight, especially when we realize that today, even half a century after him, a theoretical approach of the type he recommended cannot be found in the currently valued reflections of the often-cited authorities in the areas of pragmatics, developmental linguistics, dominant semantics and discourse analysis. Let us focus here simply on the connection between meaning and text: far from treating sentence as 'the lowest unit in language' as Malinowski suggested, the main preoccupation of semantic experts until very recently has been with isolated words. Thanks to logic and philosophy, progress has meant a shift of interest from words to sentences, or to be accurate, more frequently, simple clauses. But these too now receive attention each in isolation from its textual environment. In fact, since most examples are conjured up by linguists trying to prove a point, these can have no natural textual environment; they arise out of nothing, lead into nothing and themselves are nothing compared to the naturally functioning sentences of a 'live tongue' used in the service of natural human activity.

2.6   Meaning, text and context in Malinowski

What is most remarkable about Malinowski's hypotheses regarding meaning, text and context is the fact that his approach spans rather than exaggerates the distance between *langue* and *parole*. He views social context as playing a crucial role in the transmission of language to the next generation; in this process, by implication, text functions as a bridge between the context and the system: it is thus easier to see the dialectic between parole and langue whereby the system is shaped by the process while the process itself is an instantiation of the system. That the hypothesis of some such dialectic between *langue* and *parole* is essential to the theory of linguistics has been implied by the convincing arguments by sociolinguists (Labov 1972a, Weinreich, Labov and Herzog 1968); that it is also essential to the solution of at least some of the problems in the study of meaning is rarely recognized (Halliday 1973a, 1978). To set up a dissociation between system and process – between *langue* and *parole* – of the kind that Lyons appears to recommend (1977: 622 ff.) leaves us in the midst of many problems. His strong classification between *system-sentence* and *text-sentence* appears to be motivated by a desire to maintain a clear boundary between competence and performance; and there is more than a hint in Lyons that 'linguistics proper' is concerned with competence alone, while performance is the domain of stylistics and sociolinguistics (Lyons 1977: 585).

It is clear that such a view runs counter to Malinowski's position; for him context is not something to which one appeals simply in order to find the appropriate interpretation of some multivalent lexeme such as *plant* (Lyons 1977: 582) or *put on* (Leech 1974: 80); nor is it a device for simply sorting out the local situational referents of deixis or ellipsis. Malinowski's view of how context functions in the creation and use of the verbal symbolic system would do all this, but more. For him it constitutes the ever-present series of semiotic frames in conjunction with which the signification of the linguistic signs is defined. It is the wide social matrix within which the sign operates, and by doing so, acquires a value in the system while reinforcing a signification in the world of active experience.

It is difficult to accept Lyons' contention that a set of system-sentences constitutes the 'language system' (Lyons 1977: 586). There is no advantage in thinking of language as a set of sentences of any kind, even if we add the qualification of infinity to the set. Rather, language is a network of systemic relations, the systematicity of which permits the generation of any number of sentences – *the language system is not a product; it is a principle*. There is sufficient evidence in our ignorance of how to account for comprehension and production of ordinary day-to-day discourse to permit the claim that this undue emphasis on sentence as the central concern of linguistics has been unfortunate for the development of the field of linguistics. It is now widely recognized that no matter how rich our description of the sentence might be, it can *never* hope to throw light on the real unit of human interaction – namely the *text* (van Dijk 1977; Petofi 1978; Hasan 1979b). Even more importantly, no framework for the description of the sentence can be complete, without the means of relating it to its environment, both linguistic and extra-linguistic. This naturally implies that there has to be some kind of systematic relationship between a system sentence and its analogous text-sentence. If this relationship is one of abstraction whereby system sentences are 'derived from utterances by the elimination of all the context-dependent features of utterances' (Lyons 1977: 588), it is difficult to see why system-sentences must be regarded as central to 'linguistics proper', while text-sentences are not. After all, the text sentences would have to be understood and analysed in a principled manner to enable the abstraction of the system sentences from them. If so, it seems more reasonable to suggest that the text sentences should be the focus of the linguist's attention since they would subsume the properties of the system sentences – not the other way round.

In the Malinowskian conception of the relation between sign and context, there is no aspect of the meaning of a sign, its value or signification, that is, as it were, constructed by the speech community in isolation from the context. For example, according to this view, the interpretation of the so-called 'de-contextualized' declarative sentence type – i.e., its semantic value, as STATEMENT is based simply on the fact that in a wide range of actual contexts, this sentence type most frequently has the function of STATEMENT. In other words, it is how this sentence type typically functions as a text-sentence that gives its analogous system-sentence a particular value. A more powerful, because more comprehensive, model of semantics would, in my opinion, be one that provides a systematic account of how classes of text-sentences are interpreted by normal speakers; it is this which, of necessity, provides the foundation for the identification of the heart of Lyons' so-called 'linguistics proper', i.e., the system-sentences.

And, again, Lyons' concept of 'decontextualization' is intriguing; he defines it, at least implicitly, (1977: 589) as 'the elimination of all the context-dependent features of utterances' (p. 588), and later in the discussion of the interpretation of an elliptical sentence it is said to 'consist in supplying some element or elements from the preceding co-text' (p. 589). In other words, the de-contextualization of a text sentence consists in the explicitization of all implicit encoding devices whether ENDOPHORIC or exophoric (Halliday and Hasan 1976, 1985; Hasan 1973a, 1973b, 1979b, 1984a). But surely this explicitization is subject to as regular rules as any other set of 'grammatical rules'. More accurately, while the most specific interpretation of, say, the pronoun *he* would vary from one context of situation to the other, there is no doubt that *he* has a general meaning, which transcends instantial details (Hasan 1984a). This general meaning may be stated as 'one (co-)textually identified human male', where (co-)textual identification would equal co-reference to the nearest explicitly mentioned one human male, unless there is good reason to reject this equation. The good reasons for the rejection of the equation, if any, will be found within the accompanying text of the sentence under focus. Thus decontextualization is not merely local and random; a large part of decontextualization – which in everyday contact with language amounts, after all, simply to principle based 'interpretation' – is entirely systematic even if the details of the system may not be entirely obvious to us at this point in the development of linguistics. From whatever point of view one looks at the distinction between system-sentence and text-sentence, the theoretical value of this distinction appears questionable, unless one were to trivialize the notion text-sentence to mean sentences which contain errors of performance *á la* Chomsky. Sentence, after all, is just a sign – though one of an order different from other orders of signs; it seems more viable to think of language as a set of concurrent systems of options, where the selection of some path(s) is actualized as a particular sentence, this actualization itself being motivated by the context of situation in which the speaker happens to find himself. Whatever Malinowski's shortcomings as a theoretician, for him context of situation was not simply a cure for ambiguity, nor a searchlight for picking out the specifics; for him, it was integral to the study of language since in his view the creation of semantic competence depends entirely on the systematic operation of language in social context – and, more basic than that, it provides a viable hypothesis of how the signification of signs is established for the members of a speech community. At least at the moment we have no better theory of signification, even though I might concur with Palmer (1981) that Malinowski's pronouncements lacked theoretical coherence.

2.7   Malinowski, a shallow pragmatist

I hope I have demonstrated both Malinowski's contribution to the Saussurean theory of meaning and his far from naive view of the nature of the linguistic sign system. It seems amazing, then, that instead of getting acclaim and recognition, he has more often earned criticism. Consider, for example, E. Leach who upbraids him for the shallowness of his pragmatism. Tracing the origin of the movement of pragmatism to C. S. Peirce, Leach comments highly favourably on the quality of Peirce's work, which, according to him, is:

now recognized as one of the major influences leading to the development of mid-twentieth-century logical positivism. William James was a friend and colleague of Peirce … Peirce was austere, retiring, philosophic, [*while*, RH] James was a public figure, a missionary propagandist with a wide popular appeal. James' pragmatism is a creed rather than a philosophy. … Malinowksi's pragmatism is that of James' rather than Peirce. (Leach 1957: 121–122)

Regretfully, I was not able to consult Gallie (1952) whom Leach quotes as an authority on this issue, but my reading of Ayer (1968), Moore (1961) and of Smith (1978) does not agree with Leach's reading of Gallie to the extent that James should appear shallow by comparison with Peirce. These scholars draw attention to the difference between the two in the following terms: Peirce is more arcane and possibly more abstract but there seems to be no suggestion that James is to be regarded as no philosopher, at all.[13] So if Malinowski's pragmatism is shallow it seems to me the blame cannot be laid at James's door. But is Malinowski's pragmatism shallow?

Ignoring his application of pragmatism to his theory of needs and to culture and cultural institutions in general, if I ask the above question simply with regard to language. my answer would be: 'no'. And the best I can do to prove the validity of this answer is to compare Peirce's ideas with those of Malinowski's on the child's 'acquisition of semantic competence'. Further, a comparison of Malinowski's pragmatism with that of modern pragmatists – i.e., the speech act theorists, should be of interest. So first, here is Moore's view of Peirce's position on the child just learning to speak his mother tongue:

Suppose some fine autumn day that his (i.e. the child's) father takes him out for a walk. They climb a hill and at the top of the hill, the child encounters an object which he touches and finds to occasion an experience of roughness. He says to his father, 'what's that?'. His father replies. 'That is a tree.' Thus the word 'tree' now means to the child something such that if he touches it he will have an experience of roughness. The child leans against the tree to rest and finds that the tree supports him. He now adds to the meaning of the tree the idea that a tree is an object such that if he leans against it he will have the experience of being supported. Suppose his father now cuts the tree down and takes part of it home and puts it in the fireplace from which there presently comes warmth. The child's meaning of tree now grows to include the idea that a tree is an object such that if he cuts it down and puts it in the fireplace he will experience warmth. The next summer he learns that objects called trees are green in summer, that if one sits under them in summer he will feel cooler etc. etc. Thus what the child means by a tree continues to grow as his experiences grow. When he gets to the point where he has had all of the commoner experiences of a tree, his meaning of 'tree' will coincide with that held by most people, and he will have no difficulty knowing what they mean by 'tree'. (Moore 1961: 50)

Comparing this with the earlier citations from Malinowski, at least on this issue, if there is some difference between the austere philosopher Peirce and the shallow pragmatist Malinowski, it is to the latter's advantage than otherwise. Malinowski's pragmatic contexts, having their origin in the wider context of culture, appear far more natural than Peirce's imaginary situations which have a certain degree of artificiality, common to events conceived of a-socially. This is not to claim that Malinowski is a better semiotician or a deeper philosopher, but simply to say that on the question of how the linguistic conventions are learnt by a child, if I had to choose between the two – definitely Malinowski would not be a bad choice.

2.7.1 Malinowski and the speech act theorists

When we turn to a comparison of Malinowski with the speech act theorists, not surprisingly, we find passages in the former which could easily have occurred in the writing of, say, Austin. This is perhaps to be expected, for after all *How to Do Things with Words* is a collection of Austin's William James Lectures. Austin would have no hesitation in accepting Malinowski's claim (1935: 9) that 'Words are parts of action and they are equivalents to action', or that '... in all communities, certain words are accepted as potentially creative of acts. You utter a vow, or you forge a signature and you may find yourself bound for life to a monastery, a woman or a prison' (Malinowski 1935: 53).

Again, the aim is not to give the impression that there is no difference between Malinowski and speech act theorists: they are after all philosophers, not anthropologists. The speech act theorists have been much concerned with enquiry into the linguistic realizations of classes of speech acts (Austin 1976; Cole and Morgan 1975; Sadock 1974; Searle 1969, 1979, etc.); Malinowski never worked at that level of detail, but on the other hand, it should be added that his main aim in writing about language was not to present a detailed description of any part of the system of language, but to insist on the close relation between the social and the linguistic. Another quite important difference that springs to mind in comparing Malinowski with philosophers of language is that he does not share the philosophers' distrust of ordinary language. He would agree with Austin when the latter claims that 'words are our tools' (Austin 1976: 181). But there they would part company for Austin (1976: 181) goes on to add '… and as a minimum, we should use clean tools … and we must forearm ourselves against the traps that language sets us.' Such *logo phobia* is entirely absent from Malinowski.

Perhaps, at the risk of stereotyping, there is a generalization to be made here. Just as philosophers characteristically display a distrust of ordinary language (Halliday 1977b), just as they find it inadequate, full of traps and prone to falsity, so sociologists and anthropologists treat the ordinary language as an institution largely above question. One consequence of this difference is manifested in their respective views of reality. The philosopher's reality is given by nature; and is made up largely of physical phenomena. It makes contact with man through individual minds, while, being universal, each individual mind is in many ways simply an echo of the other individual minds – this despite the marked worship of the individual. Not so with the anthropologist. For him the world is largely made up of and through the symbolic systems for communication. So reality is inter-subjectively defined. In this respect, Malinowski and the speech act theorists are true to type. Austin, perhaps one of the few socially aware speech act philosophers, maintains (1976: 182): 'Words are not … facts or things: we need therefore to prise them off the world, to hold them apart from and against it, so that we can realize their inadequacies and arbitrariness and can re-look at the world without blinkers' (1976: 182).

This type of orientation is responsible for creating a thoughtless gulf between 'the knowledge of the world' and 'the knowledge of language'. Malinowski's position is radically different. Astonishing as this claim may sound to those whose acquaintance with Malinowski is second-hand, for him the world was made of language – at least those parts of the world which are crucial to the living of life. I am aware this reading goes against the popular view voiced by Leech who claims that for Malinowski 'meaning is reducible to observable context' (Leech 1974: 74) but a reading of section IV of the Ethnographic Theory of Language in *Coral Gardens and their Magic, Vol 2*, leaves me no option but to reject Leech's view. Let me present a few segments from this section:

Let us first consider the power of words in their creative supernatural effects. Obviously we have to accept here the intent and the mental attitude of those who use such words. If we want to understand the verbal usage of the Melanesian we must … stop doubting or criticizing his belief in magic, exactly as, when we want to understand the nature of Christian prayer and its moral force, or of Christian sacramental miracles, we must abandon the attitude of a confirmed rationalist or sceptic. *Meaning is the effect of words on human minds and bodies and, through these, on the environmental reality, as created or conceived in a given culture.* (Malinowski 1935: 53; emphasis added, RH)

Having attempted to show how tenuous the distinction between the imaginary and the real is, Malinowski goes on to conclude:

in every community – among the Trobrianders quite as definitely as among ourselves – there exists a belief that a word uttered in certain circumstances has a creative, binding force.

This creative function of words in magical or in sacramental speech, their binding force in legal utterances … in my opinion constitutes their real meaning.

Take again the verbal act of repentance in the Roman Catholic confession of sins, or again the sacramental act of Absolution administered verbally by the Father Confessor: here words produce an actual change in the universe which, though mystical and imaginary to us agnostics, is none the less real for the believer. (Malinowski 1935: 54–55)

With these statements so clearly speaking for Malinowski, I find it difficult to imagine how he could be accused of 'crude contextualism'.

One explanation for misreading Malinowski might lie in the meanings he ascribed to certain words he used frequently: they may not necessarily mean the same thing to linguists today. For example in talking of 'meaning as function of words', he opens the discussion as follows:

All our considerations have led us to the conclusion that words in their primary and essential sense do, act, produce and achieve. To arrive therefore at an understanding of meaning we have to study the dynamic rather than the purely intellectual function of words. Language is primarily an instrument of action, and not a means of telling a tale, of entertaining or instructing from a purely intellectual point of view. (Malinowski 1935: 52)[14]

Most pragmatists would agree with Malinowski when he declares that 'language is primarily an instrument of action', but it is not 'acceptable' to the modern scholarly sensibilities to appear to deride 'a purely intellectual point of view': I suspect the distinction Malinowski was making had to do with using language for living and using language as a 'language of description' for analysing certain objects of enquiry such as social organization or, indeed, language. I doubt if any pragmatist would accept the examples he provides of the 'two peaks of this *pragmatic* power of words' (emphasis added): but a contemplation of his examples might clarify the point I am making. According to Malinowski, the first 'peak of pragmatic power' is 'to be found in certain sacred uses', for example in '… magical formulae, sacramental utterances, exorcisms, curses and blessings and most prayers. All sacred words have a creative effect, usually indirect, by setting in motion some supernatural power, or, when the sacramental becomes quasi legal, in summoning social sanctions.' The other peak is to be found in environments where characteristically one may find a high frequency of directives. Examples would be: 'An order given in battle, an instruction issued by the master of a sailing ship, a cry for help, are as powerful in modifying the course of events as any other bodily act' (Malinowski 1935: 52–53).

Passages such as these lead one to suggest that it is probably not Malinowski's view of verbal meaning as such which is problematic; the real problem might lie in his use of such words as 'intellectual', 'reflection' and 'abstract contemplation', as it might do also in his insistence that the function of language as the creator of reality is simply an instance of language in action. Malinowski's usage of the words 'pragmatic' and 'action' is at least as idiosyncratic as Peirce's use of the expression 'practical consequences' in the definition of meaning. Such a wide domain of signification for the word 'pragmatic' is definitely at variance from the practices of most modern pragmatists, as a brief glance at their handling of meaning in literature will easily demonstrate (Levin 1976; van Dijk 1976; Searle 1979).

One of the most outstanding differences between Malinowski and the present day speech act theorists lies in Malinowski's idea that an isolated sentence is a fiction, since the natural unit of interaction is a text. This implies that sentences are neither comprehended nor produced apart from their context where the word 'context' subsumes both verbal and extra-verbal environment. Such an orientation to sentences would have been useful to the speech act theorists, since the speech act status of utterances quite often cannot be determined entirely by examining the sentence-internal properties (Hasan 1982). This much is quite obvious from the current discussions of the indirect directives (Searle 1979; Sadock 1974). Although most descriptions of indirect speech acts must make a reference to the co-text, such reference remains a-theoretical and ad hoc.

These same remarks can be made with regard to the speech act theorist's view of social context. It has been obvious, from the very inception of speech act theory (Austin 1962), that the notion 'context of situation' is absolutely crucial to any reasoned description of speech acts; nonetheless there is an *ad hoc* quality to their invocations of this concept. If we accept with Palmer that Malinowski's context is 'pre-theoretical', then we would have to say that the speech act theorist's concept of context is far from theoretical. For them too context is a 'bit' of real situation; there is, of course, the difference that for Malinowski situation was fundamentally a social entity, for the speech act theorist it is more physical/physiological than social, which is to be expected from their orientation. These comparative remarks are not intended to suggest that the work in speech act theory is less worthy of our attention or that as a semiotician Peirce is not an important figure. The aim has been simply to argue that when it comes to a comparison of Malinowski with these scholars in respect of their treatment of context of situation they have no edge on Malinowski. To ask the question: how is it that a hearer knows that a promise is a promise? and to answer that he does so because he knows the set of conditions that must be satisfied by an utterance before it can be taken as a promise, is only half the story. Malinowski tried to demonstrate how it is that a listener gets to 'know', i.e., gets to deduce the set of conditions whose satisfaction counts as a promise. Naturally the question is important only if you believe that the rules for promising are not universal: we do not come into the world with the defining features of speech acts.

I have argued so far that Malinowski has been misrepresented; that his contribution to linguistics has been undervalued; that his concept of context of situation is much richer, and his views on its place in the modelling of language is far more viable than he has been given credit for. I have suggested that the reason behind this misrepresentation is his unfashionable adherence to 'anti-mentalism', and that this anti-mentalist stance appears to be exaggerated by his rather idiosyncratic usage of a certain class of words. With some degree of goodwill, such as we exercise in the reading of many modern favourites, his writings would not appear as unreasonable, or as 'crude' as they have been made to appear through the standard short quotes and the traditional comments included in most writings dealing with his work. Certainly, once his orientation and the aim of his endeavour are taken into account, Malinowski's achievement does not appear mean. He was, after all, no linguist; his aim was not to produce viable descriptions of specific classes of linguistic units. More sobering, the entire debate on the centrality of context of situation to the theory of meaning was activated simply by his desire to show that the translation of ethnographic data consists in the difficult task of encapsulating a series of cultural contexts which may be quite foreign to the language in which they are being translated. To my knowledge no one has yet presented a better definition of an adequate translation: a successful translation reconstitutes the verbally encapsulated context in the original. Much work in the processing of information by AI specialists would imply that comprehension could also be defined by measuring the degree of success in reconstituting the verbally encapsulated context of the text one is 'processing'. That Malinowski arrived at important theoretical conclusions from the consideration of a purely practical problem is of interest to those of us who prefer to think of the relation between theory and practice as a constant dialogue, each contributing to the improvement of the other by a continued interaction. In this view, linguistics is not an intellectual game concerned with superbly organized form without content; it is a field of knowledge eminently useful to mankind. In the words of Whorf (1956: 232): 'the forces studied by linguistics are powerful and important … its principles control every sort of agreement among human beings, and, … sooner or later it [i.e., linguistics, RH] will have to sit as judge while the other sciences bring their results to enquire into what they mean.'

To some readers these pronouncements might sound romantic fantasies; but that might be because, at heart, many of us remain such confirmed believers in the sens-ible, what is here and now or can be easily and quickly created to be witnessed. The fact is that there is no hope of developing linguistics in the ways that Whorf had in mind unless we are willing to assign as great an importance to meaning as we have done to form, until we are willing to see language not simply as a species-specific phenomenon, but also as one which is equally importantly culture-specific, until we can think of language not simply as a mental organ, ours despite our valued unique individualities, but also as a social institution shaped according to our cultural identity while playing a major part in shaping that culture: in short, until we are willing to recognize the implications of linguistics being a powerful semiotic system. Perhaps, anthropologists, whose main stock in trade is culture, are more willing to grant that the variables across cultures are as significant as the universals of the human species; Malinowski was no exception.

2.8 Malinowski: critique and appreciation

No scholar is perfect no matter how ardently worshipped by his followers. The flaws in Malinowski's programmatic design for the description of language to which I now turn, arise precisely because he is first and foremost an anthropologist, and only secondarily a linguist. That his notion of the context of situation was not abstract enough to be used as a general framework was first pointed out by J. R. Firth (1957, 1964), who commented that Malinowski's context was 'only a bit of the social process', an actual 'set of events in rebus'.[15] It is certainly true that Malinowski never focused on extra-linguistic situation with a view to systematically abstracting from it just those factors which would be always relevant to language in use. Thus a systematization of the type we find in Firth (1957), Halliday (1957, 1959), Halliday *et al.* (1964) and Hymes (1968, 1971, 1986), and following them, others, is not to be encountered in Malinowski's writings; while he was fully alive to the elements of the context of situation which interact with an instance of language use, he simply failed to create a 'schematic construct'. Critical remarks such as these are sometimes understood, as, for example, by Leech and Palmer, to imply that for Malinowski context equalled actual observable situation. This is a misrepresentation in my view since observations such as the following cannot be reconciled with a 'crude contextualist' position; (the comments below are with reference to the interpretation of the term *buyagu*):

> First we had to remind the reader of the general context of situation ...; that is, to indicate the social, legal and technical arrangements by which a portion of cultivable soil is ear-marked for next year's gardens ... Then I give the ... approximate. ... English label 'garden-site' ... But this ... term has to be redefined by fuller English circumlocutions. ... These circumlocutions obviously derive their meaning from the reader's knowledge of how land is cultivated in the Trobriands. ... Throughout its analysis ... the word is progressively defined by reference to the ethnographic description, supplemented by additional information concerning linguistic usage. ... Thus the definition of a word consists partly in placing it within its cultural context, partly in illustrating its usage in the context of opposites and of cognate expressions. (Malinowski 1935: 15–16)

Again the power of words to create reality as in magical incantations and religious rituals to which Malinowski draws attention (1935, Div. V), can hardly be reconciled with a 'crude contextualist' position, in which the linguistic sign and the physical thing named by the sign are held to be in a one-to-one (observable) correlation. I would suggest that such a misinterpretation might conceivably arise from Malinowski's failure to draw a clear distinction between context as a schematic construct and the material situational setting (Hasan 1973c) within which an interactive event takes place. It is obvious that such a distinction is essential not only in the description of displaced language but also in throwing light on the ancillary function of language which is characteristically associated with predominantly pragmatic environments (Halliday 1977a; Ure 1971; Halliday and Hasan 1985, etc.).

Perhaps the problems inherent in Malinowski's account of how a narrative, whether historical chronicle, fiction or myth, comes to be understood by the listener, arises partly from the above failure. While he is to be commended for pointing out the necessity for recognizing more than one contextual frame in the description of the narrative, his treatment leaves much to be desired. Malinowski separated the context of narration, i.e., the outer context, from the context which is encapsulated within the narrative itself, i.e., the inner context of the story; this can be reconstituted from the language of the narrative. Malinowski referred to the former context as 'primary' (or 'direct') and to the latter as 'secondary' (or 'indirect'), justifying the usage as follows:

> When incidents are told or discussed among a group of listeners there is, first, the situation of that moment made up of the respective social, intellectual and emotional attitudes of those present. Within this situation, the narrative creates new bonds and sentiments by the emotional appeal of the words. (Malinowski 1923: 312–313)

As to the secondary context, using his words again:

> A narrative is associated also indirectly with one situation to which it refers ... the words of a tale are significant because of previous experiences of listeners; ... narrative speech is derived in its function, and it refers to action only indirectly, but the way in which it acquires its meaning can only be understood from the direct function of speech in action ... the referential function of a narrative is subordinate to its social and emotive function. (Malinowski (1923: 313)

The above extracts present all the essentials of the Malinowskian view of how a narrative is comprehended. There appears to have been no advance on this position though it is, perhaps, more lucidly expressed a decade later in Coral Gardens. Much can be said in criticism of this stance; in fact, much has already been said though sometimes the basis for the criticism itself does not appear justified. Consider, for example:

> ... he discusses narrative, the telling of stories; but here surely, *the context is the same at all time*s – the story-teller and his audience, whatever the story. If context is to be taken as an indication of meaning, all stories will have the same meaning. Malinowski's solution was to invoke 'secondary context', the context within the narrative: but that has no immediately observable status and can no more be objectively defined than the concepts or thoughts that he was so eager to banish from discussion. (Palmer 1981: 53; emphasis added, RH)

This extract makes three claims. In the first place, Palmer assumes that the outer, primary context for story telling is invariable; secondly he claims that Malinowski's secondary context is created to repair the 'deficiency' arising from the invariable quality of the primary one. And, finally, he discounts the secondary context on the ground that for Malinowski, context always had to be 'immediately observable', which quite obviously would not be the case with the secondary context. So the entire framework is faulty. I think Palmer can be refuted on all counts, without necessarily having to accept that Malinowski's account of storytelling is above criticism.

Palmer's assumption that Malinowski's primary context would be invariable is open to question. True that what is called 'agentive role' (Hasan 1978), i.e., story-teller and audience, is invariable. But this does not argue that everything else in the primary context would be also invariable, quite apart from the fact that differences in the nature of the carriers of these roles would itself create variation. Malinowski does allow for this by recognizing the importance of the 'social, intellectual and emotional attitudes of those present'; but apart from this, he also draws attention to the variety of purposes for which stories may be told and the difference that variations in this contextual variable would make to the wording of the story in order to be understood by the listeners (1935: 46 ff.). These are perceptive remarks on Malinowski's part as can be shown if we take an example from the familiar Western culture: Hamlet in the bush (Bohannan 1971) is different from Hamlet on the Elizabethan stage; and Hamlet in the modern classroom is different from both – it is a moot point how far the 'story' remains the same for these varied audiences. Malinowski's framework for the primary context takes into account many of the sources of such differences. But not having a schematic construct, he is unable to clarify how despite the identity of the agentive role and of the activity itself, what other contextual variables are likely to exist which could, from one occasion to another, make some significant differences to the actual 'contextual configuration' relevant to the narration (Hasan 1964, 1978, 1981, 1984b, 1984c). For this he can certainly be criticized, but it is wrong to suggest that his account of primary context presupposes uniformity of meaning.

Malinowski does not appear to be aware of the implications of his own comments. Although in *The Problem of Meaning* he was concerned mainly with pre-literate communities, the later work (1935) often makes comparative statements involving literate communities as well. He never seems to have recognized that at least in literate communities, and possibly also in the pre-literate ones, two outer contexts rather than one would have to be postulated: one, the context of story-creation, including two separable strands – the biographic and the artistic, and secondly the context of story-narration (Hasan 1964, 1979a, 1984c). All else being equal, the greater the distance between these two outer frames the greater the difficulty in comprehension; and if this is the case, it does support Malinowski's hypothesis of the relevance of the outer context(s) to understanding the meanings of the story. Thus Palmer's contention that the postulate of an outer context implies invariance is quite without any basis; the criticism that Malinowski failed to follow his own lead is far more justifiable, but, to my knowledge, has never been made. And since the problem of invariance does not exist, the notion of secondary context could not be seen as a solution to it! Rather, the postulate of secondary context is needed in order to account for a relationship between language and context which is different from the primary pragmatic type of relationship. As Malinowski commented

> In a narrative words are used with what might be called a *borrowed or indirect meaning*. The real context of reference has to be reconstructed by the hearers even as it is being evoked by the speaker. (1935: 46)

It is true that, as Palmer claims, 'the context within the narrative ... has no immediately observable status' and cannot be 'objectively defined'. So what is Malinowski's own account of this relationship?

> ... the real meaning of words, the real capacity for visualizing the contents of a narrative, are *always derived from a personal experience*: physiological, intellectual and emotional ... *such experience is invariably connected with verbal acts. A narrative type of utterance*

is, therefore, comprehensible by the reference of the statements to past personal experiences in which words were directly embedded within the context of situation. (Malinowski 1935:46; emphasis added, RH)

I have claimed above that Malinowski is not a crude contextualist for whom context has to be always observable. The above extract argues that the 'invoked context' can be reconstructed *only if the hearers have had a direct experience of the words of the story within a pragmatic context prior to encountering them in the story.* The acceptance of this position does not commit one to meaning as 'concept or thought'; it simply commits one to a memory for the meaning of signs previously encountered and understood through the mediation of a pragmatic context of situation. Thus once again Palmer's criticism is not to the point. This does not mean that Malinowski's position is unassailable. There are at least two very serious objections to his formulation.

First, it is not at all obvious to what extent the reconstructed context has to be identical to some directly experienced context. If a close degree of resemblance is a necessary condition for the ability to comprehend the meanings of the 'narrative utterances', then the more fantastic the tale, the more problematic the Malinowskian solution. How could one account for the hearer's comprehension of Dylan Thomas' *Adventures in the Skin Trade* or for Kafka's *Metamorphosis*? And we would definitely have to write off James Joyce as sheer nonsense, unless we turned our backs on Malinowski at this point. If resemblance between the reconstructed context and directly experienced context is not necessary, Malinowski's account has offered no hypothesis how the words of the narrative can be used to reconstruct a context in which they were never experienced.

Secondly, if it is true that the meanings of the narrative utterances are derived from a primary pragmatic context, it follows that stories could not be used for the learning of new meanings. In fact, Malinowski acknowledges this to be the case; having described a variety of pragmatic contexts, he goes on to add: '… in such situations we have speech used in a primary, direct manner. It is from such situations that we are most likely to learn the meaning of words, rather than from a study of derived uses of speech' (Malinowski 1935: 46–47; emphasis added, RH).

Anyone who has ever taught a foreign language knows very well that this claim is untenable. Stories can be used and are used for the teaching of new words, which, in the last resort, means for the teaching of the meanings of these words. It is at this point that I would like to make my major criticism of Malinowski. His main fault lies in the fact that he was never able to visualize the implications of language being a system. This is not to say, of course, that he did not see language as a system – he certainly did as I have tried to argue earlier with reference to his treatment of the semantic field of garden-site. He, however, did not seem to realize that *the very inter-relatedness of the terms within the linguistic system acts as an advantage, once an effective entry into the system has been made.* To give a very simple example, if the sign system of Urdu is likely to be a closed book to most readers, it does not help if I say that /tʃhori/ is synonymous with /leRki/ while /tʃora/ is an antonym to both. But if I were to add that the value and signification of /tʃhori/ covers approximately the same area as the sign *lass* does in English, the rest would be clear. Although my example assumes a foreign language learning situation, this does not affect the main point I am making here. It is this systematicity of language which also permits its use as a metalanguage, permitting paraphrase, explication, etc. And these too are ways of learning meaning, even though these means of learning how to mean cannot be used with the infant. It may be that having defined for himself a position which was indeed novel in linguistics, for let us not forget that *The Problem of Meaning* was first published in 1923, when Saussure was not a familiar name to even linguists, Malinowski felt impelled to single it out as the 'important unrecognized'. Further, as I pointed out earlier, Malinowski was after all not a linguist by training; it was only through his professional practice as an anthropologist that he entered the field. Be it as it may, this failure to recognize the full implications of the systemicity of language constantly mars his statements about the relation of language to context. It is this fact, rather than his insistence on the primacy of the pragmatic function, that acts as a hurdle to our complete acceptance of the Malinowskian position.

It is in keeping with this underestimation of the importance of 'systematicity' that Malinowski never raised the question: what aspects of the context can always be reconstituted by the language of a narrative utterance, more generally, any displaced text? Little wonder then that his context is not a schematic construct. Further, there is no occasion for raising the subsequent question which modern systemicists following Halliday (1970a) ask: why is it that the language of a displaced text invariably permits the reconstitution of these and no other contextual phenomena? In a sense, to ask these two questions is to complete the circle of interdependence, or better still, the dialectic, between text, meaning and context.

In his Introduction to *Man and Culture: an evaluation of the work of Bronislaw Malinowski,* Raymond Firth, the editor of the volume, makes the following comments:

... the main task Malinowski had set himself (was) – a dynamic interpretation of human behaviour in the widest range of cultural circumstances, in terms which were at once more theoretically sophisticated, and more realistic, than any then current. At that time, the tradition was that an anthropologist was primarily either a theoretician or an ethnographer, and that the theory should be kept separate from the facts. It was part of Malinowski's contribution, not only to combine them, but to show how fact was meaningless without theory and how each could gain in significance by being consciously brought into relation. The main theoretical apparatus which he constructed over a decade and a half has proved unable, in the end, to bear the systematic weight he wished to put upon it. But much of it is still usable, and it has given many ideas to others, often unacknowledged by them.

The Malinowski legend sometimes takes an extreme form – as expressed in this student's examination answer: 'Because of his views Malinowski did not make abstractions and was at best a misguided theorist.' Such a distortion of his theoretical position ignores his keen preoccupation with methodology, and indeed his general interest in philosophical issues. (R. Firth 1964: 2)

These remarks are made about Malinowski the anthropologist; but with very few alterations, they would express the position regarding Malinowski the linguist. I have attempted to show in this essay how the 'legend has taken an extreme form' in linguistics, and how 'too little attention has been paid to the work of Bronislaw Malinowski'. Unlike the authors of *Man and Culture*, I have no personal or professional allegiance to Malinowski, but in the light of revived interest in the so-called pragmatics and 'contextualism', it seems appropriate to point out that we gain nothing by either ignoring him or by keeping alive legends which smack of unscholarly reading. The handling of the concept of context in present day speech act theory, which appears to me in no way better articulated than Malinowski's, should give us a pause if nothing else does in riding roughshod on the Malinowskian heritage. Even if we are willing to ignore Malinowski's achievements, and these, as I have argued, were considerable, let us at least not ignore the real shortcoming of his position, i.e., the inability of recognizing system as a resource. It can only lead to retracing an erroneous path with great aplomb, and this is far less excusable than making mistakes in the very first exploration.

Notes

1   The original version of this paper did not have section headings. The introduction of these has led to a few minor changes in the interest of maintaining continuity. References have been updated and some new ones have been introduced, especially in the endnotes; the original version had no endnotes.

2   Though more recently the overwhelmingly psychological tradition of the formalistic linguistics – and those parasitic on it – have begun to pay some attention to social issues. Note for example the title of J. R. Searle's latest publication *Making the Social World: The Structure of Human Civilization.* London: Oxford University Press, 2010.

3   In the quarter century since the publication of this chapter, the results of empirical research have become available which give us a better idea about how human brains function and what transforms brains into minds. The findings do not support the innateness of language; on the contrary the primacy of experience of living is taken as essential to the making of mind. See Deacon (1997), Greenfield (1997), Edelman and Tonini (2000).

4   In this connection it is important to recall the careful research and debate conducted by the psychologist Vygotsky (1978) and his colleagues: these together with Luria's research are highly relevant to the present debate.

5   My use of the word 'rational' is very close to 'material' as Halliday uses that term today, e.g., Halliday (2005). It is indeed a matter of interest how close the concepts of rational, logical, and natural in philosophy, logic and often psychology are to that which is sensible, or physically based. For some discussion see Hasan (2005, 2009a).

6   One reason for this might have been that signification can occur naturally only in the course of parole, and for reasons discussed elsewhere (Hasan 1987a; See also chapter 1 in this volume (Ed.)). Saussure was less interested in the systematic study of parole.

7   Lamb (2004) (Part Two) offers an account of language as a network of relationships.

8   And today I would have liked to know: how did anyone get to know about those relations? where do signs enter into relations with other signs except in parole? (See also chapter 1 in this volume. (Ed.)).

9   It had not struck me earlier that Leech's claim is truly surprising in view of the fact that meaning-in-context is precisely what truth functional or 'correspondence' based semantics was all about. [RH 2011].

10   Even though voicing such an opinion may not be politically correct.

11   It is interesting to recall that Luria, a contemporary, was around this time engaged in observing the language of another primitive group, namely the Uzbeks (Luria 1976; see esp. the Preface).

12   Today, just 25 years later, in view of modern neurological findings such as Deacon (1997), Lamb (1998), Edelman and Tononi (2000), the 1960s

     objectification of linguistic form as 'dictionaries' or 'grammars' held in the brain appears pretty archaic. [RH 2011]
13   In any event, when it comes to what Bernstein calls 'horizontal knowledge structures' (1999), most of us could be described as 'preachers' since meticulous argumentation and comparison are not virtues of the social sciences.
14   The formulations here often criticized are not objectionable if we remember Malinowski's concern with the evolution of human speech as a social institution.
15   Curiously, today scholarly interest in 'multimodality' and insistence on treating text/discourse as pan-semiotic favours the Malinowskian approach which insists on bringing in a bit of raw situation as a way of ascribing sense to signs which are not part of language.

3 What's going on?: a dynamic view of context in language [1981]

3.1 Introduction

The basic concern of this paper is with the relationship between text and context of situation.[1] But CONTEXT OF SITUATION, sometimes called just 'context' or 'situation', means different things to different people. I believe my use of the term to be in keeping with the Malinowski-Firth-Halliday tradition. The half century between Malinowski (1923) and Halliday (1974a) has seen a radical shift in the concept, in precisely the direction in which Firth (1950) seems to have pointed it. For Malinowski context of situation was just that: 'the situation context'. For Halliday, following Firth, it is an abstraction from the cultural institutions; and if situation may be said to accompany the text, then this is more by virtue of the functional nature of language than by virtue of an accidental physical spatio-temporal co-occurrence of the two. The word 'accompany' has undergone an important re-interpretation. Halliday's context of situation (1977a, 1978) captures what Goffman (1975) refers to as the 'motivational relevancies' in as much as they bear upon the talk in all its aspects. The interaction as it unfolds through the mediation of the various modes of meaning, verbal and non-verbal, is an evidence of such relevancies. It, therefore, provides an in/direct account of its creators' answer to the question: What is going on here?

3.2 Context of situation: a subjective reality

The racy idiomaticity of this question raised in everyday usage might deceive us into thinking that the question is a simple one, with a meaning obvious to all. But as several scholars have pointed out we are faced here with an inherent indeterminacy; at any time that the question is raised, the answer to it can always be some other than that which is given, for there is a considerable latitude in the interpretation of 'what', 'here' and of 'going on'. Obviously, then, none of the answers is a 'slice of reality', something that is physically obvious here and now at the time of asking; rather the answer must refer to some elements abstracted from reality seen from some perspective which is itself furnished in response to some domain of experience. The reality captured by the answer is filtered reality, and the active agents here are the speaker and the addressee: it is their focus and their cultural orientation and their language that prompts the answer: the information is derived from their texts and its social context. So, although the answer may be rooted in the objective, its point of departure is in the subjective. According to this line of reasoning, the word 'situation' in the expression 'context of situation' refers to that part of reality which is filtered through the interactants' focus upon some aspect of their environment in performing some social activity. Were we to leave the story off at this point, each context of situation would appear to be a unique creation by some unique individual, and what could be more gratifying than the belief that one's self is indeed the centre of the universe?

3.2.1 Context: inter-subjective frame for interaction

However, we do have to take into account the fact of interaction, the presence of which argues that the subjective must somehow be turned into the inter-subjective. Perception, individual focus, one's own view of what is relevant, these are private things. To be shared, they must be made public; and some form of sharing there must be as that is a necessary condition for the unfolding of interaction even where deception is involved. The means whereby the private is rendered public is provided by the semiotic codes. My focus on the situation can become your focus on it, if we so wish, only if common to us is some means of representing that focus. A shared situation is by definition a coded situation, a fact to be kept in sight whenever we are reminded of the uniqueness of individual experience. For if emphasis on the subjectivity of focus highlights uniqueness, the need for coding functions as a corrective, indicating the limits on this uniqueness: whatever can generally function as a medium of communication must necessarily be a system of social conventions. So what is shared between individuals is conditioned not only by the unique identities involved; rather the filtering of reality is two-fold. Reality is thus and thus because *I* see it thus and thus but the *other's* perception of my perception of the thus-ness of reality must be filtered through the coded messages that connect us, which in any such process are conditioned by the nature of the code. And more important still, this sharp division between the individual and the social, the unique and the conventional, is perhaps only an artefact of our analysis. For even though we may choose to begin with the individual, there is an important sense in which the individual can be seen as a being who has been actively shaped by the sum of his own interactions and hence by the nature of the multiple semiotic codes prevalent in his community (Bateson 1942; Whorf 1956; Bernstein 1971).[2]

3.2.2 Context: a social semiotic construct

The total set of semiotic codes in a community serves to define the nature of the 'world' for its members. Each code has a role in the mediation of meanings but it would be naïve to imagine that there are no differences between them. I would suggest that distinct semiotic codes carry distinct representational capacities; the accounts of recent research in non-verbal communication would certainly appear to support this hypothesis (Argyle and Kendon 1967; Argyle 1972). Clearly, despite overlaps, what can be said through the resources of the verbal code is not co-extensive with what can be 'said' through eye-contact or gesture code or the code of dress. But in my view the difference between the codes goes beyond the matter of 'how much' can be said; it extends to what may be described as the partiality of a specific code to certain kinds of relevance (Bateson 1968). For it would appear that the functional nature of each code predisposes it to the encoding of certain relevancies rather than others. So, the code of eye-contact *must* convey an interpersonal type of meaning, and it would be a mistake to imagine that either eye-contact avoidance or the 'impersonal look in the eye' fail to convey some meaning. Certainly when it comes to the filtering of the interactive situation through the verbal code, there would appear to be certain aspects which, by the nature of the code, are treated as being relevant, as being a part of the interactants' subjective focus. Whatever else the interactants may attend to or not, these are factors which they cannot choose to ignore; their conception of what is relevant to the interaction must contain these elements within it.

(a) the nature of the SOCIAL PROCESS – what is being achieved through the acts of verbal meaning;

(b) the nature of the INTERACTANT RELATIONSHIP;
(c) the nature of the modes of MESSAGE TRANSMISSION.

These factors correspond to Halliday's parameters of the context of discourse, i.e., FIELD, TENOR and MODE of discourse. In principle it is possible to deconstruct each member of this tripartite set by reference to the different value of its parameter; it thus encompasses other contextual frames presented by other scholars (e.g., Gregory and Carroll 1978; Hymes 1968, 1972; Hasan 1973c; Martin 1979). Halliday's schematic construct is followed here because it appears to be the most highly motivated, being placed simultaneously in relation to both the social systems and the verbal codes as shown in Figure 3.1.

3.3 Culture, context and text

Figure 3.1 presents some of the most important elements which influence the habits of verbal interaction in the majority of social beings; at the same time it provides a theoretical context for the interpretation of the expression 'context of situation'. In what follows I shall restrict myself to a small corner of this broad canvas, relevant to the lives of all social agents: I will deal only with certain aspects of the context of situation and the text as if all else were equal.

3.3.1 Context and material situational setting

If we accept the view of context of situation, which is schematically presented in Figure 3.1, certain implications will follow. In the first place, we must make a distinction between what I am referring to as 'context of situation' and the actual physical setting in which a text might unfold. Let me refer to the latter as *'material situational setting'* (Hasan 1973c). The material situational setting always include elements that are not part of the context of situation; this is the reason why the question: what's going on here? has so many legitimate answers. The overlap between the two can vary according to the role that the language plays in the performance of the social process; when the process is defined by reference to language, as in the case of activities such as *seminar, lecture, lyric,* then the material situational setting in which the text actually gets produced maybe largely irrelevant to the text. Someone producing an advertisement for publication must sit somewhere at some time in or out of others' company; but these

Figure 3.1: Text positioned in social system [adapted from Halliday 2007 [1974b]: 141]

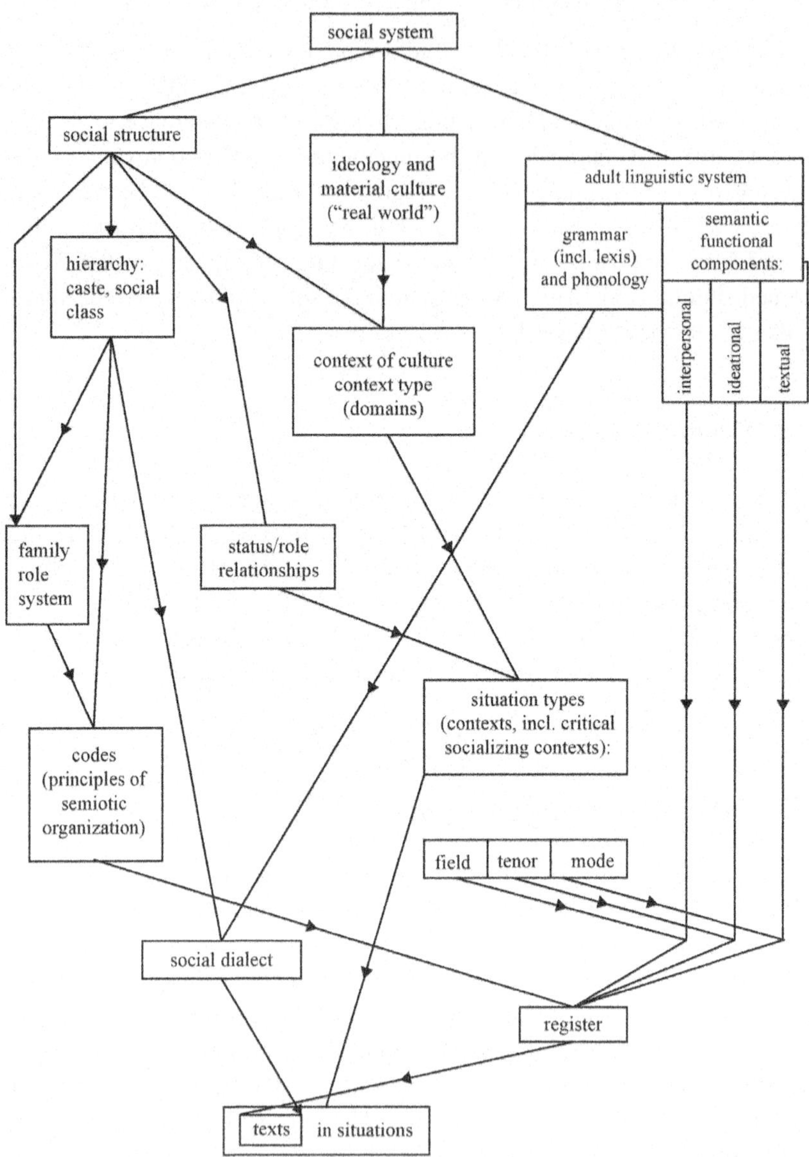

aspects of the material situational setting need not impinge upon the text in any way. By contrast, if the role of language is subsidiary, the social process being defined without reference to the language, as in the case of activities such as moving furniture around in a room, preparing food for the family, then some elements of the material situational setting are very likely to be actively picked up as the ingredients of the context of situation.

In principle, then, we can think of the material situational setting as a dormant force, which is capable of affecting the verbal goings on. Elements of this dormant force are available for activation; it is a different matter whether such activation would entail a change in the context of situation or not (Hasan 1985b). I shall return to the role of the material situational setting and the 'contextual construct' in determining the nature of the context of the situation for the observer at a later point.

3.3.2   Text in context in text

A second implication that follows from my view of the context of situation is the nature of the relationship between it and text. If context of situation is an account of the interactants' motivational relevancies, then it must be seen as a dynamic force both in text creation and text interpretation. Context is not an ad hoc, a-theoretical notion that one can appeal to when it suits one's convenience or in as much as it suits one's convenience, as in most speech act analyses (Sbisa and Fabbri 1980); it is a prerequisite of all language use.[3] I would like to dissociate myself from that use of the term context which treats it as the explanation of whatever cannot be explained through the analysis of the form of the message; for such a use of context is hardly any more viable than that of 'performance'. And in any event there exists a catch-all phrase in the expression 'knowledge of the world' which is surely a wide enough basket to take in any number of failures of analysis.

That context is pertinent to interaction is a widely held view; in recent years its relevance to specifically the verbal aspects of interaction has received a great deal of attention. However, most studies have approached the analysis in terms of the sequencing of speech acts, thus concentrating on what is often referred to as micro-analysis of interaction (Dore 1980; Labov and Fanshel 1977; McTear 1979). Yet another recent development is the attempt to synthesize both the micro- and macro-analysis (Sinclair and Coulthard 1975). Such studies have contributed a great deal to our understanding of text construction and text interpretation.

3.3.3 Context and the generalized structure of text

In my own work I have argued that context can be seen as the major determinant of the defining characteristics of text genres (Hasan 1973c, 1978,
1979b, 1985b); given the nature of the context of situation, perceived as
the contextual configuration in a specific instance, we can predict the crucial semantic elements of the embedded text as well as the permitted range
for the over-all message form.[4] For example if we know that the social
process is that of advertising, this simple fact permits us to predict that the
message form must contain an element of structure whose function it is to
attract attention. Let us refer to this element of text structure as Capture
(short form of 'capture attention'); it is this element that is realized in the
written mode through the management of the visual lay-out, the type face
patterns and/or the presence of pictures; and in the spoken mode through
the introduction of music or other acoustic effects. Further, the tendency of
advertisements to use puns, e.g., *Go to Work on an Egg*, alliteration, e.g.,
Top People Take the Times, and such apparently preposterous locutions as
Go jump in a New Zealand Lake is functionally motivated; they are there
as (part of) the realization of the element Capture. A second obligatory
element of structure may be referred to as Focus. The crucial semantics
of this element are to single out that which is being advertised. The cap-
tion *Go jump in a New Zealand Lake* adorns the top of the picture of a
beautiful lake; underneath the picture a discrete legend announces *Air New
Zealand*. This is the Focus of this particular advertisement. This beauty of
New Zealand as displayed by the picture constitutes the Justification for the
Focus. Space does not permit a more detailed account of other elements of
structure for an advertisement; but hopefully this brief introduction lends
support to the hypothesis that the contextual configuration can be used to
predict the structural potential for texts belonging to specific registers, or
genres, if that term is preferred, except that the tradition of linking genres
to any social contextual phenomena seems to have died with Bakhtin. The
notion of appropriateness would be inapplicable to the text without the
prior assumption that the meanings of the text are in some manner controlled by the occasion of talk. And by the same token, the ability to infer
the contextual configuration of a text is an essential part of its interpretation; if we read *Go jump in a New Zealand Lake* as a gratuitous insult,
we are definitely far from interpreting successfully the text or its social
context. Thus, for the acculturated reader, the relationship between text and
context is two-fold: if we have access to the context of the social practice,
we can predict the essentials of the text; if we have access to the text, then

we can infer the context from it. In both cases we proceed from that which is present to that which is not present but which stands in some causal relation to the former.

3.4   On the validity of norm as a descriptive concept

The above view of context is often seen as normative (Sbisa and Fabbri 1980; Cicourel 1980) and as such undesirable for the following reasons:

(a) that it implies the presence of a social contract;
(b) that it postulates an ideal for human behaviour;
(c) that it does not permit variation;
(d) that it denies individual autonomy; and
(e) that it presents context as a fully evolved object prior to the creation of the text, while the fact of the matter is that contexts and texts evolve together.

3.4.1 A word on norms

Let me deal with the first two objections very briefly. The recognition of a norm does not imply the presence of a social convention; we may use the metaphor of social contract to refer to the fact that members of a community follow a set of conventions which are essentially arbitrary in nature, but in saying this we claim no more than that the actual practices of a community indicate how a convention should be read; and this includes the reading of all its values, not just one. A convention is made legitimate through practice, not through amicable discussion as the metaphor of social contract might sometimes misleadingly incline us to think. The actual practices of a community are often a means for the categorization of its members; this is borne out by the researches of anthropologists of very different ideological persuasions. I would suggest that the concept power in sociology is very closely related to the concept of norm; however, to describe social norms is not to side with the group wielding power any more than to describe working-class dialects is to bring about a social revolution whose benefits are reaped by the downtrodden. The recognition of norms would naturally be misleading if, for some reason, a scholar chose to ignore the presence of conflicting norms; but such shortcomings in the practice of some scholar cannot invalidate the concept of norm itself; what is invalidated is that particular description.

3.4.2 Norms and ideals

Nor does it appear to me that norm entails idealization of relevant behaviour. Some idealization must always exist in any general statement, and when we talk about occasions of talk and how people tend to act verbally on such occasions we must make an effort to distinguish between what is inside the frame, what outside (Bateson 1955; Goffman 1975). But with reference to the occasion itself, it is not necessary to postulate one invariant mode of behaviour as the only correct possibility. In fact the question of evaluation need not enter into the concept of norm, for a norm may be established on a purely statistical basis; to say that something happens typically is not to claim that it is therefore good, or beautiful, or correct. Nor does it necessarily entail a monolithic view of 'it' whatever that 'it' may be; variants do occur; they are normal but it is also normal for variations to occur systematically. These points have been argued admirably by Labov with specific reference to language (Labov 1966, 1972a); and there seems little reason to suspect that behaviour in other semiotic codes, or in respect to other aspects of language, or the location of the speakers is likely to be radically different. Behavioural norms have little to do with the kind of idealization entailed by such theories as that of innate competence, which logically permits one single blue-print; by contrast, norms of behaviour considered appropriate to specific contexts of situation are more readily relatable to the notion of acculturation. In not a few communities, bargaining is the norm for the occasion of buying and selling; in others the fixed price prevails. Neither is ideal behaviour; but we would think that a buyer who tried to bargain in Saks is certainly behaving in an a-typical way while refusing to bargain in an African shop was once described to me as 'somewhat insulting to the shopkeeper' by one of the shopkeepers himself. It is not a question of correctness or morality: simply an observation of what people *do* do in order to accomplish a certain something. The confusion of norm with idealization is based on a misconception; the typical is only the most frequent, it is therefore bound to be socially significant; but it is not obligatory as a reflex action is or as behaviour might be which is genetically pre-programmed. Judgements concerning the appropriateness of behaviour always make appeal to the relevant culture and this appears entirely consistent since specific contextual configurations are validated only culturally (Goffman 1975; Bateson 1955; Hasan 1984a, 1985b; Malinowski 1923; Firth 1950; Halliday 1974b).

3.4.3 Norms, systems and variation

Obviously then, if context is being employed as the rationale for a prediction of the *typical* patterns of behaviour, this is not tantamount to a claim of *absolute* determinism. Although invariance may be said to imply typicality, the reverse is not true; typical behaviour is not invariant behaviour even within the context of the same culture. But to claim that variation can happen anywhere, anyhow, anytime, or that the individual is equally free to negotiate a situation in all environments, is to vulgarize the notion of both variation and individual freedom.[5] Even those scholars who talk most about the individual's negotiation of context use the habitual tense, which one might argue gives a lie to the overt rejection of norms! But it may be useful to think of variations as falling into two major categories: those which are within the system and those which are external to it. Examples of the latter type are such happenings which are often interpreted by the members of the community as 'disruption', 'interruption', 'postponement', etc., while a sub-category of this type of variation might arise due to some pathological inclination arising from whatever cause. Of these, disruption – or at least some forms of it – would appear to be the most complex as it is here that distinct foci on the situation have to operate side by side, with the participants inhabiting distinct universes simultaneously.[6]

Variations which are within the system have been described (Hasan 1978) as arising from the local, non-critical properties of both the text and the context. What one says now influences what one might go on to say next; this is obvious from the readiness with which we note mixed metaphors, inconsistencies and 'forgettings' in our own speech even as we are speaking. There is a sense in which the *processual nature of the text* is an important source of its uniqueness. Equally important is a second fact; each contextual configuration is predictive of a range of possible behaviours; this 'tells the organism among what *set* of alternatives he must make his next choice' (Bateson 1964): it does not detail what each particular choice must be. A third point that needs to be taken into account in considering variation in behaviour is the flexibility of the notion of 'context'. It is perfectly obvious that specific contexts cannot be hermetically sealed off one from the other; nonetheless, it is also an empirical fact that we recognize 'difference' in contexts. I have argued that each particular category of context contains elements whose presence or absence is non-critical to the identity of a register (Hasan 1985b): for example, the identity of the context 'shopping for food in a personal service store' does not alter either because of how well one knows the store-keeper or what particular items of food one buys. But these are certainly the elements in the context of situation whose presence or absence correlates with difference in typical behaviour. If the store-keeper is well known to us, we would normally, i.e. without 'good reason', not start off on our business of shopping without some sociability (Hasan 1978; Ventola 1979), though of course there is nothing to prevent us from being unpleasant, snobbish or eccentric, except perhaps the weight of social opinion and the part it plays in the formation of our egos. Thus it is obvious that there are variations in behaviour within the same context which are susceptible to systematic explanation in terms of more delicate details in the field, tenor and mode of discourse.

3.5   Contextual norms and individual autonomy

Let me turn now to the question of individual autonomy. It is well to recognize that there is a close relationship between individual autonomy, variation and acculturation: variation is a constant of learnt behaviour and individual autonomy operates only in the realm of learnt behaviour, not in that of automatic, genetically controlled activities. A hypothesis about the relationship between text and context must provide a systematic account of both variant norms and individual autonomy not because failure to do so is reactionary, but because these concepts are essential to our understanding of how contexts, behaviours and cultures are related to each other, and how any change ever occurs in any of these. But what does individual autonomy mean? None of us is ever totally free (Douglas 1966); this is truer still in interaction. The very recognition of the other's identity is a constraint on our own; and while it is true that to have the speaking turn is to have power, it is perhaps no less true that to be speaking is to be vulnerable: there is good folk wisdom in the saying: if speech is silver, silence is gold. To speak is to declare our relationship to our social universe; even if we flout authority, ignore peer relation, construct a new set of rights and obligations for roles with old labels, we still take cognizance of the social mores around us, for these roles and relation have already been defined without references to our own specific individualities. Thus individual autonomy cannot mean total lack of social constraint. However, in the present context it may be reasonable to suggest that individual freedom consists in freedom to negotiate a frame of relevance, a context of situation, suited to the given contextual configuration of the interaction. That one has this freedom is quite evident. But to claim just this much is not sufficient since it is equally available to all at all times. Rather, there are certain environments which permit such negotiation more readily than others and certain roles allow one to exercise this privilege more than others. So the more interesting question is: how can these latter environments be characterized? Obviously the answer would bear relevance to whether text and context evolve together or whether some perception of relevancies must precede text construction in real time just as meaning must in some sense be 'prior' to the commencement of utterance. If it is true that the subjective focus is made inter-subjective through the mediation of the semiotic codes, then it would follow that wherever the context is individually negotiated, it must evolve with the text, since the verbal code would itself play a crucial role in mediating the frame of relevance.

3.5.1 Socio-semiotic systemicity and negotiating 'new' contexts

It is best to be explicit about 'individual negotiation' before addressing the above question. To me two considerations appear relevant to the concept: first, negotiation implies face-to-face interaction; it follows, the concept is not applicable to contexts with monologic mode. Second, negotiation of context implies that one party to the interaction could not have predicted the nature of the context with a significant probability of being correct without the benefit of access to what the other party is saying. Individual negotiation is a meaningful concept only if the negotiated context is not directly supported by the weight of conventionally interpreted environment. Therefore, if we can characterize those environments which as they stand permit us to predict with a significant probability of being correct what the frame of reference is likely to be for the embedded interactions, then we shall have located the very domain in which individual negotiation of context has the lowest probability of occurrence. This is where by implication individual autonomy would be under strain; and variation in behaviour would be highly systematic. I suggest that such characterization of environments is possible; and that it can be made in terms of the three parameters of the context of situation, namely, field, tenor and mode introduced here.

3.5.2 Negotiating context in monologues

Recall that in contexts with monologic mode, the possibility of individual negotiation does not arise. Interactions embedded in such contexts do not present a genuine possibility of turn-taking; so naturally the possibility of negotiating co-operation does not exist; rather, there is from the receiver's point of view a presentation of the context as a 'fait accompli'. Typically the text is so constructed here as to verbally encapsulate its own context maximally, and barring the inherent indeterminacies of the verbal code, the reader/listener is typically presented with a frame of relevance which is now an integral part of the text. I would suggest that for texts in the monologic mode, the maker of the text must proceed from some notion of his frame of relevance. This is to say, in real time, context must precede the text. I do not imply by this that all the details of the text are, as it were, pre-planned by the speaker; this would be like claiming that a reification or an overburdening of the speaker's already too overburdened mind![7] I mean simply that the speaker must have some notion of what he is attempting to achieve, who his audience is and what strategy he is about to employ to achieve his ends. It is a common mistake to imagine the 'what' in question has to be of a practical, informational kind; this is by no means necessary. The saying of sweet nothings or even of non-sweet nothings is just as much directed to an achievement of something as the writing of a manual for the repair of a machine. Nor is there any implication of explicit awareness any more than there is of an awareness of meaning as distinct from verbal realizations in normal, everyday speaking.

3.5.3   Negotiating context in dialogues: institutions and individuals

In contexts with dialogic mode, the possibility of genuine turn-taking exists; therefore, a cooperative negotiation of context can occur. But not all contexts are equally amenable to this; as I suggested above only those contexts genuinely lend themselves to negotiation where the environment is interpretatively neutral. To state this more explicitly we have to introduce certain attributes by reference to which both field and tenor can be further sub-categorized. One such attribute is 'institutionalization'. We may think of this as a continuum extending from most institutionalized to least institutionalized – or 'individuated'. I believe that my use of these terms is in keeping with that of Bernstein (1971). Thus a process may be ranged anywhere on a cline from *most institutionalized to most individuated.*

Social processes which are most institutionalized would logically be multiply coded semiotically; that is to say, the fact that they are institutionalized would be indicated by the fact that the many different modes of meaning would single them out, and the boundaries set for a social process by one mode would be commensurate with those set by another mode of meaning. As example consider the social process of marrying or the dispensing of justice. Both these processes are towards the institutionalized end of the continuum and accordingly both are multiply coded through ways of dressing, ways of conducting oneself, performance of a set of ritual actions, the presence of a set of recognized locations for the carrying out of these ritual actions and by a communally recognized set of the rights and obligations accruing to participants who enter the various stages of these processes in various capacities. These nonverbal codings become diagnostic of the nature of the process, and this has a serious consequence for the prediction of interactants' frames of relevance. The unfolding of institutionalized processes involves *convergent coding*, with several modes of meaning operating visibly and simultaneously so that there is a great deal of redundant information. And what, from the point of view of verbal coding, may be seen as just a material situational setting, can from the point of view of the social process be seen as context semiotically coded through a series of distinct codes. Whenever there is evidence of convergent coding, we tend to interpret the context for verbal interaction by reference to these multiple frames and our interpretation has a significant probability of being correct. This is true even when an institutionalized process is under strain, since the erosion of multiple convergent codes is of necessity slow: whatever the crisis for marriage as a social process may be, even *today* if we find a young woman in a wedding dress being led towards a church the common inference is that a wedding is about to take place; and this common inference has a high probability of being correct. It is not outside the realm of possibility that she is on her way to, say, a fancy dress party but few people would infer this; and what is more such inference would have a considerably low probability of being correct.[8] Equally, when we see someone enter a shop or a bank and walk up to the counter and engage in a verbal exchange, we infer this to be a service encounter and there is a very high probability of our being correct in this inference, although again it is not entirely impossible that the person is at that moment engaged in threatening the assistant in a quiet, non-histrionic way to blow up the bank unless some demand is met.

Let me add in passing that the different participants of a social process do not have the same 'attitude' to the process: the priest does not feel the same way about this wedding as the bride and groom do, just as the golfer does not feel the same way about the game as the caddy does (c.f., Goffman, 1975).[9] But in my view this does not mean that two distinct processes are going on side by side. We must see the tension of distinct views as inhering in the nature of that process; and these tensions contribute to the form of verbal interaction if and when it takes place, e.g., in the case of the caddy and the golf-player. We can conclude then that *when the material situational setting displays a series of convergent codes, then the probability of the individual negotiation of context is appreciably reduced.*

3.5.4 Dialogic mode and social distance in negotiating context

This prediction can be made more precise if the remaining parameter is also taken into account: i.e., the tenor of discourse. Recall that tenor is concerned with role relations. Roles can also be sub-categorized by reference to the institutionalized-individuated continuum. Institutionalized roles are normally hierarchic, while the individuated ones even if inherently hierarchic, e.g., parent-offspring or teacher-pupil, permit greater discretion to the role holder.[10]

If the role is institutionalized and hierarchic this implies non-reversibility of roles: distinct rights and obligations ascribed to the roles and the boundary between them are clear.[11] The carriers of hierarchic roles cannot assume just any role except under a certain condition, provided by 'social distance' (Hasan 1973c, 1978, 1985b). *Social distance between the interactants is determined by reference to the range and frequency of their interaction*: the wider the range and the more frequent their mutual interaction, the less the social distance between them.[12] The quality of social distance modifies the role: the greatest degree of role reversibility occurs where the role is individuated and the social distance minimum, such as a *friend* or *close colleague* or *close sibling*. Here whatever one can do, the other can too; the rights and obligations are equal: a great deal of discretion is available to both. The lowest degree of role reversibility occurs with hierarchic and institutionalized roles and maximal social distance, as for example with an interviewer and a job applicant as the interviewee.

3.6 Conclusion: a systemic functional hypothesis on con/textual variation

We are now ready to make the final generalizations. In any situation of interaction in the dialogic mode, whatever other information may or may not be available to the interactants, this much they must know for it pertains to their personal history: what kind of social distance obtains between them, and therefore how far along the institutionalized end of the continuum they would be located.

If the material situational setting is convergently coded, and if the social distance is tending to the maximum, then we have an environment which is hostile to individual negotiation of context. This is not to say that one cannot attempt it, but such attempts are viewed with suspicion or anger or explained away as a joke in bad taste. If I go to get a visa at a foreign Consulate and am called to an interview with the Assistant Consul, I really do not have the privilege of negotiating a context of casual chat with him; that dance is led by him. Of course, I could always try leading, but if I did so, it would either say something about my intelligence, if you are uncharitable; or about my ideological stance; or cast doubt upon my real motive in applying for the visa.

The environments in which cooperative negotiation of context is genuinely achieved most often can be described as one where the material situational setting is not convergently coded as pertaining to some specific social process and where the social distance between the interactants is near minimum. For example upon meeting a close colleague in the Central Quad on my Campus, I can negotiate a context so that we may end up either going to the bar for a drink or we may settle down to a discussion of the latest manifestation of academic bureaucracy or whatever. Seeing us together in the Central Quad gives no one any ground for predicting what our specific frame of relevance might be at that moment. It is, however, worth pointing out that even in such an open and potentially variable environment, certain aspects of the form of our interaction is still generally predictable (Ventola 1979). When the context is cooperatively negotiated, the text and the context evolve approximately concurrently; each successive message will function as an input to the interactants' definition of what is being achieved.

I hope that I have succeeded in showing how within a conception of contextual norms, both variation and individual autonomy can be systematically treated so that they become useful theoretical tools in the discussion of text creation and text interpretation. The nature of interaction is inherently social, no matter how personal the ends it is made to achieve.

Notes

1   The talk on which this paper is based was presented at the Seventh LACUS Forum 1980 at Rice University, Houston Texas. The published paper had no section divisions. These were introduced by me for the present publication; that is when the following notes were also inserted.

2   This view predates by a good many years, the neurologist's view of the human mind as a 'personalized brain' (Greenfield 1997).

3   In other words, context is relevant whether language is being used in producing text or in interpreting it or critiquing it.

4   Today I would have used the term GSP an acronym based on Generalized Structure Potential, which is designed to represent the possible range of the structure available within a given register to the range of the texts capable of instantiating that register. (For a synopsis of the concept, see the last chapter in this volume.)

5   One of the terms current in the late 1970s and early 1980s for what I described later as 'contextual shift' (1999) was 'negotiating situation', i.e., attempting to change a situation by some semiotic action whereby the ongoing situation would change. To me it has always seemed that throughout an ongoing interaction the discursive context changes constantly, and that this change may be instigated by any feature of the context of situation; i.e., it may or may not be introduced by the interactants alone. To me the real question has always seemed to be: what kind of change becomes notable to the analyst and what does it reveal about the orientation of the analysis and/or about the nature of linguistic interaction.

6   More simply, their concepts of what is relevant to some activity at some stage of its progress differs whether in respect of the action, or the relation or the mode of contact.

7   I no longer have access to my original manuscript, but this last clause I find difficult to interpret at this stage. It is likely that what I meant was something like: 'this would be to reify the speaker's thought processes as the contents of an already preoccupied mind'.

8   The inferences seem plausible since today church halls can be 'hired' for certain types of ceremonial gatherings e.g., birthday parties.

9   Their frames of relevance have to be responsive to those of the others otherwise they would be unable to play their own specific part in the activity: this can certainly happen if the two began with a 'sour' relationship, which is not true in the majority of cases.

10   With hindsight it seems clear that what is called 'social distance' is quality 'added' to the hierarchic role: whatever the meaning of a hierarchic role, its meaning appears to be 'changed' by the application of the category of social distance.

11   In my most recent work (see Chapter 8 in this volume), I have abandoned the features called institutionalized or individuated with reference to tenor. The idea is that with the inclusion of the features as at present in the systems of social positioning, the choices spell out degrees of individuation/institutionalization; this coupled with social distance seems to do the same job with greater ease.

12   That is to say the degree of familiarity is greater: social distance between them is reduced. In my later work I described the degree of social distance as indicative of the 'interactive biography' of the interactants.

4 Wherefore context? The ontogenesis of meaning exchange[1] [2001]

'The tongue finds the aching tooth,' said Lenin, meaning that the constant return to a teasing question indicates that 'there is something behind it', it bears witness to the non-resolution of the question. (Pêcheux 1983: 55)

4.1 Introduction

There is no discourse analysis in this paper. Nor is it concerned with that enormously popular topic, namely discourse and social change. The paper thus offers neither any technicalities that can be readily borrowed and quickly applied to the analysis of another text of one's choosing, nor does it make an appeal to our moral sense of responsibility, which is such a vogue in the social sciences today. Instead its interest lies simply in considering certain fundamental questions in the so-called 'context theory'. Here too the problems I raise are not entirely novel, though I believe despite their importance, they are much misconstrued. The fundamental problem addressed by this paper has to do with the very basis for the recognition of the category of context; why is it necessary for a linguistic theory to recognize this category? And what are the attributes of this category? What justification is there for suggesting a particular set of attributes as essential to it? One might object that these questions have already been asked (e.g. see Halliday 1970a, 1975a, 1979b, etc.) and that we know all the answers. True, we do in a way; but I believe our approach to context has been a halfway approach. In this paper I will suggest a way of conceptualizing context which will hopefully enhance our understanding of the place of context in the system and process of language.

To this end, I will begin my discourse by first presenting in Section 4.2 a very brief and focused view of how the recognition of context has been validated in two major linguistic approaches. This will allow me to draw attention to a fundamental lack in the popularly held views. Following on this conclusion I will suggest that to understand the full significance and value of the category of context, we need to look into the early acts of communication by neonates. I discuss this activity in Section 4.3. Recent research in the domain of human brain/mind suggests that human beings are not so much *homo grammaticus* as they are *homo semioticus*. There appears to be a (bio)-logical necessity for semiosis, i.e., exchange of meaning: the human neonate is genetically predisposed to social acts (Brothers 1997). What this means is that the *homo semioticus* is, just as importantly, also the *homo sociabilis*. This close relation between sociality and semiosis offers a valuable insight into the category of context.

Current literature on context overwhelmingly supports the view that language in use presupposes an environment, a context for interacting. I will argue that neonate semiosis is no exception to this general principle: it too presupposes a social environment, a context, as has been demonstrated by the research conducted by several scholars e.g., Bateson, Bullowa, Brazelton and Trevarthen, to name a few. Their research is on pre-linguistic interaction – or more accurately, on proxemic semiosis – which provides valuable insight into a socio-historical stage necessary to the development of (proto-)linguistic semiosis such as recorded by Halliday (1973a, 1975a), Painter (1984, 1989, 1996), Torr (1997), which in turn is the foundation for the development of communicative competence examined by several other scholars writing within the framework of pragmatics (see, for example, Ochs and Schieffelin 1979). In my view, these researches argue for the centrality of context to the evolution and development of all semiotic modalities, not just language. The perspective thus offers a direction for answering the questions raised above. Having discussed these themes in Section 4.3, I will go on to present some implications of treating context as a phenomenon that is as much responsible for the development of language as it is for the formation of the human mind. These implications cover a wide range of linguistic theory, including of course the origin of the functional nature of languages as well as linguistic variation.

Section 4.4 will briefly address the question of linguistic functionality. If functionality in semiotic systems originates in the role of context in shaping the semiosis, then logically the principle of functionality should extend to all primary semiotic modalities, not just language. The important question for linguistic functionality is how it is articulated within the system, and what we take to be the justification for its recognition. Is it something as local and piecemeal as words for snow and camel and colour, or is it something that characterizes the form of language in a deeper sense? Most readers will be familiar with Halliday's hypothesis (Halliday 1970a, 1973a, 1975a, 1977b, 1979b, etc.), according to which there exists a realizational relation between the contextual frame and the metafunctions of language. The view of context offered here presents a compatible perspective.

Due to its origin in context, linguistic metafunctionality is a universal feature of human languages. Moreover its articulation within any one language is likely to be invariable: no matter what variety of English you use, its metafunctional make up will be the same as that of any other variety. On the other hand, the principle of variation in language by definition argues that systems within the same language will differ from each other significantly. In Section 4.5, building mainly on the work of Bernstein (1990, 1996), I will attempt to show how variation is an invariable condition of the linguistic process, affecting aspects of text formation.

4.2   Wherefore context? The traditional response

In the 1960s, context was a notion remarkable by its absence from the discourse of dominant linguistics: to express concern with context was to banish oneself to the outer periphery of the legitimate boundaries of that discipline. Today, except perhaps for a die-hard minority, the notion of context has captured the centre-stage position so that concern with context – or more accurately, the perspective adopted on context – defines one's location within the now much more enriched discipline of linguistics. To those interested in the study of language as a social process, today's popularity of context is certainly preferable to yesterday's resounding silence. But interestingly at least in one respect, the two situations appear curiously alike: today when so much is being written on and around the notion of context, the question of the basis of its relation to language still remains almost precisely where it was in the era of its neglect. In fact it would not be an exaggeration to say that despite many very significant developments in the so called context theory, there has been almost no change so far as ideas about *the place of context in the system and process of language* are concerned: context still remains overwhelmingly a category whose recognition in linguistics is made necessary by the exigencies of language use – by the fact that people talk to each other. From this point of view, the concept has stayed pretty much where Firthian linguistics, building on the work of Malinowski, placed it some seventy-odd years ago.[2] To appreciate the thrust of the above remarks, consider two accounts of the role of context in the study of language. The first is an extract from Firth published first in 1950:[3]

> In the most general terms we study language as part of the social process, and what we may call the systematics of phonetics and phonology, of grammatical categories or of semantics, are ordered schematic constructs, frames of reference, a sort of scaffolding for the handling of events. ... Such constructs have no ontological status and we do not project them as having being or existence. They are neither immanent nor transcendent, but just language turned back on itself. ... 'context of situation' is best used as suitable schematic construct to apply to language events, and that it is a group of related categories at a different level from grammatical categories but rather of the same abstract nature. (Firth 1957: 181–182)

> The context of situation is a convenient abstraction at the social level of analysis and forms the basis of the hierarchy of techniques for the statement of meaning. The statement of meaning cannot be achieved by one analysis at one level, in one fell swoop. ... Descriptive linguistics is a sort of hierarchy of technique by means of which the meaning of linguistic events may be, as it were, dispersed in a spectrum of specialized statements. (Firth 1957: 183)

The second is a contemporary statement from Goodwin and Duranti (1992: 3) following Firth (1957) some forty years later:

> When the issue of context is raised it is typically argued that the focal event cannot be properly understood, interpreted appropriately, or described in a relevant fashion, unless one looks beyond the event itself to other phenomena (for example cultural setting, speech situation, shared background assumptions) within which the event is embedded, or alternatively the features of the talk itself invoke particular background assumptions relevant to the organization of subsequent interaction (...). The context is thus a frame (Goffman 1974) that surrounds the event being examined and provides resources for its appropriate interpretation: ... The notion of context thus involves a fundamental juxtaposition of two entities: (1) a focal event; and (2) a field of action within which the event is embedded.

To be sure, there are some important differences in the way that the category of context is conceptualized in these two approaches, but what I wish to draw attention to is the factor common to both: whether context is viewed as an abstraction as in Firth, or as an objectively real phenomenon as in Malinowski or in Goodwin and Duranti, the justification for the recognition of the category is that it is needed in order to make viable statements of meaning about (speech) events: attention to social environment is necessary *simply because this is where the social process of language manifests itself; it forms the natural background for the event.* It should be added that ascribing this remark to either Firth or Malinowski without further elaboration would be somewhat unfair since they were concerned with the wider reach of the notion of context, not simply with context as a back-drop (see Section 4.3).

That there is truth in this claim is self-evident; and the work developed over the last few decades, particularly in SFL, has amply demonstrated the truth.[4] I would argue we are dealing only with half the truth: to view the relations of context and language in this limited way has, in general, obscured a crucial part of the story. By focusing on context from solely the point of view of language as process, much modern linguistics has unwittingly been led into ignoring the equally important question of the relations of context to the system of language. Context has remained a category whose place in linguistic theories is just to illuminate the nature of *parole*, not of *langue*. The implication is not far behind that language as system has a being outside the context of the social conditions of human existence. This perspective on context would obviously be welcome to those linguistic theories which actually do locate the genesis of the language system entirely outside communal existence.[5] For such theories, the category of context is a good device for 'mopping up' some of the problems that inhere in an essentially extra-social view of language: to bring back the banished realities of language use, all one needs to do is to, say, postulate a communicative competence side by side with the biologically bestowed linguistic competence, and suddenly the problems seems to be resolved. This is the kind of approach where context becomes a mundane 'reality', language a mysterious mental organ, and grammar becomes knowledge encrypted in the human brain at birth.

Clearly in theories of this kind, context, in the true Derridean fashion, can only act as a supplement for a lack in the theory itself. But it is the nature of supplements that they only do local repairs: context viewed simply as the frame for some focal communicative event is no exception to this rule. The most crucial problem it leaves unresolved is, ironically, the problem of the theoretical status of context itself: if context has no part in the genesis of language as resource for exchange of meaning, how come it possesses such wide efficacy in revealing the nature of that same language when it occurs in actual uses of decidedly varied kind? What is the mechanism that enables an *a-social linguistic/grammatical competence* to become socially responsive to the varied uses of language? How does communicative competence arise?

Of course there is no logical necessity for mutual exclusion of *parole* and *langue*: they are not like conceptual allophones incapable of existing in the same theoretical environment. Viewing context as necessary to the explication of language use in no way excludes the possibility of its intervention in the genesis of language. Quite the contrary: it does appear reasonable to assume that there must exist some principled relation between use and resource – the actual and the potential, the instance and the system, the *parole* and the *langue*, call it what you will. And if that is the case, then it appears more than likely that a theoretical category such as context possessing the potential of identifying what meanings might be relevant and appropriate to a given occasion of talk, might at the least have some interesting contribution to make in illuminating the nature of language as a resource for meaning. I suggest that both Malinowski (1923, 1935) and Firth (1957) must have reasoned along these lines. I say this because, although I myself have not come across any such explicitly expressed arguments in either scholar, it is an assumption of such reasoning that would explain their efforts to link context to the ontogenesis of language.[6] Through his notions of variant speech fellowships, and of social variation in language use, Firth (1957: 177–189) seems in particular to draw attention to the problem of the relation between the language one uses in language events and the language that grows with one as one grows into a member of a his/her speech fellowship. Goodwin and Duranti arrive at a compatible conclusion though their point of departure is somewhat different:

> If indeed language development starts as part of a social matrix and the child's egocentric speech is in fact internalized social speech, we should be questioning the adequacy of child language acquisition models based on a notion of linguistic structure as an independent level, not affected, in its most basic nature, by the conditions of linguistic performance. Indeed, it would seem that any kind of language acquisition device would have to be able to both read, i.e. interpret, and reformulate (or filter) some aspects of the context that give meaning and form to speech signals. (Goodwin and Duranti 1992: 21)

Following Malinowski and Firth, Halliday had reached the above conclusion some 25 years ago in his study of an infant learning how to mean (1973a, 1975a). This account of language development is in harmony with the claim about linguistic functionality (Halliday 1970a): *the nature of language has to be functional since language grows out of languaging and languaging itself is a form of social life.* Valuable as this work is, I suggest that to appreciate the part that context plays in shaping the language of individuals in a community, we need to go beyond (proto-) linguistic semiosis to the earlier stage of proxemic semiosis.

4.3   Context in early semiosis

Despite the popular appeal of Pinker's (1994, 1995) 'quaint' expression, recent research in neuro-science (Edelman 1987, 1992; Dennett 1991) suggests that it is not the grammar of human language as such that could possibly be viewed as a 'human instinct': rather, it is, in fact, the predisposition to semiosis which deserves that nomenclature. The research reported by Brothers (1997) on the genetic basis of human sociality makes a strong case for an inborn urge for semiosis, since the sociality of a specifically human variety is impossible without semiosis of a specifically human kin.[7] Systematic observation of neonates has established convincingly (Bateson 1975; Brazelton 1961; Brazelton, Koslowski and Main 1974; Bullowa 1979b; Lewis and Rosenblum 1974; Shotter 1978; Trevarthen 1974; Halliday 1975a; Reddy, Hay, Murray and Trevarthen 1997) that babies are born communicators, engaging in what has been variously described as 'pre-speech' (Trevarthen 1974), or 'exchange of attention' (Halliday 1975a) or 'proto-conversation' (Bateson 1975).[8]

4.3.1   Two conditions for the development of language

However, it is also quite obvious that for their early semiotic acts babies do not use the semiotic system of language in the ordinary sense of that term. What they use, instead, is the proxemic modality, enlisting their bodies as their expressive resource. This is not surprising given the state of the neuronal and organismic maturity of the neonate (see, especially, Edelman 1987, 1992 on the pre-requisites for linguistic semiosis). What this suggests is that it is not grammatical structures such as NP, VP, or transformational algorithms which are likely to be the biological 'given':

recent research in the formation of 'mind' makes it difficult to believe that a neonate's brain could act as a material container housing pre-packaged categories of grammar as implied generally by the dominant model of linguistics. It seems considerably more likely that what the infant brings at birth is something much more basic and general – some neuronal affordance that enables the brain to function as a resource for supporting the inherent design features common to all human semiotic systems including language.[9] The postulate of a biologically endowed faculty of this abstract nature suggests, in turn, that at the highest level of abstraction, semiotic systems must be alike, which is of course not to claim syntactic identity. Given the scope of this paper, I shall not develop this claim any further, but note recent descriptions of certain distinct semiotic systems (O'Toole 1994; Kress and van Leeuwen 1996; van Leeuwen 1991a) which appear to support this position.[10]

What does it mean to claim that babies have a natural predisposition for semiosis, so that from a few weeks old, they appear to engage another in pre-speech conversations or in interactive exchange of attention? In answering this question, we need look no further than ordinary everyday experiences: most of us have noticed a baby perhaps just a few weeks old focusing on some person or even an inanimate object, with her tiny body straining in an effort to address – or at least, this is how we adults, who happen to be around the baby, interpret that physical posture. And it is here, in this tendency to interpret the baby's focusing of attention as a meaningful episode, that context first impinges on the ontogenesis of semiosis. The physical posture of the baby is but a material phenomenon – what Harré (1993: 19) might call *action* of a kind. It is only when this material phenomenon can be treated *jointly* – by the baby and the immediate others in the baby's life – as a device for making some meaning that its status changes from the material to the semiotic: Harré (*ibid.*) would call this an *act*, something that is significant in the literal sense of the word as Vygotsky (1962) argued; it signifies something but its becoming significant requires the joint participation of an acculturated other and the baby learning how to mean like other members of the speech fellowship. Let me emphasize two points here. First, there is the adult's pleasure in participating in this dialogue, which is important, for it may be that *so far as the neonate is concerned presence or absence of satisfaction is perhaps the most general meaning in all interactive activities*. Second, it goes without saying that the neuronal make-up of the neonate brain is such as to support these early acts of semiosis (Edelman 1987, 1992): as some scholar remarked somewhere no amount of cooing to a cat/dog is going to enable the animal to develop human language, even though it may display a certain degree of comprehension. Brothers (1997) claims a genetic basis for attention to human (-like) faces, to hand and eye movements in all higher primates. In other words, the scene is set for the early proxemic engagement which is a necessary basis for the ontogenesis of all human semiotic systems (Halliday 1995a).

Notwithstanding Pinker (1994), the meanings babies mean cannot already be there inside their brain ready and packaged in innate syntax. In any event, the brain at birth cannot contain all the essential structures and evaluations arbitrarily associated with those meanings just straining to get out on exposure to the sound of someone speaking. Rather babies are, in fact, *born* meaning-makers in the following specific sense: as pointed out by the many scholars already mentioned, a neonate is as likely to initiate the exchange of attention as to respond to it. In other words, babies independently and non-randomly take the first step towards actions to which some meaning can be assigned. But even so, meaning making is essentially a joint activity: validation by an other is essential for seeing the action as an act, so turning the material into the semiotic. You need not, in fact you *cannot*, deliberately teach the baby to adopt the physical postures that she adopts as she begins to engage in this primary form of semiosis; nor can you teach the baby how to arrive at what I have called the principle of the conjunction of dissimilars which binds the signal and its meaning into a unity (see note 9): this is part of the biogenetic capital that the baby has inherited as a member of the human species; it forms an element, amongst some others, of the biological basis of her language development, and is far removed from the Chomskyan notion of innate grammar. But to build on such biogenetic foundation (Vygotsky 1978), to get it to function as a resource for her, the baby needs other social beings (Hasan 2005, 2009a, 2011b). Unless her physical moves are validated as moves having some semiotic value there is no reason to suppose that the baby would experience what I am inclined to call 'interactive satisfaction' – a sense of 'semiotic success'. Indeed, in this sense, the very significance of what it is to engage in semiosis is jointly created by the baby and her caregivers, and I would suggest that, if for some reason, none of the baby's initiatory attempts at engagements of this kind received any response, it is very likely that she would herself not develop a sense of those physical postures, those vocal patterns as some kind of semiotic move. To see some sensori-motor phenomenon as having a specific semiotic character, the baby needs an acculturated other as caregiver. In other words, the sociogenesis of meaning begins at a very early stage indeed and it typically takes the form of the caregivers playing what are essentially *their* semiotic games, while passing them off as really the baby's games, which turn into meaning because they are ratified by the baby's state of satisfaction.

The importance of validation and reciprocity does not disappear as the child moves into language. In any event as many scholars (see, for example, discussion in Halliday 1973a, 1975a, 1995a; Trevarthen 1974; Lock 1978; Bullowa 1979b; Painter 1984, etc.) have pointed out, the move into language does not represent a sudden and sharp discontinuity: the baby is not propelled suddenly from silence or senseless babbling to linguistic semiosis, as was implied in the 1960s accounts of language acquisition. Under normal conditions, an 18-month-old infant has had an 18 month experience of being systematically engaged in semiosis (which is not the same as babbling), and to the extent that language is one semiotic system among many, the child's familiarity with the most abstract design features of semiotic systems extends back to her first weeks of life. Some of the ways in which reciprocity by an other becomes integral to the development of language is well recorded by many scholars (Halliday 1973a, 1975a, 1979a; Trevarthen 1974; Trevarthen and Hubley 1978; Bruner 1978; Painter 1984; Torr 1997), to name a few. That this pattern of validation and reciprocity continues much longer than the very early stages of natural language development is borne out by Painter's case study of a child beyond the age of four – the magic age at which according to the innatist model, the child is supposed to have already 'mastered his mother tongue' (Painter 1989, 1996). And so he has if 'mother tongue' is equated with basic structures of simple clauses: this simply reveals the impoverished sense of what it is to learn a mother tongue.

In the nativist model of language acquisition, validation and reciprocity are assigned no importance. The other is reduced to a vocalizing mouth producing the language data against which the child can test her innate grammars to select the right grammar to which she is exposed. The mind-making features that underlie the language 'data' – its reciprocity, its role in 'scaffolding' the child's knowledge of language, in validating her developing sense of its practical power, i.e., what you can do with it, its inter-subjective nature – are all trivialized and made irrelevant in that frequently repeated phrase 'exposure to language'. As I pointed out elsewhere (Hasan 1973c) if the reductive hypothesis supported by invoking this phrase were at all viable, then it would follow logically that if you played an audio recording of, say, Urdu day in and day out to an 18-month old living in a Chinese speaking family in some remote part of China, the baby would learn the language spouting forth from the audio recording just as well as she would learn the Chinese of her speech fellowship. The absurdity of such a supposition can be ignored only by very committed theoreticians of language! Unless it can be established as an empirical fact that mere 'exposure to language' in isolation from its social context is sufficient for the ontogenesis of language, one is justified in maintaining that *even in normal humans, language will not develop without contact with some culturally specific other(s),* for the simple reason that it is only such a being who can validate, it is only such a being who will have the ability to reciprocate. As Brothers (1997: 68) points out 'the human brain stripped of its intrinsic sociality, is in fact mindless'. *Whatever the biogenetic capital that the neonate brings from birth, the complicity of the social is required to enable the child to develop a sense of the identity of an act as a semiotic act.* The baby's completely unconscious working out of the abstract design features of the semiotic systems (including the system of language) is predicated on sociogenetic intervention, and this implies the centrality of context in the process.

4.3.2   What does proxemic semiosis tell us about context?

The above account presents the barest outline of the essential nature of language development. However in this skeletal account of the ontogenesis of language two themes have been reiterated which are immediately relevant to our concerns with theorizing context. The first of these is the double condition for semiosis. On the one hand there is an affirmation of *a biological basis for sociality*: the human infant is genetically other-oriented. On the other hand, there is *a biological basis for semiosis*: the human infant is biologically programmed to cope with the basic content-expression principle, which is fundamental to all semiotic systems. The conjunction of content and expression at this early stage is likely to be entirely physiologically mediated – a pairing of the baby's emotion and bodily action and ministrations is what signing is likely to implicate at this stage; and the locus for both is the neonate's body. The second theme derives from this double foundation: *the biological resources are a necessary condition, but not sufficient in themselves, for the ontogenetic development of a human semiotic system such as that of language.* This biogenetic capital cannot be put to use without an interactive other.

It is in this second theme that I would locate the justification for the claim that context must form an integral part of any viable theory of language. Assuming that the foundation of linguistic semiosis is built on proxemic semiosis, which itself cannot develop without interaction, we may claim that *the category of context is needed because human languages as we know them cannot come about without context.* Context can so effectively resolve the many problems in the study of language use because context is, from the very start, implicated in the genesis of language system. This goes some way towards answering the question included in the title of this paper: '*wherefore context?*' At the same time, an examination of the neonate's interaction allows us to identify those elements of the social environment which are essential for the coming about of these acts of semiosis.

Taking the fact of sociogenetic intervention as the starting point, we note that the engine for this intervention is the biogenetic urge for creating intersubjectivity, which implies, first and foremost, the recruiting of an other to act as an accomplice. This other stands in some social relation to the baby – parent, sibling, hired care-giver, and so on. From the very beginning then human semiosis occurs within a social frame, and this has far reaching consequences. The interacting adult is already socially positioned, and in time the effects of such positioning rub off on the growing infant (discussion Section 4.5), whose relation to the adult is continually (re-)defined, maintained and reinforced in and through these joint acts of semiosis. The implication is that the primary condition of human interaction is some variety of relation with an other: we must therefore take social Relation to be one main element of the neonate's communicative environment. This aspect does not cease to have importance for the individual in any of the proverbial seven stages of human existence: communication always implies some variety of social relation between interactants.

Second, interaction presupposes Contact. In the first place there is the material aspect of contact – how the interactants are materially located *vis-à-vis* each other. In the case of interaction with a neonate, clearly this aspect is, as it were, predetermined: typically the interaction occurs face-to-face, implying the material co-presence of the interactants. But apart from this aspect, there is the semiotic aspect of contact – what sign systems are employed for reaching the other semiotically. In the early days of the neonate's life, contact with the body of the other, including vocal contact, is the main means of semiosis. But it is the semiotic aspect of contact that becomes the means of bringing about sociogenetic intervention: adults all over the world use the modalities of communication that they are themselves most comfortable using. Which means, of course, that from a few days old, the neonate encounters not only paralinguistic noises of one kind or another but also the language of her speech fellowship, sometimes cut to suit the consumer's size as for example by using 'motherese'. But the ordinary adult, who most probably knows nothing of Vygotsky's principle of the 'proximal zone of development' is not daunted by the fact that the baby is as yet without language. The caregiver puts into practice the principle underlying this theory of development: together the care-giver and the baby take a linguistic tour of the baby's immediate social world. It is thus that in time the baby gains familiarity both with the language of her speech fellowship and the worlds that this language construes. The socially positioned adult attending to the neonate is the most powerful device for the transmission of ideology though his behaviour towards the baby is hardly ever recognized as 'teaching' ideology.

Third, and last, interaction occurs with reference to some action: there has to be some perturbation in the even tenor of existence to bring about the convergence of interactants' attention. In most adult interactions, this initial stage typically takes the form of verbal action, such as greeting and/or forms of address or other attention-enlisting moves. The neonate is unable to use the system of sign that we normally think of as language, but this does not mean that avenues of initiating action are closed to the infant. The simplest act on the baby's part is to express her inner state, e.g. to cry, to gurgle. I am not suggesting that such actions either have a purpose in the sense we understand that term or that they are necessarily directed towards another with the intention of producing a reaction, though the work of Brazelton, Bullowa, Trevarthen and others does suggest that even a-few-weeks-old babies display remarkable evidence of interactive intentionalities. Whatever the case, it is some initial action on the part of the baby and/or the adult which brings about the convergence of their attention and acts as the occasion for creating contact, and where there is contact, there will be relation. And, of course, action and relation are two sides of the same construct: action without relation is strictly speaking impossible, while the quality of joint action produces what we see as some relation.

Action, Relation and Contact (ARC, for short) are thus the three essential components of context: they are quite literally a condition for the occurrence of any joint social activity irrespective of the semiotic system employed for creating and maintaining contact. These contextual parameters relate systematically to what systemic functional linguists have known since the early 1960s as Field, Tenor and Mode. Action, relation and contact are more general in nature: I think of ARC as relevant to any form of joint social practice, whether this involves language or not. By contrast, field of discourse, tenor of discourse and mode of discourse are, as the name suggests, specifically discourse related, and so would appear to imply language as the main, if not the only, sign system for creating and maintaining contact, though in recent years these concepts have also been used to describe 'texts' produced in systems other than that of language (O'Toole 1994; Kress and van Leeuwen 1996). Whether the terms should be seen as interchangeable or not is, in any event, a minor matter; what is much more relevant is the set of arguments through which the structure of interactive context has been established here as relevant from day one of an infant's life. The scenario I have sketched, seeking support from Edelman, Dennett, Brothers, Brazelton, Trevarthen, Halliday, etc., has suggested a fundamental role for context in the genesis of language: *there can be no language without context.*

4.3.3 Context and the system of language

This way of validating context as a fundamental theoretical category in linguistics appears to redress the balance. By emphasizing the centrality of context in the processes of the evolution and development of language, I am arguing the importance of context both in the shaping of language as system and in the working of language as a process. There is no exaggeration in the claim that the modelling of language as a social semiotic is impossible without invoking context as a primary base for semiotic activity (Hasan 2009a, 2013, 2014b). Context becomes the force which unites the biogenetic and the sociogenetic elements in the working of language whether seen as an ontogenetic process as in the above account or as a phylogenetic one (Halliday 1995a; Williams and Lukin 2004; Hasan 2004b). This in turn has important implications, some of which may be listed as follows.

First: context seen from this perspective has sufficient power for acting as the mechanism for the co-genesis (Marková 1990; Hasan 1992a, 1995, 1999b) of *parole* and *langue*. The role of context in the dialectic of instance and system (Halliday 1999; Hasan 2009a) suggests that, contrary to the popular view on linguistics, the metaphors of 'execution' and 'score' for *parole* and *langue* are a serious misreading of this relation (Halliday 1992a, 1996; Hasan 1996a).[11] Although arguably there appear to be early hints in Firth, it is in fact Halliday (1992a, 1996) to whom we owe a fuller explication of the dialectics of system and instance. This is how Halliday puts it:

> Saussure problematized the nature of the linguistic fact; but he confused the issue of instantiation by setting up *langue* and *parole* as if they had been two distinct classes of phenomena. But they are not. There is only one set of phenomena here, not two; language (the

linguistic system) differs from parole (the linguistic instance) only in the position taken up by the observer. *Langue* is *parole* seen from a distance, and hence on the way to being theorized about. (Halliday 1996: 30)

Second: given the basic attributes of context derived from an observation of neonate semiosis, and given the dialectic of instance and system, it seems reasonable to deduce certain features whose presence in language is logically predicated by the fact that for interaction to continue, the interactive means, here language, must be contextually sensitive. This allows an alternative approach to the validation of the claim of linguistic functionality, which is based on the exotropic nature of the linguistic theory (Hasan 1999c), and it adds a further dimension to the criteria suggested by Halliday (1970a, 1979b). There follow some theoretically interesting consequences, particularly for ideas on the relations of context, semantics and lexicogrammar which are briefly discussed in Section 4.4.

Third: since semiotic acts realize some cultural practice performed jointly by individuals in contexts that are specific to their own living of life – their own social positioning – it follows that every semiotic act is simultaneously both socio-historically unique because it is an individual's act operative at a specific spatio-temporal location and also socio-historically recognizable because socially regulated and culturally positioned. *Both variance and invariance can thus be found in the language of a community*, and, in the last resort, both these attributes of language are due to the contextual shaping of language. This on the one hand suggests that social context is the indispensable basis for studies in linguistic variation, and on the other hand points to the possibility of exclusive focus on the homogeneity or heterogeneity of language: this focus is an artefact of the analyst's point of view, not inscribed in the nature of language system as such, nor is it necessarily descriptive of a scholar's approach.

Finally: register or speech variety emerges as but one principle of variation in language – what Gregory (1967) referred to as *diatypic variation*. In the nature of things, this variation is not unrelated to other principles of variation – those of accent, dialect and semantic orientation (as defined in Hasan 1989, 1992b, 1992c). These different principles of variation are not segregated one from the other: they are simply the expression of the various facets of an individual's social conditions of existence, which implies that they inform the individual's system of language. Not surprisingly, each principle of variation is typically manifested within one and the same instance of language use (discussion, Section 4.5).

The following section shows the relevance of this way of context validation to the postulate of linguistic functionality.

4.4   Context and metafunctionality: instance and system

I have argued above that the three essential attributes of context – Action, Relation and Contact – form the very basis on which, for the neonate, some bodily behaviour receives its definition as a semiotic event. This is bound to have repercussions for the semiotic systems since they evolve epigenetically with each occurring instance of interaction. An indication of this is provided, for example, by Brazelton and colleagues who describe infant strategies for regulating semiotic interaction, whereby the infant controls both the course of the (inter)action and her accessibility for contact with the other. In other words, within the semiotic systems there develop features which act as a resource for the management of action, relation and contact. Of interest is Brazelton's view that disregard for the infant's interactive rhythm tends to be dysfunctional for the development of her psyche, damaging the prospects of future interaction. Similarly studies conducted by Trevarthen and his colleagues reveal the infant's sensitivity to the other and to her material environment of objects, processes and circumstances. As Reddy *et al.* point out:

> … from the first weeks of life infants are highly sensitive to the quality of adult communication. Further, they respond not only to simple alterations in form (for example, from an active and responsive partner to a still, blank face), but appear to process manifold parameters of adult displays in unison, treating each complex whole as specifying distinct interpersonal positions. The strong affective quality of infant response to the adult's unavailability or incomprehensible behaviour attests, too, to the fact that infant emotionality is intimately bound up with the state of mutual engagement, and there is a focused investment in achieving particular forms of contact. (Reddy *et al.* 1997: 257)

It seems to me that these and other such features of infant communication are an early manifestation of the functionality of the semiotic systems being used by the infant. Features of this kind which act as the resources for ensuring mutual engagement in interaction must keep pace with the increasingly complex changes in the developing patterns of interaction.

And there is every reason to suppose that as the maturing infant moves from the pre-speech proxemic semiosis to proto-linguistic semiosis, her developing semiotic system maintains the same regard for the important elements of the social environment. The seminal work of Halliday cited here and its replication and development by Painter (1984) and Torr (1997) demonstrates the trajectory of this development as it continues from proto-language into adult language.

The development of regard for the three basic elements of context is an essential condition for interactive satisfaction, and this is ultimately the basis for functionality in language: a semiotic modality which lacks efficacy for the conduct of semiotic acts is an anomaly, especially in view of the neonate's genetic bias toward social semiosis. In systemic functional linguistics, the term 'metafunction' is used to refer to that inner organization of language whereby its form acts as a resource for construing meanings relevant to the parameters of Action, Relation and Contact (i.e. Field, Tenor and Mode). Much has been written on the realizational relations of contextual parameters and texts. The questions that have been raised are: what attributes of language justify the postulate of field, tenor and mode (Halliday 1975a: 130)? Or coming at the issue from the other direction: why is the structure of language as it is (Halliday 1973a)? While appreciating the importance of both these perspectives (Hasan 1993, 1995), in what follows I want to raise a slightly different question: what does language have to be like if it must satisfy the necessity of responding to the interactive context – what the speakers are doing, with whom, and how they and their communicative modalities work to organize the social relation and the practice? The asking of this question takes for granted the fact that the responsiveness to the elements of context displays itself in some manner in the instances of use, but the question shifts the focus of enquiry from instance – from individual texts – to system. The question may, thus, be rephrased as: given the dialectic of system and instance, what sorts of features may be expected to appear in the language systems over time as a logical corollary of the fact that language must, of necessity, continue to be responsive to action, relation and contact, as it keeps pace with the communicative needs of the interactants? So the perspective is from above, and what is under focus is the system – *how the elements of context activate the elements of the semantic level, and meta-redundantly those of the lexicogrammatical level.*

We may turn for this discussion to the contextual parameter of social Relation, i.e., tenor with specific reference to discourse. Like the other two elements of context, the parameter of relation is itself a complex of factors, each of which is equally relevant to how the interactants see themselves *vis-à-vis* each other. Specifically, these factors have to do with the location of the interactants: (a) with respect to the action – what I have referred to as the *agentive role relation*; (b) with respect to power – i.e., *hierarchic role relations* based on, say, age, kinship, expertise, control of resources, and so on; and (c) with respect to the degree and quality of familiarity – what I have called *social distance*. However, the most general and pervasive factor locating the interactants *vis-à-vis* each other is with respect to their social positioning, using the term largely as in Bernstein (1990, 1996).[12] The importance of this factor resides in its relation to the social subjects' ideological stances (Section 4.5 for a more detailed discussion), through which all aspects of the interactive context are refracted. The implication is that what from some point of view might be thought of as the same social relation, e.g., that of authority as in mother-child relation, would invoke distinct orders of meaning depending upon the ideological stance of the adult. This implies in turn that if one wishes to specify the semantic features of the language system of the various speech fellowships in a community, these have to be stated at a certain degree of delicacy to permit the possibility of such non-random variation.

In being responsive to the interactants' need to manage their social relation with the interactive other in the ways discussed above, language must develop meanings and wordings which construe the interactants' discursive and evaluative attitudes in keeping with their perception of their location *vis-à-vis* the other. Some categories of meaning relevant to the realization of these attitudes would be such as the following:[13]

- categories of 'rhetorical stance' whereby an exchange of messages is brought about;
- categories of a logic based on rhetorical stance which underlies exchange structures such as the nexus of command and its compliance/rejection; question and its answer/disclaimer, etc.;[14]
- estimates of certainty, possibility, probability, obligation, discretion, etc.;
- perspective on phenomena, their evaluation as normal, positive or negative.

The lexicogrammatical resources for the realization of the above categories of meaning are found in the systems of mood, modulation, attitudinal modifications, and in evaluative prosody in the lexical items of the kind that Martin (1996) has discussed under the label of appraisal. It is not difficult to see how patterns such as those listed above might play an important part in creating, maintaining and changing the interactants' social relations. This can be appreciated by examining just a very short extract from a naturally occurring dialogue between a mother and her child. In this examination I will focus on one aspect of meaning-wording relations identified above:

Example 1:
mother   (1) put it on the stove (2) and leave it there
child   (3) why?
mother   (4) 'cause

In her first two messages the mother's rhetorical stance is exhortative (Hasan 1992b; Cloran 1994; Williams 1995), which is realized as imperative mood. The mother offers the child no discretion for rejecting, demurring, or considering other options. This does not mean that the child is prevented from doing any of these things – simply that from the point of view of the mother the situation is clear-cut; it admits of no such challenge as is obvious form her response to the child's *why?* in message (3). Compare the following possibilities any one of which might have been used instead of the original message (1):

Example 2:
(1a)   let's put it on the stove
(1b)   let's put it on the stove, shall we?
(1c)   how about putting it on the stove?
(1d)   why don't we put it on the stove?
(1e)   shall we put it on the stove?
(1f)   could you put it on the stove?
(1g)   I'd like you to put it on the stove
(1h)   it would be better to put it on the stove

There are of course other possibilities open to a speaker in roughly the same action environment. But examples (1a–1h) are enough to allow one to appreciate the contribution made by each in implying a subtly different social relation between interactants. Of course natural discourse is not like examples in a linguistic presentation: it normally consists of a large number of messages each of which carries information relevant to the social relation between the interactants; and typically each message sets up certain expectations about what is likely to be meant and worded thereafter. The liaison between social relation and patterns of meaning-wording discussed above is known as the 'interpersonal metafunction'.

In this discussion, instead of looking at the metafunctional organization of language from below, I have examined it from above. As widely recognized in the systemic functional theory, these two ways of examining a linguistic fact are not in mutual exclusion; rather they form part of the 'trinocular perspective' for validating categories of description (Halliday 1979b, 1984a, 1996). Remarkably, the conclusions I have reached are in agreement with those suggested for example in Halliday (1973b, 1979b), Hasan (1993), Martin (1992), Matthiessen (1995), etc.: tenor of discourse activates the interpersonal metafunction. The reason for the agreement is simple: the same phenomenon, i.e. metafunctionality, is the focus of attention, though from a different perspective. That being the case, rather than repeat the details of the liaison for the other two contextual parameters here, I would like to take my description of the origins of interpersonal metafunction (see also Hasan 1993, 1999b) as indicative of how one might go about describing a similar liaison between the contextual factor of Action with the patterns of wording-meaning which have evolved specifically in response to dealing linguistically with action. The resonance of action with a certain patterning of meaning and wording is what is known as the 'ideational metafunction', while a similar liaison between the contextual factor of CONTACT with certain patterns of meaning and wording is known as the 'textual metafunction'. Figure 4.1 represents this metafunctional resonance.

Figure 4.1: A co-genetic perspective on context and content

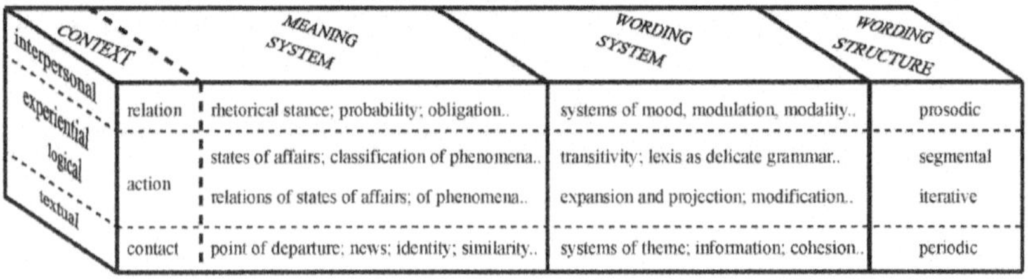

CONTEXT		MEANING SYSTEM	WORDING SYSTEM	WORDING STRUCTURE
interpersonal	relation	rhetorical stance; probability; obligation..	systems of mood, modulation, modality..	prosodic
experiential	action	states of affairs; classification of phenomena..	transitivity; lexis as delicate grammar..	segmental
logical	action	relations of states of affairs; of phenomena..	expansion and projection; modification..	iterative
textual	contact	point of departure; news; identity; similarity..	systems of theme; information; cohesion..	periodic

It is, however, important to ask what, if anything, has been gained by introducing the perspective from above? One might add that there has already been a perspective from above for some time on the relations of context and metafunctionality in the systemic functional model: this is implicit in the dialectic of realization whereby context is said to activate the semantic and lexicogrammatical choices in a text (Halliday 1977a, 1992a) while the latter are said to construe the context relevant to the text (Halliday 1973a). What is perhaps somewhat different here is the status of context itself: I have argued that the centrality of context is predicated on the genetic basis of social semiotic activity by the neonate: the relevance of context begins at a pre-linguistic stage. This is significant for it suggest that the justification for the recognition of the category of context in the last resort does not lie in the shape of the system of language; on the contrary, it is the shape of the system that depends on context – this as I have said before is the meaning of the claim of functionality in language. So the approach here is not simply from above – from context to linguistic meaning and form – but also it is thoroughly exotropic (Hasan 1999c); on the one hand, some inner properties of language are being examined from the point of view of a phenomenon – social context – which, though it is intimately bound up with the evolution of language, lies nonetheless outside language itself and has its roots in human nature; on the other hand, the validity of the postulate of context itself does not have to depend on the internal structuring of language. As I see it, *context is a pan-semiotic notion*. In the end, the justification for postulating this category takes us back to the biological make-up of the human organism: in this sense context is the bridge between the biogenetic and the sociogenetic foundations of language. What is justified by the functional organization of language is the *relevance* of context, not its epistemological status. The internal structuring of language goes a long way in supporting the claim of the epigenetic evolution of the language system.

If these views are accepted, then it seems that the discussion bears relevance to the old debate about the problem of validating the role of context in the genesis of linguistic metafunctionality (Hasan 1995, for some discussion). In the first place, such a relation is already indicated IF the internal structure of language shows fairly clear demarcations of system networks and structural patterns as suggested in Figure 4.1. Further, considering the way context operates in interaction, there is every reason to suggest that in a specific instance of language use the three parameters of Action (= field), Relation (= tenor) and Contact (= mode) will be perceived by the speaking subjects as integrated, presenting themselves as a seamless structure, an interactive occasion in which *what, who*, and *how* are not separate things; rather together they create a discursive unity. And this to my mind argues, first, that in the process of language, the correlation between these elements of context and individual metafunctions can only be probabilistic, not mechanically determinate: this is in complete agreement with Halliday's claim of several years ago (Halliday 1977a, 1979b). It is pointless to strain for an absolute one-to-one relation between, say, the field of *each* specific text and the meaning and grammar that defines the ideational metafunction. The more important question is: *are there any semantic (and lexicogrammatical) choices in texts which cannot be shown to be relatable to these three parameters of context*? Only if the answer to this is in the affirmative can we doubt the validity of the metafunctional hypothesis, and/or our description of the context based on the pattern of early semiotic practices. It seems to me that the separation of the parameters of context is inherently probabilistic. As such they are likely to be permeable – a point that I have emphasized since almost the very beginning of the discussion of context (Hasan 1973c, 1995, etc.). We cannot expect that one of these can have an instantial reality without the support of the other two: just as the instantiation of the category clause is impossible without the simultaneous mapping of each metafunction, so it seems that texts are realized by the whole metafunctionally informed ideational, interpersonal and textual semantics and grammar as a whole.

4.5   The heterogeneity of system: context, interaction and linguistic variation

Any mention of the system of language has to come to grips with the empirical fact that a living language has no other mode of existence except as an embodied semiotic resource, a point that Firth often emphasized. This fact would be quite irrelevant if the languages of individuals in the community were entirely homogeneous as postulated by Chomsky in the early 1960s: in that case, to describe one person's language would be tantamount to describing the community's language. But linguists have long recognized that language varies, both across individuals and within the one individual: 'unity' said Firth (1957: 29) 'is the last concept that should be applied to language. Unity of language is the most fugitive of all unities.' Naturally then language as in *the language of a community*, is a theoretical abstraction, not an actual fact, even if 'our language' has a reality that impinges strongly on us, its speakers. The pertinent question is how this reality is experienced by the members of a speech community. Observation of our language use suggests that typically individuals do not believe that everyone in their community has exactly the same language: we tend to act as if we believe that the most natural way of speaking is naturally ours; so far as others are concerned, they speak '*posh, proper, slovenly, crude, with an accent*' and so on. These evaluative characterizations refer simultaneously to two 'facts': in the first place, they refer to something experienced in the flow of speech, and second, they refer to something in the living of life, something in the context of members' social existence. In this section I will briefly discuss how the intervention of context in the ontogenesis of language brings heterogeneity into the developing system of the growing individual's language.

4.5.1 The larger canvas of human time and space

In talking earlier about the parameter of relation, I commented that social relation is really about the location of interactants *vis-à-vis* each other. Infants are born in a community that is always already there; and the care-giving adult is always located *vis-à-vis* others in a number of ways. Most variation in language is directly related to the contextual parameter of relation (tenor), but relation when it refers to human relation is a relative term. So far as variation is concerned, the perspective on relation may extend from the widest to the narrowest. From the wider point of view – call it the context of human history – there is the location of a community in time and space. So for example, in both these respects the Australian English speech community is located differently *vis-à-vis* other speech communities. The Australian English of today is considerably different from that spoken a century ago in Australia; and Australian English, at any time, thrives in Australia as it does nowhere else, notwithstanding the fact that speakers of this geolect will be found in nearly every corner of the globe. The Australian English of today represents a specific 'geolect' and 'chronolect', and no matter what other differences we might note within Australian English, in this respect all varieties of Australian English today are alike: each is a kind of modern Australian English. In this sense, a geolectal and chronolectal variety covers the speech community as a whole.

But hardly any aspect of language has sharply determinate boundaries. A fuzziness enters into the above situation due to language contact. Throughout human history, members of one speech community have come in contact with those of another. The twentieth century is perhaps extraordinary in the extent and intensity of exodus to the English speaking West, and Australian is no exception. Such contact typically produces types of English normally known as 'migrant English'. It is however worth noting that the migrant English of a Vietnamese in Australia is likely to be notably different from the migrant English of a Vietnamese in the United States. To have the status of an Australian citizen is not the same thing as being a member of the Australian English speech community, and at what point a migrant Asian becomes a member of, say, the Australian speech community is a moot point. The complexity of this situation is an indication of the complexity of the concept of speech community, which does not simply have to do with speech but also with affect to that speech and its speakers. Witness the language riots in various parts of the world.

4.5.2   Variation and speech fellowship

In most official literature on sociolinguistics, linguistic variation is viewed from a more local perspective: the geolect in the sense described above is taken as the starting point, whether this is ever explicitly stated or not. The fact that today's Australian English represents the same geolectal and chronolectal variety does not mean that it is one monolithic, homogeneous system: the work of Mitchell (1946) and that of other sociolinguists has demonstrated this quite clearly. So, to begin with, there are varieties of accent (Abercrombie 1951) – a term that refers to approximately the same aspect of linguistic variation that Labov was later to call 'social dialect'.

With some oversimplification, one might say that accent/social dia-lect – henceforth, *sociolect* – is on the one hand typically phonologically expressed: this is what constitutes its linguistic character. On the other hand, it is a linguistic means of 'bonding' to one's primary community, i.e. Firth's speech fellowship: this is what constitutes its contextual character. 'A speech fellowship sees itself and hears itself as different from those who do not belong' (Firth 1957: 186). Sociolects are one device for establishing such identifications. In the case of sociolects, what makes it obvious to an observer that someone does not belong is the fact that the patterns of noises they produce by way of speaking are not the same as that of the observer's speech fellowship. In this sense, sociolectal features are indexical: they become a means of signalling who you are, i.e., where you and your speech fellowships are located *vis-à-vis* the wider speech community. This loca-tion is simultaneously identified by reference to a variety of interactant attributes such as social class provenance, gender, ethnicity, age, and so on. It is not necessary to emphasize the obvious fact that, on the one hand, these attributes are significant in the social organization of a community and on the other, they are relevant to the parameter of social relation. In fact, Bernstein (1990, 1996) would claim that what we are concerned with here are not two distinct things, namely, social organization and social rela-tion: they are simply two perspectives on the same social phenomenon.

The infant's first bond with her speech fellowship is mediated by her immediate contact with her caregiver, typically her parents and more spe-cifically the mother, who in the nature of things is herself a member of some speech fellowship. If it is true that the neonate's semiotic systems

– and that means all primary semiotic modalities not just the system of language, which arrives later on the scene for the child – receive their definition and identity in interaction with an other, then from the very moment of birth when the infant's body comes in contact with the maternal body the infant is learning her speech fellowship's way of being, doing and saying, in the sense of meaning. This is where the first early lessons about bodily behaviour begin to be learned; this is where the unconscious, the deepest stratum of *habitus* (Bourdieu 1990) begins to take shape; this is where the legitimacy of desire is established; and later, this is where the child's identity as a member of a speech fellowship is confirmed, at least partially, by her adherence to sociolectally specific forms of speech. The ultimate principle that sets these practices in motion is social and semiotic, but what carries it on is *affect* – the intimate relation between the child and her caregiver, which is reinforced by the child's semiotic successes, her interactive satisfactions. It has been often observed that accent – the expression of one's sociolect – is the most persistent element of one's being. This is not surprising: one would hardly expect anything else given the role of context, especially the deeply personal relations, in the ontogenesis of vocal semiosis which begins as early as the first 6–8 months of a child's life (Halliday 1973a, 1975a).

4.5.3 Social control, ideology and semantic variation

Sociolectal variation, as I just remarked, is indexical in nature: whatever significance is attached to it is due to the prestige of the speech fellowship that owns up to the sociolect in question. Because its expression typically implicates the level of phonology – particularly the segmental features of phonology – sociolectal variation in itself is not directly relatable to the construal of meaning. It is thus not competent in itself to bring about material changes in the social environment; nor can it participate in the construal of the mental landscapes of its speakers, which depend on ways of meaning: whatever effect a sociolect creates in the life of the speaker is created entirely through the association of the sociolect with its speech fellowship. If members of the speech fellowship are underprivileged then the sociolect is so, too; and *vice versa*.

Not all linguistic variation is of this kind. In this respect 'semantic variation' (Hasan 2009a for discussion) is maximally different from sociolectal variation. Using Whorfian metaphors (Whorf 1956), one might say that semantic variation is realized *cryptotypically* by patterns of *configurative rapport at the level of semantics.* Whorf, as is well known, identified his patterns of configurative rapport at the level of lexicogrammar, and proceeded to provide their semantic interpretation, which he linked to the construal of an ideology. By contrast, semantic variation identifies patterns of configurative rapport at the level of semantics: it looks below for lexicogrammatical realizations and above to the construal of ideology as the higher level contextual phenomenon (see Hasan 2009a; Cloran 1994; Williams 1995, etc.). From the perspective of the contextual parameter of relation, what semantic variation construes is the interactants' ideological stances. Unlike sociolects, semantic variation does not simply *signal* ideology; rather, *this is how language participates in creating, maintaining and changing ideological stances.* The condition of material social existence to which ideological variation relates may most succinctly be described in Bernstein's words as 'social positioning'.

Social positioning is socio-logically related to control over the production and distribution of communal resources, whether the resources are material or symbolic. It is the quality of this control that underlies the relations of class, race, gender, age, expertise, and so on. The implication is that one's relation to the communal resources is one's relation to power: this, at the deepest level, is what social positioning is about.

Member's social positioning, in turn, underlies their ideological stances. Ideological stances do not so much determine the nature of *what* one views as content, as they determine *how* that content will be viewed. They are thus the regulators of relevance. It is a member's ideological stance that furnishes the principles through which a social context is seen for what it is for that member, both from the point of view of the recognition of the occasion and from the point of view of participation in it – the modes of being, doing and saying that are ideologically legitimate. What enables language to participate in construing distinct ideological stances is the possibility of semantic choice, which is what underlies semantic variation. The claim is then that speaking with reference to context presupposes a recognition of that context; to recognize a context is to recognize what would be the appropriate ways of being doing and saying in that environment, and these perceptions are far from uniform in any speech community. In other words, there are variant performances, variant text types, relating to what from some point of view is the same context, the same register at the primary degree of delicacy. The gist of this discussion is presented in Figure 4.2, which is a distillation from and an adaptation of some figures in Bernstein (1990: see esp. 13–62; 165–218 and 1996: 17–34 and 91–144).[15]

Figure 4.2: Social structure, variation and text in register

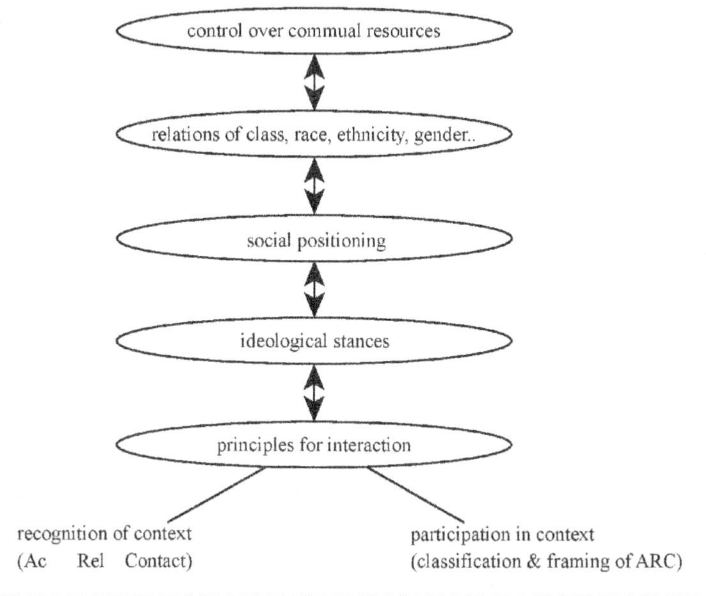

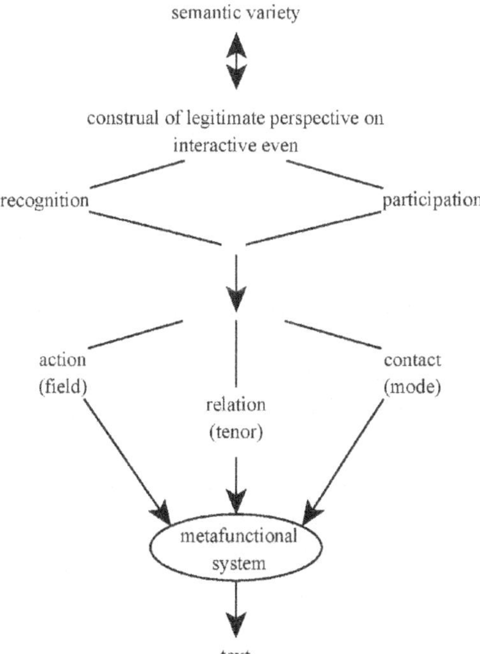

I want to make five interrelated observations with regard to the model represented in this figure. The first is the relevance of semantic varieties to the growing child's ideological stances. In adult-infant interaction, the ideological manifestations of social positioning naturally flow in one direction, namely, from the adult to the infant. However, there is evidence that the situation changes very soon: toddlers at the age of approximately three and a half years already display significant evidence of having been enlisted into the ideological stances of the speech fellowship to which the significant adults in their life belong (Hasan 1989, 1992b, 1992c, 1993; Cloran 1994, 1999b, 2000; Williams 1995, 2001). This demonstrates the efficacy of interaction in inculcating the growing child's own ideological stances – her cultural affiliation (Hasan 1986, 1996b).[16] The results of these researches strongly support the view that the ontogenesis of ideology begins very early indeed. And there again what is responsible for the success of this ontogenesis is the relation between the child and the care-giver. Through participation in these everyday ordinary interactions the child shapes her own consciousness in the image of her interactant, and this is possible only because of the special relation that holds between the child and the care-giver. The evidence of our research suggests that a grid is already being laid for the child for perceiving the world. I should emphasize that a semantic variety and the ideological stances that it construes are no more immutable than, say, Bourdieu's *habitus*; nonetheless the ideological stances developed in early infancy are the most potent because like the sociolects, they are buried below the surface of consciousness. What we take as natural is largely what has been nurtured in everyday ordinary interactions of no exceptional significance.

This leads me to the second point: the child's experience of everyday linguistic interaction is highly relevant to the development of her discursive potential (Hasan 1996c). Often, as Painter has shown (1989, 1996), adults take deliberate steps to guide the child's production of text, but most often it is the invisible local pedagogy of active participation in ordinary interactions that inculcates children into the principles and practices of discourse formation common to their speech fellowship. It stands to reason that the principles for the recognition of and for participation in contexts that the child grows up with are those of her speech fellowship, and therefore informed by its ideological stances. The child's response to ARC of context – to the action, the relation and modes of contact in any one instance – is as it should be in light of her developing ideological stances. This point is brought out clearly by Cloran (1998) and Williams (1998) who demonstrate from the different perspectives of their distinct studies that in interacting the child is learning ways of being, doing and saying common to her immediate speech fellowship; that the development of discourse does not follow a universal invariant trajectory. The mundane line of discursive development socio-logically schools the child in discourse practices informed by one particular semantic variety – that of her speech fellowship.

In view of the discussion in the last paragraph, it does not seem unreasonable to suggest that adopting a model of context along the lines developed here would be quite relevant to the arguments used for supporting the case for a genre-based pedagogic programme. As I understand, this programme emphasizes the need of those children whose mundane discursive development varies considerably from the discursive principles favoured in educational sites. The model presented here provides the socio-historical antecedents of the problem that the genre based pedagogic programme attempts to address. In addition, if the importance of control over symbolic resources is accepted (which is argued in the model), it seems highly desirable that the mundane line of discursive development should be further supplemented by a line that from the point of view of the learner is bound to be exotic. This would suggest that educational sites need to concern themselves not simply with schooling pupils in what is traditionally thought of as the favoured educational genres but the real task of literacy development consists in enabling insight into all forms of discourse prevalent in the community – whether they are currently educationally favoured or not.

The fourth observation is as follows: if we argue, as we do in systemic functional linguistics, that a context of situation is an instance of the context of culture, then it seems desirable to consult compatible existing theories which model those processes whereby the system of culture and the instance of a specific situation are brought into relation. I have argued elsewhere (Hasan 1992a, 2001b) that the most compatible theory of the social is that of Bernstein's, and in broad outlines, Bourdieu's, though the views of the latter on language do leave much to be desired (Hasan 1999a). It seems fair to suggest that if stratification of context is required to elaborate some aspect of this complex area, then abstractions of the type presented in Figure 4.2 might be better suited than those current in the connotative semiotic modelling of genre and context, which do pose problems in a functional model of the type that SFL is (Hasan 1995).

Finally, Figure 4.2 ultimately brings the highest level of cultural organization in relation to a text. The trajectory of this relation schematically covers a vast space. If it is accepted that cultures are created in and by persons being, doing and saying in the living of life, then it would seem to follow that the instance must carry some traces of this process. In this sense, each situation and each text has a long history – and it is a history that one needs to understand whether one's perspective is ontogenetic, phylogenetic or logogenetic. In my view this nicely captures the significance of context in the system and process of language. It is important to emphasize that the different kinds of variation, including the ones that I have not focused on specifically, namely that of register or (to use Gregory's term) diatypic variation, interlock: each kind of variation finds its expression within the process of language; this is because each typification vector applies to the entire system of language, and each is relevant to the interactants' location *vis-à-vis* others in the community. The system of language, whether individual or communal, is neither static nor invariant: what gives it its identity as system is in fact its systematicity. To quote Firth (1957: 185) again: 'experienced language is universally systemic'. Rather than invariance, identity or homogeneity, perhaps it is this systematicity that is a necessary though not sufficient condition for semiotic success.

4.6 Concluding remarks

As I remarked in the opening sentence, this paper contains no discourse analysis. Perhaps I should qualify this remark. The paper does not contain an example of actual analysis of some given piece of discourse such as I and many of my systemic colleagues have attempted a number of times. However, what I hope the paper does do is to chart out the sorts of considerations that are relevant to the analysis of discourse. Academic discourse is as subject to fashions as the hemline of women's skirts. The point I would like to emphasize is that all aspects captured within Figure 4.2 are relevant to discourse analysis: each aspect opens up an area of complexity in this enterprise, irrespective of whether it is in fashion today or not. This does not mean of course that every analysis needs to address every one of these aspects, simply that the analysis should be aware of their relevance. The multiplicity of aspects relevant to discourse production and comprehension should be no cause for dismay so far as the systemic functional model is concerned. One of the notable contributions of this model has been a willingness to include rather than exclude, to overview wide expanses rather than draw hard and fast lines around tiny little parcels of the intellectual landscape. When it comes to society, semiosis and the brain, we have a trinity no one member of which can exist without the other two. And this is the real context for the conceptualization of the category of context in linguistics.

Notes

1   This chapter is an elaboration of the introductory section of the plenary talk presented at The International Conference on Discourse Analysis, held at the University of Macau, October 16–18, 1997. It first appeared under the title 'Wherefore context? The place of context in the system and process of language'.

2   It is worth remembering here that for some scholars context is a category in pragmatics NOT linguistics, which simply supports my characterization of views on context (Leech 1983; Sperber and Wilson 1986).

3   Firth's paper 'Personality and language in society' first appeared in 1950 in *The Sociological Review, Journal of the Institute of Sociology*, volume XIII, section two. Page references here are to Firth 1957.

4   For some accounts of these developments within the Malinowski-Firth-Halliday tradition, see Martin 1992; Matthiessen 1993; Hasan 1981, 1995. For a state-of-the-art account of the anthropologically inspired scene in America, see Goodwin and Duranti (1992).

5   As for example in theories inspired by Chomsky's nativist approach where 'exposure' to language is provided in social context, but context is no more than 'material surroundings'.

6   It is in this sense that one would have to grant that both Malinowski and Firth at least hinted at a wider theoretical reach for the concept of context.

7   It is important to stress the difference between human sociality and animal sociality as manifested even in the higher apes. The enormously elaborated ways of being, doing and saying that human beings have evolved all over the world are as far removed from the communal 'interpersonal' behaviours displayed by the higher apes as the specificity and flexibility of human language is from the pre-programmed patterns of their language.

8   (p. 5) Halliday (1995a) has referred to it also as 'pre-meaning': this description might be open to objection unless the word 'meaning' were to be universally understood as 'linguistic meaning'.

9   In a plenary talk at the 23rd ISFC 1996 (Sydney) I suggested that a basic biological condition for semiosis is the ability to perceive a principled relation that brings together two phenomena which are otherwise quite unrelated. I referred to this as the principle of 'the conjunction of dissimilars', a requirement from which a surprising number of properties common to semiotic systems may be logically derived, such as recognition of 'sign-unity', sign functions, stratification, realization, and so on.

10   For the semiotic description of some sign systems, Hasan (2016).

11   I refer to Saussure's analogy of *langue* as the score on a music sheet, which is executed in *parole*.

12   I take social positioning to be a universally relevant aspect of human relation: although the instantial impetus and the manifestation of this social positioning might vary from one stage of human social evolution to the next, the fact

remains that from the very start social agents are placed *vis-à-vis* each other whether the basis for this is a sense of distinction due to some biological attribute (e.g. skin colour) or due to an attribute that is socially manufactured (e.g. the power that comes from control over the resources for the production of knowledge in academia).

13   Needless to say that the choice from these categories of meaning is coloured by the interactants' ideological stances.

14   It seems appropriate to refer to this way of relating one message to another as a kind of 'interpersonal logic' which is essential to the connectivity of discourse, especially in the dialogue mode.

15   The responsibility for the adaptation is entirely mine, without necessarily implying agreement on Bernstein's part. Compare this with a more elaborate systemic representation of the context of culture in Hasan (1999c: figure1).

16   There is of course no implication that social positioning is relevant to every participant in a linguistic interaction; however, all semantic modalities, including the proxemic, are sensitive to adult speakers' social position.

II
Towards a System Based Account of Context

Editor's introduction

Explaining the word *Functional* in *Systemic Functional Linguistics,* Professor Ruqaiya Hasan, in **The Conception of Context in Text (1995),** notes the relation between the metafunctions, on the one hand, and the contextual parameters of field, tenor and mode, on the other, such as is accounted for in the CONTEXT METAFUNCTION HOOK-UP HYPOTHESIS (or CMH HYPOTHESIS), i.e. the speaker's perception of field, tenor and mode, i.e. context of situation, activates the choice of certain meanings. As Hasan explains, 'On the one hand, a speech event is meaningful, because, as talk, it is answerable to the system of language. But on the other hand, the very motivation for the speech event has to be attributed to the fact that it impinges on human beings because, as action, it has a concrete social basis.' The key to identifying context types then is to identify text types – i.e. *what various texts hold in common and what they do not share.* In her words 'by virtue of its meaning-wording choices, each text announces itself as an instance of some registral variety whose correlate is some specific category of context.'

In **Speaking with Reference to Context (1999),** Hasan acknowledges instances, however, where contextual/registerial constancy across a text can be called into question, i.e. where 'the integrity of a text survives certain kinds of contextual/registerial changes.' Rather than describe the relationship between context and text in deterministic terms, Hasan instead describes the relationship as being more along the lines of a 'realizational dialectic'.

The 'well regulated nature of parole', i.e. naturally occurring discourse involving 'exchanges of meaning between *ordinary* speakers as participants in "concerted social activities"' (Malinowski 1923) should, argues Hasan in **The Place of Context in a Systemic Functional Model (2009),** 'put both language use and context centre stage in linguistics'.

In **Towards a Paradigmatic Description of Context: Systems, Metafunctions, and Semantics (2014),** Hasan illustrates how a paradigmatic

description of context can be accomplished using a system network, i.e.
sys-net. Sys-nets, which have successfully been used to account for variant
possibilities, i.e. choices, specific to parameters in other strata, e.g semantics and lexicogrammar, may also be applied to the stratum of context. As
Hasan points out, however, 'The problem is to establish their calibration in
a way that the realized actuals agree with the experience of the community
whose language and culture are under description.'

5 The conception of context in text[1] [1995]

A text *is created* by its context, the semiotic environment of people
and their activities that we have construed via the concepts of field,
tenor and mode; it also *creates* that context. The relationship that
we refer to as 'realization' between 'levels' of semiosis – situation
(doing) realized in lexicogrammar (wording), and so on ... is a dialectic one. (Halliday 1994)

5.1 Introduction

Nothing is more evident than the fact that most human activities 'involve
the use of language' (Bakhtin 1986: 60). The truth of this observation
together with the success in achieving those activities explains a taken-for-
granted assumption, namely that speakers have a reasonable idea of how
language is to be used by way of performing an activity. For example, it is
only on the basis of such an assumption that Grice (1975) could state his
conversational maxims as he does: they are worded as if what counted as the
desirable 'quantity', 'manner', and 'relevance' of one's sayings was so very
self-evident and non-problematic that its details could be taken for granted,
further enquiry into the concepts being a mere formality: the reader, rational
by nature, would surely know all details. And yet, there could be strong
arguments against this position: to think of the relation between language
and human activity as simply natural, as something that needs no explanation, could be in the words of Pierre Bourdieu (1977) a 'misrecognition.'
Certainly behind this seemingly non-problematic, self-evident naturalness
lie some of the most intractable problems in explaining the nature of human
language and human cognition. On the one hand, we need to be clear about
the very origins of this ability to use language appropriately, an ability that
we so obviously possess and that is so essential to successful performance:

what does it mean to treat this ability as something that is ours in the nature of things? On the other hand, we need also to explain that equally obvious capability of language as a potential for meaning which seldom, if ever, leaves its speakers 'speechless'; in fact, the speechlessness of speakers is seldom, if ever, construed as an inherent insufficiency of the language itself. What are the grounds for our faith in the infinite capacity of language to meet the demands of its speakers? These issues are of even greater interest to linguistic models that claim to be functional. Linguistic functionalism of any kind logically presupposes an involvement of language in human social life. However, the manner in which this involvement is interpreted will often be indicative of differences in the conceptualization of language. Witness, for example, the differences in 'ideas about language' between pragmatic functionalism, such as professed by Leech (1983), and systemic functionalism, such as advocated by Halliday (1970a, 1973a, 1975a, 1979b, etc.): the former views this relation as consisting in a language's usefulness for the performance of acts, while the latter considers it to be a process of symbiosis, in which the existence of one is the condition for the existence of the other.

In this chapter, I intend to re-examine the relations between concepts such as CONTEXT OF SITUATION, TEXT, REGISTER, and TEXT STRUCTURE. Two reasons for doing this stand out: first, the concepts are important to the claim of symbiotic relations between language and human activity. And second, this examination will serve the purpose of showing why the alternative CONNOTATIVE SEMIOTIC modelling of GENRE, REGISTER, and language as proposed by Martin (1985a, 1985b, 1992) is neither necessary nor viable. My claim will be that Martin's framework for the study of text is inconsistent with the systemic functional model.[2] The re-examination of these concepts will take the form of tracing their development through the work of three important scholars: Malinowski, Firth, and Halliday. Into this historical account, I shall project my own views of the implications of the claims made by them. Instead of setting aside separate sections for discussing either Martin's views, or my own, I shall introduce both our views and some important issues of disagreement between us as and where they appear relevant by the developing discourse. This presupposes a familiarity on the reader's part with Martin's views as well as mine, since they will not be systematically described in any one place, though I shall signal such digressions wherever possible. Any discussion of Martin's position involves an understanding of at least some aspects of Hjelmslev's theory known as GLOSSEMATICS. I shall introduce these aspects as they become necessary to the discussion. It does not need to be pointed out that, when I make claims about the SFL model as a whole or about aspects of glossematics, this is naturally based on my interpretation. In making these interpretations, I have drawn heavily on what I believe to be the authors' own views; but the responsibility for my interpretations as also for the extrapolations from them lies with me.

An ever-present danger in this form of discourse is its somewhat negative quality. Neither Martin nor I have lightly adopted positions on text studies; the discussion here is an attempt to show why I find it difficult to accept Martin's framework. This could be read as denigration. So it is important to emphasize that the only purpose for going into these issues is to clarify, perhaps even to myself, the implications of adopting certain theoretical 'positions'. Further, there are equally important if not weightier issues in the study of language on which I believe both Martin and I are in complete agreement; so this is not intended as adversarial discourse. I do not subscribe to the convention, fashionable though it is, whereby the development of disciplines is seen to depend, not on the search for clarification, but on confrontation.

5.2   Context of situation: (1) the practical basis of discourse

SFL's interest in the relations of language and human, i.e., social, activity has its origins in the pioneering work of Malinowski (1923, 1935), who foreshadowed many of the avenues of research in this area (Firth 1957, 1968; Halliday 1973b, 1975a, 1975b; Halliday, McIntosh and Strevens 1964; Halliday and Hasan 1985). Malinowski was attempting to resolve problems in interpreting the meanings of a fairly distant culture – namely, that of the Kiriwinian – to the European. However, while that was his immediate concern, the implication of his efforts extended the fundamental problem of linguistics: how the exchange of linguistic meanings can come about in the first place. The concepts CONTEXT OF CULTURE and CONTEXT OF SITUATION were postulated to resolve that issue. Malinowski argued that, just as textual context illuminates meanings, so also situational context facilitates the apprehension of the meanings being meant in any given instance. For him, context of situation was essential to any explanation of the possibility of the ontogenesis of meaning: it was in the frames of social context that signification (as the term is used in Saussure 1966) could initially take root; and it was here that the INEFFABLE VALEUR of the linguistic signs becomes palpable as indicated by the significance of the sign (Hasan 1985c). In this view, language as a semiotic system develops only through its connection with the living of life.

5.2.1   Context as subjective experience

Malinowski's context of situation referred to everything significant that was going on concurrently with the speech activity. Notwithstanding his idea of context of culture, the immediate context of situation itself was often presented as something that surrounded the speaking subjects materially and directly: the apprehension of the environment seemed to be as natural as breathing. As Firth pointed out:

> In the work of Gardiner and Malinowski, there are distinct traces of the realist approach which is in strange contradiction, in Malinowski's case, to his repeated insistence on the need for theory. He seems to imagine that there is such a thing as the 'existence' of the brute 'fact'. … 'To us' he says, 'the real linguistic fact is the full utterance within its context of situation.' There is a belief in the 'concrete situation', the 'situation of action' in which the utterance is 'directly embedded' and he even uses the phrase 'environmental reality' (Malinowski 1935, Volume II, p. 57). The word 'utterance' seems to have had an almost hypnotic suggestion of 'reality' which often misleads him into the dangerous confusion of a theoretical construct with items of experience. (Firth 1968: 154)

I would draw attention here to two points. First, in Malinowski's work a separation is implied between text and context, i.e., between language and social activity. I believe this separation is still widely accepted in SFL. Second, and by contrast, the realist view of situation criticized by Firth has been largely abandoned, partly thanks to Firth's own contribution.[3] In fact, today this realist view appears to be characteristic of 'the current pragmatic based approach to discourse analysis' (Cook 1990: 1), where, again like Malinowski, the expectation seems to be that the interactants' primary experience of the situational context can be described in totality without the mediation of theory. But to describe all that enters into the primary experience of the speakers in any single instance of interaction amounts to 'transcribing infinity' in terms of Cook (*op. cit.*). Reasonably enough, Cook considers this as not feasible. However, this lack of 'feasibility' does not arise from the inherent infinity of the data of 'context' *per se*, as Cook's comments appear to suggest. To accept that explanation would be to believe that context of situation, as a category, presents data that, by its nature, are different from data of some other kind: the latter happen to be objectively well defined, whereas the situational data inherently lack these properties. From the perspective of a competent linguistic theory, this stance is questionable. I, therefore, prefer Kitching's explanation offered in a different debate: according to him 'concepts of "explaining the world" or "describing the world" left in this unqualified form are simply incoherent' (Kitching 1988: 34). All description involves selection: the effects of selectivity do not disappear simply because, as describers, we may not be aware of the principles underlying the selections. These remarks are relevant to my disagreement with Martin, which leads me into the first excursus of this chapter.

5.2.1.1 *Excursus A: subjective experience and dynamic description.*

In an important sense Firth's criticism of this aspect of Malinowski's approach amounts to the claim that *to describe is to theorize*: it is reasonable to expect the theory's ability to furnish an argued set of principles for recognizing that which is to be described as well as the rationale for why it should be described at all. These comments are relevant, since certain interpretations of what is today called DYNAMIC DESCRIPTION, or *the description of process, rather than of text*, encourage the belief that we can describe things as they are in themselves. So for example, in commending on Ventola's (1987) flow chart as an example of dynamic description, Martin claims: 'There [i.e., in Ventola's flow charts, RH] *genre is viewed subjectively, in the process of manifestation, full of interacting decisions, dependencies, choices and the like*' (Martin 1985a: 259).

This, according to Martin, contrasts with the 'linear representation' of discourse such as in a GSP (i.e., generalized structure potential; Hasan 1978, 1979b, 1984c, 1985b, etc.).[4] In Martin's view, in the GSP approach, 'genres are viewed objectively, after the fact, as things, with particular relations to each other in our culture' (Martin 1985a: 259). Martin suggests that we need a dynamic perspective in order to view language as process. But if Martin's view of what constitutes the dynamic quality of discourse (e.g., Martin 1985a: 254ff.) is correct, then it would seem that any reliance on theoretical categories will have to be abandoned since that would inevitably lead us to viewing verbal interactions synoptically, simply as 'finished or frozen' instantiations of SYNOPTIC categories. This follows from the fact that *theoretical categories are by necessity abstractions, generalizability being a necessary property of theoretically motivated description*; these abstractions, which form the substance of a synoptic system, are validated by their renewal of connection with data. *The price one pays for the power gained from abstraction is to have to define data under focus in such a manner that it does not include everything that may be going on, for in 'nature' there are no clear-cut, given boundaries.* We create the interlinked theoretical categories because they contribute to the power of description: the more general a category is, the less likely it is to fit the instance in its entire specificity as it occurs in the natural course of happenings (Cartwright 1983). While acknowledging the danger in abandoning synoptic categories, Martin (1985a) has never given any indication of how he proposes to overcome the paradox.[5]

Although Martin allows the static/synoptic perspective to be one of the two possible perspectives on semiosis it is certainly my impression that in *his* framework the static perspective is neither privileged nor privileging. Note that, if Martin's view of the synoptic system is accepted, then the very conceptualization of the nature of talk in the synoptic perspective will have to be seen as defective: for according to Martin, in the synoptic approach, talk is seen 'simply' as product (Martin 1985a; Ventola 1984, 1987). The implication appears unavoidable that, through the kind of approach advocated by Hasan (1978, 1979b, 1981, 1984c, 1985b, etc.) in general, and through the notion of GSP in particular, that essential quality of talk which makes it talk, i.e., its moment-by-moment evolution, cannot be described. By contrast, the active perspective produces the DYNAMIC SYSTEM, Ventola's flow charts being one example of such a system. The latter is capable of doing all the things which the former approach, being synoptic, fails to do. So, although *ostensibly* the synoptic approach exemplified by the GSP type of analysis is ascribed an equal status in 'the two modes of human semiosis', *rhetoric apart*, the synoptic approach could hardly be desirable, since it cannot respect the very defining features of what constitutes its object of enquiry, namely 'talk'. Claims that the two approaches are viewed as complementary appear to me as so much lip-service to complementarity; in actual fact, if we accept Martin's argument, then we would *have to* treat the dynamic perspective as better worthy of attention, since it is presented as revealing the true nature of talk as talk.

The sorts of demands that Martin's projected dynamic analysis is required to satisfy can be inferred from his approving tone about what the flow chart is capable of representing. I read Martin as claiming the *centrality of real happenings – linguistic or extra-linguistic – in real space and time as the object of study in the dynamic perspective* (Martin 1985a, 1991). But this poses some problems. To elaborate, if an essential property of dynamic description is to describe happenings as they happen in real time and space, then to me one obvious implication seems to be that *in such a dynamic perspective, the describing system must be capable of evolving at the same moment in which the described process occurs.* This seems to follow from the fact that the focus of dynamic analysis has to be on the instance-as-it-is-evolving, not on an already completed product that is just 'a thing, in relation to other things'. I do not doubt for a moment that each speech event is unique: it will, in the nature of things, never be exactly identical to any other instance (Hasan 1985b; especially, chapter 6). The norms/types to which these unique instances nonetheless pertain can be established by the synoptic system (e.g., Hasan 1978, 1979b, etc.). The dynamic analysis will focus on what makes the instance unique.[6] In maintaining the active dynamic perspective, this kind of 'analysis' is committed to foregrounding how each text is itself. It seems to follow from this perspective, that the analysis will be locked simply into describing an 'infinity of individual texts', one by one. Naturally, the dynamic perspective has no use for GENERALIZATION, nor would the concept of TYPE or CATEGORY be of any consequence; *types, by definition, can never be equated with actual occurrence.* If this is true, then the dynamic system can hope to present an analytical perspective only if it can describe every discursively relevant aspect of the infinity of texts without making use of any generalization. There seems to be an inherent contradiction in this programme: the fact is that there can be no purely dynamic *analytic* perspective; to know that there is departure from the usual – that texts are being characterized by their 'twists and turns' – one would need to know the properties whose presence indicates the norm/the usual – we have accepted this since Firth. The categories of the synoptic system have been devised to identify text types in a *non-ad-hoc* way: they are designed systemically to account for varying norms of the registers that can vary between the types as well as within each type (Hasan 1985b). These categories function systemically. It seems clear from the above discussion that, to identify what can count as data for the dynamic perspective, the dynamic aspects of a text as process must depend on synoptic categories![7]

It is clear from the above discussion that the requirements imposed on the so-called dynamic analytical perspective are contradictory: it is supposed to identify the culturally recognized 'stages of talk', that is to say, their 'frozen regularity' (which it could not do without being 'synoptic'), but at the same time, its mode of engaging with the text-as-process is to focus on the uniqueness of each unique individual text's process here and now. And from this latter perspective, it is not sufficient to stipulate, as Martin does with respect to the flowchart, that at each step/stage of the continuing interaction, there are many choices, including that of opting out, and that the speaker is free to choose any one of those choices. This can scarcely count as description of any kind, for it claims, in effect, that *anything goes in linguistic interaction*, which, as experience tells us, is *not true*. A dynamic description, worthy of the term 'description' will describe adequately only if it will both analyse and predict the possible vicissitudes, the turns and changes at each possible point, clearly specifying the conditions under which unpredictable things may be predicted to happen (!). These are indeed extraordinary demands, which have but one merit: they can keep any number of linguists busy in the futile search for such a dynamic frame of description, since the contradictory demands of this position make the achievement of the goal clearly unlikely.[8]

My comments do not mean that I am opposed to a dynamic perspective; indeed, I welcome it, but under a different interpretation of the term 'dynamic'. The perspective of my chosen interpretation would account for the conditions under which interdependencies, novelties, and changes are likely to occur (as, for example, Halliday 1991b; Hasan 1981; 1994: chap. 3). However, 'dynamic,' as used by Martin and his followers, strikes me as badly in need of further reflection. Martin quotes Bourdieu as the source of his inspiration in condemning the synoptic, but in fact, the perspective that comes closest in Bourdieu to the dynamic analysis of data in Martin's sense of the term, is the ethnomethodological one; and it is instructive to examine Bourdieu's (1977) critique of that framework as 'naturalizing' precisely the phenomena that it aspires to analyse. What Bourdieu puts in its place, while rejecting the subjective as lacking viability, has the ultimate backing of 'structured structuring structures' which explains the power of his concept of 'habitus.' To those who are familiar with these concepts in Bourdieu's writing, this will not sound much like Martin's idea of the active and the dynamic, though it is pretty close to a description that incorporate systemic variation.

5.2.2   Context as a schematic construct

Firth criticized Malinowski for describing the context of situation as consisting of the participants' or the observer's actual actions, their direct perceptions, sensations, and reactions. This is not because Firth denied the existence of subjective experience; he simply assigned it a different status: '*The factors or elements of a situation, including the text, are abstractions from experience and are not in any sense embedded in it, except perhaps in an applied scientific sense, in renewal of connection with it*' (Firth 1968: 154).

The distinction appears valid: communication presupposes, not only the inter-subjectively objective meanings for the lexicogrammatical units of the language; it also presupposes an inter-subjectively objective construal of the occasion of the participants' verbal encounter.[9] What is construed in saying and understanding is neither the reality of the speaker's direct experience nor the addressee's, nor even that of the observer: rather, it is something removed from this primary domain of reality, and is best seen as an abstraction. Similarly what is construed as the context of situation by co-acting participants is not the sensuous reality of any actual participant: it is something abstract. It could hardly be otherwise, since construal of meanings from wordings, and construal of context from worded meanings, are not dissociated activities; one is a continuation of the other, as is implied by the SFL claim of the symbiotic relation between language and human activity. Note that the abstract nature of context of situation was a recurrent theme in Firth's writing.[10] For example, '... "context of situation" is best used as a suitable schematic construct to apply to language events, ... it is a group of related categories at a different level from grammatical categories but rather of the same abstract nature' (Firth 1950/1957: 182).

Firth's account of the categories of the context of situation, what he described sometimes as 'the interior relations of the context of situation' (Firth 1968: 155), are reproduced below:

A.   The relevant features of participants: persons, personalities.
   (i)   The verbal action of the participants.
   (ii) The non-verbal action of the participants.
B.   The relevant objects.
C.   The effect of the verbal action.

To Firth, the incorporation of context of situation as part of the apparatus of 'linguistic techniques' for making 'statements of meaning' was simply a logical extension of a concept necessary for the description of linguistic form: for example, to say that something is a phoneme is to say that *that* something functions in the environment of a syllable. Seen from this perspective, context of situation is not an oddity; it is simply that environment by reference to which one might describe how sentences-in-use function in situation. Firth often referred to these sentences-in-use as LANGUAGE EVENT or SPEECH EVENT. I shall treat these Firthian terms as roughly synonymous with text in context, where text is an 'instance of living language that is playing some part in a context of situation' (Halliday and Hasan 1985: 10).

Context of situation, as a category of linguistic analysis, was analogous to other linguistic categories in yet another respect: Firth saw concepts such as 'syllable' and 'phoneme' as 'schematic constructs' for the description of language. They are theoretical fictions; they do not name any physical object having an existence apart from the theory itself. Much less could they be regarded as phenomena of primary experience. Thus he maintains that 'such *constructs have no ontological status and we do not project them as having being or existence.* They are neither immanent nor transcendent, but just language turned back on itself' (Firth 1950/1957: 181).

Since the context of situation with its 'interior relations' is a theoretical category for the description of language, logically it too has to be viewed, like the other categories, as a theoretical construct, which had no 'ontological status', no existence apart from the theory itself. Its only claim for recognition is that together with those other traditional categories of linguistics, it forms part of the linguist's technique for the description of meaning; and the significance of this claim itself rests on the assumption that the aim of linguistics is 'to make statements of meaning':

> The context of situation is a convenient abstraction at the social level of analysis and forms the basis of the hierarchy of techniques for the statement of meaning. The statement of meaning cannot be achieved by one analysis, at one level, in one fell swoop. Having made the first abstraction and having treated the social process of speaking by applying the … set of categories grouped in the context of situation, descriptive linguistics then proceeds by a method rather like the dispersion of light of mixed wavelengths into a spectrum. … Descriptive linguistics is thus a sort of hierarchy of techniques by means of which the meaning of linguistic events may be … dispersed in a spectrum of specialized statements. (Firth 1950/1957: 183)

5.2.3   Context and autonomous linguistics

These Firthian themes are familiar enough. Let me raise a question here that has seldom been asked: why did Firth so readily embrace the Malinowskian framework? why did he feel the need for the 'social level of analysis'? It is obviously not sufficient to say in response that for Firth 'linguistics without "meaning" is sterile' (Firth 1968: 160), for we can readily think of any number of linguists who have professed interest in meaning without also accepting the importance of context or of the social level of analysis. I suggest that the answer to these questions can be found if we enquire into the basis of Firth's critique of what he called 'fossilized formalism' (Firth

1950/1957: 178) which he associated with traditional historical philology, and of 'static structural formalism' (Firth 1950/1957: 180). He traced the origin of both to Saussure's narrow conception of what counted as *doing real linguistics.*

The impetus for Firth's critique of contemporary linguistics were varied. First, there was his commitment to the centrality of speech, i.e., parole, banished by Saussure from internal linguistics due to its allegedly unstructured nature. Firth saw speech as orderly, a site for creativity, and a necessary process in the development of language:

> Every time you speak you create anew, and what you create is a function of your language and your personality. ... In the process of speaking there is pattern and structure actively maintained by the body which is itself an organized structure maintaining the pattern of life. (Firth 1948/1957: 142)

It would seem that, on the one hand, Firth had some inkling of the development of ideas about the interconnectedness of the universe of human experience, ideas perhaps foreshadowing today's theory of the 'butterfly effect' (Gleick 1987), and on the other hand, he was well ahead of his time in appreciating the close relationship between parole and the dynamics of language maintenance and language change:

> Linguists and sociologists have to deal with systems, but systems very different from physical systems. Personal systems and social systems are actively maintained (with adaptation and change) in the bodily behavior of men. Most of the older definitions (and de Saussure's must fall in this category) need overhauling in the light of contemporary science. ... But from what we already know it is clear that we must expect human knowledge to be a function of that [i.e., bodily] action. Language and personality are built into the body, which is constantly taking part in activities directed to the conservation of the pattern of life. We must expect therefore that linguistic science will also find it necessary to postulate the maintenance of linguistic patterns and systems (including adaptation and change) within which there is order, structure, and function. Such systems are maintained by activity, and in activity they are to be studied. It is on these grounds that linguistics must be systemic. On these grounds the phonetic and also the systematic phonological study of one person at a time is not only scientifically justified but in fact inevitable. (Firth 1948/1957: 143)

Firth's focus on language as part of the social process wherein the social beings are the active agents inevitably led him to regard language as an inherently variable system, a view that he considered incompatible with that of Saussure's. 'Unity is the last concept that should be applied to language. Unity of language is the most fugitive of all unities, whether it be historical, geographical, national, or personal. There is no such thing as *une langue une* and there never has been' (Firth 1935/1957: 29).

These were not signs of idiosyncrasy or of personal whims, as has sometimes been implied: to his credit, Firth was sensitive to the political implications of scholarly attempts to discover that language which could be regarded as the original for all its transformed variants. He would have regarded with disdain the practice of postulating 'universals' on the basis of a handful of (usually) Indo-European languages, not so much because this would be empirically unsound, but because of its subtle ideological dangers. Witness his remarks about 'theorists who enjoy Indo-European fantasies and from *Ursprache* go on to speculate on the *Urvolk* and the *Urheimat*' (Firth 1950/1957: 178).

Given Firth's own convictions, he was particularly receptive to criticisms of Saussurean linguistics: amongst his contemporaries, he is the only linguist who acknowledges the force of 'the Russian objection that this theory [i.e., Saussure's] leads to static structural formalism, to mechanical structures, to mechanical materialism in linguistics' (Firth 1950/1957: 181). Like Vološinov (1973) and the Prague School linguists (Vachek 1964), he attributed this to Saussure's strong classification of LANGUE and PAROLE. And thus, like them, he anticipated by a couple of decades the single most serious criticism of structuralism, which was to be put forward with much éclat by the post-structuralist and the deconstructionist movements, as if the criticism had never been voiced before (Hasan 1987a). Firth was anxious to point out to the critics of structural linguistics that, structuralist though he was, his work 'is certainly not Saussurean in the Russian pejorative sense, nor is it "autonomous" linguistic structuralism, without sociological component' (Firth 1949/1957: 170). In Firth's vocabulary, autonomy of linguistics was bad news; and from this point of view, he differed, not only from Saussure, but also from Saussure's interpreter, Hjelmslev, while fully appreciating the excellence of his coherent structuring of his theory as a theory of the form of language.

Firth was not an orthodox Saussurean (Butt 2001). He negated the sanctity of some important Saussurean boundaries. Where Saussure found nothing but chaos, flux, and irregularity, Firth found order, structure, and function. This was not accidental: the apparent irregularities of language, the ones Saussure considered incapable of being described, become amenable to description when seen from the perspective of the higher order systems of human social existence.[11] The incorporation of the higher order of the social is precisely what Firth saw as the social level of analysis; and the concept most relevant here is that of the context of situation. Firth points explicitly to what, in his linguistics, 'makes sure of the sociological component' (Firth 1950/1957: 182) is the notion 'context of situation'. In so arguing Firth implies that, if a linguistic theory is designed to describe language both as system and as process, if it is designed to treat variation as an inherent and necessary attribute of language, then it *must logically invoke a sociological level of analysis and that invoking this level of analysis entails a recognition of the notion 'context of situation'*. Firth embraced and developed Malinowski's context of situation, because he believed that it would serve to introduce that dynamic element in his linguistic model the absence of which had rendered formal linguistics static and sterile.

5.2.4 Language and social context: Malinowski and Firth

Although Malinowski commented repeatedly about the relevance of context to the language of speech events, not surprisingly, these remarks are hardly systematic enough to present a framework for analysing the language of speech events so as to reveal the solidary relation of language to the features of the context of situation. And even though Firth's approach to context of situation is informed by theory, the same criticism can be levelled at his writings as well. When it comes to actually showing how language and context cooperate, Firth is often given to episodic remarks, presenting comments on some imaginary example rather than offering principles which would apply to a class of speech events, rather than offering principles which would apply to some particular class of speech events.[12] For example, *first* there are statements on the effect of ongoing verbal action on participants as exemplified below:

> The moment a conversation is started, whatever is said is a determining condition for what, in any reasonable expectation, may follow. What you say raises the threshold against most of the language of your companion, and leaves only a limited opening for a certain likely range of responses. (Firth 1935/1957: 33)

The *second* topic concerns the possibility of variation from the expected pattern of behaviour, e.g.:

> It is true that in everyday life we generally say what the other fellow expects us, one way or the other, to say, but this expectancy is the measure even of our most delightful surprises, and good personal style is highly valued. (Firth 1950/1957: 186)

And the *third* set of observations relates to the ritual quality of language in routinized situations as shown in the following:

> A study of the jargon of contemporary book reviewers in the press shows how all such routine situations involving public judgment tend to produce stereotyped forms of language. This does not mean that such reviews are become meaningless, but rather that a fairly simple set of stock indicators are practically convenient. (Firth 1935/1957: 31)

On the basis of some of his examples, it would also appear valid to suggest that Firth saw the relation between language and situation bi-directionally: given 'bits and pieces' of language, an expression fairly common in Firth, you could be expected to gather what the context of situation might be; similarly, given a context of situation, you could be expected to predict, within reason, what sort of language use will ensue. Apart from such general comments, most of Firth's remarks on how the language of speech events is to be studied in relation to social context are fragmentary and usually concern specific linguistic items. For example, he comments on an Englishman's reactions to 'a good man', 'a good chap', 'a good fellow', 'a good sort', 'a good scout' (Firth 1935/1957: 31), or uses the sentence 'Ahng gunna gi' wun fer Ber' as the text from whose linguistic characteristics some features of the context could be predicted (Firth 1950/1957: 182). It is impossible to distil a general framework from these chance examples. If it is true that Malinowski was a realist in regard to situation, Firth could fairly be said to have been a realist in regard to 'linguistic items': these engaged his attention to the exclusion of more abstract linguistic patterns, such as those we would today describe as systemic choices in mood, modality, expansion, or transitivity, correlating systematically with certain meanings.

Mention should be made here of Mitchell's classic study of 'The language of buying and selling in Cyrenaica' (1975). It follows Firth faithfully and could be treated as a demonstration of how, in the Firthian framework, one would describe the language of a speech event in relation to its context. But as Sinclair and Coulthard (1975) noted, the study follows the practice of listing the actual items that are typically associated with the different stages of the specific social activity under focus. Mitchell's study is certainly a step towards the description of the structure of (a) social activity, which, in my view, is somewhat different from claiming that it presents a systemic framework for describing text structure (Martin 1992; Ventola 1984, 1987).

5.2.5   The contexts of Malinowski and Firth

Some important conclusions can be drawn from this rather detailed discussion of the Firthian position. First, Firth's theorization of Malinowski's context of situation transmuted that concept. The difference between the two is comparable to that between naming and the valeur-mediated theories of meaning. Once Firth's arguments are accepted, context of situation can no longer be confused with direct, subjective experience of reality, despite the dynamic quality of such descriptions as implied by Martin (1985a); instead, it is a theoretical construct that turns the individual's sensuous perception into an inter-subjectively objective reality.

Second, a level of description has been added to linguistic theory, but not to language. Firth's context of situation, like Malinowski's, is distinct from language itself, no matter how analogous the techniques for the description of context may be to those for the description of the formal elements of language.

Third, whereas in Malinowski, the basis for the separation of language from context is the common sense observation that language just is a separate thing from action, in Firth's treatment this separation is theoretically demanded (see Section 5.2.3). Without this higher level, the diversities in language will appear chaotic, as they did to Saussure, prompting him to reject synchronic variation as a fact of language. The alternative approach is Hjelmslev's, who works 'with the premiss that the given text displays structural homogeneity', while accepting that 'this premiss, however, does not hold good in practice' (Hjelmslev 1961: 115).[13] The cost of this solution is high: it is to counteract the consequences of this false premise of homogeneity that Hjelmslev needs to invoke the notion of a connotative semiotic whereby language varieties, for example, dialect, rhetorical styles, and presumably registers, become content for which his 'denotative language' is the expression:

> Stylistic form, style, value-style, medium, tone, vernacular, national language, regional language, and physiognomy are solidary categories, so that any functive of denotative language must be defined in respect of them all at the same time. ... The individual members of each of these classes and the units resulting from their combination we shall call connotators. (Hjelmslev 1961: 116)

The result, in this case, is a structural formalism that denies speech its central role in making, maintaining, and changing language, *either* by excluding language in use from consideration altogether *or* by treating all that is done only in language use, e.g., style, dialect, register, etc., as something that is other-than-the-real language. The idea that there is such an invariable homogeneous core of language is open to question, as, perhaps, decades of unsuccessful effort to exclude parole from langue would suggest. When, by contrast, a higher level of social context is introduced in the theory, the two, i.e., the system of language and the systemically governed use of language form part of a dynamic open system:

> the level of social analysis provides a motive for rejecting the view of language as homogeneous or autonomous; at the same time it also furnishes categories by reference to which the different kinds of synchronic varieties are given orderly significance, and need not be seen as outside linguistics as the comprehensive study of language.[14]
> (Lemke 1984b: 24ff)

Let me say quite clearly that I am not objecting to treating language as the expression plane in a higher order semiotic, as such; but one needs to understand the problems that inhere in Hjelmslev's notion of connotative semiotic. If that metaphor pleases, and if it fits the theoretical requirements, then, certainly, language – both as system and process – can be viewed as the expression of something, but in that case, that something being expressed is not-language: for example, one could say that context of situation is the CONNOTATOR for which the DENOTATIVE SEMIOTIC SYSTEM OF LANGUAGE acts as one form of expression, provided one is willing to accept the consequences of such a claim (for further discussion, Section 5.3.2.1). But there is hardly any justification for suggesting, as Hjelmslev does that varieties of language, per se, are the connotators: this is to suggest that they fall outside language (as the denotative semiotic), *for in such a denotative semiotic there is nothing that can be language as a functional resource*. It seems to me that the Hjelmslevian premise of homogeneity, introduced on a *pro tem* basis as a convenience, ultimately exacts a heavy price by forcing a conception of language which is surely not acceptable in SFL. It may well be that Martin believes those tenets *need* to be abandoned, but if so, there should be some discussion in support of Martin's view: those basic principles should not be abandoned in silence.

It may be argued that linguistic varieties are not an internal fact of language in the sense that they cannot be explained without invoking extralinguistic context. This is certainly so; but, in essence, this is not very different from the need to invoke the concept of context in order to *explain* the nature of language; and without question, this latter need is well recognized in the systemic functional model (Halliday 1970a). Without invoking context, it may be possible to *describe* the structure of language but it will not be possible to *explain* it. For example, suppose that Halliday's claims about the metafunctions are empirically true; then it should be possible, without invoking context, to show that there are only four types of lexicogrammatical structures (Halliday 1979b), and that lexicogrammatical options are most economically organized into four relatively independent system networks; we could conceivably also demonstrate (though this seems to me problematic) that, at an abstract level, each such network has a semantic character which differs from that of the other three. But we could *never* hope to *explain* why the structure of language is as it is, without invoking context. As in linguistic variety, so here too, context is an explanatory factor: it is not simply a notion that permits effective description of linguistic varieties (Hasan 1973c, 1989, 2009a); it is also a concept without which the inner structure of language remains unmotivated. My claim is that Hjelmslev's language as denotative semiotic is nothing other than Saussure's *langue*. And I am arguing that, in a functional theory, language cannot be equated with *langue* without causing inconsistencies.[15]

Clearly these remarks are germane to my debate with Martin (1985a), who, it appears, has accepted Hjelmslev's notion of connotative semiotic without enquiring sufficiently into the conditions that logically drive Hjelmslev to introduce this concept in his theory, which is essentially nonfunctional. It is difficult to interpret Martin's representation of language as for example in Martin (1992: 496). In Martin's case, the claim would be that register (aka, context) is a connotator, with the denotative semiotics of language as its expression.[16] This proposition leads to further complications, because genre equals context, what Martin has done is to collapse Halliday's concepts of register and context as one undifferentiated phenomenon. It would be one thing to agree that language participates in a connotative semiotic, functioning as the *expression form* of what Halliday calls 'context of situation'. But it is quite a different proposition to suggest that language itself is the *expression plane* of its own varieties; this would run counter to the notion of register in the sense in which that term has been used by Halliday from the early 1960s to date; and it certainly does not agree with the Firthian approach. And no one to my knowledge has yet shown any reasons for thinking of register as context rather than as referring to language variety. In recognizing context of situation as an abstraction, one would imply that the interior relations of context of situation are grounded in the conditions of human social existence. For the present, we may think of the human social conditions of existence – the entire material and cultural universe – as analogous to Hjelmslev's content-purport. Like content-purport, human social conditions of existence are also 'an unanalysed, amorphous continuum, on which boundaries are laid' by the semiotic system of language (Hjelmslev 1961: 52). 'The purport is ... in itself inaccessible to knowledge, since *the prerequisite for knowledge is an analysis of some kind; the purport can be known only through some formation, and thus has no scientific existence apart from it.*' (Hjelmslev 1961: 76).[17] I would, however, reject Hjelmslev's idea that all purport is necessarily universal, 'the factor ... *that remains common to all languages, however many languages are drawn into comparison*' [p. 50; emphasis added]. This Hjelmslevian position is thrown into doubt in his own words when he goes on to suggest:

> The description of purport, in respect of both the linguistic expression and the linguistic content, may in all essentials be thought of as belonging partly to the sphere of physics and partly to that of (social) anthropology. ... The substance of both planes can be viewed *both as physical entities* (sounds in the expression plane, things in the content plane) *and as the conception of these entities held by the users of the language.* Consequently for both planes both a physical and a phenomenological description of the purport should be required. (Hjelmslev 1961: 77–78; emphasis added)

To a certain extent, the debate hinges on the interpretation of the term 'phenomenological'. But if purport is the unformed reality, it does not seem reasonable to suggest that this reality is universal, except in a highly reductive sense. (Compare Hjelmslev's discussion of purport, pp 51–52 and pp 76–78.) Human reality cannot consist of just the physical; and the social (anthropological) reality is quite clearly not universal. As Firth always insisted, nature and nurture combine to produce this 'kaleidoscopic flux', that is to say the content purport, which in my view comes nearest to the conditions of human social existence. The interior relations of context of situation provide one means of making sense of this amorphous continuum.

To wrap up this debate, if it is true that speaking and the context of speaking furnish two perspectives on the speech event, then a recognition of the social level of analysis in linguistics is an explicit recognition of the necessary link between language and human social conditions of existence. (Compare Kress and Threadgold 1988, or Thibault 1989.) The implications of this observation need to be spelled out. It is that a speech event is not first and foremost a linguistically defined structure with which some situation has come to be associated: rather, it is talk that receives its motivation and is accorded recognition primarily because it has a place in the living of life. Certainly, a speech event is meaningful, because, as talk, it is answerable to the system of language, by virtue of both its conformities to and its departures from the system. But at the same time the very motivation for the speech event has to be attributed to the fact that it impinges on human beings because, as action, it has a concrete social basis, irrespective of whether it conforms or diverges from the existing ways of being and doing. One may liken the speech event to the linguistic sign, a unity of signified and signifier, of social content and linguistic expression. The talk aspect of the speech event, i.e., the text, is the signifier or expression, while its concrete aspect, i.e., the social context, is the signified or content. So, as the title of this section suggests: discourse, that is, the speech in a speech event, has a basis in human social practice and hence in human social existence. But, at the same time, in as much as the context itself is construed through acts of meaning, these acts of meaning play a part in producing the social conditions of human existence within which speech is rooted.

5.3   Context of situation: (2) the discursive basis of social practice

In closing the previous section, I have again anticipated myself. Even if, as I hope, the reader agrees with me that the implications I indicated are 'in' the Firthian approach, this by itself is not enough. For example, to the 'initiated' it may make perfect sense to say that language-in-use construes context: but how does this actually come about? What categories and relations are necessary? Here Firth's own contribution could be seen as negligible.[18] I believe I am right in saying that such questions did not get clear or elaborate answers. True, Firth insisted that the interior relations of context of situation were theoretical constructs; but there is still an unanswered question: What motivates these particular interior relations? Why these parameters, why not some others?

And while there may be no quarrel with the assertion that the concept of speech event, i.e., of text in context, brings the relations of language and human social conditions of existence closer, implicit in the acceptance of this principle is a practical problem for anyone attempting to describe speech events. More often than not, human actions proceed in a continuous flow, and, in this seamless progression, human actors are unceasingly implicated both as agents of some actions and as the bearers of the consequences of those actions. Is it possible to identify in this continuous flow something that we may see as an instance of 'a construct' to be known as 'context of situation'? Perhaps, this is what Rorty (1982: 191) might describe as a 'bad question'. However, if we are about to make statements of meaning about speech events by placing the talk within its social context, do we not need to know what constitutes *that specific speech event*? Granted the fuzziness of boundaries, nonetheless, do we not need to explicitly state ways of recognizing the specificity of the many speech events that might occur within the continuous flow of human social practices? These demands seem perfectly reasonable; in the end, in terms of Halliday (1988: 28), all one is asking for is just the 'encoding definition' of the two critical concepts in the study of discourse analysis: how do I recognize a context when I come across it? and, how do I know a text when I come across it?

Many of the problems in the study of text that have claimed our attention in recent times are not without some foundation in the past studies – I am thinking of such issues as the relation of registers to each other, within which falls the issue of genre agnation, (c.f., Martin 1985a); the explanation of diachronic change in a community's register repertoire (Lemke 1985); the relation of language to ideology (Threadgold, Grosz, Kress and Halliday 1986); the role of everyday talk in maintaining and changing the character of human conditions of existence (Hasan 1988, 1989; Hasan and Cloran 1990); the question of dynamic and synoptic perspectives (Martin 1985a, 1992): these and many other questions could not have been asked, leave aside answered, without assuming some answer to those raised in the last two paragraphs. Halliday's elaborations of the notions of text, context and register have made the greatest contribution in providing directions for viable answers to these and other such questions. I will devote the subsections of this section to develop this claim by examining Halliday's answers to some of the questions raised earlier.

5.3.1 On realization and the construing capacity of language

In turning to the first issue, i.e., the capacity of language for construing context, one should begin with a word of caution. In the study of text and context, there is need to keep simultaneously in view both the textual and the contextual perspectives, not just as a combination of two co-occurring things, but as two interacting, mutually influencing factors, each developing in response to the other.[19] I understand the claim of symbiosis between language and human activity as implying here that, if perception of context motivates the talk one talks, i.e., one's text, then the comprehension of the developing text construes the perception of the context as it appears to be evolving. Notwithstanding this need to keep both perspectives in view simultaneously, in practice it is difficult, if not impossible, to describe both at once. In what follows, the focus is on texts construing contexts, without any implication of the priority of this perspective in the study of texts. More specifically, the question is: how does the SFL model theorize that crucial capacity of human language by virtue of which a language construes 'the interior relations' of the 'schematic construct' we are calling 'context of situation'? Halliday's answer to this important question should be examined by reference to three developments in SFL: (a) the conceptualization of language as a multiple coding system; (b) the recognition of the relation between the upper levels of coding as a dialectic; and (c) the introduction of a functional hypothesis. I begin by examining the first two points together.

The question of the relation between strata is naturally important to stratal linguistic theories. The theory where this relationship is perhaps most meticulously thought out and explicitly stated is Hjelmslev's Glossematics. SFL initially borrowed some of these notions; the most relevant to our discussion are STRATA and REALIZATION. I hope to show that certain developments since the late 1960s have made SFL sufficiently different from Hjelmslev's model so that one cannot treat the terms as referring to the same theoretical notions without causing confusion. A few words then on my understanding of how Hjelmslev theorizes the relations between strata, particularly because it is relevant to my debate with Martin.

The notion of realization is not extensively discussed in Hjelmslev's Prolegomena. I take that use to be closest to Firth's exponence.[20] Thus a class will be 'called realized if it can be taken as the object of a particular analysis and virtual if this is not the case' (Hjelmslev 1961: 40); this suggests perhaps a relation between realization and 'presence in substance'. If my reading is correct, then realization demands the concrete manifestation of a system by a process: unless such a process exists, its actual analysis is impossible even though 'the linguistic theoretician can indeed consider the existence of such texts as a possibility' (loc. cit.); however, such imaginary texts are virtual, not realized. This notion of realization was never adopted in SFL, and, as will be seen below, it is certainly not present today: no distinction is made in the theory between realized and virtual texts, though the adoption of the metaphor POTENTIAL covers all events, the actual as well as the systemically possible. Before turning to a discussion of strata, it will be useful to present diagrammatically my understanding of the two models in this respect.

Figure 5.1: Language as a multi-stratal coding system

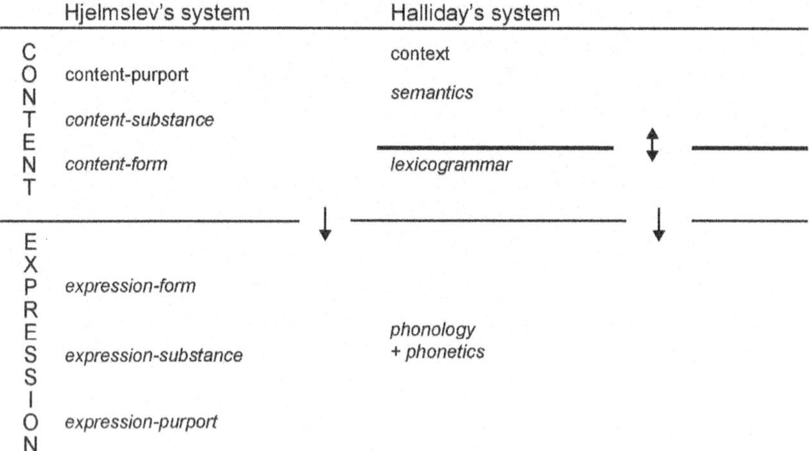

As Figure 5.1 indicates, Hjelmslev's language as denotative semiotic consists initially of two PLANES, which he refers to as CONTENT and EXPRESSION. The relationship between them is one of interdependence: that is, in the theory, it is not possible to postulate the one without the other.[21] Analysing these two planes further, Hjelmslev introduced a three term division on each plane (as shown in the left column of Figure 5.1). Restricting myself, for obvious reasons, to the content plane, the divisions, beginning from the top, are CONTENT-PURPORT, CONTENT-SUBSTANCE, and CONTENT-FORM. I have already said a few words about content-purport (extracts from Hjelmslev in Section 5.2.4). To those let me add the following on the relation between the three terms:

Purport remains, each time, substance for a new form, and has no possible existence except through being substance for one form or another.

... We, thus, recognize in the linguistic content, in its process, a specific form, the content-form, which is independent of, and stands in arbitrary relation, to the purport, and forms it into content-substance. (Hjelmslev 1961: 52)

On the strength of such comments, I take the relation between content-form and content-substance to be one that is nearest construal, as the term is used in SFL: thus, on the content plane, content form construes content substance. I shall return to the conception of purport, substance and form at a later point. And while I accept that this account of the conception of strata and their relations in Hjelmslev's model is pitifully condensed, I believe it does not misrepresent, and will form a sufficient basis for comparison. One point is immediately obvious: there is no simple one-to-one correspondence between Hjelmslev's planes and strata as they have developed in SFL (as shown in the right column, Figure 5.1). Whereas Hjelmslev's system is bi-planar, with divisions within each plane, Halliday's *system* has four strata, and there are no further divisions on any of the four strata. But this simple and obvious fact has some serious consequences. In the interest of clarity, I shall from now on refer to Hjelmslev's content and expression as **planes**, and to the levels of context, semantics, lexicogrammar, and phonology + phonetics in SF as **strata**. I shall use the word **level** to refer to the three-term divisions within planes in Hjelmslev's system.

5.3.2 The nature of coding relation: expression and realization

If, to begin with, we ignore partitions within the planes of Hjelmslev's denotative semiotic, then it consists of one single cycle of coding: the relation across the levels is symmetrical, content coded as expression. And although the planes are interdependent, the explanation for their interdependence is conventional association as in Saussure. In other words, it could not be maintained that the expression plane in some sense orders, articulates, forms the content plane (cf. the discussion of purport, substance and form; see Hjelmslev 1961: 5l ff.). So, in its nature, the line dividing content and expression is precisely the same as that dividing the Saussurean SIGNIFIED and SIGNIFIER, despite Hjelmslev's rather dismissive comments (1961: 50). Where Saussure spoke of the sign, Hjelmslev spoke of the system:[22] and this is certainly a significant difference, but in both cases the coupling of inter-dependence is arbitrary as demonstrated by Saussure; the sole reason for their association is social convention. What is the position in SFL?

Here, arguably, the conception of components of the system closest to the Hjelmslevian design is perhaps the earliest one (Halliday *et al.* 1964: 18; and a revised version, entitled 'figure 1: Levels of language' in Halliday 1961). Note in passing, that at this early stage, the term 'context' was used approximately in the sense of semantics, and situation is something comparable to today's 'context of culture and situation'. However, in the late 1960s, this practice underwent a change: language, in the SF model, came to be conceptualized in Halliday's words (1984b, 1992a) as a 'multiple coding system'. There three strata were postulated as modelling human language as such; the fourth, i.e., context, is not an inner stratum of language, though it forms part of the theoretical model. The obvious result is that more than one cycle of language-internal coding had to be recognized, semantics coded as lexicogrammar, coded as phonology+phonetics. But like most changes, this change too did not occur all at once: while this development was occurring, the terms 'content' and 'expression' were often employed to refer to the strata; and the relation between the strata was variously referred to as expression, manifestation, or realization, the last being the most popular. Even today, when the multistratal conception of the inner structure of language is well established, SFL practitioners still find it convenient to make use of the metaphors of content and expression.[23] Thus in my own writing I have referred to the semantic stratum as the content whose expression is lexicogrammar, and the latter as the content whose expression is phonology (see, for example, Hasan 1988, 1989; Hasan and Cloran 1990).

The convenience of this continued usage lies in the *non-delicate, undifferentiated notion of coding*, which permits one to draw attention to a certain similarity across all strata: the higher plane/stratum is knowable *only* 'as' the lower plane/stratum. However, the convenience of this similarity should not allow one to forget that the postulate of expression/coding by itself does not cover everything about the nature of that process. When language is conceptualized as a simple coding system, that is, as a binary structure with just the content and expression planes, as in Hjelmslev's model, then it is valid to conclude, as indeed the majority of autonomous linguistic models have done, that the coding relation is throughout conventional, based on a regularity of association. But when language is conceptualized as a multiple coding system, this same position cannot be taken as a foregone conclusion: it becomes theoretically impossible to maintain this view if the multiple coding model is also functional. These comments are relevant to how the notion of realization came to be seen in the SFL model.

It will be obvious that in the SFL model as well, the explanation of arbitrary, conventional association will apply to the primary planar division between the strata of phonology-phonetics (as expression) and those of lexicogrammar-semantics (as content). However, serious theoretical inconsistencies will arise if the same explanation is applied to the cycle between lexicogrammar and semantics, which are comparable to levels of content-form and content-substance in Hjelmslev: in SFL the relations of lexicogrammar and semantics are crucially different from that between content and expression. Lexicogrammar **construes** semantics; it is thus a resource for construing the semantic potential of a language; it is the recognition of this relation that, in the words of Martin, allows language to be seen as a 'meaning-making system' (Martin 1986).

If the term realization is used as simply synonymous with 'coding' (as indeed it was in SFL through the 1960s), then the important difference between the two cycles of coding does not become evident. I believe that the recognition of the qualitative difference between the two cycles of coding was present even in the late 1960s; but the full force of its implications became obvious only as the model began to develop an explicitly functional perspective. Concurrent with that development, a view of realization began to emerge which could support the functional hypothesis of a 'natural' relation between lexicogrammar and semantics. This involved the recognition that important as the notion of construal is, it needs to be complemented by yet another notion, that of **activation**:[24] in other words, realization had to be seen as a dialectic at the 'content' strata/levels. By the early 1970s, Halliday can be found claiming explicitly that, when it came to lexicogrammar coding semantics, realization was not just a matter of conventional association between the two. He presents these in a relation that could be viewed as a **dialectic**: the higher stratum, i.e., semantics, activates the lower one known as lexicogrammar, as the latter construes the semantic potential of language:

> the concept of the social function of language is central to the interpretation of language as a system. The internal organization[25] of language is not accidental; it embodies the functions that language has evolved to serve in the life of social man ... (the) sets of options, which are recognizable empirically in the grammar, correspond to the few highly generalized realms of meaning that are essential to the social functioning of language – and hence are intrinsic to language as a system. (Halliday 1973a: 42–44)

According to this view the lexicogrammatical form of a language cannot be validly viewed as evolving independently of what people do when they engage in speech events. This aspect of the form had to be seen as NON-ARBITRARY i.e., NATURAL; in short it was functional: 'The relation between the meaning and the wording is not ... an arbitrary one; the form of the grammar relates naturally to the meanings that are being encoded' (Halliday 1985b: xvii).

It seems to follow from this view of meaning and wording that construal and activation are necessary kinds of relations in the cycle of stratification seen as internal to language, that which relates meaning and wording. This conclusion is important to my argument, first for the consequence it has for the stratum of context, and second for drawing attention to an important difference between SFL and Hjelmslev's Glossematics model. As the right column of Figure 5.1 shows semantics, lexicogrammar, and phonology + phonetics, represent Halliday's modelling of the inner strata in language. Apart from these, the theory postulates yet another stratum: this is known as the context of culture and situation, and it is external to language. Given the conception of realization above, Halliday is able to integrate this stratum into linguistic theory by arguing that, in the theory, the relation between the strata of context and semantics is the same as that which obtains between the language internal strata of semantics and lexicogrammar (see, for example, Halliday 1973b). This is reminiscent of Firth, who argued that context of situation was simply an extension of the category of context, which is already in use in the description of language (c.f., syllable as the context for phoneme; see 5.2.2 above). For Halliday too, the relation of realization is not something that has to be recognized purely in order to bring context into the theory: the notion is already necessary if analysis is to culminate in synthesis.

5.3.2.1   Excursus B: connotative semiotic in a functional model

Return now to the Hjelmslevian model. I have argued that here we have: (a) a bi-planar organization of language; (b) a three-level organization inside each plane; (c) the relation between the planes is arbitrary; and (d) the relation between the levels at least of substance and form is one of construal. Accordingly, content-substance is construed by content-form. However, if I understand Hjelmslev correctly, it would be wrong to suggest either that an expression plane construes a content plane, or that content-substance activates content-form: the relations between the strata within content plane is exactly the same as that between content plane and expression plane. With these understandings, we may now examine the notion of CONNOTATIVE SEMIOTIC. The abstraction primarily relevant to this notion is that of planes. In Figure 5.1, the planes of content and expression are functives of that sign function (Hjelmslev 1961: 47ff.) to which we refer as 'language'. Speaking informally, there can be no language such that it lacks either of these two planes: the postulate of one necessitates the postulate of the other. Note that, on its own, neither content nor expression can be thought of as a semiotic. Language, as a semiotic is created by the interdependence of content and expression. For Hjelmslev, such a semiotic is a denotative semiotic: the crucial attribute of a denotative semiotic is that neither of its planes is itself a semiotic.

If such a denotative semiotic acts as the expression plane of some content, thereby, presumably, creating another sign function, then this latter sign function is referred to as connotative semiotic in the theory, provided its content plane itself is not a semiotic. If a sign function is created such that both its content plane and its expression plane themselves have the status of a semiotic, then, in Glossematics, such a sign function is to be known as a METASEMIOTIC (see discussion in Hjelmslev 1961: 114 ff.). Both these concepts – connotative semiotic and metasemiotic – remain underdeveloped in Hjelmslev's theory; by this I mean that there does not exist enough theoretical discussion or application of either concept to enable them to act as a means of explanation. Thus a crucial question that arises is: are the planes of a connotative semiotic and/or metasemiotic arbitrarily related to each other? If so, I foresee problems in any application of these concepts in Martin's framework; and certainly Hjelmslev's idea of language varieties as connotators would be quite unviable for yet another reason. If the relation is no longer arbitrary, then we need to know how the relation of planes differs from the relation of levels in the Hjelmslevian theory. Further, if the relation of planes to each other is the same as that postulated for levels in the theory, then the definition of connotative semiotic and metasemiotic calls for revision. Such a revision is not a minor matter in a theory that is as elaborately and explicitly articulated as is Glossematics. So one reason for my discontent with Martin's framework is that his use of the notion of connotative semiotic without further theoretical development is a source of obfuscation rather than explanation. None of the issues raised above has ever been broached; certain notions have been taken for granted, without examination and with the assumption that they are not incoherent when inserted into the SFL theory. These comments call for attention because, if Martin's assertions are taken at face value, there is no reason to suggest that he is working within SFL. By contrast, once we ignore the claims about genre necessitating the recognition of language as the expression of a connotative semiotic, his model resembles SFL to a large extent; the departures from it appear to be based on confusion.

Focusing on what I have called the levels does not appear to bring greater joy to connotative semiotics. Here the concept that seems to raise the greatest number of problems is that of purport. The first question one needs to ask is whether language as denotative semiotic is represented in Figure 5.1 by all the levels in the left column, stretching from content purport to expression purport. Limiting the discussion to content-purport alone, could one say that purport is internal to the sign function? If so, what would it mean to make this claim? I interpret this as a claim that the sign function necessarily extends beyond language as such to physical and phenomenological reality; that without such 'reality', language as a sign function would not have its universe of reference. We could argue then that purport is a part internal to language as denotative semiotic. This, in my view, has a disastrous effect for the notion of connotative semiotic as employed in Martin. Recall that Martin's use of the term 'register' often stands for both what Halliday would refer to as 'context of situation' and also what is known in SFL as 'register'. Now if we accept with Martin that his register is a connotator, and, as a denotative semiotic, language is its expression, then we are implying that the context of situation aspect of Martin's register is not any part of that kaleidoscopic flux, that reality which is purport, (aspects of) which are turned into content-substance by the boundaries laid upon it by content-form. So then, naturally the question arises: What sort of abstraction is Martin's context of situation, which he confusingly calls 'register'?

In Glossematics, the notion of purport is so wide that no extra-linguistic reality can be said to exist beyond it, over which language could have any jurisdiction. If purport is part of language, and it is so wide in its scope, then there can be no context of situation left outside the denotative semiotic of language to play the (partial) role of connotator to it. In that case, if Martin maintains his connotative semiotic claim without changing his concept of context of situation, then either he is being illogical in that there is nothing whatever outside the denotative semiotic of language that could be said to be context of situation; or he is making a false claim in saying that the context of situation aspect of his register is even approximately the same as that of Firth or of Halliday. I am assuming that, whatever else context of situation may be for Malinowski, Firth or Halliday, it is some abstraction from raw reality: it can hardly be otherwise. If an important aspect of context of situation is its status as an *abstraction* from purport, and if purport is part of the denotative semiotic of language, then clearly we cannot have a connotative semiotic of Martin's kind.

We can get out of this impasse by saying that Hjelmslev's theory of language consists of only two levels per plane, namely the form and substance pair both at content and at expression plane in Figure 5.1. I am inclined to this view for two reasons. First, it seems to me to agree with the spirit of Hjelmslev's claims. It simply makes no sense to say that raw reality, an expression often used as an alternative for referring to purport, is internal to the denotative semiotic of language; and certainly one would be totally unjustified in imputing to Hjelmslev a view of language in which mountains, chairs and rings, feelings and sensations were to be considered as inside the ds-language, i.e., as elements of linguistic form/substance.

A second desirable side-effect of this revised conceptualization of ds-language would be to make the models of language in Glossematics and SFL more comparable, with content-form and content-substance of the former corresponding, respectively, to lexicogrammar and semantics of the latter. Note also that the two models of language are alike in another respect: just as content-form construes content-substance, so lexicogrammar is said to construe semantics in SFL. However, the major difference that still remains is in the overall conceptualization of realization: for SF, realization at this point is a dialectic, wording construes meaning, and meaning activates wording. This is not true of the Hjelmslevian model: the model does not allow content-substance to activate content-form. This position is entirely consistent with the view of language as an autonomous system. But, coupled with the problem of the relation of planes to which I drew attention earlier, the position has consequences for the notion of connotative semiotic as used in Martin's model, so long as that model aspires to remain functional as well. Let me elaborate.

Grant that purport is not part of language as denotative semiotic: if so, then this has the effect of leaving Martin free to affirm both that the context of situation aspect of his register is an abstraction from purport (which is now outside ds-language), and that this abstraction, together with the register varieties (*aka* 'genre') acts as the connotator in a connotative semiotic. In other words, Halliday's context of situation, plus Halliday's register as one indivisible bundle, become a functive in a sign function whose other functive is language as denotative semiotic: this seems an unavoidable reading *if* connotative semiotic is a semiotic and *if* a semiotic must be a union of content and expression planes/levels. This position appears to me entirely unsatisfactory on many counts, though here I shall consider only those issues which are germane to the relations of planes and levels (see Section 5.5 for a discussion of further problems).

First, we have here the same problem which exists in Hjelmslev's suggestion. Now that, in Martin's framework, register as one significant dimension of language variation is abstracted from language as denotative semiotic and is exported to the content plane of a connotative semiotic, it is reasonable to ask: what is this denotative semiotic like which is a functive of the sign function whose other functive is context plus genre? How come a language variety is being seen as a connotator in a connotative semiotic whose expression plane is a denotative semiotic, namely, language? Both Firth and Halliday argue that the structure of language is essentially hetero-geneous (Halliday 1974a, 1975b, etc.). In this they differ from Hjelmslev's 'working' assumption of homogeneity. Their position is validated by the fact that it has not been possible for any linguistic model to demonstrate the existence of a single, homogeneous system for any language. Language is poly-systemic in more than one sense; it is certainly poly-systemic in that neither its meanings nor its forms can be described as constituting a single, invariant system. I believe the most sympathetic reading of Martin's position could be that it is not the actual register/genre categories but the abstract fact of a specific dimension of variability and its situational cor-relate that is the connotator, but this reading is not supported by Martin's own analyses, and it does not resolve the problems mentioned here. We are still left with a language as denotative semiotic that is an idealization in much the same way as Saussure's *langue*; this ds-language is not what people use for the living of life.

This is not the end of the story. If Martin's register (seen as equal to Halliday's context) is the content plane of a connotative semiotic whose expression plane is what we know as language, it becomes important to ask: is the relation of these planes arbitrary? It is worth noting that, in his earlier writings, Martin often referred to the so-called denotative system of language as the phonology of register (in Martin's sense of the word). This is precisely what the Hjelmslevian theory suggests; so it was clearly not a capricious move by Martin. But if we think of the relation as arbitrary, we are faced with two questions. First, what is the semantic level of language as a denotative semiotic like? We may wish to claim that the valeur which is the content-substance i.e., the semantics, is created entirely by the relations of content-form, i.e. lexicogrammar. This, however, is not a completely sat-isfactory account of meaning in human languages. In fact, even Saussure acknowledges the need for situationally motivated paradigms (e.g., 'teach-ing,' 'lecture,' 'learning,' in Saussure 1966: 126), as an important aspect of the valeur construction of a sign. I have pointed out elsewhere (Hasan 1985b) that Malinowski's thinking about context of situation arose mainly because he wanted to provide an opening to that formal closure of language, which is the inevitable result of the equation of linguistic meaning solely with language-internal valeur-based relations. In a bi-planar semiotic such as suggested by Martin, the problem of how language comes to mean is just as severe as it was for Saussure, and precisely for the same reasons. Further, if the semantic level of Martin's language as a denotative semiotic is just a valeur system, then natural language development will be as much a problem for his framework as it is for any autonomous model. The hypothesis of language as an innate system is, after all, not based on a miraculous revelation; it is the most logical move in autonomous models.

The second question in accepting the arbitrary relation is: what becomes of register in Halliday's sense, where it has been conceptualized as a lexicogrammatically/semantically defined variety (Hasan 1973c)? There are enormous difficulties in maintaining that register is arbitrarily expressed by whatever we conceive to be the nature of Martin's level of discourse, which is said to be comparable to Halliday's semantic level (Martin 1992). From the tenor of Martin's current writings, I assume that he would wish to deny the possibility of language as denotative semiotic being arbitrarily related to his register (which is equal to Halliday's context and register put together). [26] I am suggesting that he would see the relation between the content and expression planes of his connotative semiotic as qualitatively different from that between the content and expression planes of the linguistic theory where Hjelmslev first introduced it (1961: 47 ff). If so, it is legitimate to ask where, when, and how was this relation re-conceptualized? with what result? Is it more like the relation of construal now? If so, why is Martin's register a plane, not a level that is construed by his level of discourse, just as discourse is construed by lexicogrammar? But if it is, then what becomes of the connotative semiotic claim? Does connotative semiotic involve levels rather than planes? I am not convinced that these serious theoretical problems are resolved by the simple device of talking about communication planes, as Martin has recently begun to do: the issue is not nomenclature; it is, rather, the structure of the theory that needs to be reconsidered.

These seem to me to be important questions, in need of discussion; but suspending them for the moment, let it be granted that, in a connotative semiotic of the type postulated by Martin, the relation between planes is more like that between Hjelmslev's plane-specific levels of substance and form, but that nonetheless they must be viewed as planes rather than levels on some ground or other that we are not aware of, though Martin is: where would that leave the connotative modelling of register? I think, so long as Martin wishes to remain functional, he would still face a serious problem, since in the framework he has adopted, the only possibility of bringing any two planes together is that of conventional association, while a relation of construal is accepted between the higher level of content substance to the lower one of content form. The theory has, to the best of my knowledge, never suggested that the higher level of content substance activates the lower one of content-form. So even if the planes of a connotative semiotics are level-like, activation of the lower plane by the higher is not a possibility. Speaking informally, within the framework of Glossematics, there seems to be no coherent way of asking: why would a speaker choose these meanings rather than those others? This non-recognition of activation as an important part of the relation between levels is again perfectly coherent with the postulates of an autonomous, perspective on language, but it is a serious problem in conceptualizing context-register in relation to language as a denotative semiotic. Whatever Martin's discourse level is like, choices from it can hardly be activated by this hybrid category of context-register without a radical revision of the Hjelmslevian model. How does this state of affairs compare with the relations between the strata of context, semantics, and lexicogrammar in SFL?

I have suggested already that purport is a more inclusive concept than context: this is implicit in the claim that an alternative term for describing 'the social conditions of human existence', would be 'situation purport' (see Section 5.2.5). If purport is thought of as *external to language*, and if it is granted that acquaintance with purport implies some mode of its systematization, then we must ask how this systematization comes about? What turns the social condition of human existence into knowable reality? In Hjelmslev's model, where content-substance lays the boundaries over purport through the workings of content-form, there exists no other means for the systematization of purport. However, as I have pointed out earlier, in this model content-substance itself is entirely construed by content-form, and there seems no reason to imagine that the content-substance construed purely by language-internal relations would be more than a set of isolated units of meaning or at best a set of semantic fields (this I deduce from various examples offered by Hjelmslev, e.g., colour, kinship terms, etc.). Clearly, purport has to be more than just this. It would follow then that whatever of purport exists beyond the reach of content-substance of language as denotative semiotics must be an undifferentiated, uncharted universe, at least so far as the linguist is concerned. It is also clear that in Glossematics, there exists no other level of patterning between the kaleidoscopic flux of purport and the formed content-substance of language. The systemic functional model differs remarkably from Glossematics in the conceptualization of the relation between human social conditions of existence and language.[27]

Here, because of the functional nature of language, semantics is not to be viewed as either isolated units of meaning or as sets of semantic fields. The net that the semantic stratum of language casts on purport is more extensive: where Hjelmslev's purport stands at primary delicacy being linguistically under-analysed, SFL has arguably made some progress. It splits Hjelmslev's purport into at least three orders of abstraction. Thus there are the multiple worlds of human experience, what I have called the human social conditions of existence, or 'reality' if one prefers that term. This is the order of abstraction that is unknowable except through semiotic construal. The second order of abstraction is the context of culture; it is through the study of culture that reality is refracted for the analyst: culture, thus, represents the meaning of that reality. And the third order of abstraction is the context of situation. The latter instantiates choices from the cultural systems as a clause instantiates choices from the lexicogrammatical systems. In this view then, metaphorically, context of situation is to culture as instance is to its potentiating system. Thus contrary to the impression given by Figure 5.1, in SFL context is not so much comparable to Hjelmslev's purport as a whole, as it is to one of the levels of abstraction in purport. And given the concept of realization in SFL, we would say that the instantiating context is construed by the meanings construed by wording: the meanings are specific to some variety of language, while the (wording of the) meaning is itself activated by those cultural choices which underlie the relevant context and function as the activators of meaning.

The point I am emphasizing is that the developments in the concept of realization and functionality in SFL allow the construction of a DYNAMIC OPEN SYSTEM that permits exchange across three strata, from lexicogrammar right through to the context of culture, embracing the system and its process. Needless to say, culture is not reducible to simply linguistically construed phenomena; other modalities, other semiotic systems, although not discussed here, play their part in culture-construal (see, for example, O'Toole 1990; van Leeuwen 1991a, 1991b; Kress and van Leeuwen 1990; Cranny-Francis and Martin 1991). We can then say with Firth and Halliday that, in SFL, lexicogrammar orders, forms, articulates semantics, the latter orders, forms, articulates context of situation, which in its turn is an instantiation of the context of culture. This is the construal perspective of realization. But at the same time, the notion of realization must include the relation of activation especially where the higher strata are concerned. Choices at the stratum of context activate choices at the stratum of semantics, which in their turn activate choices from the systems at the stratum of lexicogrammar.[28]

This continuity of relation from content-form to purport is not attainable in Glossematics because of the non-dialectical nature of the relation between Hjelmslev's levels of form and substance, both at the content and expression planes. Even if we grant that the relation between the two planes of Martin's connotative semiotic is one of construal, the problem remains unsolved, because it is not at all obvious that, without revising the Glossematics theory in fundamental ways, Martin would find it possible to show that in his connotative semiotic, context (Martin's 'register') can activate content-substance; or that an answer can be found to the question: what activates the choice of meanings in a speech event? In fact, it is from this perspective, that the metaphor of sign, as much as that of sign function, becomes problematic when applied to speech events. Thinking of the speech event as a unity of signified and signifier, or as a function of content and expression working together (see Section 5.2.5), far from explaining the relation between the two, seems rather to obscure it. It is to be noted that activation as a form of realization relation is an embarrassment to the connotative semiotic modelling of Martin's genre, register, and language. Different metaphorical locutions have been used. So in the early 1980s, Martin and others working with him talked about 'genre negotiating with register' (Ventola 1987) as if there was some conflict of interest; more recently Martin has claimed that 'mode is oriented to both interpersonal and experiential meaning' (Martin 1992, chap. 7, section 7.2.1). What does 'oriented to' mean in such claims? Is it a theoretical term, with general application? Can we for example also claim that the experiential metafunction is oriented to transitivity? Is it, in short, one aspect of the dialectic of realization and therefore just a terminological variant of activation? Or is something other than that intended?

In the final analysis, we must return to the meaning of planes, levels and their relations in Glossematics. As the Hjelmslevian theory stands in Prolegomena, the cases of connotative semiotic postulated by both Hjelmslev and following him, Martin, are untenable. So, Martin's connotative semiotic will work only if the relation between its two planes is conceptualized precisely as that of realization in SFL. To conceptualize the relations in this way does violence to Glossematics; further it simply recreates SFL under another label. The gratuitous multiplication of labels is not desirable in any theory. My discontent with connotative semiotic is deeper: readers acquainted with Martin's writings will most probably agree with me that Martin presents his connotative semiotic as a model which solves certain problems that in his view are not resolvable in SFL without the importation of the notion of connotative semiotic. But if it is only a terminological variant then this claim is misleading; if it is not a terminological variant, Martin has yet to show how he solves the problems to which I have drawn attention (for further discussions of some of these issues, see Section 5.5).

I would conclude this discussion by suggesting that if the relations of planes and levels are not revised, then theoretically the kind of connotative semiotic Martin proposes is impossible. If the relations do get revised enough to make their relations more like realization is in SFL, then the notion of connotative semiotic becomes unnecessary. Of course, having introduced these metaphors of negotiating, orienting, and so on, one can say, if it pleases one, that context of situation is the connotator for which the denotative semiotic of language is the expression plane, but it is not at all obvious to me that importing the Hjelmslevian notion of connotative semiotic has any advantage whatever: in fact, if my arguments are correct, then it poses serious difficulties. Since I believe my arguments are cogent, I am puzzled by the fact that Martin's suggestion has been so unquestioningly embraced by other linguists (e.g., Hammond 1989; Rothery 1989; Ventola 1984, 1987; and others).

5.3.2.2 Excursus C: realization and meta-redundancy

In the preceding discussion of realization across strata, I have limited my comments to the realization relation of immediate stratal dyads. Is talk in terms of such dyads viable? Could my arguments and conclusions have arisen from ignoring what Lemke refers to as meta-redundancy? Would Martin's model become more viable if the notion of meta-redundancy were to be applied to Martin's strata? There are good reasons against this supposition: meta-redundancy is active only in a 'non-minimal semiotic' (Halliday 1992a). So the concept is irrelevant to Hjelmslev's various categories of semiotic, including language seen as a denotative semiotic without the content purport: it would be an odd use of the term meta-redound to suggest that the pair form and substance at the plane of content meta-redound with the pair form and substance at the plane of expression. The notion of meta-redundancy requires at least three strata in succession, which is not found in Hjelmslev's framework of language as a denotative semiotic, since purport appears best located in above the denotative semiotic. The structure of that semiotic ordering appears to be bi-planar, quite irrespective of whether the planes are referred to as communication plane or as content and expression planes. It therefore does not seem viable to suggest that meta-redundancy across the Hjelmslevian planes/levels is going to resolve any problems that can be resolved by meta-redundancy.

Halliday (1992a) points out that realization can be thought of as a reversible relation. So if p, q, r is semantics, l, m, n lexicogrammar, and a, b, c phonology, then either of the following abstract statements of realization relation holds:

(1) p, q, r ↘ (l, m, n ↘ a, b, c)
(2) (p, q, r ↘ l, m, n) ↘ a, b, c

I believe reversibility is the logical outcome of conceptualizing realization as the main relation across strata in a non-minimal semiotics that allows the scope for meta-redundancy. While the reversibility of realization is an important fact, I believe it is equally important to note that in a functional model, the meaning of the arrow inside the bracket of (1) will not be the same as that of the arrow inside the bracket of (2). Halliday has remarked that if the expression **a**, **b**, **c** realizes wordings **l**, **m**, **n** with the latter realizing meanings **p**, **q**, **r**, then 'in terms of redundancy' we would not view this as two dyadic relationships. 'Rather there would be a META-redundancy such that **p**, **q**, **r** redounds not with **l**, **m**, **n** but with the redundancy of **l**, **m**, **n** with **a**, **b**, **c**.' (1992a: 24). But in drawing attention to this property of realization, it is equally important not to forget that the bond between **p**, **q**, **r** and **l**, **m**, **n** is critically different from the bond of **a**, **b**, **c** to the other strata whether the picture is as in (1) or as in (2) above. I see statements (1) and (2) as neatly capturing the two aspects of the process of speaking. In the active aspect of the process of speaking as the message is being produced, the speaker's starting point is meaning in context; here the bond between lexicogrammar and phonology appears so tight that the awareness of linguistic form, as it were, disappears. As evidence, note that speakers are seldom aware of ambiguities in their sayings (Hasan 1971a). It is typically when one is editing one's own sayings that ambiguous expressions suddenly become noticeable, which is not surprising, since in editing one is playing the role of an attentive addressee to oneself. The second abstract statement represents the other aspect of the process, where one's focus is on understanding. To make sense of the stream of events, the listener has to proceed from the sens-ible to the intellig-ible. This situation is captured in (2): the listener's awareness is of that which impinges on the senses and of that which is understood. In both these perspectives, what is hidden from awareness is the role of lexicogrammar. Thus the common sense view of language as a pairing of meaning and sound, where the lexicogrammatical stratum is the invisible one, is well represented in the two abstract statements of meta-redundancy in realization.

The not-so-hidden thesis of this rather lengthy section has been a very simple one: the concept of realization as a dialectic at the higher strata of coding, and the postulate of language as a multiple coding system in the SFL theory, make the notion of connotative semiotic *à la* Martin, not only unnecessary, but also unviable. It is not simply that with these developments the invoking of connotative semiotic in the specific sense in which Martin invokes it is superfluous; it is also the case that the invoking of it creates problems without yielding benefits. We cannot pretend that, just because Hjelmslev's ideas were important to the development of SFL, present day SFL is therefore a variety of Glossematics, and that theoretical concepts can be transferred with impunity from one to the other. SFL does not need a connotative semiotic of this kind; the two major developments in SFL named above have enabled the theory to model the processes whereby language might be implicated in the construal of context and whereby the perception of a context might be an essential condition for both speaking and understanding. If my arguments are correct, then nothing in the notion of connotative semiotic improves on this; quite the contrary. I shall have to return to connotative semiotic at a later point; here I turn now to the significance of the functional hypothesis.

5.3.3 Language defining context

The claim that language construes context as wording construes meaning is far too abstract; to be able to make use of it descriptively, more specific statements are needed. If those statements not only specify the how of the details of construal but also why this is how it is done, this would be a major step forward in the theory. Halliday's second important contribution to the study of speech event was to secure just such a resource. Before considering this aspect of Halliday's contribution, his concept of context of situation should be presented.

The three components of Halliday's context of situation, field of discourse, mode of discourse, and tenor of discourse, are well known. At this abstract level, the concept of context has undergone no change since Halliday *et al.* (1964), though the details of how the three parameters are to be conceptualized has been subject to considerable elaboration. I use the term elaboration deliberately, because the original interpretation has, in my view, never been abandoned, though over the years as work in textual analysis has progressed, and as others have attempted to use Halliday's concepts, Halliday and other colleagues have added more information, in many cases identifying the intended reading of some feature previously stated cryptically or ambiguously.

I am aware of the criticism that Halliday's view of context has not been constant, but I shall ignore it. In the first place, theories are not born readymade; when they are no longer subject to change and exploration, they are already close to being obsolete: scholars who try out alternative solutions are not mentally deficient, or necessarily ad-hoc or a-theoretical as a narrow interpretation of Popper's view of how theories are produced and validated would imply; rather, alternative solutions indicate the nature of knowledge as process. The obvious and frequently experienced fact is that two opposing positions can appear valid, depending on one's point of view. It would indeed be convenient if scholars always explicitly argued out the reasons for and against taking certain positions: at the least this would absolve the reader from having to work hard. But in the history of the production of knowledge, the number of scholars who have failed to argue the implications of their position or failed to accurately present their claims far exceeds the number of who have done so without exception. Popper himself is a case in point: does he really recognize and argue out the full implications of his claims about the importance of language in gaining access to his World 3 (Popper 1972)? Does he recognize, leave aside reconcile, the contradictions involved in his view of language as irrelevant to real ideas, knowledge, and so on, and his view that language is central to World 3? This is not simply a *tu quoque* argument. Requirements of this kind, which sound so clearly objective and rational, on examination, turn out to be edicts from the dominant modes of thinking and reasoning. It is through these 'rational', 'objective' edicts that those whose position is not dominant may be forced to comply with a standard which hardly any naturally occurring production of knowledge has ever met. Of course, it would be useful if Halliday put out a flag every time he considered an alternative position, but so would it be for Chomsky (see Lakoff 1990), for Popper (see Feyerabend 1976), and for Lakatos (see Berkson 1976; Toulmin 1976). So the more important issue is not whether the view has remained unchanged, but rather how has the view changed, and what did it have to do with the development of the theory.

My second reason for wishing to ignore this inconsistency critique is that, empirically speaking, it is at least exaggerated, if not entirely without basis; to me the consistencies from the 1960s (Halliday *et al.* 1964: 90ff.) to the present (e.g., Halliday and Hasan 1985) appear more remarkable than the imputed differences. For example, at this level of abstraction, the 'inconsistency' in Halliday's view of context has to do with the position of rhetorical mode, to which I shall return at a later point. First let me simply represent a more recent formulation of context; hopefully, during the discussion consistencies might become evident:

1. THE FIELD OF DISCOURSE refers to what is happening, to the nature of the social action that is taking place: what is it that the participants are engaged in, in which the language figures as some essential component?
2. THE TENOR OF DISCOURSE refers to who is taking part, to the nature of the participants, their statuses and roles: what kinds of role relationships obtain among the participants, including permanent and temporary relationships in which they are involved?
3. THE MODE OF DISCOURSE refers to what part the language is playing, what it is that the participants are expecting the language to do for them in that situation: the symbolic organization of the text, including the channel (is it spoken, written or some combination of the two?), and also the rhetorical mode, what is being achieved by the text in terms of such categories as persuasive, expository, didactic, and the like. (Halliday 1985c: 12)

Though Halliday does not explicitly discuss how he sees his own schema of context in relation to Firth's, this much is clear: in setting up the three parameters of field, tenor, and mode, from the very beginning, Halliday has appealed far more consistently than his two predecessors to the operation of language itself. He is keen to differentiate his theory of register, that is, the theory of speech events that explains how context and text are related, from Firth's RESTRICTED LANGUAGES. Halliday's field is not necessarily co-extensive with Firth's 'nonverbal action':

if two people discuss politics while doing the washing up. ... the language activity does not form part of the washing up event, and the field of discourse is that of politics. (Halliday *et al.* 1964: 91)

If the field is not 'washing up,' this is because language is not figuring as an essential component relevant to that physical activity: it is doing something else. So, even this early, language is the critical factor for construing this parameter of context; by comparison, Firth's 'nonverbal action' remains somewhat vaguer. Why should the question of playing at darts, being inside or outside a pub, etc., arise at all in attempting to state the meaning of '*Ahng gunna gi' wun fer Ber*' (Firth 1950/1957: 182)? How far does the notion of nonverbal action extend, and on what basis shall we answer that question?

Similarly, the notion of 'relevant objects' in Firth gives way in Halliday to that which is constituted by linguistic signification. So there may be *situations 'in which the language activity accounts for practically the whole of the relevant activity'* (Halliday *et al.* 1964: 90), as perhaps in writing an essay on biology, in which case the things relevant to the discourse are 'things' in biology, and their character as object is hardly a straightforward concept. Starting from the notion of activity and objects relevant to it, one might argue that, to undertake the physical activity of writing the essay, the writer would need such objects as pen, paper, chair, table, etc. If these would not be part of Halliday's field described as 'writing an essay about biology', then this is because he has already stated what the principle of inclusion is.[29] The point is not that Firth would necessarily have included these objects among his category of 'the relevant objects' (although see Mitchell 1975), simply that he gave no guidance how his sense of the 'relevant' was to be recognized. I am not claiming that such tangentially relevant objects, for example, pen, paper, and so on, here, can be ignored. In fact, I coined the term MATERIAL SITUATIONAL SETTING (Hasan 1973c, 1981) precisely in order to admit such facts into the theory of register while precluding the possibility of their being mistaken as part of the RELEVANT CONTEXT of a text. But this development, which I believe does make some contribution to understanding the nature of contexts (Cloran 1987; Hasan 1981), was itself made possible because of the clarifications provided by Halliday.

To Halliday, we owe, then, the perspective that the meanings we produce by virtue of our lexicogrammatical acts help to delineate for us the values of the parameters of relevant context of situation. If the term 'relevant context of situation' does not refer to all of human social conditions of existence, to all situation-purport in Hjelmslev's sense, then some principle for abstraction is needed, as Firth was the first to point out. The principle Halliday provides, from the construal point of view, is that of consulting the text: *relevant context is that part of the extra-linguistic situation which is illuminated by language-in-use, by the language component of the spatio-temporally located speech event*, the other name for which is 'the on-going text'. Expressed formally, context meta-redounds with meanings construed by wordings (see Section 5.3.2.2). And if relevant context has been construed by language in such a way that it has this tripartite structure, then on this basis, an encoding definition of relevant context would be: relevant context is a verbally construed three part construct composed of some doing, by some doers in some verbal mode of doing. Just as we do not know what the variant categories of the Latin noun look like without 'hopping along the realizational chain,' (cf. Halliday 1984a), so here too we do not know the variant categories of the context of culture and situation without hopping along the realizational chain and ultimately appealing for evidence in the text's wording that construes meaning. From its early stages, SFL has assigned lexicogrammar a central role in the recognition of register, which is defined as a linguistic variety that correlates with variation in the context of situation:

> It is by their formal properties that registers are defined. If two samples of language activity from what, on non-linguistic grounds, could be considered different situation-types show no difference in grammar or lexis, they are assigned to one and the same register: for the purposes of the description of the language there is only one situation type here, not two. (Halliday *et al.* 1964: 89)

A register is a variety of language which with some context of situation, but not any context can correlate with just any category of register. And by virtue of its meaning-wording choices, each text announces itself as an instance of some registral variety whose correlate is some specific category of context. A claim of this kind demands the ability to specify what aspects of language will correlate with the three contextual variables. In the 1960s these statements tended to be made in terms of patterns of lexis and of grammar, which were as yet not systematized by the meta-functional hypothesis. The measures used were crude (for one critique of which, see Hasan 1973c). With the development of the functional perspective, Halliday's claims become more precise about the details of how the language of a text construes its context and how context might become an explanatory principle in the functional hypothesis itself.

5.3.4 Context in text: a functional perspective

These more specific statements (e.g., Halliday 1977a, 1985a) have certainly caused some debate (Berry 1982, 1989; Butler 1985a, 1985b; Martin 1984, 1985a, 1992), though regrettably they have not incited any actual experiments, which might have been better. In what follows I shall assume acquaintance with Halliday's metafunctions, interpersonal, namely, EXPERIENTIAL, LOGICAL, and TEXTUAL; increasingly detailed descriptions of these have become available in Halliday's own work, and more recently in other linguists' writings (such as Halliday and Fawcett 1987; Martin 1991). Since the metafunctions are organizing concepts at the semantics stratum (Halliday 1977a: 176–177), to validate them one needs to examine them in a trinocular perspective: from above – how the metafunctions might realize elements of the context of situation by choice of certain meanings; from their own stratum – how the metafunctions account for the phenomena we think of as linguistic meaning; and from below – how the lexicogrammatical realization of meaning impacts on the metafunctional hypothesis. Each of these perspectives is equally important, and the evidence from each carries equal weight. But in maintaining this multiplicity of perspectives, which is one important source of the richness of SFL descriptions of language, there arises a problem. The origin of this problem is in the requirement that strata must be non-conformal: the strata are realizationally related, in the sense that there exists a stronger than chance relation between them. However, if the two strata conformed completely, it would be theoretically unviable to postulate distinct strata:

> The prerequisite for the necessity of operating with two planes must be that the two planes, when they are tentatively set up, cannot be shown to have the same structure throughout, with a one-to-one relation between the functives of the one plane and the functives of the other. We shall express this by saying that the two planes must not be conformal. (Hjelmslev 1961: 112).

This situation leaves the possibility open that the evidence from the three distinct perspectives will not always point in the same direction (see, for example, Halliday 1977a: 179, on the conflicting evidence for the relation of the logical metafunction *vis-à-vis* the experiential and the textual). Any discussion of the metafunctional hypothesis would be incomplete unless all three strata, are examined taking into account the non-congruent evidence.

Since the above demands cannot be met within the confines of the present chapter, one might note that the evidence from below is already positive: Halliday has claimed since the introduction of his metafunctional hypothesis (1970a) that the organization of the lexicogrammatical level supports the hypothesis of just these metafunctions in just that sort of relation (Halliday 1970a, 1979b, 1985b; Halliday and Matthiessen 1999). I shall also assume that the evidence from the level of semantics itself positively favours just these metafunctions: indeed as the indicative work on semantic networks (Hasan 1983) has demonstrated the four metafunctions suggested by Halliday appear to be adequate to account for the *kinds* of meaning we exchange linguistically.[30] So of these three validating moves, I shall be concerned immediately only with the first one, that is, *how the metafunctions are realizationally related to context*. Given the meaning of the term 'realization', there will have to be a dual perspective: how are metafunctions related to contexts? And how does context support the metafunctional hypothesis: in other words, how is the nature of linguistic meanings explained?[31]

On the realizational relation between context and metafunction, Halliday's claim is well known: he suggests that the three elements of context, i.e., field, mode, and tenor, correlate with the metafunctions; there is a tendency for the experiential metafunction to realize field, for the interpersonal to realize tenor, and for the textual to realize mode. This represents the heart of the hypothesis that has become known as the CONTEXT META-FUNCTION HOOK-UP HYPOTHESIS (abbreviated by its critics as CMH HYPOTHE-SIS).[32] Halliday (1977a: 201–202) presents the situation as follows:

semiotic structure of situation	associated with	functional components of semantics
field (type of social action	" "	experiential
tenor (role relationships)	" "	interpersonal
mode (symbolic organization)	" "	textual

The selection of options in the experiential systems – that is, in transitivity, and in the classes of things (objects, persons, events, etc.), in quality, quantity, time, place and so on – tends to be determined by the nature of the activity: what socially recognized action the participants are engaged in, in which the exchange of verbal meanings plays a part. …

The selection of interpersonal options, those in the systems of mood, modality, person, key, intensity, evaluation and comment and the like, tend to be determined by the role relationships in the situation. ...

The selection of options in the textual systems, such as those of theme, information and voice, and also the selection of cohesive patterns, those of reference, substitution and ellipsis, and conjunction, tend to be determined by the symbolic forms taken by the interaction, in particular the place that is assigned to the text in the total situation. ...

Let me point out, first, that, although Halliday uses the word 'determined' in talking about the relationship between the situational parameters and the metafunctions, typically he views this relation as *probabilistic*. Second, more often than not, Halliday does not mention the logical metafunction in describing the 'determination' of context by metafunctions, leaving open the question of its relationship to the situational parameters. Finally, in the above extract, the realizational relation is viewed from the point of view of process: The speaker's perception of field, tenor, and mode is such and such, and this perception of the situation, as it were, activates the choice of certain meanings, which are realized by her choice of wordings. That is to say, context is presented here as an activating force. Note then that the first two characteristics to which attention is drawn are typical of Halliday's presentation, while the last is simply incidental to the needs of that piece of writing from which the passage has been extracted. That Halliday conceives of context-metafunction relation as a dialectic is borne out by such comments as the one which opens this chapter. In fact without recognizing such dialectic Halliday could not claim that the nature of language is as it is because of the functions it is made to serve. That the correlation between context and meaning-wording is viewed probabilistically and the logical metafunction tends to be ignored can be seen again from the following extract:

the contextual features ... under the 'field' of discourse are by and large reflected in just one of the modes of meaning of the poem, namely that which we referred to as the 'experiential' mode. ... just as we were able to recognize certain lexicogrammatical features as *particularly reflecting the field*, ... so also we can recognize other lexicogrammatical features as *particularly reflecting the tenor*, namely those that we identified as carrying the interpersonal meanings, ... we can make a general observation that the mode is *typically reflected* in the lexicogrammatical features that we were able to identify as carrying textual meanings. (Halliday 1985b: 25; emphasis added)

If Halliday's hypothesis about the typical realizational tendencies is correct, this would have some notable implications: (a) that the abstract structure of the context of situation is as it is because meaning-by-wording is so organized as to constitute precisely these elements of situation and no other: from the myriad of extra-linguistic phenomena that surround us at any occasion of talk, these are the phenomena that would have the privilege of being invariably highlighted through linguistic meanings; (b) this, in turn, would imply that (i) in the construal of culture human relations, human actions and the linguistic patterns associated with the enactment of relations and construal of actions have equal importance: the organization of these parameters and so also the associated realizational patterns of language would therefore be called for; and that (ii) from the amorphous flux of human social conditions of existence, it is these parameters rather than any others that would emerge as critical to shaping the nature of verbal interaction; (which of course does not mean that these are the only phenomena that will be relevant to other modes of semiosis as well); (c) it will follow from (a) and (b) that conceptions of context such as presented by Firth (1957, 1968), Gregory (1967), Gregory and Carroll (1978), Hymes (1971, 1972, 1986), Jacobson (1966), Cook (1990), Hasan (1973c), Fawcett (1980), Martin (1985a, 1985b, 1986, 1992) would have to be viewed as theoretically less well motivated; and finally (d) if the hypothesis is correct, it will support the central claim essential to the functional component in the SFL model, namely that the structure of language is as it is because of the functions it is made to serve in the life of a community, because of how people use their language for living. Human subjects respond to semantic pressures (Butt 1989) occasioned by the daily concerns of living because they are beings with a predisposition to sociality. The metafunctions have evolved in response to the pressures in the exchange of meaning; in no sense can they be said to solely and simply emerge from the structure of language, though that is where we find the most tangible proof of their existence. This is in contrast to the most abstract structural capacity of language, i.e., its paradigmatic and syntagmatic nature, which cannot be said to emerge from the human predisposition to sociality.[33]

What these implications show is that the claim about the relation of metafunctions and contextual parameters, which have sometimes been referred to as the CMH hypothesis, is theoretically critical to the inclusion of the word *Functional* in the title of *Systemic Functional Linguistics*. It is, therefore, not surprising that its discussion has excited interest; what is surprising is that not many SFL practitioners who are critical of others for not substantiating their arguments have failed to devise ways of testing Halliday's hypothesis. It is no exaggeration at all to say that the context metafunction relations as presented by Halliday are either acceded to without any such testing, presumably because either it satisfies our intuitions or, more disappointingly, it has been quietly put aside without a fair trial, for example, in Martin's work, whose theory of genre (Martin 1985a, 1985b, 1986, 1992) is partly predicated on the assumption that: (a) in its original form the CMH hypothesis is untenable; and (b) that the modifications suggested by Martin would rescue the hypothesis by validating the metafunctions from above with a different view of context.[34] The final sections of this chapter will examine some of these claims. In the following section I shall conduct an indicative experiment to examine the validity of what I described as the heart of the claim regarding the relations of context and metafunctions.

5.4   Language making contexts: the process of the text

The CMH hypothesis implicates the strata of context, semantics, and lexicogrammar. I have already assumed as my starting point the claim that such and such metafunction is typically realized by such and such lexicogrammatical system(s); so for example, I will posit with Halliday (1970a, 1979b, 1985c) that the experiential metafunction is *typically* realized by options in the transitivity system and by reference to entities, processes and their incumbents (see Figure 5.2).

Figure 5.2: Relation of the text to the context of situation (from Halliday 1985c: 26)

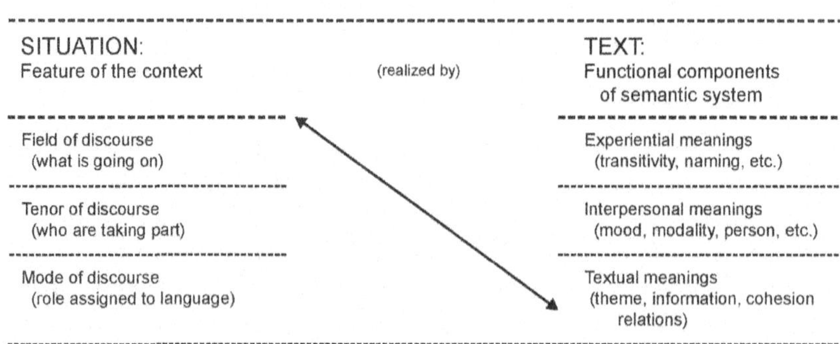

Given this assumption, if I simply alter the transitivity and reference choices of a language piece, leaving the coding of the other metafunctions largely unchanged, then I can ask: is my understanding of the situational context relevant to the second passages different from the original? If it is different, what exactly does that difference consist in? Obviously, whatever difference is found between the contexts relevant to the original and its transformed version would be attributable to the experiential metafunction via its lexicogrammatical coding. There would then be ground for maintaining that those aspects of context in respect of which the two pieces differ are construed by the coding of the experiential metafunction. One can then ask: are these construed contextual phenomena such that one could think of them as (components of) field? In other words, did the worded meanings alter what we refer to as field? If so, this could be taken as some indication that Halliday's CMH hypothesis is valid.[35] If there is doubt that what is being altered is field, then the next questions are: what is the nature of that situational 'correlate' which is construed by this altered wording-meaning? And equally significantly: what is the basis on which we are able to say that the difference is constitutive, not of field, but of something else? Before proceeding with this mini experiment, let me say: first, I realize of course that a small attempt of this kind is far from deserving the name of even a mini experiment; but one has to begin somewhere. Further, it is necessary to say a words on Halliday's formulation of the hypothesis: framed in terms of tendencies, it has been criticized as not exact enough to be scientific.

5.4.1 Hypotheses and conjectures

Halliday does not claim a categorical or absolute correlation between some metafunction and some specific parameter of the context of situation. Although there remain some linguists who still cherish categorical statements as the only desirable mode of describing linguistic phenomena, with recent developments in the sociology of knowledge (Barnes and Edge 1982; Berger and Luckmann 1967; Bloor 1976, 1983; Feyerabend 1975, 1976, 1978; Knorr-Cetina and Mulkay 1983; Latour and Woolgar 1979), it is now becoming increasingly unnecessary to argue the case for the scientific character of non-categorical, probabilistic hypotheses. But scholars accepting probabilistic hypotheses as valid differ in another respect: there are those who do their science *à la* Popper, who, while accepting probabilistic statements, might still wish to impose the requirement that probability statements should be so expressed as to be susceptible to refutation.

This requirement entails a problem. A definite statistical claim, which is what is needed to make refutation possible, can only be made on the basis of large-scale empirical studies; no such studies have yet been carried out with reference to the CMH hypothesis, which makes the statement of such a definite probability problematic in practice.

But is it a theoretically sound requirement that, before making such probabilistic claims, a scholar must carry out an empirical investigation? An affirmative response would be hasty. Quite apart from the hidden intuitivist assumptions behind this requirement, which are surely quite contrary to Popper's ideal of the hypothetical-deductive nature of science (Oldroyd 1986), it is both contradictory and arbitrary. For in order to hypothesize that the probability of field being realized by experiential meanings is such and so in exact terms, one first needs to have conducted an analysis. But, there is a problem: analysis presupposes some hypothesis underlying it. Clearly, then, an infinite regress would be the natural outcome of this contradiction. The arbitrariness of the requirement can be seen from a consideration of the history of the development of science: for example, Eddington's observations did not precede Einstein's predictions concerning the gravitational deflection of light. In fact, this *risky* quality of the hypothesis, whose backing was deductive, was the measure of its brilliance (Oldroyd 1986: 299).

Speaking from a deductive perspective, Halliday's CMH hypothesis is well grounded in his proposal that language and the speaking subject's sense of the world are related to each other.[36] The world, which we live in and act on, is knowable only as construed by some system capable of laying a grid on it; language is one such perspective on the basis of which hypotheses about the nature of reality are made (Firth 1957; Halliday 1974a, 1975a, 1975b; Hjelmslev 1961; Whorf 1956). If it is true that experiential meaning specifically provides a perspective on processes, their participants and circumstances, on things, their non-attitudinal qualities, quantities, and so on; and if it is true that transitivity and reference, to a large extent, encode such meanings; then the correlation between these meanings and our perception of the nature of social activity is logically likely to be significantly above chance level. The hypothesis has to be formulated in probabilistic terms, because, no matter how strong this probability, it seems also logically impossible to claim a one-to-one relationship across strata (discussion in Section 5.3.4 above). Probabilistic statements are desirable also because there can be both orderly and non-orderly variation in how the social activity is realized by transitivity and reference choices. While it is possible to both describe and predict on the basis of theory the patterns of orderly variation – e.g., variation of the kind involved in writing a fragment of the history of aviation as a way of advertising air travel – it is not possible to make a predictive statement about non-orderly, chance phenomena, no matter how critical they may be from the point of view of indicating social change. And yet chance is something you can by definition neither anticipate nor eliminate.

The aim of this discussion has been to argue that probabilistic statements are not 'defective' statements: they are not probabilistic simply because, due to our human infirmities, we have not been able to find the facts as they always happen in reality. Rather, the statements are probabilistic because such indeterminacy inheres in the nature of things; it is in the nature of content-expression relation that it does not just tolerate but actually requires this lack of exact fit. In the examination of the language piece below, I shall adhere to the probabilistic nature of Halliday's claims; there will be no effort to alter everything that appears to realize the experiential metafunction.

5.4.2   A text and its context

The language piece to be used for this purpose is taken from one of the many dialogues recorded for a large-scale sociolinguistic research that has been conducted at Macquarie University (Cloran 1994; Hasan 2009a). In order to simplify the issues, I have edited out all features indicative of social dialect, e.g., double negatives, lack of concord, and certain lexical forms, e.g., *nah* as opposed to *no*. The transcription is made as non-exotic as practicable. The conventions worth noting here are: (a) the numbers in parentheses refer to messages (Hasan 1973a, 2009a); (b) dots such as those between (54) and (55) indicate a pause greater than would be normally expected at that particular point in the dialogue; (c) writing in the upper case in parentheses indicates some interpretation which is based on acoustic information; and (d) the *asterisk at the beginning of words *in contiguous turns* indicates utterance overlap, as in Ventola (1987), but without the convention of underlining. Message can be glossed here as the smallest semantic unit that has the potential of realizing an element of a text's structure (Hasan 1978, 1979b, 1981, 1985b, etc.) and is typically lexicogrammatically realized as an instance of the unit clause, irrespective of patterns of ellipsis:[37]

Extract 1:
A: (42) this baby shampoo doesn't go in your eye, does it?
B: (43) no

A: (44) baby *shampoo –
B: (45) *it doesn't hurt –
A: (46) *no
B: (47) *does it
A: (48) and some doesn't fall into your eye, does it Mum?
B: (49) no
A: (50) 'cause this is a good one (51) and some of them are naughty ones, aren't they?
B: (52) yes (53) this is your shampoo
A: (54) yes … (55) this is the kind for little girls, isn't it? (56) not for babies
B: (57) mmm (AGREEING WITH A) … (58) this one's just all for you … isn't it?
A: (59) yes
B: (60) OK, lie down (61) and I'll get the soap off you

As a normal speaker of English language, I am able to construe certain kinds of contextual information from this piece of language, even though I was not present at the time of recording. In fact to say that I understand the meanings of the sentences and words of this piece of language is to say that I can use them to interpret, and infer, in short, to construe, the situation relevant to this discourse: what is going on, who are the 'persons' involved, and what part language is playing in it.

In describing these aspects of the relevant context of situation for extract 1, I shall also make certain general points about the nature of the three parameters postulated by Halliday. So, starting with who the speakers are, most listeners/readers would agree that the dialogue is between a little girl and her mother: A refers to B as *Mum* in message (48), and identifies herself with *a little girl* (55) as opposed to *babies* (56); A and B are daughter and mother, respectively. Our experience of the relevant culture leads us to see this as a permanent social relationship between these two interactants. But being able to identify an 'institutionalized' relation of this kind does not tell all about the social relations of the interactants. Speaking more delicately, on this particular occasion, the daughter and mother are acting in a mutually supportive and companionable way. However as would be readily recognized there are occasions when a mother and her child do not speak to each other supportively, the mother perhaps asserting her authority, and the child perhaps rebelling against that. In fact, if I had not cut the dialogue off at message (61) in extract 1, this same mother would be heard in approximately 8 minutes following message (61), using a very different tone, ordering her child to get out of the bath immediately and threatening her with dire consequences if she failed to comply.

The mutually supportive engagement of A and B is not all that is relevant to what is going on. There is reference in the extract to such objects as *shampoo* and *soap*; the appropriateness of this particular shampoo which is not a 'naughty one' and will 'not fall in your eye' and it 'doesn't hurt'. There is the offer from B to get the soap off A. From these references to entities and processes we gather that there is also a less permanent relation between them which is based on the practical activity that is taking place: the mother is bathing the daughter. So at a more abstract level, the social process may be described as that of care-giving/receiving, which places them in a 'temporary' relation: the mother is the caregiver and the child is the receiver. Like their mutually supportive social relation this caregiver-receiver relation too can be viewed as transitory. Mothers do take on the role of instructor, entertainer, and so on (Hasan 1986). So the fact that A and B are daughter and mother does not mean that is all there is to their social relation; there is a gamut of varied social relations into which they enter from one occasion to the next. This clearly raises a problem. It is highly unlikely that mothers and children in any culture, no matter how egalitarian, how non-paternalistic, how universally benign, could conceivably assume or enact just any social relation whatever. If the choice of relations is wide, on what basis is it typically made?[38]

As to the social activity in which the mother and daughter are engaged, two simultaneous things seem to be going on: on the one hand, the main thing being discussed relates it to the social activity of caregiving, more specifically mother amicably bathing her daughter. Concurrent with the bathing activity, there is something else going on, which can be described as the maintenance of social relation: the mother is humouring the child along, supporting her positive face (Levinson 1983), and maintaining the mutual relation of supportive, amiable companionship. Each social activity has a corresponding participant relation; and just as, from the activity of a mother bathing her child, we cannot deduce the concurrent activity of maintaining amiable social relations, so also from the caregiver-receiver relation we cannot deduce the supportive, amiable companionship relation: both the social activity and the social relation can co-occur with other kinds of social activity and social relations. An interesting question is: what kind of theoretical framework do we need in order to be able to predict which social activities are typically combined, and what constraints there are on the range of combination?

Before turning to that question, let me say a word about the part that language is playing in the activities identified above. It is obvious that one of the social activities in which the mother and child are engaged, namely that of the maintenance of amiable social relations, becomes accessible even to the participants by their acts of languaging: the role of language is constitutive of this enactment of relations precisely in this sense. Had either participant used language differently not affirming, agreeing, or appearing solicitous or complying, no one listening to them or even actually engaged in the social process would have the sense that the relation of amiable companionship is being maintained. The emotions, states of mind, the right attitude and so on are construed for the interactants largely through what goes on by way of saying and meaning: in other words the *role of language is constitutive*.

By contrast, in the practical social activity of caregiving-and-receiving, e.g., bathing the child, does not depend solely on language, though typically language is used if two or more persons together engage in doing something. Here the same words are performing a different function: they are 'referring' to 'relevant objects, actions and persons' in the sense of 'signifying' them in Saussure's sense of the term. In this sense the role of language is not 'constitutive' but 'ancillary'. It is ancillary because, so far as the participants are concerned, they do not *need* languaging in order to perceive themselves as engaged in the activity of caregiving and receiving. The mode is dialogic: there is the immediacy of the interactants' co-presence, which allows sharing in the social process of the text.

5.4.2.1 Excursus D: context: combination versus configuration

At this point what becomes obvious is the *interdependence* between the three parameters of the context of situation. This interdependence can be viewed from two perspectives. Let me comment first on the nexus (or tie-up) of the three parameters, for this will lead to the consideration of the first perspective. I have shown above that there is a close connection between the social relation of the interactants and the social activity in which they are engaged. This close relation is not fortuitous. When a relatively permanent social relation, for example, mother, is examined analytically, it becomes obvious that, in all communities, such terms as mother, husband, teacher, judge, policeman, and so on, 'describe' social relations, and are themselves socially constructed. Part of the means by which this construction of social identity comes about is the range of social processes in which persons are observed to participate; in other words what persons do with other persons is part of the enactment of their social identity *vis-à-vis* this social other; the interaction *enacts* elements of their identity, who they are in respect to those other. This being so, it might seem viable to claim that engagement in social processes is an explanatory factor in the construction of social relations.

But to put it thus is to oversimplify and to act as if social process has a *sui generis* existence, like a piece of physical reality, e.g., 'landmass'. It is true that the social construction of motherliness depends on the identification of certain social processes which are viewed in the community as typically those in which mothers are likely to engage qua mothers. I am not concerned here with the feeling of distaste that many scholars feel with regard to *established* social expectations: *my aim is to describe what passes, not what should pass, in the living of life with others.* In a specific instance then, one may claim a mother to be in the relation of caregiver to her daughter on the basis of her engagement in the social process of caregiving. But caregiving is not all that mothers do; and it is not only mothers that give care. Mothers qua mothers engage in other processes; and caregiving is practised not just by mothers but also by such social identities as a social worker, a paramedic, a geriatric companion, a house-help, and so on. This has two consequences: engagement in processes cannot be the sole definer of social relation; and the nature of social processes must be affected by who engages in them. The caregiving that a mother does is qualitatively different as a social process from that social process of caregiving which is undertaken by, say, a geriatric companion. So just as social process may be said to act on social relation, so also the social relation of participants acts on the nature of social activity. Equally, how the activities are enacted is an important part of the construction of both social process and social identity. One may, for example, teach through demonstration or through exposition: to use Halliday's terminology, the rhetorical mode may be practical or expository. The way that Kristy's mother 'teaches' her the meaning of the verb 'grease' is different from the way that Amie's teacher teaches her the meaning of 'infected': Kristy's mother employs a rhetorical mode that is practical/commonsensical, whereas the teacher employs an expository/argumentative one (for discussion of the examples, see Butt 1989; Hasan 1984e). *There is no such thing as the social activity of teaching in the absolute* such that it retains its inherent integrity irrespective of who is doing the teaching and in what way.

We may refer to both the social activity undertaken by Kristy's mother and that undertaken by Amie's teacher as 'teaching', but in referring to social process in this way we are making an abstraction, which is a necessary condition of analysis. But analysis, as Firth commented, needs to be complemented by synthesis. If the synthesis aspect of social process is disregarded, then the true dynamics of the context of situation relevant to verbal interaction would also be disregarded. The treatment of each single parameter as scaled from the other two ignores one of the most potent sources of the dynamic quality of human interaction: an important part of what makes one instance of interaction at once the same and different from another is in how the values of the contextual variable configure. The CONTEXTUAL CONFIGURATION that results from the choice of symbolic mode, social process, and social relation is not a simple combination: its meaning is not additive, not just the sum of the meanings of the three. Rather, contextual configuration is like a chemical solution, where each factor affects the meaning of the others. This is then the first perspective on my claim of interdependence of the three parameters of Halliday's context of situation. Many of these ideas were presented in an incipient form in Hasan (1973c: 274ff.), where the issue of the interdependence/independence of the contextual parameters *vis à vis* each other was first raised. (Compare and contrast the dialectic nature of the relationships and the configuration of parameters in Gregory 1986, 1995.)

For the second perspective, let us begin with the assumption that, in any community, there is a fairly extensive range of social processes in which persons in some specific social identity may engage. This is again an abstraction, for in actual fact no one single person in any community has a clear idea of the total range of social processes from among which he or she is able to choose. But if the range of social processes in which persons can engage is wide, then it is valid to ask: on what basis would a person choose one social process as opposed to another? One answer to this question is implicit in the claim that social identity is constructed partly through engagement in certain social processes. If mothers qua mothers could engage in just any social process, then social process would be immaterial to the construction of that social identity. Choice from a wide range of social processes is choice viewed as the prerogative of some social relations itself. (Naturally I am not implying that such choice is conscious and deliberate, though some time it could be.) If persons are unaware of the total range of social processes in their community, this is because access to social process itself is regulated via social relation. If the probability of engaging in this or that process can be derived from this or that social relation, then it is just as true to say that the choice of social activity depends on the social relation of participants as it is to say that engagement in a social activity puts one in some specific relation to an other.

The enactment of the mother relation via social process engagement logically implies that in the relevant community a valuation is placed on processes: only some processes are 'naturalized' as 'motherly'; others are not. But to look at engagement in social process purely from the perspective of one participant is highly misleading, for it is not simply motherhood that is socially constructed; obviously, the concept of 'mother' without 'child' is vacuous. There is then a calibration of several factors in the valuation of motherly social processes, i.e., those that may be appropriately undertaken by mothers. The sorts of things mothers do with sons differ from those they do with daughters (Cloran 1989); what they do with 16-year-olds differs markedly from what they do with 16-month-olds. Since none of these factors operates in isolation, the possibility of systematic variation built into this account of the interaction between social relation and social process is as impressive as the capacity of language to produce an infinity of 'new' sentences. However, this account of what motivates the choice of social process is still incomplete until we add the most fundamental aspect of human social existence: how speakers are positioned by virtue of their place in the social structure. The valuation of certain social processes as the most likely ones for mothers and children to engage in as well as the valuation of what is owed to which sex, what to which age group, and so on, is refracted through their social positioning in the sense Bernstein (1990) uses the term 'social positioning'. Implicit in the social positioning of the speaking persons within the socioeconomic structure of the society are both the valuation and the recognition criteria for possible social relations and social processes they may engage in. This conception of the relation of social positioning and human social actions is widely accepted in sociology, and there seems to be strong empirical evidence for it in the results obtained in my sociolinguistic research (Cloran 1989; Hasan and Cloran 1990; Hasan 2009a).

If this analysis of the relationship of the parameters of relevant social context is correct, then it might answer the questions I posed earlier: Which social relations combine? Which social activities co-occur? How is choice of social activity made? The answer depends on the specific makeup of the contextual configuration: who you are, what you are doing, with whom, and how. Engaging in a social process as mother to her young child, the mother can combine only certain activities, because the activities are, in a manner of speaking, dedicated to certain social relations. So a critique of Hamlet is not a possible activity that B could have undertaken together with bathing her small daughter; but if a mother were engaged in the practical activity of eating dinner with a 16-year-old, this could be one possible option, depending on her social positioning. It is clearly a somewhat pointless question to raise: which comes first, the idea of engaging in a social activity or the perception of one's social relation to the other?

The presentation of the CONTEXTUAL CONSTRUCT as a structure with three separate parameters has had one undesirable consequence mainly because each parameter has been separately glossed and discussed in the literature; so it has been too easily assumed that each is a totally self-enclosed, autonomous element quite independent of the other two. There has been hardly any discussion in SFL about the relation of the contextual parameters to each other, though many have bemoaned the tendency of others to move some contextual factor, often without any explanation, from one parameter to another. This tendency is probably indicative of an intuitive recognition that the parameters are permeable: it is difficult to ignore for long the fact that choices in one parameter attract or repel those in the others. The choice of a certain social relation is a predictor of the range of choices at risk so far as social activities are concerned; the combination of social relation and social process is a good predictor of the range of options available in the part language can be made to play though that is said to be the purview of mode. The total configuration of contextual choices produces an entity that will always be unique in some respect, because the possibilities of configurations are pretty close to infinite. This infinity of contexts has some serious consequences, both from the point of view of statements about the classification and realization of contexts as they present themselves as textual attributes. If the exact statement of the realization of the configured values defies prediction, this is because realization statement depend on what else appears in the configuration; and the possibilities of configuration are almost inexhaustible.

5.4.3   Creating text paradigms: the meaning of variation in wording

To return to extract 1, my remarks on its relevant context were based on an informal scanning of the way language is used. Extract 1a is a transformed version of extract 1.

Extract 1a:
A: (42) these antihistamine tablets don't cause any side effects, do they?
B: (43) no
A: (44) antihistamine *tablets –
B: (45) *like they don't make you feel sick –
A: (46) *no
B: (47) *do they?
A: (48) and they don't make you sleepy, do they Sister?
B: (49) oh no
A: (50) 'cause the kind I had before really knocked me out
    (51) but this lot's been great, hasn't it?

B: (52) yes (53) they were rated the best in the review
A: (54) yes ... (55) they're used for all sorts of allergies as well, aren't
    they?
    (56) not just for dust or pollen
B: (57) mm ... (58) they're the best choice for you
A: (59) yes
B: (60) OK roll up your right sleeve for me please (61) and I'll do the
    blood-pressure for you.

Extract 1a was created by introducing changes in the transitivity and reference choices of the original piece, retaining only the 'yes' or 'no' clauses
unchanged. These clauses are elliptical; and since their interpretation
is ENDOPHORIC (Halliday and Hasan 1976), the coding of their experiential and interpersonal meaning can be deduced from their INTERPRETATIVE
SOURCES (Hasan 1985b). In altering the transitivity and reference choices
of extract 1, I have tried to hold constant most of the choices in mood,
theme and cohesion. The degree to which I have succeeded in maintaining
the similarity of coding in the realization of the interpersonal and textual
metafunctions while introducing significant changes in the coding of the
experiential metafunction, can be judged from the series of tables that are
presented below. These tables give a comparative account of the choices
in the two extracts, often by assigning distinct columns to extracts 1 and
1a, and sometimes by presenting separate tables, e.g., 5.3 and 5.3a. With
the exception of Table 5.1, the elliptical clauses have not been analysed
because either their relevant choices are fully deducible, as in Table 5.1a, or
because the choices under focus are not relevant, as in Table 5.2. Table 5.1

Table 5.1: MOOD options in extracts 1 and 1a

Number	Extract 1	Extract 1a
(42)	declarative:tagged:reversed	declarative:tagged:reversed
(43)	elliptical (42 dec:untagged)	elliptical (42 dec:untagged)
(44)	*incomplete*	incomplete
(45 + 47)	declarative:tagged:reversed	declarative:tagged:reversed
(46)	elliptical (45 dec:untagged)	elliptical (45 dec:untagged)
(48)	dec:tagged:reversed:vocative	dec:tagged:reversed:vocative
(49)	elliptical (48 dec:untagged)	elliptical (48 dec:untagged)
(50)	declarative:untagged	declarative:untagged
(51)	declarative:tagged:reversed	declarative:tagged:reversed
(52)	elliptical (51 dec:untagged)	elliptical (51 dec:untagged)
(53)	declarative:untagged	declarative:untagged
(54)	elliptical (53 dec:untagged)	elliptical (53 dec:untagged)
(55)	declarative:tagged:reversed	declarative:tagged:reversed
(56)	elliptical (55 dec:untagged)	elliptical (55 dec:untagged)
(57)	elliptical (55 dec:untagged)	elliptical (55 dec:untagged)
(58)	declarative:tagged:reversed	declarative:tagged:reversed
(59)	elliptical (58 dec:untagged)	elliptical (58 dec:untagged)
(60)	imperative	imperative
(61)	declarative:untagged	declarative:untagged

displays the mood options in the two extracts: here, the similarity in mood choices between the two pieces is obvious at a glance.

Table 1 does not explicitly include information about the Mood or the Finite element which in Halliday's analysis may be inferred from the analysis in terms of MOOD. The information about the choices in primary tense (at Finite) and polarity are presented in Table 5.1a: the analysis excludes the non-elliptical clauses.

In Table 5.1a, two points of difference between Extract 1, i.e., the original and its transform, i.e., Extract 1a, will be noted, one at message (50), the other at (53); in both cases, in Extract 1 the primary tense choice is 'present', while in Extract 1a it is 'past'. The polarity choice is identical in all cases. With so many similarities in mood, finiteness, modality, and polarity, it appears viable to claim that on the basis of the lexicogrammatical coding the interpersonal metafunction associated with tenor should be pretty alike across the two extracts. Table 5.2 shows theme selections.

Table 5.1a: Primary tense and polarity in extracts 1 and 1a

	Extract 1		Extract 1a	
Number	*Clause*	*Tag*	*Clause*	*Tag*
(42)	pres;neg	pres;pos	pres;neg	pres;pos
	doesn't go	*does it*	*doesn't cause*	*do they*
(45 + 47)	pres;neg	pres;pos	pres;neg	pres;pos
	doesn't hurt	*does it*	*don't make a sick*	*do they*
(48)	pres;neg	pres;pos	pres;neg	pres;pos
	doesn't fall	*does it*	*don't make sleepy*	*do they*
(50)	pres;pos		pres;pos	
	is	*had*		
(51)	pres;pos	pres;neg	pres;pos	pres;neg
	are	*aren't they*	*is*	*isn't it*
(53)	pres;pos		pres;pos	
	is		*were*	
(55)	pres;pos	pres;neg	pres;pos	pres;neg
	is	*isn't*	*are*	*aren't they*
(58)	pres;pos			pres;neg
	is	*isn't it*	*do seem*	*don't they*
(60)	imp;pos		imp;pos	
	lie down		*roll up*	
(61)	fut;pos		fut;pos	
	'll		*'ll*	

Table 5.2 displays the simplest METHOD OF DEVELOPMENT (Fries 1981) in both extracts; the same experientially described Thing is topicalized in all non-elliptical clauses, except the last two. The single point of difference is at message (45), where, in Extract 1a, a textual theme realized by the word 'like' (= I mean) is selected, while there is no textual theme in its counterpart in Extract 1. I have ignored the analysis of 'OK' in both extracts.

Table 5.2: Theme options in Extracts 1 and 1a

Number	*Extract 1*	*Extract 1a*
(42)	single:topical:unmarked *this baby shampoo*	single:topical:unmarked *these antihistamine tablets*
(45)	single:topical:unmarked *it = this baby shampoo*	multiple:textual;topical:unmarked *like: they = these antihist tabs*
(48)	multiple:textual;topical:unmarked *and;some (+ shampoo)*	multiple:textual;topical:unmarked *and; they — these antihist tabs*
(50)	multiple:textual;topical:unmarked *'cause; this = shampoo*	multiple:textual;topical:unmarked *'cause ; the kind (+ of antihist tab) I had before*
(51)	multiple:textual;topical:unmarked *and; some of them — shampoo*	multiple:textual;topical:unmarked *but; this lot (+ of antihist tabs)*
(53)	*single:topical:unmarked* *this = shampoo*	*single:topical:unmarked* *they = antihist tablets*
(55)	single:topical:unmarked *this = shampoo*	single:topical:unmarked *they = these antihist tablets*
(58)	single:topical:unmarked *this one = shampoo*	single:topical:unmarked *they = these antihist tablets*
(60)	single:topical:unmarked *lie down*	single:topical:unmarked *roll up*
(61)	multiple:textual;topical:unmarked *and; I*	multiple:textual;topical:unmarked *and; I*

One other aspect of the textual metafunction is lexicogrammatically coded as cohesive relations in a text. The analysis of cohesive relations for Extract 1 and 1a is presented in Tables 5.3 and 5.3a, respectively. It will be noted that the number of componential devices (Hasan 1973b, 1979b, 1984d, 1985b) functioning cohesively in the two extracts is roughly the same: Extract 1 has 16 cases of reference, 3 of substitutes, and 1 of nominal ellipsis, all functioning endophorically, while in Extract 1a there are 20 cases of reference, 1 substitute, but no componential ellipsis. In both extracts, the first and second person pronouns refer to speaker A, up to the very last turn of the dialogue. Together these pronouns form an IDENTITY CHAIN (Hasan 1973b, 1979b, 1984d, 1985b) the forms *you, your* in Extract 1 (42) and (48) and in Extract 1a (48) are analysed as institutional EXO-PHORIC (Hasan 1984a) and are excluded from the above counts). Another identity chain is made with (*this*) *baby shampoo* in Extract 1, and with (*these*) *antihistamine tablets* in Extract 1a; in both cases the initial member of the chain is itself exophorically identified; that is to say, the question *which baby shampoo/which antihistamine tablets* can be answered only by reference to the immediate situation, not by reference to any earlier verbal description of the same entity, but the remaining members of the chain are endophorically related by privilege of CO-REFERENCE to *this baby shampoo* in Extract 1 and to *these antihistamine tablets* in Extract 1a.

Apart from identity chains, usually some chains of SIMILARS are also found in normal non-minimal connected pieces. This kind of chain, I have referred to as SIMILARITY CHAIN (Hasan 1973b, 1979b, 1984a, 1985b). They are formed by the mutual prehension of lexical items which are paradigmatically related. The members of the chain are not implicit devices such as 'he, she, it', and so on, but would be traditionally described as content words (lexical items, in SFL). Without attempting an exhaustive analysis, the similarity chains found in Extracts 1 and 1a are presented in Tables 5.3 and 5.3a respectively.

Table 5.3: Lexical cohesion and their relations in Extract 1

(42)	go into your eye			shampoo
(44)				shampoo
(45)	hurt			
(48)	fall into your eye			
(50)		is good		
(51)		are naughty		
(53)		is	you	shampoo
(55)		is	for little girls	
(56)			for babies	
(58)		is	for you	
(61)				soap

Because of variant experiential coding, the actual choice of lexis in the two extracts must obviously be different. But chain formation is based on relations that account for relevance; at this level of abstract relations, in the grammar that realizes this aspect of textual metafunction, similar patterns are found in both pieces as can be seen from a comparison of Tables 5.3 and 5.3a. Members of the chains relate either as reiteration, e.g., shampoo in Extract 1, or as hyponyms, for example, 'go in your eye' and 'fall into your eye' which are arguably hyponyms of 'hurt'.

Table 5.3a: Lexical chains and their relations in Extract 1a

(42)	antihistamine tablets	cause	side effects		
(44)	antihistamine tablets				
(45)		make	feel sick		
(48)		make	sleepy		
(50)		knocked out		had	
(51)				wonderful	
(53)				rated best	
(54)				used	all...allergies dust(")
(56)					pollen(")
(58)				best choice	

In both Tables 5.3 and 5.3a the chains are entered on the vertical dimension. On the horizontal dimension can be seen the other axis of cohesive relation, namely, CHAIN INTERACTION (Hasan 1973b, 1979b, 1984a, 1985b). Thus, for example in Table 5.3, the reiterated cases of 'be' in its FORMAL SCATTER of 'is, are, was' are to 'good, naughty', and 'for little girls, for babies, for you' (= a little girl), as ATTRIBUTIVE PROCESS is to ATTRIBUTE and CIRCUMSTANCE (benefactive). This aspect of the analysis of cohesive relations, what I have referred to as COHESIVE HARMONY (Hasan 1973b, 1984a), yields information about the organization of a language piece which is similar to that provided by PHASAL ANALYSIS (Gregory 1986, 1995). This aspect is only partially displayed in the tables (for details see Hasan 1984a, 1985b), but there is hardly any doubt that the measure of cohesive harmony for the two extracts will be more alike than different.

As for the ORGANIC RELATIONS within each piece, that is to say those relations which hold between one whole message to another as a whole message, note first the PAIRING (Hasan 1979b, 1985c), which is typical of dialogues.[39] In fact the eight cases of clausal ellipsis (see Table 5.1) indicate this relation of pairing, each elliptical clause functioning as VERIFYING RESPONSE to the preceding VERIFICATION SEEKING DEMAND FOR INFORMATION (Hasan 1988, 1989; Hasan and Cloran 1990). In addition to this, we find JOINING (Hasan 1979b) by such conjunctions as 'and, but, and (be)cause', etc. In monologues joining is the most typical means of relating messages to each other; in dialogues such relations may occur turn-internally, but also as joiners of the messages either in two adjacent (AB) turns or in two consecutive turns by the same speaker (i.e., either AA or BB, skipping the intervening B or A turn; e.g., see the relation between messages (48) and (50) in Extract 1a). In the former case, they are typically read as an indication of the incorporation of some part of the preceding turn; in the latter case, the relation is as in monologues. These organic relations qua relations are identical for both the extracts (see Table 5.1 for details of pairing, and Table 5.2 for structural conjunctions, which usually create the joining relation).

We may conclude then that the lexicogrammatical patterns realizing the textual metafunction are just as similar across Extracts 1 and 1a as they had been in realizing the interpersonal metafunction. If worded-meaning construes context, then it should follow that any difference between the construed contexts of Extracts 1 and 1a can be attributed to such differences as may be found in the coding of the experiential metafunction. The two such aspects of coding are transitivity and reference signifying things, processes, and circumstances, etc. Table 5.4 presents the transitivity choices in the two extracts.

Table 5.4: Transitivity in Extracts 1 and 1a

Number	Extract 1	Extract 1a
(42)	material;middle	material;effective;active
(45)	material;affective;active	intensive;attributive;active
(48)	material;middle	intensive;attributive;active
(50)	intensive;attributive;middle	material;effective;active
(51)	intensive;attributive;middle	intensive;attributive;middle
(53)	possessive;attributive;middle	intensive;attributive;passive
(55)	intensive;identifying;active	material;effective;passive
(58)	circumstantial;attributive;middle	intensive;attributive;middle
(60)	behavioral;middle	material;effective;active
(61)	material;effective;active	material;effective;active

As Table 5.4 indicates, the transitivity choices are substantially distinct across the two versions: only two SELECTION EXPRESSIONS are entirely identical at messages (51) and (61); two options are shared in the selection expression for message (58); and one each in the selection expressions of messages (42), (45), and (53). The extracts are too short to make quantitative statements meaningful, but it needs to be pointed out that, at the primary degree of delicacy, while there is a substantial difference in the choice of voice options, there is not much difference in the overall choice of process options. So Extract 1 has roughly the same number of MATERIAL PROCESS instantiations as Extract 1a, though there are differences as well. But if we move to greater delicacy in process, the choices would be seen as different. And the deepest degree of delicacy would take us to distinctions in signification of doings, happenings, etc. (Fawcett 1987; Hasan 1985a, 1987b). In describing the cohesive chains in the two extracts, I have already described this aspect of the lexicogrammatical coding of the experiential metafunction, although selectively from the point of view of their cohesive relations, and covering other classes of signification than just doing, happening, and so on. A comparison of Tables 5.3 and 5.3a with the discussion of identity and similarity chains shows the difference in cohesively relevant lexical choices that refer to things, processes, circumstances, qualities, and other such experiential phenomena. In fact, the choices differ to such an extent that we can no longer interpret 'you' of Extract 1a, e.g., in message (58) as referring to the same person as the one to whom you in Extract 1 (58) refers. We do not know which specific individuals are being referred to in either case, but we do know with complete certainty that they cannot be the same individuals. If the differences in transitivity are substantially greater than the similarities, and if the two extracts also differ substantially in their signification, then it follows that, if the options in transitivity are related realizationally to some feature of the context, there should be some significant differences between the relevant contexts of Extract 1 and Extract 1a.

5.4.4   Contextual reality in the grammar of experiential meaning

Before examining the relevant context of la, first note that my 'experimental ploy' has produced in Extract 1a a piece of dialogue that, to me at least, seems to lack authenticity. It lacks authenticity perhaps not to the same extent as those sentences of Jespersen's – *a charming woman dances* and *a dancing woman charms* – that Firth described somewhere as 'nonsense' but for roughly the same reason. Extract 1a has been produced using the lexicogrammatical forms as the focus of attention; I was trying to either maintain or alter certain given formal patterns, just as a linguist producing a paradigm introduces alterations to make a formal point. Meanings were being entrained here by a conscious manipulation of the form of language rather than the reverse. As pointed out above (see Section 5.3.2.2, Excursus C), in the natural process of producing an utterance, particularly as in everyday un-self-conscious interaction, a speaker begins with the perception of relevant meanings, rather than from a conscious choice of lexicogrammatical form: the unnaturalness of the meanings configured in Extract 1a as a result of focusing on lexicogrammar is therefore interesting for theoretical reasons. It draws attention to the difficulty of creating authentic register paradigms. So, even though the present manipulation of Extract 1 may be unimpeachable as a primarily metalinguistic activity, it lacks the authenticity of a naturally occurring dialogue. Nonetheless it is interesting to ask whether in the properties of the context construed by Extract 1a there is a culturally recognizable element which explains my reaction to the interaction as somewhat odd.

What reading can we make of Extract 1a, and how does it differ from that of Extract 1? Because there is a great deal of similarity between the two extracts in the part played by language, let me first say a few words about mode in Extract 1a. Language plays an ancillary role in the action based activity of dispensing these antihistamine tablets, just as it plays this same role in Extract 1 in respect to the action-based activity of bathing. By contrast, languaging is the means by which A and B in Extract 1a recognize the nature of the other aspects of the activity, namely, maintaining an amiable, supportive social relation: this too is reminiscent of Extract 1, where a similar relation-based activity was wholly constituted by language. The dialogic nature of the interaction is equally obvious in both. There seems to be no difference between 1 and 1a in respect of their mode of discourse. If the CMH hypothesis is tenable, this state of affairs would be expected on the basis of the near invariance of choices from the textual metafunction across the two pieces.

On the same grounds, one might expect a similar situation with regard to the tenor of discourse. However, this expectation is not satisfied. I infer from Extract 1a that both A and B are adults. Notably, this inference is not made on the basis of any interpersonal choices expressed by mood, modality and modulation; rather, all the necessary information comes from the choices in transitivity and reference (aka 'signification'). So speaker B is referred to as Sister, and the fact that in some way B is involved with the dispensation of medical prescription leads to the inference that most probably B is a professional member of some medical establishment, not of a religious denomination (although, of course, the religious and the medical can combine in an altruistic enterprise of caregiving). This argues that Sister is not used as a kinship term, but as a term for someone whose status is identified as a member of a medical institution. The expectation is, then, that B is probably a female adult nurse while A is a patient. As for speaker A, this interactant is not construed as a little girl; instead, he or she, I would say *she* rather than *he*, seems to know about all sorts of allergies, and generally displays concern about the medicine being dispensed. Both A's locutions and A's understanding of the situation as inferred from those locutions are more typical of adults than of children. What we are witnessing here is the linguistic face of the mutuality between actors and their actions.

This nurse-patient relation can be thought of as a caregiver-receiver relation specific to medical institutions. So B is the caregiving nurse, A the care-receiving patient. As in Extract 1, so here too, there exists another relation between A and B: that of mutual support. So at the primary level of delicacy, the social relation construed by the two extracts is very alike: (a) the nurse-patient relation is as institutionalized as the mother-child one, with the significant difference that the former is official while the latter is local; (b) the caregiver-receiver relation is up to a point identical; the interactants have an asymmetrical relation; (c) despite this, the amicable social relation suggestive of near minimal SOCIAL DISTANCE also seems similar. However, at a more delicate level, the relations are different. So in 1, A is a child and B an adult; in 1a, both A and B are adults. In 1, the mother-daughter relation in our community would be viewed as closer, particularly given the age of the child; in 1a, B representing the nurse-patient type relation would be considerably less close.

Since the only part of the lexicogrammar that varies across the two extracts is that which is said to be realizationally related to the experiential metafunction, and since, according to the CMH claim, field is realizationally related to the experiential metafunction, then, on the assumption that the CHM hypothesis is correct, it would be reasonable to expect that the greatest differences between the two extracts would be in their field of discourse. In examining, the similarities and differences between the field of discourse which is construed by the language of the two extracts, I will also offer an explanation for my perception of Extract 1a as somewhat odd. The first point to note is that the similarities and contrasts between the construed fields of Extracts 1 and 1a largely parallel those found in the construed tenor of discourse for the two extracts. Just as in Extract 1, so also in Extract 1a, there is evidence of engagement in two distinct social processes, one action based and the other relation based. An action-based social activity may be described as that of caregiving: the essence of care-giving is providing a service needed for the well-being of another. And in Extract 1a, B is certainly providing a service, which is presumably needed for A's well-being. So it is legitimate to think of it as a caregiving activity. But beyond this primary level of delicacy, there are also differences, and notably these cannot be discussed without invoking facts about tenor. As pointed out earlier, the speakers' transitivity and reference choices in Extract 1a construe B as a nurse involved in providing A, an adult patient, with medical care. This in turn implies important facts about the nature of that activity, making its character qualitatively different from the action based activity of Extract 1. Bathing and giving health care are considerably different in themselves, but what makes this difference even greater is that the social relation of caregiver-receiver, at a more delicate level, is differ-ent. A mother dispensing medical attention to her own small child would be different in any case from a nurse doing so to an adult patient (see Section 5.4.2.1, Excursus D); naturally then the activity of a mother bathing her small daughter is bound to be even more different from that of a nurse giv-ing health care to an adult patient. In my understanding, this latter activity is officially institutionalized as opposed to the local institutionalization of mother-child relation.

The second social activity relevant to Extract 1a is relation based. The nurse is not dispensing medicine as an automatic dispensing machine might have done; instead the nurse and the patient speak to each other in an amica-ble, supportive kind of way, just as the mother and daughter do in Extract 1. Through her observations about the medicine, the patient seeks the nurse's concurrence. The nurse, in her turn, is obliging and solicitous: She concurs with the patient; so whether she says yes or no, the meaning conveyed is 'I agree with what you have just said'; and at the same time, she herself says things which both reassure the patient and show concern, for example, in (45–47), (53), and (58). So just as in Extract 1, here too the second aspect of the activity could be described as the maintenance of social relationship in which a dependent, in this case a patient, ingratiatingly seeks reassurance from an authority, here a nurse. Note that the dependent participant, speaker A, in each case, seeks reassurance, twice as often as speaker B. And yet, despite this close similarity, it would be inappropriate to describe this second social activity in 1a as phatic communion. The reason why it would be unviable to think of this activity as phatic communion is also the reason why the interaction itself appears odd.

My reason for suggesting why it would be inappropriate to describe the relation based activity of 1a as phatic communion is derived ultimately from a consideration of the significant difference in the social relation of the two dyads: the rights of the dependent participants across the two interactions are not commensurate; the daughter does not have the same rights *vis-à-vis* her mother as the patient has. Given the cultural background of the interaction in 1a, the nurse is both morally and legally responsible for the information that she gives out about any medicine she might be involved in dispensing. So whether she simply concurs with the patient or she expresses approval of the medicine as in (53), she can be held responsible for the factual accuracy of what she is saying. I doubt if this could be said about the mother's responses in Extract 1. The small daughter has no court of appeal if the mother makes misleading/false assertions; by contrast, the patient has such a right of appeal. This I suggest prevents the nurse's reassurances from being a case of phatic communion (I realize that this implies a particular interpretation of the term 'phatic communion,' but I believe this is precisely how Malinowski intended it). Due to the difference in the basis of their social relation, the nurse's reassurances about the medicine, unlike the mother's comments about the shampoo, go beyond personal matters. The socially recognized relation of nurse-patient is a public one; that between the mother and her child is largely personal: in the latter case, social institutions have little or no right of intervention except where the behaviour of one toward the other denies their rights as human beings (e.g., as in child abuse; geriatric neglect, etc.). We may grant also that intimacy is typically congruent with nonpublic relations. This conclusion raises some interesting questions. Assuming the nurse-patient relation is public, would it be correct also to claim that 'in our culture' it must be seen as a relation that is unsuitable for intimacy in all cases? Does the culture in which we live prohibit absolutely the conjunction of public relation with reduced social distance? Is the oddity of this extract attributable to the conjunction of disjunct contextual choices?

5.4.4.1   *Excursus E: the conjunction of disjunction*

In raising these questions, I am assuming that my perception of Extract 1a as somewhat odd is not idiosyncratic; that most people would see it as not a very typical sort of interaction. By claiming that the degree of dependence and reliance, the patient here shows the nurse, and the degree of obliging reassurance and concern displayed by the latter will be perceived by most members of my community as not normal of nurse-patient relationship, I am attempting to explain the oddity of the extract as arising from the conjunction of two values of the context of situation which typically do not combine in one and the same situation in our culture. Later in this excursus I shall modify this somewhat bald characterization. At this point I wish to use this feature of Extract 1a to do three things: (a) show the place of disjunction in my approach to textual analysis; (b) question Martin's claim that a model of the type he proposes has an advantage in this respect; and finally (c) question the conception of disjunction and its role in social change as propounded by Martin (1985a). I will first discuss the first two points together, but to do this I shall need to refer to terms such as genre and register. And as I have pointed out earlier, Martin's understanding of these terms is crucially different from Halliday's, and I believe from mine (see discussion in Section 5.5). From now on, to avoid confusion, when these terms are used in Martin's sense I shall call them **m-genre** and **m-register**, using **h-register** and **h-context** to refer to my usage, which I believe is largely compatible with Halliday's usage.

Martin (1985a) draws attention to a point that I myself made some years ago (Hasan 1973c): despite the conception of the three contextual variables as distinct, the selection of values from one variable tends to act upon the selection of values from the others; that is, their combination is not entirely independent of each other. According to Martin, this situation creates 'holes in a culture's register paradigm' (Martin 1985a: 250) and 'some of the holes in a culture's register paradigm ... appear at a first glance arbitrary. Others are more obviously highly functional' (p. 251): They support taboos, conventions, and the like. 'At other times, functional holes in a culture's register paradigms seem to exist for the purpose of ensuring that culture's survival' (p. 251). I admit that I find the development of Martin's argument somewhat confusing at this point. I have interpreted him as claiming that the 'rules' whereby the combination of some values in one contextual configuration is naturalized while that of some others is constrained, are counterrevolutionary in that they maintain status quo. They thus contribute to 'invisible semiotic repression' and are 'immensely useful to those benefiting from this repression'. Following Lemke (1985), he refers to such holes as DISJUNCTIONS; 'if holes like this are filled, a culture is bound to change, quickly and radically' (Martin 1985a: 251). Since most socially responsible linguists would wish to change those conditions of the society which contribute to the invisible semiotic repression, and since most would welcome change in the 'right direction' (the trick is to know what will count as the 'right direction'!), clearly that model would be deemed better which can 'account for' such disjunctions.

One reason offered by Martin for the separation of m-genre and m-register is that, without this innovation, it would be impossible to account for naturalized conjunctions and repressive disjunctions of contextual features. The context of Martin's discourse seems to suggest also that the GSP approach either prohibits any consideration of such disjunctions or is incapable of throwing any light on its nature. It is not clear to me why he supposes this. In the GSP approach one possible direction for attempting analysis is that of working from a certain configured set of contextual features to ask how these are expressed in the overall structure of the relevant discourse (as in Hasan 1978, 1979b, 1981). Perhaps this was misread by him either as implying that: (a) all configurations of situational values are equally typical; and/or (b) what is not typical is not important or worthy of attention. It is true that, in my presentations, I worked from typical configurations, but the decision was tactical: it was methodologically convenient in trying to invent a framework where none had existed; to begin with problematic cases particularly within the scope of slender articles did not seem practical. It would be sociologically naive to imagine that describing something as normal or typical is to say that it should be regarded as normal, or worse still, that there are no conflictual models present within the community under description. I suggest that nothing in my writing is susceptible to this interpretation: there is no foundation for suggesting that the GSP approach either prohibits or is inherently incapable of drawing attention to disjunction, while Martin's own conception of genre would lead the community to desirable social changes. Such interpretations of my work could arise from a genuine lack of understanding, for quite clearly to demonstrate that something is normal in a culture is to say simply that 'this is how things are done in our culture', a locution much to Martin's liking. With this matter out of the way, the only material issue that now remains is whether Martin's 'stacking up' of m-genre and m-register as (communicative) planes in a connotative semiotics provides a surer, better, more theoretically viable explanation than would a GSP approach.

In resolving this issue, I am hampered by the fact that, to the best of my knowledge, there has been no demonstration whatever of how separating m-genre from m-register and both from language as a denotative semiotic helps in bringing disjunctions to light, or in describing them insightfully. True, that Martin (1985a) claims: 'one of the principal descriptive responsibilities of genre is to constrain the possible combinations of field, mode and tenor variables used by a given culture' (p. 250).[40] But to understand this claim requires an understanding of Martin's conceptualization of m-genre itself, which differs crucially from the conception of h-register in the GSP approach. In the latter, the overall structure of talk is said to realize the configuration of choices made from all three variables: the configuration of field, tenor, and mode choices activates the elements of the structure of the text, while the elements of the text structure (at least partially) construe the context of situation as discussed already. To the extent that h-contexts are similar across two socio-historically located instances of talk, to that extent the overall shape of the two instances of talk would be similar. Thus the structure of the texts is not something separate from the text functioning as an instance of h-register that realizes some h-context; in this view, textual structure becomes simply one feature of diatypic variation. By contrast in Martin's model, this relationship is reversed, so that what Martin calls the SCHEMATIC STRUCTURE of the text is not activated by the contextual configuration as a whole. Rather, his schematic structure is the expression of PURPOSE or the GOAL of the social activity. It is this single abstraction from the variable of what would be field in h-context that is critical for schematic structure (for further discussion see Section 5.5). What is amazing is Martin's suggestion that these purposes expressed as elements of a schematic structure 'constrain a culture's legitimate combinations of field, mode and tenor variables' (Martin 1985a: 252). Speaking informally, the claim is that the speaker's conception of the overall shape of her talk determines what she is going to do, who will be other participants in it, and what role will language play. The question naturally arises: where does the speaker's conception of the overall shape of his or her talk come from? I am at a loss to understand how this conception of genre is less static, and why Martin's approach is not guilty of treating text as a finished product rather than as a process. Serious implications arise also from abstracting from h-field all else except what is being talked about. And an important question is how, in Martin's model, one moves from purpose to elements of schematic structure and to tenor, mode and field (reduced to 'what'). Why should appeal to one single factor from h-context be a more powerful way of locating the disjunctions in a culture's register paradigms than would be appeal to what I have called the contextual configuration (Hasan 1978, 1979b, 1981, etc.)?

Putting aside these details, if my reading of Martin is correct, then for Extract 1a, m-genre selection will constrain the choice of m-register. (Which genre should be selected in this case, the action-based one or the relation-based one? Which genre is the purpose?) Presumably, in general terms, this constraint will specify that, in m-genre of type so-and-so, only the selection of m-register features of such-and-such type(s) is legitimate (conventional?). It would follow that the selection of any other kind of m-register features will count as the conjunction of the disjunction. So if my explanation of Extract 1a is correct, then in Martin's terminology, the interactants A and B are 'filling a hole in their culture's register paradigm' by their talk! But, with apologies to Martin, surely in this description, disjunction is being 'viewed objectively, after the fact, as things with particular relation to each other' (Martin 1985a: 258). Where is the dynamic element in this? Surely, it is useful to be able to say: this state of affairs has happened; here are certain contextual features combined whose combination in the culture is not typical. But what we need is an adequate model with some indication of where these disjunctions are likely to occur as the much maligned GSP model does (Hasan 1981), not simply the assertion that this is where the disjunction has occurred. It is not clear to me how such a specification could be made from Martin's so-called dynamic perspective. Martin emphasizes the need for m-genre networks; according to him, it is through these networks that elements of the schematic structure of an m-genre would be 'generated'. (Martin creates such a network, which he wrongly imputes to me; see Figure 3 in Martin 1985a: 253.) But it is not clear how these elements come in contact with the m-register features, or how the legitimate combinations can be predicted by appeal to purpose. For the sake of argument, assume that attached to each element of structure will be a realization statement specifying what m-register feature may or may not be selected at that point, but what is such a statement grounded in? Clearly, this way of identifying the possibility of disjunctions would succeed, if it does, only because in the behaviour of the community there is systematicity (Firth 1950/1957; Frake 1972): so it turns out that *to describe what forms the dynamic aspect of an interaction, the framework must be synoptic!* Since the GSP approach, by Martin's own declaration, is an epitome of the synoptic perspective, it is reasonable to suggest that far from being unable to draw attention to disjunctions, this approach will offer a framework well suited to making such statements about disjunctions.

In fact the GSP approach might provide a better framework (e.g., Hasan 1981), because it will allow relative rather than absolute statements about both conjunction and disjunction. To think of the conjunction or disjunction of certain contextual features in the absolute appears quite undesirable, for constraints on what can combine, thus by implication naturally indicating what would be excluded, are subject to certain features of environment. This environment is not supplied simply by what Martin calls PURPOSE but by the entire configuration of contextual features ranging over the three parameters. This is what one would expect if Firth and Halliday are right in claiming that, in many ways context is 'organized' as language is, and can therefore be described by categories that are created following the same principles that underlie the categories for the description of the internal structure of language, its lexicogrammar and its phonology. The reader may compare this position with that of Martin's, who is scathing about the possibility of using the theoretical insights gained from the description of clauses and sentences for the description of text (Martin 1985a).

Taking 1a as a specific example, it might be said that in our culture the m-genre of medical encounter (if that is how Martin might describe the genre of Extract 1a), the conjunction of nurse-patient relation and formality are legitimate features of m-register, while intimacy is not permitted. However it would be rash to suggest this without qualification for indeed nurse-patient interaction *can* combine with intimacy, but only under certain conditions. Intimate discourse with this social relation in this type of m-register is likely if speakers A and B know each other quite well, and it is highly probable that while they are in a nurse-patient interaction, they have also been friends, good neighbours, or have some other basis for interaction which warrants intimacy. The fact that here they are interacting as nurse-patient does not negate their histories as if they had not existed. To use a technical term, the SOCIAL DISTANCE (Hasan 1973c, 1978, 1981.) between the participants would have to be close to MINIMAL. So the constraint on the conjunction of contextual features can be overridden by the personal interactive history of the interactants: talking intimately in a public pursuit is not odd, not disjunction, provided the public relation is tempered by the personal one. A moment's reflection will show that this is logical, if public and private are to be socially produced as opposites. The very form of the system network at the level of context, if such were being drawn, should specify those conditions under which certain less frequent options become viable.

As to Martin's revolutionary project of filling 'functional holes in a culture's register paradigms' (Martin 1985a: 251), I have three comments. First, if the idea is that all disjunctions should/could disappear, then I suggest it is a contradiction in terms to imagine that we can have culture. If culture is a complex system of systems, then it must involve disjunctions, even as there are 'disjunctions' in the grammar of the clause. There can be no sense of the possible, if everything were to become equally possible. Second, that being so, whatever 'new' conjunctions are being 'pushed' by making disjunctions combine will certainly help in creating a new order, but the disjunctions of that order will also be disjunctions; their status as disjunctions will not change simply because these particular disjunctions do not worry those who have brought in the new order. Both Douglas (1975) and Bernstein (e.g., 1987, 1990) have, in their different ways, commented on the impossibility of eliminating the 'dark side of the moon' where social structure is concerned. We know no society in which some segment of the community or some set of ideas are not repressed. It may be that the existence of this situation fills us with revulsion but one important question is: can we conceptualize a society where nothing is barred, and everything is possible for everyone? Such a society, I suggest, could exist only where there is total consensus, where there are no differing points of view, no differing grading of values. This 'brave new world' could be quite frightening when experienced from close quarters. My third point has to do with the social consequences of 'doing linguistics': a linguist as a linguist is (hopefully!) trained to present a clear and well-reasoned analysis of language in use, which, among other things, also shows to what extent the 'reality' that surrounds us has been 'naturalized' through semiosis, and particularly through verbal semiosis. To be able to show this is to create a condition for self-aware reflection; this could possibly lead to action. But to imagine that, by revealing disjunctions, we could bring about revolutions, does appear to me somewhat grandiose. It suggests quite wrongly that the material effects of past semiosis, i.e., the institutions, practices, and systems of beliefs that have been created through interactions using various semiotic modalities, are so insubstantial as 'to keel over' at our new daring verbal semiotic adventures in combining what in our culture is considered uncombined!

If my explanation is correct, then the oddity of Extract 1a does not consist simply in the conjunction of disjunctions, i.e., in combining choices that are not permitted in our culture. The interaction appears odd, not because it overrides a 'sacred' aspect of our culture; it appears odd because it does not 'ring true' either as a public discourse or as a personal one, or as a public one tempered by private relations.[41] The expectation in the culture we are familiar with is that the social distance between a representative of some public institution and a client of that institution, for example, the nurse and patient here, would be typically not minimal: rather, we expect it to be NEAR-MAXIMAL. Interpersonal closeness, particularly indulgence in any behaviour that might indicate dependence on another's goodwill in such environments, is in fact likely to be viewed generally as a sign of immaturity, and efforts to span social distance are typically unwelcome (Cloran 1981, 1987). Thus it is alright for a little daughter to show this degree of dependence on her mother, but it is rather atypical, if not impossible, for an adult patient to enact this same relationship towards a nurse. I realize this is tantamount to claiming that the social activity of maintaining a supportive relation depends on the quality of the relation at the initiation of the interaction. However, relations do change in some interactions; and there has to be some point in it where change sets in, is maintained and/or augmented. But I doubt if change begins quite the way that the patient and nurse are talking here. What strikes the loudest false note in Extract 1a is A addressing B as Sister. Forms of address today grow informal in our culture much before a true interpersonal dependence/equality can be indicated by an adult towards another adult. Thus it appears that the authenticity of Extract 1a can be attributed to the implausibility of combining disjunct features of context without evidence of good reason for doing so: the patient's address form construes a relation that is formal and public; her discourse construes a relation that is intimate enough to permit the presumption of personal dependence. In the last resort, in making one's judgments one is listening to the speech in the speech event, and, with apologies to Sinclair (1990), one is 'trusting the text', though not exactly in the sense he intended.

5.4.4.2   *Excursus F: field and the concept of social activity*

In the discussion of contexts inferred from 1 and 1a, I have suggested that two simultaneously occurring social activities are relevant to both extracts. This raises a question: are there two fields of discourse in each of these extracts, or simply one? My own view is that there are *two activities going on* here, but that they are *integrated into one field*; in other words, we do not have two contexts operating side by side, but simply one. An alternative perspective would be to maintain that each such social activity 'is' a distinct field, so underlying each of the extracts are two goals and so two fields (and therefore possibly two separate m-registers?). On what basis might one choose between these alternatives? Is the idea of either social activity or of field so self-evident that it can be taken for granted? What kind of intuitions do people have about such abstractions? Are such intuitions more reliable than are those about a sentence or a word? In SF literature, there are complaints about inconsistencies found in others' treatment of field, tenor, or mode, but no explorations of any such questions, much less answers to them, which supports my earlier comment that there has been either an unquestioning acceptance or a hasty dismissal of the CMH hypothesis.

Field as postulated in Halliday has a central importance in Martin's framework, since it is largely the factoring of this parameter that results in his stratified m-genre and m-register, as indicated in the above excursus. But Martin's analysis of field hardly distinguishes itself as deeper than my own initial efforts (Hasan 1973c): my term SITUATIONAL SETTING corresponds quite neatly with purpose by indicating what the goal is likely to be (Martin 1985a, 1985b) or why (Martin 1991), while my term subject matter is as close to 'what about?' (Martin 1991) as makes no difference. In neither case is there an analysis of the notion of activity itself; it is as if the meaning of this contextual parameter held no problems at all. In fact, in criticizing my GSP framework, Ventola complains that 'even *a slight value change* in a variable is sufficient to alter the structure of the GSP' (Ventola 1987: 52, emphasis added.). Since Ventola does not specify exactly on what basis she would consider some value change as slight, the implication is that the slightness or otherwise of a change in context is a pretty obvious thing, so that anyone with a modicum of common sense can see that buying vegetables is only slightly different from buying a stamp, a present, a ferry passage to some place, or even perhaps a house: after all, there is only a difference of one lexical item in the expression describing 'the social activity', and the purpose is clearly 'buying'. I suggest that this is an outcome of naturalization; and the place of individual features in a contextual configuration needs to be argued in a theoretical model. In what follows, I intend to theorize the notion of social activity and its relation to field, tenor and mode. There are three motivations for taking this step. *First*, since the CMH hypothesis proposes that variation in experiential choices would correlate with variation in field, it is important to unpack the notion of field; *second*, as we have seen, Martin's notion of genre cannot be discussed without an understanding of what h-field is like and how it differs from m-field; and *finally*, a discussion of the concept of field will also provide an opportunity for reviewing Martin's concept of genre-combination. This is important, since one of the shortcomings of GSP approach according to Martin is that it cannot account for genre-combination.

Let me begin by looking more closely at the two social activities identified for the two extracts. In each case, activity (i) is action based or practical, whereas activity (ii) is relation based or relational. Turning to the first one first: action-based activity reflects the fact that many of the social practices of a community are essentially of a physical nature. Languaging enters into these activities almost as an extra limb with which the interactants can perform the activity, and bring it to its completion. It is this relation to which we refer in claiming that the role of language in action-based activity is typically ANCILLARY. The relevant domain of experience for these activities is historically specific: a specific person P undertakes a specific activity A at a particular time T, and the relevant objects, persons, and actions are all specific to that particular moment, that particular case of that class of action by those particular participants. Now I have argued earlier that engagement in activities of any kind engenders some social relation; the social relations that are logically entrained by the social activity are inseparably related to it. I have referred to these relations as AGENTIVE ROLES (Hasan 1978, 1979b, 1985c). Given the historically specific nature of the action-based activity, it is not surprising that the agentive roles entrained by it are themselves of a temporary nature. So *bather* and *bathed* may appear to some readers as social relations so obvious and so temporary that they need no mention: they could simply be taken as an aspect of the activity itself. I believe, though, that their recognition is useful in any attempt to throw light on those other social relations that are seen as more or less 'permanent', without being logically entrained by it, such as for example mother and child. The permanence of mother-child relation is simply one aspect of its institutional character; but institutional social relations are socially constructed by the innumerable instances of nonpermanent social relations of precisely the type 'bather'. It is noteworthy that the conjunction of 'mother: bather' or 'house-help: bather' is so ordinary that it appears trite until we begin to ask why the agentive role of bather did not combine, until quite recently, with the institutional role of father; or why even today, this conjunction is typical of only a specifiable segment of the Western community; or why 'neighbour: bather' appears less odd than 'vendor: bather'. This discussion once again reinforces the claim of the permeability of field and tenor. The permeability may be described in different ways: that, if the activity is such and so, then the agentive role will typically combine with institutional roles such and such; or that, if the institutional role is such and such, then activities so and so are more likely to be undertaken. A third possibility is to say that there is no directionality; no mutual constraint can be inferred either from the doer or the doing. I believe that Martin's position is the last one while my own is the first mentioned.[42] Martin implies that using social activity (aka 'field') to 'constrain' the choice of what about, who with whom, and how is somehow more explanatory. I believe this is an illusion.

The second social activity is relation based. Unlike the action-based activity: it does not always have a relevant physical action, though aggression, caressing, kissing, the sharing of valued resources and so on can be viewed, where appropriate, as the relevant nonverbal action for a relation-based activity. It follows that the role of language in this sort of activity is constitutive; in the context of h-register, a relation-based activity depends on languaging, though paralinguistic modalities such as facial expression, voice quality, eye contact, and so on, could be relevant to its inception and manifestation. *This activity is essentially an enactor of personal relationships, influencing the quality of human interactions, no matter what their nature.* Thus quarrels, confrontations, love scenes, humouring, sarcasm, humiliation, friendly chats, compliance, rejection, and so on, are activities engagement in which 'marks' (the nature of) a person in relation to an other: their future engagement with each other is coloured by virtue of the previously enacted personal relation. The recognition of this sort of activity is then another affirmation of the permeability of field and tenor. This permeability is indicated, not so much by the need to recognize the entrained agentive roles of, for example, antagonists, friends, intimates and so on, as it is by the fact that the consequences of relation-based activities are in the end woven into the interactive biographies of those who are carriers of the agentive role. Where a history of relation-based activities of a particular kind exists, the carriers of the agentive roles do not view themselves as simply actors of certain actions with other co-actors. Rather, the action-based activity of bathing might get perceived as 'problematic' because the child 'is difficult'; the discussion on linguistics threatens to become a confrontation because the colleague is 'argumentative'. In other words it is from their experience of such tenor-enacting activities that the participants assign a specific 'character' to the other carrier of the agentive role as well as to their action-based activities. Relation-based activities are typically integrated with some other type of activity. So even though a quarrel may tend to take over everything else once one has embarked on it, one does not typically set out with the purpose of having a quarrel; sarcasm is seldom the beginning and the end of an occasion of talk.[43] Quarrels, sarcastic jibes, humouring, and so on, usually happen, as it were, a propos of something whose own *raison d'être* is of an entirely different nature. It would therefore be a somewhat superficial analysis to treat activity (ii) of Extracts 1 and 1a as an instance of a distinct field from that which is instanced by activity (i). A better solution would be to think of the two as INTEGRATED, together forming the field of discourse. In fact, the supportive, amiable talk between the mother and the child in Extract 1 plays an important part in the conduct of activity (i): it FACILITATES the activity of bathing the child by keeping her happy and satisfied.

Let me draw attention now to a third type of social activity, which does not actually occur in Extracts 1 and 1a. I shall refer to this third type of activity as REFLECTION-BASED SOCIAL ACTIVITY. This kind of activity is construed by wording-meaning (though pictorial material, formulae, etc., may occur in specific cases), so the role of language is CONSTITUTIVE. In this respect, reflection-based activity is like the relation-based one. However, its nature is entirely semiotic: whereas with relation-based activity, there can be some relevant nonverbal physical action, with reflection-based activity such action, even if it occurs, for example, consulting a dictionary, drawing a figure to represent what is being discussed, or making a system network, and so on, is not simply accompanying the reflection-based activity: rather it is a manifestation of the fact that such reflection-based activity is occurring. So a reflection-based activity becomes materially visible only through the mediation of some semiotic modality or other, language being the most powerful and pervasive of these because of its design features. An example of such an activity would be (re)producing knowledge, say, as in the presentation of new concepts, as in a classroom lesson.[44]

At this point it is important to draw attention to the 'misrecognition' that could result – and in fact has actually done so – from describing the activity in this way. We have to formulate it this way – and the grammar of this descriptive expression makes it appear as a Process^Range structure – because this is the way one has to speak because one is speaking English. The same is true of *caregiving*, which is quite clearly not *giving plus care*; no action of the 'giving' kind enters into it: instead, it would be better to say *relating-by-caring*. Producing knowledge, by the same token, is not producing plus knowledge: it is in actual fact *knowledging*. Used this way, *knowledging* runs parallel to other such actions as regulating, facilitating, bathing, cooking, and so on.

Mainly because of its essentially semiotic nature, the perception of a reflection-based activity is entirely engulfed by what is known in SFL as the RHETORICAL MODES, that is, ways of saying where the wording alone indicates what reflection-based activity is being undertaken. Certain rhetorical modes become associated with certain reflection-based activities, so much so that terms such as EXPOSITION, ARGUMENTATION, EXPLANATION, NARRATION, and so on, actually function as the name of the activity one is actually engaged in. The fact is that when didactic, argumentative, or explanatory ways of wording occur as typically in teaching grammar, sociology, or geography does not really mean that there is an activity of, say, explanation or exposition, and distinct from it there is a body of knowledge such as say geography or grammar, which the activity of exposition or explanation is about. Since reflection-based activity is essentially semiotic, the only way one can 'geography' or one can 'grammar' is by languaging in a geography-kind of way. The important question here is: why has this pattern of association grown between a particular kind of reflection-based activity and a style of wording? And in answering that question, it is relevant to remember that the didactic modes of exposition and explanation is as atypical with the practical activity of buying, as the dramaturgical mode is atypical with the activity of geography-ing or grammar-ing. I find such probing of the interdependence of contextual features far more revealing than the rhetoric of 'filling holes in the register paradigm' in a culture. And contrary to Martin's claim there is no impediment in my framework that prevents the asking of such questions or speculation on the consequences of abrogating what we have regarded as typical conjunctions whether in acts of linguistic analysis or in actual life.

While, in 1 and 1a, a reflection-based activity does not co-occur with the others, this is not to say that such co-occurrence is impossible. In fact, if primary socialization is viewed from this point of view, mothers often engage, and particularly middle-class ones in all three types of activities concurrently (Cloran 1999b; Butt 1989; Hasan 1986). Classroom interaction is a particularly interesting example of an integration of the three types of activities so far discussed. That it is both reflection and relation based is recognized in Bernstein's description of teaching as an INSTRUCTIONAL DISCOURSE embedded within a REGULATIVE DISCOURSE (Bernstein 1990); and this integration of the two is the essence of educational socialization. This is a complex situation, and its complexity becomes obvious when we probe further into the meaning of 'instructional.' The term 'instructional' typically refers to an integration of a reflection-based activity of knowledging and an action-based activity of facilitation. Teaching as a social activity is a complex concept, because it refers to the integration of all three kinds of activities discussed so far. So the social activity of teaching involves a person knowledging to/with someone whose knowledging is being facilitated and whose behaviour is being regulated, ostensibly at least, for the creation of an environment in which knowledging and facilitation can occur.

Even though classroom teaching is culturally and perforce semantically an exceptionally complex activity, and so, perhaps, it should not be used as the prototypical case, the fact that different types of activities co-occur is fairly common. In fact, it is very likely that many of the culturally crucial activities will display a similar type complexity. If the co-occurrence of two or more types of activities is always seen as a case of 'combining distinct fields', and if the activity aspect of field is abstracted out as m-genre, then it follows that for Martin there will be a large number of cases that will need to be seen as m-genre-combination. But m-genre-combination as a problem surfaces only because of entertaining a particular perspective on field/genre; it is not something like gravity, or heat/cold, that everyone is likely to encounter ordinarily. As Firth pointed out all analytical categories are constructs; they have no *sui generis* reality. What makes a category useful is what one can do with it to illuminate the nature of their object of enquiry. I do not find the concept of genre combination *à la* Martin illuminating: certainly that perspective has no edge on the one I have developed above and that was implicit in the conception of h-context.

The notion of FIELD INTEGRATION is useful in another way. It will probably be granted that there is a qualitative difference between the sort of co-occurrence of activity types that I would refer to as integration, and those co-occurrences of activities where they are simply running parallel. As an example of the latter, one may talk about the ingredients of a dish one is cooking, and the next moment about some problem in linguistic description, which might have been engaging one's attention before the interruption caused by the need to cook this dish. It is possible, though not very likely, that these two activities, the first action based and the second reflection based, will integrate in the same way as the enactment of relation and the bathing do in Extract 1, and as regulation, facilitation, and knowledging do in the classroom. Where there is integration of activities, the various activities interpenetrate: what one is doing in the relation-based activity has some consequence for what one is doing in the action-based one. If the values of the relation-based activity were to be different, then this would affect the perception of the performance quality of the action-based activity as well. So, for example, when later in the dialogue from which Extract 1 is taken, the mother refuses to grant the daughter's request to let her have her toys in the bath, the character of the relation-based activity changes. A serious altercation ensues, and because the relation- and action-based activities are integrated rather than parallel, the action-based activity of bathing is affected: it remains arrested at a particular point. Where activities are not integrated but simply interspersed, the process of interaction as it were runs in parallel; the disruption of one does not necessarily imply a disruption of the other.

If it is accepted that there are different types of activities, at least some of which may be sometimes integrated so that it is not possible to view them simply as social activity 1 + social activity 2, while others may at other times be simply running parallel, then certain consequences follow. First, the realization of field, if activity is allowed to remain within field, unlike in Martin's model, could be a complex affair rather than a simple calibration of denotative reference. Where a complex field integration occurs, we should expect a complex mode of realization. Second, *the idea of one single purpose for the interaction becomes somewhat questionable*; in complex integrated activities, we would not be justified in picking out just one purpose as the only relevant one. The idea of genre as goal-directed, staged social activity will become problematic. For example, if we take what the community refers to as teaching, which of the goals should we recognize as the one relevant to the pedagogic genre(s)? Anyone who has looked carefully at classroom interaction will agree that all three activities shape the overall structure of the talk. Moreover, it is not simply, the social activity such as h-field alone that motivates the structure of classroom talk: a comparison of an upper secondary classroom interaction with a lower primary one will show that the maturational stage of the addressee also plays an important part in activating some aspects of what Martin calls the schematic structure of the text. If m-genre is purpose driven, how do we theorize multipurpose genres? The problems inherent in this situation lead one to seeing them as a combination which entrains other problems. So, finally, the theory will require some method of distinguishing activity-integration, which yields a single context, from the case where activities run in parallel, which logically calls for as many contexts as the configured activities, interactant relations and modes. It is obvious that, as a concept, genre-combination is hardly capable of satisfying the needs. In as much as the account of activities given above appears to have any merit from the point of view of explaining the nature of social action in society, and to the extent that the semantic realization of these activities also justifies the conception of social activity offered here, to that extent the present approach to the concept of social activity is to be preferred to the somewhat reductive notion proposed in Martin's model. Let us ask, then, whether the semantic realization of the construed h-contexts will support my view of social activity, and whether in doing this it will also permit an evaluation of the CMH hypothesis.

5.4.5   Paradigms of context: the reality of construed meaning

For ease of discussion, I have summarized the inferred context of situation for both Extracts 1 and 1a in Table 5.5: as stated earlier, this inferred context is based on the meaning-wording that forms the text of the dialogues.

Table 5.5: Context construed by meaning-wording

1:	**WHAT IS GOING ON?**
	Extract 1:
(i)	care-giving: mother bathing her small daughter;
(ii)	phatic communication: mother and child maintaining an amiable . cooperative social relation
	Extract 1a:
(i)	care-giving: nurse dispensing prescription to patient;
(ii)	nurse and patient maintaining an amiable, cooperative social realtion
2:	**WHO ARE TAKING PART?**
	Extract 1:
(i)	mother care-giver, i.e., bather; daughter care-receiver i.e the one being bathed
(ii)	daughter seeker of reassurance; mother supplier, concerned with her well-being
(iii)	social distance: near-minimal
(vi)	status: personal relation; hierarchic: mother in benevolent control, daughter subservient
	Extract 1a:
(i)	nurse care-giver, i.e., dispenser of prescription; patient care-receiver, i.e., receiving prescription
(ii)	patient seeker of reassurance; nurse supplier, concerned with her well-being
(iii)	social distance: ??
(vi)	status: public relation; institutional rights and obligations; nurse in control, patient acting as subservient
3:	**WHAT PART IS LANGUAGE PLAYING?**
	Extract 1 and 1a:
(i)	language used as means of identifying objects etc relevant to activity (i)
(ii)	language used to constitute the whole of activity (ii)
(iii)	language used is not *book language;* it is everyday colloquial speech
(vi)	language is used dialogically, with equal privilege of sharing in the talk

The table is organized around the three contextual parameters proposed by Halliday *et al.* (1964): (1) what's going on?, i.e., the field of discourse; (2) who are taking part?, i.e., the tenor of discourse; and (3) what part is language playing?, i.e., mode of discourse.[45] These parameters remain identical for both Extract 1 and Extract 1a: in the first and the second parameters, each extract receives a slightly different description; the third parameter, that of mode, is exactly the same for both extracts. Let us ask now whether the CMH hypothesis is supported by these findings. Very briefly, three pieces of evidence from Table 5.5 are relevant to the CMH hypothesis: (a) that, at a secondary level of delicacy, the action based social activities of 1 and 1a vary; (b) that the relation-based activity remains invariant; and (c) that social relation varies in complex ways. I suggest that, while the similarities and differences between the inferred contexts are quite obvious, the interpretation of this finding is itself not simple.[46]

One interpretation of the evidence could be that it indicates the invalidity of the CMH hypothesis: the arguments for this would be as follows. On the one hand, choices from the experiential metafunction do not lead to variation in *every aspect* of field, and on the other hand, what they construe is some phenomena pertaining to tenor (cf. agentive roles), which according to one interpretation of the CMH hypothesis should be construed always and only by choices from the interpersonal metafunction. In this interpretation, call it the *negative interpretation*, the experiential metafunction curiously ends up doing less as well as more than it is supposed to do. From this negative conclusion would follow the need for fundamental modifications in Halliday's theory, such as those introduced by Martin, at the least. I would argue that this negative conclusion about the validity of the CMH hypothesis itself depends on the validity of certain assumptions; these are, first, assumptions about how the contextual parameters should be interpreted and how they are related to each other, and, second, what counts as correlation; and what is it in the wording-meaning that is differing. So it might be thought that in considering the negative interpretation, the arguments in its support should be examined in the light of those assumptions. However, if the assumptions underlying the negative interpretation are themselves untenable, then, it would seem the negative conclusion is thrown into doubt. I believe this is indeed the case: to me, the negative conclusion appears hasty; my own interpretation on the same evidence, call it the *positive interpretation*, would be that there is a strong likelihood of the CMH hypothesis being valid. To argue out my case, I shall consider the doubtful credentials of the two assumptions in support of the negative conclusion. The discussions in Excursus D, E, and F have hopefully paved the way to an understanding of my position on the question of interdependence between the values of a contextual configuration, on disjunction, and on the nature of social activities.

To begin with the favourable evidence, first a brief word about the realization of activity (i): at a secondary degree of delicacy, the action-based activity of care-giving differs across the two extracts; this difference is directly construed by the difference in the choices of transitivity and signification: whatever the wording-meaning all it does is to construe field. Up to this point the CMH hypothesis appears to encounter no problems. But what about, the second aspect of the field, i.e., the social activity (ii)? This relation-based activity remains identical for both extracts, whether one views it as appropriate to Extract 1a or not. Its invariance implies that it cannot be an activity that has been construed through the workings of transitivity or signification. I suggest that for the construal of this relation-based activity, the facts presented in Tables 5.1 and 5.1a are relevant: what are referred to as relation-based activities are largely construed by the workings of the interpersonal metafunction. This claim may be tested by changing just the mood and finiteness choices in Extract 1, while holding all else largely constant. If my claim is valid, then the text so produced would differ from the original precisely in respect of the relation enactment, which I have referred to as relation-based activity. In a solidarity-affirming interlude integrated into a dissertation defence (see, for detail, Hasan 1994) similar MOOD selections were found; the interpersonal meaning construed by the selection was 'we agree', just as it is in 1 and 1a. The choice of transitivity and signifying reference across that dissertation defence and these minute pieces varies vastly. On this evidence, clearly, the experiential metafunction is irrelevant to what has been described as the relation-based activity in the field of 1 and 1a. Before interpreting this evidence, let me consider also the question of the realization of the third type of social activity discussed above. Even though reflection-based activity does not occur in the extracts under focus, the question of its realization is pertinent to the examination of CMH hypothesis.

It has been assumed in the literature generally that in the cases I refer to as reflection-based activity, the *real activity* is that of explanation/explaining, exposition/ expounding, or argumentation/arguing, or some such 'genre'. I have argued above that this misrecognition arises from our ways of talking. If cases of mode such as explanation, etc. are to be seen as social activity, which, I suggest is not an entirely preposterous idea, for what else is mode except verbal activity of some kind, then the activity of a revision lesson as well as of a consultation in the surgery should be simply described as dialogue. The problem with this view of activity is that it explains very little. If, on the other hand, it is accepted that reflection-based activity is altogether semiotic, then clearly signifying reference will be required for such objects, relations, processes, and circumstances as are relevant to any instance of it: in such activities, these are comparable to 'relevant non-verbal objects, actions' and so on, as Halliday *et al.* (1964) remarked. So one would predict that, as with the action-based activities, so also with the reflection-based ones, there will be a direct positive correlation with the experiential metafunction. From this perspective, doing geography, which is a more specific instance of knowledging, is expressed congruently at the semantic level by choices in the experiential metafunction right down to the relevant lexical items (Hasan 1985d, 1987b). I am suggesting that, on this interpretation of social activity, two out of three types identified are directly realized by the choices in the experiential metafunction. I, naturally, do not wish to imply that only these three types of social activity exist, but it should be the concern of those who argue against the CMH hypothesis to show what other types of social activity, with what realizational probabilities, can be said to exist, or why the present analysis of social activity is not tenable on some theoretical or empirical ground.

I proceed then on the assumption that both action-based and reflection-based social activities will be realized by the experiential metafunction, while the relation-based activity will be realized by choices in the interpersonal one.[47] In support of that assumption, let me briefly examine the social process of teaching, because all three types of social activity are integrated into one field in this occasion of talk. If my claims are correct, then its realization must involve, not only the interpersonal metafunction, but also the experiential one. Since teaching is a complex process, my arguments suggest that we should expect a complex realizational statement. This is indeed the case. To the extent that classroom teaching is relation based, whereby the teacher is the regulating agent and the pupils the regulated ones, this aspect of the field will itself place little constraint on the choice of the experiential meanings, but there will be a direct positive correlation between it and the interpersonal metafunction. To the extent that classroom teaching is reflection based, whereby, say, knowledge of geography, more specifically, of water cycle, is being constructed, there will be positive correlation between it and a specific domain of the experiential metafunction (Cross 1991). Finally, to the extent that classroom teaching is action based, so that the teacher is the facilitator, there will again be a direct positive correlation between this activity and another specific domain of the experiential metafunction. In other words, the suggestion is that the action-based activity of facilitation in the field of teaching will be construed by choices in transitivity and signifying reference, which pertain to a domain of experience that would be distinct from, say, 'knowledging: geography: water cycle'. In the construal of the facilitative activity, it is not the relations of evaporation, condensation, and precipitation that will be constructed; rather, for the activity of facilitation, the 'relevant nonverbal objects' are likely to be such as the blackboard, the desk, the book, diagram, map and so on, the relevant actions are likely to be opening, copying, writing down, looking, tracing, and so on. An examination of such classroom data as presented by Sinclair and Coulthard (1975), Mehan (1979), Hasan (1987c, 2004a), Christie (1988), Lemke (1990), and Williams (1990), and so on, would substantiate my claims that: (a) in any classroom interaction, three 'strands' of social activity intertwine; and (b) that in their construal, the interpersonal metafunction regulates while choices from distinct domains of the experiential metafunction facilitate and construe knowledge.[48]

Faced with this complex situation, we could certainly point out that while there is one single social activity, known by the name teaching, in its realization are implicated other metafunctions than the experiential one, and that this fact invalidates the CMH hypothesis. But, as I suggested earlier, this reasoning would be valid only if it is assumed: (a) that, just because there is a lexical item in the language called teaching, therefore underlying it there must be a single social activity, in other words *that field must be a simple concept necessarily consisting of only one activity*; and (b) that correlation between an activity and the experiential metafunction must always be simple. I have argued that the former assumption is not justified (see excursus F). The same can be said about the second assumption regarding correlation.

The standard and fairly simple interpretation of correlation is that of direct reflection: according to this view, if social activity is AX, then the only way its correlation with the experiential metafunction will be established is by demonstrating that only meanings EX occur. But what happens if it so turns out that, whenever the social activity is AY, we cannot have meanings EX; instead what we need is EY? This is not like saying that the relation between a value of the field and experiential meaning, as such, is random: on the contrary, it is a claim that, when field has a specific class of value, then and then only is it the case that choices from the experiential metafunction will not be primarily relevant to its construal. In this interpretation, there is still a systematic relation between field and experiential metafunction. Would such systematic exception invalidate the hypothesis that, generally, field is construed through experiential choices? Would the acceptance of systematic exceptions imply that correlation is 'anecdotal', and that one is simply creating 'intuitively satisfying pigeon holes for describing diatypic patterns' (as Martin has sometimes remarked)? Should one recognize correlation only if it is absolute?

I suggest that the demand for a 100% correlation is based on a misunderstanding of the meaning of correlation in linguistic variation. Register variation is a kind of linguistic variation; there is no reason why this kind of variation should differ markedly from other kinds of linguistic variation. Where in language variation do we find a correlational statement that stands without exception? Should all quantitative sociolinguistic studies be simply dismissed? I would reject the demand for absolute determination as based on lack of sufficient understanding, and offer here a strong argument against this demand. If the CMH hypothesis is interpreted as implying that field must always and invariably be realized as experiential metafunction, tenor as interpersonal, and mode as textual, there would obviously be no need to recognize both the notion of metafunctions as organizing concepts at the semantic level and contextual parameters at the social level of analysis. In the interest of theoretical economy, they would need to be collapsed. Separate strata are necessarily non-conformal (cf. discussion in Section

5.3.4). The most that we can require is that the relation be systematic; this I have shown to be the case: the relation between the experiential meta-function and the various types of social activity that may be chosen as integrated in the same field can be stated entirely systematically.

But there still remains another fact that is of interest to the meaning of the CMH hypothesis: the exception, namely, that relation-based activities are realized by the interpersonal metafunction, is not random. Instead, this realizational tendency is precisely what one would have expected in the light of the predictions of the CMH hypothesis! So the finding is not that the correlation between social activity and metafunction is random, nor that the correlation between the experiential metafunction and field is less common than that between field and any other metafunction, simply that relation-based activities are realized by interpersonal meaning and gram-mar. Since the correlations are systematic, and since both for action-based activities and for reflection-based ones the correlation with the experiential metafunction is positive, and since, moreover, for the exceptional case of relation-based activity both the condition of exception and its metafunc-tional realization can be systematically stated, it would be a theoretical extravagance to claim that the CMH hypothesis is not valid.[49]

One motive in unpacking the social activity of teaching was to show that what we see as one social process because it is expressed by one lexical item, e.g., teaching, does not necessarily make teaching an unanalysable concept. Obviously the realizational statements for such a complex field cannot be simple. The solution to the problem posed by this complexity is not to destroy the concept of field by subtracting social activities from it and leaving it simply as an entry point for the construction of lexical taxon-omies (as in Martin 1992). The stratagem of exporting the so-called activ-ity of exposition somewhere else in order to permit the field of geography to be realized by the experiential metafunction so as to preserve the CMH hypothesis is like curing the patient of a sickness that is simply imaginary. What is needed is a more careful analysis of the notion of social process: an insistence that complex phenomena should be describable by simple categories is reminiscent of the debate that raged in the early 1960s in linguistics.

But what about the fact that there is variation in the tenor choices under-lying the two extracts? According to the CMH hypothesis, tenor variation should have correlated with variation in interpersonal choices, but since this was invariant it is obvious that the experiential metafunction must construe more than just certain types of social activity. Two points appear relevant: first, the aspect of tenor that is at issue is what I have called the agentive role; this social relation is logically inseparable from social activity itself. If one is willing to accept that soap and shampoo are 'relevant objects' for the action-based social activity of bathing, then there is hardly any ground for excluding the bather and the bathed as relevant agents entrained by the activity of bathing. It is at this point that I would suggest the CMH hypothesis needs to be scrutinized carefully. The most powerful realization of the experiential metafunction is to be found in the grammar of transitivity. However, this grammar, though its nexus is process, involves, not simply process, but also participants. Transitivity is not simply about disembodied goings on; it centres around PROCESS-PARTICIPANT CONFIGURATION (Hasan 1987b). It does not seem reasonable to require that the only situational fact it should construe should concern just the social activity, without bearing implications for the nature of the participant relation.

The conventional assumption that h-field and h-tenor are two entirely independent parameters of the context of situation appears untenable. It seems to me that one way of conceptualizing the context of situation is to see it as a simultaneous mapping of choices that are social-activity-related, choices that are social-relation-related, and choices that are mode-related: Like the clause, each contextual variable might conceivably be seen from the perspective of the three metafunctions. The three contextual variables do not just remain compartmentalized into their neat little boxes of field, tenor, and mode: the nature of field-as-social-activity pervades tenor-as-social-relation and mode-as-symbolic-social-contact, just as the nature of tenor-as-social-relation pervades field and mode, and so on. From this point of view, one would be asking: how are social-activity-related phenomena, such as entrained roles, expressed, rather than simply how is field-as-social-activity expressed? In testing the validity of the CMH hypothesis, it seems important to examine the ways in which values of the contextual parameters may be independent of each other and the respects in which they may not be (Hasan 1973c: 273).[50]

The contextual construct is a highly complex phenomenon. The integration of different types of activity into one field is not the only source of its complexity. The interdependence of the values of the various parameters is just as important, if not more so. But if the variables are interdependent, then in any given instance they will naturally influence each other. So it would not be surprising to find that statements about the configured values a, b, and c are not just the sum of the realization for each value considered in isolation. Even in the physical sciences, the principle is accepted (Cartwright 1983) that the sum of, say, two laws that efficiently describe two phenomena, each in isolation, does not necessarily describe that phenomenon which is created by the coming together of the two iso-lates. The specific problem of testing the CMH hypothesis is to know what it means to test the realization of some contextual parameter. The prob-lem is severe, because the steps in neither direction of approach are self-evident. So if we consider, say, field, then on the one hand we cannot take the nature of this contextual variable for granted, this is not because 'other' systemicists are carelessly inconsistent; the inconsistency draws attention to the inherent complexity. On the other hand, we cannot take the mode of its realization for granted either, for there just have not been enough empir-ical studies so designed as to test hypotheses about the realization of field. But it seems to me that a mechanical interpretation of the CMH hypothesis defeats the very purpose for which it was designed: after all, it is meant to be a step on the way to the important claim of symbiosis between verbal and nonverbal praxis. If in testing the hypothesis, one creates an interpre-tation of context which is qualitatively different from Halliday's, one can hardly be said to be testing his hypothesis, whatever else one may be doing. I am inclined to suggest that what is needed most at the moment is not innovations based on the assumption that the CMH hypothesis is invalid; rather, my inclination would be to engage in a deeper exploration of the kind of issues I have raised about the nature of contextual variables and their realizations.

5.5   The conception of context in text: systems of registers

A re-examination of Tables 5.1–5.4 draws attention to another important point: linguistically speaking, Extracts 1 and 1a are members of the same paradigm. This claim is based on the commonality of the lexicogrammat-ical choices found in the two pieces; these choices are so close that we might be justified in referring to them as members of a minimal textual pair. If this is accepted, then in view of the SF claims about the relation of strata above phonology, certain other consequences would follow logi-cally: being lexicogrammatical agnates, Extract 1 and Extract 1a are also very likely to be semantic agnates; and, if meanings construe contexts, then their semantic agnation makes it highly probable that the contexts relevant to 1 and 1a are also agnates. This, it may be said, is borne out by Table 5.5. The two contexts are systematically related. However, the relation of agna-tion, or what Wittgenstein called family resemblance (Baker and Hacker 1980; Wittgenstein 1953), is not an all-or-none affair: there can be degrees of family resemblance covering the entire range between complete identity and complete nonidentity. Agnation is a variable relation. Moreover, it is not simply the degree of family resemblance that is variable; there is also a similar discretion in respect of the basis on which resemblance is examined. So, for example, while a clause might resemble another more or less, depending upon how much it shares in common with this other, it is also the case that the fact of this sharing does not imply a sharing from all points of view: criteria for family resemblance can be in conflict. So the same item may be viewed as members of one paradigm from one point of view, but of another from another point of view. So, two clauses might bear very close resemblance from the point of view of their mood choices, but they may have nothing whatever in common from the point of view of their transitivity choices, as for example with 'you are singing a song, are you?' and 'I bought a book yesterday'. These clauses are agnates in terms of their mood choices declarative, but fairly distant relatives indeed when it comes to transitivity.

These remarks apply, in general terms, equally well to context and register agnation. Two registers may resemble each other in respect of simply some one underlying value of a variable, or in respect of all values, though the most common experience is that of variation in some underlying contextual values but resemblance in others. Like dialect, register is inherently indeterminate. We speak of British English as opposed to American English as opposed to Australian English; but at another level of delicacy, we may also just as validly speak of Scottish English as opposed to Cockney or Yorkshire dialect. Similarly, we may speak of mother-child register as opposed to pupil-teacher register; or we may speak of control register as opposed to companionship register; dialogic registers or monologic ones. As register variation correlates with variation in three interacting situational parameters, each of which can be described with a lesser or greater degree of delicacy, the question of agnation for both the linguistic varieties and their contextual correlates poses some interesting problems. What will constitute the basis for agnation? At what point would one say: this is not simply a case of resemblance; it is a case of identity, where two instances betoken the same type? The GSP approach grew out of my concern with these questions regarding the recognition of register types. One of its aims was to show on what basis we may claim that two texts belong to registers that display a close family resemblance, as opposed to registers that are far removed. If agnation in linguistic units is variable both in extent and in the point of view from which it is being studied, then the expectation is that the same situation would hold for the semantic unit of text and the social unit of situation type.

5.5.1   Context, text and register in a stratal model

As implied in the above discussion, the question of agnation can be approached from different points of view: the families of agnates constructed by reference to distinct points of view would naturally be distinct. Thus we may postulate contextual paradigms purely on the basis of how far the values of two contexts resemble each other. This would be looking at context from one single stratum; the classification of contexts from this perspective is capable of generating an infinity of context types, because of the multiplicity of the parameters and the open-ended nature of DELICACY OF FOCUS. Elsewhere, I have discussed some of the textual phenomena that can be explained through the postulate of such highly delicate contextual paradigms (Hasan 1985b). If, however, our interest is in the form of interaction, i.e., in how the interaction is structured, and the hypothesis is that speakers fashion the form of their interaction on the basis of their perception of the nature of the occasion of their talk, then an alternative perspective on family resemblance of contexts becomes available to us. We can ask: what are the necessary and sufficient features of context whose realization can be effected by this or that text structure? At a fairly early stage of the inquiry (Hasan 1973b, 1978), it became obvious that the answer to this question identified contextual paradigms by reference to relatively less delicate situational features: the features of context which, as it were, motivated the structure of interaction were not those specific to a unique occasion of talk; rather, they were general in nature, for example, care-giving, rather than bathing or dispensing medicine. To predict the structural shape of an interaction, it was not necessary to know each and every value of the three variables: the more delicate values might differ without any substantial consequence for the overall structure. The question was: what is the nature of the principle by reference to which one might specify the type of contextual information needed that was sufficient and necessary to predict the structural features of the interaction? It was the exploration of this issue that resulted in my GSP hypothesis.

From the beginning, then, my approach to the analysis of the structure of interaction has been problem oriented: I was attempting to answer a question that seemed important to the theory of register variation. Both Ventola (1984, 1987) and Martin (1985a, 1992) have taken it upon themselves to write my intellectual history, tracing the influence of Mitchell (1975) on my thinking. Of course, one can never be certain where one's ideas have originated from, but most readers will hopefully note a substantial difference, despite certain superficial similarities, between Mitchell's concerns and mine. So far as I myself am aware, I saw myself as addressing problems that arose from the sort of hypotheses that are implicit about the relation of context and text in SFL. Whether Halliday said it in as many words or not, it seemed to me that the model would make sense only if it is assumed that speakers' perception of context plays a critical role in the form their interaction takes, just as the addressees' understanding, validation or rejection of the speakers' position plays a critical role in the construal of the shared context.

In saying this, I am claiming that there is some kind of awareness in the speech (sub)community about context types; and that such awareness is made manifest by the (sub)community's interactive behaviours. Let me add also that, just as the awareness is a condition of recognizably different behaviours, so the interactional practices are the condition for the recognition of contexts of talk. Created socially, these occasions of talk become social facts, having a quality that Durkheim might have described as *commes des choses*, for which Berger and Luckmann (1967) devised the term 'facticity'. To say that there are these socially constructed occasions of talk, just as there are also conventional labels prevalent in the community to refer to some of these types of talk (although not all by any means), is to claim no more than that there are communal frameworks for verbal praxis. This, I assume Martin would refer to as a synoptic perspective on contexts and text types (although I am at a loss to see how his conception of genre as 'the way things are done in our culture' is any different!): whether one talks about text types or of context types, in both cases, we are concerned with 'things' the sense of whose existence already exist as *commes des choses*. It is not possible to begin by looking at the unique, if that is really the essence of dynamism; but as I have argued in the discussion of disjunction, it is impossible not to implicate the normal in the discussion of the unique. And methodologically, in developing a theory of context construal such that context construal can be seen also as playing a part in culture construal, one's emphasis cannot be on the unique. It seems necessary to devise some method for identifying text types and context types, so that in the seamless stream of social practice, it may become possible for an investigator to '... segment and classify the events of this behaviour stream so that he [i.e., the investigator] can say, for example, of two successive events, that one is "different" from the other and, of two non-successive events, that they are repetitions of the "same" activity' (Frake 1972: 110).

To inquire into the criteria by which text types or context types may be recognized as types is to subject communal intuition to analysis: one is not presupposing that either text type or context type can be taken for granted. Naturally, I do not reject the idea that, depending on their social positioning, members of a community recognize both the context and the text types prevalent in their community. I agree with Frake entirely that the types the analysis postulates must renew contact with communal experience: we must ask how members of some community whose language one is describing 'talk about talking' (Frake 1972: 110): a presumption of such knowledge can hardly be an adequate point of view for a viable 'register theory'. A basic concern is to explain how and why the members of a community come to talk about talking in these ways. The fact that people know what counts as a promise in their community does not absolve the linguist from providing a description which states rigorously the conditions under which some saying is typically so regarded. If context or text type is to be taken as a theoretical concept, then it must be validated. Following the principles of SF, this can be done by looking above the stratum of context, if one exists, and at the same stratum as context, as well as below the stratum of context. In developing my theory of text structure, I had attempted to do precisely this.

It is in the first requirement that we encounter the most serious problem: at least in Halliday's model, there is no recognized stratum above the stratum of context (Halliday and Hasan 1985: 7 and 100). The stratum of context can be conceptualized as a system of systems the totality of which represents the context of culture, just as the totality of the lexicogrammatical networks represents the grammar of a language. A context of situation is simply a SELECTION EXPRESSION from this vast system network; technically, it is an instantiation (Halliday 1999). A given GSP is the structural output of such a selection expression; it is related to the context of situation as the elements of the structure of a clause are related to some selection expression. I do not wish to give the impression that, in my writings, these perspectives have been articulated clearly. At the same time, the idea is not novel (Hasan 1984c, 1985b) to my work. Note, for example, the manner in which I have tended to specify the contextual features I considered necessary to some contextual configuration: these formulations have followed the formalism of selection expression statements, even though I have seldom if ever presented system networks representing some aspect of culture as a set of interlocking choices.

One persistent problem in the exploration of context agnation from the stratum of context alone is as follows: while in theory the relation of context of situation to context of culture seems clear, the description of the options in the context of culture has never been articulated in any detail.[51] Perhaps one is tacitly saying with Hjelmslev that, at this point, the sociologist and/or anthropologist will take over. Certainly, linguists as linguists are not able to analyse, or are at least limited in the extent to which they can analyse, the crucial properties of culture; *the most that a linguist can hope to achieve is to draw attention to those phenomena which are partially construed via their linguistic realization.* This may be a good deal; but it certainly cannot be all. A very important reason why one needs to go beyond linguistics is precisely that those very institutions the creation of which could not come about without the complicity of language, once having been created become like 'objects', and 'forces' over which language cannot have *immediate* control. Perhaps it is worth adding that, in a functional stratal theory of the type that I take SFL to be, where the theoretical model attempts to model the permeability of human conditions of social existence and the system of verbal semiosis, there will inevitably arrive a stage where the instantiations of the highest stratum would not be wholly describable in terms of language use. This seems to be entailed by the structure of the model. One might therefore conclude that appeal to the context of culture, at least at present, is not likely to give clear and decisive answers to the kind of questions that engaged my attention.

This is certainly a legitimate conclusion. But the acceptance of this position does leave one with the problem that, above and around context, there is not a clearly articulated set of abstractions by reference to which we may talk about the agnation of context of situation. True, we may appeal to the community's 'intuitions' about the types of talk and talk occasions; but appeal to intuitions must be substantiated somehow. So the most theoretically developed means of arriving at specific context types appeared to be: look below the stratum of context, by examining those semantic units called texts (Halliday and Hasan 1976). This is reasonable: register is variation in language correlating with variation in context of situation; text is language operative in a context of situation. It follows that every text, every interaction, must be an exemplar of some register(s), and every register must have some contextual correlate. So *to identify what various texts hold in common and what they do not share, i.e., to identify text types, would also be to move a long way in the direction of identifying context types, particularly if one asks what accounts for the commonality, and what for the variation, of the texts under examination.*

It goes without saying that 'looking at' is an informal expression for examining paradigmatic and syntagmatic relations: in a systemic functional model, the description must be systemic. And while it is true that having system networks represented materially is a great asset in this enterprise, it is not the case that paradigmatic and/or syntagmatic examination cannot be carried out without such a material representation. The system network is an abstract entity, a form of prediction regarding possibilities within some environment; it should not be confused with its own material manifestation. One can be systemic without having systems on a piece of paper. I would add also that to differentiate texts from interaction by saying that text is something that is already produced and static, while interaction is ongoing and dynamic, is not nearly as profound a statement as one is led to believe; dynamic and static are not properties of data: they are ways of looking at data. A critical question then is: what is the nature of those properties of text by reference to which their family resemblances are to be established? What shall I consider as members of the same h-register paradigm, and why? The theory assumes that looking from below, the worded-meanings will provide the requisite information. But speaking is dense with meaning: what kinds of meaning are we looking for? What aspects of the worded-meanings provide evidence for generalizations regarding contexts (Hasan 1973c: 274ff.)? With hindsight I see that I might have expressed my position perhaps more clearly by claiming that, of the two essential attributes of texts, their texture, and their structure, it is the latter that correlates with context type; and it is the specific details of the former that realize the context's specificity as an instance. Although such wording was not used in my writing, this reading is decidedly not precluded; on the contrary, it is in fact actively encouraged (Hasan 1978, 1979b, 1984b, 1985b, 1994).

My answer to the problem of the identification of contexts via the notion of GSP is not different from the kind of criteria one employs at the lexicogrammatical stratum, the stratum that, together with phonology, has the advantage of having more precisely defined analytic relations than any other. The postulate is that the elements of the structure of interaction are realized semantically: in the meanings of any text, there are certain 'bundles of meaning' about which we are able to specify within reason where each such specific bundle would occur *vis-à-vis* some other. Such ordering is not absolutely determinate, but it is not entirely free either. These bundles of meaning in that specifiable order *vis-à-vis* each other is the structure of that talk, each such bundle representing a stage. These semantic attributes of talk are realizationally related more specifically to certain grosser, more abstract properties of the occasion of talk. *The expression of textual structure is semantic in nature; but the activation of this structure is contextual.*

Turning to the contextual phenomena, it is a tacit assumption of the GSP approach that only certain categories of the values of contextual parameter motivate forms of talk structure (Hasan 1985b). I could have then stated that text structure is that aspect of h-register that defines a register variety from the point of view of the overall organization of the texts that might instantiate that register. The GSP specifies the possibilities of textual structure available to texts bearing close family resemblance, i.e., being members of very similar registers, so similar that from this point of view they could be thought of as the same family of register. It is important to point out that this claim does not imply that all texts belonging to the same register will be identical; nor does it imply that register paradigms are unviable, far from it. This method created a fluid mode of identifying register paradigms, in order to account for the well-known fact that varieties cannot be sealed off from each other. The one question which I did not explicitly address, and which is fundamental to this approach, was: what is the generalization that will capture those aspects of the contextual configuration that will motivate the structural aspect of a register type? As the reader will appreciate, Martin has answered this question; and I shall be pointing out my reasons for rejecting that answer.

It is Martin's claim that my approach to the analysis of text is typical of the synoptic perspective: if I do not misrepresent him, he sees the GSP approach as modelling itself rather naively and shortsightedly on lexico-grammatical analysis; in his opinion there is no reason to suppose that the problems in the analysis of text are the same as or similar to those in clause analysis (Martin 1985a: 254). In other words, *once we enter into the study of what Firth called the speech event, the apparatus developed by the science of speech, namely linguistics, particularly in its systematic, generalizing aspect, is no longer capable of dealing with speech!* So then, one question is: why should the analysis of speech event be part of linguistics? If the nature of categories relevant to the analysis of speech is not relevant to the analysis of speech events, why does SFL, which is supposed to explain 'how language works' concern itself with register? Why does it treat register as an integral element of the theoretical model?

In Martin's view another shortcoming of my approach was that I had presented no system networks whose output would be the elements of the structure of texts in some register(s). I have already commented on this: it seems to me that Martin read my work, slight though it is, in a rather superficial manner. Further, *there is an element of self-contradiction in his claim that, on the one hand, my work is synoptic and, on the other, it does not have the backing of systematicity.* How can both be true, particularly in the systemic model? It has to be conceded that the account could hardly be synoptic without generalization; and the SFL framework has an assumption that generalization is essential to systemicity. The omission of system networks from my work on text analysis is deliberate: I am perhaps even more clearly aware of the limitations of system networks at this stratum, particularly given the state of the art in the analysis of text and context. The history of the development of system networks in SF will show that the lexicogrammatical system networks in SF truly took off as the functional semantic perspective evolved; and that the latter probably would not have evolved without a critical achievement in the description of linguistic form. I would claim that system networks representing choices at the stratum of context will become nontrivial and deep only as we develop more revealing analyses of discourse, and as these allow the creation of some similarly productive perspective on the stratum of context.[52] Constructing systems for abstractions from a culture implies that linguists have to look to the relations of language to the material social aspects of human life: the socially positioned and positioning conditions of interaction (Bernstein 1975, 1990), to what Bourdieu describes as 'habitus' and 'disposition' (Bourdieu 1977, 1981), to what Vygotsky calls the development of higher mental functions (Wertsch 1985a, 1985b, etc.), and, not least important, to the nature of the phenomena of Popper's World 1 (Popper 1972), what physicists, chemists, and biologists, and so on, study. A viable analysis of the context of culture in SFL, thus, calls for a truly transdisciplinary approach (Halliday 1991b). *Nothing will be gained by pretending that, once all the verbal semiotic phenomena have been described, the residue at this level of analysis will be zero*; and it is even less justifiable to expect that every important phenomenon of human existence is a linguistic phenomenon per se. What has evolved through semiosis comes to have a facticity which, for practical purposes, is as real as the experience of a physical touch or taste so much so that in the affairs of humanity its semiotic origins are submerged and its 'realness' is foregrounded; without this feature, it would perhaps have been easier to bring about cultural change.

A study of the context of culture along these lines is an exciting prospect; but let us not forget that so far it is simply a 'gleam' in the systemicists' eye (Berry 1987). When I argued that, in recognizing context types, the relations: (a) between the contexts; and (b) between the texts are the most accessible means available to linguists, I was simply following the predictions of SFL theory. The theory made certain claims about the nature of the relation between strata; it postulated context as one of the strata; it claimed register as a linguistic variety correlating with variation in context; and it provided a better developed set of abstractions at the level below context than at the level of context itself. So a reasonable course was to proceed with the inquiry from a general acceptance of these conditions. This was one legitimate response, even though somewhat pedestrian; but there is yet another possibility, and that is to extend or revise the theory by postulating a different set of strata. Martin has adopted this latter strategy. Although there are some important differences between our approaches to the study of text, Martin's goal in attempting to explain how m-genre and m-register are related is not too different from my concern with the relation between texts and contexts. The major difference between his approach and mine, according to Martin, is that his approach is dynamic, whereas the GSP approach is synoptic. I have already argued that, on the basis of his sayings, *Martin's notion of the dynamic appears is both contradictory in its demands, and incapable of supporting the weight he places upon it.* Of course it is always possible that I have misread him. So a closer examination of Martin's alternative framework might enable me to see what this dynamic quality consists in. Not only does Martin (1985a) claim that his alternative framework complements Hasan's synoptic approach by being dynamic, but his claim is that it also solves problems that Halliday's stratal hypothesis fails to: in particular, his model 'preserves' the CMH hypothesis, whereas, if the relation of context and text is conceptualized, as in Halliday or Hasan, the CMH hypothesis is said to be doomed. These are important incentives for looking closely into Martin's theoretical framework, to which I turn below.

5.5.2   Genre and register in a connotative semiotic model

With the development of Martin's connotative semiotic framework, the representation of the proposed strata and communication planes has become more and more complex. With apologies to Martin, I have not reproduced the more recent diagrammatic representation (but see Martin 1992; Ventola 1987: 58). As in Figure 5.1, so here too, I have simply used columns to represent the theoretical models of both Halliday and Martin in Figure 5.3, where the left column represents strata/planes in Martin's model, while the right one represents Halliday's model. The broken lines between strata/planes indicate separation of planes and communication planes; there are no breaks in the right column since in Halliday the strata are in the similar realization relation.

Since the relations between the levels, strata, and planes shown in Figure 5.3 are important to the claim of Martin's connotative semiotic (from now on, MCS), I shall first say a few words about these. I shall refer to the levels in Halliday's model as strata. Following Martin's own practice, I shall use the term strata for the lower three levels in MCS. Thus (3) discourse,

Figure 5.3: Strata in Martin's connotative semiotic and in SFL

Martin's CS	Halliday's SF
6 ideology	
5 genre	context
4 register	
3 discourse	semantics
2 lexicogrammar	lexicogrammar
1 phonology	phonology

(2) lexicogrammar, and (1) phonology are strata of language as denotative semiotic according to Martin's interpretation of Hjelmslev; by contrast semantics, lexicogrammar, and phonology represent the internal structure of language for Halliday.

There seem to be some differences between Halliday's semantics, as I understand it, and Martin's discourse stratum, but for this discussion I shall ignore these differences as they are not clearly articulated. Following Martin, (4) m-register, (5) m-genre, and (6) m-ideology will be referred to as communication planes. I have also retained the planar division between (1) phonology and (2–3) the upper two strata in MCS. While the strata (1–3) represent the make up of language as denotative semiotic for Martin and the relation between (1) and (2–3) is in his framework is the same as in Hjelmslev, the relation between (2–3) in Martin is not as in Hjelmslev's content-form and content-substance, but more as in Halliday's lexicogrammar and semantics. Martin makes a distinction between planes and communication planes, the nature of which is not very clear. I have already discussed many of the problems from the incorporation of the theoretically underdeveloped notion of connotative semiotic (see Section 5.3.2.1). Here I draw attention to some other additional problems that arise directly from Martin's conceptualization of m-register and m-genre, in themselves and in relation to each other. Let me turn first to m-register.

M-register differs in important ways from h-register. To respond to the tensions that arise from the fact that '… each separate utterance is individual … but each sphere in which language is used develops its own relatively stable types of utterance' (Bakhtin 1986 as cited by Martin 1992: chapter 7), Martin makes the following proposal: 'The tension between these two perspectives will be resolved by including in the interpretation of context *two communication planes*, genre (context of culture) and register (i.e., what SFL calls 'context of situation'), functioning as the *expression-form of genre, at the same time as language functions as the expression-form of register* (emphasis added).[53] Note in passing that the tension to which Bakhtin draws attention is precisely the same as that which formed the focus of my attention (Hasan 1978, 1979b, 1981). I paraphrase Bakhtin as asking: how can we explain the fact that distinct texts are at one and the same time unique, possessing a specificity, and also non-unique, functioning as tokens of some identifiable register type? Martin's answer to this question is to make two orders of abstraction from Halliday and Hasan's context of culture and situation: m-genre, which is glossed as context of culture; and m-register, glossed as context of situation. The relation between these and language as conceptualized in SFL is created on the analogy of phonology, so we can say: for Martin phonology is to lexicogrammar and semantics, as language as denotative semiotic is to the connotative semiotic of m-genre and m-register. In the midst of this the question of genre *à la* Bakhtin seems to be lost, unless Martin's view is that Bakhtin like Martin views culture as 'm-genre'!

On the basis of this extract, one might assume that both m-genre and m-register are therefore not levels of language, just as Halliday's context is not a level of language; rather, language realizes the social level of context of culture and situation. If that were the case, we would have simply a terminological variant, with perhaps a minor difference, where what is being proposed is that h-context should be seen as a stratum composed of situational features that construe the schematic structure of the text, and yet another stratum that does not play this role. This solution would not have been very different from that I adopted in GSP, except that I found no justification for dividing context into two distinct strata. But as I have pointed out, Martin's connotative semiotic is not a terminological variant; instead it proposes some very radical modifications to SFL in my understanding of the model. I am not suggesting that modifications to the model should be avoided; what is to be avoided is the adoption of alternatives without a serious discussion. This discussion is missing from SFL literature. Let me quote another extract where Martin draws attention to how m-register and h-register differ:

English Text [i.e., Martin 1992] extends the use of the term register as defined by Halliday. Halliday uses the term [i.e., register] to refer to language as context's expression plane, the linguistic meanings

> (entailing their expressions) at risk in a given situation type. English Text extends the notion to cover in addition part of context's content plane; register is used, in other words, to refer to the semiotic system constituted by the contextual variables field, tenor and mode. (Martin 1992, chapter 7.1.2; emphasis added)[54]

In other words the h-registers, which are linguistic varieties, and their situational correlates are collapsed by Martin under one term, which confusion is hailed as a great advance. Where Halliday uses one distinct term to refer to an abstraction at the social stratum of analysis and another to refer to its realization at the semantic stratum, Martin uses just one term. I am surprised that he refers to this as an 'extension'. To me it has the extraordinary consequence that I can never be sure when Martin is talking about one kind of abstraction, namely, the nonlinguistic conditions, and when about the other, namely, the linguistic features identifying some linguistic variety. Consider, for example, the quote from The English Text. If m-register is both h-context and h-register, then how should one interpret the use of the word context in this quote? This kind of objection appears simply formal, as if it were all about terminology. The appearance is false, for underlying it is serious lack of understanding on Martin's part. The very first issue is that of stratification in linguistic models. Although the relation of realization is conceived of as a dialectic in SFL, the division between planes/ strata is important; for example, it would be odd to claim that h-register is linguistically realized, when in actual fact the register repertoire is simply one dimension of variation in language: the register-repertoire of Urdu is the language Urdu; there is no other Urdu except that which is a system of its own varieties (cf. Firth on the unity of language; see Section 5.2.3). Abstracting register variation from language which is viewed as a denotative semiotic implies that varieties are not inherent to language (e.g., there is a semantics other than that which has evolved in the course of realizing register); and, indeed, this seems to be close to Martin's view, for he does refer to genre and register as parasitic on language as is evident from the following: 'Linguists, especially those with an interest in why language is the way it is, have probably been remiss in ignoring these semiotics [i.e., connotative semiotics]; since it is the function of language to realize them; both of *these parasites, register and genre, have profoundly affected the nature of language itself'* (Martin 1985a: 249; emphasis added).

This is a curious conception of language, and certainly, in my interpretation of SFL, it is at odds with its tenets. What does it mean to say that both the linguistic variety and its nonlinguistic correlate are, on a communication plane, distinct from the strata of semantics and wording in language? If varieties, whether according to use or to user, are not constitutive of language as denotative semiotic, what exactly is that language like? Language as conceptualized by Martin is in the first place would have to be autonomous; its genesis, and therefore its development, would not be tied to the sociality of human beings; it is, in fact, Hjelmslev's overly homogeneous system, which just happens to satisfy the need of its speakers by there somehow arising a connotative semiotic. How either the connotative or the denotative semiotic manages to do this, Martin does not ask.

If stratifying implies something, then it is equally true that collapsing two levels or strata into one, or expanding one into two has implications. First, there is the general issue: how far can we carry the business of collapsing strata, and does the collapsing have any consequence? To answer this we need to have some idea about the conditions that have to be satisfied before stratification may be deemed viable. Criteria for stratification have to be commensurate with the shape of an overall model. For SFL, my understanding is that strata are separated only if the 'facts' of one stratum are demonstrably related above chance level to the 'facts' of another by some specifiable relation, for example, that of conventional association as is the relation between phonology and the rest 'above' it or that of construal-activation, as between wording and the rest 'above' it; and only if the 'facts' of the two strata are not conformal; there should not exist a one-to-one relation, between facts a, b, and c at stratum X and facts p, q, and r at stratum Y, such that a 'is always' p, b is q, and so on. From the point of view of the relations between strata as they are postulated in the SFL theory, it makes no sense to collapse h-context and h-register but not h-register and lexicogrammar. If any two strata above phonology can be collapsed, then in SFL, through the entailment of the realization relation, everything above phonology should be collapsed, unless some good reason is produced to make an exception. Each stratum above phonology is related to the other(s) by construal-activation relation, a relation which is incidentally typical of all socially constructed semiotic systems. So the only un-collapsible planes would be the planes of phonology/phonetics (Hjelmslev's 'expression plane') and the rest of language (Hjelmslev's planes). So from the point of view of SF, collapsing two strata into one necessarily implies certain things about the 'facts' relevant to the two strata.

These implications are not removed by the choice of nomenclature for the collapsed abstractions. For example, the collapsing of h-context and h-register has the same implications whether it is referred to as a stratum, as a plane, or as a communication plane; and once the two have been collapsed, it makes little difference whether it is called context or register! By the logic of the proposed criteria for stratification, non-stratification of abstractions will imply that conformality is a necessary condition of the relation between the two. Context 1 must be expressed as register 1, context 2 as register 2, and so on: the possibility of non-conformality would be completely absent. By stratifying context and language, Halliday is implying that context 1 is not always and invariably realized as just this semantic configuration; there are possibilities of incongruent realization through metaphorical means. Disjunction gets a chance! Further, it is being implied that, just as a slip of the tongue gives information about mismatch between the speaker's intended meaning and the speaker's encoded meaning, so also the possibility of viewing context and register as distinct though realizationally linked phenomena allows the perception of how, perhaps, my view of what is appropriate differs from someone else's, or how, perhaps, a context would be 'read differentially' by one or the other of the interactants. If these are virtues of the SFL model, and I tend to believe they are, since they allow the possibility of systematically explaining variation, then Martin's connotative/denotative semiotic model is a poorer substitute to SFL, for it must be unable to do any of these important things.

There is nothing novel in thinking of the language as a denotative semiotic as a variation-free system. In most formal models, variation is a feature of the use, of process, of performance, not of the system, the linguistic competence as such. This is not news: ever since Saussure, we have heard of *langue*, of autonomous and homogeneous system, of competence. We have, in the last three decades, also witnessed evidence that this view of language is not viable even for formal linguistics. The postulate of a homogeneous system is an idealization that severs language effectively from what people do with their language. If such a view is unacceptable even to formal linguistics today, I doubt very much that a functional model would be able to accommodate a division between language as a denotative semiotic for its varieties which form its connotative semiotic. In one way, of course there can be no quarrel with Martin that the possibility of renewing variation inherent in the system lies with the active speaker in the process of speaking; when the speech community is dead, the language ceases to vary. But to say that diachronic variation and evolution depend upon synchronic variation is to affirm that, at any given moment, language as a system is a dynamic object: it is not the grammar that is synoptic; it is our grammatics that is synoptic. *The irony here is that to banish variation from the system is to aggravate the synoptic quality of your concept of the system;* and this runs counter to Martin's avowed aims! (I wonder, incidentally, whereabouts in MCS one would locate dialect variations that correlate with time and with geographical and social space.)

Now, if the recognition of variation is also the recognition of at least one dynamic perspective on the system of language, then, by refusing to recognize variation, either by collapsing h-context and h-register or by stratifying register variation and language, one would be actively constraining the dynamic study of language rather than adopting an active perspective. On what grounds can Martin claim, then, that Martin's connotative semiotic model provides a dynamic perspective?

Perhaps to answer this question one should turn to m-genre which is curiously absent from this debate; it is possible that the answer is concentrated there. As I begin to discuss m-genre, the reader will note that the differences between m-register and h-register have not yet been fully expounded. One of the earliest accounts of m-genre is as follows: 'Genres are how things get done, when language is used to accomplish them. They range from literary to far from literary forms: poems, narratives, expositions, lectures, seminars, recipes, manuals, appointment making, service encounters, news broadcasts and so on. The term genre is used here to embrace *each of the linguistically realized activity types* which comprise so much of our culture' (Martin 1985a: 250; emphasis added). It is possible to read this formulation in two different ways. One, that genre is not an aspect of language (cf. the emphasized words in the quote from 1985a: 249): in that reading the m-genre is an activity type, which happens to be realized linguistically, with language functioning as a separate semiotic with its own semantics, lexicogrammar and phonology. The other reading suggests that it is itself a linguistic entity, although underlying it is some other entity which is itself not linguistic. Again this is not simply a matter of terminology; it seems reasonable to insist that we recognize the distinction between a variety of some language and an entity that is expressed by language. Even though each member of such a pair may be considered as the *raison d'être* for postulating the other, the two are not identical abstractions, especially if possibilities of parodies, of diachronic evolution, etc., are to be considered. The ambiguity of the prior quote is systematic. As in the case of m-register, m-genre too collapses what I perceive to be two distinct orders of abstraction. In m-genre, as in m-register, two things combine: there is the overall form of the discourse, its structural shape; and there is, correlating to this form, some abstraction from situation. This abstraction is sometimes a part of h-field; at other times it is a part of h-mode, specifically its rhetorical component. To this Martin refers, somewhat confusingly to my mind, as purpose (Hammond 1989; Martin 1985a, 1992; Ventola 1984, 1987). It may be best to present this complex situation diagrammatically.

It needs to be noted that in Martin's connotative semiotic modelling of genre and register, there is yet another plane; that of IDEOLOGY above the communication plane of m-genre, but I shall only say a few words in passing about that here and so it will be excluded from Figure 5.4. I believe the figure as presented here displays Martin's model faithfully, even though the diagram is not as impressive as most of the recent visual representations have been with staggering levels stacked step-wise.

Figure 5.4: Planes/levels in connotative semiotic

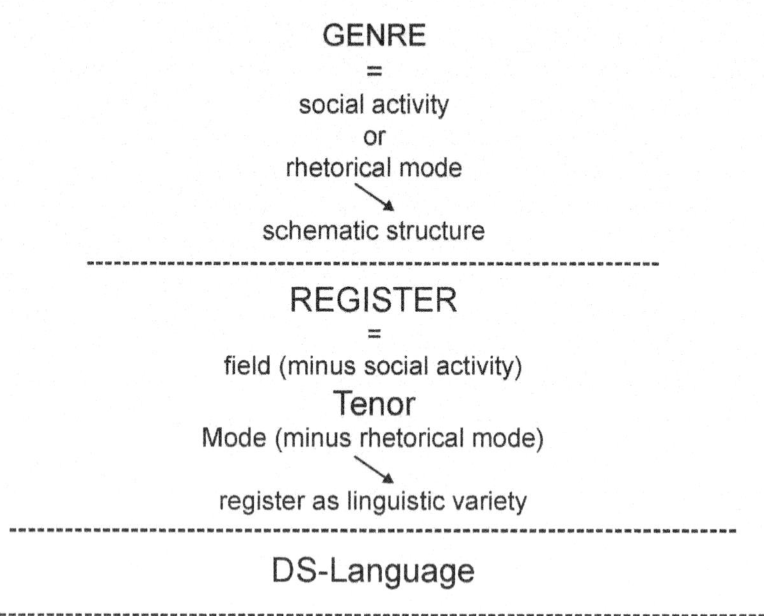

Genre we are told is a complex *situational/cultural* phenomenon, call it purpose, which corresponds to Halliday's social activity plus his rhetorical mode and is realized as SCHEMATIC STRUCTURE, that aspect of text which can be seen as organized in stages, each stage having a definite relation to the others. Schematic structure in Martin's connotative semiotic is thus very much like my concept of ACTUAL STRUCTURE. But unlike Martin's notion of purpose, in the GSP approach there is no single separate situational abstraction that by itself 'generates' text structure: instead *in the*

GSP approach the overall structure of talk is activated by the configuration of the selection of relatively more primary situational choices, from field, tenor, and mode (Hasan 1978, 1979b). By contrast, in Martin's connotative semiotic model, the schematic structure of the text is 'predicated' by single, one might say simple, considerations. One problem in the GSP approach is that the situational phenomena that correlate with textual structuring are not easily nameable: they are difficult to specify accurately, the most that *I would claim is that the combination of primary values of the three variable will explain why the textual structure is as it is.* By contrast, as Figure 5.4 shows Martin makes a clean and clear statement: underlying m-genre – a situational phenomenon – is social activity, alias goal alias purpose. The communicative plane of m-register mimics the situation at the communicative plane of m-genre: there is both stratification and collapsing of distinct orders of abstraction. This feature is important, and Martin claims for his connotative semiotic modelling are closely dependent on it. Both m-genre and m-register are 'structured entities' (whatever that might mean); in fact Martin often refers to them as a semiotic. At each of these communicative planes, abstractions of two types exist: one abstraction must be seen as an abstraction from situation, the other as having something to do with the verbal system, for no matter how we conceptualize m-registers and m-genres, their expression is (genre-less) language. Language as a denotative semiotic is itself a separate entity from whatever it is that is language-like that functions as the realization of the situational abstractions at the two communication planes. Martin presents the justification for the stratification of m-genre *vis-à-vis* m-register as follows:

> the fact that notions of purpose and effect do not correlate with any one metafunctional component in language and have been associated at one time or another with different variables in the development of register theory suggests that a teleological perspective on text function might be better set up as superordinate to – rather than alongside or incorporated in – field, mode and tenor. The register variables field, tenor and mode can then be interpreted as working together to achieve a text's goals, where goals are defined in terms of systems of social processes at the level of genre … genres are social processes, and their purpose is being interpreted here in social terms, not psychological terms. Nor does the model imply the cultures as a whole are goal-directed, with some over-riding purpose governing the interaction of social processes. Social processes negotiate with each other and evolve. (Martin 1992: chapter 7.1.2)

I would like now to raise a few questions about the concepts of m-genre and m-register.

(a) What sort of connotative semiotic do we have when a semiotic is expressed by one which is itself expressed by another one?

(b) Does the strategy of stratification of genre and register as shown above serve the purposes it is claimed to be able to do: the purposes as enumerated are that first the connotative semiotic modelling of genre and register is dynamic; second, that in it the disjunction is easily/better explained; third, that 'context metafunction hook up hypothesis' is preserved; and

(c) Is the assumption empirically true that the forms of the over-all structure of interaction are sensitive only to 'purpose', neither to tenor nor to other features of mode which are still not abstracted away from h-context?

It is possible that I am missing some very fundamental point made by Martin, but I must admit to being bemused by the situation created by the collapsing of situational and linguistic phenomena in m-register and similarly in m-genre. The problem of the relation between Hjelmslev's planes of the connotative semiotic was severe enough. To me it seems that here we have even worse problems. First, if the communication plane of register is itself a semiotic, then, technically speaking, Hjelmslev's model gives us a METASEMIOTIC, not a CONNOTATIVE SEMIOTIC. But there is a problem even in that conceptualization: what is that semiotic some part of whose expression-form is not a semiotic but the other is, for this seems to be the situation with respect to m-genre and m-register? If we take m-register, which is a complex entity wherein some situational phenomena and some sort of linguistic phenomena are solidary, then we can only hold the following positions: that both its components are semiotic; that neither is, but that their coming together makes them into a semiotic; or that only one is a semiotic. If field, tenor, and mode as situational abstractions are themselves a semiotic, and so is their verbal expression, then that communication plane itself is a metasemiotic. If only one of the component levels on this communication plane is a semiotic, say the verbal expression of field, tenor, and mode, then the said communication plane itself represents a connotative semiotic. Does it matter which of these is the case? Would the description be any different? I am not able to answer these questions, because, important though they are to Martin's theorization, they have never been discussed in any detail. Let me remind the reader that the question of the clarification of the relation between communication planes is as crucial in

Martin's connotative semiotic as that of the relation between Hjelmslev's planes. If a serious claim of connotative/metasemiotic is to be sustained, work needs to be done to show why there is not a succession of similarly related strata; what gain is there in not having the kind of stratification as is found in SFL. My reaction is that the edifice of the series of connotative semiotics postulated by Martin would be a harmless game if it were not being implied as it is that somehow this feature, which is so remarkably without demonstrated theoretical basis, is a revolutionary innovation as a result of which Martin's model manages to do things that static systems such as Halliday's, Bernstein's, Hasan's, and so on, are incapable of doing. Let me then turn to some of those claims.

On what basis can one claim, as Martin continues to, that Martin's connotative semiotic views in a dynamic perspective the question of Halliday's contextual parameters and register variation? I have shown that it has no edge in describing disjunction; I have pointed out that by collapsing abstractions such as h-context and h-genre it creates a situation that is severely synoptic. The same can be said about the collapsing of social activity and schematic structure. The collapsing of situational features, i.e., purpose or goal, with schematic structure implies a one-to-one correlation, and yet empirically the claim does not seem to be tenable; for example, in what sense is it true to claim that, whenever social activity is [encountered], there will be an element of structure GREETING (cf. Figure 5.3.3 in Martin 1985a)? One may define encounter in this way. This may be offered as a definitional fact: whenever we have something languaged that can be called GREETING, we shall say that the purpose is [encounter]. However, if that is the case, then how does this claim differ from mine that a certain contextual configuration is to be seen as identifying a context type if its realization is such and so? Just because I did not draw a network with a lexical taxonomy does not mean that all the elements of the GSP descended together from some mysterious source. The source both for Martin and for myself as SFL linguists should be the same, namely, the speech community's sense of the occasions of talk, and that is to say the basis of description is a generalization, not unique instances.

One other question puzzles me: what motivates the gloss of genre as context of culture? True, much of culture is construed semiotically, but certainly not simply through parole and much simply through the schematic structure of talk. That there is no mechanism of any kind in MCS by which choices at the level of m-genre can be shown to be realized in a principled way by choices at the level of m-register is quite obvious. The appeals are, as they have to be in the nature of things, to what is the norm in the community. Metaphorical expressions whereby genre negotiates with register, or genres negotiate with each other, or social processes do, are all very well; and one must accept the difficulty of talking about complex phenomena. Nonetheless, when one attempts to deconstruct these expressions, what is the result? Hiding behind the metaphors does not make the concept of m-register or m-genres less norm bound.

Then, exporting all variation from the perspective of language as denotative semiotic is not calculated to make that language description extremely dynamic: rather it is calculated to insure that the description of that language will be in a maximally synoptic perspective, because there is no principle for creating the possibility of change in that kind of conception of language. I have discussed above the question of 'preserving' the 'context metafunction hook-up hypothesis', drawing attention to its complexity. Martin claims that, by stratifying language as denotative semiotic, and m-register, and m-genres its connotative semiotic, he would be able to create a situation whereby his field now is always realized by experiential metafunction, and tenor by interpersonal. I would be surprised at this outcome, and there is no evidence to support it. For example, there is the question of the realization of mode: what realizes mode? Is dialogic mode purely realized by the textual metafunction? Does the logical metafunction play any role in construing the distinction between written and spoken mode? Then, too, it is not true that such textual phenomena as the degree of cohesive harmony is entirely a realization of some mode choice. The sort of cohesive harmony one gets in geography is not really the sort that one gets in, whatever it is in Martin's field that corresponds to the social process of bathing a child. Martin himself mentions (Martin 1992) that mode is oriented to both interpersonal and textual metafunctions. How, then, has Martin's connotative semiotic modelling of genre and register 'preserved' the endangered 'context-metafunction hook-up hypothesis'? So far as I can see that model has proliferated strata/communication planes, without explaining anything whatever either in the language of the interaction or in its so-called schematic structure, or in any clarification of the metafunctional hypothesis.

Turn now to the empirical validity of the claim that purpose, i.e., social activity and rhetorical mode, are good predictors of the forms of talk structure. One does not have to look very far to see that, quite apart from the theoretical and conceptual objections to the dissociation of activity from agents of activity, it just is not true that tenor plays no part in motivating text structure. Consider the marked difference between three classes of advertisements: those that promote corporate image (e.g., the image of the national defence corps); those that promote some goods to those who are not necessarily seeking those goods (e.g., estate agent advertising house sale); and those that promote some goods to persons actively looking for those goods which are being purveyed by some private provider (e.g., private house sale). The last category is referred to in our community as classified advertisement. We might say this is a candidate for m-genre. But if so, what is hidden in the name? And if we find that the structures associated with the last two are critically different, as they will be found to be, shall we say that is because the social activity is that of producing classified advertisement? What does this kind of statement illuminate? How does it help us to understand how speaking persons co-act with each other? Take another example: the nursery tale and the short story for the adult are different in their schematic structures, but is that because the social activity of narration is different? What in any case is the social activity in these genres; what is their purpose? Presumably the purpose underlying a fictive narrative is to produce a fictive narrative! A narrative structure of the type Martin uses for the analysis of stories is not always activated by one single purpose; much less frequently is it activated simply by the purpose of entertainment. I have discussed the problems arising from stratification and level collapsing. Consider another effect of stratifying m-genre and m-register. If these communication planes have an activation-construal relation, model would seem to suggest that a social activity activates the narrator's social relation to the addressee as also his/her choice of mode. I have argued that the three parameters are interdependent, without being entirely predictable on one another. It is difficult to differentiate between the evidence for this claim and the evidence for Martin's claim that it is social activity as such that, as it were, motivates the choice of social relation and symbolic contact. But there are some situations in which the reverse is quite obviously true: we may look to the mother-child relation; do we choose that relation on the basis of the social activity? Assuming that activation is not denied in Martin's model, then does the communication plane of ideology motivate schematic structures? An affirmative answer would be amazing, because the schematic structure of a Marxist's chapter will be pretty much along the same lines as the ultraconservative's! To treat ideology as a disembodied abstraction, separated from the speaking subject does not suggest it is being viewed in a dynamic perspective. In my view a true dynamic perspective on the ideological base of discourse resides in the socially positioned perceptions of the interactants; the relations they construe between themselves, their interpretation of what needs to be done and how, are phenomena that are refracted through the speaking subject's consciousness. What places restraint on the individual, and what creates normalization, appear unavoidable socially, necessary by the creation of inter-subjective objectivity.

5.5.3 The conception of language and social action

In discussing Martin's approach I have tried to give mostly reasons for my disagreements which are based on SFL theory. Martin's work in language education has made noticeable impact: many of his arguments there are unimpeachable. And the kind of pedagogic programmes Martin and his immediate colleagues have introduced certainly appear to me to have a lot to recommend themselves. It is sometimes said that the proof of the pudding is in the eating, arguing that if Martin's approach to discourse analysis has been so successful in its practical application, then this shows that he must be right. I disagree with the logic of this approach. On this basis the continuation of traditional grammar for pedagogic purposes could be said to be a proof of its desirability. We do not know when exactly we have met the end of eating which can point to quality of the pudding!

Practice can hardly be better than the theory permits; otherwise, the practice is better despite the explicitly held theory. My own view is that the stratification of genre and register, the collapsing of the social and the verbal, at both these planes, which in turn entails a questionable view of language, is far from desirable: it moves the whole issue of text structure and its activation from active, feeling, reacting interactants to culturally given forms of talk in agreement with 'how things are done in our culture', as if the culture is unchanging and as if the interactants are simply preprogrammed. This is somewhat ironic, for it was precisely to avoid these sorts of outcome that Martin professes to reject the GSP approach, which in fact does not suffer these problems. But I do not think that Martin, or any of his colleagues, for that matter, have produced a better alternative where the reasoned and reasonable analysis of text structure is concerned.

Martin has made considerable contribution to SFL. In disagreeing with him, and in provoking him to clarify his views, I believe I am taking a useful step. I believe that the usefulness of his genre-based work might gain if attempts are made to respond to some of these critiques. If that happens, the chapter will have achieved its purpose even though its schematic structure defies description!

Notes

1 I thank Carmel Cloran for comments on the first draft of this chapter. The responsibility for views presented here is mine. The chapter was submitted for publication in February 1991. Endnotes have been added to this reprint in order to update certain relevant developments in ideas and positions over the last two decades. A few changes have been introduced in the chapter in the interest of clarity and/or brevity.

2 With hindsight I see that this in itself is no objection: I should have added that therefore the acceptance of Martin's move requires a clear indication of how and why the model needs to be modified. This has never been attempted.

3 However, with recent interest in multimodality all the elements of the material situational setting (Hasan 1973c, 1981, 1999b, etc.) seem to have become the focus of interest in discourse analysis. As I myself have remarked, what is seen as 'raw situation' by the linguist interested in the analysis of the language use may turn out to be the domain of other 'modalities' as if the specifically linguistic meaning was incapable of being studied: texts must be analysed multimodally; semantic analysis has become suspect.

4 In the first published account of this approach (Hasan 1978) I had used the term 'generalized structural formula'; this was revised to 'generalized structure potential' (=GSP). Since then it has been variously known as GSP, generic structure potential or generalized structure potential; I prefer the last reading.

5 A cursory reading of the literature suggests that this comment holds true even today.

6 Recently I have wondered if there is a case for making a distinction between 'instance' and 'occurrence': the latter term would refer to such data of language use which is being viewed without the eye of any categories consciously and deliberately created in a theoretical frame. The 'instance' that just instantiates a systemic path would clearly be a synoptically identified product: it would be the exemplar of a type. By comparison, the object of study for Martin's dynamic theory would be an actual occurrence: this would be a 'real event' which is clearly not to be confused with something that simply conforms to some systemic representation; that would naturally call for analysis in synoptic perspective. The focus of Martin's dynamic perspective has to be on entirely serendipitous properties, be it an error, a turning back on oneself, an incomplete utterance, or a deliberately crafted innovation. It is this latter type of semiosis that Martin's dynamic system prioritizes.

7 This and the next paragraphs have been revised in this edition. I have been always puzzled by the inherent contradictions in Martin's position, but the original rendering of my puzzlement was far from easy to interpret. My excuse is that the earlier intended content has been perhaps more clearly worded this time.

8 Over the years, I have noted that the concept of 'order of sequence', of the 'optionality of elements' as well as optionality of position with reference to

other elements of the GSP have been quietly borrowed from the 'frozen' synoptic GSP approach apparently without the need for acknowledgement.

9   When in early 1991, I submitted the manuscript of this chapter to the editors of Discourse in Society, the terms construe and construal though 'around' were not established as technical terms in my own parole.

10 All page references for the extracts taken from Firth's earlier publications are to Firth (1957).

11 On the basis of Firth's insight into the importance of the social in the description of language, I argued that to be adequate and explanatory linguistic theory needs to be 'exo-tropic' (Hasan 1999c, 2005).

12 For a critique of Firth's methodology to 'secure' the analysis of meaning see Hasan (2009a, 2010).

13 Hjelmslev used the term 'text' to refer to *any actualization of the Danish potential,* irrespective of whether it was a syllable or a phoneme or morpheme or sentence. I admit I have no clear idea about exactly where Hjelmslev would position Martin's genres.

14 Let us not raise the question as to how the CONNOTATIVE SEMIOTIC categories avoid being synoptic.

15 Relevant to this discussion is Hasan (2014b).

16 Martin has stated that under a misunderstanding of Halliday's views, he misinterpreted register as more or less synonymous with context.

17 Does this suggest that connotative semiotic phenomena lie somewhere between content purport and content substance? If so, this makes the connotative system that much more mysterious!

18 'Negligible' is too strong: careful studies (e.g., Butt 2001) have established the richness of Firth's schema; even so, I would still maintain that Firth's account of how 'you mean' needs a good deal of elaboration. In my view that elaboration will extend beyond simple additions of strategies for description.

19 The dialectic of text and context has been a constant theme in my writing as evident from the volumes of my collected works, especially this Volume and Volume 6: Unity in Discourse: Texture and Structure (forthcoming).

20 In the original version I had suggested Hjelmslev's use of 'realization' might be analogous to Halliday's 'instantiation'; I now believe this was not the case; see for example the discussion of the latter term in Hasan (2009a) chapter 1.

21 The best explanation for this requirement can only the provided by reference to the Saussurean claims about the structure of a sign, which Hjelmslev criticized, in my view wrongly, and un-necessarily sharply (1961: 47 ff).

22 See however Saussure (2006) for an interpretation in relation to SFL Hasan (e.g., 2013, 2014b).

23 For a long time SFL used 'phonology' as 'subsuming both phonology and phonetics'. More recently (e.g., Halliday and Greaves 2008) 'the tri-stratal conception of the inner structure of language' has shifted: the division between phonology and phonetics has been explicitly recognized as forming distinct strata.

24 I began using the 'two-way' relationship between the upper strata from a fairly early stage as can be seen from Hasan (1973c, 1981); but the explicit elaboration is more recent, e.g., Hasan (2010).

25 At this point, a one page analysis of some clauses is presented to show how grammar is a device for 'hooking up together the selections in meaning which are derived from the various functions of language, and realizing them in a unified structural form'. It would appear Martin's notion of 'context-metafunction-hook-up device' is a misapplication of this passage.

26 I am here referring to Martin's Figure 2 in 1985a: 250, which offers a modelling of 'language in relation to its connotative semiotics'. While writing this chapter I had to focus mainly on Martin (1985a) since this was the only *published* account available to me containing Martin's reflections on register in a connotative semiotic perspective. Martin (1992) differs significantly from that document but by then copies of the present chapter had become available in manuscript form to many colleagues including Martin.

27 If as 'shown' by Taverniers (2016) Halliday has abandoned the Hjelmslevian model of stratification, this may be because in interpreting it he found it incompatible with a functional modelling of language.

28 In other words, no one uses a lexicogrammatical structure for any other reason than that it construes a chosen meaning.

29 In fact 'writing' is not part of the field at all; if anything it is referring to a feature of mode. What is the basis for deciding that some 'action' refers to some feature of field or of mode.

30 The claim is not that Hasan (1983) covers the entire range of linguistic meanings but simply that the kinds of meanings we habitually mean match postulated metafunctions.

31 It is obvious that my own sense of the relationship of semantics, lexicogrammar and context to metafunctions was not fluent enough to allow me to state the issues more clearly. In the last analysis, the three contextual parameters arise from the nature of 'social practice', i.e., by doing something with an other where the doing must necessarily involve language relevant to that social practice, since as linguists the basis of our interest in context lies in the job of linguistics to explain how language works. A social practice must involve some sort of action which implicates at least two interactants, and interaction demands a sense of relevance in relation to the task in hand and then to the 'other' concerned party. I hope this is explained more clearly here in the Introduction.

32 I use context-metafunction hook up device following Martin's usage. To me this metaphor does not appear well suited for characterizing the relation suggested by Halliday in 1973a, 1977a and elsewhere.

33 This suggests that language is based in the human body and it needs other human bodies for interactive undertakings as Thibault has argued (Thibault 2004b).

34   I do not think it is unfair to add that the decades since 1992 have not at all shown any evidence of the genre theory contributing anything to context-metafunction relations.

35   I would much rather not use the word 'hook up' in referring to the 'CMH hypothesis': this formulation significantly changes the probabilistic nature of Halliday's claim; but that is precisely the point; colleagues have first rejected probabilistic statement as lacking in theoretical power, so they take it as a 'one-to-one relation'; when that does not work in actual use of language, they reject the hypothesis.

36   For additional support developed over the last three decades see, see Hasan (2001a, 2014b).

37   There are exceptions (Hasan 2009a; Cloran 1994; Williams 1995); but they need not concern us here.

38   This does not mean we leave the description by saying 'talk is dynamic; anything can happen' even though this is true to a certain extent: to describe means to identify the limits of variation, and the conditions in which the limits are tested as for example in Hasan (1981) (chapter 3 here). These steps are important for understanding the meaning of the term 'register variation'.

39   By organic relation, I meant relations between two or more whole messages. At that time no comprehensive lexicogrammatical account existed. At present, Cloran's (1994) work on RHETORICAL UNIT has offered an account at the semantic level with its lexicogrammatical realizations, and Mann, Matthiessen and Thomson (1992), etc., have produced a RHETORICAL STRUCTURE THEORY, which could be said to be based on logical relations (whether realized explicitly or implicitly). There is room for a good deal of discussion and development in this area, which is central to the issue of textual unity.

40   I reiterate the remarks on Martin's framework are based on Martin (1985a); I did certainly have access to many pre-publication drafts of Martin (1992). But to critique unpublished material would have been neither helpful to the reader nor friendly to the author. In any event, the published form of those chapters is not necessarily the same as the earlier versions.

41   Which is to say I did not do a good job in 'transforming' Extract 1 into Extract 1a.

42   There was a mistake at this point in the original, which makes nonsense of the sentence that follows; this has been corrected here.

43   Note that all such statements have to be probabilistic: of course one is not very likely to begin an interaction with the intention of quarrelling; but it is not beyond possibility that one may go to see someone with the intention of 'having it out' with someone and end up shooting them.

44   At this point it is important to draw attention to the 'misrecognition' that could result from describing the activity in this way: the grammar of English forces us to say 'give care' or 'produce knowledge' and other such expressions. But quite clearly we are not talking of two different phenomena: there is no such activity as that of giving in 'giving care' any more than there is something that

is being given. Producing knowledge, by the same token, is not producing plus knowledge: it is in actual fact *knowledging*. Knowledging used this way is parallel to regulating, facilitating, bathing, cooking, and so on, which puts the expression on a par with other (action-based) activities.

45 For some decades now I have thought of mode as concerned with the quality of contact, which depends on the relevance established both by the material and semantic contact (Hasan 1999a, 2001a, 2014b).

46 There is much in the discussion in Section 5.4.5 that I would view somewhat differently today: for one thing, the grammatical description has become more, and secondly our understanding of the relations of the parameters has developed considerably.

47 This conception was developed to a certain extent in Hasan (1999b) (here chapter 6) and the last two chapters.

48 In Hasan (1999b) both these aspects are included in field; the various forms of pedagogic action and the sphere to which the action relates are separated as two distinct vectors of field.

49 Today I would reject my own argument as defective; instead I would suggest that texts are multilayered organization of meaning and wording like the clause (Halliday 1991b): the same rhetorical units and messages realize field, and tenor and mode as analysed from different semantic and lexicogrammatical perspectives. Therefore every text will display all three metafunctions.

50 This as I now see destroys the whole hypothesis and must be resisted in favour of 'research first'. However nearly two decades after the publication of this chapter, the so-called *context-metafunction-hook up hypothesis* still remains untested. At least to the best of my knowledge, there have not been any serious experiments to test the hypothesis. To be fair it is very difficult to get 'true' minimal pairs of some parameter in texts holding other parameters constant (as the transformation of Extract 1 into 1a has demonstrated).

51 In a manner of speaking this lack is being rectified by such writings as Hasan (1999b), Butt (2004b), and Bowcher (2007).

52 It was nearly one decade later that I published a system network representing the potential of the contextual parameters (Hasan 1999b); I had however indicated the systemicity in the realization of the elements identified as GSP relevant to some specific register type (1985b). In 1985 my then doctoral student Linda Gerot presented a seminar at Sydney University on a systemic representation of the parameter of mode. And in any event I had been using system networks for teaching about context. In one respect, from early on these networks are very different from Martin's: unlike his m-register networks (Martin 1992) they are not taxonomies of relevant lexical items; they represent the systemic relation of the values pertain to the parameter in question as in Hasan (1999b).

53 Reformulated in terms of Hasan's GSP approach the suggestion is: (1) m-genre is equivalent to 'context of culture' as in Halliday and Hasan (1985); (2) m-register is equivalent to 'context of situation' as in Halliday and Hasan (1985); (3) except that now h-register has disappeared or become equal to

context of culture which is instantiated as context of situation (4) these 'communication planes' (i.e., m-genre and m-register) are external to language; (5) borrow from Hjelmslev the notion of connotative semiotic; (6) view these two communicative planes as a connotative semiotic that is *expressed* by language, consisting of strata (1–3), which shall now be known as a denotative semiotic. Deconstructed in this way, the suggestions leave one gasping with surprise: where did text as the instantiation of register as the realization of context of situation go? What happened to Martin's ideology? Anyone who is familiar with Hasan's conception of the relation between language and the context of culture and situation must wonder if greater comprehensiveness, clarity, or descriptive coverage has really been brought to the study of discourse analysis. How the CMH hypothesis can possibly be resolved by this confused set of relations and how this makes Martin's so-called genre theory approach dynamic are issues that remain mysterious.

54   I have left the bibliographic reference to Martin as in the original just as a reminder to the reader that at the time of writing this paper I did not have access to Martin's 'more developed thesis' as presented in Martin (1992). This often made it difficult to even understand what Martin's real claims were, especially since he is fairly economical in providing justifications for the importation of the Hjelmslevian model.

6 Speaking with reference to context [1999]

The aspects of things that are most important for us are hidden because of their simplicity and familiarity. (One is unable to notice something – because it is always before one's eyes.) ... We fail to be struck by what, once seen, is most striking and most powerful. [Wittgenstein 1953: 50]

6.1 Introduction

As the title suggests the talk in this chapter is about context; more specifically, the aim is to present my understanding of what is involved in *speaking with reference to context*; we are enquiring into the relation of text and context, as seen from the viewpoint of systemic functional linguistics (henceforth SFL).[1] That the characterization of this relation is not a new problem is obvious from the fact that ever since Malinowski (1923) first introduced the topic some 75 years ago, linguists too numerous to name here have turned repeatedly to reflect on it. That the problem is complex is evident from the fact that while conceptions of context have developed considerably over this period (for some accounts, see Martin 1992; Hasan 1995; Lecki-Tarry 1995), at least some fundamental issues still remain unresolved. So not only does the conceptualization of the category of context prove descriptively inadequate when it confronts certain classes of data (see Section 6.2.3), but also the answer to a fundamental question in linguistic theory remains in need of elaboration, namely, given that speaking is done with reference to the contexts of social living, what if anything does this signify for the relations of language and culture? Failing to maintain a sustained focus on this question, we have failed also to appreciate that its exploration has the power to define the very nature of the linguistic enterprise by identifying the nature of its object of study, i.e., how should 'the science of human language' conceptualize language? Is language simply an invariable set of rules written into the human DNA? Is it just a cultural product with no basis in the cultural history of the species? Addressing these questions seriously, we might have succeeded in abandoning the age old polarization between the biological and the cultural; we might have instead adopted a view put forward by Vygotsky (1978) according to which there is no *conflict* between the biogenetic and the sociogenetic: the sign system of language, rooted in human biological affordances, grows only by cultural intervention. This postulate permits the claim that language is an inherently variable meaning potential (Halliday 1978) which varies with variation in its speakers' material and social conditions of living. The exploration of context along these assumptions would have developed the explanatory reach of the concept; instead, what has happened is that context has become more or less an a-theoretical appendage which functions as a 'disambiguator' of ambiguous sentences – a trouble shooter for inadequate theories of language.

On reflection, none of this should appear surprising. In fact the developmental trajectory of the concept of context proves the truth of the adage that the point of departure is never irrelevant to the point of arrival. From the very beginning of the development of ideas about the relations of context and text, two claims have been universally assumed: first, that appropriate speech is speech suited to the social context in which the speaker finds himself, and second, that the impetus for speaking does not originate in the knowledge of language whether it is seen as practical knowledge gained in LANGUAGING with others or as innate knowledge that consists in naturally knowing that language has such and such rules and regularities. In citing these assumptions I am not implying there is no truth in them, though with hindsight I would reject the belief that these are the only relevant or even most important considerations when it comes to reflections on the relations of text and context. Nor does it seem fanciful to suggest that at least some of the unresolved issues have remained with us because we have tended to take these truisms as our point of departure, allowing them to steer the enquiry in particular directions. For example, if we begin with the assumption that speaking is simply fashioned to suit some given social context, then it does not seem unreasonable to suppose that *context must come before text*; and by the same token, language is powerless to create contexts for speaking. If to this piece of 'reasoning' we add also an unquestioning belief that the innate knowledge of the 'rules' of language is prior to its practical knowledge, implying that you need to have the essence of language before you can use it in practice, then the deterministic perspectives typically adopted on the relations of context and text becomes easy to understand. What is implied is a unidirectional logic: the innate rules of the grammar of language are taken to be in the brain as a prior condition for languaging, and languaging is in its turn treated as a prior condition for the emergence of the practical knowledge of language in the speaker; 'performance' naturally presupposes the existence of natural competence; the reverse cannot be true. In terms of Marková (1990), the 'reasoning' here is MONOLOGIC: in this narrative, context is *always already there* even before any speaking has been done. These intellectual stances create gaps between context, language and speaking, and the only resource our unquestioning assumptions have provided for coping with the situation is the principle of a monological determinism, according to which context of situation 'determines' the meanings you might mean, while the system of language 'determines' the wordings for expressing the meanings which are already 'dictated' by context. Speaking is thus in a double bind: its meanings are bound by an already existing context, and the expression of those meanings is bound by the already existing system of language with its pre-existing rules. Meanwhile continued adherence to this 'reasoning' has turned context and language into the mundane and the mysterious: context resurfaces in linguistics as a material backdrop for performance, leaving its own origins shrouded in mystery, while language resurfaces as a mental organ, the issue of whose evolutionary impetus remains equally mysterious.

It is important to emphasize that, despite the critical overtones of the above comments, there is enough truth in the truisms as well as in the arguments derived from them to make their simple outright rejection problematic. The fact that the assumptions are not outright false explains their hold: it explains why even today with very few exceptions ideas about the relations of context and text continue to be largely 'deterministic', thus stunting the growth of the concept. The persistence of this perspective does not mean that our predecessors foolishly failed to recognize the power of language to create context; quite the contrary, the theme is as old as the debate on context itself. For example, in developing his seminal ideas about the relevance of context to text, Malinowski (1935: 52ff.) very clearly identified 'two peaks of … [the] pragmatic power of words'. One of these peaks was to be found in the role of language as an instrument in carrying out some 'concerted human activity' and the other in its role 'as potentially creative of acts', such as the sacred language in magic, religion, law, etc. around which evolve a large number of social activities.[2] And Malinowski was by no means alone in drawing attention to both aspects of the relations of context and language: other scholars such as Firth (1957) and Halliday (1974b, 1975a, 1975b, 1978) have reiterated these views; I myself have echoed the theme from time to time (Hasan 1981, 1984a, 1984b, 1984c). In fact it is not difficult to find both the determinative and creative perspectives within one and the same piece of work, not reconciled in a dialectic mode but co-existing almost unaware of each other. The *emphasis* has, however, continued to remain on the role of context as the determinant of texts and this is so even where the professed aim is to abandon it in favour of a more 'flexible' view. Examined impartially, most SFL literature would bear out the truth of this generalization.[3] In recent years, fuelled by the postmodernist faith in the efficacy of actual practice as the most important explanatory principle, critics of the determinative perspective have suggested a shift of the analytical focus: it is recommended that instead of focusing on text, which according to them is a 'rule-governed product', the analytic eye should turn toward the rule-defying serendipity of real process located in real time carried out by real individuals (e.g., Martin 1985a, etc.). This shift in focus, it is argued, would constitute a DYNAMIC PERSPECTIVE; taking as its object of analysis the particularities of a unique occurrence/process, the dynamic perspective is said to be capable of revealing the role of individual desires and decisions in contributing to the uniqueness of the *praxis* which unique social subjects engage in; actual process is thus raised above system.

Whatever the merits of this recommended focus (Hasan 1995, 1999a), employed by itself, it too would suffer from limitations: its MONOLOGICAL character will allow it to tell a story even more partial than that told by a synoptic analysis.[4] I say this because in the current conception of the dynamic perspective which has become popular in SFL during the last decade (Martin 1985a, 1992; Ventola 1987), the relations of a unique instance and a non-unique system remain entirely unclear, not to say incoherent; and this remains true despite recent attempts at justification (e.g., in Martin 1997). It seems reasonable to conclude then that escape from one set of truisms into another is no recipe for producing a more efficacious solution to the problem of creating a better description: what the situation calls for is a move out of the monological perspective into a dialogical one; instead of privileging either the system or the process as temporally and/ or logically prior to the other, a better solution is to investigate *how the two perspectives cooperate* in a CO-GENETIC LOGIC (Marková 1990; see also Marková and Fopper 1991): it has to be a cooperation that makes intelligible the uniqueness of process by relating it to the general regularities of a shared system, familiar to some speech fellowships, while foregrounding

Figure 6.1: Realization and instantiation as dialectical relations [Adapted from Halliday 1999: 8]

<pre>
                              instantiation
          SYSTEM ——————————————————————————————— INSTANCE

                    context of   context of
CONTEXT   culture   situation
    | (situation
    | (cultural   type)
 realization   domain)
    |
    | (register)   (text type)
    | language as   language as
LANGUAGE   system   text
</pre>

Note: Culture instantiated in situation, as system instantiated in text.

Culture realized in/construed by language: same relation as that holding between linguistic strata (semantics: lexicogrammar: phonology: phonetics).

Cultural domain and register are 'sub-systems': likeness viewed from 'system' end.

Situation type and text type are 'instance types': likeness viewed from 'instance' end.

also the system's ability to appropriate innovation and change as these arrive in the form of innumerable unique acts of meaning by innumerable social beings engaged in the interactive living of life.

Over the last two decades Halliday's SFL has moved steadily towards the dialogical perspective: what this means with reference to the relations of text and context, language and culture, is that each has begun to be seen as active in the definition and development of the other. I have argued elsewhere (Hasan 1995) that the critical step in this enterprise was the rethinking of REALIZATION and INSTANTIATION as bidirectional relations rather than as unidirectional ones.[5] In principle, the postulate of bi-directionality invokes a dialectic which, on the one hand, engages the notion of context and language as a meaning potential, and, on the other, the system and instance of culture and language, as represented in Figure 6.1 borrowed from Halliday:[6] it is this dialectic that distinguishes current SFL views of realization and instantiation from Hjelmslev's EXPRESSION/REALIZATION (1961) or Firth's (1957) EXPONENCE.

Thus, for example, if in speaking,[7] the speaker's perception of context ACTIVATES the speaker's choice of meanings,[8] then also the meanings meant in speaking contribute to the CONSTRUAL of contexts; and the same relation of activation and construal holds, *mutatis mutandis,* between meaning and lexicogrammar. The working of realization as a dialogical principle, i.e., as a dialectic, limits the scope of the operation of arbitrariness in language. The significance of this observation is that arguably arbitrariness is the other face of a determinative MONOLOGICAL relation across strata. I am aware that in this age of 'post-everything' much has been made of *l'arbitraire du signe* by respected masters in many social fields. However, there is reason to believe that the interpretation of the Saussurean principle has in fact been based on partial readings by partial readers (Hasan 1987a, 1999a) as implied in Thibault (1997): arbitrariness in language is far less pervasive than current academic fashions would suggest. For example, it is only a certain class of phonological pattern, namely, the segmental ones such as the syllable, that relates uni-directionally and arbitrarily to linguistic form.[9] By contrast, the categories of context, meaning and lexicogrammar are related realizationally, not arbitrarily: a contextual category, unlike sens-ible items in the material situation, acquires part of its identity by its semantic construal just as a linguistic meaning exists by virtue of its activation by context *and* its construal by some lexicogrammatical form. This is not to deny that the categories of linguistic meaning do bear a necessary relation to the categories of speakers' subjective experience. *Subjective experience is a necessary, but not sufficient condition for* SIGNIFYING *some linguistic meaning.*

The move towards a dialogical orientation has proved profitable for the SFL model: this has opened up the possibility of providing a more powerful account of the relations of context and text, culture and language (Halliday 1999; Hasan 1995); and it has also provided a sound basis for the much needed clarification of the role of text production in fashioning the system of language as it is, a functional system that simultaneously displays stability and variation, flourishes on the seeming contradictions inherent in the co-presence of HOMOGLOSSIA and HETEROGLOSSIA, and is as cognizant of communally accepted regularities as it is permissive of individual liberties. The limitations and determinism we ascribe to the system are not so much *in* the system as they are ingredients of our own modes of analysis.[10] Thanks to its dialogical perspective SFL is today better able to locate human language as an element in what Lemke (1984, 1993) refers to as *a dynamic open system.* However, SFL's adoption of a dialogical perspective does not mean that all descriptive categories have already been re-thought in light of that theoretical move: the processes of the development of a theory, much like the process of speaking, are full of unexpected turns, twists and even internal inconsistencies. In asking what *speaking with reference to context* means I will be exploring some categories that are specifically relevant to the relations of text and context in a dialogical perspective. This, as the introductory comments have suggested, will involve making the assumptions briefly stated below:

- that in order to describe its nature, human language needs to be placed in its social environment; that this environment, call it context, must be taken as referring to an integral part of linguistic theory;
- that the linguistic theory is stratal, consisting of four strata: context, semantics, lexicogrammar and phonology (which subsumes phonetics). These represent four distinct orders of abstraction, which are both necessary and sufficient for a satisfactory description of language;
- that the first three strata in the linguistic theory, namely, context, semantics, and lexicograrnmar, are realizationally related; by contrast, the relation of phonology to the other strata is in part expressive and in part realizational;[11]
- that language and text – system and process – are related by instantiation (Halliday 1992a, 1992b, 1996; Hasan 1996a) just as the context of culture and situation are (c.f., Figure 6.1); that, therefore, the critical relation between language and context can be expressed in terms of two proportionalities: (1) from the point of view of instantiation, situation is to culture as text is to language; that is to say, the first term of each proportion instantiates the second:

  situation: culture:: text: language

- and (2) from the perspective of realization, language is to culture as text is to situation; that is to say, the first term of each proportion presented below realizes the second:

  language: culture:: text: language.

So identified, my focus is on the second term of the last proportion displayed above, i.e., the realizational relations of context and text in a dialogical modelling that takes the other three terms of the proportions as essential to the argument. I shall continue to use the term *context* to refer to *context of situation;* the term (*context of*) *culture* will be used to refer to *context of culture* when needed.

6.2 Context making text

In this section I will first present three cases of speaking, followed by an informal commentary on each, which will furnish an occasion for making observations and raising questions that are relevant to the discussion in hand. Using the currently *prevalent* SFL model of context description, I will specify the relevant context for each of these cases of speaking

(Sections 6.2.1–6.2.3). My aim here is to highlight step by step a shortcoming in the prevalent descriptions of context in SFL: (a) the descriptions are based on an assumption of CONTEXTUAL CONSTANCY across a given text: this, for example, is the assumption that underlies Halliday and Hasan's (1976: 23) statement that a text is 'a passage of discourse which is coherent ... with respect to the context of situation, and therefore consistent in register.' While the claim of contextual/registerial constancy is empirically validated in the majority of cases, it is apparently not universally true: cases are found where the integrity of a text survives certain kinds of contextual/ registerial changes (c.f., Example C, in Section 6.2.3). (b) This being the case, the question arises: what would one mean by 'coherent with respect to the context of situation' in the latter type of cases? Current SFL models possess no satisfactory means of answering this question or of specifying the nature and character of those contextual and/or registerial changes which do not disturb the contextual unity of the text, nor can they specify *where* i.e., in what kind(s) of discursive situation, such changes are most at risk. (c) By the same token, the systemic accounts of context fail to provide the formal means for indicating the potential for such changes; and finally (d) current contextual descriptions fail to indicate the essential unity of the social process which lies at the heart of the notion of context, tending to treat each component of context as if it were a *thing in itself.* In order to overcome these shortcomings, in Section 3 of this chapter I shall attempt to follow an alternative path for the development of contextualizing descriptions, while subscribing to the general delineation of context as presented in Halliday *et al.* (1964). This will involve departing from certain assumptions so far never questioned in SFL. First then, the examples of speaking:

Example A:[12]

Emile Durkheim: Selected Writings
Edited with an introduction and notes by
ANTHONY GIDDENS
University Lecturer in Sociology and Fellow of King's College, Cambridge

Durkheim's writings have exerted a profound influence in modern sociology. Many of his ideas have been incorporated into the conventional wisdom of the subject; others have remained controversial, and are a matter of continuing debate. The reception of Durkheim's views in the English-speaking world, however, has suffered from the inadequacy of certain of the existing translations and, while most of his major studies are now available in English, a considerable number of his writings – particularly his shorter articles and reviews – have still not appeared in translation.

This is the first collection of Durkheim's writings to draw upon the total corpus of his work. All the texts included in the book have been newly translated, about a quarter of them for the first time. This selection thus offers a comprehensive survey of Durkheim's contribution to sociology and social philosophy. The book is organized in terms of the substantive themes in Durkheim's writings, rather than following the chronology of his intellectual development; but since it contains selections from every phase of his intellectual career, giving the date of their first publication, the interested reader can easily trace the evolution of his thought.

Mr. Giddens' Introduction identifies the leading themes in Durkheim's work, and offers a critique of previous interpretations of his theoretical standpoint.

Example B: [Text 1: Post office][13]

01 Server: yes please (CUSTOMER STEPS FORWARD)
02 Customer: can I have these two like that? (HANDS OVER TWO LETTERS)
03 Server: yes (... SERVER WEIGHS ONE LETTER)
04   one's forty-five (... SERVER WEIGHS THE OTHER LETTER)
05   one's twenty-five
06 Customer: and have you got.. the.. first day covers of..
07 Server: yes
08 Customer: [? Anzac] ..
09 Server: how many would you like?
10 Customer: four please
11 Server: two of each?
12 Customer: what have you got?
13 Server: uh there's two different designs on the – (... SERVER SHOWS CUSTOMERS THE COVERS)
14 Customer: I'll take two of each
15 Server: uhum (... SERVER GETS THE STAMPS FOR THE LETTERS AND THE COVERS)
16   right, that's a dollar seventy thank you
17   (SERVER PUTS THE COVERS INTO A BAG; CUSTOMER GETS THE MONEY)
18   here we are
19   (... SERVER HANDS OVER THE STAMPS AND THE COVERS; CUSTOMER HANDS THE MONEY TO THE SERVER)
20 Customer: *thank you*
21 Server: *thank you*
22   (SERVER GETS THE CHANGE)
23   dollar seventy that's two four and one's five *thank you* very much
24 Customer: *thank you* (... CUSTOMER REACHES FOR THE LETTERS)
25 Server: they'll be right I'll fix those up in a moment
26 Customer: okay (CUSTOMER LEAVES)

Example C: [extract from a dialogue][14]

01	Mother:	now Stephen, do you want a sandwich for lunch?
02	Stephen:	yes
03		and some passionfruit
04	Mother:	and some passionfruit
05		where is the passionfruit?
06	Stephen:	um .. Um the passionfruit is um .. Um [?]
07		do you know where the passionfruit is?
08	Mother:	no
09		you were walking around with it
10		what did you do with it?
11	Stephen:	I don't remember
12	Mother:	is it on the table?
13	Stephen:	let me see .. It is under the table
14	Mother:	under the table!
15	Stephen:	yes ..
16		here it is
17	Mother:	ok .. right .. peanut butter sandwich?
18	Stephen:	yeah ..
19	Mother:	you go to the table
20		and I'll bring it in ..
21		there aren't many passionfruits out there at the moment
22	Stephen:	why?
23	Mother:	because .. passion fruit usually come
24		when its warm
25		here, you sit here in Nana's seat
26	Stephen:	why –*
27	Mother:	*I'll put –
28	Stephen:	why does Nana like to sit here?
29	Mother:	I'll put –
30		oh it's easy for her to get up
31		if she's sitting there ...
32		we have to go to Chatswood this afternoon Stephen
33	Stephen:	why?
34	Mother:	um .. to .. Peter has to have injections ..
35		[?]
36	Mother:	and we might – if we've got time
37		we might go to the library
38		to see if we can get a book on goldfish
39	Stephen:	why?
40	Mother:	Richard wants to know about how to keep goldfish ...
41		ah I have to ring up that lady about the music class, don't I?
42	Stephen:	what music classes?
43	Mother:	um the music classes that Daniel goes to

44 Stephen: oh .. you mean the um the dancing class .. Mummy
45 Mother: yes
46   I'll see if she's got room for you .. in the class, will I?
47 Stephen: Mm
48 Mother: ok .. what would you like to drink, Stephen?
49 Stephen: um orange juice ..
50   and I want some vitamin C
51   I want one –
52   I want*
53 Mother: *you can have one tonight, darling!
54 Stephen: why? (WHINGEING)
55 Mother: well, they're very big tablet, sweetie
56   very big tablets
57   five hundred milligrams there are in those
58   that's twice as much as any other tablets ..
59   so you really had two tablets this morning ..

6.2.1   Context and text: Example A

I came across A as a blurb on the back cover of the book entitled *Emile Durkheim: Selected Writings*. It is the kind of place where, as a buyer somewhat undecided about the purchase of the book, I might have turned for information on its orientation and content. Given the practices of the publishing industry, it is highly likely that the blurb was produced at least in consultation with Giddens himself; but if not, it would certainly have been okayed by him. In any event, it is not the specific identity of the 'speaker' of this written text that is critical; what is more important is the fact that the interests of the author and the publisher coincide in producing information which presents the publication as attractive: the voice of the composer is the voice of collaboration between the intellectual and the economic. It is also certain that in composing the blurb, the writer could not have been thinking of any particular person as the intended reader except in the capacity of a prototype: the intended addressee of this text is an imaginary being. He is the anonymous prospective buyer, whose face is refracted through the author's text as an educated adult with a serious (i.e., near-professional rather than dilettante) interest in sociology. This is borne out by the fact that the positive evaluation of the information presented to attract buyers depends on the buyer's (desire for) familiarity with the field of sociology. The producer of this text would have been aware also that such intended addressees will come in contact with the text through writing (what I have referred to technically in Hasan (1985b: 58) as the *graphic channel*) encountering it as the product of an already completed process. The addressee's absence from the scene of the text's production naturally implies that he would be unable to share in the process of text production: thus, the use of strategies such as *probe, repair* and *realign* (c.f., Hasan 1985b: 66), in fact the possibility of any *immediate* response, would be unavailable. Here it is essentially the writer's privilege to decide what information and from what perspective, the reader needs to know, though this privilege is constrained by the writer's need to capture and enlist the reader's interest. The social relationship of the speaker and addressee is thus balanced as peers. It is notable also that on the basis of the language of this blurb, no reader of Text *A* would be able to judge whether or not the original composition of the text was interrupted at any point, and if so, how often, on what ground and at what 'stage' in the production. The text's seamless appearance suggests that *if* there were such interruptions, then at each resumption, the writer's sense of the social activity he was engaged in and his sense of the addressee he was addressing had remained the same as when the interruption(s) occurred. In other words, the writer's perception of the context relevant to his composition did not undergo any registerially significant change during the process of production. The text bears no proof of emendations which, judging by common experience, are very likely to have been made, nor does it carry any indication of the specific location or time of its original composition. Much of what I would call the text's *material situational setting* (Hasan 1973c, 1981) is destined to remain unknown to the addressee of this blurb.

The above comments on text *A* are one reader's 'reading' of that text's relevant context as inferred from the text itself, but it is highly probable that the reading would be shared by a good number of other persons in the community. What does it take to make this kind of reading? and on what basis is it performed? It is a commonplace of discourse analysis that the ability to read a text in this way implies familiarity with the functioning of the text types in the reader's culture. The LINGUISTIC HABITUS for such interpretation shapes itself through the processes of communal living which is saturated with speaking. And it is very likely that as a social subject the RECOGNITION RULES for interactional practices (Bernstein 1990) become a part of one's being considerably earlier than do those REALIZATION RULES (*ibid*.) which enable 'appropriate' discursive performance. In fact, for certain text types, the realization rules may never reach that stage of felicity where they are able to translate themselves into an actual text. This, as scholars of literacy have testified, is very often the case when speaking concerns the SPECIALIZED not the QUOTIDIAN sphere of social activity.[15] To sum up then, those who can provide this kind of reading of the context from text *A* are persons familiar with the family of this text type as its purveyors or/and its consumers and the basis on which they are able to do this reading resides: (a) in their practical experience of speaking with reference to such contexts; and (b) in the language of the text itself. As Bernstein (1971) could have put it, the language of a text encapsulates its own context, though to be sure the quality of this encapsulation varies across texts as the discussion of Examples *B* and *C* will show. One important factor relevant to this variation is how much is shared between the speaker and the addressee: the greater the reliance on the shared *material situational setting* (Hasan 1973c, 1981; Cloran 1994, 1999a), the less, and the less explicitly, will the language of the text encapsulate its context (see Section 6.2.2 for some examples). Variable though the degree of context encapsulation is, *complete* inability to construe anything at all from the language of a naturally occurring text would normally be an indication that the speaker and/or the reader of the text suffer from some variety of language disorder. But of course what makes an enormous contribution to the reader's ability to go beyond the text in making contextual inferences, is the quality of the reader's own experience of participation in the processes of text production, the embodiment of the cultural ways of being particularly by speaking and being spoken to. If I am a reader of books, if I have an interest in sociology and/or allied areas, if as an author or a publisher's editor I have monitored such compositions of this kind, then I will read the context from *A* in a way that is likely to be qualitatively different from the reading made by those who do not have such experience.[16] With practical involvement in this variety of speaking, one would have an idea rooted in experience about what information might be foregrounded and why; and one would have a fairly good understanding of the extent to which the activity of producing such a blurb might be responsive to the writer's image of his virtual addressee, i.e., the prototypic reader/buyer. One's own experience of producing such texts might lead to the recognition that, behind its seamless facade, the blurb on Giddens' book is very likely to be the product of several tries at speaking.

This brings us to an interesting question: are those trial runs whose existence and nature will never be revealed to anyone purely on the basis of contact with the text significant to an understanding of the relations of text and context? If so, in what way? The real issue in general terms is as follows: experience of making sense of texts tells us that some of the situational details are invariably encapsulated with varying degrees of explicitness in the language of the text,[17] others, such as the trial runs and interruptions, might do so only under certain circumstances (see the discussion of *B* and *C* in 2.2 and 2.3; for the discussion of one relevant parameter, see Halliday 1985a), while information about many other situational features such as the specific time or place of textual composition, the body posture of participants, their general appearance and so on may be encapsulated in the text's language even more rarely if at all. The question is whether we need to treat all these sets of situational details alike in describing the relations of text and context. If so, our description of context runs the danger of being as unmanageable as 'transcribing infinity' in the words of Cook (1990); if we decide to be selective, then the question arises: on what basis can we justify the inclusion of all such details? More important still: would we really know what the expression 'all such details' refers to? How do we conclude that enough has been said about some specific context of situation? If to make context an effective tool for text analysis, it has to be 'contained' in some respects, then we need to be clear what aspects of the interactants' material and social conditions of existence are integral to the concept and why? (see also Levinson 1992).

This dilemma about what should be taken as the content of the category of context and why, has been with us ever since the introduction of the concept (for discussion, Hasan 1995). Firth (1957, 1964) criticized Malinowski for taking context as 'an ordered series of events considered as in *rebus*' (Firth 1957: 182); Halliday (1964) modified Firth's construct and was the first to indicate the grounds for his choice; others, such as Gregory or Hasan have attempted to modify Halliday's constructs.[18] But there still remains room for discussion and I shall return to this problem below (Section 6.3). I adopt the SFL view of relevant context as a construct with three variables:

- FIELD OF DISCOURSE (the nature of social activity relevant to speaking),
- TENOR OF DISCOURSE (the nature of social relation relevant to speaking), *and*
- MODE OF DISCOURSE (the nature of contact for the conduct of speaking).

I have referred to this tripartite structure as the CONTEXUAL CONSTRUCT (Hasan 1978, 1981, 1985b, etc.) and to the totality of its detailed features, i.e., the specific configuration of the values of field, tenor and mode relevant to any particular instance of speaking, as the CONTEXTUAL CONFIGURATION (=CC): the CC is thus an instantiation of (some category of) the contextual construct. Since language in use realizes some given CC, any variation in CC will naturally activate some variation in the language used; it is this kind of variation that in SFL we refer to as REGISTER VARIATION. According to the

Table 6.1: Reading context from text A

FIELD OF DISCOURSE:
>   promoting a sociological publication: giving overview of content: foregrounding distinctive qualities...

TENOR OF DISCOURSE:
>   *agentive relation*: promoter addressing prospective buyer: virtual addressee imagined prototype: adult; educated; interested in social questions ...
>   *social relation*: institutionalised; peer: promoter dependent on buyer's goodwill, buyer dependent on promoter's service...
>   *social distance*: near maximal...

MODE OF DISCOURSE:
>   *role of language*: constitutive...
>   *channel*: graphic; no visual contact; monologic: no process sharing...
>   *medium*: written...

SFL modelling of the relations of context and text, which approximates Halliday's framework, each specific instance of language in use, would be seen as a text that realizes one CC and in so doing, also instantiates some diatypic variety (Gregory 1967), i.e., some specific category of register.

The contextual configuration (CC) relevant to Text *A* is presented in Table 6.1. The description itself is modelled on Halliday and Hasan (1985).[19] According to SFL, descriptions at any level of language can vary in detail of focus: the specification of a CC is in principle no different in this respect; it too can be always extended in delicacy. The dots in Table 6.1 indicate this open-ended-ness of the description of Text *A*'s contextual configuration as presented here.

6.2.1.1   The field, tenor and mode values of text A

As the foregoing discussion of Text *A* suggests the contextual configuration presented in the table is relevant to the entirety of that particular process of speaking which we have encountered as Text *A*. The text is thus a paradigm instance of 'a passage of discourse which is coherent ... with respect to the context of situation, and therefore consistent in register' (c.f., Halliday and Hasan 1976: 23) exemplifying what I will from now on refer to as the principle of CONTEXTUAL/REGISTERIAL CONSISTENCY in text production. It is a principle that is highly likely to apply where the channel of communication is graphic, i.e., where the addressee's contact with the text is in writing, as in the present case. However, this generalization is neither invariable nor is it exclusively applicable to contexts with graphic channel alone,[20] as will become obvious from the discussion of Text *B* (see Section 2.2). In the following two subsections, I review the implications of some of the specific terms used in the description of the CC of Text *A*.

6.2.1.2   *The social process of speaking: goals, outcomes and designs*

Turning first to the parameter of field in Table 1, consider the description 'promoting a sociological publication'. A view could be taken that, strictly speaking, promotion is the *goal* of the social activity; the actual activity itself is simply that of informing. The goal of promoting should therefore be recognized as separate from the act of informing. But to accept this view would be to assume that informing can be done without any underlying principle for selecting and organizing information, which is hardly credible. From this point of view it would seem that goal or motivation must be regarded as an inherent aspect of human social action, and as such an important component of a text's relevant context. This view has been tacitly accepted in SFL, both in Martin's CONNOTATIVE SEMIOTIC MODEL boasting a dynamic perspective and in Halliday's variation based model, though the treatment of goal is somewhat different in the two (compare, for example, the use of the term *goal* in Hasan 1985b and in Martin 1985a). This claim about the relevance of the notion of goal seems to be relatively simple and obvious but its simplicity is deceptive: as a concept, goal/motivation in social action is riddled with problems, which despite the long tradition of philosophical discussion, have remained unresolved. So it is, clearly, not a matter that can be pursued here in much detail; however it will be useful to highlight some of the most crucial considerations, which a competent description of context cannot afford to ignore.

In the first place, it is notable that social agents' awareness of the goal/ motive of their action is variable: agents are more overtly conscious of goals in certain types of activity than in others. As a rule, this awareness is at its lowest when the activity is RELATION BASED, and at its highest when the activity is ACTION BASED.[21] Thus, agents are typically well aware of the goal of their activity when engaged in such actions as, say, buying stamps or getting lunch for someone than they are when having a chat with the neighbour or building a Lego model with a child. There is thus a cline of goal awareness, the two endpoints of which range from VISIBLE to INVISIBLE GOAL. Visible goals tend to be SHORT TERM: they are achieved (or not) typically within one interaction; by contrast, invisible goals tend to be LONG TERM: their achievement occurs, if it does, over a series of interactions bearing some logical relation to each other. However, the two sets of terms are not always paired or synonymous: they refer to different aspects of an activity, and their conjunction is not pre-determined but simply a tendency, otherwise only one pair of features would be needed. For example, by contrast with chatting to a friend on the phone, a short term activity, with invisible goal, the buying of a car or a house is a long term social activity with a visible goal. Reflection suggests that the goal of social activities might also differ in its complexity: in some activities there may be 'an array of goals', in others just a simple one. For example consider again the social activity of buying postal goods: its goal is typically simple as stated in the name of the act itself, which contrasts with the social activity of telling a joke, where the joke teller may have the goal of just 'going along' with other members of the group who are swapping jokes, and/or of amusing his company, and/or showing off his verbal proficiency, and so on.

As practised social actors with rich experience of engaging in social activities, we would have no difficulty in granting the truth of the above observations, which throws doubt on the easy use of the unanalysed concept of goal as a descriptive tool in discourse/genre analysis. Take, for example, the notion of invisible goal. If it is true that social agents are not *always* aware of the goal of their activity, this poses some serious problems: throughout the long history of this concept, it has been taken for granted that goals/motives are conscious mental states even though side by side there have existed such familiar expressions as 'hidden motive', or 'covert goal'. To attribute an invisible goal to some activity of a social agent's is to ascribe him a conscious mental state of which he is not conscious, and that is patently self-contradictory, unless we change the meaning of the word 'goal' by fiat! A possible solution is to claim that there exist some goal-less social activities in which subjects engage without any purpose whatever. But this again seems far from satisfactory especially if the goal of the activity is what determines its staging or structural shape (as in the so-called dynamic perspective): after all a friendly chat, a casual conversation are social activities with maximally invisible goals unless somewhat speciously the goal is taken to be to chat, to converse. If the speaker's goal/purpose is what really organizes (the shape of) his sayings, i.e., its genre, then it is remarkable that there is such a thing as 'conversational structure' or 'conversational logic'; certainly ordinary conversations are far from being incoherent or disorganized, and this organization goes beyond the mere creation of a series of what is known as EXCHANGE STRUCTURES. An additional problem with goal is that to have a goal is not necessarily to achieve it: one may start off with the goal of persuading, but end up with a quarrel on one's hands.

This brings us to a notion closely allied to that of goal, viz., OUTCOME. From the interactants' point of view, outcome is to goal as the present is to the future. Unlike goal, outcome is not a subjective phenomenon: rather, it is an emergent, discursive 'fact', so it is inherently objective. Irrespective of whether and to what extent the social subject is aware of the fact, every social activity has some outcome(s), not excepting even those which might have been prematurely terminated: social action always produces something, though *this something need not be the same as the goal with which the subject started.* It seems to me that the discussion of goal as a necessary feature of a text's context has most probably been subject to some confusion: what has been actually described as the goal of a social activity is in fact nothing else than what we have perceived or assumed to be the *outcome* as indicated by the text that is produced in the context of that social activity. In other words, our analysis of goals and social activities has always been *post hoc,* and based mostly on our reading of the text: as analysts, we have never been innocent of a text's outcome. *Irrespective of whether as analysts we claim to employ a dynamic perspective or a synoptic one, what we analyse is not text-in-process*; it is, by necessity, a text whose process is already a past event, and typically its outcome is easy to perceive or infer, the inference being semiotically engendered. One might be tempted to treat this as a reason for replacing the notion of goal by that of outcome as perhaps a more viable descriptive tool than goal. But outcome under any name is not a very satisfactory tool for analysis: for one thing, it is logically unknowable until the process of the text's production is well under weigh or terminated; and, besides, it makes no concession at all to the interactants' sense of the nature of their social activity, i.e., what they think of themselves as being engaged in achieving. What we need is a concept that is open to both the subjective intentionality typically associated with goal and the objective distancing implied in the outcome, allowing us to invoke either member of the pair as and when needed without taking either member as the critical basis for describing its register/genre.

I suggest such a concept may be DESIGN. *Design is not an expression of field alone*: it is associated with the social process as a whole (i.e., as a contextual configuration of the values pertaining to field, tenor and mode), and is independent of any one individual's desires, intentions and/or decisions, having been negotiated between at least two interactants. These designs have come about because through the long history of the communal living of life, in every culture there have evolved recognizable ways of being, doing and saying communally deemed relevant to those occasions where social subjects have co-acted. *The design of a social practice is nothing other than a near ritualization of ways of doing something with other(s) by using such semiotic systems as are at the community's disposal*: the more culturally significant a social process, the more ritualized it gets (Hasan 1981, 1994; further discussion, Section 6.3 below). It is in this sense that specific social processes have 'become' the *raison d'être* of specific designs. And all things being equal, interactants will choose to engage in a social process whose inherent design promises to best satisfy their own desires/intentions, their own sense of what they are attempting to do in their interactions with others. The verbal behaviour of social agents suggests that during their engagement in a social process, interactants tend to monitor it from the perspective of its efficacy in the actualization of their goal(s) and purpose(s), hence we come across corrections, clarifications, and debates on the use of some different strategy when those so far employed have failed. This monitoring is clearly important since the speaker's goals/motives would remain unknown to others unless they are embedded within the design of a social process. If 'an intention is embedded in its situation, in human customs and institutions' as Wittgenstein (1953: 337) claimed, this is because any other objective mode of the intention's existence is not available; the design of a social process as a whole is taken as an enunciation of the interactants' (intended) goal. As acculturated persons, speakers have (varying degrees of) awareness of the design of a social process and its relation to whatever they perceive as their own desires/motives: they know also how the process should begin, how it should end and what may or may not come in between the two ends under what circumstances if the design of the social process and their own intention are to be calibrated. So one way of paraphrasing *engagement in social process* is to say that it is a *continuous struggle on the part of the speaker(s) to calibrate their perceived goals with the perceived design of the social process so that the outcome matches the goal*, with the implication that interactants must also have a pretty good idea of when the social process they are engaged in is being suspended, diverted, jeopardized or abandoned before the completion of its design. A full understanding of the outcome of the social processes we engage in is perhaps even more rare a phenomenon than the full awareness of why we engage in certain types of these social processes.

6.2.1.3 *The social process of speaking: social relation and modes of contact*

Turn now to the parameters of tenor and mode. The channel of discourse relevant to Text *A* is graphic, i.e., the text producer's languaging is accessed via graphological representations. Typically such texts are (meant to be) received in displacement from the location of their production. And, again, typically they may be accessed not only by the intended addressee but by whoever has physical access to it and the desire and power to actually use it. But the relation of these different categories of 'readers' to the text is never the same, and it is useful to make a distinction between the technical term *addressee* and everyday words such as *listener/hearer*. The most significant difference is that *the addressee is built into the text as a prosody of the text's meaning and structure*: that is to say, what meanings will be at risk and how the social process will be conducted is responsive to the speaker's relation to the addressee. No such relation exists between the speaker and the (merely casual) listener/hearer: the latter lack *textual recognition*. As implied above, when the channel is graphic, the addressee is typically not co-present with the producer of the text, as is the case with Text *A*. But the context of Text *A* possesses another feature, which does not logically inhere in the graphic channel: the addressee of this text is not simply absent from the moment of production, but he is also an imaginary being, corresponding to the text producer's idea of the type of person who might be interested in purchasing the publication in question and therefore perhaps in reading it. Let me refer to an imaginary addressee of this kind drawn in the image of some prototype as a VIRTUAL ADDRESSEE: in addressing such an addressee, a speaker speaks to a stereotype, a socially defined category. This contrasts with other addressees who, though they might be materially absent from the scene of the text's production, are in fact ACTUAL ADDRESSEES of whom one has some actual experience, such as one's friend or one's lawyer/employer being spoken to in writing. This distinction is textually significant: where the addressee is virtual, all aspects of the interactant relation such as their respective status, their social distance, the specific attributes of such an addressee are *created* entirely by the language of the text; for obvious reasons none has a material basis. The relations of language to context are here highly complex, and it makes little sense to ask whether it is (a pre-existing) context that is determining the language of the text or whether it is the language itself that is creating (an important part of) the context of discourse relevant to this text: the process and the product become inextricably intertwined. And by the same token, irrespective of the fact that the speaker must have had some sense of the context as he began composing this blurb, for others, including his virtual addressee, the context relevant to the production of Text *A* is unknowable except on the basis of the language of the text; interestingly, in terms of the dynamic perspective as defined by Martin, the text here is a so-called static product, encountered objectively after the fact when the text's process has been completed. So it might be claimed that the process of the text is irrelevant to such 'genres' or texts of this type furnish their own process! Does the concept of dynamic perspective apply to their analysis?

Obvious as the point is, it is important to underline its implications. First, if it is true that in arriving at the contextual configuration relevant to Text *A,* its language has played an important part, then this is because *language has the potential for construing context*: this is a principle that applies invariably, irrespective of whether the moment of a text's production and its reception by the addressee are the same or not and whether the addressee is virtual or actual. The construing power of language is equally relevant where both the speaker and the addressee are co-present as they engage in an on-going social process, including unexpected moves, changes and surprises that might suspend, divert, or force the interactants to entirely abandon the social process before the completion of its design associated with that practice. The critical difference between the two is that where the interactants are CO-PRESENT, there *the text's context is construed for both interactants in the very moment of speaking being done*. By contrast in cases where the text is interpreted in displacement, the moment of the construal of the context by language is different for the producer and the receiver, for the speaker and the addressee. Whichever is the case, in an important sense *textual* context is not something that is knowable with certainty, or guessable to any significant extent in the text's absence. The basic reason for this lies in the nature of linguistic meaning: text is a unit of meaning and linguistic meaning is not knowable without the lexico-grammatical resources that construed it. This follows logically from the dialogism of realization.

The second point follows directly from the first: since language has this creative, construing power in relation to context, it seems best to abandon the popular though pejorative term *product* for text, or at least to elide the notion of *stasis* from it: what is text except language in use possessing certain properties such as that of texture and structure? And what is language in use except a process? Whatever is thing-like about a text, i.e. the substance of its expression, is strictly immaterial to its quality of text-ness: a transcribed lecture is no more a product than lecturing itself. The text is the voice of some social process/practice: it is through this voice that a social practice becomes known as the social process it is (Hasan 1978): it follows that analysis in a dynamic perspective too will depend on language in use, i.e., the text. Drawing a firm line between a process and what specifies the recognition criteria of the process, gives rise to an unnecessary complication in the context of semiotic activities.

Third, while the practical experience of speaking is important in inferring a text's context, *it is in fact the text's language that acts as the essential crystallizer of that experience*. As acculturated adults, our discursive and practical experience of social life clearly surpasses particular texts or text types, and not all of this experience is equally relevant to reading a specific text's context. It follows that in interpreting some particular text/context, some discriminating device is central: it is this device that calls to consciousness only those aspects of practical experience which bear directly on that text/context. I suggest that whatever the nature of this device, it must be set in motion by the language of that particular text: whether in its completed form or in its on-going state, it is the text's language that summons up that part of a speaker's experience which has bearing on the reading of that text. If this view is accepted, it provides a principle for resolving, the problem of the 'content' of context raised earlier (see Section 6.2.1). From this perspective *the concept of context must include all those features of the interactants' material and social conditions of existence which are necessary and sufficient for the explication of what is said, whether directly or by implication.*

Finally, it should be noted also that the context with reference to which the writer produced Text *A* would be rather different from the context of the text's reception by a genuine user of the blurb, who could, after all, be an approximation of the virtual addressee: in the ordinary everyday sense of reading, this genuine reader will use Text *A* as a resource for making decisions about whether to invest time and money in acquiring and reading the Giddens volume. And as part of this enterprise it is useful for the genuine reader to be able to 'place' the blurb in its relevant context: is it an advertisement? Does it provide trustworthy information?, and so on. This understanding is important to the genuine reader only in so far as it serves his practical purposes: his interest is neither in theorizing the relations of context and text in general nor in discovering the motivational relevancies underlying Text *A* just out of simple curiosity. Natural texts are not created with analysis in mind: speakers do not speak with reference to context nor do addressees attend to speaker's speech with the aim of enabling an analysis of the relations of text and context. The one who aims to do this is the 'impartial spectator', i.e., the analyst, whom Bourdieu has derided (1990: 31) because he 'seeks to understand for the sake of understanding'. There is thus substantial difference between the genuine speaker's/addressee's practical understanding and that of the analyst's 'purely theoretical relation' (*ibid.*) to the object of analysis. The interactants' practical angle is limited by the specifics of the social process precisely because it concerns only specific subjectivities, specific instance. The analyst aims to go beyond; he wishes to describe elements of the linguistic HABITUS in some section of the community. It is possible to produce a subjective account and it is possible to produce an objective analysis, whether good, bad, or indifferent would depend on the analyst's and evaluator's conception of the task, but to ask for subjective *analysis* is to produce an intellectual oxymoron: analysis demands generalization; the subjective is by definition NOT general.

6.2.2 Context and text: Example B

Example *B* differs from *A* in several obvious ways. One simple difference, though with far reaching consequences, is that while Text *A* belongs to a category where in the nature of things the speaker and addressee will never find each other in the same place at the same time, with Text *B* the interactants must be co-present. With this co-presence comes the possibility of sharing material environment, which implies a qualitative difference in the conduct of speaking at least in three significant ways.

First, the physical actions of each are visible to the other as are many surrounding material objects, whether immediately relevant to the ongoing activity or not: these constitute part of the MATERIAL SITUATIONAL SETTING. It follows that in referring to these phenomena the interactants can rely on this sens-ibly shared information to assist in an understanding of what is going on, a facility that is not available to the analyst *qua* analyst. Consider in this light the interpretation of *these two like that?* (line 2, Text *B*): the density of EXOPHORIC REFERENCE (Halliday and Hasan 1976; Hasan 1984a, 1984d) in this message poses no problem of interpretation to the server, who completely undaunted by it, answers in the affirmative (line 3) and goes on to inform the customer that *one's fortyfive one's twenty five* (lines 4–5) where again the material situation assists correct interpretation. By contrast, without some external help the meaning of these utterances must remain opaque for the analyst, who lacking co-presence would be unable to share the material environment. The reading provided by an analyst who is herself absent from the scene of the social process, is likely to be retrospective, supported either by what the interactants go on to say after line 2 and/or by reliance on the analyst's own experience of conducting business in a post office, the latter can happen only when it becomes obvious to the analyst that the speaking is in fact *a propos* postal goods. In Text *B*, the first such clue comes in line 6, with the customer's *and have you got ... the ... first day covers of ...* where, for an acculturated speaker, the enquiry about the availability of *first day covers* clinches the issue of locating the social process.[22]

Second, the complex structure of multimodal semiosis is immediately accessible to co-present interactants. The human body is an amazing system for engaging in multimodal semiosis and co-presence provides the best environment for an effective exercise of that potential (Hasan 1973c, 1981, 1996c; Ventola 1987). Speaking becomes only one aspect of face to face social interaction, and may not be easily intelligible in dissociation from the workings of other modalities and/or the sharing of material environment.[23]

Speakers make use of the kinetic semiotic system, access to which is lost with the loss of material situation; also there occur acts which may not pertain to a specific semiotic system but which may come to be seen as having some particular significance due to their contiguity with linguistic acts: for example, in *B* the act of getting the stamps and day covers (line 15) would be interpreted as Compliance in an environment where Sale Request (line 2 and line 10; 14) for these items has already been issued. The same act of getting stamps, etc. out of a drawer in the absence of a Sale Request is not very likely to be interpreted as an act of Compliance. It follows that the context of situation (partially) realized by the language of Text *B* cannot be successfully read by the analyst without knowing what meanings are construed jointly with other modalities: in the words of Bernstein (1971) the language of Text *B* is CONTEXT DEPENDENT (for some discussion of the terms context dependent and context independent, Hasan 1973c; Cloran 1994, 1999a). The information provided in parentheses in Text *B* by the transcribe records the interactants' physical actions, which are clearly not part of their *speaking* though they are part of their social interaction. Naturally the provision of such information is strictly for the benefit of the outsider/ analyst: so far as the interactants themselves are concerned, their use of other modalities and of their shared information is as much part of their social performance as is their use of language. If by text we mean *just* speaking with reference to some context, then strictly speaking, example *B* is not just a text: it includes also a meta-text, i.e., an informal commentary from the transcribe on what else is going on in the text's process. It is this commentary that gives the analyst access to (part of) the material situational setting, though the power of language in construing the details of a situation should not be underestimated (see note 24).

Finally, although phonic channel does not *require* the interactants' co-presence since telephonic mediation is possible, it is nonetheless the default choice in such contexts: this, in turn, opens up the possibility of dialogue, which is hospitable to PROCESS SHARING, as process sharing can come about only in environments permitting immediate SEMIOTIC RECIPROCITY between interactants. So far as languaging is concerned, at least *in theory* each can speak and by speaking contribute to the social process in which they are jointly engaged dialogically.[24] For example, if necessary the server can, and in Text *B* does, ask the customer for further information by saying *how many would you like?* (line 9)? *two of each?* (line 11) where the use of these questions positions the customer into construing the identity and quantity of goods that she is interested in buying.[25] I have suggested that these meanings are crucial to the realization of the element of text structure called Sale Request in the environment of a certain CC (see for details, Hasan 1985b). The customer in turn asks *what have you got?* (line 12) which construes a variety of Sale Enquiry where information about the goods on sale is exchanged while the actual conduct of buying/selling is held in abeyance until by these semiotic acts the nature of the goods under consideration has been established.

It is already implied in the above discussion that the social activity relevant to Text *B* is economic in nature. In fact from this point of view Texts *A* and *B* are distant relatives, at once similar and different. The speaking in Text *B* is with reference to the purchase of goods by an actual buyer who is involved in the activity of buying goods from a real salesperson at a real location. This contrasts with Text *A*, which is concerned with promoting the goods to a potential buyer anywhere, any time. In Text *B* the goods are material, in *A* essentially intellectual which implies a relatively restricted category of buyers for *A*. The interactant relations relevant to Texts *A* and *B* are also 'distant relatives'. To appreciate this, compare the social activity of selling postal goods with that of, say, selling fruit and vegetables by the owner of a small shop. The crucial difference lies in the relation of the two salespersons to their work place and their work activity, which bears also upon their social relations to their clients: given the socioeconomic infrastructure, the small shop owner is dependent on being able to serve his customers to their satisfaction; it is in this environment that 'the customer is always right'. By contrast, neither the post office salesperson nor the composer of Text *A* are dependent on their clients' satisfaction in this way, and understandably the relation to their (actual or prospective) clients is of neither case that of subservience. Despite this similarity in tenor between *A* and *B* at a primary degree of delicacy (see Table 6.2), differences in the attributes of the addressees emerge as we look deeper into the categories of goods the disposal of which is the concern of the blurb producer in *A* and the postal salesperson in *B*. Since Text *A* realizes an activity that is ultimately related to the marketing of intellectual goods, the buyer is likely to be someone who, in terms of Bourdieu (1991), has already invested in the intellectual capital of his culture. So he is likely to be educated and probably informed in the field of the study of social problems. The buyer of stamps is not known by any such specific attributes; and while the prospective buyer of a Durkheim anthology is likely to be an adult, this is not a requirement for buying stamps. Table 6.2 summarizes the relevant contexts of Texts *A* and *B* at a primary degree of delicacy.

Table 6.2: Contexts in texts A and B

	text A	text B
field:	economic: goods promotion by foregrounding distinctive qualities goods: sociological publication	economic: goods disposal by buying and selling goods:postal items
tenor:	promoter & potential buyer addressee virtual; adult; educated relation institutional nonhierarchic social distance maximal	salesperson & actual buyer addressee actual relation institutional nonhierarchic social distance maxiinal
mode:	role of language: constitutive channel: graphic; monologue no visual contact no process sharing medium: written	role of language: ancillary channel: phonic; dialogue visual contact present active process sharing medium: spoken

As the description in Table 6.2 indicates Text *B* too observes what I have called the principle of contextual/registerial consistency: just like Text *A,* the context of Text *B* too 'covers' the whole text. As with *A,* so also with *B,* we have one single text that realizes one single context and instantiates one single category of register. Further, a comparison of the two columns in Table 6.2 shows quite readily that the most outstanding differences between the contexts relevant to these two texts are to be found in their mode of discourse. I have already pointed out that this difference is realizationally related to the quality of texture, which is in turn crucial for the outsider's or the analyst's ability to interpret the speaking. Note at this point that features in mode are also significant to the realization of a register's GENERALIZED STRUCTURE POTENTIAL (GSP). In fact, we can generalize quite safely that the selection of mode features is systematically related by realization: (a) to texture in texts and so to variation in the degree of context-dependence in the text's language; and (b) to the actual global structure of texts instantiating the structure potential associated with a given register type. We can raise this generalization to a higher level of abstraction: there exists evidence for claiming that the actualized GSP of a text is realizationally related to its entire CONTEXTUAL CONFIGURATION (CC); the features of the three parameters, field, tenor and mode, are in principle capable of making some contribution to this structural shape (Hasan 1978, 1979b, 1985b, 1994). In light of this fact, models such as Martin's which claim that the structural shape of texts in a genre is activated by a single parameter, sometimes simply by (the goal of) an activity and sometimes simply by particulars of mode, have some explaining to do.

A final point to be made before leaving this discussion is that the cc relevant to Text *B* shows even more emphatically than that of *A* that although each contextual parameter has a separate identity of its own, the three do permeate each other. The contextual parameters, field, tenor and mode, are not, to use Bernstein's (1975) terminology, three strongly classified domains, each with a clear-cut boundary of its own: they are in fact permeable. What choices are made in field is relevant to some extent to the choices in tenor and in mode. Thus, as discussed above, the social activity of promoting a sociological publication by producing a blurb has implications not only for (some of) the attributes of the promoter and prospective buyer (i.e., tenor) but also for some features of mode. Naturally, the interdependence across the three parameters is partial: the choices in one parameter do not 'determine' or fully 'predict' all the choices in the remaining two, otherwise we would not have needed to recognize three separate parameters. What happens typically is that they display (with apologies to Firth 1957) a 'mutual prehension': the echoes of a choice in one are found to some extent in the choices of the others.[26]

Before leaving this discussion, let me point out two curious characteristics of systemic relations amongst contextual choices which have been foregrounded here. First, SFL assumes that choice paths in a system network typically display genuine dependency. Idealizing a little, if entry condition *a* then options *b or c*, if entry condition *b* then options *d* or *e;* and if entry condition *c* then options *f* or *g*; and so on. This illustrates a relation of genuine dependency, encountered fairly typically in lexicogrammatical system networks (for some examples, see Hasan and Fries 1995; Hasan, Cloran and Butt 1996; Matthiessen 1995, etc.). It seems to me that at the level of context, in addition to such a relation of genuine dependency, there also exists just as often a relation of DEFAULT DEPENDENCY, that is to say, choice in one system might bear implications for some other system. Take, for example, the phonic channel: though it is hospitable to dialogue, it also provides a genuine choice between dialogue and monologue (compare a conversation with a lecture). But in the environment of graphic channel, monologue is the default choice. It is not that we do not find dialogues *simulated* in the graphic channel, but when we do, we find also that it relates to a contextual feature we may describe as AS-IF: some examples of text types that realize such contexts are dialogues within novels, drama, or a news story reporting a dialogue. In other words, the value of dialogue in graphic channel is significantly different from that of dialogue in the phonic channel where it is a genuine option. Default dependency relations are not unknown at the level of lexicogrammar, but they are far less frequent. This suggests to me that the organization of the level of context may differ in subtle ways from that of the language internal strata e.g., semantics and/or lexicogrammar, which would not be entirely surprising: after all, context may be (partly) construed by language, but it can never be dissociated from the material and institutional aspects of a culture.[27]

The second characteristic of systemic choices at the level of context has to do with the way that probabilities function. For example, it will be found that in the phonic environment, the probability of the choice of dialogue increases IF the field choice is a quotidian activity such as buying stamps or having a conversation: the more specialized the social activity the less likely it is that the choice of dialogue will be taken up; thus the activity of presenting a keynote address or a sermon is not likely to 'go with' a dialogue: in pronouncing his sentence, the judge is not really engaged in a dialogue. If, however, with phonic mode and quotidian social activity, the social distance in tenor is minimal, the probability of the choice of dialogic mode increases considerably: unlike a keynote address or the judge's summing up of a case, telling your friend about a serious surgical operation you had to undergo is highly likely to be in dialogue mode rather than in monologue. We are familiar with the concept of CONDITIONAL PROBABILITY at least at the level of lexicogrammar,[28] but it seems to me that interestingly, conditional probability there tends to implicate choices within the same general system network: for example conditional probability operates within the larger system network of mood, modality and polarity; it does not go across to, say, the system of transitivity. At the contextual level, however, conditional probability is quite likely to implicate features *across* the systems of field, tenor and mode. I suggest that this pattern of conditional probability at the level of context can be explained by the fact that the three contextual parameters are in fact permeable. When as analysts we talk of context as a tripartite structure, it is important to remember that so far as the interactants are concerned, the social activity and the interactants' relation to each other as well as their mode of jointly carrying out the activity are one integrated whole: unlike a character in an absurd farce, a speaker does not first choose to carry out an activity such as buying stamps and then look around to determine what his relation to the addressee, i.e., the salesperson, might be, whether greeting is in order or not, and whether he should talk to the addressee or write, something that is implied by the dynamic flowcharts which employ the metaphor of decision making to report on the process as it occurs in real time (Martin 1985a; Ventola 1987). This kind of conception of context in the study of text is certainly at variance from our experience of how things are done in our culture.

6.2.3 Context and text: Example C

Perhaps most readers would agree that Example *C* differs crucially from both *A* and *B*. The most pressing problem we face here is whether a reading of the context for *C* can be provided that will display the principle of contextual/registerial consistency at work as in the case of Texts *A* and *B*. Certainly at a particular degree of delicacy the tenor and the mode appear to 'cover' the entire example: throughout the example, a mother and her son are engaged in face to face dialogue. Their relation is hierarchic, based on kinship and age, especially since the son is no more than 4 years old.[29] This in turn implies a fairly minimal social distance: supporting this conclusion, their talk shows them at ease with each other, able to address questions, requests and comments to each other with equally relaxed facility. In *A* and *B*, a particular aspect of interactant relation, namely, their *agentive role* (Hasan 1978, 1985b), derives logically from what they are engaged in doing, e.g., salesperson or publication promoter talking to actual or virtual buyer (see Table 6.2). For *C*, it is difficult to identify one single relation of the agentive kind which would apply constantly to the entire dialogue: the interactants are, in fact, engaged not in just one activity but several. So far as the features of mode are concerned, *C* resembles *B* a good deal. Like *B*, *C* too is a dialogue between interactants who are co-present; there is visual contact between them, and also good evidence of process sharing; the medium is throughout spoken and the channel is phonic. However the role of language appears to shift in keeping with the shift in their activity: what it is that the child and his mother are engaged in doing. I examine these shifts briefly below.

The dialogue opens (line 1) with the mother asking Stephen if he would like a sandwich for lunch; Stephen accepts the sandwich but asks for some passionfruit as well. The social activity, call it care giving, takes up lines 1–4 (segment i), at which point mother and child engage in a hunt for the missing passionfruit (lines 5–17 segment ii). When the passionfruit is relocated, the mother turns again to the business of providing Stephen his lunch, eliciting more information from him about what particular sort of sandwich he would like and advising him on where to sit to have his lunch (lines 17–20 segment iii). There is a short pause (see line 20) before the mother comments on the scarcity of passionfruit and states the reason for it. This happens most probably as lunch is being taken to the table (lines 21–24 segment iv).[30] She turns again to the management of lunch (lines 25; 27; 29 segment v: a) but is diverted from it by Stephen's demand for information regarding Nana's preference for a particular seat (lines 26; 28;

30–31 segment v: b). As their talk overlaps, the mother and the child engage in rather different activities: the mother is concerned with getting Stephen to sit somewhere suitable to eat his lunch, and the child with getting the mother to explain his grandmother's seating preference. Obviously sitting is not a physical action that requires help from the use of language for its performance; we assume that Stephen is getting himself seated in compliance with the mother's advice while she is giving the explanation required by him, since after this he ceases to ask about Nana's seating preferences and the mother stops guiding him to sit in a specific place. Thus two related but somewhat different actions co-occur. In lines 32–47 (segment vi) the mother and Stephen talk about something which is not connected with any aspect of the lunch even tangentially: here the mother reveals her plans for their visit to Chatswood. In the absence of any comments to the contrary from the mother, we assume again that as the mother and child discuss their Chatswood plans (32–47), Stephen is seated as mother desired and is eating his lunch. So it is not surprising to find talk of lunch reasserting itself at line 48. But a potential conflict appears on the horizon as the mother rejects Stephen's request for vitamin C (line 54–59 segment viii). From the child's point of view, the concern is perhaps still with lunch: vitamin C which Stephen apparently likes to eat is another thing he could have at lunch (48–53 segment vii). But from the mother's culturally informed point of view the situation is different: as medication, vitamin C cannot be eaten just any old time and Stephen must be made aware of this. The mother is thus engaged in classifying the activity of medicine-taking, framing Stephen's performance relatively strongly (Bernstein 1990): she rejects his request, and when Stephen appears disgruntled, she offers a rationale for this rejection (lines 54–59 segment viii). Again as the child does not continue to 'whinge', it appears reasonable to assume that he has accepted the

Table 6.3: Shifting fields of discourse in Example C

Segment i:		lines 1–4	**organizing lunch**
Segment ii:		lines 5–17	finding the passionfruit
Segment iii:		lines 18–20	**organizing lunch**
Segment iv:		lines 21–24	Commenting on scarcity of passionfruit
Segment v:	a:	lines 25, 27, 29	**organizing lunch**
	b:	lines 26, 28, 30–31	explaining Nana's seating preference
Segment vi:		lines 32–47	planning visit to Chatswood
Segment vii:		lines 48–53	**organizing lunch**
Segment viii:		lines 54–59	explaining about vitamin C
Segment ix:		lines 60–61	**organizing lunch**

mother's reasoning, and we return once again to talk that concerns lunch (lines 60–61 segment ix). The dialogue between the mother and her child continues (see a larger extract in Cloran 1999a), though for my purposes this much is enough.[31]

Table 6.3 presents a schematic account of the social activities I have read in Example *C*. If a given contextual configuration consists of the total set of the values relating to each of the three parameters, and if *any* change in these values automatically spells a change of relevant context, then clearly the speaking in Example *C* does not realize just one CC, but several different ones; by the same token, it does not instantiate just one register but several different ones. If we insist on the principle of registerial/contextual consistency as an invariable attribute of text-hood, we would have to treat Example *C* as a succession of distinct texts realizing distinct registers. This is tantamount to abandoning the principle of registerial/contextual consistency and treat Example *C* as one conversation which nonetheless realizes different registers, a solution which I believe might be favoured in the framework suggested by Martin (1985a, 1992) who has used the term GENRE COMBINATION for similar cases of speaking, in referring particularly to Ventola's (1987) data. But both these positions leave something to be desired. According to the first position Example *C* consists of either nine (and a half?) different texts, or at least of six, five of which (segments ii, iv, v-b, vi and viii) just interrupt the text that opens the interaction in Example *C* (segments i, iii, v-a, vii and ix); the latter are all concerned with organizing lunch, and the different parts of this lunch text simply leap-frog over the interrupting segments (see Table 6.3). Whatever the number of texts we claim to find in Example *C*, according to position one, each text is, as it were, on its own; none bears any relation whatever to the others, and this surely goes against our intuition as makers and receivers of texts. The second choice of seeing Extract *C* as a genre combination is marginally better as it suggests at least a sequencing of genres/registers. However, it leaves the concept of text-hood dangling in the air: is genre combination a feature of one text? If so, what is the difference between a text and a verbal interaction? Then again it offers no principle underlying the combination of genres as if it is equally possible for any genre/register to combine with any others, and as if there exists no other basis for their affinity. This is manifestly not the case: consider that neither any part of Text *A*, nor even a substantial portion of *B* could combine with *C* to produce a credible case of genre combination representing a real interaction.[32] Nor could we claim with justification that amongst the nine segments of *C* identified in Table 6.3, there exists no other relation than that of temporal sequencing: in fact, perhaps all segments except one, viz., (vi: lines 32–47) can be shown to be related to each other not by the accident of their spatio-temporal co-location but by *the function they serve in the ecology of the primary text* concerned with lunch. I develop this theme in the following subsections.

6.2.3.1   *The concept of primary text*

A textual concern that runs intermittently through Example *C* centres around the mother providing lunch for her son, Stephen: intermittently but coherently, segments (i, iii, v-a, vii and ix, highlighted in bold in Table 6.3) voice the concern of the interactants with this activity. As Cloran (1999a) points out this is a variety of care giving activity, whose various elements (or, *stages* if you prefer) the mother negotiates with her child. So in segment (i) (lines 1–4) she consults Stephen about what he wants to eat; in segment (iii) (lines 17–20), having finalized the lunch menu, she tells him where she would like him to sit to eat. Segment (v-a) (lines 25, 27, 29) actually guides him to this location while segments (vii) (lines 48–53) and (ix) (lines 60–61) establish what more he might or might not drink or eat. Together the segments realize, albeit with certain 'interruptions', what at some degree of delicacy can legitimately be seen as just one contextual configuration, consisting of the details of one activity which involves the same interactant relation; and their mode of discourse remains the same throughout. From now on I will call the strand of the context relevant to this identified part of Example *C* the MAIN CC; and the segments which together realize it will be referred to as the PRIMARY TEXT. Table 6.4 presents the details of the main CC.

Table 6.4: Main CC realized by the primary text in example C

FIELD OF DISCOURSE:

care-giving: negotiating the mean for lunch, indicating location for its consumption & presenting items on mean, attending to child's lunch needs…

TENOR OF DISCOURSE:

mother care-giver & preschool child recipient of care: age-relation institutionalized as hierarchic: acculturated mother & apprentice child; social distance; minimal…

MODE OF DISCOURSE:

role of language ancillary; channel phonic; dialogue; process sharing; visual contact present; medium spoken…

6.2.3.2 *Integration: dependent context and complex text*

What about segments (ii, iv, v–b, vi) and (viii) which fall outside the primary text? Clearly in some way they do interrupt the realization of the main CC. The idea that a text/context may be interrupted is familiar in SFL: it is implied in the observation that texts may be enclosed or interspersed (Halliday 1964; Hasan 1968). But when a text/context is enclosed within another or when two (or more) texts/contexts are interspersed, there is no departure from the principle of contextual/registerial consistency: each such text stands, as it were, on its own, without contributing to the conduct and/or structure of the other(s). The situation is different, at least in part so far as Example *C* is concerned. Here all the segments, except perhaps segment (vi) (lines 32–47 planning a visit to Chatswood), make a substantial contribution to how the interactants themselves experience that social context which is realized in the primary text. In fact the very *raison d'être* of these four segments (ii, iv, v–b, and viii) lies in the management of the conduct of the main context realized in the primary text; and it is some aspects of this context that, in a manner of speaking, provoke the segments into existence.[33] Their occurrence acts on the overall nature of the social process, modifying the very character and structure of what is referred to here as the primary text. When a segment contributes to the character of the primary text in the way(s) I have just outlined, I will refer to it as a SUB-TEXT.

A sub-text relates to (some part of) the primary text in certain clearly specifiable ways, and in so doing it creates a complex text, much as the relation of *taxis* creates a complex unit, such as the clause complex at the lexicogrammatical level. And just as in a clause complex, semantically the secondary clause 'tempers' those clauses to which it relates by taxis, so in a complex text such as presented in Example *C*, the sub-texts temper (aspects of) the primary text, changing its nature substantially for the interactants. To appreciate some of the specific ways in which sub-texts relate to (aspects of) a primary text, I will begin by considering segment (ii) (lines 5–16) in *C*. Segment ii will be referred to as SUB-TEXT$_1$ from now on.

It is obvious perhaps that the field of discourse construed by sub-text$_1$ is subservient to that construed by the primary text: if passionfruit is one of the relevant objects for lunch, its whereabouts are bound to make a difference to what the interactants might do and/or say *a propos* the provision of lunch. The search for the missing passionfruit 'arrests' the actual progress of the primary text much as a *side sequence* (Goffman 1981) arrests the progress of an exchange or adjacency pair consisting of, say, a question and answer, and just as a Sale Enquiry arrests the design of a buying text (see discussion of Example *B*). The 'ARRESTIVE' nature of a sub-text such as sub-text₁ is independent of what may or may not be achieved in the text's make up by it, since irrespective of that it will have a modifying effect on the structure of the primary text. If the material outcome is successful, and notably success and failure in this context will be defined entirely by reference to the (details of the) main CC, this will contribute to the completion of an on-going element/stage in the structure of the primary text, which is what happens in Example *C*.[34] If the material outcome is unsuccessful, this will still impinge on (some) details of the main CC, giving rise to further negotiation, revision and/or even termination of the main context altogether. This suggests that the occurrence of sub-text₁ is not a simply temporal sequencing of a text of one register/genre with that of another as the term 'genre combination' appears to imply; rather it performs a FACILITATIVE function in the economy of the primary text.

A facilitative sub-text realizes a dependent context, which typically varies from the main context in a limited way. The critical feature of a *dependent* context is that it is subordinated to some feature(s) of the main CC which is in the process of being construed when the dependent context first appears. For example, sub-text₁ construes a dependent context the details of which are identical to those of the main CC except with respect to its field: it is the field of the dependent context realized by sub-text₁ that is different, while its tenor (except for the agentive role) and mode remain constant. As Table 6.4 shows one feature of the field in the main CC is *presenting (to addressee-recipient) items (which by mutual agreement have been placed) on the menu.* By contrast, the field of discourse relevant to sub-text₁ could be described as *locating the whereabouts of an item on the menu which the interactants expect to be presented to the recipient.* It is this relation of contextual dependence that underlies its facilitative function whereby a sub-text and a primary text become functionally integrated into a complex text. Approaching the problem from the related perspective of textual constituency, Cloran (1999a) interestingly suggests that the part here identified as sub-text₁ in Example *C* is an embedded constituent of a rhetorical unit which realizes (part of) the caregiving activity.

FACILITATION is thus a functional relation of (some) elements of the (global) structure of a COMPLEX TEXT. What passes here between the mother and the child by way of sub-text₁ is in its function very much like a category of an optional element that I have referred to as Sale Enquiry (Hasan 1979b, 1985b, and elsewhere): both contribute to the conduct of the activity specified in the main context and both get integrated into the primary text. Whereas the principle for the production of SIMPLE TEXT such as exemplified by *A* and *B* is that of contextual/registerial consistency, an alternative principle for text production is at work in the case of a complex text: I will refer to this principle as the principle of CONTEXTUAL/REGISTERIAL INTEGRATION.[35] Whether the principle for the production of a text is that of contextual/registerial consistency or of integration, what is not in doubt is the fact that whatever is perceived as a text typically displays two kinds of unity: that of texture and that of structure.[36] The operation of the principle of contextual/registerial integration does not negate this generalization, which I believe applies almost invariably except in pathological discourse (Armstrong 1987, 1992). It needs to be said quite clearly that the dependency of a 'dependent context' as being described here is a functional relation: there is nothing inherently dependent in the features of a context described as dependent, *except their dependent relation to (some) component of the main context.* Thus a search for missing objects does not have to be subordinated to some other on-going context as it is in Example *C*; it could just as well have been (part of) a context operative on its own: clearly, then, it is not its own internal make up, but only the positioning of sub-text$_1$ *vis à vis* the on-going interaction, that denies it the status of realizing a text with the same independent status as that of the primary text. When the term 'genre combination' is applied to a complex text such as in Example *C* which is embedded in one spatio-temporally identified interaction, there is an implication that all segments of such an interaction are genres/registers each equal in status with the others. At best, this is to equate a spatio-temporally identified unit such as *interaction* with a descriptive semantic category which I am calling here a complex text; and at worst, it is to view the discourse from a morphological perspective only, i.e., on the basis of what the various parts look like in their own make up, rather than from a functional one, based on what, if anything, the segments of the talk do in the context of the other co-occurring talk. This is not to deny that within the same spatio-temporally identified interaction there may be found a text instantiating a register which does not 'combine' functionally with the other co-located texts/genres: as I said earlier 'interruptions' can and do occur, but interruption is a rather different kind of phenomenon. In the following section, I will draw attention to one such example, while identifying other forms of contextual/registerial integration.

6.2.3.3 Contextual/registerial integration: collaborative contexts, complex texts

Not all sub-texts are facilitative in the sense described above. Thus although segment (iv) (lines 21–24; see segment iv in Table 6.3) is integrated into the primary text in Example *C*, its relation to the latter differs significantly from that of sub-text$_1$. Just before the four messages of this segment occur, the mother has identified the place where she would like Stephen to eat his lunch (lines 19–20 part of segment iii). The short pause (indicated by the dots at the end of message 20 in Text *C*) suggests that most probably, segment (iv) is produced as the mother is carrying the lunch to the table with Stephen in tow, a reading further supported by the fact that the segment is the joint work of both participants in the dialogue, Stephen and his mother. Moreover immediately following its close, the mother is able to point precisely where Stephen is to seat himself (line 25, segment v-a), a feature that in this context suggests their co-presence. So unlike sub-text$_1$, segment (iv) occurs at a moment when the mother's action of carrying food to the table is 'silently' i.e. purely physically, contributing to the realization of the main CC: the mother is actually presenting Stephen items on the previously agreed menu. It can hardly be denied that the discourse on passionfruit in this segment is materially not essential to carrying out the particular series of actions necessary to the completion of the activity of the main context. The mother's physical action of presenting food and her verbal action of telling Stephen about the fruit-bearing conditions for passionfruit vines are independent activities pertaining to different spheres and running side by side: so segment (iv), unlike sub-text$_1$, is not arrestive but concurrent with the non-verbal manifestation of some action predicated by the main CC. From now on I will refer to segment (iv) as SUB-TEXT$_2$, and to the type of context it has construed as a COLLABORATIVE context: this context type is construed by a sub-text and runs together with the conduct of (some part of) the main CC.

Collaborative contexts differ from the dependent ones in significant ways. A dependent context is by definition dependent on the main context; a collaborative context is not. Further, during the operation of the dependent context, the conduct of the activity in the main CC is arrested as exemplified by sub-text$_1$ (c.f., 6.2.3.2 above); by contrast, this is not necessarily the case with the collaborative context where two (or more) contexts may run side by side, a characteristic exemplified by sub-text$_2$. However, if the matter is left at this point, then we would have to grant that the context construed by segment (vi) (lines 32–47) is also collaborative. It is fair to assume that while in segment (vi) the mother reveals her plans for her visit to Chatswood that afternoon, the physical activity of attending to the child's lunch, an aspect of the activity in the main context, is 'silently', i.e., physically, going on without any verbal realization at that point. So is segment (vi) also just like sub-text$_2$? Does it construes a collaborative context with respect to the main CC? In my view, there are good grounds for arguing against a positive response: the similarity between sub-text$_2$ and segment (vi) is in fact superficial; segment (vi) is neither a sub-text, nor does it construe a collaborative context, though it does share with segment (iv) the characteristic of being concurrent. To justify these assertions, I will first examine the function of sub-text$_2$ *vis à vis* the primary text.

As argued above (in 6.2.3.2) a facilitative sub-text, which construes a dependent context, contributes materially to the conduct of (some part of) the activity in the main CC. Generally speaking the same is true of a sub-text which construes a collaborative context, such as sub-text$_2$: it too contributes to the conduct of (some part of) the activity in the main CC, *but it does this with a difference*. The facilitative sub-text contributes via an action that, as it were, assists whatever activity is being carried out; sub-texts such as sub-text$_2$ contribute not via an action but by *managing the affective tone of whatever is going on,* either tending to make the wheels of on-going (inter)action turn smoothly or tending to create/ intensify obstructions. In short, it affects the manner in which the activity of the main CC is conducted not by contributing directly to the activity in a concrete, physical way but *by acting on interactant relations.* I will refer to this function as TONE SETTING, which explains my choice of the term 'collaborative' for the context that is construed by such sub-texts. Taking the variation in the quality of interpersonal relation as a cline, I will refer to its two endpoints as the 'relaxed' and the 'strained'. The tone setting enacted by a sub-text may be said to be 'positive' when the sub-text construes a (near) relaxed relation, and 'negative' when the relation construed is (near) strained. Sub-text$_2$ belongs to the former category: it performs the function of POSITIVE TONE SETTING; its relaxed friendly nature further cements the relation of social solidarity between the interactants that is evident from the very beginning of their dialogue. That sub-text$_2$ does have a positive tone setting function is perhaps clear from a comparison of this sub-text with cases quite easy to imagine where the mother may simply put the food down on the table without saying anything, or more likely, where whatever she says is directed towards getting the child to eat in a particular way, at a particular pace considered appropriate by her (e.g., *Now, don't play with your food just sit down properly and eat up your lunch,* as many mothers do say; for some naturally occurring examples of this type, see Cloran 1999b; Hasan 1992b). Segment (viii) (lines 54–59 in Table 6.3), the last sub-text in Example *C* where the mother explains her rejection of the child's request for 'some vitamin C', teeters very close to a NEGATIVE TONE SETTING: the child is clearly unhappy; their relations are more strained than at any other time in this extract. The mother rescues the situation by the strategy of explanation which, on the basis of her prior experience she most probably expects to be effective with her child.

The genesis of facilitation is in what main action is being performed, and what the 'ingredients' of that action are: it arises from some features of the field choices in the main context and is typically ACTION-BASED; the genesis of tone setting is not so much in *what* is being done but in *who* is doing it: it arises from some features of the tenor choices in the main context, and is typically RELATION BASED.[37] Note that tone setting sub-texts are more likely to occur where the social distance is (near) minimal; and whether the tone setting will be positive or negative depends typically on the inter-actants' ideological orientation, their view of what constitutes legitimate forms of the living of life, which view is in turn related by social logic to their social positioning. This ideological orientation is expressed, amongst other things, in the way the interactants FRAME their interaction with their interactive other. In SFL, we often talk about the power of language to enact social relations: the tone setting function is one highly effective and relatively more visible means of enacting social relations.[38] If interactants experience positive tone setting in their interaction with each other, their mutual relation over time is likely to develop an evenly relaxed tone which will, all things being equal, carry over from one interaction to the next: when we talk of positive affect, what we really mean is that the mutual interactive history of those interactants has hitherto not given rise to any significant anticipation of conflict or strain.

One may quite reasonably ask why segment (vi) should not be said to have a tone setting function: after all, it fills the silence in companion-able talk while the child is eating his lunch and the mother is attending to his needs. Wouldn't this companionable talk act positively on the affec-tive tone of whatever other activity is going on? On these grounds, we might conclude that broaching the plans for the visit to Chatswood has the function of positive tone setting. So why did I reject this analysis above? My rationale is to be found in a comparison of the language of sub-text$_2$ with that of segment (vi). I have argued earlier (Section 6.2.1) that speak-ing, i.e., language in use, is not simply activated by context: it also con-strues context on-goingly, and that evidence from language is decisive in the inter-subjective construals of context. It follows that if I claim that the context construed by sub-text$_2$ differs qualitatively from that construed by segment (vi), then by my own argument the language of the two segments in question should show some significant difference. This is indeed the case. In citing such evidence, let me reiterate first that of all the contexts construed in Example *C*, the only one that is considered not integrated into the main CC is the one relevant to segment (vi): this context of (vi) is an *independent context,* albeit its realization runs side by side with the conduct of the main CC. The remaining segments (ii, iv, v-b and viii) all construe INTEGRATED CONTEXTS, and only sub-text$_1$, i.e. segment (ii), is facilitative; the remaining three segments, (iv, v-b, and viii) have a tone setting function, and represent sub-text$_2$, sub-text$_3$, and sub-text$_4$, respectively. A look at the language of all those segments which I am claiming to be functionally related to the primary text, construing contexts integrated into the main CC will reveal that each one of these enjoys textural unity with the primary text: irrespective of whether their function is facilitative or tone setting, each is *cohesively multiply related* to the primary text. This point is brought out excellently by Cloran (1999a: 177–217): she presents a fairly detailed analysis of much of what is presented here as Example *C* with reference to cohesive chain formation and cohesive harmony (Hasan 1984d). For ease of ready reference, her analysis of cohesive harmony is presented here as Figure 6.2.[39]

Appendix II in Cloran (1999a) shows that amongst all the segments, the one I have referred to as 'segment vi' consisting of (lines 32–47) is the only one which displays negligible chain relation to the rest of extract (Example *C*): the boxes containing lines 32–40 and 41–46 are closed; no arrows show any connection to the preceding or following segments. This is precisely the segment that according to my analysis has no functional relation to the primary text nor does it construe an integrated (collaborative or dependent) context. Further, in approaching Example *C* from the point of view of textual constituency analysis, Cloran finds linguistic grounds, both semantic and lexicogrammatical, for treating the entire segment (vi) as an independent, free-standing RHETORICAL UNIT (RU), which does not function as a constituent of some other larger unit (for further details, Cloran 1999a discussion 177–217). This is in substantial agreement with my analysis according to which segment (vi) is not a sub-text: its status is that of a PARALLEL TEXT, which runs parallel to the complex text, represented by the remainder of Example *C* within which this parallel text is ENCLOSED.

Due to the lack of its textural unity with the primary text, the speaking in segment (vi) could just as well have happened somewhere else, either alongside of some other discourse or singly on its own: from the perspective of the complex text made up of the primary text and its various sub-texts, there is nothing that links segment (vi) specifically to it, except its quite fortuitous spatio-temporal co-location with it. This contrasts with the four integrated segments (ii, iv, v-b and viii) each of which acts as a

Figure 6.2: Cohesion in Example C [Adapted from Cloran 1999a: 190 (Table 2)]

chain interaction in the dialogue

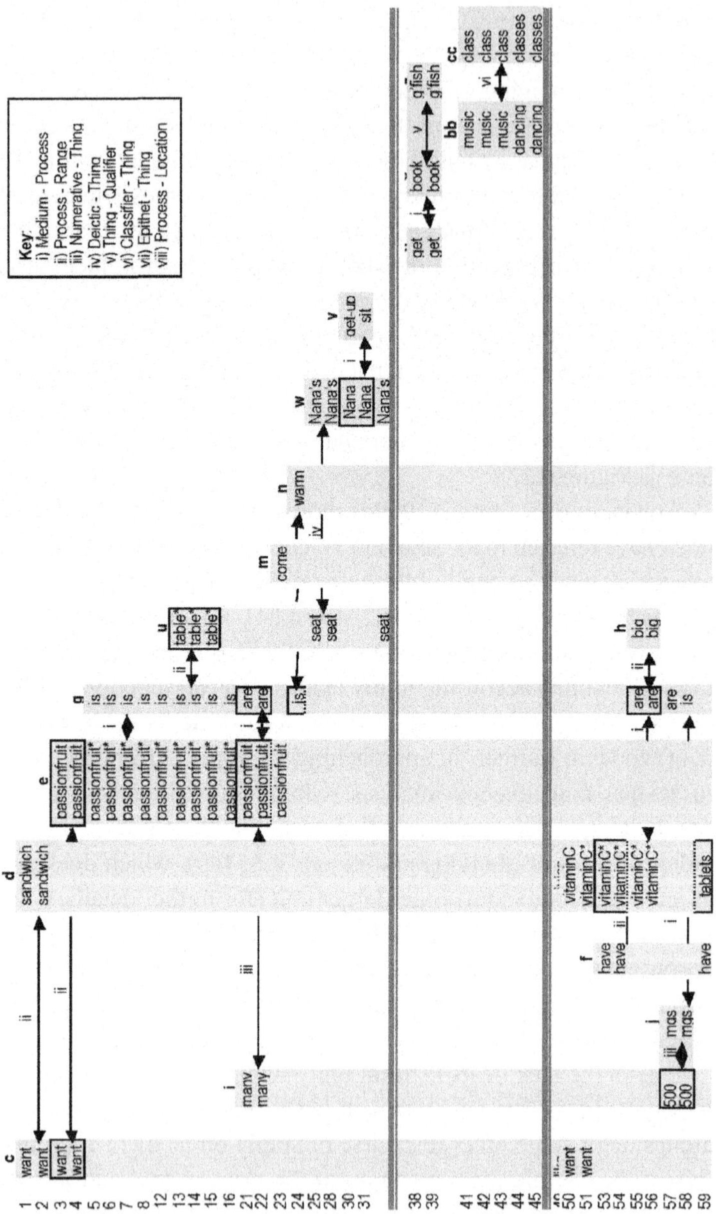

sub-text and each displays points of cohesive continuity with the primary text. These threads of continuity which unite the other parts leap over segment (vi), leaving the latter unconnected to the rest of the dialogue (see the iconic representation in Cloran 1999a:Appendix II: 212). And again it is significant that whatever new cohesive chains are formed in segment (vi), they are restricted to just that single segment; they do not continue beyond it (see chains labelled l–q in Table 3: 191 in Cloran 1999a). In common parlance, segment (vi) has nothing to do with any concern raised in/by the features of the main context realized by the primary text. And this is my justification for describing segment (vi) not as a sub-text but as a text parallel to the complex one, within which it also happens to be *enclosed.* The context construed by this enclosed parallel text is not collaborative but *independent.* This analysis is further supported dramatically by the cohesive harmony analysis,[40] which iconically separates it from the remainder of Example *C.* By contrast, the textural unity of the primary text with the four sub-texts is a strong justification for treating them as one complex text. In common parlance, the discourse in each of these sub-texts arises from the discourse in the primary text: this is what underlies the substantial threads of textural unity amongst them. Generalizing from this, I would claim that textural unity is as crucial a condition for postulating contextual/registerial integration between segments of speaking within a single interaction as is the function of the segments to the conduct of the main CC: this follows from the logic of realizational relation across context, semantics and lexicogrammar. Below in Table 6.5 I present my summary of the relationship of segments (ii, iv, v–b, vi and viii) to the primary text.

Since textural unity bears so much 'responsibility' for the analysis of con/textual relations as proposed above, it is relevant to comment briefly on those cohesive chains and their interactions that apparently link the parallel enclosed text (segment vi) to the primary one. Notably there are only two such chains: the chain with the lexical repetition of *go* and the identity chain referring to the mother and Stephen (c.f., Table 2 in Cloran 1999a).[41]

Table 6.5: The relation of primary text to the remaining segments in Example C

segment	status *vis à vis* primary text	function in primary text	context construed	chain interaction with primary text
ii: 5 - 17	sub-text1	facilitation	dependent	present
iv: 21 - 24	sub-text2	tone setting	collaborative	present
vb: 26 - 31	Sub-text3	tone setting	collaborative	present
vi: 32 7	**parallel text**	**none**	**independent**	**none**
viii: 54 59	sub-text4	tone setting	collaborative	present

I will ignore the former, since hardly any weight can be attached to one single lexical cohesive tie across segments of an interaction, especially since the tie does not interact with any other chain than the identity chain just mentioned. One might argue that because the referents of this identity chain are Stephen and his mother the context of the enclosed parallel text (segment vi) does, after all, make contact with the main CC: contextually, Stephen and his mother are the interactants in segment (vi) as they are in the main CC as well as the CCs of all segments. Should this be taken as justification for treating segment (vi) as a subtext that construes not an independent context but a collaborative one?

There are good reasons against claiming cohesive continuity between two cases of speaking *simply* on the basis of reference to the same interactants in both (Hasan 1979b, 1985b): it potentially extinguishes the claim of individuality for texts and contexts, since such reference is likely to pervade over a wide range of cases of speaking by the same person(s) forming an interactive dyad. Of course at one level of analysis, anyone individual's actions and locutions throughout their life do possess a historical continuity. But in this holistic perspective whereby everything in life could be seen as related to everything else, not only in one individual's life but in the whole community's life, and perhaps even beyond that in the history of the entire universe. The fact remains, however, that register analysis cannot be effected without devising some basis for the recognition of historically distinct individual discursive events: we do need to identify the singularity of episode in the life of even the same person. This necessarily implies ignoring the identity of an interactant across distinct episodes and attaching greater importance to phenomena that lead to the coherence of the outcome. The relation between individual and collectivity is perhaps best decided not by the swings of academic fashions but by the nature of the problem to be solved. The notion of individual contexts and texts, whether simple or complex, forms the centre of the problem here.[42] And from the perspective of that problem, any relevance construed by any form of cohesive continuity based *only* on the spatio-temporal or historical continuity of specific interactants is of no consequence (Hasan 1994): it is thus immaterial that the language of segment (vi), like the language of the primary text, was produced by (the same) Stephen and his mother: as argued above such an identity chain cannot be used for recognizing what constitutes one individual text. The basis for textural unity cannot be said to reside in the identity of the referents of *you, I, me* and *we* when they refer to the speaker and the addressee; it lies in a textured reference chain to some third person entity (i.e., potentially identifiable by personal pronouns *he, she, it, they*).[43] Such a third person entity is either actually indicated in the speaking, e.g., *passionfruit* or *Nana's seat* in Example C or its potential relevance is implied by some aspect of the main CC, as for example the relevance of shampoo to the activity of bathing someone (c.f., an extract from a naturally occurring dialogue discussed in Hasan 1995, chapter 5 of this volume). In either case, such a third person identity chain must be echoed over the entire stretch of speaking for it to treat as a focal part of the same text, as, for example, *passionfruit* does with respect to Example C or shampoo in the example discussed in Hasan (1995). It is also important to emphasize that as recognition criterion for text-hood, chain formation by itself is less decisive than the patterns of chain interaction of the type referred to as cohesive harmony: elsewhere I have suggested (1973b, 1984c, 1994) that a particular measure of cohesive harmony identifies (part or) whole of a coherent text. And by this measure, segment (vi) can be best treated as a text on its own that is not integrated into the complex text, but is enclosed in it as a parallel text. Figure 6.3 displays a schematic representation of the analysis of Example C. It includes both the enclosed parallel text and the complex text which encloses it. As stated before, the complex text itself is the integration of a primary text and its (four) sub-texts. The straight line in Figure 6.3 stands for the progress of the design

Figure 6.3: Textual integration and co-location in Example C

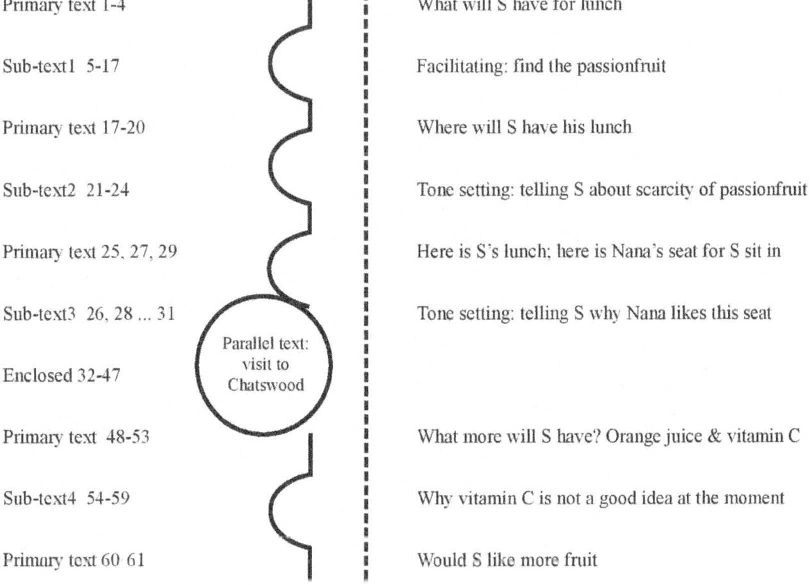

logically associated with the context of the primary text; the four sub-texts are shown as creating a shift from the direct progression of this (normal) design, producing an overall design for the complex text which modifies the primary text's character. The enclosed text is represented as a circle with a solid boundary that separates it from the complex text.

6.2.3.4   *Interactional continuities: material co-location and linguistic integration*

The problem that Example C posed was: how many texts have we got here? If more than one, what if any, is the relation between them? Problems of this kind arise only in environments of one interaction where the same interactants continue their acts of meaning without substantial change in their spatio-temporal location. And notably identical location and identical interactants both appear to be necessary for raising such questions sensibly: no one has suggested that when different groups of guests engage in conversation at the same cocktail party, they are together producing just one text with or without genre combination, just as it has never occurred to anyone to suggest that every critique of Hamlet written by the same critic on different occasions is one text. But while the continuity of inter-actants and spatio-temporal location may be good attributes for identifying an interaction, it cannot be assumed that interaction and text are necessarily isomorphic, that whatever speaking is done within the material frame of one interaction necessarily represents one text, where if activity changes then what we have is a text with genre combination. To equate interaction and text in this way may provide an easy and simple way of defining a textual boundary, but the definition is far from satisfactory. Textuality by this definition would no longer be a semiotic phenomenon, but a material one, and clearly the notion of text emerging from this kind of perspective is unlikely to prove satisfactory. [44] There is the obvious fact that an interaction thus identified could be either less or more than one intuitively perceived text. It could be less, for example, if the judge adjourns a case, resuming it the next day precisely at the same point where the case was left off; and the interaction could be more than one text if, for example, in the course of providing dinner to my child, I also help him with his homework. If as practised speakers, we perceive the continuity and/or discontinuity of texts on some principle other than that of 'same location, same interactants = one text', then the definition and recognition criteria for text-hood must lie elsewhere than in the material identity of an interaction. This makes sense: a text realizes some contextual configuration; it must, therefore, be respon-sive at once to the social activity (field), the interactant relations (tenor) and to their mode of contact (mode); in short, *the text's identity is as multifaceted as the text's context*. The structure and texture of a text are activated by the features of the CC, the details of which are construed for the addressee by certain patterns of worded meanings, i.e., by the calibrated selections at the levels of semantics and lexicogrammar. In the make-up of a text we find a classic demonstration of the co-operation of the material and the verbal: the relevant aspects of the material are linguistically validated and the crucial characteristics of the verbal, i.e., the text's textural and structural unity, are contextually motivated. This dialectic is an active force throughout the process of text production, irrespective of the channel of discourse.

The possibility has to be allowed that while an interaction is a locus for discourse, a discursive unit such as text is not necessarily co-extensive with all of the speaking done during one interaction. Within any one interaction we may have a primary text into which are integrated certain sub-texts that construe contexts which are integrated into the main CC; or we may have two or more texts each of which might construe two CCs each of which is independent of the context construed by the other: it is these latter category that I refer to as 'parallel texts'; they are parallel in status not in material terms. Whereas a primary text and its sub-texts are 'textually integrated', parallel texts are 'materially co-located'. The relation between parallel texts is not linguistic but material, and their status *vis à vis* each other is pretty much the same as that of texts arising in distinct interactions taking place in distinct locations with the engagement of distinct interactants: the only critical difference would be that the latter texts, unlike the former, would not be co-located. It is important to add that although across parallel texts there might exist some marginal textural relation for example, contiguous texts may share a short cohesive chain or two (as with segment vi in Example *C*), the perception of chaining is accentuated due to co-location; this is true especially for cohesive relations of the type that make up a similarity chain.[45] Further, there is no established pattern of the clustering of chain interaction: textural unity is by definition absent across parallel texts (as illustrated by segment (vi) in Example *C*). It is important to emphasize also that the fact of co-location itself says nothing about the internal nature of the parallel texts themselves: each parallel text co-located in an interaction may be simple or complex; or some may be simple and some complex. Thus according to my analysis, there are two parallel texts in Example *C*, one simple, instantiating one register, which is realized by the enclosed parallel text (segment vi as Figure 6.3 shows) and the other a complex parallel text made up of the remaining segments.

Note that co-location may take different forms: for example, texts may be INTERSPERSED, different parts of the speaking relevant to two (or more) texts appearing in alternation; or one text may be ENCLOSED within another, as with segment (vi); or they may appear in SEQUENCE, one parallel text following the preceding one; and of course, the three temporal arrangements may combine.[46] From a practical point of view, sometimes when extreme degrees of enclosure or interspersion occur, especially if co-located simple and complex texts combine in any of these temporal arrangements, problems of comprehension are likely to arise for listeners/analysts. We all know some speakers who give the impression of 'darting about from one topic to another', which is in fact a non-technical description of texts in close material proximity without significant textural links. In fact in its extreme condition, this may represent a form of language disorder.

Genre combination (Martin 1985a, 1992), as I understand the term, and contextual/registerial integration are not simply terminological variants. To appreciate this difference, imagine a set of parallel texts each simple, and each, therefore, displaying the principle of contextual/registerial consistency. We may, if we wish, refer to this collection of simple parallel texts as a combination or colocation of genres/registers; but if so, genre combination obviously means no more than spatio-temporal contiguity of texts instantiating different registers. By contrast, as I have argued above, the structuring of a complex text is significantly different: irrespective of whether a complex text is co-located with some other text or not, the underlying principle for its own production is contextual/registerial integration. Integration implies that *the context of the complex text as a whole has an integrated character* in which the dependent and/or collaborative contexts construed by the sub-texts are neither random nor dissonant: in the overall design of the social process, the contextual shifts construed by sub-texts have a functional place since the nature of the main CC continues to act as the denominator of the entire complex. So, for example, the context construed by a facilitative sub-text differs from the main CC *only with respect to (certain) features of field;* its tenor and mode remain largely unchanged as Example *C* illustrates. Shifts in the features, ingredients, stages (call it what you will) of action are fairly easy to observe whether the action is material and/or verbal, whereas it is comparatively less easy to observe subtle contextual shifts in social relation, i.e., in the tenor of discourse. Nonetheless as I have argued tone setting sub-texts do construe *some adjustment to (some) feature of the tenor* of the main CC.[47] In addition to acting on tenor features, the tone setting sub-text may construe a context whose field may differ considerably from that of the main CC: consider, for example, sub-text$_2$ in C, where the field choices in the collaborative context differ significantly from those in the main CC despite a functional and textural relation. That is to say, such shifts are always mediated by a reference to what Firth (1957) would have called 'relevant objects and actions': it is this joint focus by interactants on objects and actions relevant to the main CC that becomes a means of textually enacting social relations. Although these subtle shifts in the context/register of the primary text do occur with respect to its field, and/or its tenor, and/or the mode, the integrated contexts do not completely overthrow or change the character of the main CC.[48] Instead, the integration acts on the character of the entire complex as a whole, creating a unity out of diversity: what happens is that the primary text's context/register is modified, or, to use my earlier term, 'tempered', by the contexts/registers of the sub-texts. In this process, each of the involved contexts/registers loses its independence and its character as an individual; the integration, whether in progress or as a completed whole, presents itself as the unique experience of a unique context/register. In this sense, the principle of contextual/registerial integration does not negate the essence of the claim that 'a text is a passage of discourse that is coherent' (Halliday and Hasan 1976) though it certainly throws doubt on the universality of contextual/registerial consistency as a pre-requisite of text-hood.

There is, however, another side to the story: whether a context is collaborative or dependent and whether the function of the sub-text is tone setting or facilitative, the occurrence of a sub-text carries the potential of disruption for the (putative) primary text. For sub-texts can, and sometimes do, 'take over'. For example, given certain circumstances, the tone setting function can transform itself, so that the sub-text may end up construing a context which itself becomes the interactants' focus, with the main context either entirely dissipated or largely placed in the background. I would suggest that this may be less a case of integration than that of the main context/register being SUPPLANTED by another context/register following a brief interspersion of the two. To elaborate on this comment, let me draw attention to what Bernstein (1990) has called LOCAL PEDAGOGY, which often begins its life, particularly in one of its manifestations, in a tone setting sub-text, especially if the interactants are a child and an adult, and especially if the adult is a parent. The form I have in mind is the one closest to OFFICIAL PEDAGOGY as exemplified in the range of official pedagogic registers, particularly those produced by official pedagogues. Elsewhere (Hasan 1995, i.e., chapter 5 in this volume) I have claimed that a major component of official pedagogic discourse, such as classroom talk, is REFLECTION BASED:

its design is geared to creating some understanding of the world around us. Clearly, understanding of any kind is a semiotically created construct. So it is not surprising that when texts construe reflection based activity, then in terms of the current SFL terminology, in performing it typically, the choice of verbal action will be constitutive.[49] The linguistic realization of the official pedagogic discourse, particularly that produced by official pedagogues, relies (amongst other things) on generalization of one kind or another, such as we find in defining, classifying, explaining, etc. The realization of local pedagogic discourse particularly in the middle class educated families in most industrialized countries bears resemblances to this and in such families those sub-texts are at risk of developing into a local pedagogic discourse which typically construe the verbal activity of informing (whether on demand or spontaneously) by describing, classifying or generalizing about the nature of some entity or process or by explaining some form of injunction.[50] Let me illustrate this point, by considering a likely scenario, which might have come about but did not, within example C: the mother's comments on the scarcity of passionfruit could have built up gradually into a fairly detailed description of the conditions under which passionfruit might be successfully cultivated. In fact something of this kind does occur in an embryonic way as can be seen just four messages later in the continuation of the same dialogue:

Example Ca: [continued four messages later from end of C]

63: Stephen: can you get – can you get the rest out Mummy?
64: Mother: it's got very thick skin, this passionfruit, hasn't it
65: Stephen: why has it .. mummy?
66: Mother: well, it's probably taken very long time to grow
67:    see, they don't usually grow in –
68:    it's cool for passionfruit now
69:    they don't like the cold weather
70:    do you think we should plant a passionfruit vine at out new house?
71: Stephen: yes.. yes
72: Mother: I think that would be a good idea
73: Stephen: me too ..
74: Mother: all gone! ..
75:    t usually takes a couple of years before you get many passionfruit on your vine
76:    when you're six ..
77:    we'll have lots of passionfruit
78:    when you're six ..
79: Stephen: oh
80: Mother: that'd be good wouldn't it?

The resemblance of differentially distributed everyday talk to the critical qualities of official pedagogic discourse is sufficient to remind us that the early construction of knowledge is rooted in quotidian social processes of the type which enact a specific kind of social relation.[51]

Interestingly, when a casual verbal activity is on its way to becoming a local pedagogic activity, such a development activates a subtle shift in mode from dialogue towards monologue: thus in the continuation of Example *C* to be found in Cloran's text (lines 67–81) the balance of turn taking changes so that the mother's turn is considerably longer than the child's. Figure 6.3 presented above (Section 6.2.3.3) highlights a similar pattern in sub-text$_4$ represented by segment (viii) explaining the mother's rejection of Stephen's request for a vitamin C tablet (see lines 54–59): here the mother's turn accounts for most of that sub-text; in fact it is the longest turn taken by the mother in what is presented in this paper as Example *C*. I have remarked earlier that the tone setting sub-text acts on human relations: when tone setting construes a reflection based activity as for example with Stephen's mother explaining why/when passionfruit get thick skin (c.f., Cloran 1999a: Table 10, especially lines 67–69), the interaction serves to construe knowledge mediated through a specific category of interpersonal relation. In this way, learning about the world becomes not just learning about objects, activities, or concepts in isolation from one's relation to the interactive other: rather, both the world and the self become known within the frame of some human relation. The nature of these relations differs across the different segments of a community, but the fact that the first acts of construing knowledge are embedded within such relations is a constant (Williams 1999; Cloran 1999b). This close nexus between interpersonal relation and what Vygotsky (1978) calls concept automatization characterizes all acts of local pedagogy. By contrast much of official pedagogy is an effort to construe an understanding of the world, to create what we call knowledge, as if such construals and creations were dissociated from interpersonal considerations: this aspect of official pedagogy is a denial of the importance of those human relations, those discursive contexts, in which the social subject's understanding of the world historically begins. Whatever the ideological justification offered for the practice, the results are less than palatable.

Returning to the (informing) sub-text that might come to supplant the primary text, when/if such supplanting does actually come about, the common perception is likely to be that of the speakers 'moving on' to something else, because the concerns of the discourse are no longer what they were before: what might under different circumstances have been just a subsidiary event, e.g., a tone setting or facilitating sub-text, would have developed into a text that, so to speak, declares its independence from that other text where it started its life. Two observations appear important here. First, this situation closely resembles one where two parallel texts might be interspersed briefly, with one of them, the one that began first, discontinuing while the other continues in temporal sequence. After all as I have remarked earlier, the speaking that functions as a sub-text has nothing in its own make up that stops it from being a text in its own right: the line between purely material co-location and textual integration is not drawn along the morphological make-up of the sub-text, but on the grounds of its GSP and its textural relations. When speaking of this kind is not pressed into performing the function(s) which allow it to be integrated into a primary text, it logically assumes the independence which is implicit in its own make-up: realizationally its textural relations with the preceding text 'thin down'. Whether there is a substantial difference between supplanting and SEQUENCE is an empirical issue, though it appears likely that the early stages of supplanting may display a more robust cohesive linkage than would those of sequence or interspersion. In fact, supplanting of the type with relatively robust cohesive linkage 'at the edges' is the most highly favoured method of progression in casual conversations.[52] Second, a supplanting pattern of the kind described above explains the basis of the feeling interactants sometimes have of, say, a conversation having moved away from a casual affair to a serious discussion. But if speaking is subject to these vicissitudes, and if speakers for the most part successfully navigate these twists and turns in their discourse, then it follows that at some level of consciousness they must monitor the discourses in which they are engaged, for it is this on which the success of their discursive enterprise depends (Hasan 1994). It is not simply the objectivity of an analyst that makes her note the difference between the complex text and the simple parallel one, but very probably Stephen and his mother too recognize that the plan to visit Chatswood is a different kind of discursive episode compared with

Table 6.6: One interaction, different relations: complex v. parallel simple texts

	relations within complex texts	relations betwen parallel simple texts
material:	same location; same interactant	same location; same interactant (=colocation)
principle:	integration of different registers	consistency of register within each text
structural:	subtexts and primary text integrated	each text a separate structureal identity
contextual:	dependency or collaboration	each context independent of the other(s)
functional:	facilitation or tone setting	one text has no function in the other(s)
textual:	substantial textural unity present	textual unity absent or marginal
	chain sharing, chain interaction	chain sharing minimal: no interaction

Table 6.7: Forms of co-location: parallel texts within one interaction

material continuity:	same location; same interactant (= co-location)	
text type:	complex or simple	
forms of colocation:	*enclosure:*	one parallel text is preceded & followed by another parallel text
	interspersion:	parallel texts 1 and 2 occur in alternation
	sequence:	parallel text 2 follows parallel text 1; 3 follows 2 ...

commenting briefly on the scarcity of passion fruit or explaining Nana's preference for a particular chair, or the inadvisability of taking too many vitamin C tablets.

The material and textual relations discussed so far are presented in Tables 6.6 and 6.7. Table 6.6 summarizes the critical attributes of complex and parallel simple texts, in order to highlight the differences between integration and pure co-location. Table 6.7 presents a summary of the forms of co-location, i.e., the modes of material contact between parallel texts. As will be noted, whether speaking is examined from the point of view of integration or of pure co-location, the necessary assumption in both cases is that the segments occur within the outer frame of the same interaction. There is thus a material relation between a primary text and its sub-texts which together make up a complex text: each of the constituents of such a complex text has the same interactive location and the same interactants. From this point of view, the constituents of the complex text are co-located just like parallel texts; the difference is that over and above this material contact, the sub-texts in a complex text also have a textual relation. For the formation of the complex texts, the co-location of its constituents is a necessary condition but not a sufficient one. Table 6.6 is intended to bring out this contrast.

The one relation that is not mentioned in either of these tables is that of supplanting. It seems to me that supplanting represents a genuinely fuzzy category, so that the supplanting text shares some characteristics with a sub-text and others with the parallel ones. Thus, all things being equal, in a supplanting text, as also typically in sub-texts, there will occur some shared identity chain(s), whose referent will be some (third person) object or action relevant to the text being supplanted. This is what accounts for the display of early textural unity in a supplanting text. As I have argued above, this characteristic is either totally absent from parallel texts or only nominally present: the identity chain they may share with other texts will typically refer to the interactant(s) as in the case of segment (vi) in our example. However, as the field of the context being construed by the supplanting text moves further towards independence from that contextual configuration wherein it began its life, the textural unity between the supplanting text and the supplanted one weakens. In fact, the absence of textural unity and the divergence of contextual configuration are one and the same fact seen from the perspective of the distinct levels of linguistic description.

In introducing the discussion of sub-text$_1$ and sub-text$_2$ which construe a dependent and a collaborative context respectively, I used the terms arrestive with reference to the former (Section 6.2.3.2) and concurrent with that of the other (Section 6.2.3.3). These terms refer to one way social process and its realizing text impinge on another context/text along the time line furnished by the interactive frame. When the conduct of an on-going social process and its realizing text is suspended by that of another, as with sub-text$_1$, this arrests the direct progress of the design of the on-going text. For example, this is how sub-text$_1$ with its facilitative function impinges on the on-going social process being realized by the primary text in Example *C*. But arrestive contact is not limited only to facilitative sub-texts construing dependent context; a parallel text construing an independent context too could arrest the on-going social process and its realizing text. To give an imaginary example: John is engaged in a casual conversation with a friend when the postman knocks with a recorded delivery parcel for him. The casual conversation previously in progress will be arrested by the activity of receiving the recorded delivery parcel, and the realizing text of the latter context will be an enclosed parallel text, assuming that the casual conversation with the friend is resumed.

The term CONCURRENT is used when the conduct of an on-going social process continues, irrespective of the onset of another: both processes run side by side. In the nature of things, this is possible only if at the time of contact, one process calls only for verbal action and the other is at a stage where it can be continued just by physical action. This condition is met by sub-text$_2$ *vis à vis* the primary text in Example *C*. The action in sub-text$_2$ is verbal: the mother is commenting on the scarcity of passionfruit, while the action in the primary text at that point is wholly physical: a part of the design of organizing the child's lunch is to actually present the agreed lunch items to him. Concurrent contact is not limited to occur only with sub-texts: a parallel text may be concurrent with another, the context construed by the two being independent of each other. This is illustrated by Example *C*, where the complex text and segment (vi) represent two parallel texts, each with a context independent of the other (see Figure 6.3 above in Section 6.2.3.3). It appears that a sub-text with facilitative function is limited to making an arrestive contact with the primary text.[53] By contrast, tone setting sub-texts may be either concurrent or arrestive. We have already witnessed concurrent tone setting sub-texts in Example *C* (e.g. sub-texts 2–4 in Example C as shown in Figure 6.3). Examples of arrestive tone setting may be found quite regularly in classroom talk, as for example, when in the middle of an on-going lesson, the teacher tells the pupil(s) to pay attention, or upbraids them (explicitly or implicitly) for not doing so.[54] Such injunctions/observations naturally arrests the progression of the on-going lesson, and since they act on teacher-pupil relations they would be treated as a variety of tone setting sub-text: in fact, in current analysis of classroom discourse they are often cited as evidence of the teachers' will to power.[55] Table 6.8 summarizes the patterns of contact found in integration by tone setting and facilitative sub-texts as well as two forms of co-location, viz., enclosure and interspersion.

Table 6.8: Interactive time and types of contact in the process of talk

	concurrent	arrestive	contacting CC
tone setting:	✓ e.g. sub-text2	✓ e.g. classroom	collaborative to main
facilitation:	—	✓ e.g. sub-text1	dependent on main
enclosure:	✓ e.g. segment (vi)	✓ e.g. recorded parcel	independent of other(s)
interpersion:	✓ (actions material & verbal)	✓ (both actions verbal)	independent of other(s)

The notion of arrestive and concurrent contact is significant as it forces us to confront an important issue in the description of context. If, for example, we wish to make predictions about the possibilities of concurrent contact, it is important to be able to talk about both material and verbal action. Concurrent contact is possible only when the activity in *at least* one contextual configuration is essentially material; if the activity in both relevant CCs is entirely verbal, then concurrent contact for their realizing texts is logically impossible: if any contact occurs, it must be arrestive. Note that making this kind of generalization implies a recognition that social activity in the field of discourse could be material and/or verbal. In the current SFL frameworks, however, such recognition is problematic because the term *activity* as an aspect of field has been interpreted (at least by implication) as largely physical/material activity (calling upon language for assistance). The descriptor *social*, which in SFL literature often modifies the term activity simply confirms that the activity is typically SYNSOMATIC; in other words, it involves the synchronization of effort by two human agents or more: it is, in the words of Malinowski, concerted human action. So paraphrasing field as social activity does not recognize the verbal action aspect of social activity. Verbal actions such as those of explaining, defining, narrating, reporting, chronicling, lecturing and a myriad of others that I would describe as verbal actions are treated as a matter of mode in the current SFL models of context. From this perspective, the distinction between field and mode is suspiciously reminiscent of the distinction between the what and the how, the content and the style, which has been popular in literary criticism.

The history of this practice is irrelevant at this point; what is relevant is the fact that it poses serious problems in the description of context. In the first place, when all that is happening on some occasion of speaking is, say, simply the recounting of a past experience, or storying, i.e., narrating an already fashioned story, or fashioning one anew, then considerable confusion arises. Is there an activity in contexts of this kind? If not, then we are confronted with the possibility of activity-less contextual configurations,[56] which in turn raises further questions. For example, under what conditions is it permissible for a contextual configuration to have no activity? And even assuming that in some way it makes sense to have an activity-less contextual configuration, what would the rhetorical mode be a mode of? On the other hand, if we maintain that there indeed is an activity when one is storying, then it seems reasonable to assume that this activity would be named by some synonym for narrating a story.[57] In that event, we need to be clear about the nature of this activity: it is clearly not physical/material; what is it then? And what is its relation to the mode (that in this hypothetical case is very likely to be described as 'narrative')? I believe it is important for SFL to re-consider the notion of field/activity/domain, for a good deal of the complexity of field is describable by reference to the interaction of physical/material action with the verbal ones. At a later point in this paper (see Section 6.3.3), I shall propose that the presence of verbal action is an essential attribute of the field of discourse; in doing this I shall in fact be simply repeating what I had claimed more than a decade ago. As early as 1985, at a conference organized by Martin, I had suggested that the notion of social activity must be reconceptualized to cover action as well as locution, i.e., both material and verbal action.[58] My recent exploration of the relations of context and text appears to support this position.

6.2.4 Learning from instances: from texts to system

Much more can certainly be said about the three examples discussed above, but perhaps what has already been said is enough to point to new directions. On the basis of the examination of these instances, we can turn now to ask how the insights we have gained might be represented in a way that does justice to the system. In recent years system has received bad press, whether from scholars devoted to critical studies or from those who have favoured a particular interpretation of the dynamic perspective. This appears to be a hangover from those approaches which treat the system of language as synonymous with a set of invariant rules: this implies in turn that the system is static and incapable of change. If this were true then obviously there would be no question of it contributing to social change in any way. From this viewpoint, the very concept of system may be considered reactionary. However it is a view of system that is excluded logically from SFL, since it contradicts the postulated dialectic of system and instance according to which system is a resource that shapes the instance and instance in its turn is a resource for introducing innovation in the system as represented here in Figure 6.1 (Section 6.1) (see also Halliday 1992a, 1992b, 1996, 1999; Hasan 1973c, 1984e, 1996a; Matthiessen and Nesbitt 1996). If the system of language changes through time, and we know that it does; if at every stage of its history, the system of language is variable, and we know that it is; if we postulate that language as a system is fashioned by the (near) infinity of instances, and that by definition each instance is unique, then clearly it follows that these unique instances must also mediate change and variation in the system of language. System itself cannot, therefore, be either static or a body of invariable rules: the delusion is created by the trick of confusing it with Saussure's *état de langue*. Instead of being a constraint, system is in fact a resource; instead of determining what can or cannot be said, it serves as a grid for saying, whether innovatively or conformingly and for interpreting, whether the said conforms to the probabilities of the system or departs from them (Hasan 1996c, 1999a). However, at the same time it is important to note the obvious fact that no one instance by itself can ever reveal the potential of the system as a whole: it cannot reveal the range of possibilities for instantiation. Language, in the sense of 'the system of language' is the biggest abstraction made in linguistics as Firth (1957) pointed out some four decades ago: as individual speakers or even as analysts, we can never come in contact with the whole system of language; what we encounter at anyone moment is some instance of some variety of language. This gives rise to a paradox: on the one hand it is true that an instance is not a miniaturized version of the system; on the other hand it is also true that all we ever encounter at any one occasion is the instance of some one variety. As analysts, then, we are faced with having to piece together the system of language, because we are unable to encounter the system *per se* in an instance; we can and do encounter instances, but they are limited in their power to reveal. The informal analysis of three examples of speaking is certainly not sufficient ground for generalizations, but one must begin somewhere. In beginning from the analyses I have offered above, I take the following conclusions for granted as warranted by the acceptance of the analysis.

- The principles for text production are variable: speakers may produce a simple text, simply pursuing the design associated with a social process; this is the principle of contextual/registerial consistency, exemplified by Texts *A* and *B*. But it is also possible for speakers to produce a complex text, diverging from a simple design to accommodate other, subsidiary concerns; by so doing, they modify the character of the social process with which they began; this is the principle of contextual/registerial integration, exemplified by the complex text in *C*;
- An adequate framework for the analysis of context must be able to identify the environments, i.e., the (conjunction of) features where contextual/registerial integration is at risk (and, by implication, where such integration is relatively less likely to occur);
- The modelling of context must be such as to be able to explain why certain conjunctions of contextual features are typically less hospitable to integration, and others are not;
- There is reason to believe that the three contextual parameters of field, tenor and mode are not just three completely separate ingredients of social situations: it may be in fact more profitable to think of them as three interrelated perspectives on the social context with reference to which speaking is done. Activity (i.e., field), relation (i.e., tenor) and (modes of) contact permeate each other. An adequate description of context must reflect this close relation;
- The modelling of context must embrace both the material and the semiotic: to act as an adequate tool for the analysis of talk, it can neither be viewed as entirely material, an external backdrop for the enactment of the drama of speaking, nor as entirely semiotic, as something that impinges only on the intellect, not on the senses.

Current SFL frameworks for the description of context/text are unaware of the phenomenon of contextual/textual integration. The competence of these frameworks is limited to the description of independent contexts realized by simple texts as is evident from the Halliday and Hasan model used above in stating the contextual descriptions of Examples *A-C* as well as from the framework offered in Martin (1992; see especially Chapter 7). Lacking the concept of contextual/registerial integration, we have been satisfied with the sequencing/combining of registers/genres, and the only explanations offered for the occurrence of these reside in the imagined desires and decisions of unique individuals as represented in the dynamic flowcharts (Ventola 1987). [59] In the absence of the notion of integration, the question of addressing the difference(s) between integration and co-location can clearly have no meaning; nor can the issue of producing formal descriptions suited to the distinction. Further, in both models the three parameters of the contextual construct are treated as impermeable – three discrete vectors, each to be seen as the point of origin for a system of choices which pertain simply to that vector without creating any echoes in the other two.[60] In fact, I have reason to believe that to point out default dependencies across the different systems and choices, i.e., to identify 'habitual conjunctions' such as I have presented above (see Section 6.2.2), is not regarded favourably by at least some colleagues: it is said that to draw attention to the typical conjunctions of contextual features is to 'naturalize' the *status quo,* thus potentially hindering change in the system of culture by making contextual disjunctions invisible (Martin 1985a). My own view of linguistic analysis is that description is not 'injunction': to say 'this is how it is' is not to say 'this is how it should be'. Linguistic analysis is good if it makes available a deeper understanding of how language works; it does not necessarily serve as a tool for achieving an agenda for social reform, no matter how excellent that agenda might appear to those who propose it. This stage calls for a different kind of engagement with the product of that analysis. The description presented below will make connections with the material social conditions of human existence, for this is the only site for language to exist and to work. However, *on principle,* I will attempt not to exploit the fuzziness of boundaries between description and injunction.

6.3   The system of context: a dynamic perspective

It is not possible to present the description of the entire contextual construct even at the primary degree of delicacy within the scope of a paper such as this. In this section I shall focus particularly on field, since whatever the form of integration – facilitating or tone setting – some shift in the field choices is possible if not always necessary. So the description of field can provide a good starting point for representing hypotheses about contextual/ registral integration. In the course of doing that I will attempt to address the issues highlighted above at the close of the last section.

6.3.1 Field of discourse and the concept of action

The most important concept relevant to field is ACTION: what is being done. Everything else in field may be seen as an elaboration of this concept. The concept of action/activity/act is not unique to linguistics: irrespective of what label we use to refer to it, the concept is in fact crucial to most disciplines concerned with the study of human social existence.[61] As one would expect each discipline brings a different perspective for engaging with the concept, but in the majority of cases action is thought of as non-verbal, often physical. So far as the discipline of linguistics is concerned, the situation is reversed: its primary interest is in language and its framework is developed with a view to describing language; therefore its perspective on action is language based. Aphoristically, the focus of the field of discourse 'is' *doing with different degrees of speaking.* The concept of action is of interest to linguistics only because, and to the extent that, non-linguistic human action actually impinges in some way on linguistic action, i.e., on the choices in speaking and interpreting. Without this nexus between non-linguistic action and meaning, linguistics would have had little ground for interest in the concept of action as it is generally understood; and it certainly would have scarce tools, if any, for the analysis of action in that sense. But the concern with the nexus of action and language means that the perspective linguistics brings to the examination of activity is, *without apology,* centred around acts of making meanings by language, irrespective of whether this focus is shared or spurned by other human/social discipline(s).[62]

The acceptance of this position has some important implications. To begin with, if as a linguist my interest in activity stems from its relation to language, then the presence of speaking is a *sine qua non* for something to be regarded as an activity. No matter how many non-verbal actions might be going on in an interaction, if there is no speaking, then there is no object of study so far as linguistics is concerned: *in the absence of discourse, there can be no call for a field of discourse.* Linguistic analysis can assign some value to 'silence' and/or physical action only in the context of speaking, when it is surrounded by language, not when it occurs divorced from language. The significance of this claim will become obvious as the description of field progresses, but note here that if non-linguistic action enters in the conceptualization of context, and especially of field, because it impinges on speaking and interpreting, then the field of discourse, the doing with degrees of speaking has a Janus-like character. One face that field *must* present is that which consists of speaking, call it *verbal action:* the necessity for the presence of language follows from the fact that languaging is a *sine qua non* of activity so far as linguistics is concerned. The other face field *might* present is that of some doing which is basically physical/material, call it *material action:* so far as the linguistic focus is concerned, material action is not a necessity; it may be present or not; what must always be there to justify a linguistic analysis is language. However, linguistics needs to recognize both faces of action if it is to explain how the two might co-operate within the same activity when they are co-present. This co-operation can take different forms. It is certainly possible for the two kinds of action to proceed along two parallel paths. Here is an imaginary example: John is driving a friend to work, and as they drive they also discuss the recent reports on 'road rage'. So the two actions simply run parallel to each other, and it is possible at least in theory that neither helps or (significantly) hinders the performance of the other: the material action remains purely material, the verbal, purely verbal. But anyone who has participated in such a situation will readily accept that the conduct of each activity could impinge on the other, simply because they are co-occurring; thus depending upon the state of the traffic, the discussion might be full of stops and (re-)starts, though one hopes that the driving might be less subject to distraction! However, the very fact that one is apprehensive driving with a driver who is engrossed in discourse shows that the possibility of mutual impingement is recognized. Systemic descriptions of context have no way of building such possibilities into the description, a point first made in principle by Martin (1985a), though I believe his model did not offer a solution to the problem. Then also experience teaches that material and verbal actions do not always simply run side by side with this kind of marginal contact: in fact social activities vary in the extent to which these two classes of action might coalesce in their make up. Below, I describe some of the ways in which the co-operation between these two classes of action occurs. The description is paradigmatic in orientation and will be represented in the form of a system network.

6.3.2   Verbal and material action: primary systems in field of discourse

A commonplace observation is that in every known culture a large category of social activities exist *that just cannot be performed except by languaging,* irrespective of whether or not they are also assisted by other semiotic systems, such as those of gesture or graphics. [63] In an important sense, such activities are semiotic, and more specifically the most pervasive semiotic system is verbal/linguistic. Not unreasonably, then, there are certain social practices (i.e., social activities) the recognition of which as this or that type of discursive activity depends not on what else may be going on physically/ materially at the moment of speaking but on the details of the verbal action itself. Examples of such 'decisive' verbal action are, say, defining, explaining, generalizing, narrating, lecturing, persuading, advising and so on. We may rightfully claim that in such cases, the activity (i.e., field) is realized by verbal action(s) in the sense that *there would be no activity for a linguist to analyse if there were no action of speaking.* From this point of view the verbal action in these cases is *constitutive* of the entire activity (i.e., field), which of course is not to claim that the social value of such activities, their place in the culture, is determined by speaking as such. As I will show below, the choice of constitutive verbal action interacts in interesting ways with the choice of material action.

By contrast with verbally constituted activities, there are some social activities which *just cannot be performed with verbal action ALONE*: they call primarily for material action, although many will permit, if not actively require, some speaking as an additional resource in its performance.[64] In activities of this kind, verbal and material action coalesce: the material action is *present* and the verbal action is employed as an additional resource in the performance of the activity. This type of verbal action has been traditionally recognized in SFL as ANCILLARY: *it does not constitute the complete activity, it simply assists in its conduct.*[65] Since such activities are basically material, i.e., (*action based*), not surprisingly, *their identity can be established more readily by an observation of the material action* rather than by the examination of language in use. This is demonstrated by Text *B*, which is a good example of a kind of action based field: we noted (Section 6.2.2) that it was fairly problematic to read the on-going actions in the activity of this text by reference to the text's language alone.[66] Comments by the scribe on what was going on materially were needed in addition to the ancillary use of language. Further examples of this category of action are care-giving, e.g. bathing a child, helping with household chores, such as cooking, cleaning, etc.; helping with a practical project, e.g. setting up a theatre stage, building a model aeroplane; economic transactions, e.g., buying goods of various kind from retail stores, and so on. These are the sorts of actions that Malinowski (1923, 1935) might have described as 'concerted human activities'.

It follows from this discussion that ancillary verbal action will occur *only if* a material action is present; but the reverse is not true: it is not the case that whenever material action is present the verbal action will be ancillary (c.f., earlier example of driving a car while talking about 'road rage' supports this). So in the first place, there is the possibility that material action may be present without any verbal action whatsoever; *in that case the situation is not one that linguistics can be concerned with* (see Note 65); there will be no displaced text if text is defined as language in use. However, another possible scenario is that the material action may be physically present, and some verbal action is occurring; in that case, the language would be constitutive, IF it is, in no way, instrumental in the performance of the material action. It is this kind of conjunction of material and verbal action that is implied in the imaginary example of John driving (material action: PRESENT) while discussing road rage with his friend (verbal action: CONSTITUTIVE, i.e., NOT ancillary): constitutive verbal action of discussing does not *require* the material action of driving for the conduct of its design or vice-versa: strictly speaking they are 'irrelevant' to each other (as indeed Butt 2004a maintains). It is perhaps for this reason that SFL has never incorporated the scenario into its model of field. But in principle with this sort of conjunction what we have is two on-going activities, the co-performance of which creates a tension in the situation: though they are unrelated, the possibility is open that one could impinge on the other as suggested earlier, and if so this would definitely be manifested in some way in the speaking. In other words, the conjunction of two different activity types identifies an environment where the field is left open to shifts and changes of one kind or another, which might lead to textual colocation and/ or integration: this is where the possibility of *iterative field choice* exists (discussion in Section 6.3.1.1). For example if there is an accident on the road ahead and John has to stop at the tail of many waiting cars, the discussion activity is bound to be interrupted by some language use which will ordinarily not pertain to the course of the 'discussion on road rage'. Note another interesting fact about the ancillary verbal action: typically it tends to be intermittent; it comes in spurts, along which the conduct of the material actions 'silently' being manifested by physical actions; this is demonstrated both by Example *B* and *C*. This fact is significant because such 'silent' spatio-temporal *loci* offer another environment that is hospitable to recursive field choices which underlie textual integration and/or co-location, as shown by Example *C*.

As implied above, when material action is NON-PRESENT, so far as the linguist is concerned this is of no consequence from the point of view of register: the linguistic expertise is called for only when *there is some verbal action occurring*. But in this case, for obvious reasons the verbal action running independent of the material action would be [constitutive] as for example discussing road rage while driving: this is the *default choice* in the environment of [non-present] material action. The non-presence of material action might itself mean that it is genuinely ABSENT. With absent material action, the constitutive verbal action must be CONCEPTUAL as when one is writing an exam paper. Such [conceptual] verbal actions construe verbal semiotic constructs, something that must be processed by the intellect; it calls for mental work, without implying any physical sensuous action. And if any physical action does occur, it is typically an adjunct: the point of such action is the performance of the primary verbal activity, as for example teacher displaying a map/figure to the class. The choice contrasting with [absent] material action may be called DEFERRED material action. When material action is [deferred], the constitutive verbal action must more delicately be feature PRACTICAL: verbal actions with this feature specify the details of the material action that is to be performed at some time following the production of speaking. The feature [practical] verbal action is thus related by default to the feature [deferred] material action, and itself functions as an entry point for more delicate choices, to be described in Section 6.3.5 below. The hypotheses discussed above about the interaction of material and verbal action in the field of discourse suggest that the (co-)selection of the various features from the two kinds of action is non-random and systemic. The possibilities of their conjunction are represented in the form of a system network in Figure 6.4a.

Before turning to a discussion of some issues arising from Figure 6.4a, let me emphasize that the hypotheses underlying this system network and all those presented hereafter in this chapter are only partially tested against data: they are both tentative and lacking in depth of delicacy. The selection expressions based on these networks will provide a reasonable (though not thorough) indication of the *structure potential of register varieties*.[67] Typically, however, the structural aspect of a text (type) is activated by relatively less delicate features; nonetheless, the networks will need to be developed a good deal in delicacy before we can specify the kind of semantic and lexicogrammatical features which are critical to the creation of textural relations in a text.[68]

6.3.3 Default dependency in the system of field

The network in Figure 6.4a represents choices at the stratum of context. Its point of origin is social activity; that is to say, the parameter under discussion is field of discourse, and it displays the two simultaneous systems of MATERIAL ACTION and VERBAL ACTION, whose primary options are

Figure 6.4a: Primary systems of action in field

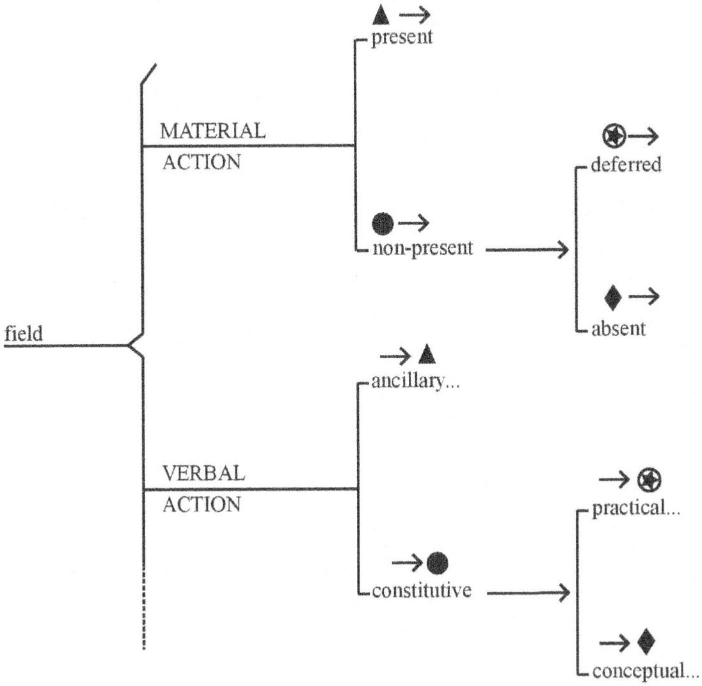

paired by default dependency: such default choices are represented by a complex pair of matched symbol: thus the marking →▲ appended to the choice [ancillary] in the system of verbal action is paired with the marking ▲→ appended to [present] in the system of material action. This is to be read as 'if the feature [ancillary] is chosen in the system of verbal action, then in the system of material action the feature [present] *must be chosen*': schematically 'if feature is marked →▲ then select feature marked ▲→'. The option that is being constrained is the one marked by the 'if' symbol: so it is the option [ancillary] that is constrained to be co-selected with what is shown here as [present]. Earlier (Section 6.2.2) I also discussed several cases of 'default dependency'; these were across parameters. The marked pairing of systemic features in Figure 6.4a–f is system internal (more discussion in the last chapter, Section 5.3.1.5). The row of dots at various points in these networks is a reminder that further networks are anticipated at that point, i.e., the networks here are incomplete and, therefore, tentative.

Default dependency translates 'possibility of conjunction' into 'necessity of conjunction'. This is demonstrated by Table 6.9a which takes the constraints imposed by default dependency on the possible conjunctions of material [present] v. [non-present] with verbal [ancillary] v. [constitutive] (note the use of modals in this table). Default dependencies thus limit the conjunction of systemic features. This can be seen from a comparison of Tables 6.9a and b: in Table 6.9b the constraints imposed by default dependencies on the conjunction of the same four terms have been ignored, which produces four possibilities with each term combining freely with the others as normally expected with simultaneous systems. However, of these, statement (iii) is clearly problematic: to put it informally, verbal action cannot assist a [non-present] material action. Note also that (ii) is a valid conjunction, illustrated by the example of John driving a car while discussing road rage or Stephen eating lunch while discussing plan to visit Chatswood in Example *C*.

Table 6.9a: Default dependencies in Figure 6.4a primary systems

(i)	*if* verbal action is ancillary, then material action *must* be present:
(ii)	*if* material action is non-present, then verbal action *must* be constitutive:
(iii)	material action *may* be present while verbal action *is* constitutive

Table 6.9b: Systemic option in Figure 6.4a (ignoring default dependencies)

(i)	material action present; verbal action ancillary;
(ii)	material action present; verbal action constitutive;
(iii)	material action nonpresent; verbal action ancillary; *and*
(iv)	material action nonpresent; verbal action constitutive.

Table 6.10 presents the possible conjunction of all of the systemic features displayed in introducing, while observing the constraints imposed by the default markings.

Table 6.10. The conjunction of choices from Figure 6.4a, with default dependencies

1:	if verbal action [ancillary], then material action must be [present] as in B;
2:	if material action [non-present], then verbal action must be [constitutive] as in A;
3:	if material action [non-present: deferred], then verbal action must be [constitutive:practical]: for discussion and examples see Section 6.3.5:
4:	if material action [non-present:absent], then verbal action must be [constitutive: conceptual] as in A; for further discussion and examples see Sections 6.3.6–6.3.8:
5:	material action may be [present], and verbal action may be [constitutive]; this implies co-location as in segment (vi) example C, or aligned relation; for discussion and examples, see Section 6.3.11

Table 6.10 suggests that linguistic models of context which treat material action as a system of options in the field of discourse and verbal action as a system of the options [ancillary] v. [constitutive] in the mode of discourse might have greater difficulty in identifying those environments where textual integration or co-location might are at risk (see entry 5 in Table 6.10; and discussion above). Apart from this there are other reasons for treating material and verbal action as simultaneous systems in the field of discourse. Let me review some of these below.

6.3.4   Ancillary v constitutive verbal action: systems in field or in mode?

Tables 6.9a–b and 6.10 between them enumerate the possible conjunctions of systemic features that can possibly be derived from the system network in Figure 6.4a. As the dots following some of the options in the figure indicate these options themselves can be further developed in delicacy, but before proceeding further, some comments need to be made on the terms constitutive and ancillary (c.f., earlier discussion, Section 6.2.3), which have been used here to distinguish classes of verbal action: this is at variance from the tradition practice in SFL where for nearly two decades now they have been treated as features of mode.

From an early stage in my own writing, despite occasional misgivings, I too have typically treated the distinction between constitutive and ancillary as values pertaining to the parameter of mode: it was I who suggested that the two terms refer to the two endpoints of a cline concerning the role of language (Hasan 1981, 1985b, etc.; for further discussion and development of this perspective, see Cloran 1994, 1999a). In SFL persuasion, explanation, definition and so on are described as categories of rhetorical mode.[69] The role of language is obviously related to the rhetorical mode of language in use, if not a pseudonym for it: in fact the terms constitutive and ancillary as used typically in SFL may be taken to refer to the least delicate rhetorical mode, whose more delicate instantiation might be such things as explanation, definition, generalization and so on (see Cloran 1994; Halliday and Martin 1993; Painter 1996). However, on reflection, it seems to me, that what part language is playing or what it is doing in the social situation (c.f., Halliday's remarks quoted in Note 70) are not aspects of mode, nor is rhetorical mode really a phenomenon that belongs in mode: rather, these various cases of speaking, viz., persuading, explaining, joking, narrating are cases of verbal action: they are what language as action achieves. There seems no reason for suggesting that instead of verbal action, they are just a modality or a mode of access for bringing that action about; rather, all content being construed comes with a way of doing. Note that just like material actions, verbal actions, called in SFL terminology rhetorical mode/role of language, in fact, specify what the actants are doing: in the verbal action of explaining, one of the interactants explains just as in the material action of buying, one of the interactants buys. I suggest that the parameter of mode is concerned with CONTACT: options in the system of mode specify the way (i.e., the mode) that semiotic contact is created between interactants, or how the speaker's speaking come in contact with the addressee's intelligence. If this is the case, then considerations pertinent to mode are those of what is known as channel (phonic or graphic) and the physical contact between the speaker and his addressee (virtual or real; if real, co-present or distanced). It is worth mentioning also that the lexicogrammatical realization of mode in this sense generally implicates patterns of textual meaning and lexicogrammar, just as what I am calling verbal actions together with its sphere generally implicate patterns of ideational lexicogrammar: in other words, the claim is that it is these linguistic patterns that are most at risk of variation with variation in material and verbal action.[70] Again, the argument is convincing that an action-less field is not a field at all; and there certainly are occasions of talk when all that is being done relevant to register variation is just speaking as when one is presenting a formal lecture or writing a book. Unless we take lecturing as a kind of doing, we would be forced either to allow an action-less field, or to bring in unanalysed categories of action e.g., recount, lab report, exposition, or 'narrative'.[71] One problem with the use of unanalysed concepts of this kind is the pretence that the choice of, say, the narrative mode is independent of the choice of the activity of narrating, a stance that is clearly questionable. Certainly there exists the possibility that for example a mother might tell her child a 'story', hoping thereby to make the child draw a 'moral' from it. But this kind of *quasi* 'metaphorical' deployment is strictly a feature of a certain category of verbal constitutive action: and it is neither a free choice nor is it an unmarked one; the normal unmarked expectation is that in doing narrating the speaker would employ what we call the narrative mode. It seems to me then that the so-called rhetorical modes such as explaining, defining, generalizing, reporting, recounting, narrating, chronicling and so on are best viewed as constitutive verbal actions, and if the system of field is concerned with specifying the nature of social action, then both material and verbal actions should form part of it.

6.3.5 Practical verbal action: secondary systems

The default markings in Figure 6.4a implies that if material action is [DEFERRED] then verbal action must be [PRACTICAL] (as shown in entry 3 in Table 6.10). A constitutive verbal action with the feature [practical] construes the outline of some material action. So although [deferred] material action, unlike [ancillary] verbal action, does not require a physical action to be in progress at the time of speaking, the future occurrence of some material action is always on the cards. As Figure 6.4b shows the feature [practical] acts as the entry condition for more delicate systemic choices such as PLAN or INSTRUCT, and perhaps other options of a similar kind, a possibility indicated in Figure 6.4b by leaving the system open below the option [plan]. I use the term [plan] with apologies to Cloran (1994), who employs it to label a rhetorical unit wherein interactants speak of some intended future action of theirs.[72] The justification this can be presented in terms of the analysis being proposed here, underlying at least a subcategory of such a rhetorical unit there would most probably be the following field features:

MATERIAL ACTION [non-present: deferred]; *and*
VERBAL ACTION [constitutive: practical: plan]

It is this set of features that, for example, underlies segment (vi) of *C*, where the mother and Stephen speak about their intended visit to Chatswood. An activity with the feature [plan], as I am defining the term here, is action based in the sense that it is oriented towards some physical action of the interactants to be undertaken in the future.[73]

The verbal action with the feature [PLAN] activates a text whose STANCE semantically speaking is ASSERTIVE (Hasan 1996a) realized typically as DECLARATIVE: in informal terms the text 'states/declares' the interactants' intention of doing something. By contrast, a verbal action with the feature [INSTRUCT] produces something of a resource for an addressee: *the speaker's wordings construe a virtual design for performing some deferred material action*, specifying the various stages through which it may be performed. So, although there is no on-going physical/material action occurring at the time of speaking, the point of a verbal action with the feature [instruct] is to enable the performance of such action as and when the addressee might need/desire to do so. And it is an action that typically construes instructions either on how to CREATE some artefact or how to MANAGE an already created artefact. The feature [instruct] may thus be viewed as the entry point to a binary system with the options [CREATE] or [MANAGE]. For example, underlying texts which provide instructions on how to prepare a dish (i.e., recipes), how to knit a sweater (i.e., a knitting pattern), how to conduct a lab experiment (i.e., a lab exercise in the schooling environment), etc. have the following field features:

MATERIAL ACTION [non-present: deferred]; *and*
VERBAL ACTION [constitutive: practical: instruct: create].

Clearly the systems of both material action and verbal action must at some point come together with the sphere of the social activity: does it belong to everyday life or to some specialized aspect of it. This is discussed briefly below (see 6.3.11 below). Returning to 6.4b, here the feature [manage] offers entry to three more delicate choices: how to *install* an artefact, e.g., instruction to install a computer monitor; or how to *maintain* it, e.g., instructions for taking care of an installed computer monitor; or how to *repair* it, e.g., instruction on how to repair a fault in a printer. These systemic choices whose ultimate entry condition is constitutive [practical] verbal action are presented in Figure 6.4b.

In discussing a system at the level of context, ideally a series of actual texts should be presented each of which can be shown to realize some possible selection expression derived from the system network in question. This is obviously not possible for lack of space. So, turning to the more delicate features represented in Figure 6.4b, I will adopt what seems to me the next best solution: this will be to present in Table 6.11 all the possible SELECTION EXPRESSIONS (henceforth SE) whose entry condition ultimately requires [constitutive: practical] in its systemic history. Further, with each SE, I shall provide example(s) of text types which would construe the field features that characterize the relevant SE. Since the choice of [constitutive: practical] verbal action calls also for the selection of [non-present: deferred] material action by default, each SE in Table 6.11 will assume the latter features.

Figure 6.4b: Secondary systems of practical verbal action

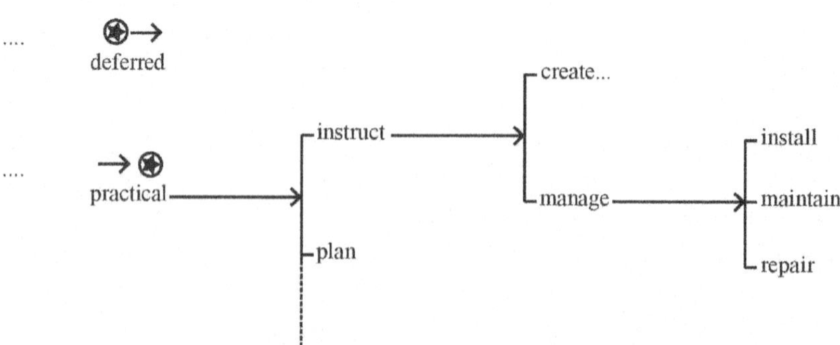

6.3.6 Types of action and the identification of register specific meaning potential

In Tables 6.10 and 6.11, all those SEs which have either the feature [ancillary] or the features [constitutive: practical] verbal action, identify contexts where the point of the social activity is the performance of a material action, which is either occurring concurrent with speaking or will occur somewhere at some later point. This is evident from the text types mentioned as examples of the SEs in Tables 6.10 and 6.11: in each of these the relevant material action is either going on in which case the verbal action is [ancillary] or the language construes the steps whereby the possibility of bringing it about is put within the addressee's reach; in the latter case material action is [deferred]. It is activities of this kind that I have referred to as 'action based' (Hasan 1995, and sections above). The choice of such options in the field always brings physical action in the picture, either as on-going performance or as a physically doable one: *this is what it means to say that the field is action based.* Typically activities of this kind

Table 6.11: Some SEs with [practical] verbal action with [deferred] material action

Assume for each SE the features: MATERIAL ACTION [non-present:deferred]

1: [constitutive:practical:plan]
realizing text construes what the interactants will do at some point in the future: e.g. segment (vi) in example C.

2: [constitutive:practical:instruct:create]
realizing text construes the stages of some action based activity as a resource for the conduct of the same if/when desired; outcome is typically a material artefact: e.g. recipes, knitting instructions: sewing patterns: model kits (e.g. for making a boat or aeroplane) etc.

3: [constitutive:practical:instruct:manage:install]
realizing text construes the stages of some action based activity as a resource for the conduct of the same if/when desired; acting of some material artefact/device to make it function: e.g. instruction on how to install a washing machine, a computer monitor etc.

4: [constitutive:practical:instruct:manage:maintain]
realizing text construes the stages of some action based activity as a resource for the conduct of the same if/when desired; acting of some already produced artefact to keep it in good order: e.g. instruction how to keep food fresh ("keep contents refrigerated once opened") or on how protect a computer monitor ("avoid exposure to direct sun, heat and dust") etc.

5: [constitutive:practical:instruct:manage:repair]
realizing text construes the stages of some action based activity as a resource for the conduct of the same if/when desired; acting of some damaged artefact to restore its original function: e.g. instruction on how to mend a torn shirt; repair a bike puncture: service a malfunctioning printer, etc.

have simple and often a fairly visible goal profiles, and significantly their (expected) endpoint, i.e., outcome, is both obvious and non-contentious.

It is possible that the early focus of discourse analysis on action based fields has encouraged the belief that the statement of the goal of an activity is a non-problematic and clear-cut enterprise: when you are buying vegetables or stamps, the goal is to exchange money for certain goods and unless the activity is terminated prematurely, the completion of just such an actual exchange would be viewed as 'goal achieved'; *ideally, with successfully conducted action based fields, the goal and the outcome are expected to be isomorphic.* Needless to say that there exist other kinds of activities that do not conform to this pattern. In particular, there is an interesting issue that needs to be discussed: each social activity in its performance not only carries information about what is being done by whom under what circumstances but also how it is being done. I am inclined to suggest that this latter aspect is part of what we refer to as 'enacting relations', i.e. performing an interpersonal function. For example 'shut that door, can't you?' construes a very different interpersonal tone than 'could you shut that door, please?' The action in signified action and object is the same, but what has been set in motion is not just shutting the door; at the same time the interpersonal strand of information helps change, maintain or enact a relation. [74] The metafunctions are equal and simultaneous; they do not come one at a time.

Wherever the activity (i.e., field) is action based (as in entries 1 and 3 in Table 6.10 and in all of the entries in Table 6.11), there for obvious reasons the 'relevant objects' and processes as well as the attributes and circumstances attendant on them e.g., the weight and size of objects, and the degree and extent of actions, etc., will have a basis in physical reality. The details of such physical reality are construed by language, as something that is either being done at the moment of speaking or can be brought to the stage of being done at some point in time. This in turn implies that certain categories of semantic and lexicogrammatical choices are relevant to the performance of such verbal action: for example, in a text of the type that instructs how to install some device (see Table 6.11, entry 3), semantically the *event* will be of the *doing* type, which will be realized lexicogrammatically by *material* processes. Example *D* presents an actual example of just the first two steps for the installation of a computer monitor.

Example D:[75]
Chapter Two: Installation
Connecting Your Monitor to a Computer
1 Turn off your computer and unplug its power cord.
2 Connect the signal cable to the signal port on the back of your monitor.

All three processes occurring in this extract *(turn off, unplug, connect)* are material action, each construes an event of the doing kind. Most of the relevant objects are semantically speaking physical entities and belong to the category of artefact; they are realized lexicogrammatically by concrete nouns functioning as Thing with or without Classifier *(computer; power cord, signal cable, signal port, back, monitor).* This is of course not an original insight; other systemicists have commented on such features of this text type known in the genre based descriptions as the PROCEDURAL GENRES. My purpose in highlighting this observation is to use it as a necessary step towards a more general claim about context, meaning, wording and register type. In my understanding the latter category comes nearest to genre when referring to some text.

The choices in the systems of field of discourse are relevant to the specification of what I have elsewhere called the *domain of signification* (Hasan 1985b), i.e., the domain of experience, i.e., the entities, events and their incumbents to which the wordings of the texts are expected to refer. The description of field in Figure 6.4a–b, the history of whose SELECTION EXPRESSIONS is indicated in Tables 6.10 and 6.11, is at a fairly primary degree of delicacy. Using these SES as the basis for making realizational claims, we can only specify the *general* categories of meanings/wordings that the given contexts will activate, such as *doing events* and *material processes:* it does not enable the identification of the *specific* domain of doing or the *specific* lexical taxonomies the members of which might be expected to realize those doings lexicogrammatically. However, *the inability of the present networks to make contact with actual language is a practical problem, not a theoretical one.* There is every reason to believe that as the description of the field of discourse progresses in delicacy, it would become possible to identify the specific lexicogrammatical and semantic domains at risk in the realization of specific choices from the systems of field: such work is in fact well under weigh (see Halliday and Martin 1993). This claim takes us to a higher level concept, to what I have called GENRE SPECIFIC SEMANTIC POTENTIAL elsewhere (Hasan 1985b: 98ff.) which consists of the meanings and wordings that are crucial to the recognition of a register type, which is naturally related to domain of signification. Clearly the more delicately specified the features of the field, the more specific will be our information about the domain of signification, what objects, circumstances, and events are at risk of being referred to. Information of this kind constitutes an important part of the profile of a register. It is, however, important to emphasize that since the domain of signification is stated here by the features of field alone, it forms only a part of some register specific semantic potential: however, the latter is not specified simply by the field but by the values of the contextual configuration as a whole. Important contributions to it are made by the features of tenor[76] and of mode (e.g., Cloran 1994, 1995, 1999a) as the discussion of the three examples in Section 6.2 has already indicated. In principle, *each parameter of the contextual construct, and each value in each parameter acts as the activator of some meanings/wordings that contribute to the formation of a text's identity, which naturally includes its register identity.* However, the required degree of descriptive detail that would allow us to make such specific statements is daunting. Certainly, this chapter will not be able to reach even that stage in the delicacy of description which might enable identification of the specific components in the domain(s) of signification.

6.3.7   Conceptual verbal action: the creative power of language

In the system of verbal action the feature [practical] is in immediate contrast with [conceptual] (see Figures 6.4a and 6.4b). Verbal actions with the feature [conceptual] are maximally different from material action: while material activities are, to use Russell's well known terms, *sens-ible* (i.e., they can be sensed) and physical (i.e., they call on the body as resource for performance), the conceptual ones are *intellig-ible;* instead of calling for physical action, they demand mental action. Just like the feature [practical], the feature [conceptual] too acts as the entry condition for a systemic choice: the terms of this secondary system are [RELATION BASED] v [REFLECTION BASED] (Hasan 1995 for some discussion) as shown in Figure 6.4c. In exploring these choices further, I will first consider the first mentioned, namely, [relation based] verbal action.

Engagement in *any* social action, quite obviously, contributes to the enactment of social relation: this is what forms the foundation of degrees of SOCIAL DISTANCE (Hasan 1973c, 1981, 1985b, 1995). However, perhaps no category of action is as potent in the enactment of social relations as those I have called relation based. Examples of relation based activities would be chatting, swapping jokes, satisfying the other's need to know or to have, consulting, insulting, quarrelling, sarcasms, explicit show of agreement in opinions and perspectives, or of disagreement, emphasizing differences of perspective, and so on. Generalizing from this and many other such verbal actions we may say that the feature [relation based] is the entry condition for a choice between [*cooperative*] v [*conflictual*]. Three quick comments on [relation based] action. First, one might suppose that in the everyday meaning of these terms, cooperation and conflict do not necessarily have to be enacted by verbal action: they can be just as well enacted non-verbally, for example by nodding, smiling, handing over something that someone desires, looking angry, pushing, hitting and the like. Up to a point this is true but [relation based] verbal action, being a variety of semiosis can import into the enactment of social relation such nuances as would elude purely material actions such as those of hitting, shoving, spitting and so on. When seen *in dissociation from verbal action,* the enactment of social relation purely by material action is qualitatively different: the elaboration of the interpersonal relations that comes from [relation based] verbal actions is in a class by itself. Second, it is a notable characteristic of [relation based] verbal actions that between the same interactants they typically tend to follow a trajectory, which has become a part of the speakers' interactive history. Thus typically the same interactants will engage in the same/similar category of [relation based] action, whether [co-operative] or [conflictual] (see Cloran 1994, 1999b; Hasan 1989, 1992b, 2009a; Williams 1995, 1999). This is partly because such activities are particularly sensitive to the ideological orientation of the interactants: underlying what Bernstein (1990) calls (strong/weak) framing are in fact [relation based] actions of specific kinds. Third, and last, [relation based] action seldom appears as a feature of the field in the main context: though this is not impossible (what is odd in a clause such as *he kissed her angrily*? Action can have positive or negative value, entraining certain choices of manner and such like), what typically happens is that the [relation based] verbal action whether [co-operative] or [conflictual] – runs side by side like a prosody of the on-going main activity.[77] Though as briefly discussed above, it has its own grammar derived from its own metafunction. It follows that this feature tends to be rather foregrounded in collaborative contexts which are construed by tone setting sub-texts rather than by a primary or independent one. The frequently prosodic appearance of [relation based] action is noteworthy since it agrees well with the observation (Halliday 1979b, and elsewhere) that interpersonally sensitive patterns of meaning and lexicogrammar tend to occur prosodically. I have suggested that [relation based] action is highly relevant to interactant relations; it is thus a feature of context that is likely to be realizationally related crucially to the interpersonal semantic systems of punctuative message (e.g., address, feedback devices, ritual civilities and so on), to the system of attribution particularly ascription of state (Hasan 1983); prefacing (Hasan 1989, 2009a; Cloran 1994; Williams 1999); appraisal (Martin 1996) and to the lexicogrammar of mood, modality, and modification which construe those meanings.[78]

If [relation based] verbal actions enact social relations, those that are [reflection based] produce semiotic constructs such as explanations, generalizations, classifications and descriptions of phenomena in the world of experience and imagination as well as various forms of moral rules: they thus underlie all institutions and all 'knowledging' whether in its mundane form *(local pedagogic discourse),* as when Stephen's mother explains why Stephen's passionfruit had thick skin or in its esoteric form as when Ian Stewart (1989) explains the new mathematics of chaos *(official pedagogic discourse).* Esoteric knowledging, be it primitive magic or modem day science, the elders' code of conduct or what we know as jurisprudence, in all its forms, production, reproduction, and evaluation, is created when [reflection based] verbal action occurs in conjunction with the sphere feature [SPECIALIZED]. Both [relation based] and [reflection based] actions are inherently creative activities: they are instrumental in creating something that could not be created in that form without such verbal action. This is not to claim that the actions create interpersonal relations or knowledge *ex nihilo* simply 'out of words': clearly social relations are created in the context of human communal existence, just as structures of knowledge such as physics, chemistry take for granted the existence of a physical world.

Despite this similarity, [reflection based] action and [relation based] action do differ from each other: to express this difference in terms of Halliday (1975a), if the latter type of activities position the speaker as an intruder *vis à vis* his environment, the former, i.e., [reflection based] conceptual verbal actions, position the speaker as an observer *vis à vis* the already existing material and social world. This is perhaps one reason why [reflection based] action is often treated not as a creative action but as exposition of some pre-existing phenomena. Since the semiotic constructs produced by the [reflection based] activities either take as their point of departure the physical phenomena of the sens-ible universe or the (existing) codes of communal conduct, the ordinary perception of such activities is that they are 'about' something which already exists and whose identity is independent of [reflection based] verbal actions as such. Thus geography is taken to be about the physical features of a land that exists; history is about what some real people are supposed to have really done in real time; science is about what the physical world is like; jurisprudence is about what is just and fair conduct; and so on, *as if the human intellect were a replicator of whatever exists* and language is the device by which the existing phenomena can be 'expressed'. It is this belief that underlies the ancient views about reference/correspondence whereby language is just a mirror held against the pre-existing material/social realities (for critical comments on this position, see Hasan 1984a, 1984e, 1999a). However, in a very important sense, we never come to know the universe as it *really* is: the world we know is the world uttered by language. Any sensuously validated knowledge of the world that cannot be exchanged with an other is of little consequence to human social existence; the universe *in* which and *with* which we live and act is that which is inter-subjectively objective. And this inter-subjectively objective universe is defined by, grows out of, the [reflection based] verbal actions of the human race. The feature [conceptual] identifies that family of context which Malinowski would have described as the peak of creative action.

6.3.8 Conceptual verbal action: informing and narrating

The feature [conceptual] acts as the entry condition for another system which is simultaneous with the system described above. The terms of this second system of the [constitutive: conceptual] verbal action are [NARRATING] or [INFORMING]. I use these common currency words in a rather abstract and technical sense here: one way of clarifying the underlying principle of this abstraction would be to say that the options capture respectively the significant division between already experienced time and time that is in some sense present. The feature [narrating] thus activates the construal of goings on supposed to be located *in time that has already been experienced* whether in reality or in imagination: examples of text types construing the feature [conceptual: narrating] verbal action would be an autobiography or a research report construing events which have already been experienced in real time, or it could be a story or a nursery tale construing events that have already been experienced in imaginary time. It is interesting to note that in the construal of the field feature [narrating], the semantic concept 'experienced time' is, as it were, more clear-cut than the lexicogrammatical feature known as 'past tense': there is no one-to-one relation between 'experienced time' and the tenses. Thus the so-called 'narrative/historical present' is simply a present tense which construes 'experienced time', albeit introducing a tone of immediacy when this tense is used in company with other semantic and lexicogrammatical features activated by [narrating].

By contrast with narrating, the feature [informing] activates the construal of events perceived to be current at the time of speaking, e.g., in observations, comments, descriptions, and so on. Clearly there is much scope for the development of more delicate choices which depend on the feature |informing| and |narrating|. I will return to these presently (Section

6.3.10), but first a further system which depends on the feature [conceptual] verbal action.

6.3.9   Conceptual verbal action: discourse as object

One respect in which language differs from most other semiotic systems is its ability to 'turn back on itself'. This capacity of language is rooted in the possibility of [constitutive] verbal action, and more specifically in the feature [conceptual]: it is a sub-category of this kind of verbal action that possesses the potential of being reflexive in character. This presents a systemic choice: a [constitutive: conceptual] verbal action may be a [FIRST ORDER] verbal action or a [SECOND ORDER] one.[79] The entry condition for this system is the feature [conceptual]. To indicate what these choices refer to let me use as an example the simple case of a nursery tale, which realizes the selection expression (see Figure 6.4c): [… conceptual: narrating; first order …]. The activity described by this SE would produce an instance of a narrative text type, say, a nursery tale. This would be the [first order] activity of [narrating]. But once this verbal action has been accomplished, then by definition there exists a semiotic artefact, viz., a nursery tale (expressed in graphic substance covering some pages, or in phonic substance occupying time and recording space), and this first order narrative can itself become the relevant object in some other verbal action. This latter verbal action, though still [conceptual] in character, will differ from the [first order] action of narrating inventively (see Figure 6.4d and the discussion of the feature [narrating] below in Section 6.3.10). For example, one might simply reproduce the tale, either replicating it by, say, reading it; or one might condense it as in a summary; or one might transform it in the true sense of the word, by changing its form: for example, the tale of Snow White might become a 'little' stage play. These reproductive actions have the feature [second order] conceptual verbal action: they are [second order] in that for their own conduct, they depend on the existence of a text produced by the first order activity; this somewhat parasitic relation to the discursive product of the first order activity is a necessary condition for the second order activity to come about. But [second order] verbal action is not restricted to being reproductive in the sense just described. It may, in fact, be META-DISCURSIVE, examples of which would be analyses, critiques, history of that text type and so on, the variety that is reflexive in character. This implies that the feature [second order] functions as the entry condition to a systemic choice between the features [reproductive] v [meta-discursive]. Figure 6.4c incorporates these systems.

Figure 6.4c: Secondary systems of conceptual verbal action

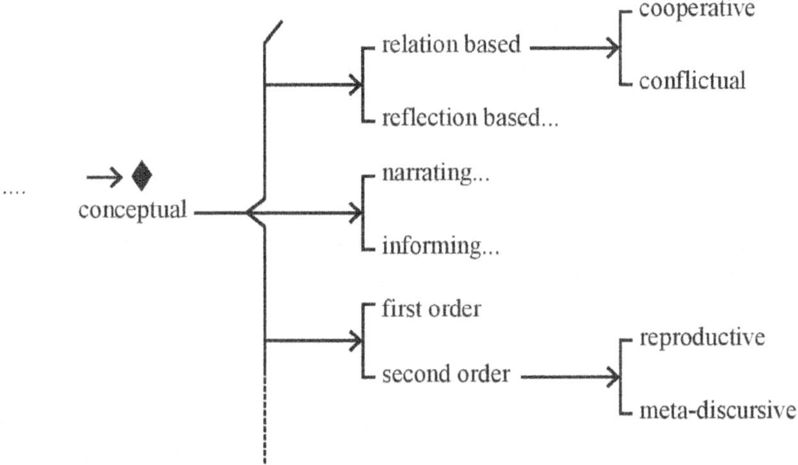

6.3.10 Narrating and informing: some secondary systems

In Section 6.3.8 I presented a very brief discussion of the contrasting features [informing] v. [narrating] whose entry condition is the feature [conceptual] (see Figure 6.4c). I want to suggest that between them these two features identify the majority of constitutive contexts that are not action based, and as such their more delicate description in terms of secondary systems is crucial to an understanding of the nature of verbal action in the make up of the field of discourse. The claim must, unfortunately, remain speculative since any attempt to substantiate it by discussion and/or exemplification will go far beyond a paper of this scope. At this point, I present, purely by way of a brief example, certain systems of choices whose entry condition is [narrating].[80] The systems are presented in Figure 6.4d below.

The verbal action [narrating] offers a systemic choice between two rather transparently labelled features called [INVENTING] and [RECOUNTING]; [inventing] is verbal action creating an *as-if* universe, while [recounting] is verbal action capturing experienced events as refracted from the interactants' point of view. The option [inventing] in turn gives access to a choice between [SIMPLE] or [COMPLEX].[81] The highly tentative more delicate 'systems' of [TALE], [FABLE] and others which depend on [simple] and those of [STORY], [NOVELLA] and others the entry condition for which is [complex] are more in the nature of an indication of the power of the systemic description: the system of options presented here, although highly condensed and lacking elaboration, does allows an initial systemic view of the discursive universe in western cultures. What I am suggesting is that there are constitutive conceptual verbal actions (where material action is [absent]) such as those of 'storying', 'fabling' and so on which are as much action as, say, 'playing cricket' or 'drilling' the soldiers where verbal action is [ancillary], and material action [present]. In the latter cases, language is incidental: the physical activity is the main thing. In the former cases, anything physical (if it occurred) would be incidental: verbal activity is the main focus.

Although at first glance it seems somewhat strange to treat [narrating] and [informing] as terms in a system dependent on [conceptual] verbal action, these two features belong to the same family. They also seem to bear a rather intriguing relation to each other. For example, like a tale or a short story, the early myths too realize the feature [narrating]; but it seems that these myths have a specific kind of function in human history: they as it were 'explain' and construe the cosmology for some (section of a) community, though they do it quite differently from the way that a modern physics text realizing the feature [informing] might do from the perspective of science today. Nor has this close relation entirely disappeared. It is present, even if as a trace, in the behaviour of mothers who in trying to explain some principle to their young children, are just as likely to use a narrative of some kind as they are to offer well argued information. It may be that behind the distinction between [narrating] and [informing] there is the implied diachronic development of ways of 'knowledging', something that is central to the evolution of human cultures. I suggest that it might be useful to recognize a system with the terms [CONGRUENT] v. [METAPHORICAL] with the feature [narrating] as the entry point; thus the system would be simultaneous with the system of [inventing] v. [recounting] as shown in Figure 6.4d.

The selection of the feature [informing] verbal action activates reference to current time: examples of text types that realize this feature are comments, observations, generalizations, explanations, definitions, descriptions and so on. As these examples suggest the currency of the states of affairs is variable. Thus on the one hand the [informing] verbal action may construe states of affairs that are as it were located within the spatio-temporal confines of the on-going interaction, e.g. telling someone what is happening here and now. Let me refer to this feature of [informing] as

Figure 6.4d: More delicate options in narrating and informing

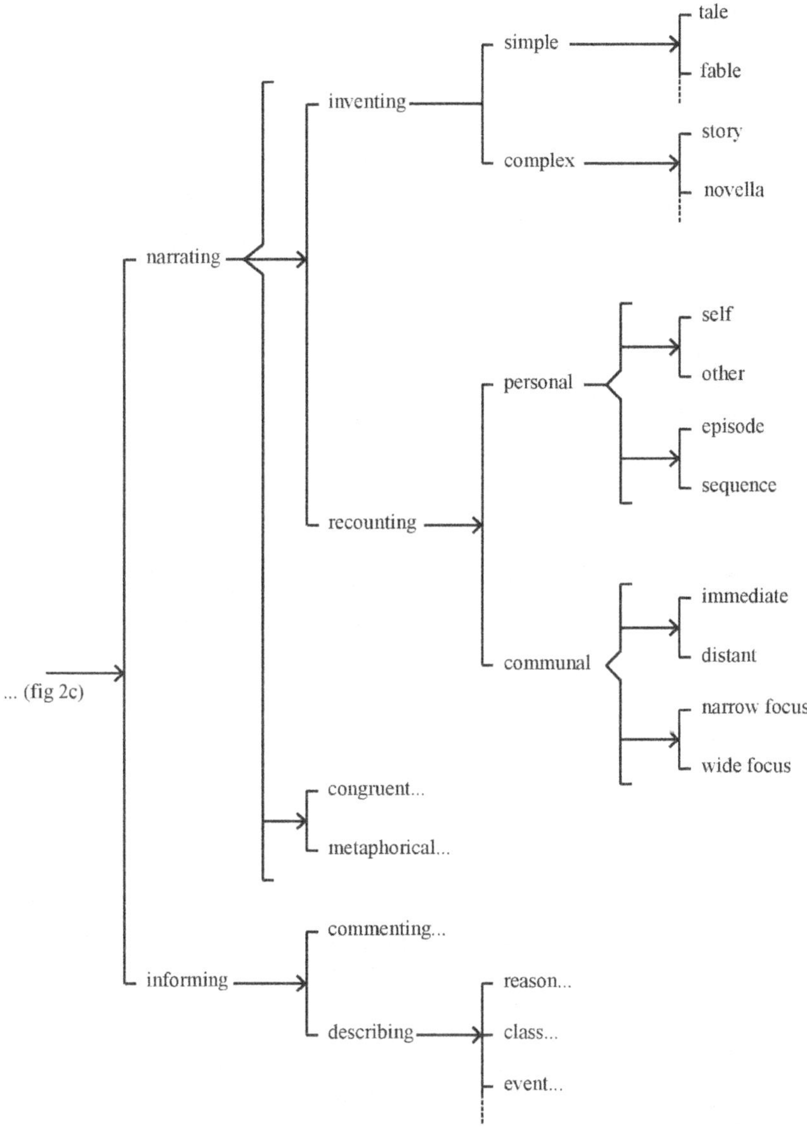

[COMMENTING]. One rather established variety of register that realizes this feature is in fact known as commentary, where the speaker comments on some on-going sport/spectacle. Nearer our everyday experience would be someone in the middle of a conversation suddenly pointing out to something that is going on around them. So the currency of the states of affairs in [informing: commenting] is fairly constrained: they belong to the speaker's here and now.[82] By contrast, the [informing] verbal action may also construe states of affairs whose currency goes beyond the here and now of the speaking moment. For want of a better term, I will refer to this feature of the [informing] verbal action as [DESCRIBING]. It is a feature that may be realized by such texts as describe, say, the circulation of blood, the hydrological cycle, the activity of atoms, the structure of society, the relations of supply and demand, the laws governing the transfer of property, the nature of language and so on. In informal terms, what we have in such text types is *a description of what is a usual state of affairs*: the currency of the event at the time of speaking is implicit in the so-called time-less or universal statements. In terms of the distinction being made here, various kinds of verbal action such as explaining (describing reason) defining (describing classification criteria), generalizing (describing habitual/universal categories), and so on would be viewed as some kind of 'description', even though in common parlance the word 'description' has a much more restricted meaning. What is at issue, however, is not the label but the distinctions being made here: one implication is that at a certain degree of delicacy texts such as the exposition of hydrological cycle and those which classify and/ or define are being seen as belonging to a category that differs from those which comment on the on-going states of affairs. More delicate features will have to be used to make further distinction, as indicated by the dots following the options.

6.3.11 The sphere of action: one aspect of the cultural status of an activity

Let me return briefly to the set of actions listed in Table 6.11 as instances of the various selection expressions from the system as shown in Figure 6.4b. One respect in which the examples of some of these SEs differ systematically from those of the others has to do with the sphere of a community's social life in which the actions are located: the actions might be *quotidian,* i.e., they might pertain to everyday, mundane living or they might be *specialized,* which would pertain to areas of life that are rather exotic and remote from unselfconscious everyday living. As such they would typically be carried out not by just anyone in the community, but by especially designated members. As some actions appear more specialized than others, we are in fact talking about a continuum rather than a binary division. For example, according to Table 6.11 SE 5 might be instantiated by instructions to mend a tom sweater, to repair a punctured bike, or to service a malfunctioning computer printer. Of these the last is the most specialized, the repair of a punctured bike is, by comparison, less so, and mending a sweater even less so. Certainly, someone capable of servicing a malfunctioning printer would, in our community, be expected to have undergone some training or apprenticeship which is designed to bring about some understanding of how the printer is put together and how its various parts function; this is not true of repairing a bike puncture, which requires no extensive training or apprenticeship and so far as mending a torn sweater is concerned, like many of the chores silently set aside as 'woman's work' it is seen as a job that calls for no expertise because anyone can do it![83] It is instructive to compare here the mending of clothes as part of 'woman's work' with the mending of clothes performed by a trained 'accredited' tailor: in talking of sphere, we are talking also of communal perceptions of the value of certain categories of action. The more specialized the action, the higher the 'cultural capital' in Bourdieu's (1991) term and the greater the profit to the actants; by contrast, the more quotidian the action, the further removed it is from locations of social power; and by the same token, the less privileged or privileging (Bernstein 1990) any participation in it will be. It is my understanding that when constitutive verbal action is co-selected with quotidian sphere, the speaking it activates is in terms of Bernstein (1990, 1996, 1999) *horizontal*: such discourses, according to Bernstein (mimeo), tend to be context-specific and segmentally organized. From this point of view *local pedagogic discourse* is a kind of horizontal discourse. By contrast, when the verbal action is constitutive and the sphere is specialized, this activates the type of discourse that Bernstein (ibid.) would refer to as *vertical*: according to Bernstein knowledge worded in such discourses are hierarchically organized with an 'explicit systematically principled structure'. Bernstein's 'official pedagogic discourse' (1990, 1996) is a variety of vertical discourse. Inherent in these systemic distinctions is a remarkable power for indicating the crucial realizational choices in the texts, which for lack of space cannot be described here; but it is important to add that vertical discourses, with their systematically principled structures, are far less hospitable to the occurrence of co-location or integration.

It appears then that the description of field can achieve a greater depth if the contrasting choices of the sphere of action are included in the system network. Its inclusion into the field, just like that of material and verbal action systems, adds to our understanding of 'discursive dynamics' by identifying those attributes of the field which open it to co-location and/ or integration. At the same time, the system of sphere in reflecting on the nature of evaluation; the consideration of the objective basis of the distinction between the specialized and the quotidian highlights at least one basis for ascribing higher value to the activities of the specialized type, and this links the evaluation of action unmistakably to issues of power and control. Naturally the systemic description offered here simply says 'this is how it is', without in the least implying a moral stance that 'this is how it should be'; after all analytic discourse does not consist of moral exhortation, no matter how highly valued the stance of morality may be. Figure 6.4e takes us back to the primary systems represented in Figure 6.4a in order to incorporate the system of SPHERE as a third system simultaneous with the systems of MATERIAL and VERBAL ACTION. The terms of this third system are [QUOTIDIAN] v [SPECIALIZED].

If I am right about the evaluation of an activity, then it follows that in general the more specialized the activity the greater the sense of authority it will bestow. Without doubt, various communal institutions collaborate in the performance of specialized activities: what this means is that around specialized activities there grow not only inter-textually related discursive corpora but also functionally inter-related institutions and personnel; the feature specialized thus has material and semiotic manifestation. For example around the specialized activity of 'trying a case in court' we have a network of resources the complexity of which is quite staggering. Consider simply the body of discourses which cumulatively support such activities: the body of law including legislation and precedents drawn from the actual 'practice of law', the lawyer-client case preparation, the prosecution of the case, its defence rebuttal, witness interrogation, cross-interrogation, the briefing of the jury, the jury's deliberation, the jury's decision, the sentence.[84] And attached to each of the immediate 'relatives' of the discourse of legal trial are physical locations for the enactment of the process; these are often accompanied by specific designs for space management, spatial disposition of personnel, their clothing and control on forms of behaviour; thus the list of 'related' behaviour potential, location and design of activity continues. This multimodal coding, which gives a social process a relatively 'ritualized' character, is what I identified as the defining characteristic of institutionalized activities and relations (Hasan 1981). The more specialized an activity, the more it will tend to be institutionalized in this sense. But it is worth noting that even quotidian activities differ in how far they are, as it were, shored up by communal conventions and institutions. It seems for example that one is free to wear whatever one likes wherever one likes 'within reason', but the very meaning of the expression 'within reason' is spelt out by communal institutions: note, for example, how we have had to legally nominate nude beaches. What I would suggest is that certain quotidian activities are more institutional than others: consider from this perspective the social activities associated with giving birth (e.g. baptism in Christian communities; *aqiqa* amongst the Muslims, and so on) eating with others, marrying, exchanging goods and services, dying, and so on. This suggests that the feature [quotidian] acts as a genuine entry condition for a more delicate systemic choice between [INSTITUTIONAL] v. [INDIVID-UATED]. This is shown in Figure 6.4e. Note also the default relation that obtains between the feature [specialized] and [institutional]: as indicated by the markings *if* the feature [specialized] is selected, *then* the feature [institutional] will also be present by default.[85]

Since the three systems, viz., material action, verbal action and sphere – are simultaneous, the choices in the system of sphere just discussed are applicable to the (permitted conjunctions of) material and verbal action (see Tables 6.10 and 6.11). Clearly the number of SES yielded by the network represented fragment by fragment in 4a–e is already too large to discuss or exemplify even though the description of field is at a fairly low level of delicacy. It is perhaps obvious, though, that the more delicate identification of the 'domain of signification' will be arrived at by consideration of the conjunction of choices from the system of verbal action and of sphere. It might be easier to determine the considerations that would apply in a more delicate description of cultural domains such as those of jurisprudence, religion, pedagogy, aesthetics, commerce, politics, and some other domains by relating them to the features of the systems of sphere and verbal action. For example, the existence of some domains, such as jurisprudence appears to be at the conjunction of [specialized] and [conceptual: reflection based; informing], whereas others such as pedagogic action are not limited to just the [specialized] sphere. The realizations of actions from the domain of religion as well as pedagogy are very likely to differ depending on whether the sphere is [quotidian] or [specialized]. The development of an analysis of the field of discourse along these lines will certainly present problems; but the struggle to solve those problems will most probably be a major step in producing a language based description of social actions and institutions. When a similar systemic approach is brought to bear on the system of tenor and mode, the description of context will cease to rest on uh-theorized notions of the context of culture and situation.

Contexts can differ from each other in a variety of ways: first, there are the three parameters, each with multiple systems of differentiating features, then also the selection of different value combinations has the potential of producing an infinity of contextual configurations. However, the attributes that are describable linguistically and relevant to a language based theory

Figure 6.4e: Primary field systems: sphere of action, material action and verbal action

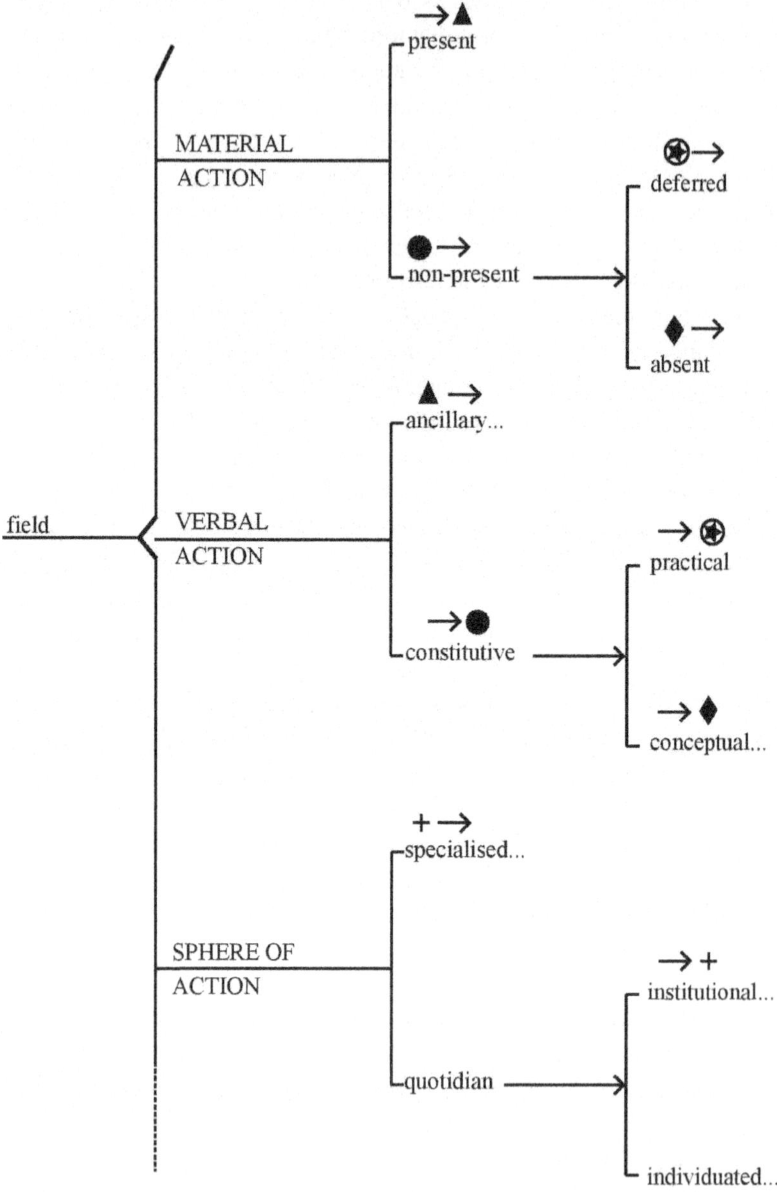

of context are those which activate linguistic meaning and wording in text types: it is worth repeating that not all differentiating features of a context of situation are equally relevant to language and/or describable by the tools of linguistics. From this point of view, the choices in the system of sphere are as significant as those of material and verbal action. For example, to say that activities with the feature [institutional] tend to have a more ritualized design is to say that associated with them is a fairly clearly defined design, with a relatively determinate sense of a beginning, a middle and an end, as for example in a court trial of a case. And, as I have suggested elsewhere (Hasan 1981), this makes it relatively more problematic and therefore considerably rarer to find such contexts/texts supplanted, or co-located with parallel texts.[86] Integration certainly occurs but it is possible to narrow down fairly easily what sort of speaking can be integrated with what class of institutional activity. For example, when a classroom lesson is being presented, a pupil has just so much leeway and no more for her speaking to be seen as facilitative: the pupil's speaking must always link itself to some aspect of the lesson, otherwise it turns into disruption. But even fields with the feature [quotidian] are not free to accept 'genre combination' just anywhere, anyhow: for example, Cloran's empirical research has shown (1982, 1987) that an answer to a question in everyday talk can be just so detailed and no more; otherwise it tends to be seen as an effort at supplanting, a shift towards teaching rather than telling: 'What is this? A lecture or a conversation? as one of the outraged subjects in her experiment asked at the occurrence of such a deliberately created shift!

6.3.12 Contextual iteration: material situational setting and contextual multiplicity

In speaking with reference to context in real life situations, we manage the calibration of material and verbal action without a moment's thought, but the constraints and freedoms enjoyed by the terms related by default in the system network in Figure 6.4a are in fact highly complex. Let us return briefly to Figure 6.4a and to Table 6.10 which presents some selection expressions, with a view to spelling out one outcome of the workings of default dependencies as displayed in Figure 6.4a. The claim that *if* there is [ancillary] verbal action, *then* material action *must* be [present] (see entry 1 in Table 6.10) clearly places a constraint on the feature [ancillary] verbal action, leaving [present] material action free to combine with [constitutive] verbal action. At the same time, Figure 6.4a claims that *if* material action is [non-present] *then* verbal action *must* be [constitutive], thus placing a constraint on the feature [non-present] material action, not on [constitutive]. Similarly with the next step in delicacy, the default pairing constrains the features [deferred] and [absent], not [practical] or [conceptual], which are the more delicate categories of [constitutive] action (see Figure 6.4a). A moment's thought will reveal that this creates a paradox: how can material action [present] be relevant to a field with [constitutive] verbal action? Unlike [ancillary] verbal action, the genesis of [constitutive] verbal action is not in material action [present]: in fact material action is irrelevant to the recognition of any activity characterized as [constitutive], and it is highly likely that so far as that particular activity is concerned material action is of no consequence to its formation, as for example in inventing a nursery tale.

Could we not reverse the default relation, claiming that if the verbal action is [constitutive], then material action must be [non-present]? This would remove the paradox at the stroke of a pen by restricting the feature [constitutive] and its more delicate categories, suggesting that the co-selection of [constitutive: practical/conceptual] verbal action and [present] material action is unlikely. This is fine so long as it is taken for granted that a field with the option [constitutive] is impervious to shifts, changes, etc., which is of course not always the case. So the solution is problematic in that the potential of impingement between, say, John's material action of driving and his constitutive verbal action of discussing road rage with his friend can no longer be accounted for with this alternative framework. In other words, this alternative description on the one hand is observationally inadequate since such 'conjunctions' are fairly common, and on the other hand, we block the possibility of revealing those attributes of a field that leave it open to co-location and/or integration.[87] In the discussion of the various systems in field, I have informally identified three profiles of field which make it relatively more susceptible to co-location and/or integration; these scenarios are

(a) verbal action [ancillary]; material action [present] by default and ancillary verbal action intermittent;

(b) verbal [constitutive]; material [present], where material action is not germane to the conduct of the verbal action itself; and

(c) sphere [individuated].

The probability of co-location and/or integration in the presence of these field attributes is considerably higher. This, however, does not mean that all other categories of field are absolutely *disallowed* such shifts/changes. Whether at a particular moment in its history a field is independent or already displays integration, the possibility of iterative choice cannot be said to be completely restricted to the three 'high risk' scenarios identified above. Keeping these considerations in mind, I now propose a fourth system simultaneous with the systems of MATERIAL ACTION, VERBAL ACTION and SPHERE (see Figure 6.4f). I will refer to this fourth system as the system of ITERATION.

Like systems of iteration elsewhere (e.g. taxis or tense at the level of lexicogrammar), the terms of the system are [STOP#] v. [GO]. The selection of the former term is realizationally related to the closure of further field choices: it thus announces the end-state. The selection of the term [go] enables re-entry into the three simultaneous systems of field viz., sphere of action, material action and verbal action. Further, at this point simultaneous with the re-entry into the three main systems of field, certain other choices become available but only to the field that is being newly instigated by the choice of [go] in the system of iteration: in other words the term [go] is the entry condition for re-entry into the field systems and also to any other system such as those of tenor and/or mode. To facilitate the discussion of the latter, let me refer to the first field construct as an α-field, and to the subsequent ones re-entered with the choice of [go] as a β-field. The terms α and β are used purely by reference to the iterative system, whatever field has the choice [go] is also a β-field without any necessary implication that it is subordinate to the co-occurring fields.

Figure 6.4f: Primary systems of field in relation to the system of iteration in action

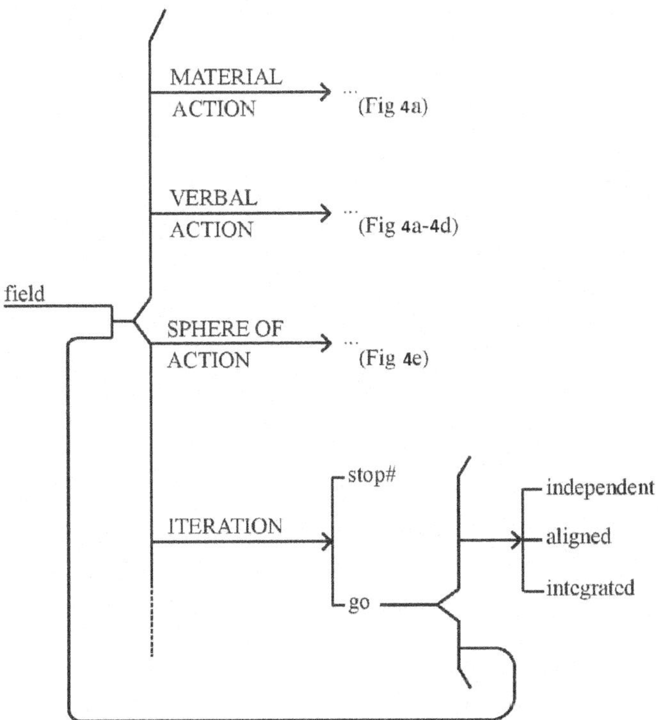

As the discussion of segments (ii, iv, and vi, etc.) from Example *C* has already shows, the selection of a β-field offers a systemic choice, two of which, co-location and integration, have already been discussed in some detail in Section 6.2.3. I suggest that in fact three options are available to the newly instigated field at the point [go]: it may be *independent,* or *aligned,* or *integrated.* Since the first and the last terms are already familiar, let me say a brief word about these before turning to the middle feature [aligned]. To begin with the feature [INDEPENDENT]: we have already encountered two instances of field with this feature – first, segment (vi) of Example *C* (plan for visit to Chatswood) which construes a field that is [independent] *vis à vis* the field construed by the complex text (a friendly and relaxed management of providing lunch); and, second, the imaginary case of John interrupting his conversation with a friend to receive a recorded delivery parcel; here too the two activities are independent of each other as in the first example. The difference is that the first is largely material, while the second is purely verbal. In both cases, the co-located fields simply occur within the time frame relevant to one interaction, but the design of neither is relevant to the conduct of the design of the other.[88] This is what it means to say that they are [independent] of each other and that their only relation to each other is entirely physical. Their co-location is adventitious, and even if they impinged on each other, which they well might do by creating distractions of one kind or another, this would be a matter of chance: there is no basis of a functional relation between them. The choice of the feature [independent] means that the text activated by that β-field would not enter into the structure of another one as its sub-text, and all things being equal it is more likely to function as a simple text than (part of) a complex one.

In contrast with the above situation, a β-field may itself become 'amalgamated' into some already on-going field: as demonstrated by the sub-texts in Example *C*. This is what happens when the option [INTEGRATED] is taken (for discussion, see Section 6.2.3). Clearly, the physical fact of co-location within the same interaction applies here too, but when the β-field has the feature [integrated], this means a relation to the α-field, the basis of which is not physical but discourse functional. What this means is that such a β-field contributes to the conduct of the design of the α-field, the two together activating a complex text, as with Example *C*. The feature [integrated] itself acts as the entry condition for a choice between [DEPENDENT] or [COLLABORATIVE], terms which have been discussed informally in Section 6.2.3. In Example *C*, the β-field construed by sub-text$_1$ had the feature [... integrated: dependent] while the β-fields construed by the other sub-texts would be described as [... integrated: collaborative]. In integration, the verbal action in the α-field may be [ancillary] or [constitutive]. In Example *C*, it was [ancillary]. An imaginary example of an α-field with [constitutive] verbal action is that of a teacher giving a presentation lesson. Imagine that during the course of this lesson, she presents some visuals relevant to the lesson: in that case, she may engage in the material action of adjusting the display screen, switching on the overhead projector and checking with her pupils if the display is clearly visible to all, and so on. If there is use of language during the performance of this activity, this will constitute a β-field with material action [present] and verbal action [ancillary]. Like the field of subtext₁ in Example *C*, this β-field too would be [dependent], its realizing text would function as a facilitative sub-text to the primary text of the lesson, while the α-field itself would be [constitutive].

We come now to the middle feature [ALIGNED]. The placement of this feature as the middle term of the system is iconic, for it appears that the feature shares some qualities with the [independent] and others with the feature [integrated]; while there are other qualities which it shares with neither. Here too, just as in the case of [independent] field, the actual conduct of one field is not affected by the conduct of the other. On the other hand, just as in the case of [integrated] β-field, so here too there seems to exist an intrinsic connection between the two that is over and above the simple fact of co-location. As an example, take the activity of broadcasting cricket commentary in its relation to the cricket game. I will refer to the game and the commentary as α- and β-field, respectively. Here the α-field has a material action [present], namely that of playing a cricket game, accompanied most probably by its own [ancillary] verbal action which is realized by intermittent cries such as 'Out!', 'How's that?', etc. The features of the β-field are [constitutive: conceptual: informing: commenting] verbal action of broadcasting a cricket commentary on a game that is in progress; needless to say that the two activities – the commentary and the game – run side by side just as co-located [independent] fields might do, but this co-location of the commentary and the game is actuated by a necessity that is missing from pure co-location of independent fields: the cricket game is, in fact, the *raison d'être* of the commentary to the extent that every cricket commentary broadcast presupposes a cricket game in progress, though the reverse is not true. So the element of pure chance that underlies the feature [independent] is absent; the commentary is rooted in the game. The on-going cricket game becomes a reference point so far as the β-field of commentary is concerned, which treats the game as an object to which it must (selectively) refer.[89] So the on-going cricket game, the actual play, the players, and what the players do and what they say turns into 'relevant objects and activities' to be referred to by the β-field of commentary. We recognize this situation informally by saying that the commentary is *about* the game in progress: the game being played is the 'topic' of the commentary. This is precisely why it seems appropriate to say that the β-field of commentary is [aligned] to the α-field of the cricket game: the two are logically associated. In this respect the relations of the [aligned] α- and β-fields appear to resemble somewhat those of the [integrated] β-field to the primary α-field: the game is logically relevant to the commentary; the [integrated] sub-text is functionally relevant to the primary text. But this is where the resemblance stops; unlike the [integrated] field it appears to have no bearing upon the structure potential of commentaries: the design of one turns out not to be relevant to the conduct of the design of the other, a situation that is more like the co-located [independent] field than the [integrated] ones. The structure of commentaries displays a number of preoccupations: a commentary moves between the recall and evaluation of other games, the evaluation of various players present and past, the expectations of the outcome of this play, what other games of similar salience are being played where, and what's going on in the game in progress on the field; in short, the complex movements of the commentary range not only over the game but also over the game's cultural domain. And yet the game has nothing much to do with this complexity, the sources of which lie elsewhere: so far as the design of the commentary is concerned the game scarcely plays any role in its shaping. And despite the multiplicity of the concerns the commentator manages in his discourse, technically speaking, the commentary would be a simple text, not a complex one; this is in contrast with those texts whose field has the feature [integrated].[90] So we have an interesting situation: the game must be there, an on-going material action, separated from the commentary but what happens in the game what the players do in the field is relevant to the commentary only as the appearance of an entity or event is relevant to a text that describes it conventionally and faithfully. Conversely, *what the commentator does in his commentary matters not a jot to the conduct of the game*: the game is impervious to the commentary. The two activities are neither [independent] nor [integrated]: they are simply [aligned], or more precisely, a commentary is logically [aligned] to a game; no one has yet presented a commentary either in anticipation or in retrospect! The game has to be co-located in the same space-time environment as the commentary. This brings us to an additional characteristic of [aligned] fields: unlike the other two options, the fields with the feature [aligned] are not part of the same 'interaction'. They are in fact two parallel interactions, each with its own separate activity, its own interactants, its own modes of contact, and yet the existence of one, i.e., of the commentary, unilaterally presupposes the existence of the other, i.e., the game. In this respect to the feature [aligned] differs from the other two in the system. Figure 6.4f has presented these features of the system of iteration along with an indication of the other three simultaneous systems with their primary terms.

The above discussion of the feature [aligned] might bring to mind another feature discussed earlier (see Section 6.3.8), viz., [second order] as at first glance the two features might seem to describe the same phenomenon. I have argued above that with the feature [aligned], the two fields are linked by a presupposition: to say that a particular activity (of a small subclass) has occurred is to say that concurrent with it must have been another specific activity, though the two are necessarily not part of the same interaction. Further, one field in this relation is, as it were, objectified, in the sense that what is said or done in that field becomes (part of) the potential domain of reference for the other field. It might appear at first glance that the above characterization fits also those activities which have the feature [second order]: activities with this feature too presuppose another activity. Thus the [second order] activity of reading a nursery tale to a child presupposes someone somewhere undertook the activity of inventing that tale, of narrating inventively, and the trace of that activity is the nursery tale being reproduced. There are, however, some important differences between the feature [aligned] and [second order]. First, as the network in Figure 6.4f claims the feature [aligned] can only occur in the environment of field re-entry, which implies that the logically related activities must occur concurrently (for the most part) as the game and its commentary do. By contrast, with the feature [second order] there is no such constraint. For example, the activity of, say, creating a nursery tale will typically have occurred in the past before the activity of reading it is undertaken. Although the possibility of the co-location of two activities does need to be granted (if only to account for such activities as 'repeating' after the teacher!), it is not a requirement the way that it is with the feature [aligned]. Further, the [second order] activity act with/on the product of some activity which functions as the/a relevant object for the [second order] field. Moreover, crucially, the class of the product is restricted: it must belong to the specific class *semiotic verbal product*. A [second order] activity either re-discourses an already existing discourse (c.f., the feature [reproduction]) or it discourses *on* an already existing discourse (c.f., the feature [meta-discursive]). This has an implication: both the [second order] activity and the activity whose product it focuses on must have the feature [constitutive] verbal action, because it is only the latter that is capable of producing a semiotic verbal artefact and it is only a [constitutive] activity that is capable of either 're-working it' or of 'working on it'; these requirements are not applicable to the feature [aligned].

6.3.13 Using the field network: some examples

Section 6.3.1–6.3.12 have presented an indicative account of the system-ization of the Contextual construct. Incomplete as they are, the systems of choices pertaining to the parameter of field discussed so far will be brought together one (incomplete) system network pertaining to the parameter of

Figure 6.5: Field of discourse: some systemic choices in a language based conception of social practice

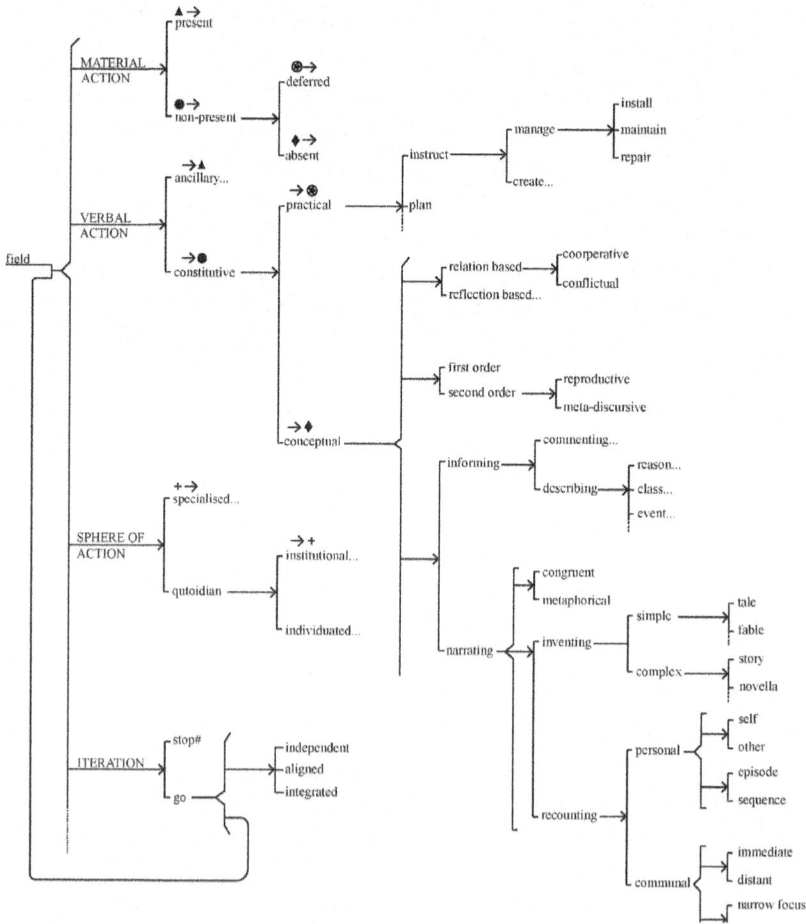

field of discourse. I will close the discussion with a few examples of activity types and their description in terms of the features networked in the system presented in Figure 6.5, without any claim that they represent an exhaustive, perfect and/or final representation of the contextual potential of field. These are offered more in a spirit of exploration than as finished and tried account of field.

First, then, I return to Example *C*, particularly to the main and the first two integrated fields realized by sub-texts$_{1-2}$.

> (i) Example *C*: describing **integrated field**
> **α-field: primary text**
> material action [present]; verbal action [ancillary]; sphere [quotidian: individuated]
> **β-field: sub-text$_1$**
> [go: integrated: dependent]; material action [present]; verbal action [ancillary]; sphere [quotidian: individuated]
> **β-field: sub-text$_2$**
> [go: integrated: collaborative]; material action [present]; verbal action [constitutive: conceptual: relation based; informing: describing; first order]; sphere [quotidian: individuated]

The feature [integrated] activates the COMPLEXIFICATION of the primary text. Note that details of the field such as [care giving; providing lunch and negotiating menu for lunch...] and so on (see Table 6.4) are not included in the above description since the network in Figure 6.3 was not developed far enough in delicacy to reach this point; there is, however, no reason to doubt that such systems, which in a manner of speaking are much closer to the situational and linguistic coal-face, can be built into the network without much problem. But until the description is developed to this degree of delicacy, the inclusion of such features would, in principle, be intuitive and comments on their realization would have no explicit basis in the descriptive methodology. Martin (1992, Chapter 7) presents many system networks which appear to me to relate to the delicate end of field specification without building in any primary systemic choices such as those represented in Figure 6.5.

> (ii) Example C: describing **parallel fields**
> **α-field: complex text**
> (as described above with ref to Example C (i))
> **β-field: independent text**
> [go: independent]; material action [present]; verbal action [constitutive: conceptual: practical: plan]; sphere [quotidian: individuated]

The choice of the feature [independent] in a field implies that the text it activates would be simply co-located with the other(s) in the same interaction.

(iii) Broadcasting cricket commentary: describing **aligned fields**
α-field: playing cricket
material action [present]; verbal action [ancillary]; sphere [specialized]
β-field: cricket commentary
[go: aligned]; material action [present]; verbal action [constitutive: conceptual: reflection based; informing: commenting; first order]; sphere [specialized]

The choice of the feature [aligned] in a field implies that the activity as a whole is relevant to the other co-located field as a (main) specifier of its domain of signification; each activated text may be simple or complex depending on further iterative choices:

(iv) Minute taking at a meeting: a variant example of **aligned field**
α-field: a meeting
material action [absent]; verbal action [constitutive: conceptual: reflection based; informing; first order]; sphere [specialized]
β-field: taking down the minutes
[go: aligned]; material action [absent]; verbal action [constitutive: conceptual: reflection based; informing; second order: reproducing]; sphere [specialized]

Taking down the minutes of a meeting is something like broadcasting a cricket commentary: both presuppose another on-going activity: both have the feature [aligned]. However, with minute taking, the presupposed activity, i.e., the process of the meeting, is verbally constituted, whereas the commentary as we saw above presupposes an activity which is characterized by the presence of material action and ancillary verbal action. Note also that whereas broadcasting a commentary is described in example (iii) as a [first order] activity, the activity of minute taking is [second order: reproducing]. Informally speaking, what the analysis claims is that (a) the activity of minute taking and the process of the meeting co-occur (feature [aligned]); (b) the wording in the minutes will re-construe (at least partially) what was going on at the meeting, not just what they said but what actions the sayings constituted e.g. proposing a motion, seconding it, voting and so on (feature [aligned]); (c) the minutes must attend to what is being produced verbally by the meeting, e.g. decisions, objection, suggestions (ignoring such material actions as those of sneezing, fidgeting, laughing ..., etc. (feature [second order]); (d) the minute must schematically reproduces (some part of) the verbal product of the meeting (feature [reproductive]). The features [aligned] and [second order: reproduction] will most probably prove useful for the description of other such activities, e.g. simultaneous translation, taking down dictation, prompting actors during a performance, repeating after the teacher, and (with a slight stretch of imagination) language lab practice and so on. In a rather important sense, much of what goes on in schools by way of education is [second order: reproduction] activity: this is partly what it means to say that all educational knowledge is re-contextualized (cf. Bernstein 1990, 1996). The catch is, of course, that reproduction is never equal to replication; rather it is a selective reorganization of information that has already been produced by someone somewhere. The problem of education is not that knowledge is re-contextualized; in fact, the very condition of human social existence is that discourses must move around, being discoursed, re-discoursed and meta-discoursed: rather, as Bernstein has suggested, the problem so far as education is concerned is who controls the re-contextualizing function and what principles they use for this process.

6.4 Concluding remarks

Any attempt to account for the categories of the context of situation along the lines adopted here is an attempt to account for a language based theory of culturally significant action. In the context of this wide canvas, the (incomplete and somewhat rudimentary) descriptive categories represented in Figure 6.5 are only a small beginning. The impetus to re-think contextual description came from a specific problem: how to describe context so as to provide a principled basis for the description of dynamic moves which might occur during the process of speaking. Does the present approach appear promising from this limited perspective? On the whole I am inclined to think that it does. It differentiates casual co-occurrence of texts from those co-occurrences which have a functional significance (cf. features [integrated] and [aligned]). On the basis of the possible conjunctions of the features of the primary systems in Figure 6.3, it is possible also to identify some of the environments where dynamic moves are at higher risk. And on the way to doing these things, the description enables us also to theorize at least some aspects of inter-textuality (cf. the features [aligned] and [second order]). It opens up the possibility of describing educational registers (or genres, if you prefer) in a way that allows a better perspective on their social location (cf. the features of the system of sphere; [reflection based], [informing] [first order] [second order] and so on). To my mind, the description has taken a significant step forward in theorizing the dynamics of discourse in culture.

A system network designed along these lines could very well be shown to be realizationally related to what Cloran calls rhetorical units. This is significant in that from the point of view of constituency her claim is that a text may consist of one or more than one rhetorical unit. Further although in her analysis Cloran has displayed tactic relations between rhetorical units which she sees as making up one text, it is only with a descriptive framework such as the one presented here that these relations can be further clarified. That a development of this kind has been necessary for some time now is never as obvious as when one encounters casual conversation. It is quite normal for SFL scholars to elide contextual descriptions when describing conversation (see Lemke 1990; Eggins and Slade 1997), as if conversation is a freakishly random social activity which is free to occur in any cultural context. To specify the contextual choices which are realized in a conversation is definitely not an easy task, for as Martin rightly pointed out (1985a) this is the environment *par excellence* for dynamic moves in speaking. It seems to me that a framework such as has been initiated here could help provide a deep analysis of conversational contexts.

The approach presented here has also exploited the dialogical perspective: we do not take it for granted that process comes ahead of product, and even if it does, this, in a semiotic environment, would be no reason for discounting the importance of that which realizes (substantial part of) the process. The mark of context on text is indelible, just as the mark of text on situations in culture is not negligible. It is therefore important to examine process to see what sort of expectations it gives rise to just as it is important to examine the product to see how/why it helps in (re-)construing its own context. The perception of the occasion of talk is an important element in shaping the speaker's meaning making acts and to this extent context may rightly be said to 'determine' the initiation of discourse. The semiotic act, however, has the power to redefine the initial context, and in this sense context may be rightly said to be 'determined' by speaking. My own inclination is to speak of realizational dialectic, rather than of determinations. For lack of space, I have not been able to show how the structure potential of a text type/register/genre is realizationally related to the systemic features of context: after all a text's actual structure provides an important recognition criterion for the category of register which the text instantiates, while the underlying contextual features are the defining criteria for the categories of register. The connection between a text's structure, its register and its context is logically predicted by the theory of realization.

A step toward further development of the framework is presented here. I would like to draw attention to two shortcomings of the description that I am already aware of. In the first place, although it has been possible to point out *informally* the conjunction of systemic features where the phenomena of colocation, integration and alignment are more likely to occur, despite several efforts I have not succeeded in alighting on a formal systemic representation of these generalizations. Second and equally severe is the problem implicit in the shape of the network as presented here. The system of iteration allows a free re-entry into the systems of material action, verbal action, sphere and of course again iteration: this, in my understanding, is normal in all iterative systems. But there is a serious problem in implying that on re-entry all choices are equally possible: this is certainly not the case. If the α-field is the material action of playing cricket, the choices in the β-field are far from open; similarly if the α-field is a meeting in progress, the β-field is not likely to have the feature [… practical: manage: install …]. The way the probabilities of various choices might be indicated appears so complex as to be daunting. I believe these are problems that have not arisen simply from a defective hypothesis on my part. But if I am right in believing this, then could it be that a system network is not the optimal means of representing hypotheses in the language based theory of social action in culture? Or do we need other formal tools to add to the tool provided by the system network?

Finally, before closing this long discussion it is important to clarify two points. First, it is very likely that the *location* of the system of iteration in Figures 6.2f and 6.3 is simply an artefact of the context of this paper. Clearly when from the system of iteration, the choice [go] is made, it is very likely that re-entry will involve not only field systems but also those of tenor and mode: one would hardly expect anything else in view of the reciprocities across the three parameters of context. So for example: the interactant relations in the cricket game are quite different from those in the commentary; and the mode of minute taking is clearly different from that of the meeting. Here is another respect in which the present account is simply an opening. Second, and related to this: all through my focus in Section 6.3 was deliberately limited to field. In closing this paper I want to say quite unequivocally that the dynamic possibilities of context do not inhere in field alone: both mode and tenor are important. But if any one parameter has to be singled out as the most relevant one it has to be that of tenor. For it is the perspectives that interactants bring to the actions they engage in, which act on the probabilities of grasping the chances of making dynamic moves. But entry into this discourse will have to await another occasion. (See Chapter 8 in the present volume.)

Acknowledgements

This paper contains some of the material first presented at the 22nd ISFC (Beijing University 1995), a revised version was presented also at the 8th I-ESFW Nottingham University, Trent campus (1996). Thanks to Flo Davies' workshop group who helped by applying my hypotheses as represented in the system network of field by attempting to analyse naturally occurring data from the domain of business communication. Special thanks to Margaret Berry for thoughtful comments not only on my two presentations but also on Hasan (1995). My thanks are due to Carmel Cloran who commented on an earlier draft of the present paper. [with her permission I have borrowed her analysis presented as Figure 6.2 in this chapter. Note added 2012].

Notes

1   The resurgence of interest in context over the past three decades has resulted in much scholarly discourse: today there are at least logical, sociological, pragmatic, linguistic, ethnomethodological and psychological theories of context. As an aspect of the relations of culture to language, discourse on the relations of context and text takes us back to the great American masters such as Boas, Sapir, Whorf and G. H. Mead. Then there is the work of contemporary scholars such as Garfinkel, Goffman, Gumperz, and Hymes, not to mention the many scholars who are devoted to speech act and conversational analysis. My decision to limit the discussion just to one corner of the SFL model has arisen from two considerations; first, by the space allowed to this chapter: though generous, it would not be sufficient to attend to the achievements of all these scholars; but even more important is my belief that I know a little more about context in SFL than the other models. I hasten to add that the interpretation of SFL presented here is mine, and as such it may or may not be in agreement with other scholars' interpretation of the same model.

2   For a discussion of Malinowski's contribution to this debate, see Hasan 1985c (here Chapter 2). Earlier I treated these as the *two peaks of the contextual efficacy of language*. The last two chapters of this volume present the elaboration of the two peaks *as contextual options in verbal action*: either verbal action is 'ancillary', in which case, it typically co-occurs with material action

that is 'focal': language use assists some on-going face to face material action in the performance of some social practice, or it is 'constitutive', in which case the identity of the social practice can be established only by languaging, the addressee is typically 'materially absent' and any co-occurring material actions is peripheral, whether it occurs 'automatically' or 'illustratively'.

3   The comment applies also to the 'dynamic' approach introduced by Martin (1985a, 1992). (For discussion, Hasan (1995, presented here as Chapter 5).)

4   It is fair to point out that in launching the so-called dynamic approach in SFL, Martin's recommendation, at least in theory, had been for texts to be studied from both the synoptic and the dynamic perspective; in practice, however, matters were rather different: the synoptic became the 'underprivileged' member of the pair. (See Martin 1985a, 1992 as evidence; and Hasan 1995 as a critique of Martin's perspective.)

5   For a discussion of these concepts, see Halliday (1992a, 1992b, 1996, 1999); Hasan (1995, 1996a, 2009a); Matthiessen (1995, 2007); and Matthiessen and Nesbitt (1996). The move towards a dialogical approach is foreshadowed as early as Halliday (1970a, 1973b, 1975a).

6   The chapter as presented here differs from the original at some points in its composition. For example: in the original publication, Figure 6.1 had been presented in Chapter 1 of the anthology (Ghadessy (ed.) 1999: 8); in the present version, it has been added for ease of reference (for further discussion of the figure see Halliday 1999; also Hasan 2009a and 2012). Attention will be drawn to another such addition at a later point. These have inevitably caused some re-arrangement of the original wording, and numbering of figures.

7   The word *speaking* is used throughout this chapter as approximately synonymous with *the act of verbal semiosis,* what Halliday (1993 and elsewhere) has called *the act of meaning.* It encompasses the processes of text production, activated by any category of activity (field), any class of social relation (tenor) relayed in any variety of *phonic* or *graphic* channel. In other words, speaking does not refer to only oral-aural discourse.

8   The word 'context' has normally been used in linguistics to refer to the context of situation but, of course, every mention of situation implicates culture: just as behind every text lies a language system so also behind every situation lies the context of culture. See Halliday (1999) for discussion. Throughout this paper I shall use the term context with these assumptions.

9   The syllable is typically activated by some category at the stratum of lexicogrammar; the relation of the syllable to semantics is too complex to describe here. It is, however, highly unlikely for the syllable to construe a lexicogrammatical category *simply by virtue of its phonological patternment. So* consider the lexicogrammatical status of the vowel in the second syllable of the following patterns: /beike/, /seife/, /leibe/ (baker, safer, labour). I would suggest that instead of *construing* a lexicogrammatical category, a segmental phonological pattern simply *signals,* or in the words of Hjelmslev *expresses* some

lexicogrammatical category, by virtue of a conventional (arbitrary) association under certain conditions.

10   To extrapolate by analogy to Halliday (1996: 2–3): the GRAMMAR of a language system is not a static set of invariable rules; however the account of that grammar, i.e., our GRAMMATICS, is often presented as a determinate, static set of rules, and we fail to make a distinction between grammar and grammatics.

11   The main line of arbitrariness lies between the planes of content and expression (for discussion, see Chapter 5). The dialectic of activation and construal works only at the content plane.

12   This is a complete reproduction of promotional material (the 'blurb') on the back cover of Giddens (1972).

13   This example is taken from Ventola (1987: 239–240); each dot represents 1 second of pause: the dash shows that the utterance was left incomplete; the start of overlapping utterances is identified by an asterisk and its extent is indicated by italicizing the relevant part of the two utterances; other transcription conventions are the same as for Example *C*.

14   This extract is taken from data of naturally occurring everyday talk between mothers and their 3;6–4;0 year old children, collected for a sociolinguistic research at Macquarie University, Australia. For a brief account of this research see Cloran (1989), Hasan (1989, 1992b), and Hasan and Cloran (1990). A larger extract of this same dialogue is discussed from a related point of view by Cloran in Ghadessy (1999). The transcription conventions are the same as in Cloran.

15   For an interpretation of these terms, see Figure 6.4e, and the relevant discussion in Section 6.3.10.

16   The socio-economic infrastructure needed to support the production of a blurb obviously depends on a 'book culture'. For an interesting account of the production of a book in a community lacking a book culture, see Cerón and Canger (1993).

17   When the language of the text is such as to permit one to infer most of the contextual features relevant to the text, it is somewhat unfortunately described as *context independent* or *de-contextualized language;* conversely, when the possibility of such inference is low, the language is said to be *context-dependent*. For some further discussion, see Cloran (1994, 1999a).

18   It is my understanding that Martin's connotative semiotic modelling of genre and context (Martin 1985a, 1992 and associates) does not modify the *content* of context; it presents a rather confusing picture of genre, i.e., text type, to context, but that need not concern us here.

19   See especially Halliday (1999: 14) and (Hasan 1992a: 59). A similar account of context is also presented by those following the connotative semiotic model. See for example, some of the contributions in Hasan and Williams (1996).

20   For example consider the novel as a text type which displays coherence typical of longer texts such as a description of the immune system but at the same

time, unlike the latter, a novel construes many distinct contexts (Hasan 1964; Bakhtin 1986).

21 For a discussion of these terms, see Hasan (1995); see also the discussion of Figures 6.4a–c in Sections 6.3.3 to 6.3.9 here.

22 The ready availability of the information in parentheses in texts such as supplied here, which have been prepared this way for analysis, prevents us from appreciating these facts at first glance.

23 It is however remarkable how little problem of interpretation arose in the face-to-face dialogues between mothers and their children, audio-recorded by mothers for my research (see details in Hasan and Cloran 1990, etc.).

24 In this sense, a distinction must be made between Bakhtin's (1981) use of the term *dialogic* and my own. I agree with Bakhtin that in principle all interaction is dialogic in his sense. But being dialogic in the sense of being aware of and responding to the other's perspective, which I believe is what Bakhtin has in mind, differs from dialogue in the sense of the immediacy of semiotic reciprocity. The former is *a condition of all non-pathological interaction* while the latter implies in addition both co-presence and also a certain variety of social action and relation. Consider in this light the co-presence of counsel and jury, where despite co-presence there is no dialogue, though it would be rash to say that in his speaking the counsel is not guided (to some extent) by his sense of the Jury's perspective. Thus there is dialogism in the Bakhtinian sense but hardly any dialogic engagement.

25 In terms of Hasan (1985b: 66) and elsewhere, a demand for information such as is made here functions as *repair*. This strategy calls for the construal of meanings which as yet have not been produced by the buyer-speaker but which are required for the realization of the design of the on-going social process if it is to be continued.

26 For a discussion of permeability see Hasan (1995), and for an early discussion Hasan (1973c).

27 For examples of default dependency in the systems of activity, i.e., *field of discourse,* see Figure 6.4a and its discussion in Section 6.3.3 below, where default dependency is discussed again.

28 For a discussion of transitional and conditional probability in systemic choices, see Halliday (1992b).

29 Note that so far as the outsider is concerned, a good deal of this information, e.g., kin relation, becomes available only retrospectively and some information such as the actual age of the child, is never provided in the dialogue from which Example *C* is extracted; my source of information is extra-textual.

30 It is notable that Example *C* does not contain as much specialized language as Example *A* does; this may be because the interactants were not co-present, or because the social activity calls for different kinds of interactants – not a child but an adult receiver.

31 For further continuation of this dialogue see especially Tables 10 and 11 in Cloran (1999a: 203–204); she has used a larger portion of this interaction to

illustrate her analysis of RHETORICAL UNIT as an immediate constituents of text. As will be noted her analysis and that presented here complement each other.

32   The identification of this 'substantial portion' is made by reference to the meaning potential specific to the register/genre in question (for *genre specific meaning potential* see Hasan 1985b; further comments in Section 6.3.4).

33   A comparable contribution is made by the optional elements of text structure: texts whose actual structure contains only obligatory elements will normally appear more brusque than texts which contain (some) optional elements in addition to the obligatory ones. (For actual examples of both, see Hasan 1978, 1985b.)

34   Note the significant fact that in this case of speaking, the determination of Stephen's lunch menu is completed almost immediately after the successful search of the missing passion fruit.

35   There are most probably other principles for the production of text, e.g. the artistic principle which would exploit all known principles of text production in the interest of realizing the deepest theme of the work (Hasan 1964, 1971b, 1985c, 1996c).

36   I suspect that the most complex forms of text structuring are to be found in the domain of literature and religious registers. The generalizations and discussions offered here are not expected to cover all forms of text structuring in these two domains, though the principle of unity (with varying manifestations) is expected to hold.

37   For a discussion of these terms, see Hasan (1995), and Section 6.3 below.

38   See Bernstein (1975, 1990) and elsewhere for the concept of framing and its relevance to the creation and maintenance of social relation as well as its activation by speaker' ideological orientation.

39   Since Cloran 1999a was published in the same volume as 'Speaking with reference to context' (i.e., this chapter), what is presented here as Figure 6.2 was simply referred to; it is a new insertion here. The analyses most relevant to the present discussion in Cloran 1999a are found in Tables 6.2–6.3 and Appendices I and II (pp 211–213). Figure 6.2 presents the upper half of Cloran's Table 2 on p. 190. I am grateful to Cloran for permission to include this part of her analysis of cohesive harmony as Figure 6.2 here.

40   Cloran has in fact analysed the chain interaction right up to message 88; the portion presented here concerns only the messages of Example *C*. It is clear at a glance that sub-text4 (lines 54–59), occurs after segment (vi); it is nonetheless connected by chain interaction to the other parts of Example *C* without showing any textural unity with segment (vi).

41   For the notion of identity and similarity chain and for chain interaction, Hasan (1979b, 1984d, 1985b). For the display of chain conjunction and disjunction in the identity chain referring to Stephen and his mother, see Table 2 in Cloran 1999a: 177–217.

42   One may of course argue that the problem is not worth addressing, that in this fragmented, post-modernist universe the idea of attempting to specify

the definition and recognition criteria for text-hood is a pointless pursuit. However, if the notion of genre is important, as it seems to be in the different varieties of post-modernist discourses, then, criteria for text-hood are obviously a relevant concern if one is interested in serious research.

43 I find this requirement interesting in view of the notion of 'secondary intersubjectivity'. According to Trevarthen and Hubley (1978), the baby moves from 'primary intersubjectivity' where interaction concerns only one 'person', the baby, to 'secondary intersubjectivity'; at this stage the baby is able to interact with an 'other' by bringing into their 'conversation' a third entity, i.e., at least another human and a material object: this move represents a major maturational step. Textual integration too appears to demand a coming together of interactants around a third relevant object, namely an activity that instantiates a distinct cultural domain from other activities that the same interactants might have been engaged in.

44 Some of these points are discussed in Hasan (1994) *Situation and the Definition of Genre.*

45 The same/similar similarity chains are logically expected to occur in texts instantiating the same register, especially where the domain of signification (Hasan 1985b) is same/similar. For this reason, I have suggested elsewhere (Hasan 1979b) that similarity chains constitute part of the recognition criteria for a register, whereas a specific sub-class of identity chains (those not referring to the interactants) constitute part of the recognition criteria for language functioning as one text within one interaction. These principles are not affected by whether texts are co-located or not.

46 For further comments on text sequencing, see the discussion of text integration with reference to Example *C* (2.3.2–2.4) and (section 3.12–3.13) below.

47 Shifts in tenor are easier to notice where tone setting is negative rather than positive (for discussion, see Section 2.3.2). It is not easy to determine if a generalization of this kind is ideologically conditioned whereby conflict becomes more noticeable than conformity.

48 See, however, the discussion of the term *supplanting* in the following paragraph.

49 Reflection based activity may be facilitated by an action based one, as for example in guiding pupils to physically carry out an experiment or in helping them make groupings of objects as a step toward classification. For the terms action, reflection and relation based, see Hasan (1995).

50 See Tables 11 in Cloran 1999a, especially lines 67–69. Analysing these messages in terms of rhetorical unit, she assigns them the function of generalization; this, she suggests, construes an instructional context.

51 Though the focus of Painter's study (1996) is somewhat different, her account of how children begin to use language for learning agrees with my analysis, and her data would corroborate the claims I am making here.

52 What we call *a* casual conversation is often more accurately described as a dialogue, co-extensive with one interaction (on the distinction between

dialogue and conversation, see Hasan 1994): in fact a dialogue might consists not of one conversation but many, where one conversation supplants another, which is supplanted by a third, and so on. This is not to deny that other co-locational arrangements may also be present.

53   There seem to be good reasons for this. First, facilitation is typically action based, even though it is accompanied by language; secondly, it involves undertaking some action which is deemed essential to the conduct of the activity in the main context. This implies a delay, a fracturing, so far as the latter is concerned until this subsidiary essential act is completed. And this is the essence of arrestive contact.

54   See Lemke (1990: 73), especially Chapter 3 for good examples of such tone setting sub-texts and for an interesting discussion. Lemke refers to such sub-texts as 'admonitions of side talk'.

55   Needless to say that in my view the analysis of classroom discourse is lacking both in critical insight and methodological *finesse* if it stops at this attribution.

56   In practice this option is never explicitly adopted in SFL, though most probably it is implied in certain descriptions where mode takes over in lieu of activity.

57   Of course we may say that *narrative* in the sense of *narrating a story* is really the mode; the real activity is that of, say, *entertaining or teaching*. But this is really treating the goal/outcome of an activity as the activity itself and that has its own set of attendant problems, attention to which was drawn earlier (see Section 6.2.1.2 above). Besides, to maintain consistency of analysis, we could argue that the activity in Text *B* should be described not as that of *buying postal goods* but of *maintaining an economic institution,* and buying postal goods is a mode of such maintenance. That solution would really put us in a quandary!

58   The conference with the title *Writing to Mean* was held in 1985 at Sydney University; the title of my talk was *Shapes in Narrative.* The proceedings appeared as Painter and Martin (eds) (1986) though due to certain circumstances, I was unable to write up my own contribution for publication.

59   To make this evaluation is not to deny that in our understanding of the conceptualization of context, each of these frameworks/tools has represented an important step forward when first introduced. I acknowledge my debt to both Martin and Ventola: Martin's idea of genre combination (1985a) and Ventola's flowcharts (1984, 1987) presented as methodological tool at once drew attention to problems in SFL text analysis, specifically in GSP analysis (Hasan 1978, 1979b, etc.), and at the same time gave rise to new problems.

60   At the level of context, representation of description in terms of system networks is not as common as it is at the level of lexicogrammar. Nonetheless there have been sporadic attempts since the late 1970s, e.g., in my own teaching (Cloran 1982, 1987) or conference presentation (c.f., note 59 above). In recent years Martin and colleagues have presented many system networks

purported to be at the level of context (see especially Ventola 1987 and Martin 1992).

61 In my work I have often used the term social activity as a concept that is at the same level of abstraction as field of discourse; action itself is a lower order concept than social activity.

62 I am thinking here of such critiques which find fault with linguistics for focusing on language, describing it as 'privileging language'. This is as absurd as it would be to blame physics for being concerned with physical phenomena.

63 As a semiotic system, language seldom operates in independence from other semiotic systems: in fact this statement is generally true of *all* semiotic systems; they all work co-operatively, as I have pointed out elsewhere (1973c, 1996b, 1999a). I will henceforth take it as given that wherever the term 'verbal' is used the possibility of such 'collaboration' between the various semiotic systems is to be assumed. See also Note 67 below.

64 Given our declared perspective, we have already excluded from the purview of linguistics those cases where there is only material action *without any verbal action whatsoever:* doubtlessly such cases exist and they most probably are socially significant, but the tools of linguistics are not (nor should be) competent to describe or analyse them. It is possible of course that the basic concepts of some linguistic theory may be useful in suggesting a framework for the description/analysis of such purely material action, but this does imply that the derived theory is *not* part of linguistics; it is a branch of semiotics. O'Toole (1994) is a good example of a theory of a non-linguistic semiotic system based on linguistic theory: the theory of 'displayed art' he has created is derived from SFL but it would be wrong to view it as a part of SFL.

65 It is not an accident that vending machines or supermarkets can be used for selling certain categories of goods. The speaking relevant to material action is typically minimal and routinized; consider for example Wittgenstein's bricklayer. Routinized verbal action can be 'mechanized' fairly easily. Compare this with some imaginary device for lecturing which excludes and/or minimizes verbal action. Any such device with the least chance of success will have to utilize other semiotic systems and even then it is highly doubtful that lecturing could be accomplished without a good deal of verbal action.

66 The fact that in such environments verbal action is ancillary is significant: being ancillary to a material action, the language is likely to carry some evidence of its nature. So although the recognition of the activity on the basis of language alone may be problematic in such cases, it is a fair assumption that this would not *always* be entirely impossible.

67 I use this term interchangeably with my earlier term generalized/generic structure potential (GSP), which was designed to capture the structural potential applicable to a particular category of register. (discussion in Hasan 1978, 1979b, 1981, 1984c, 1985b, 1994).

68 It is interesting to compare the semantic unit 'text' with the lexicogrammatical unit 'clause'. The structure potential of clause types can be stated quite

confidently by reference to fairly primary systemic choices in, say, the system of MOOD and/or TRANSITIVITY, just as the structure potential of a registerial category can be stated fairly confidently by reference to primary choices of field, tenor and mode. However, specifying the lexical shape of a clause calls for infinitely more work, just as specifying the textural content of a text calls for a much more delicate description (Hasan 1995).

69   According to Halliday (1985b: 12) 'mode of discourse refers to what part the language is playing, what it is that the participants are expecting the language to do for them in that situation'; the concept of mode includes 'the rhetorical mode, what is being achieved by the text in terms of such categories as persuasive, expository, didactic, and the like.' (*ibid.*) For statements in agreement with this position, see also Hasan 1985b, 1995, and for the notion of *genres based on mode*, see Martin (1992).

70   As an illustration of this point see Hasan (1995). For actual descriptions of ideational lexicogrammatical patterns implicated in the realization of, say, definition or generalization, see Martin (1993)

71   I call them 'unanalysed' because we do not appear to have asked: what kinds of activity these are.

72   Cloran (1999a: Table 9) makes very fine distinctions across rhetorical units; it is however likely that underlying some of her rhetorical units which involve future action is the feature [practical].

73   I believe that the presence of specifically material action has not been mentioned as a necessary condition in Cloran's rhetorical unit called plan. However, rhetorical unit is a semantic category, not a contextual one.

74   At this stage the semantic network of messages treated the exchange of information and goods and services as 'enacting speaker stance' (Hasan 1983, 1996a; Hasan, Cloran, Williams and Lukin 2007); more recently this has been re-labelled as 'relation enactment' (Hasan, 2013; also Chapter 8 here, especially c.f., Figure 8.7). It is clear that options in this system do more than indicate stance.

75   Taken from: SyncMaster 500s Color Monitor: Owner's Instructions. Samsung Electronics (Australia) Pty Ltd.

76   For example Cross (1991) has shown convincingly that the semantic and lexicogrammatical potential of registers/text types/genres, call it what you will, is just as clearly activated by the features of tenor. (For some indication of the important contribution to the texture and structure of a text made by the values of tenor, see Chapter 8 in this volume.)

77   In commonsense terms, only a very small proportion of our actions are *purely* for making someone feel good or bad, though clearly flattery and condemnation could occur intermittently as features of the main context, and they would enact a relation between the interactants.

78   For an early indication that mood and modality might be pertinent to the realization of certain activity types, see Hasan (1995).

79 The choice of the terms [first order] v. [second order] by me was rather an unfortunate oversight; the terms have sometimes been confused with Halliday's use of these expressions (1977a) to characterize field. What Halliday calls first/second order fields is different from my definition as offered here. For example first order field for Halliday would be a football game, and the commentary on that game would be the second order field. My definition as offered here is closer to 'object text' e.g., a nursery tale (whether known as spoken text or written); the second order would be a discussion about the nursery tale, or making its summary, etc. So it might have been better to use the terms DISCURSIVE and META-DISCURSIVE, respectively.

80 This system was first presented in essentially this form in my paper called Shapes in Narrative at a conference convened by Martin in 1985 with the title Writing to Mean. For a system network in roughly comparable area, see Martin (1992: 522, Figure 7.11).

81 Clearly these terms are not very desirable now in view of the development of the notion of simple and complex text as discussed in Section 6.2 above; I leave the terms here just to indicate the ideas introduced in my (1985a) presentation.

82 I believe this characterization of [commenting] verbal action is applicable to Cloran's (1994, 1995) rhetorical unit which she refers to as *commentary*, though the categories she suggests are generally more delicate (cf. her distinction between commentary and observation).

83 This description of less specialized activities e.g., repairing bike puncture or mending a torn shirt perhaps gives the impression of 'no training at all'. Objectively speaking, all social practices involve some expertise including those of bathing a child, putting her to bed, laying the table and so on. I want to suggest that the degree of specialization is greater with the need for greater organization in the training/apprenticeship and it calls for more mental work.

84 These are just the immediate 'relatives' of a legal trial. In discussing the lexicon, linguists often talk about the complex mosaic of lexical relations: however, this complex mosaic is far surpassed in complexity by the mosaic of the inter-connectedness of discourse types and institutions where the field is specialized.

85 Today I would reject this default marking for reasons discussed elsewhere (Hasan, under preparation); moreover, I think a better label for the option called [institutionalized] here is [conventional].

86 While I did not use the terminology of textual co-location and integration, Hasan (1981) was very much concerned with an objective theory of the conditions under which such patterns may be said to be at risk.

87 Needless to say that such generalizations are also possible with respect to tenor and mode. Thus minimal social distance in tenor and phonic channel with dialogue are relatively more hospitable to co-location and/or integration (for early discussions, see Hasan 1981).

88 Note that the condition of 'same interactant' is not met in the second case, or at least met only partially.

89 Halliday (1977a) draws a similar distinction, but perhaps because his point of departure is textual, he refers to the material action of the game as secondary field and to the constitutive verbal action (e.g., a commentary or instructions on playing the game) as the primary field, the one that language-wise is far more substantial.

90 In actual practice it usually turns out to be complex because there is usually more than one commentator and exchange of opinions between them, banter and joint recall contribute to the design of the commentary turning it into a complex text.

7 The place of context in a systemic functional model [2009]

> ... 'context of situation' is best viewed as a suitable schematic construct to apply to language events ... it is a group of related categories at a different level from grammatical categories but rather of the same abstract nature. [J. R. Firth 1957: 182]

7.1 Introduction

Some fifty years ago, any mention of the term CONTEXT was in effect an identifier of the kind of linguistics one professed. Today the situation is reversed: except for one or two restricted models, the word is currency in the discipline of linguistics. This does not mean, though, that meaningful dialogue between different models is now free of problems: despite a substratum of some commonly accepted meanings, the term continues to have different value in the many current linguistic models.[1] This chapter will be concerned primarily with an examination of the category of context in Halliday's systemic functional linguistics (henceforth, SFL),[2] where the concept has played a crucial role throughout the development of SFL from general linguistics to scale and category to system and structure to the model's present position as a systemic functional theory whose aim is to offer a scientific description of the nature and function of language. Inherited from Malinowski (1923, 1935) via Firth (1957) at its general linguistics stage, context has been greatly elaborated since Halliday first used it in his early writings (1957, 1961).[3] Perhaps the most decisive step was taken in Halliday, McIntosh and Strevens (1964), where the 'scientific study of language' was said to depend on an understanding of 'how language works' in the social processes of life. The authors theorized context of situation in terms of the three parameters of the MODE OF DISCOURSE, FIELD OF DISCOURSE, and STYLE OF DISCOURSE; following Gregory's suggestion

(1967), the last label was later changed to TENOR OF DISCOURSE; the authors related these contextual parameters to a kind of language variety, which they called REGISTER.

What was remarkable about this theory of context was not the abstraction of these three parameters from the referential domain of the word 'context' in its 'ordinary' usage, for some abstraction of this kind had already been made by Firth (1957, 1964).[4] Rather, *The users and uses of language* (1964: 75–94), the section of Halliday *et al.* most relevant to this discussion, was remarkable for its methodical establishment of the relationship of what Austin (1962) called 'words and vocables' or Firth, 'bits and pieces of language' to each contextual parameter and for an explicit indication of their place in the ecology of text in context, suggesting that distinct varieties of text could be recognized by reference to variation in language use correlating with variation in values of these parameters. Equally clear was the implication that the authors' perspective on the context of culture and of situation is founded primarily on the centrality of discourse, i.e., on the process of 'language as text', a principle that holds true to this day: the SFL description of context has been overwhelmingly socio*linguistic* rather than socio*semiotic*[5] or socio*logical*. Partial accounts of some of the developments following upon Halliday *et al.* (1964) may be found in Butt (2001); Butt and Wegener (2007); Cloran (1994, 1999a); Halliday (1973b, c, 1977a); Halliday and Hasan (1976, 1985); Hasan (1973c, 1978, 1979b, 1984c, 1994, 2009c and chapters of this volume); Martin (1992, 1999); Matthiessen (1993, 2007). The aim of this chapter is to explore two major issues: (a) the place of context in the theoretical framework of SFL, and (b) its descriptions in relation to the linguistic analysis of the uses of language.

7.2   The place of context in scientific linguistics

According to my understanding of SFL, the acceptance of linguistics as a scientific study of language implies that such a study will be comprehensive: not only will it offer a coherent and viable account of 'the architecture' of language as system (Matthiessen 2007), but also the offered account will have the potential of making sense when confronted with the social practices whereby language is maintained, including both its phylogenetic and ontogenetic development (Painter 2009); it will also permit a viable account of language change, thus including both the descriptions of synchronic variation and diachronic change.

7.2.1 Context and the system and process of language

Context as a theoretical category is crucial to any coherent account of all the above aspects of the study of language, though its origins lie primarily in its contribution to a principled study of PAROLE. When examined with reference to its context, parole *contra* Saussure (1966, 2008), provides irrefutable evidence of its orderliness. A large number of studies of naturally occurring discourse establishes beyond doubt the well regulated nature of parole.[6] This orderliness depends not on the whims of a single individual, i.e., Saussurean '*sujet parlant*' nor the Chomskyan 'ideal native speaker', but on the exchanges of meaning between *ordinary* speakers as participants in 'concerted social activities' (Malinowski 1923).

This finding should have put both language use and context centre stage in linguistics, but the dominance of the idea that 'linguistics proper' has to be concerned solely with *langue*, or worse still, with competence, has led formalistic linguists to believe that in the words of Leech (1974: 80) they have 'a justification for ignoring as far as possible the study of context where it interferes with the study of competence'.[7] One severe problem with this conception of 'linguistics proper' was to deny it the possibility of explaining coherently either synchronic variation or diachronic change, making the so-called 'linguistics proper' a rather undesirable framework for the comprehensive scientific study of language (Labov 1972b). It seems obvious that for an account of language as system and process, linguistics needs to take as its object of enquiry both these aspects of language in its social context as Halliday *et al.* (1964, 1971) had suggested; in fact, it can be claimed quite confidently that there can be no comprehensive scientific linguistics without parole, and no study of parole without context: a viable linguistics needs to incorporate both. And indeed soon after Halliday *et al.* (1964), the category of context, which since Firth 1957, had appeared as something of a surrogate for semantics, became recognized in SFL as a stratum in its own right in the theoretical linguistic framework.[8] Clearly, the integration of some category into a theory is not a magical single step affair: a category grows slowly into an element of the theory as the understanding of its nature and function grows; and the justification for its integration lies in the work it does (Butt and Wegener 2007) in generating the explanatory and descriptive power in the theory. Figure 7.1 presents a view of Halliday's integration of the categories of parole and context into SFL.

Figure 7.1: Language and context: system and instance (Halliday 1999: 9)[9]

<pre>
                              instantiation
           SYSTEM ——————————————————————————— INSTANCE

              context of _________________________ context of
 CONTEXT   culture   situation

                           (cultural   (situation
      c   domain)   type)
      realization

                           (register)   (text type)
 LANGUAGE   language as _________________________ language as
              system   text
</pre>

Note: Culture instantiated in situation, as system instantiated in text.

Culture realized in/construed by language; same relation as that holding between linguistic strata (semantics: lexicogrammar: phonology: phonetics).

Cultural domain and register are 'sub-systems': likeness viewed from 'system' end.

Situation type and text type are 'instance types': likeness viewed from 'instance' end.

7.2.2   The relationship of language and context

Figure 7.1 displays four categories, and two relations, one on the vertical axis, called REALIZATION, the other on the horizontal, called INSTANTIATION. The four categories can be organized into two distinct sets by reference to each relation. Thus, set (1) consists of the members (a) CONTEXT OF CULTURE and (b) LANGUAGE AS SYSTEM (see the left column). Set (2) consists of the members (a) CONTEXT OF SITUATION and (b) LANGUAGE AS TEXT (the right column). The two members of each pair are related to each other realizationally, so that 1a is to 1b as 2a is to 2b. These same four categories can be re-classed by reference to the relation of instantiation: set (3) shown along the top line of the rectangle consists of the two members, (a) CONTEXT OF CULTURE, and (b) context of situation, while set (4) shown along the bottom line of the rectangle consists of (a) LANGUAGE AS SYSTEM, and (b) LANGUAGE AS TEXT. The two members of each pair are related by instantiation, so that 3a is to 3b as 4a is to 4b. Thus each category enters directly into two relations, and also indirectly into some relation with the remaining other category. To understand the significance of this dense pattern of relationships it is necessary to understand the meaning of instantiation and realization, and what is implied by this mode of integration for the 'architecture of language' according to SFL.

Instantiation is the relationship between a potential and its instance, so in set 3, context of culture is the potential, i.e. the system, while a context of situation is an instance of that potential. Halliday (1988, 1992a, 1993, 2008) points out that instance and system are not two distinct kinds of phenomena: they are in fact the same thing viewed from different time depths. Instance is what is immediate and capable of being experienced; system is the ultimate point of the theorization of what has been experienced and is imaginable by extrapolation. System thus takes shape through the distillation of the relations among the significant properties of instances: the system of culture is not simply an inventory of all its situations; it is an organization of the possible features of all possible situations in all their possible permutations, where 'possible' means socially recognizable: it is something that the acculturated can interpret, act on and in, and evaluate; in addition, both system and instance are sensitive to perturbations in each other's properties.[10] What this means is that anything new entering the system of culture will enter only through variation in the properties associated with some context of situation, i.e., cultures change through human social practices. The same observations apply, *mutatis mutandis*, to the categories of set 4, i.e., language system in relation to its instance, language as text. One reason 'linguistics proper' is unable to account for language maintenance and language change is its banishment of language use, i.e., parole; this logically prevents it from recognizing any category comparable to that of instantiation. If systemic change and innovation depend on language use, then in such models language system cannot claim access to the resources of parole, which is where texts manifest their properties maintaining the existing patterns and innovating new ones. There exists a dialectic between language system and language use: the system furnishes resources towards the formation and interpretation of the process, and the process furnishes resources towards the system's maintenance, innovation, and change.

The relation of realization is inherently semiotic: its roots lie in the nature of the sign itself, which being a union of CONTENT and EXPRESSION (Hjelmslev 1961) is necessarily stratified. The concept of realization refers to that relation whereby the stratified phenomena are calibrated permitting language in use to be subjectively experienced as a seamless flow where meaning, wording and sound work together (Halliday 1992a; Hasan 1995, 2009c; Matthiessen 1995, 2007; Butt 2008). With years of experience of working with a stratal model, today SFL recognizes five strata: context is the 'highest' stratum in the theory, and it is language external. The remaining four strata are language internal: SEMANTICS and LEXICOGRAMMAR are the elaboration of what Hjelmslev called content, and PHONOLOGY and PHONETICS, that of expression.[11] The most important to the present discussion are the first three strata in the theory, viz., context, semantics and lexicogrammar: the functioning of realization across these strata is critically different from that across the last two.[12] At the three higher strata of context, meaning and wording realization functions as a dialectic: looking from above, contextual choices ACTIVATE semantic choices activate the lexicogrammatical ones; looking from below lexicogrammatical choices CONSTRUE semantic choices construe contextual ones (Hasan, Cloran, Williams and Lukin 2007; Hasan, 2016). To put it simply, to explain why anyone says anything one must appeal to the context which exerts pressure on the speaker's choice of meaning; and to explain why these patterns of wordings appear rather than any other, one must appeal to the meanings which, in response to the context, activate those wordings: semantics is thus an interface between context and linguistic form.[13] This activation-construal dialectic does not extend to the strata below lexicogrammar: one may claim that lexicogrammar activates phonological choices, but it would be clearly wrong to claim that phonological choices construe lexicogrammatical choices: they simply signal it, which is in keeping with their status as an aspect of expression; the signalling sound pattern, i.e., Saussure's 'sound image', simply identifies something as a sign; its status as a category of lexicogrammar is defined by reference to its relation to other categories at the level of lexicogrammar, as is evident from examples such as *a whiting couldn't possibly be singing.*

7.2.3   Context, language system and linguistic theory

There are some significant implications of this mode of integrating context of situation and parole into the linguistic theory. Briefly, the recognition of the instantiation relation opens a legitimate avenue for the description of practices that contribute to language maintenance, the two faces of which in a living language are manifested as stability and change, regularity and variation.[14] SFL anticipated Weinreich, Labov and Herzog (1968), in recognizing systemic variation as an inherent attribute of language system (Halliday *et al.* 1964). Thus one face of language maintenance is presented in language use as an overwhelming endorsement of systemic regularities, and the other, as selective departures from them. These departures do not simply take the shape of replacement of this signal by that as usually documented in diachronic phonetic changes: very much more important are the phenomena we might describe as 'expansion' or development. Two processes significant for language development are: (1) 'semo-genesis' (Halliday 1992a, 1995a); and (2) variation be it 'user based' i.e., dialectal or 'use based', i.e. registerial. Context is pivotal to the study of both kinds of variation (Hasan 2009c): it is the locus of variant occurrences, and speakers are located by reference to context within their social world. At the same time, being an instance of culture, it carries the potential of tracing the work that varieties of a language do in the maintenance and change of cultural patterns of life. One pay off for the integration of context into a linguistics thus is that it allows a logical basis for entry into the valuable field of the sociology of language as a natural step in the theory.

Seen in this light, register variation gains a central position both in the life of a language and that of the speaker as well as her speech community. Based on the range of social processes in which the individual participates, her register repertoire acts as a significant indicator of her SOCIAL POSITIONING (Bernstein 1990) and her social positioning is at least partly a function of her register repertoire (Hasan 1999a/2005; 2016): register repertoire is in fact a cog in the social wheel of what Bourdieu (1990) used to call 'structured structuring structures'. It follows that what is true of the individual, is also true of the speech community, whose socio-political positioning *vis à vis* other communities is indicated by a comparison of their respective register repertoires, as even a cursory enquiry into the current political situation of the world will quickly show: it is not an accident that international/world languages have always been languages of powerful speech communities, certain segments of which logically participate in considerably wider range of social processes. While the potential for development is identical across the languages of the world, their actual state of development can and does vary: communities with less developed languages are also communities with fewer material resources.[15]

The varieties of language begin life as acts of parole, but through the working of instantiation and realization, they eventually end up enriching the system of language. Nowhere is this more obvious than in the functional character of language. Since the early 1970s Halliday has drawn attention (e.g. in 1970a, 1971) to the fact that the contexts of language use leave their indelible impression on the inner structure of language: the structure of language is as it becomes in meeting the demands its speakers make on it, the functions it is made to serve in their life. Simplifying, in SFL, the arguments for the recognition of the metafunctions rest on what is revealed by the analysis of language use in natural context. In this examination, the tripartite structure of the context of situation is significant; it emphasizes the nature of talk as a form of social action. The parameters are in fact the three most obvious aspects of linguistic action. Thus field of discourse refers to the nature of social action, apropos which language is being used. Tenor of discourse refers to the nature of social relationship amongst those involved with the action, not concerned with the identity of specific individual, but how the individuals are socially positioned *vis à vis* each other, since this is what will impinge on the production and reception of the messages. Mode of discourse refers to the mode of contact for the actors in the discourse event, since clearly the nature of the message will be different for a co-actor in absentia compared with that for the co-present interactant. As the last comment implies, the nature of the text changes as the values of the contextual parameters change: this is what it means to claim that language in use is responsive to the speaker's socio-semantic needs.

It follows that given a substantial quantity of naturally occurring use of language in context, and given a viable method of analysing this data, the question can be meaningfully raised: is there any specialization of meanings in relation to the three different contextual parameters. It would clearly be impossible to give an answer in terms of specific meanings of lexemes or syntagmatic structures: the former is too sensitive to variation in contextual values; the latter, very much less so. But if the question is answered in terms of classes of meanings, and if paradigmatic analysis provides a viable ground for the classification of those meanings, as is the case in SFL, then the answer to the question may be given in a meaningful way. Figure 7.2, borrowed from Halliday (1973b: 101), is a schematic representation of the results of one such examination.

As the legend in Figure 7.2 shows, the first column represents raw data of text as language in use, the second represents the situation types relevant to some specific group of texts – the instances of text types/registers: from each bundling of texts in some situation type radiate three lines representing each of the three vectors of tenor, mode and field in that order. The formal resources of worded meanings that realize the features of each vector have been identified by specific labels in Figure 7.2: tenor is associated with INTERPERSONAL worded meanings, mode with TEXTUAL and field, with IDEATIONAL ones. These are the labels Halliday uses for the three metafunctions of language recognized in SFL. The remaining columns in the Figure represents the paradigmatic resources of the language system at the stratum of meanings and wordings, which the hearer encounters as syntagmatic structures: the latter are represented in the form employed which, in the 1970s, was overwhelmingly to represent such structure.

This analysis casts a new light on the work being done in the 1970s in the analysis of lexicogrammar especially with reference to CLAUSE: it became obvious that, seen in a paradigmatic perspective, the lexicogrammar that

Figure 7.2: Arguments for context metafunction resonance [Halliday 1973b: 101]

		i n s t a n t i a t i o n		
	SYSTEM	⟶		INSTANCE
CONTEXT				context of situation
	context of culture	cultural domain	situation types	
LANGUAGE	language as system	register	text type	language as text

Note: Both culture and language are systems, relations of relations of relations …
Culture is instantiated in situation as language is instantiated in text
Culture is realised/ construed as language as situation is realised/construed as text
Realisation relation relates culture to expression plane via content plane
Cultural domain and register viewed from the perspective of system
Situation type and text type viewed from the perspective of instance

construes interpersonal meanings forms itself into a complex of system networks, options within which are closely related to each other by dependency and simultaneity, e.g., the systems of MOOD, MODALITY, PRIMARY TENSE, EVALUATION and GENERAL QUANTIFICATION. By contrast, the lexicogrammar which construes textual meanings organizes itself into another complex of system networks, options of which are similarly closely related to each other by dependency and simultaneity within that complex but show relatively fewer relations to other complexes – the systems in question are such as those of THEME, INFORMATION FOCUS, PHORICITY and KEY. The same is true *mutatis mutandis* regarding the ideational lexicogrammatical resources, which are called upon for the construal of ideational meanings – such as those of TRANSITIVITY, REFERENCE, EXPANSION, PROJECTION, and TENSE. Halliday suggests that this characteristic organization of the semantic and lexicogrammatical resources, whose internal organization is shaped in response to each of the three contextual vectors, can be interpreted as a validation of the hypothesis (see also Halliday 1979b) that: (a) the form of human language is necessarily functional; and (b) that this functionality of form has arisen in response to the evolution of human language as a resource for acting semiotically in social contexts. Functionality in language thus resonates primarily throughout the strata of context, semantics and lexicogrammar; albeit, traces of functionality are found also at the stratum of phonology where segmental phonology is overwhelmingly ideational, while the prosodic is overwhelmingly interpersonal and/or textual. All said, the metafunctional resonance is clearest at the higher three levels which, as pointed out earlier, enter into realizational dialectic. This appears reasonable since the postulate of functionality in language does depend to a large extent on the dialectic of realizational relations linking context, meaning and wording mutually. Before leaving this discussion, it should be added that here, as also in the preceding paragraphs, the focus has been on the analysis of situated language use, but what the analysis has revealed is the way in which parole in context contributes to the shaping of the resources of the system. As Halliday (1971: 62. italics original.) says:

> The image of language as having a 'pure' form (*langue*) that becomes contaminated in the process of being translated into speech (*parole*) is of little value ... We do not want a boundary between language and speech at all, or between pairs such as langue and parole, or competence and performance, unless these are reduced to mere synonyms of 'can do' and 'does'.

7.2.4   An appliable theory for the study of language in its social context

The sections above have attempted to provide an account of the space that Figure 7.1 opens up for the exploration of the category of context: it has presented what Dawkins (2006) might describe as 'mutually buttressed evidence' in favour of the SFL modelling of language and the need to integrate context and parole in linguistic theory; without this inclusion a comprehensive scientific description of language is not feasible. The integration is critical to the conceptualization of functionality in language, and makes possible a coherent description of not only the inner structure of language especially its semantic and lexicogrammatical organization, but also of the system's maintenance and development: diachronic change is an important aspect of these processes. Language development is supported by the relations of realization and instantiation which link language and society, system and instance: they allow an evidence based account of ontological development, and help explain the significance of patterns of language development in the community, especially their relevance to the community's social positioning *vis à vis* others. The cogenetic relation between language and society is in fact the foundation of a viable discipline of sociolinguistics, which needs not only naturally occurring data; it needs also the appropriate theoretical apparatus for perceptive interpretation (Hasan 2009c). The appliability of linguistics to any field of human endeavour depends on this open-ended view of language and society, system and instance, semiosis as social practice. Formalistic linguists have sometimes deridingly described SFL as 'applied linguistics': an alternative view is that the explanatory and successful application of linguistics to a wide range of social practices demonstrates the probity of the theory's modelling of language. Just as the exploration of space would have been impossible without a good modelling of the earth in its physical context, so also successful applications of linguistics would be impossible without a good modelling of language in its social context.

7.3 Describing context in textual processes

This section attempts to discuss issues in the description of context in SFL: how is context described, with what implications for understanding its nature, and, for expanding its potential for application to diverse categories of discourse analysis. According to SFL, there exist two possible perspectives for the description of context, which can be identified by reference to Figure 7.1: the description may be from the point of view of instance, or from that of system. The former is concerned with what is going on here-and-now in the social situation where language is being used on a specific occasion; the latter, with a description of context in any case of language use whatsoever, i.e. with the potential of context. A good deal of ink and energy were deployed in SFL in the 1980s in praising the former, and downgrading the other as incapable of describing instances (Martin 1985a). With hindsight, it seems clear that both perspectives have to work together: to demand only the dynamic perspective is to say by analogy that the lexicogrammar, which after all is a description of language from the perspective of the system, is incapable of describing the linguistic patterns in the instance, i.e., the text; further, it is to deny, by implication, the possibility of a theoretical basis for discourse analysis (Hasan 1995). In the event, the dynamic approach did not remain truly as dynamic as first mooted; and the synoptic was never really synoptic despite repeated cries of stasis. In actual practice, in the work of all SFL scholars, the description of context has *always* straddled the two perspectives. The reason for this inheres in the system-instance relation: an orderly description is a step toward 'systemization'; and linguistics is about orderly descriptions. The dual perspective has been beneficial to the study of context: it has, in a manner of speaking, enabled the description to be 'tested' by patterns in large scale studies of instances, thus contributing to the understanding of both its system and instance.

7.3.1   Concept 'relevant context'

Both Firth and Halliday began with the system perspective and, one might say, moved too quickly to the instance, a necessary step perhaps, because that's where the immediately visible pay-off is. Firth explicitly built in the attribute of 'relevance' thus implying that there was somewhere in the environment something that might not be relevant. His categories for context description were worded as follows (Firth 1957: 182; emphasis added):

A.   the *relevant* features of the participants: persons and personalities.
   (i)   the verbal action of the participants.
   (ii) the non-verbal action of the participants.
B.   the *relevant* objects.
C.   the effect of the verbal action.

However, it was not clear how relevance was to be established: relevant for whom or to what. Halliday *et al.* (1964) clarified this issue by suggesting that their parameters called, field, mode and tenor are relevant by virtue of the fact that they would always leave a 'trace' in the text (see especially Halliday 1977a; Hasan 1973c, 1978, etc.): what is relevant in the context of situation would be illuminated by the language of the text. In both cases, parameters of context were offered as 'abstractions from'/dimensions of the context of situation; but the relationship of the contextual parameters to what there was in the situation remained shrouded in mystery.

These uncertainties, and others related ones, were foregrounded for me in the late 1960s, when I was faced with a mass of running prose, which represented transcribed discourse produced in the oral mode by children for one of the research projects conducted by Bernstein's Sociological Research Unit. The children had responded to a request to tell a bed time story to 'this teddy bear' about 'this sailor, this boy, this girl, and this dog'.[16] What was one to describe as the relevant features of the context? Who were the relevant participants? What could be anticipated about the children's language use if one took the requesting researcher and the responding child as the relevant interactants? Were the sailor, the boy, etc. relevant participants/ objects? If not what were they doing in the children's stories? How was it to be established that the children had really told stories? Was everything they said part of one story? What intersubjectively objective recognition criteria could one offer for the resolution of any of these issues to those research assistants who were to actually engage in the analysis of the data?

In Malinowski's ethnographic descriptions (1935) narrative function and its dual context had been highlighted: the fact that the language of the story 'referred to' a separate context, an imaginary one of the story itself, and another relating to the actual process of telling the story to someone. With hindsight, I recognize that the solution to some of my research problems was achieved by putting together Malinowski and Halliday *et al*. The latter implied that 'context' refers to selective phenomena in the total speech environment which is ratified by the language of the text; and the traces of these selective phenomena are found in text as an instance of language in use. The former suggested the simultaneous operation of two contexts, which though related were yet distinct. It appeared reasonable to suggest (Hasan 1973c) that the IMMEDIATE CONTEXT of discourse has two aspects, viz., a MATERIAL SITUATIONAL SETTING and a RELEVANT CONTEXT. Hasan (1973c) had briefly referred to the material situational setting, identifying it as a 'dormant' force. Elements of this dormant force enjoy the possibility of impinging on the ongoing parole (discussion below). By contrast, relevant context refers to that frame of consistency which is illuminated by the language of the text.

This conceptualization of relevant context immediately raises certain issues: (a) are the elements of a relevant context referred to by the language of the text always materially present in the speaker's speech environment? The answer is 'no': for example we do produce written instructions, where the addressee is materially absent; so, how should the theory interpret the everyday word 'environment' or 'situation'? (b) if relevant context is recognized only by reference to 'the text', then what are the recognition criteria for the boundaries of a text? Unless we know what the reliable source of evidence is, we can hardly use it to recognize that which is made evident by the source; and (c) what exactly is going on when two distinct relevant contexts are operating simultaneously, as in the data representing children's attempt to tell a story on demand from an interviewer? Are the two contexts related? And, if so, how? The first two issues are briefly addressed below;[17] for the last issue see Hasan (1971b, 1985a, 1999b, 2011b), Halliday (1977a).

7.3.2   Relevant context and material environment

Hasan (1973c) and Halliday and Hasan (1976) had suggested that a register is known by the meanings at risk in that environment: a register is what meanings in text are supposed to instantiate.[18] If relevant context is that which is based on the interpretation of the language of the text, then, clearly, it is something at least partially 'made of (worded) meanings', which is to say that it is a SEMIOTIC CONSTRUCT. It is this semiotic construct, that is being abstracted from other elements of the situation and it need not consist merely of those elements of the material situation that may be present here and now as the process of text is occurring. The tripartite structure consisting of field, tenor and mode is assigned to this semiotic abstraction: it cannot sensibly be assigned to 'the material situational setting', which consists simply of material objects, person(s), but not 'personalities', which always form part of the relevant context, and their mutual relations. The language of a text may or may not contain any traces of the situational existents, whether it will do so depends on other features of the relevant context. If traces of elements of the material situational setting are encapsulated in the text, then such tracing semantic elements become part of the relevant context.[19] So the elements of the material situational setting are a 'dormant force' precisely in this manner: they are capable of impinging on a certain class of relevant contexts, though 'conditions apply!' for this to happen.[20] If and when they do impinge, they might lead to change(s) in the context: these changes are primarily relevant to the production of sub-texts, i.e. they are in some specifiable manner connected to the text already in progress; or they function as an independent, parallel text, which in the end acts as an interruption of the text already in progress (Cloran 1999a; Hasan 1999b),[21] though there are registers where the global structure of the text moves via what might be called 'associative movement', as for example in informal conversations between friends, where 'one thing leads on to another'; one part of on-going conversational text is supplanted by a new one by association.

7.3.3   Relevant context

The clarification of the relationship between material situational setting and relevant context proves helpful in providing an orderly way of describing the 'unexpected', encountered under certain conditions. It can also be used to suggest a viable classification of relevant contexts; relevant contexts may be:

(a) capable of being perturbed by their material situational setting, informal conversation being a quintessential example; or

(b) not subject to such perturbation – except in serious emergency – the production of verbal art, or the presentation of speech at a convocation being quintessential examples.

Taking language in use as verbal action in service of some social activity, the three parameters place a grid on the space occupied by its relevant context: this space may be seen as exhaustively describable in terms of the three parameters called field, tenor and mode of discourse, on which the description of relevant context depends.

Relevant contexts differ from each other by the particular configuration of the values of the three named parameters specific to a particular occasion of language use. Each parameter is, in effect, treated as a reservoir of 'values', only a selection of which characterizes one instance. From this perspective, the make up of a specific relevant context consists of all the values 'selected' in each of the three parameters that 'apply' to the text, which is a semiotic representation of the relevant context: such a set of values specific to a relevant context has been referred to as a CONTEXTUAL CONFIGURATION (Hasan 1978) (acronym CC). An indicative account of some values ascribed to each in SFL is provided below.

7.3.4 Relevant context and contextual configuration

Beginning with field, which concerns the nature of social ACTION, we might think of the many different actions we undertake by using language, such as shopping, teaching, telling a bed time story; playing a board game; giving someone a bath; attending to a patient; making an appointment for consultation; supervising a child eating food, and the list just goes on. Clearly, there are an enormous number of actions, any of which could be unfolding at the same time: the only condition for the linguist's interest is that the action must necessarily involve some use of language. The GOAL or PURPOSE of action is quite often mentioned in the CC. Here too one might elaborate on the kind of goal as, say, visible/invisible, for example, the mothers talk to their children while giving them a bath: describing the context of such talk we might note that the visible goal is to engage/entertain the child; however, a number of such verbal actions over time lead to 'socializing' the child in a particular way of being, doing and saying, and this could be treated as an invisible goal. Parents are often aware of this goal as they speak though an onlooker might not be. The recognition of goal/purpose as separate from the action itself often poses problems: for example could you be engaged in pedagogic action of lecturing with the goal of exchanging material commodities? As work on discourse analysis continued, higher level generalizations were also made, e.g., 'service encounter' which could be instantiated by buying food, or stamps, or tickets for a trip, etc.; or, say, 'pedagogic action' which would 'cover' teaching, revision, discussion, exams, orals and what not.

Tenor, concerned with social RELATION, early on lent itself to descriptions of ROLE. Thus such roles as mother-child; teacher-young pupil; lecturer-adult student; customer-vendor, doctor-patient; friend-friend were used as implying a certain kind of relationship between the interactants. Contact with Bernstein's work brought further vectors of classification such as ASCRIBED and ACHIEVED roles; further, SOCIAL STATUS was introduced though selectively to handle symmetrical/asymmetrical discourses: examples of values would be PEER or HIERARCHIC; in some cases the vector of hierarchy was further elaborated. DEGREES OF FORMALITY have also been used as an attribute of relation. SOCIAL DISTANCE, introduced in SFL early (Hasan 1973c), attempted to capture the interactive biography of the specific interactants, as this modified the tone of agentive and semiotic roles. The character of their interactive biography, i.e., how often they have interacted and in how many different kinds of social processes they have participated together; as well as what social status they carry *vis à vis* each other, these and many such features are all essential to how the interactants are likely to relate to each other.

Mode of discourse, concerning CONTACT, was seen as a two part affair: MEDIUM and CHANNEL. The values of channel refer to how 'the said' was to be accessed. Two obvious values were AURAL or VISUAL (from the addressee perspective) or PHONIC or GRAPHIC (from the speaker perspective). Medium referred to what 'language was doing', and the early examples consisted of such values as SPOKEN, WRITTEN; DIALOGUE, MONOLOGUE; WRITTEN-AS-IF-SPOKEN; (e.g., in drama; novel, etc.) WRITTEN-TO-BE-READ-ALOUD, such as sermon; EXTEMPORE, e.g., informal conversation or PREPARED, e.g., a paper presented at a conference; ANCILLARY language used as an instrument for assisting material action, e.g., directing arrangement of furniture in a room, helping someone cook something for the first time or CONSTITUTIVE, e.g., seminar discussion or writing a paper, where the activity is primarily conducted by languaging (and some other signing system; though unless there is language, the linguist qua linguist has hardly a part to play in its professional analysis). Clearly, 'what language is doing' was an informal description and as such, was subject to one's interpretation. In time, mode began to include labels of genres, e.g., discussion, moral fable, humour, letter, application and so on.

What is interesting in the above description is its vagueness, the absence of 'checkable' criteria, and the reliance on 'common sense'. It is as if, other than the context's tripartite division, its description has no underlying regularities, and no reasoned framework to work with: the assumption seems to have been that being acculturated persons the linguists would know what the occasion of talk was and what meanings were being exchanged, just as one might assume that native speakers 'know' the grammar of the clauses they are producing and comprehending. So faced with a text already there, the SFL linguists have largely been doing what any ordinary speaker of language would do, i.e., construing from the language of the text what the text is all about, who was doing what to/with whom and why, when and where. And conversely, when it came to predicting an example of the relevant context for an *imaginary* language use, a text not yet there, one did the same, supposedly, in reverse. Whether the perspective was claimed to be dynamic or detected to be synoptic made no difference whatever to the practice. As an example of the description of such an imaginary context, consider Hasan (1978: 231):[22]

Table 7.1: A partial account of an imaginary contextual configuration

VARIABLE	VALUES OF THE VARIABLE
Field	professional consultation: medical: application for appointment ...
Tenor	client: patient as applicant; receptionist: agent for consultant; social distance maximum
mode	aural channel; minus visual contact; telephone conversation; spoken medium

The account in Table 1 is highly selective, guided solely by the imaginary text I wished to analyse. In this description of relevant context, the only items that have the status of a theoretical category are those found in the left column. They alone have 'an abstract nature' such as the 'grammatical categories' are expected to have (see Firth quoted, p. 365); the others are intuitive, based on (the memory of) experiences. I am not implying that such descriptions are *ipso facto* incorrect in the details they offer; or that partial descriptions must necessarily be unacceptable: simply that such descriptions are not based in any consciously and carefully prepared framework for what, for want of an established term, one might call CONTEXTUALIZATION system networks. What has been attempted so far by way of contextualization is a common sense account: if, by analogy, the same types of conventions were applied to 'doing the description of a clause', a description *essentially without grammatics*, then the linguist would be reduced to simply identifying the 'doer', the 'doing', the 'when', the 'how' and so on by way of '*doing* transitivity'. Naturally systemic linguists would not approve of this practice – and they are rightly critical of it, when it is used, as often, in some educational sites.

There is much in this situation to cause discomfort. More recently efforts have been made to find perhaps better alternatives. The following section is a brief exploration of what is involved in such an effort.

7.3.5   Is a systemic description of the contextual parameters possible?

Given the discussion of Figure 7.1, it would be tautological to say that linguistic descriptions in SFL are made from a system perspective. For example, the lexicogrammar in SFL is unquestionably a grammar of the language seen from the system perspective.[23] When it comes to describing the grammar of an instance, this same lexicogrammar functions largely adequately as a resource: we do not go looking for a 'dynamic system' – a phrase containing a contradiction in terms (cf., Chapter 5 here).[24] This is not surprising: system and instance are not two totally different kinds of phenomena, and the very effort to move towards an orderly description is a move towards the system perspective (Hasan 1995; Halliday 1999). It is also to be noted that, although the distinction between grammatics and grammar is valuable, grammatics, if it is to account for the process of hearers understanding and of speakers speaking, must strive to a state of close iconicity to grammar. The same has been taken to be true *mutatis mutandis* for the other strata in the theory – there is however one exception and that exception is the level of context: SFL linguists have in general treated context description qualitatively differently from description at other strata, for example, that of lexicogrammar; in fact the effort is rejected as unsound.

There are two possible reasons for this: first, perhaps there is no agreement with Firth's (1957: 182) suggestion 'that "context of situation" is best viewed as a ... schematic construct to apply to language events, ... it is a group of related categories at a different level from grammatical categories but rather of the same abstract nature'. Although no one has so far explicitly disputed this Firthian claim, suggestions have been made that discourse analysis is indeed a very different kind of thing from doing grammar (Martin 1985a). However, no proof has been forthcoming that context is more different from meaning than meaning is from grammar, or grammar from phonology in respect of requiring 'schematic construct'; nor do we know how to measure the degree of these 'different differences'. The second reason for the reluctance to create a systematic framework might lie in a feeling that as an instance of the system of culture, the description of context of situation is probably better provided by sociology or anthropology. Certainly this is an important object of enquiry for those two disciplines, and it does form the object of enquiry for both the sociologist and the anthropologist, but not from the perspective of language. SFL, on the other hand, does attempt to describe instances of registers, i.e., texts, and it defines text by relating it to relevant context. And since, undeniably, a register's structure potential is the realization of its contextual configuration, it seems important to be able to provide a theorized framework for the description of the prime mover in the shaping of the discourse. It is important to remember also that although relevant context may in specifiable cases be linked through reference to the material situational setting, what relates to the discourse as relevant context is itself a semiotic construal, and as such it should be within the descriptive orbit of linguistics. Relevant context refers to a semiotically mediated universe; and it is one important function of SFL as a social semiotic theory of language to throw light on this construct. As it is, there are hardly any system networks in SFL concerning contextualization. In fact, partial contextualization system networks comparable to the lexicogrammatical ones are in a nascent stage; so far only three such have appeared in print (Cloran 1987; Hasan 1999b; Bowcher 2007).[25] David Butt's set of contextualization system networks (2004a) is the most exhaustive attempt in the sense that it includes an account of the largest number of contextualization options; but this remains in mimeo form.[26] What is in common to all these contextualization system networks is a characteristic in common, namely, that instead of taxonomizing realized meanings, they actually systemize the realization-instigating contextual features; and an attempt is made to relate context to wording via semantic categories which act as the interface between the two strata of context and lexicogrammar. In so doing these networks are building on similar efforts by Halliday in Halliday and Hasan (1985: 34ff; and elsewhere). There have also existed partial system networks with reference to the features of the contexts of some specific genres (Martin 1992; Ventola 1987); but here it is often difficult to decide whether we are dealing with lexical taxonomies pertaining to some 'registerial semantic potential' or with features of the potential of discursive contexts that instantiate some culture. To actually create a substantial, i.e., theoretically argued, contextualization system network of all three parameters with realization statements that reach lexicogrammatical choices via the semantic ones is a huge enterprise requiring a lifetime of work: what I hope to be able to do here is to give some example that might indicate: (a) that a paradigmatic description of the context of discourse is possible; and (b) that its options can be shown to be realizationally related to lexicogrammatical choices: clearly in taking a lexicogrammatical pattern as the realizationally relatable to meaning, the linguist must process with the semantic mediation; the relation of signification is much wider than 'lexis'.

7.3.5.1 *The point of origin for contextualization system network*
The total set of primary systems in the contextualization network as postulated so far (Hasan 1999b) opens as represented in Figure 7.3a.

Figure 7.3a: Parameters of contextualization systems (Hasan 1999b)

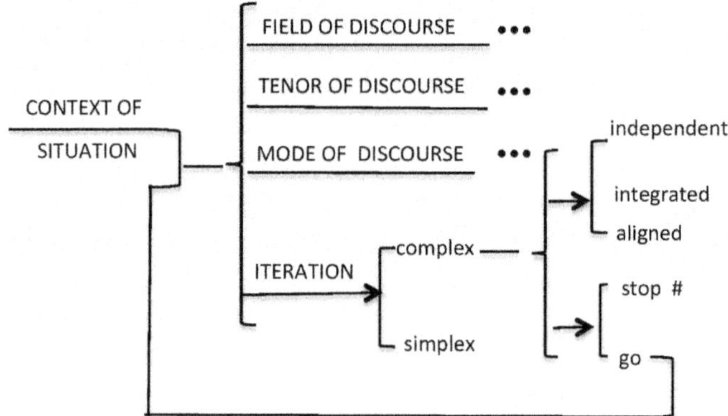

The point of origin for Figure 7.3a is context of discourse: it is the potential of context that the contextualization system networks are meant to describe. The system allows entry into four simultaneous systems, relating to the three parameters of the context of discourse as already described, namely, field of discourse, tenor of discourse, and mode of discourse. Some options will be chosen from each of these to account for the context of situation. However, as Hasan (1999b) has suggested, a fourth system, called ITERATION, is needed in addition. The primary options in this system are [simplex] realized as a simple text, or [complex] which would need to be chosen under certain circumstances: these circumstances are specified in general terms if the option [go] is chosen. This will allow simultaneous re-entry into field, tenor and mode permitting the selection of options that

are specified by a system which runs simultaneously with [stop] or [go].
Each time [go] is selected a choice must be made by the simultaneous
system indicating the kind of contextual shift that may be being called for –
either [independent] or [integrated] or [aligned]. That the to-ing and fro-ing
between the 'main text' and its 'sub-texts' is neither restricted to just one
'departure' from the original/ main 'contextual configuration' (= CC) nor is
it ransom, is indicated by the simultaneity of these two member systems.[27]
In displaying the options in the first system, the description specifies by
implication the reason underlying the departure from the original CC,
while the second system allows choice between recursion whereby either
the recursion continues or it is arrested by the choice of [stop]. Underlying
a complex text will be con/text conjunction (more than one context and text
are being brought into relation) such that as new contexts are introduced
the integrity of the original alpha-context is maintained by the working
of the sub-text, with the new contexts playing a functional role *vis à vis*
the alpha-context. The choices in the system of iteration are also designed
to account for con/text disjunction, where either a parallel or interrupting
discourse might occur (some discussion and illustrations of these statement
will be found in Hasan 1999b, and the next chapter of this volume).

7.3.5.2 *Field of discourse*

In this section, I would like to examine critically one segment of a system
network presented in Hasan 1999b (p. 279) as (2b).[28] In problematizing
certain features of this fragment, which will be referred to as 'Hasan Mk1',
I hope to put on display some of the considerations that prompted its creation and some arguments that one might raise in accepting, rejecting or
partially modifying Hasan Mk1. The aim is to offer some indication of
what might perhaps count as evidence for accepting or rejecting an option
as worthy of inclusion in a descriptive framework.

Figure 7.3b displays some of the primary options that were considered
pertinent to the type of action in the field of discourse as developed in
Hasan (1999b: 279). This original Figure 7.2b – Hasan Mk1 – provoked
some serious problems: the least significant of the errors was the reversed
markings on the options [present] and [ancillary].[29] This error has been
corrected here. But the more instructive problems were of a different kind:
although marking of this kind is not unknown in SFL lexicogrammatical
descriptions, it had fallen somewhat out of use, and in any event, the density of marking within a small number of options within the same system.
As will be noted field Mk1 puts the vectors of material action and verbal action on par as two simultaneous systems. This makes it necessary

Figure 7.3b: Some primary systems of field: Mk 1 [Hasan 1999b: 279]

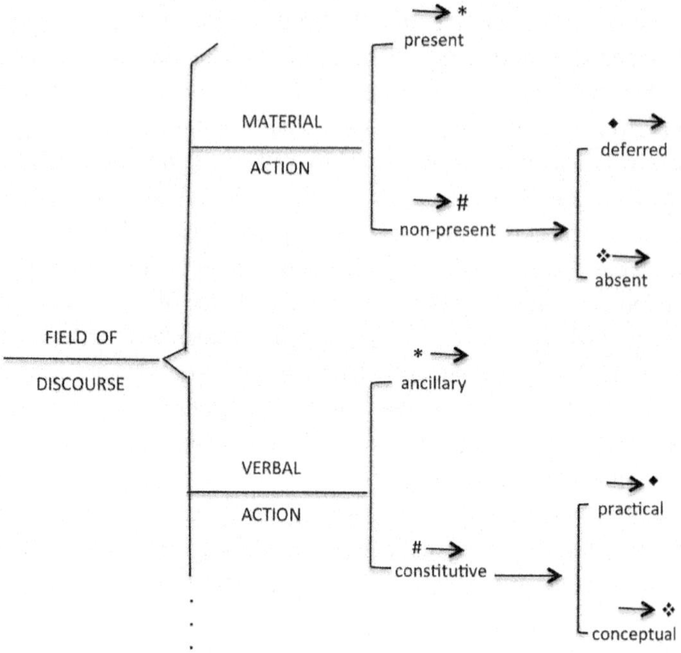

to build in a large number of constraints on the possible combinations of choices from these two ACTION types. As pointed out by Halliday, this is not a desirable situation:[30] options within the same systems being affected by each other raise doubts about the independent status of systems. It was natural to ask: what motivation is there for including both actions?

In postulating two action types, I was attempting to account for the fact that register variation is recognized by the systematic variation in meaning-wording; that meaning-wording varies often in response to material situational setting; that material action forms a part of such material situational setting. The impressive fact is that a material action which has nothing whatever to do with what is going on by way of some verbal action, till has the power to disrupt the on-going discourse. A couple are washing up and discussing some political issues; suddenly a glass slips down to the floor. What happens next has very little to do with politics; the event catapults both interactants into a very different – an independent – text. Less cataclysmic interruptions in a situation of two concurrent actions – one material one verbal – are familiar to not only all adults, and even to children who are old enough to play and talk simultaneously.

More importantly, there are some social activities that can only be performed with language assisting in its performance, such as shopping, booking for journeys or entertainment, helping small kids to put on their clothes. Here the domain of reference is constrained by the details of that social activity; this is one property of [ancillary] verbal action. These have typically entrained face to face interaction, leading into dialogue, which in turn implicates a momentum quite different from that of a monologue. A large number of these are being mechanized into varieties of robotic interaction; thus now one gets one's bottle of coke and bag of pretzels from a machine, or from supermarkets; online purchase is changing the shape of economy. But an equally large number of such activities will retain their usual character. Recognizing material action explicitly as the source of certain features of interaction allows the possibility of rationally anchoring those properties that characterize these sorts of speech events. These considerations apart, there was the attraction of bringing together all material action based activities (for discussion, Chapter 6 here), whether pertaining to the present, the future or the past, and irrespective of their SPHERE as the local or communal arena of life. This situation is reasonably well described in Hasan Mk1 (presented here as Figure 7.3b). Whether some material action is anticipated, as in recipes, instructions, etc., or has already taken place, as in lab experiment, report on accidents, etc., the recounting of which is being carried out now, in both cases the verbal action would have to be [constitutive]. Bringing them together as in Figure 7.3b Hasan Mk 1 here would provide an elegant way of bringing this large family of activities together, showing what is in common to both as the [practical] (action based activities) and the [conceptual] (reflection based activities).[31] However, the critique about the density of marking had needed to be addressed.

The above issues are not as simple as they sound; in fact, they call for a detailed discussion.[32] The suggestion by colleagues in discussions in a discussion group was to try excluding material action from field resources by bringing these in into realizational statements.[33] Figure 7.3c presented here as 'some primary systems of Hasan Mk 2' is an attempt to explore the possibility of just invoking material action through realization by excluding the vector of MATERIAL ACTION altogether. A strong justification for this would be that unlike VERBAL ACTION, MATERIAL ACTION by itself could never represent *all* of the action in 'field': what is in field is reference made by the language of the text to or traces of material phenomena. Figure 7.3c is a *tentative* revision of 'Hasan Mk1' (Hasan 1999b: 279).

In Figure 7.3c, called here 'Hasan Mk2', only the vector of VERBAL ACTION is brought into the network; two other vectors are shown. Of these, the second vector, called SPHERE OF ACTION, had been recognized in Hasan (1999b), though not explicitly brought into play in linking MATERIAL and VERBAL ACTION types; the primary options of SPHERE are shown [quotidian] v. [specialized]; the latter is the entry condition for the options [official] v. [private] avoiding the earlier ambiguous terms (see Figure 5 in Hasan 1999b: 311) [institutional] v. [individuated]. The third vector is new: nothing comparable to this can be found in Hasan (1999b); it was called PERFORMANCE OF ACTION, with options [bounded] v. [continuing]; the latter allows entry into a more delicate system [sequenced] and [conditional]. Time and space will not allow any detailed discussion, but a brief word on each of the vectors of choice in the system of field is called for.

Figure 7.3c: Some primary systems of FIELD: Hasan Mk 2

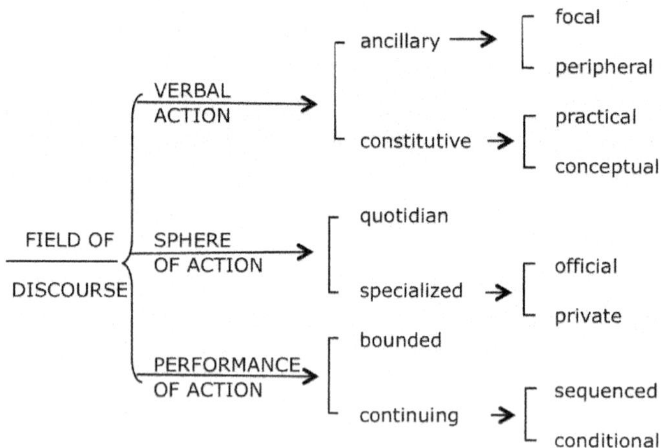

For the linguist the importance of material action is subsidiary to the verbal one: a material action without some choice from verbal action is irrelevant to the discussion of register, and the parameters of the context of situation are proposed only as a means of describing situations which realizationally relate to some register variety or another. The primary options in VERBAL ACTION remain the same as in Hasan Mk1 (= Figure 7.2b 1999b: 279); these are [ancillary] or [constitutive]: what has been elided is the vector of MATERIAL ACTION, which is now completely absent from the field network. If verbal action is ancillary, the realizational prediction would be that reference to some elements of the Material Situation Setting is mandatory; the nature of the relevant interactants, actions and objects (c.f. Firth, p. 372 above) must be inferred by the meaning-wording constitutive of the text. This could introduce some problems in analysis, but in the last resort, no analyst analyses any text as it is being produced: what is normally realized is the meaning-wording which is some sort of 'surrogate' of what was going on. If verbal action is constitutive, material action may or may not be present, depending on the evidence from relevant context, i.e., the meaning-wording. However, it is on the cards that there may be no direct reference to that action but simply indirect indication by way of interruption of some kind. Figure 7.3c shows [ancillary] and [constitutive] verbal action as mutually exclusive, and so, in general; there are, however, occasions of language use where quite regularly, [ancillary] verbal action will occur sporadically in the midst of dominant use of [constitutive] verbal action: consider for example, a classroom presentation of information in some knowledge domain where the teacher may issue such utterances as 'take a look at this map!' or 'look at page 16 in your textbook'. These sayings contribute to the ongoing activity, and the issue that one faces is what importance to attach to such sporadic 'textual shifts': at what point does it become necessary to say that the context has changed; another action that is material, whether we acknowledge this or not, is on the floor. This issue has been discussed sporadically in SFL.

The primary options in the SPHERE of action are called [quotidian] or [specialized]. This systemic contrast makes a distinction between such actions as cooking, bed-making, bathing the child, cleaning the house, shopping for food and so on, which are all daily actions, into the performance of which we are invisibly inducted through the processes of daily life; these contrast with specialized actions such as mending a punctured tyre of a bicycle, servicing an automobile, instructing others on how to explain something, whether concerning conceptual or practical matters, and so on: clearly this represents a continuum; all of these require some specific environmental training whether given in an [official] context or a [private] more local one; girls all over the Indo-Pakistani continent learned sewing, cooking, child minding in a [private], i.e., locally demonstrated way; 'home science' on the other hand was a different matter, you learned it at school and explicitly how you cook rice, and so on. The specialized activities tend to vary in the degree of institutionalization: the more specialized an activity is the more multiply coded it is in a culture (Hasan 1981 and elsewhere); and so at the increased degree of specialization it would be expected to maintain a certain routine of design – what is the sequencing of actions, what constraints if any are there on the doer's age, sex, status and so on. The variation in the degree of specialization is reflected in the option OFFICIAL v. PRIVATE. The former are more ritualized e.g. court proceedings; medical procedures, police interrogations; by contrast, actions in the private sphere will have a relatively relaxed routine within a framework of fixed expectations: consider for example the daily national news, the TV interview, the newspaper feature articles, and so on. Together with the options that depend on conceptual constitutive verbal action, they will account for a large number of actions for which we use language.

The third systemic vector is called PERFORMANCE: its primary options are shown as [bounded] v. [continuing]. A [bounded] action will by default complete in one spatio-temporally located interaction, for example shopping for fruit, bathing the child, getting the child a snack and so. By contrast, [continuing] performance of action will call for intermittent actions, each of which requires a distinct spatio-temporal location; for example, buying a car or a house is a different kind of action from that of buying vegetables; it will require different occasions for different so called 'stages' of activity, and some stages may occur more than once each on a different spatio-temporal site. The continuing action could be either SEQUENCED as in buying cars or as CONDITIONAL, e.g. a certain repeated effort and physical presence of the pupil form a condition for entry into final test; the revision action in the classroom presupposes that earlier an action of presentation of concepts/information has occurred.

The problem in constructing a system network of this kind is to keep in mind on the one hand the large variety of instances of language use, and on the other, the need to specify which contextual options will 'go with which other', what dependency and simultaneity relations there might exist among the various social activities in a community. For example, how realistic is it to say that verbal action in court proceedings could be ancillary? Short of some accidental occurrence, this is not likely to happen; if so, then clearly the freedom to choose between [ancillary] or [constitutive] is simply as shown in systems Figure 7.3c, i.e., Hasan Mk2, has to be a misleading descriptive statement. In this revised version, neither the nature of the social activity likely to typically select one option rather than the other is explicit, nor is it obvious that the intervention of the 'peripheral' material action is specifiable. So it does not seem very likely that excluding material action and relying totally on realizational statements to import the practical action types is going to be a very good solution. In other words much more thinking has to be done to successfully describe the contextual features whose possible combinations and permutations can be shown to occur in a the range of possible CCs familiar to us.[34]

One last point is worth making: at no point could one have made the kind of objection to any feature entered in Hasan's (1978) contextual configuration as shown in Table 7.1. In fact, disagreement with any-one's description of context presented nonsystemically is possible only if we have the meaning – wording, i.e., the specific text, in front of us and there is disagreement on the significative value of some linguistic pattern. Systemizing the possible relevant features of context makes the claims more explicit, puts the relevant environment 'on line' and raises the options to the conscious level as an object of reflection in the act of text descrip-tion. Thus the description can become a focus of discussion, and objection can be made as indeed they have been here with regard to the description represented in Hasan Mk1 as well as Hasan Mk2. For such discussion, a text does not have to be present; simply the calibration of the options on (socio-)logical grounds will point to problems if there are any. In the com-parative discussion of the two fragments of description, we have seen valid objections and an effort to pursue the solution favoured by the tradition of description. Neither account appears to be very satisfactory. Naturally whatever problems are recognized, their basis lies in familiarity with 'how we do things with words in our culture'; if the analyst is not familiar with the context of culture, the nature of the situation will not be familiar either. Much more elaborate field networks with several realization statements will be found in Hasan (1999b) and in (Butt 2004a). For work such as this to proceed, discussions such as for example Bowcher's (2007) are essen-tial. I would even add, that incomplete and inaccurate as the 1999b field network is, it is not any worse than the MOOD system networks drawn in the early 1960s SFL. This is only the beginning: *you aint seen nothin' yet*! We have to become much more clear and precise in our selection of terms and the consistency of their use. One main problem in Hasan Mk1 was unsuitable choice of words to describe MATERIAL ACTION options.

7.3.6   Contextual configuration and text structure

The role of relevant context and particularly of the contextual configuration (CC) is central to the analysis of text in Halliday's SFL (Halliday 1977a, 1985c, and elsewhere). Hasan (1973c, 1984c, 1985b, 1994 and the chapters of this volume) have already argued that the frequency of lexical and gram-matical categories by themselves might not be helpful in providing the recognition criteria for a register variety; attention to the patterns of mean-ing prove more useful in this enterprise. Based on further research, it has been argued (Hasan 1984c, 1985b, 1994, 2001a) that the best recognition criteria for a register family or variety are provided by the range of possible structural shapes of texts which are seen in the community as instantiating a particular register family or variety: THE STRUCTURE OF THE TEXT is indicative of the text's registerial allegiance. An ACTUAL STRUCTURE (AS) realizes a specific text, and is itself a sub-type of some DERIVED STRUCTURE (DS), which is capable of realizing a text type (or REGISTER VARIETY), and which in its turn is itself a subtype of a specific GENERALIZED STRUCTURE POTENTIAL (GSP) which is capable of realizing any instance of a register family. An ACTUAL STRUCTURE (AS) may be quickly described as what the formalists called schematic structure (Schank and Abelson 1977), a term that has been imported into SFL by Martin's genre based theory of language (Martin 1985a); but any one register type enjoys a range of AGS, such that they have certain distinctive patterns in common. It is this distinctive pattern that is contained within a GENERAL STRUCTURE POTENTIAL (GSP). Discussion of how the selection of contextual features will realize the ACTUAL STRUCTURE will be found in Hasan (1978, 1979b, 1985b and elsewhere; see also the following chapter of this volume). I have suggested (Hasan 1978, 1984c, 1985b, etc.) that two different kinds of elements need to be recognized for the formation of a specific GSP: (a) the OBLIGATORY elements that are to be found in every *complete* instance of a text or text type; and (b) the OPTIONAL ones which realize contextual features that are not central to the definition of that specific GSP, and might in fact be responsive to certain contextual features that are non-critical to the GSP's definition. In addition, the elements may have a FIXED order in sequence or they may be MOBILE within limits (Hasan 1978, 1984b). The critical register-identifying part consists of obligatory elements and their specifiable fixed order in sequence, while the optional elements and mobility in order of sequence in the structure is indicative of the range of variation within one register variety or family.

No two texts belonging to the same text type (= register variety) are expected to be exactly alike – a feature that many scholars have commented on. When do the differences between two texts become such that they have to be seen as instantiating a distinct register family? The onset of systemic description of contextualization, and conscious search for the relation of those features to the semantic level, suggests that the contextual features most relevant to the GSP, i.e. those that act as the recognition criterion for some specific register, are options that have primary-to-mid degree of delicacy. As we move further to the right end of the network, the options lose this power. Instead, they become critical to THE TEXTURE OF THE TEXT, emphasizing its unique instantial nature. Putting it simply, the register of two texts will not be distinct simply because in one case the speaker is buying potatoes in a retail store and breakfast cereal from another such store in the other case: but with potatoes weight and quality count and must be specified whereas with breakfast cereal, the default situation is to look for brand names and package size. It is elements of meaning such as these latter ones that will enter into texture, creating some kind of cohesive harmony pattern, which will be unique to each text though generalizations can be made about the text on the basis of the cohesive harmony patterns. In other words the semantic potential of a register family or variety is certainly specifiable. However, attempts to decide on a common-sense basis such issue as purchase of which objects will form part of the same CC, thus predicting which CC as whole would underlie which specific register family, are likely to prove a futile exercise. It is not the object itself but the density of contextual relations that foregrounds the object that will determine the matter. There is from a common sense point of view much in common between buying a blouse and a length of some fabric, but an examination of the GSP of the two will most probably put them in different categories.

7.4   Concluding remarks

This chapter perhaps raises more questions in the readers' mind than it provides answers: for one thing it is unconvincing to talk of the structure of text types on the basis of a preliminary analysis of CC features which have been only partially investigated, as it would be to postulate the structural patterns of the clause on the basis of a partial exploration of the metafunctionally regulated system network of mood, transitivity, theme, information focus or cohesive devoices. There is no CC simply consisting of the features of field: choices from all three parameters must be seen together in any statement about the text.[35] Another important issue concerns the way two or more contexts might integrate, producing context conjunction, or they might form two or more distinct contexts within one spatio-temporally defined interaction, presenting an instance of the disjunction of relevant contexts as in parallel texts (Hasan 1999b): is such conjunction and disjunction of context 'un-describable' from the system perspective? Does a dynamic perspective demand a case by case statement, without the possibility of generalizations? The arguments about the relationship of language and context and of system and instance suggest to me that this possibility cannot be entertained in SFL theory: such occurrences are not 'discursive freaks'. In fact for a long time linguistic literature has been providing descriptions (e.g., Goffman 1974; Cross 1979; Cloran 1987, 1994, 1999a; Hasan 1981, 1994, 1999b) which suggest not only is a 'systemic account' possible but its viability is quite unquestionable. Some of the most interesting areas of study are how and when an ongoing text and its context can be subverted? Cloran (1982) in her research involving a range of different contexts demonstrated that it is, in fact, pretty difficult to achieve contextual shift within an established con/text with a reasonable degree of institutionalization. In view of this, the reputed changes of conversational discourse stand in need of very close attention from the point of view of their relevant context. Is there a register change here or is there simply a con/textual supplementation?

The system based account presented here is necessarily incomplete, best seen as a preliminary to a better argued perhaps more complete systemic account. It seems true that the systemic (truly paradigmatic) description of context has not received much attention so far, but that it is a serious and seriously desirable possibility in con/text description should not be denied too easily.

Notes

1   This is also true of what Fawcett (2000) calls 'dialects of SFL', which explains the indefinite article in the title.

2   The other two prominent models of context in SFL are those of Martin's (1985a, 1992) and Fawcett's (1984, 2000); both are appreciably different from Halliday's theory of context. It goes without saying that the interpretation of the theory here is mine. Readers might compare other authors' interpretations of both, e.g., in Matthiessen 1995, 2007; Martin 1992, 1999; and Fawcett 2000.

3   As is well known, Halliday 1961 is the foundation of the Scale and Category model.

4   Before Malinowski's appropriation of the term to refer to the cultural-situational phenomena in semiotic environments, 'context' had referred to 'environment' in general or to the linguistic environment in a text, i.e., to today's 'co-text'.

5   The situation is changing with interest in multimodality; see for example Bowcher (2007).

6   Even within the limits of SFL, this literature is too extensive to be referenced here in the traditional form in a publication of this scope. Beginning with the many observations by Firth (1957), followed by Mitchell (1957), and a large scale study by Huddleston, Hudson, Winter and Henrici (1968), Halliday (1973a), Hasan (1973c), Halliday and Hasan (1976) text analysis really took off after Halliday (1977a) and Hasan (1978). By now a large number of scholars have made valuable contributions. Any bibliography of SFL publications will indicate very clearly the outstanding names in the field.

7   Saussure had offered only two reasons for the elevation of langue as the only legitimate concern of 'linguistics proper': (a) langue was needed for parole to achieve the desired effects; and (b) that the study of parole is not feasible due to its irregular nature. He undermined the strength of the first claim by granting that ultimately langue has its origins in parole; the second claim loses its force once context is integrated into linguistic theory allowing language use to be seen in the context of social practice. By contrast, the autonomy of Chomsky's competence from everything social (at least in its initial appearances) makes the exclusion of performance from linguistics a qualitatively different kind of phenomenon: it is impossible to support or refute the hypotheses about competence, since the scope of the concept has never been clear enough to be debated in any detail.

8   The reader is invited to compare the figure representing 'the complete framework of levels for linguistic description' in Halliday *et al.* (1964: 18) with later figures which show context, semantics, lexicogrammar and phonology as linguistic strata in the 1980s, with phonetics added more recently (e.g., see Matthiessen 2009: 13) .

9   The first version of this figure appeared in Halliday (1991a); the version published in 1999 is reproduced here, since here the legend is more explicit.

10   I am not implying that such comprehensive description of any system is currently available in any approach, simply that the cultural and semiotic systems must be inclusive rather than exclusive, allowing for variation and change, characteristics that pertain to both language and culture systems.

11   Despite linking the strata to Hjelmslev, it is important to point out that the stratal relations as conceptualized in SFL are qualitatively different from those postulated by Hjelmslev (Hasan 2010; 2016).

12   I have often commented (e.g., in a presentation to IESFLW, Gorizia 2006, and elsewhere) that realization is one of the hardest working concepts in SFL; it has been used for inter-stratal relations; also for the relation between system and structure; and of course as an inter-stratal relation it is both a dialectic as at the higher level three strata, but works as 'true' content expression where phonetics and phonology act as expression, as signalling the categories of form by convention.

13   For the concept of meta-redundancy, see (Lemke 1985; Halliday 1992a). To my mind meta-redundancy does not absolve one from spelling out the relations of the various strata to each other; it simply helps model the seamless functioning of a 'multiply coded' system that language is.

14   Although Marie Smith Jones, the last speaker of Eyak, died barely a month ago (Guardian Weekly, 8/2/08 pp 28–29), her language actually died with the death of her sister in the early 1990s, because that is when the avenues were closed for the language system to develop and to change.

15   The idea of 'less developed languages' has been anathema to linguistics, but this reaction is not based on careful thinking. To say that a language, such as English, was less developed in ancient times than it is today is not to imply

that it lacked the potential to develop. In fact, so long as we do not think that the system of language is hardwired in the brain, we allow it the possibility of growth and decline.

16   These stories have been discussed in Hasan (1984a and 1984b), as well as in Hasan (1973a, b) mimeo.

17   The developments in the study of context described here have been brought about with help from a large number of colleagues; so far as the development of my own thinking is concerned the most important amongst these was the work of Halliday, and my immediate research helpers. Later students such as Butt, Cloran, Cross, Bowcher, Armstrong, and a wider community of colleagues such as Kress, Martin and those led by Michael Gregory in Toronto provided intellectual stimulus. My work has from the beginning foregrounded the role of linguistic meaning, i.e., semantics, in identifying register varieties and in the realization of contextual features as is evident from my attempts (Hasan 1973c, 1981, 1984b, 1985b, 1995 and so on).

18   The term 'genre' was borrowed into SFL from Bakhtin by Martin (1985a and thereafter). The term 'register' had been deliberately preferred and 'genre' avoided because like the term 'style' it carried connotations from its use in literary studies that did not fit the concept of register as systemic variation (note also Bakhtin's modification of the term by 'speech': a scholar of literary texts, he used 'speech genre' for a good reason. Genres in literary studies were innocent of Firthian-Hallidayan conceptualization of context; they were recognized purely by the global arrangement of their form. There was no reasoning for linking a literary genre and a text instantiating it, except literary conventions that defined genres such as sonnet, story, novel and so on.

19   We do not have adequate language of description for the relations I am describing here. Reference, i.e., Saussure's 'signification', to experiential phenomena is particulate; it will concern elements of material situational setting but the latter is capable of impinging in a non-referential way (as for example in Text C in Chapter 6 here). Try helping your child solve a mathematical problem while engaged in cooking a complex dish – there will be hesitations, pauses, repetitions because the material situation is 'dividing' speaker attention. The language of the text might then bear traces of MSS, without there being any reference to any specific element of the material situational setting (=MSS). On the other hand interactant relations, by definition, might be excluded from forming part of the MSS. (See, however, the last chapter of this volume where I argue that the discursive roles of the interactant demand they should be considered to have a material presence.)

20   These were listed in Hasan (1981), and were validated in an empirical research (Cloran 1982).

21   Martin had begun referring to these as 'genre combination'; there are some obvious problems in this nomenclature (Hasan 1999b); I have preferred 'con/text integration/disjunction'.

22   Many examples may be found, for example, in Volume 2 of Halliday's Collected Works; also in the writings of other linguists avowedly holding a dynamic perspective e.g., scattered over the pages of Martin (1992).

23   Attempts to produce consistent 'dynamic' i.e. instance based or prospective descriptive frameworks have typically fizzled out. The concept of prospective grammar was introduced by John Sinclair; for an example see (Ravelli 1995).

24   Certainly there are problems especially in oral language use e.g. the *ums* and *ers*, the incomplete clause, the mid-clause changes in structure, the unmotivated repetitions, and sometimes an innovative pattern; but these have not been found to militate against either comprehension or analysis.

25   Strictly speaking, Bowcher offers valuable critique of Hasan (1999b) and attempts to extend that field network to cover multimodal phenomena; I am informed that Butt (mimeo) is being 'trialled' by researchers at Macquarie.

26   It has been circulated in selected circles, and more recently has received public discussion in the Symposia on Context and Register convened by Lukin at Macquarie University in February 2011 and 2012.

27   The technical terms used here e.g. 'contextual shift', 'main text', 'sub-text' and others have been defined to a certain extent in Hasan (1999b).

28   Hasan (1999b) is the article that appears as Chapter 6 here. As explained there the number system for figures had to be revised for Chapter 6. In order to avoid confusion I will use Hasan Mk1 for the old number (2b which is reproduced as 3b here), though the page numbers refer to Hasan (1999b). In this article Hasan Mk1 is Figure 7.3b and Hasan Mk2, Figure 7.3c.

29   In the original printing of Hasan (1999b), there was a typographic error: Table 9a (p. 280) claimed quite correctly that 'if verbal action is [ancillary], then material action must be [present]', but the marking in the figure (2b on p. 279), which Table 7 was 'interpreting' had erroneously been reversed so that the marking claimed that 'if material action is [present] then verbal action must be [ancillary]'.

30   I thank Michael Halliday who pointed out in a personal discussion that on the level of grammar or semantics this degree of constraint for choices across two simultaneous vectors would be considered 'ill-formed'.

31   I would not claim that these aspirations were actually achieved in Hasan Mk1 or even in Figure 5 of Hasan (1999b: 311). But this does not mean the resources were not being opened up. After all the system network of MOOD consisted of just two individual systems in 1962–1963. The significance of these comments is obvious in view of Halliday and Matthiessen's latest MOOD system network (see 2014: 162).

32   I must point out that due to the lack of space, the discussion on these issues had to be elided from the published version of this article in Halliday and Webster (2009). These brief remarks introduced here (in Section 7.3.5.2) are indicative of what had been written on the issues; I seem to have no copy of the original from which I abstracted the published version to conform to the chapter size required.

33   At that time David Butt, Wendy Bowcher, Carmel Cloran, Marilyn Cross, Rebekah Wegener, and I met regularly to discuss the implications of the existing descriptions of the context of situation. My thanks are due to the group as a whole, particularly to Wendy Bowcher, who gave me their valuable reactions.

34   Meanwhile I have produced a modified version of FIELD with both material and verbal action types, but, although it is displayed in Chapter 9, unfortunately, for lack of space and time, it is not discussed; only the option by option realizations are stated in a rudimentary manner.

35   For an effort of this kind see the last chapter of this volume.

8 Towards a paradigmatic description of context: systems, metafunctions, and semantics[1] [2014]

8.1 Introduction

The main aim of this paper is to contribute to the description of contextual parameters of field, tenor and mode by focusing on what each specific part each parameter plays in the production of text, which is in fact nothing more than the meaning-wording produced by the interactants in speaking with reference to some social practice. Given that these parameters were first introduced nearly half a century ago (Halliday *et al.* 1964), and that they have been in use over this long period, one might wonder why the issue has arisen now. The significant factor is the move in the last couple of decades to produce paradigmatic accounts of field, tenor and mode; and these accounts are now becoming more widely available (Hasan 1999b, 2009a, 2013, 2014b, 2016; Bowcher 2007, 2014; Butt 2004a mimeo). There are suggestions for the 'unification' of options from distinct system networks, and some evidence of disagreements as to the task that may be assigned to each of the three parameters. I hope to make a contribution to these debates: (a) by presenting a brief history of the description of context from the inception of the idea to date; (b) by exploring the bases of accuracy and consistency in paradigmatic linguistic descriptions represented with precision by using the conventions of the system networks; and (c) by pointing to the significance of the description of context in keeping with the architecture of the SYSTEMIC FUNCTIONAL LINGUISTICS (SFL): I see this model as a post-Saussurean theory whose aim is to provide a scientific account of both the system (*langue*) and the use of language (*parole*).[2]

With this aim in mind, Section 8.2 is designed to provide relevant background information about the contextual parameters. The focus here will be on certain problems in the identification of the contextual parameters which acted as the impetus for the application of the paradigmatic description to this study: I will argue that the roots of the problem go far back into the history of the contextual descriptions. The account will begin by relating the concept of context to that of register; it was the classification of register that had acted as the main impetus for the introduction of the three parameters of field, tenor and mode. Some problems in conceptualizing their role will be brought to attention together with steps to specifically address those issues. In Section 8.3, the formal conventions and the semantics of the language of paradigmatic description will be highlighted. Some important questions here are: how the domain of description is identified and how its integrity is maintained throughout the representation of the description presented as system networks; how the relevance and the validity of systemic options may be established and validated. Representing description in the form of system networks enforces order: the method is designed to create explicit and non-ambiguous relations across the options (8.3.1a–8.3.1.5). Their validation is tested by their realizational relations to language: this guards against contradictions within the description (8.3.2–8.3.2.3). Section 8.3 is in a way the heart of my argument: it presents my understanding of what doing paradigmatic description means in practice. Implicit in those statements are the reservations against some of the actual systemic contextual representations as well as the proposals for future directions. Section 8.4 closes the discussion by explicitly indicating the role of the scientific description of context in the ecology of SFL theory. Treating that theory as a post-Saussurean version of Saussure's 'linguistics of langue', I present arguments for the inclusion of parole into the modelling of language. I will argue that variation cannot be ignored because even within a synchronic '*état de langue*', it will affect the 'system', i.e., langue. It seems highly likely that without the support of a competent scientific theory of parole neither the fallout from linguistic variation can be adequately handled, nor can Saussure's 'associative bonds' receive the validation they require to fulfil the role that Saussure assigned it as the most important methodological instrument in his 'morphology of meaning'. As Section 8.3 will demonstrate the method for studying Saussure's 'associative bonds' are best developed in SFL in the shape of paradigmatic linguistic description. Apart from this, there is a significant hypothesis in the *systemic functional* model systemic functional linguistics, SFL.[3] The theory claims that there is a systematic prehension between the linguistic metafunctions and the internal organization of natural language, the basis of which lies in how language works in the life of social beings in performing the many social practices. I will close with a brief reference to an important topic in today's world – namely meaning.

8.2   Register variation and context of culture and situation

The first linguist to appreciate the rich implications of Malinowski's 'context of situation' (1923, 1935) was Firth, though he was also quick to note its 'instance based' view of 'situation' as simply 'events considered *in rebus*' (1957: 182). Halliday appreciated not only Firth's insights into the relations of context and language, but he also recognized the value of Firth's efforts to transform context from 'a bit of the social process' to a viable 'schematic construct' suitable for applying to the analysis of 'language events'. These understandings were injected into SFL by Halliday, who positioned 'text' as language event, relating the systematic textual variations to the inherent tendency of language to display systematic variation.

One cannot help but notice with interest that today it is Malinowski's concept of context, perhaps strengthened as needed with ideas from Halliday's SFL that supports the drive towards the multimodal 'text' analyses highly popular today. Halliday's method for bringing order to the chaos of situation was to focus on the 'speech event' without either ignoring or privileging the extra-linguistic information. SFL is widely viewed today as friendly to text analysis, especially where the concern is with linguistic meaning-wording. In contrast to these two frames, Firth's account falls in the middle: it rejects Malinowski's 'instance-based' 'holistic' view of the context of situation, and it fails to foreground specific methods for the linguistic analysis of '*speech* events' that would pin-point forms of its systematic variability. Not many practitioners of SFL use Firth's inspiringly rich but sprawling and sometimes contradictory framework for the contextual analysis of meaning either as instance or as system.[4] Often, even linguists, announcing a Firthian orientation, will 'elaborate' Firth's ideas *typically* in terms of Halliday's methods for register analysis.

The commitment of SFL to language as the *central* object of enquiry is evident in claiming that the goal of linguistics is to provide 'a theory of how language works' (Halliday 1961: 241). This aim is later reiterated by Halliday, McIntosh and Strevens (1964: 5): '*To study language scientifically means to construct a ... theory of how language works, and to derive from it certain exact methods for describing language.*' (emphasis introduced). It cannot be doubted that language works in time and space; nonetheless, the essence of 'situation' as in *'context of situation'* does not lie in the situation's spatio-temporal dimensions *per se*: what imbues it with relevance is the function of talk in the performance of social practices. Entry in the world of extra-linguistic phenomena has value for the linguist in as much as it helps explain the 'how' and 'why' of language: after all, that is where the data of experience will be found. The issue is not a choice between 'inside' and 'outside'; rather, it is the question of maintaining a balance in their relations while keeping the goal of the theory in view. The analysis of 'discourse' acts as the measure of the analyst's success in maintaining this balance.

8.2.1   Register as a linguistic variety and text as instance

Responding to this focus on language, the category of 'register' emerged from a concern with the *inherently variable nature of language*. Halliday *et al.* (1964) suggested that this inherent variation in language is best viewed in relation to language use and language user:

> [there are] varieties according to users (that is, varieties in the sense that each speaker uses one variety and uses it all the time) and varieties according to use (that is, in the sense that each speaker has a range of varieties and chooses between them at different times). The variety according to user is a 'dialect'; the variety according to use is a 'register'. (Halliday *et al.* 1964: 77)

The concept of register as a 'variety according to use' was developed further (e.g., 1964: 87–89):

> Language varies as its function varies; it differs in different situations. The name given to a variety of a language distinguished according to use is 'register'… It is only by reference to the various situations, and situation types, in which language is used that we can understand its functioning and its differences. Language is not realized in the abstract: it is realized as the activity of people in situations, as linguistic events which are manifested in a particular dialect or register.

As their text shows, despite the 'or' above, the authors thought of the two varieties as cutting across each other: a speaker positioned in a specific context of situation would in all likelihood speak with relevance to it; in other words, he would speak 'in' register. At the same time, speaking has also to be done 'in' dialect, whether standard or not is immaterial from the perspective of linguistic variation. Besides this, each act of speaking displays also some indication of the syndrome of linguistic features unique to an individual speaker's ways of speaking: every feature in the syndrome is part of the system; what belongs uniquely to the speaker is its formation as a particular syndrome. Linguists recognize this category as 'idiolect', though sometimes today its description is presented as the study of a speaker's *identity*. By definition, idiolects cannot be recognized in any segment of the community as a linguistic variety (Hasan 1973c).

Each of these categories represents a distinct aspect of the naturally occurring text: each text indicates some register, some dialect, and idiolectal syndrome.[5] In the early 1960s, the term 'text' had been much the same in Halliday's writing as in the other models of general linguistics. To quote, 'The data to be accounted for are observed language events, observed as spoken or as codified in writing, *any corpus of which, when used as material for linguistic description, is a "text"*.' (Halliday 1961: 243; emphasis added). The concept of 'text' has matured into a qualitatively different concept without changing the name: today in SFL, we see 'text' as naturally occurring language use, therefore having a social function, and possessing the attributes of texture and structure (Halliday and Hasan 1976, 1985; Hasan 1978); as an instance of register, the text may be simple or complex (Hasan 1999b); and, most importantly, instantiating the linguistic system, it is where every form of linguistic regularity as also every move in innovation will manifest itself (Halliday 1991a).[6] The text, thus, represents a measure of what language is able to do: it is a reliable source of insight into the power of the language system (Matthiessen 2009b).

8.2.2   Contextual parameters and the classification of register

The genesis of contextual parameters too lies in register variation. They were assigned the task of furnishing the basis for the linguistic evidence by reference to which registers may be validly classified:

> There is enough evidence for us to be able to recognize the major situation types to which formally distinct registers correspond; others can be predicted and defined from outside language. A number of different lines of demarcation have been suggested for this purpose.

It seems most useful to introduce a classification along three dimensions, each representing an aspect of the situation in which language operates and the part played by language in them. Registers, in this view, may be distinguished according to FIELD OF DISCOURSE, MODE OF DISCOURSE and STYLE OF DISCOURSE. (Halliday et al.1964: 90; original emphasis)

From the speaker's perspective, register is perhaps as remote a concept as language system: in everyday life we encounter neither system nor register but just text – the meaning – wording produced by interactants in performing some task. Concepts such as language system, register, register variety (I believe 'register variety' refer to what is called 'text type' by Halliday 1999: 9) are abstractions. Text is where the long journey towards system begins; and the concept of text is pivotal to validating the categories of register, because this is language in use which realizes systemic patterns.

Following the above extract are the *introductory* remarks on each parameter; below, beginning with 'field of discourse', a selection from each characterizing description is presented (Halliday *et al.*, 1964: 90):

'Field of discourse' refers to what is going on: to the area of the operation of the language activity. Under this heading, registers are classified according to the nature of the whole event of which language activity forms a part. In the type of the situation in which the language activity accounts for practically the whole of the relevant activity, such as an essay, a discussion, or an academic seminar, the field of discourse is the subject matter. On this dimension of classification we can recognize registers such as politics and personal relations, and technical registers like biology and mathematics.

'Mode of discourse' is the next parameter to be discussed (Halliday *et al.*, 1964: 91):

this [i.e., 'mode of discourse', *RH*] refers to the medium or mode of the language activity, and it is this that determines, or rather correlates with, the role played by the language activity in the situation. The primary distinction on this dimension is that into spoken and written language, the two having, by and large, different situational roles.

Last mentioned was the parameter called then the 'style of discourse' (Halliday *et al.* 1964: 92–93):

Third and last of the dimensions of register classification is 'style of discourse', which refers to the relations among the participants. To the extent that these affect and determine features of language, they suggest a primary distinction into colloquial and polite ('formal', which is sometimes used for the latter, is here avoided because of its technical sense in description). This dimension is unlikely ever to yield clearly defined, discrete registers.

The meanings of the word 'style' varied a good deal, especially in the field of literary criticism. It was Gregory (1967) who offered 'tenor of discourse' as a replacement for this 'undesirable' term, and the label has prevailed. Halliday *et al.*'s three parameters resemble Firth's 'categories' which he suggested could be used in 'linguistic work'; the differences between the two frames are as significant as their similarities. Let me close this discussion with what has turned out to be a highly significant remark by the authors (1964: 93):

> It is as the product of these three dimensions of classification that we can best define and identify register. ... The formal properties of any given language event will be those associated with the intersection of the appropriate field, mode and style.

8.2.3   Parameters evolving: major developments and major problems

Like most newly introduced theoretical categories, the contextual parameters as seen in relation to their linguistic correlates have also undergone changes and developments. A viable and verifiable view of this correlation is essential in view of the status of register as 'linguistic variation according to use'. Below is presented a brief history of the developments made in its pursuit. Pushed to its limits, probably each would have resulted in moving SFL towards a viable method for establishing correlation between the text's language and its context. As it happens, each to date has ended in what might be described with a touch of wry humour as 'snatching defeat from the jaws of victory'. As I commented in introducing this paper, the current problems have become more visible with attempts to describe context paradigmatically, but their genesis lies in the earlier studies of context. In the following sections, I present my views on this earlier history.

8.2.3.1   *Developments and outcomes in text-context studies: (1) early FTM*

The first development in this pursuit was the hypothesis as presented in Section 8.2.2. As Halliday *et al.* (1964: 90) acknowledge, other lines of demarcation for context of situation had been introduced, the most important being Firth's (Butt 1989; Hasan 1995). However, the parameters of discourse presented by Halliday *et al.* (1964: 89–94) do differ significantly from the earlier discussions: here, for the first time, each parameter was conceptualized as facing in the direction of *both* the context of situation, representing '*an aspect of the situation* in which language is operating' *and* of the text, representing '*the part that language is playing* as an aspect of the social practice'. This can be seen, perhaps, as an early indication of the need to use realization bi-directionally as a means of bringing context and text in reciprocal relation (Section 8.2.3.2).

The requirement of correlation between linguistic and situational features imposed a grid on both context and text by using that theoretical concept of 'realization': without this relation register classification could not get off the ground. Once the fact of correlation is accepted, all that the analyst needed to do is to find some reliable recognition criteria *either* for the features relevant to each contextual parameter *or* for those of language; either identified *correctly* would have led to the other. In fact, things did not work out this way. Below I suggest an explanation why, half a century later, SFL has still not established viable principles for the recognition of either the situational or the linguistic features, thus leaving register classification in limbo.

Eirian Davies (2014) has commented on the paucity of viable information on registers prior to the research at University College London in the second half of the 1960s. The Hallidayan conception of register required a fairly precise understanding of both situational and linguistic facts. But in the words of Bernstein, the 'language of description' had not developed as yet to enable an adequate conceptualization of either of the two unknowns. The words that named the important concepts were new arrivals in a nascent theory. It is not that words such as 'situation', 'field' and 'mode' were too exotic; their meaning in 'ordinary language' hardly seems problematic. But as Firth had warned, ordinary words, when used to construe 'schematic constructs', tend to acquire a somewhat different value and identity. They begin to act just like words naming 'grammatical categories' such as, say, the 'simple present' which is neither 'simple' nor necessarily 'present'. But the terms referring to contextual features as help for indicating their linguistic correlate needed further attention to enable them to work successfully.

The contextual term that I as a novice found most problematic in context studies was 'activity' (Halliday *et al.* 1964): in ordinary life, the word has many meanings and each seems clear in its 'context', but what exactly did it mean in the description of field of discourse? Here it seemed to have multiple values: it was not clear if the word referred to precisely the same phenomenon in its various appearances, such as 'social activity', 'relevant activity', 'language activity'. There were also 'descriptive references' such as 'what is going on', and also to refer to 'the area of the operation of the language activity'. Sometimes 'the whole activity' was said to consist of two kinds of 'activities', a 'language activity' which 'assisted' 'the whole event', in which case it would seem that the 'whole event' was to consist of both 'language activity' and some other kind of 'activity' which was not linguistic. At other times, the 'whole of the relevant activity' could be accounted for 'practically' by 'language activity' (did that mean language was fully constitutive of such a 'relevant activity', so that nothing else was needed to recognize what was going on?). Equally problematic was the word 'subject matter', a term that has continued to be used in a sense quite close to the 'content, specific to some specialized domain'; but the whole of the field could clearly not consist of subject matter. If something is going on, then some action seems to be required somewhere; and in the nature of things, the domain of activity is defined by the classification of goings on. Where did 'subject matter' fit?

The problem of the meaning of 'activity' in field was not made any easier by the account associated with the mode of discourse: this was characterized as 'refer[ring] to the medium or mode of the language activity'; 'it (i.e., mode) … correlates with *the role played by the language activity in the situation*' (1964: 91). One possible interpretation of mode is that it was a means of relay, obviously needed in 'concerted action'; but [phonic] is not identical in meaning to 'spoken' as in 'spoken style', nor does the spoken style become [graphic] when written down. How did the role of language clarify this situation? As for 'language activity', was it part of field, or of mode? What would be the 'language activity' in field, when 'interviewing' (on par with 'lecturing') is the 'role of language'?

To my mind, the entanglement of field and mode is not new; it dates back to this early stage. By contrast, tenor, a more 'exotic' term, escaped this fate, though it too was distorted in other ways; it began to be treated like a thing apart from field and mode. And yet, features of style/tenor do clearly correlate with interactant relations, as well as the kind of linguistic activity, and/or mode. In early SFL, some evidence of discussion about the scope of the parameters among interested scholars can certainly be found, but solutions usually took the form of suggesting a greater number of parameters (for example, Fawcett 1980; Gregory and Carroll 1978; Ure and Ellis 1977; Hasan 1973c). And those suggestions appear not to have had much impact except locally; the uptake in the SFL community suggests the original three parameters are more widely used – but what the users mean by them is not entirely clear.

Could one not have used language patterns as the first step in the search for correlates? When the parameters were first introduced, the register specific linguistic patterns were stated in terms of grammatical and lexical patterns, including a selection of idiomatic expressions 'strongly marked as register specific', e.g., 'how are we today?' as indicating 'a doctor-patient style'; and 'denture' as part of the language of advertisement. Hasan drew attention to the serious drawbacks in this itemizing approach (Hasan 1973c) especially restricted to 'wording' alone.[7] But by this time, Halliday had moved to a more abstract means of classifying linguistic form. This was based on the outcome of the paradigmatically oriented description of lexicogrammar. Specifically, when the system networks pertaining to the various linguistic patterns were examined, this revealed a grouping of options typically organized fairly systematically with reference to generally recognizable segments of the semantic space. This led to the 'metafunctional' perspective on language, one of the hallmarks of SFL (Halliday 1967b, 1967c, 1968, 1969, 1970a, 1970b, 1973b, 1979b). The concept of metafunction as related to the form of language had a substantial impact on the SFL view of language, with significant consequences for the three strata directly related to context, meaning and lexicogrammar. That story merges with the second development in language-context relations.

8.2.3.2 Developments and outcomes in text-context studies: (2) CMR hypothesis

More specifically, the metafunctional perspective implied that the form of language has evolved along functional lines; different systems of content are markedly oriented to different linguistic metafunctions. With this metafunctional orientation, system networks became instruments for revealing the resources that linguistic form has for making meaning: it was about this time that SFL began to view language as a MEANING POTENTIAL. This led to the second major development in the exposition of the relations of text and context.

SFL recognizes four metafunctions: (1) The EXPERIENTIAL concerns the resources for the exchange of experience: the grammar of languages encodes human experience of the external and internal world as processes of various kinds which implicate entities as participants, and specify circumstances (including time) that elaborate aspects of process-participant configurations. (2) The LOGICAL metafunction concerns the relations between the various individual process-participant configurations; it also elaborates on the properties of processes, circumstances and entities, by relating them in different ways to a range of properties (Halliday and Matthiessen 2014). According to Halliday (1973a), these two metafunctions are closely related and together they have been referred to as IDEATIONAL.[8] (3) The 'INTERPERSONAL' metafunction enacts social relations, including the speaker's assessments of possibilities, the evaluation of phenomena, attitude to self and others as well as commitment to interactive process. Finally (4) the TEXTUAL metafunction contributes to 'the creation of text' (Halliday 1973a: 99): the meaning wording patterns oriented to the textual metafunction encode 'the structure of information, and the relation of each part of the discourse to the whole and to the setting' (Halliday *ibid*.). Unlike other functional theories, SFL views them as non-hierarchic: in any use of language they act simultaneously and no metafunction is more powerful, more authentic than the others; there is no hierarchic order: 'with only minor exceptions, whatever the speaker is doing with language he will draw on all three components of grammar'. Halliday adds (1973a: 100):

> He [i.e., the speaker] will need to make some reference to the categories of his own experience – in other words, the language will be *about* something. He will need to take up some position in the speech situation; at the very least he will specify his own communication role and (will) set up expectations for that of the hearer – in terms of statements, questions, response and the like. And what he says will be structured as 'text' – that is to say, it will be operational in the given context.

Halliday has often suggested that metafunctions resonate systematically with the meaning-wording that realizes the three contextual parameters thus creating texts: Thus typically (a) the linguistic patterns oriented to the experiential metafunction would *typically* correlate with the features in the system of field; (b) those deriving from the interpersonal metafunction would *typically* correlate with the features in the tenor of discourse; and (c) the textural and organizational resources of the textual metafunction would *typically* correlate with the mode of discourse. In short, the 'default' linguistic realization of the features pertaining to the three parameters are predicted by reference to the metafunctional orientation of the lexicogrammar and semantics: the formulation leaves open the possibility of departures from the highly probable.[9] This probabilistic formulation of the context-metafunction resonance (CMR) was greeted with a lively controversy (some detail, see Hasan 1995). Those expressing objections never took any notice of the fact that in the study of sociolinguistic variation, predictions about linguistic features correlating with situational ones such as age, gender, geographical or social provenance, have typically been are stated in probabilistic terms, and continue to still do the same.

When in 1964 Halliday *et al.* had introduced the parameters, presenting a perspective on both the nature of the context of situation and of the linguistic features correlating with the three parameters, this, despite its shortcomings, had been a considerable improvement on the previous rather gross statements about the relations of situation and language. The context-metafunction resonance (CMR) hypothesis was a huge step forward. First, it had the potential of providing more specific guidance for recognizing the kind of formal linguistic features capable of acting as the *typical* correlates of the features pertaining to each situational parameters; instead of citing items, it was possible to identify them as patterns of transitivity, mood, aspects of modality, modulation, or the categories of cohesion. Second, the postulate of the contextual parameters raises a pertinent question about the proposed number of not only the parameters themselves but also the linguistic metafunctions: why this number and not any other? The CMR hypothesis offered the possibility of treating the nature of human interaction as the origin of metafunctions, thus resolving both issues at once. According to Halliday (1973a) the proposal had been based on a pilot research; that, for him, was reason enough for a cautious probabilistic formulation of the hypothesis. This naturally called for searching ways of checking on its validity. Surprisingly, instead of debating the original probabilistic hypothesis, the view among the SFL scholars was that the hypothesis had failed to provide a 'context metafunction hook up device' that could hang the three specific metafunctions in absolute terms one on each of the three contextual pegs. The more relevant need had been to search for ways of testing the validity of the probabilistic CMR hypothesis, i.e., the one that the author had actually formulated.[10] In the event, no aspect of the hypothesis received careful scrutiny: the outcome was to follows the same rather intuitive style of context description which had been in vogue since Halliday *et al.* (1964). The problem of register classification has naturally remained unresolved: lacking serious enquiries it has been allowed to lose visibility.

8.2.3.3 Developments and outcomes in text-context studies: (3) GSP hypothesis

The third move was a conscious attempt to provide a viable criterion for register classification. The approach required treating each parameter as a resource that offered choices from a large set of contextual options: the total set of options chosen from the three parameters would count together as the contextual configuration (CC) of the text. It was said to underlie the occasion of talk (aka context of situation) as a particular situation type (for some discussion, see Halliday and Hasan 1985).

Hasan (1978) was an attempt to demonstrate that a specifiable class of choices in a CC motivates the over-all structural shape of the text type. Predictive claims of this kind are based on an examination of the data of language use, whose systematic analysis must focus on the shared dis/similarities across the many events. The distinction between a *text* and a text *type* becomes critical. Every naturally occurring text is an individual; it will display some features specific to it, even if only those correlating with its material situational setting (Hasan 1985b). The study of instantial uniqueness has, no doubt, a value. But so far as the study of register variation is concerned, this is less significant than those properties shared by a number of instances: the latter alone can lead to viable statements of correlation between texts and contexts. This was the perspective adopted in the study of correlation between textual structure and the features of the CC.

The 'over-all structural shape' presented in Hasan (1978) is better treated as a generalized formula. It consists of a configuration of functional elements whose mutual relations are calibrated in such a way as to allow its use to describe the structure of not only a specific text type but also a range of other *related* text types. Each member of that *range of text types* will have some structural properties in common with other members: no individual text type will have the same structural shape as any other, and none will be entirely different. The entire range of such text types will constitute a single register family. Clearly the variations across text types are not accidental. They are based on the text-context relations: underlying these similarities and differences across the structural shapes of the members of a register family there will be specifiable similarities and differences in the selection of features from the dimension of field and/or tenor and/or mode of discourse. The actual structural shape of a text is not the achievement of that particular text: despite its uniqueness, it is recognized by its regularities which arise from the text's response to the context of situation that it is realizing in a specific case. The study of register is a study of the regularities between the features of CC and its realization as text.

  This generalized structural formula eventually got labelled as the 'Generalized Structure Potential' (GSP).[11] And from the above perspective, the GSP is clearly relevant to register classification. I would go so far as to claim that it is, in some ways, analogous to the system network (discussion, Section 8.3). For example, a system network treats its point of origin as its ultimate 'descriptum', i.e., its object of enquiry. And in the course of this enquiry, it creates a number of 'selection expressions', each of which represents the properties of one specific sub-category of the descriptum; these sub-categories are closely related to each other in specifiable ways. The GSP resembles the system network in these respects: it describes the structure of a specific register family. In the course of doing this, it produces a range of 'derived structures' each of which pertains to one and only one register variety (aka text type). It is these various text types that constitute one specific register family identified by the GSP. This allows the derivation of structural shapes pertaining to each register variety; and the register varieties are systematically related to each other. The system network displays many visibly laid out paths each of which can be represented as a 'selection expression', each specifying one specific sub-category of the ultimate descriptum. The GSP does not produce visibly laid out choice paths, but it explicitly signals those features whose selection would be the realization of some systematic variation across the derived structures: the structures do not vary accidentally; they vary with predictable perturbations in the configuration of the underlying context. In all the GSP visibly indicates three classes of phenomena:

- the status of its functional elements is visibly indicated: an element is either obligatory, i.e., defining the nature of that register family, or it is optional, i.e., elements that are subject to certain specifiable variation in the underlying CC;
- the order in sequence of the functional elements that can relate to each other is visibly indicated, some being fixed *vis à vis* others, and some free within specifiable limits;
- the possibility of recursion/reiteration for some element is visibly indicated.

Just as no systemic choice path will ever describe an ill-formed category of language, so also no GSP will accommodate twists and turns that are 'accidental'. This is for a good reason: in general, systems are known by their regularities; they are not known by their instantial variations. The accidental textual moves are not very likely to realize any part of the CC that would be recognized as relevant to any social practice underlying a register.[12]

This third development was directly focused on the issue of register classification, the quest for which had led to the postulate of the three contextual parameters. It invited research on closely related fronts, namely: (a) the derived structure pertaining to register varieties; (b) the CC features underlying its functional elements; (c) the environmental conditions for the operation of the obligatory and optional elements; and (d) their modes of realization by semantic categories which are themselves realized lexicogrammatically. The payback from the uniqueness of each GSP and its battery of derived structures appears significant for attempting register classification both at lower and higher degrees of delicacy: being unique, a particular derived structure could be tested as a *'recognition criterion' for a specific register variety*, and by abstraction, also *for a specific register family*. Underlying the obligatory elements of each derived structure of a GSP is a set (syndrome) of the CC features, and realizational pairing with meaning-wording is a critical means of testing the 1973 CMR hypothesis. So it had seemed that attention to issues raised by the GSP based analysis of register could have been valuable in view of CMR hypothesis. However, the preoccupation with the 'scientific', and the attraction of the 'dynamic' (i.e., accidental) formed the focus of attention. Register classification remained an obscure problem. The SFL research on both context and register has suffered in consequence.

8.2.3.4 *Developments and outcomes in text-context relations:*
(4) ARC hypothesis

The fourth relevant move came some eight years later in exploring Vygotsky's concept of 'semiotic mediation' (Vygotsky 1978). The questions were: how is culture mediated to the neonate?; when does the ontogenesis of semiotic mediation begin, and how? Halliday's account of protolinguistic communication between the infant and the care-giver (Halliday 1973a, 1975a, 1998) had already highlighted the central role of context in the exchange of meaning. Soon scholarly research was to focus on communication between only weeks-old neonates and their care-givers (Brazelton *et al.* 1974; Trevarthen 1974; Lock 1978). The concept of *meaning exchange* had to be reinterpreted in this context: meaning, obviously, could not have been mediated semantically, i.e., by means of language. Even those linguistic items uttered by the adult care-giver could hardly be taken as conveying 'the' semantic value of the utterance to the infant. What did the communication communicate, and how? Halliday had suggested it was an exchange of personal affect and attention – a classic 'inception of reciprocity' in terms of Brazelton *et al.* (1974). The research led to the conclusion that the ontogenesis of 'semiotic mediation' could not *begin* with language – what is needed is an embodied affordance for 'meaning/significance recognition', perhaps independent of semiological conventions, a kind of direct move from sensation to the internalization of 'meaning', significance, relevance – we just do not have the word for that meaning-like-thing-which-is-not-quite-meaning-yet. This obviously raises the question: is this communication without context? If not, then how to outline the frame for the contexts pertaining to neonate communication – which, as Brazelton *et al.* emphasize, can and do vary significantly within and across communities, if only because the adults were 'acculturated'.

So the search was for a contextual frame that could be applied to the social practice of any kind where cultural mediation was not limited only to the linguistic means or heavily dependent on 'social conventions'? Here it is relevant that social practice covers a much wider domain of human experiences than does register, simply because the latter is language specific. Clearly the 'context of *discourse*', specific to register, could not be taken as a viable frame for social practices of all and any kind for all normal human beings. On the basis of an informal survey of various types of social practices, it appeared that the undertaking of any social practice must entrain three domains of human experience, namely, Action, Relation and Contact (ARC) (Hasan 2001a: 6): a social *practice* entails some action (activity/doing/act), significant enough to the doers' co-engagement. [13] Then being *social*, some relation is implied between the doers even if just that arising from doing something together (cf., 'agentive role', and 'social distance', Hasan 1978): in the nature of things each participant is socially positioned (Bernstein 1990); they cannot but be 'related'. And there has to be some way of establishing contact between the actors of those actions, i.e., some means of enabling *access to what is going on*; in the absence of ability to indicate relevance, both continuity, and the pursuit of the shared activity would be jeopardized. The concept of ARC is relevant to the discussion since it can be used as a template specifying the triadic 'situational' support that *every social practice* requires. Using language to perform an action with an 'other' is clearly a variety of such activity: the dimensions of the context of situation, Field, Tenor and Mode (FTM), pertaining only to linguistic social practices, can therefore be viewed as a specific case of the ARC template. This validation of contextual parameters by reference to ARC has significant implications.

First, taking FTM as a more specific instance of ARC provides a clearer guide to the concerns of each contextual parameter: there is a basis in this frame for identifying certain features of the context of situation as belonging to one parameter rather than another. For example, sphere as applied to field clearly pertains to Action; mode as Contact is a way of facilitating communication, materially or/and by helping to make sense; and tenor as Relation concerns speaker/addressee as socially positioned, culturally specific co-actors of an activity requiring linguistic acts with/without physical ones.

Second, and following from the above, this conceptualization of FTM should provide a comprehensive account of the situational features relevant to speaking to an other: therefore, logically, it ought to include the valid features of other variant models such as Hymes' SPEAKING (1986: 59–65) or Gregory's 'functional tenor'. The latter for example is implicit in naming the action types in field; if the action is consultation with a doctor, you could hardly have a 'functional tenor' such as exchanging goods for money.

Third, seen in this perspective, the nature of the parameter is very likely to validate the 1973a CMR hypothesis: the metaphor of 'resonance' is apt for referring to the reciprocal relations of context and metafunction. As a linguistic resource, the metafunctions developed in the use of language as forms of action, and as a means of enacting interpersonal relations, as well as ways of creating relevance, continuity and coherence in (inter-)action. These are properties common to all languages. If field is *far more likely* to be realized by the formal resources of 'transitivity' and 'reference' (i.e., Saussure's 'signification'), which are actually derived from the experiential metafunction, this is not a statement of two facts, but of one: the resonance of context and metafunction is a good indication of how eventually what happens in the 'instance' could end up as a feature of the 'system'.

Fourth, the significance of the context of *situation* cannot be explained in terms of the material situation *as such*: the identity of the situation is created by its association with types with specific social practices. The material units of space and time are specialized by the ARC properties of types of social practice, giving them their identity; so 'classrooms' are rooms for teaching, the court for dispensing justice, the shop for shopping, the bank for a variety of financial transactions, and so on. Nonetheless, the identifications of material spaces/moments are seldom completely 'binding'; other things can and do regularly happen in most locations: so the places mentioned witness the social practice of maintenance – being cleaned and tidied up; and 'hold ups' sometimes occur in a 'bank', as do friendly chats.

Finally, social practice is as central to the development of culture as text is to that of language. Language is directly experienced only through its instantiations in texts; similarly, the working of culture becomes tangible to the social subject through involvement with the features of the social practices. Just as language is created, maintained and/or changed by social subjects participating in texts, so also are cultural institutions and domains, by the social subjects' participation in social practices. No wonder, the relations of language and culture and of text and situation as well as those of language and text and of culture and situation are so complex: they require deliberate and conscious enquiry. Considering all this, the hypothesis of ARC seems to be not insignificant. But unlike the other three moves, this one, I believe, never came centre stage to be noticed by the SFL community in general: the publication where it appeared (Hasan 2001a) was obscure, and nothing incited me to actively try to foreground its potential. So, playing on the wording of a title by Goffman (1964) the ARC hypothesis, in fact, made no difference to the 'neglected context of situation'.

As I remarked before, one might wonder if context of situation is important enough to deserve such detailed attention. I believe it is, and I will return to this issue later (Section 8.4). What the discussion shows is that underlying each move is one single issue, namely, that of precision – precision in the conceptualization of the parameters, in the specification of their features, *and* precision in identifying their linguistic correlates. I moved seriously towards the paradigmatic description of context in search of precision and accuracy: the purpose of this activity is register classification; and the success of that enterprise depends on achieving a precise means of identifying the correlates underlying that variation. It is good to live with hope: perhaps this time con/textual description will actually get there.

8.3   The paradigmatic description and its representation in system network

Paradigmatic description is probably a familiar concept to all linguists: in fact, the underlying concept can be traced back to Saussure's 'associative bonds' (Hasan 2013, 2014a). So the concept dates back to the birth of modern linguistics. For SFL, with its origins in Firthian linguistics, there had been a long tradition of orientation to these concepts (Firth 1957, 1968; Halliday 1961; Butt 2001; Matthiessen 2007, 2009b, 2015). However, the method of representing such description in the form of a SYSTEM NETWORK (= sys-net) is unique to SFL: in its form, this differs significantly from Firth's representations, and it had never been anything like Saussure's image of the 'associative bonds' (1966: 126).[14] Guided by a set of theoretical concepts, introduced in the early 1960s to the mid-1970s, the conventions of the system networks (= sys-net) have evolved a good deal from the early 1960s to the present, as evident from a comparison of Halliday 1959, 1961 with Halliday 1973a, 1975a, 1976; Halliday and Matthiessen 2014.

Three important aspects of the paradigmatic description are relevant to the ensuing discussion: (a) the conventions of the sys-net; (b) the relations that the conventions signal; and (c) the *relata* of those relations. What is being related by the conventions, i.e., the relata, is not words or even structures: rather it is those features which underlie the DESCRIPTUM, i.e., that which is being described. The conventions, i.e., the lines, arrows, brackets, braces and such-like, whose material (visually accessible) configuration constitutes the system networks, are dedicated to one specific goal, that of representing the analysis of semiological phenomena. So in its make-up, the sys-net is rather like the linguistic sign system whose description it has been designed to represent. Underlying the materially accessible lines, arrows, etc., are the relations: in this sense, the sys-net is a signing system; just as in linguistics the categories describing the language signs, has 'no ontological status' (Firth 1957: 181) and can be assigned some meaning, some SIGNIFIED in Saussure's terms, only on the basis of their relations, so also the relations signalled by the conventions, have no status except as Firth's 'schematic construct' (1957: 181). The relata in a sys-net are simply features/properties in terms of which the category under description, i.e., the descriptum, is being analysed: these feature/properties are labelled; those labels are what we know as OPTIONS. The options represent the set of possible features whose relations to other relevant possibilities (features/options) constitute the description of that category: in this sense, each option is derived from the category is analysing. In short, a sys-net is something like a document which can be read by anyone who knows the 'language of its convention'. This document is not a dictionary concerned only with part of the apparatus of the system; it is more like a thesaurus – a compendium of knowledge, contain a number of inter-related theses about some category relevant to linguistics. A sys-net offers the possibility of representing the entire set of relations or a part thereof: it can be as detailed as the analyst desires.

The sys-net was first applied mainly to the analysis of lexicogrammar (Halliday 1967a, 1967b, 1968, 1979b), the method led to the metafunctional hypothesis in SFL (Halliday 1970a, 1973b, 1979b).[15] Following Halliday (1973b), the same descriptive orientation and systemic form of representation were further developed in the early 1980s to describe the semantic unit 'MESSAGE' (Hasan 1983 mimeo). This led to other sys-nets, e.g., that concerning the RHETORICAL UNIT at the same stratum (Cloran 1994), so related by constituency to message. The description represented in these sys-nets were employed successfully as research tools for the study of socio-semantic variation (Cloran 1994; Williams 1995; Hasan 2009a; Hasan *et al.* 2007; Matthiessen, Lukin, Butt, Cleirigh and Nesbitt 2005). So far this approach has not been applied widely or regularly to the stratum of context; but it would most probably be a careless mistake to ignore it in that domain. The essence of the paradigmatic description is to navigate analytically through a set of possibilities – the potential of the category – so as to postulate which of these might be chosen in what environment, under what conditions. The description of the contextual parameters seems very well suited to such a study: it has been suggested (Halliday *et al.*, 1964; Hasan 1973c; and all chapters here) that each contextual parameter, representing a distinct area of human experience, may be usefully viewed as a variable that offers a distinct set of variant possibilities (values), specific to each parameter. The problem is to establish their calibration in a way that the realized actuals agree with the experience of the community whose language and culture are under description. The system network has so far proved versatile in representing analyses of this kind for both semantics and lexicogrammar: the question is whether it will successfully meet the requirements of describing this extra-linguistic domain. This is an empirical issue that needs to be tested.

Below, in this section, I hope to demonstrate the full range of the resource of the sys-net as an excellent device for representing explicitly and precisely, without any ambiguity, the calibrated relations of the myriad properties in terms of which a category can be exhaustively described. If the aim is to produce orderly and precise descriptions, then so long as the analyst is clear about the nature of the descriptum – what properties should be attributed to it – the conventions of the sys-nets are sure to satisfy. The systemic description of contextual parameters may be a nascent enterprise, but in general a good deal of information is available in SFL on sys-nets as the references to SFL work indicates. If Halliday (1976) is a good account of the state of the art in the early days, then today Matthiessen (2015) gives an excellent account of the significance of this method.

8.3.1   Some basic concepts: point of origin, simple system and system network

I would have much preferred to use only the contextual sys-nets for illustrating the systemic conventions, throughout the discussion of the sysnet. But the first figure, an exception, seemed better suited as an opening. Figure 8.1 will be used to introduce some 'basic concepts' in the formation of a system network. A contextual opening network (Figure 8.3) will be presented in a later section.

Figure 8.1: Point of origin and the primary system [Hasan 2013]

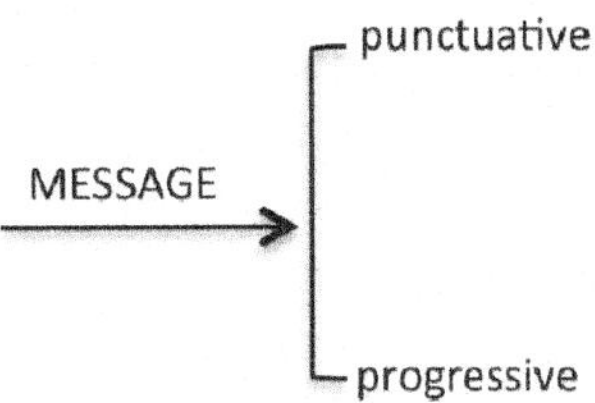

The word MESSAGE, which opens Figure 8.1, refers perhaps to the most basic concept, known as the POINT OF ORIGIN. Though sometimes an analyst might not display the point of origin materially in the system network, the context of their discussion makes its identity obvious. This is because the point of origin forms the foundation of the description, not because it is always the first to appear in a sys-net: much more important is the fact that it is what functions as the category under description; it forms the sys-net's object of enquiry; its DESCRIPTUM that will be being described in every single part of that sys-net. The sys-net following the point of origin in Figure 8.1 will be found to describe the properties of message and nothing but message (Hasan 1983, 2013).

In SFL, only a theoretically motivated category can act as the descriptum: thus message is a UNIT on the RANK SCALE of the semantic stratum, with the implication that a good deal is already known about the identity of the descriptum: the theoretical work, that the category does in cooperation with some others, positions it unambiguously, because their entire history has unfolded by reference to the theory. This is true of the message as well. For example, units on the rank scale of any language-internal stratum are in an orderly relation of constituency: so, message as a unit is made up of one or more SEMES, and itself enters into the structure of a RHETORICAL UNIT (Cloran 1994).[16] As a category at the semantic stratum, it is itself construed by some specific categories of the lexicogrammatical stratum 'lying below it', typically pertaining to the systemic properties of the unit CLAUSE; and as a semantic unit, it will realize specifiable features of the context of situation, which lies above the semantic stratum.

A quality of the point of origin is that as a term in a sys-net, its embrace is treated as comprehensive – it will cover as much ground as may be necessary to describe the descriptum exhaustively, though the analyst may curtail the description at some earlier point. So, although Figure 8.1 presents only the initial system, the fact that the point of origin is message implies that any sys-net describing any category of message would be seen as relevant, either as (potentially) complementing it or as a critique or modification of the original. This is implicit in the fact that message is an instance of a theoretically positioned category of language. Point of origin thus announces a domain of relevant discussion: obviously, the actual possibility of profitable discourse depends on a shared language of description. All the sys-nets pertaining to the same point of origin, say message, if considered valid in the theory, are logically relevant to any other sys-net declaring to be 'about' message. The concept, like other theoretical categories, has no ontological status: most probably, it would be impossible to even display an image of a comprehensive sys-net that exhaustively represents the description of its point of origin. It is conceivable that the digital media could provide an extensive and/or mobile surface for the purpose, but even so the limits of human vision might restrict its perception as one single complete visual object whose content can be appreciated as a whole. Halliday has always maintained that language is big; it seems reasonable to suggest that therefore linguistics, which describes language, should be considerably bigger.

Moving to the *open square bracket* in Figure 8.1, that shape signals a SIMPLE SYSTEM: a sys-net is simply a configuration of related simple systems. The simple system can appear in two guises: it may appear alone, having no company whatever, as does the system in Figure 8.1: these are known as INDIVIDUAL SYSTEMS. By contrast, a simple system may appear together with at least one other simple system. This will be referred to as a SIMULTANEOUS SET, and the systems of the simultaneous set will be called MEMBER SYSTEMS (= m-system). Each simple system, whether a member system (= m-system) or an individual one, must display more than one option. If only one option is shown in a system, the other being a zero or some other equivalent, then that system would be void: this makes sense since every option in the system-now always represents a distinct property of that foregoing option which acted as the entry point of the system-now. So if one option is displayed, this would be interpreted as no analysis has occurred; one might just as well not have inserted a new system. The initial system of a sys-net, i.e., *the first one to appear with displayed options after the point of origin*, is known as the PRIMARY SYSTEM of the sys-net, and will have the lowest degree of delicacy: this is to say simply that the information about the descriptum offered by the primary systemic options is at a gross degree of delicacy: it can be further explored for more delicate information. This last statement implies that the systemic options 'offer' information. But where does this information come from and how did it get into the systemic option? The answer to this question unmasks the apparently inscrutable nature of the sys-net.

In Figure 8.1, the sys-net's process is 'declared open' with the display of its first system of options. The description here begins by a primary analysis of the descriptum: this takes the form of a primary simple individual system displaying just two 'options' [punctuative] or [progressive]. These options refer to two properties of the point of origin: it is being claimed that the unit at point of origin is to be viewed as possessing two mutually exclusive properties: either the message must have the feature [punctuative] or the feature [progressive]. So logically the two properties are mutually exclusive: at this primary degree of delicacy it is being maintained that either a message will be 'punctuative' (e.g., *Hi!, you know what?, pardon! Wow!*), or 'progressive' (e.g., *didn't you talk to him? well, I wanted to, but I don't know where he hangs out these days and every time I go to his office he just isn't there…*); and there will be no third property by reference to which a third class might be created. This may or may not be factually correct, but on the basis of what is displayed in Figure 8.1, this is what the conventions of the sys-net will ascribe to the analyst. We may reformulate this analysis: in the primary analysis, message, the point of origin, has *reappeared as a system of two mutually exclusive options*. The same process will repeat itself in the next step with one difference. The primary system derives from one category, namely, that which functions as the point of origin. In the next step, the process becomes a process of multiple derivation: every simple system must have at least two options, so the option [punctuative] may be analysed as having two or more features, and so can the [progressive]. This means that after the primary system, progress from it into the second system and beyond might entail a one by one analysis of each of the options.

The above account specifies a relation basic to the progress of the sys-net: from the primary system onwards, in principle, the system begins to grow into a system network by the DERIVATION of system from each preceding set of options. The relation here is one of 'dependency' since the disposition of a system *depends* on the option that is being described. This describes the basic mode for the development of a system into a system network. To maintain an orderly description, there is a sys-net requirement that for further exploration *at any one specific point, one and only one option can be chosen* from amongst the existing mutually exclusive options (later I will need to modify these statements to accommodate more complex cases; see Section 8.3.4). This situation introduces the concept of 'choice' as an essential step in the process of the sys-net derivation past the primary system; and as just described the exploration of the chosen options 'reappears' as the options of the next simple system(s) displaying, in its turn, a number of mutually exclusive options, ready to be chosen to continue to further the cycle of the system's derivation. The origin of the derivation had been initiated with the point of origin; the analysis of the chosen category as represented in the options of each new system is taken to be exhaustive. It follows, therefore, that each next step in the process provides a more delicate analysis than the previous one(s): the information ever increasing in delicacy refers back to the descriptum, which had appeared as the point of origin. The information in the options is the product of analysis; the conventions of the network are pursuing the relations between the various options. This, in a nutshell, is how a sys-net grows: *it develops by a continued analysis of already analysed categories.*

Two related comments need to be made here: *first*, each simple system has two or more mutually exclusive options: whatever their number, the options of each simple system, are analysed from one perspective. This is why all the options in belonging to the same system bear some semantic affinity to each other, even though they are mutually exclusive. This is evident from such examples as either [private] or [public], either [graphic] or [phonic]; either [animate] or [inanimate], either [male] or [female]; either [tense] or [modal], either [singular] or [plural], and so on for each stratum. *Second*, for the description to be complete, every option of the said system must, in its turn, be chosen for analysis: no systemic option can be abandoned so long as there is anything significant to be said about it. As these 'same generation' options are analysed, the description is extended in the breadth of coverage, not in the depth of delicacy. Of course, a stage can arrive in any network where an option might fail to follow the above 'cycle of birth and re-birth'; an option might simply terminate, while others are being further described. This can happen either because the 'terminal option' has reached the limit of its description: i.e., in the analyst's view no more needs to be said about it, or for some reason the analyst might suspend the analysis at that point. For example, the systemic options in

Figure 8.1 are only at the primary degree of delicacy, so it is not very likely that their description had been exhausted; they are suspended here as of no further relevance. The measure of a sys-net's success is the extent to which it produces information in the shape of new options specifying greater descriptive delicacy at each new step, until the sum of these related options has arrived at an adequate, explicit and explanatory account of the descriptum. The conventions of the sys-net, throughout guard the transparency, orderliness and precision of the process that has moved option by option, relation by relation, system by system to represent description, turning one simple system into a sys-net.

A few words on some terms as used here in talking of some sys-net relations. The term 'option' refers to the as-yet-unexplored property of a potential presented in the system; 'choice' is option selected for further exploration of properties, in their turn ready to act as an entry point for the next system.[17] And a 'feature' is a property of the property under description, i.e., its point of origin. These descriptive categories do not name 'entities': they refer only to relations. For example, the point of origin has at least three kinds of relations: (a) as used so far, it is a unit at some stratum; (b) it is an '*initial entry point*' on which the first move in a sys-net *depends*; and (c) it is the *ultimate descriptum* whose potential is to be represented in the sys-net as a continuous set of relations across the options of the system.

8.3.2   The individual system and network derivation: an example

In describing the mechanism of the sys-net derivation, I have deliberately focused on the individual system in terms of the choice of simply one of its options at any one time whose exploration begins by treating it as an entry point to the next individual system: this was referred to as the cycle of a system's birth and re-birth, perpetuating new systems from the old. But the mutual relations of the entire set of choices from an individual system were not brought to attention. Figure 8.2 is an example of this latter aspect of a sys-net's formation: below it will be used to show how the sys-net records such derivations.

The main part of Figure 8.2 occurs on p. 42 of Butt (2004a), but its history actually begins with the MODE of discourse (2004a: 37), which specifies three terms in an opening brace, namely: (a) ROLE OF LANGUAGE; (b) CHANNEL; and (c) MEDIUM. These terms are labels for members of a simultaneous set of three systems. The m-system of MODE called ROLE OF LANGUAGE opens as an individual system (which is treated as a primary system) with

Figure 8.2: Mode: the 'ancillary' Role of Language (Butt 2004a: 42)

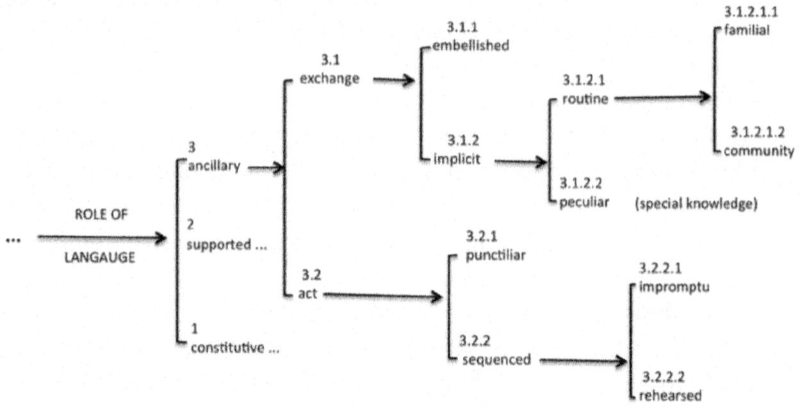

Legend for Figure 8.2:

Ref	TERM	CHARACTERISTICS
3	**ANCILLARY**	activity, as exchange or as act, which takes its course without relying on the exchange of language—the language that does occur (if it does) is merely an adjunct to activity.
3.1	exchange	
3.1.1	embellished	when ancillary language adds to the course of an exchange.
3.1.2	implicit	when the exchange is guided by local knowledge of habits based on routines of family or community, or based on peculiar idiosyncratic, insider experience.
3.1.2.1	routine	
3.1.2.2	peculiar (special knowledge)	
3.2	act	activity involves only a single act (punctiliar) or a sequence (sequenced) which can be impromptu or rehearsed.
3.2.1	punctiliar	
3.2.2	sequenced	
3.2.2.1	impromptu	
3.2.2.2	rehearsed	

three mutually exclusive options: (a) 'constitutive'; or (b) 'supported'; or (c) 'ancillary' (p. 38).[18]

With apologies to Butt, I have included this primary system, ROLE OF LANGUAGE in Figure 8.2 presented in this chapter so as to indicate the dependency relations beginning with the primary option 'ancillary'; in other words Figure 8.2 as presented here is a combination of Butt (2004a: 38+42). Its status as an individual system is signalled by the ENTRY INDICATOR, which is signalled by an arrow under the label ROLE OF LANGUAGE (Butt 2004a: 38). Choosing the option 'ancillary' permits entry into the next individual system with two options of its own, namely [exchange] or [act].

As Figure 8.2 stands, it signals that these options are more delicate than 'ancillary'. The choice of the option [exchange] in its turn leads to a new individual simple system with two options [embellished] or [implicit]. The former is here terminal option, since it is not chosen for further exploration; the latter, [implicit], acts as the entry point for the next new individual system, and so on. This account shows a method for charting CHOICE PATHS in sys-net derivation: IF the systems are individual ones and the relation is that of dependency, the cycle producing a sys-net will schematically be:

option=choice=entry point→next system of options→option=choice=entry point

When a sys-net begins life at a primary option, as [ancillary] does in Figure 8.2, and moves through the derivations system by system right to the end, the traversal of each entire path is known as a SELECTION EXPRESSION (SE). Each such SE would be a formulaic statement of the properties of one of the primary options from its appearance in the primary system right through to the end of the path without any gaps. This, in effect, implies that each SE represents the total description of one single sub-category of the descriptum acting as the point of origin. Clearly the longer the SE, the more delicate the description. So long as the relation between the option is simply that of dependency, the general shape of the SEs would be as presented in Table 8.1, which offers details of all such SEs from Figure 8.2, with [ancillary] as the starting point from the primary system in ROLE OF LANGUAGE, pursuing each of its derivations right through to the last option in each SE. As Table 8.1 shows, each SE derived from one primary option, e.g., [ancillary] in Figure 8.2, will have that primary option in common, but no SE can be a replication of any other; each must be unique in respect of at least one option. There points are illustrated by the SEs in Table 8.1. The colon between two options signals a relation of dependence: the second depends upon the first.

Table 8.1: Selection expressions initiated by the primary option [ancillary]

	Selection expressions (SEs) initiated by the primary option [ancillary]: c.f. Figure 2 (Butt 2004: 42), sys-net fragment role od language
1	ancillary: exchange: embellished
2	ancillary: exchange: implicit: routine: familial
3	ancillary: exchange: implicit: routine: community
4	ancillary: exchange: implicit: peculiar
5	ancillary: act: punctiliar
6	ancillary: act: sequenced: impromptu
7	ancillary: act: sequenced: rehearsed

A system developed entirely by a cycle of dependence relation between individual systems, as presented in Table 8.1, resembles a simple taxonomy, with one notational difference that its branches move sideways. This mode of sys-net derivation is quite the commonest: in fact, most developed sys-nets will display a number of SEs built only or mainly on the relation of dependence. However, this type system derivation is like simple taxonomies, which like the sys-nets can represent moves in delicacy ('granularity'). But sys-nets are capable of representing more complex relations such as those of simultaneity.

8.3.3   Context as point of origin of a simultaneous set: the working of m-systems

The 'simultaneous set' and its member systems (m-systems) have been mentioned briefly above (Section 8.3.1 p. 22). Systems occurring as members of a simultaneous set are not as frequent overall as systems occurring as individuals; but when they occur, they bring a multi-faceted perspective to that chosen option which has functioned as their entry point to the new systems. This is because, as pointed out in concluding section 3.1 (p. 24), each simple system has a particular point of view from which it analyses its entry point into the features of the new system. It follows that when the analysis of the chosen option is in terms of multiple perspectives, this results in the creation of a simultaneous set. This introduces a complexity in the relations of the options, thereby affecting the process of derivation, and in any event making the sys-net differ from a simple taxonomy. Figure 8.3 will be used to illustrate these points as well as to draw attention to the sys-net conventions that signal these relations. The point of origin for Figure 8.3 is CONTEXT OF SITUATION; it has been selected deliberately because it does raise some important issues. Their exploration will allow me to elaborate some necessary questions about the relations of context and language.[19]

As I see it, there are three important issues: (1) the fourth primary system in Figure 8.3: what is it and why is it relevant here?; (2) the first three primary systems cannot be said to exemplify the *systems* of FIELD, TENOR and MODE OF DISCOURSE since they display no options; what are they doing here? (3) its point of origin, CONTEXT OF SITUATION, unlike MESSAGE above (Figure 8.1) is not a unit; how is its identity established? What ground is there for assuming that CONTEXT can be actually analysed in terms of categories established for the analysis of linguistic phenomena? These issues will be addressed below in Sections 8.3.3.1, 8.3.3.2 and 8.3.3.3 respectively. It will be better, however, to first discuss the conventions that signal

Figure 8.3: Context of situation as point of origin (after Hasan 2009b: 182)

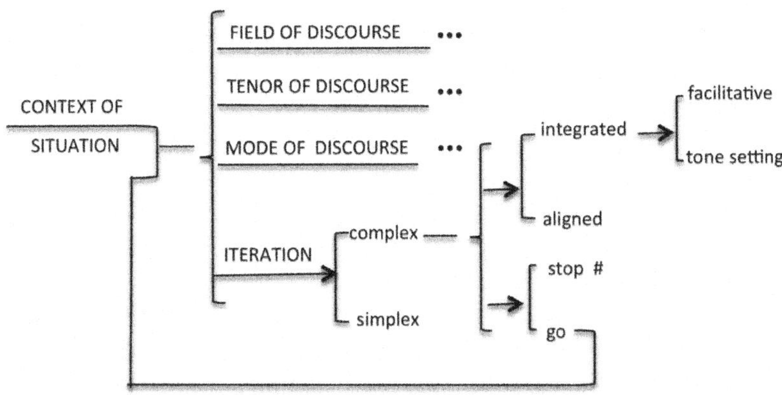

Legend:

PARAMETERS	DESCRIPTIVE DOMAIN	DEFAULT REALISATION
field of discourse	action	ideational resources
tenor of discourse	relation	interpersonal resources
mode of discourse	contact	textual resources

iteration = the possibility for a CC to reselect new environment

simplex = maintain the current CC   complex = select a new subordinate CC is selected

stop = go back to primary CC at the end of the current subordinate CC

go = open a new subordinate CC

integrated = the subordinate CC must be functionally integrated in primary CC

aligned =   two essentially separately bounded social practices A and B;
              A independent of B; can occur without B
              A must have material action focal; if verbal action, mut be ancillary;
              B must have verbal actionconstitutive descriptive of on-going action in A;
              either may make choice 'go' to introduce new but predetermined CC;
              the predetermination originates with distinct social practices.

facilitative = contributes to the action chosen in main field

tone setting = contributes to goal achievement by enacting relations the various relations associated with the working of the m-systems in a simultaneous set.

The simultaneous set is signalled by a right facing open brace that 'holds' all its m-systems. In Figure 8.3, the terms referring to the primary m-systems are shown as FIELD OF DISCOURSE, TENOR OF DISCOURSE, MODE OF DISCOURSE and ITERATION; only ITERATION, the fourth m-system, is developed as a system: it alone displays options. The other three are left just as ENTRY INDICATORS, which suggest there will be some m-system(s). The entry indicator for a simultaneous set is not an arrow but a plain line which schematically links the chosen option acting as entry point to the brace of simultaneity. In Figure 8.3, such an entry indicator links the point of origin, CONTEXT OF SITUATION, as the entry point to the big right open brace. The first three indicators in the brace are plain lines, meaning that the ensuing systems in each would form a simultaneous sets. ITERATION, the fourth and last entry indicator of an m-system is an arrow; it signals the ensuing m-system will be an individual. In Figure 8.3, this individual m-systems displays two options, either [complex] or [simplex]. In other words, the m-system(s) of a simultaneous set may allow the derivation of either a simultaneous set or individuals. Irrespective of this, simultaneity modifies the relation of the options in its member system (m-system): *only one option from each m-system must be chosen simultaneously from each member system of the set until all possible combinations are exhausted*: the options of all m-systems in a simultaneous set must combine freely while maintaining the above principles. The system of ITERATION from Figure 8.3 will briefly indicate how the combination of contemporary options works: this reveals itself in the account of possible traversals of the system. Table 8.2 displays a complete list of SEs, each of which represents a traversal of the system; that is to say each SEs shows the 'free combination' of the contemporary choices from the systems of ITERATION, wherever this is legitimate.

Table 8.2: Selection expressions arising from the system of iteration

1	simplex
2	complex: integrated: facilitative; stop#
3	complex: integrated: facilitative; go
4	complex: integrated: tone setting; stop#
5	complex: integrated: tone setting; go
6	complex: aligned: stop#
7	complex: aligned: go

As in Table 8.1, so also in Table 8.2, the colons indicate the relation of dependence between the relevant two choices, while the semi-colon signals concurrent choice of contemporary options as allowed by the disposition of the m-systems in the simultaneous set. The choice of the option [simplex] will combine with a CC that is proceeding as predicted from the nature of the social practice; there are no twists and turns. The choice of [complex] means that the main CC will be perturbed. The perturbing event is not a necessary part of the social practice as indicated by the CCs to this point, but in some way relatable to it. Details concerning this are indicated in the m-systems of the simultaneity brace which is entailed by the choice of [complex]. The first m-system in the simultaneity brace following [complex] is an individual; it depends on the choice of option complex and its options indicate the kind of contextual perturbation at issue. The option [integrated] refers to a contextual shift that in some way not only relates to the main CC but is also integrated into it by contributing to the completion of the social practice, whereas [aligned] entails the unfolding to distinct social practices deliberately being conducted at the same time; one of these practices always depends on the ongoing performance of the other for example taking down the minutes of a meeting presupposes the side by side conduct of meeting (more details below). Figure 8.3 shows that if the option [integrated] is chosen, this must lead to the choice of [facilitative] or [tone setting]. The options [stop#] or [go] make up the second m-system; [stop] requires 'return to the main CC' whereas [go] requires 'select new features' as new contextual shift which would be subsidiary to the main CC. As Figure 8.2 shows, 'integrated' or 'aligned' are options of the same individual system: they can never combine legitimately. The options 'facilitative' or 'tone setting' depend on 'integrated'; so they can combine as shown in SEs 2–5. Had any options been shown for field, tenor or mode, they would in principle be required to appear as well. Table 8.2 with its seven SEs initiated by the choice of [complex] shows very clearly how the options of the m-systems must combine. All the SEs initiated by the choice of [complex] have that option (and some others) in common; but, at the same time, each SE is unique.

8.3.3.1 *Complex contexts: system of iteration and concept 'text complex'*

The above discussion has served two purposes. *First,* the SEs reveal how the options in the m-systems of the simultaneous set are calibrated, which is different from the calibration of individual systems; the relations here are not as those of simple taxonomy, as with Table 8.2, representing SEs of

Figure 8.2 (section 8.3.2). *Second*, using the system of ITERATION to illustrate the working of m-system has brought me to the first issue raised by
Figure 8.3: what is the justification for including the system of ITERATION in
Figure 8.3 as a member of the simultaneous set containing the three well
known parameters? It does offer the convenience of using a small set of
m-systems to demonstrate the 'combination' of contemporary options in
m-systems; but this does not serve as justifiable reason from the perspective
of the sys-net. The justification lies in the function this system has in the
description of con/text. An iteration system on which this one is based, was
designed to explain in systemic functional terms the difference between
the concept of 'complex text' (Hasan 1999b: 246–273, 2000: 28–47) and
Martin's 'genre combination'. The thesis is that the complex text is based
on certain functional relations between the main text and the subordinate
(or aligned) ones whose co-selection accounts for the text's complexity. In
other words, unlike spatio-temporally based combinations, text complexity
is open to explanatory description: it is not a happenstance. Elaborating the
brief account above, the primary system of ITERATION has two options here:
'complex' or 'simplex'. The choice of 'simplex' calls for 'no change' in the
CONTEXTUAL CONFIGURATION (CC) current at that point; in other words, the
text is simple, and the evidence for this lies in the consistency of its CC. By
contrast, the choice 'complex' implies a 'con/textual shift' (or alignment).
I prefer to write 'con/textual' for the simple reason that there exists a 'solidary' relation between context and text: the text realizes the CC choices.
The choice of the option 'complex' acts as an entry condition to a simultaneous set with two m-systems. The first m-system from this brace specifies
the function of the subordinate CC: this is either 'integrated' into the main
CC or 'aligned' with it (as pointed out, Hasan 1999b: 269, other possibilities are open but not yet described to my knowledge); the options of the
second, [stop#] or [go], specify the possibilities open for iteration: if option
[stop#] is chosen, the main CC will be resumed; the option [go] will imply
that a con/textual shift is a-foot and the nature of this will be specified
by the first m-system options. Having to select these con/textual features
would obviously mean re-entry to the resources of all three con/textual
dimensions so as to access the necessary options relevant to the production
of the new subordinate CC. The signal to indicate iteration of CS is the
option [go]. The line beginning at option [go] makes its way to the point of
origin, CONTEXT OF SITUATION. The left facing elongated bracket that reaches
the point of origin is an iconic symbol showing that re-entry here via the
point of origin is accessible.

I believe viable realizational statements relevant to the option [integrated: facilitative] or [integrated: tone setting] have been presented in Hasan (1999b: 246–273; here chapter 6; Cloran (1999a)). The option 'aligned' refers to paired social practices each pertaining to distinct domains which are systematically coupled as part of the realization of the choice [aligned]. Unlike discussing politics (c.f. Section 8.2) while washing up, this pairing is not an accidental co-occurrence: in any event the co-occurrence of those is described by recognizing the material and verbal action type is m-systems in the simultaneous system (e.g., Hasan 1999b: Figure 3; here chapter 6, Figure 6.5). Instead, [aligned] demands the culturally deliberate co-occurrence of the two practices: one of the two social practices has the aim of in some way describing (call this B) whole or part of what is going on in the other (call this A): from this perspective, B depends on the performance of A. Many such aligned practices come to mind, e.g., sports commentary, A playing a game, B broadcasting a commentary; minute taking, with A the conduct of meeting, B summarizing some specific part of meeting; or taking down a dictation, with A dictating, and B reproducing the sayings. The significance of the culturally deliberate conjunction of social practice is that it is possible to predict the main CC of each up to an elementary degree of delicacy. Thus imagine that A is the activity of playing a game and B of broadcasting it live, the main CC may be described to some extent. So, in the main CC of A, field will have material action 'focal' verbal action ancillary; sphere will be 'specialized; institutional'; addressee will be 'present', social distance 'close; normal', status will be 'neutralized'; and in mode the material contact would be 'phonic; direct'; iteration choice is likely to be simplex. For B, in mode material contact would be 'phonic, mediated, congruent: synchronic: single (if radio commentary) multiple if live TV broadcast; public', in tenor addressee would be 'absent: category: actual', and field would be material action: peripheral, verbal action constitutive (the meaning of the terms for options are found in Appendix A for mode features; Appendix C for tenor features ; (both attached at the end of this chapter; for field see Appendix F attached at the end of the next chapter).

So the system of ITERATION appears to be useful: there is a range of situations, where either by alignment or by integration the functional conjunction of situational shift complex texts might come into being: a system of this kind needs to be tested against actual situations where textual complexity takes place to learn more about it. What has been described here is just a beginning. Finally, iteration is not specific only to complexity in con/texts;

all language internal units at the content plane manifest the possibility of appearing as simplex or complex. However, the same symbol as presented in Figure 8.3 for iteration is used in all cases to represent the 'combination of registers' except that these combinations are not chance affairs but based on specifiable condition. The more delicate details referring to, say what game, and options describing those differences will naturally not be statable at a near-primary degree of delicacy.

8.3.3.2   *Systems and options: density in contextual parameters*

The second issue arising from Figure 8.3 concerns the absence of systems following the first three entry indicators: these announce that a simultaneous set of m-systems will occur following each entry indicator. The process of the system can only begin when a potential of entry point can be located. Sometimes, due to practical considerations, an analyst may background some part of the information (as in Figure 8.3) in order to focus on some part – in Figure 8.3 this was the m-system of iteration. Imagine now that Figure 8.4 joins Figure 8.3 just after FIELD OF DISCOURSE the three dots are shown.

Positioned thus in Figure 8.3, Figure 8.4 will now display its previously missing steps: as a result, it now has a point of origin and the first entry indicator clearly displays a same simultaneous set. We assume similar simultaneous sets would also follow tenor and mode; each of these three simultaneous sets will have the status of m-systems. Ignore the latter two, I focus on Figure 8.4, which brings the gift of primary m-systemic options to Figure 8.3, confirming that the primary system of FIELD is considerably complex. According to Figure 8.4, the primary system of FIELD consists of simultaneous system which contains: (a) an individual m-system of ACTION with two options; (b) a simultaneous set of SPHERE OF ACTION, with three m-systems each consisting of two options; and (c) another simultaneous set called PERFORMANCE OF ACTION.[20] This simultaneous system consists of one individual system displaying two options and one simultaneous set with three m-systems, each with two options.

The complexity of FIELD is indicated by the form taken by these three arrangements of system, each of which is in the last analysis a member of one simultaneous set: each option is a contemporary of the others. Figure 8.4 has at least three layers of simultaneity. Figure 8.5 schematically represents the union of Figure 8.4 with Figure 8.3.

Figure 8.4: A field network (Bowcher 2014: Figure 9; p. 203)

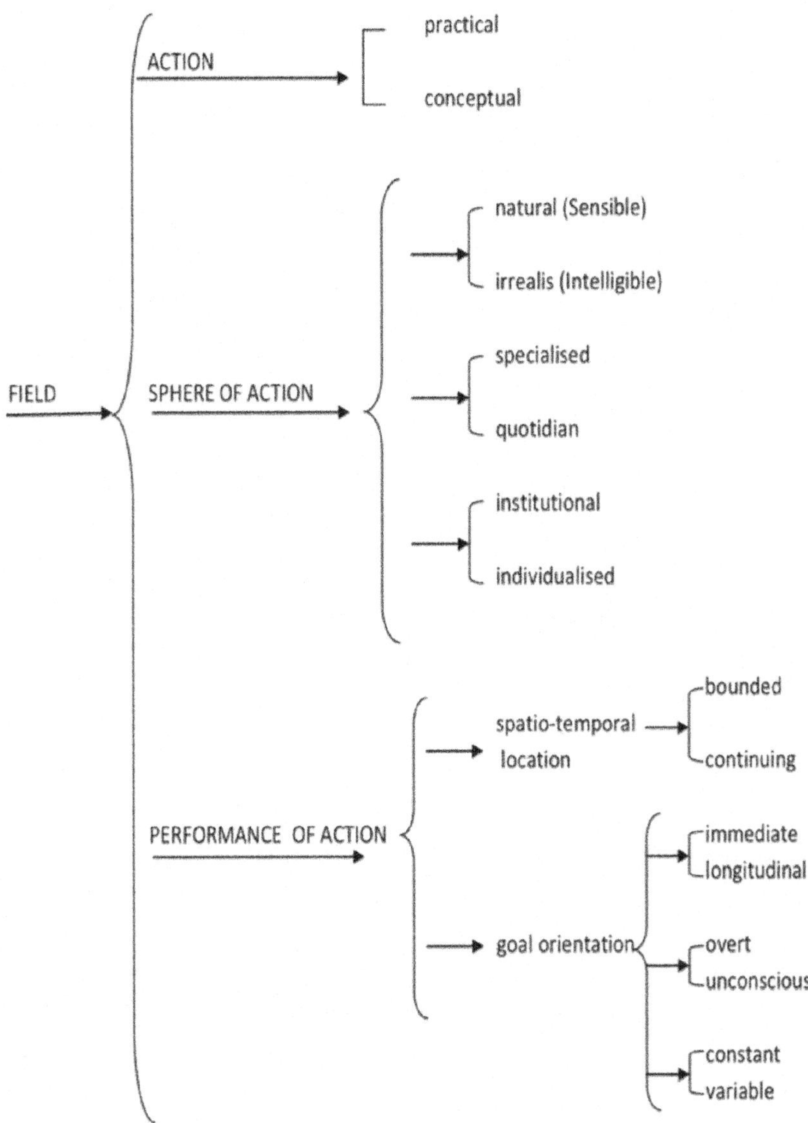

This description of field is formally equivalent to a set of eight simultaneous systems, where the options of each may combine with those of the others. So, notwithstanding the repeated nesting of simultaneous sets, all these systems would be treated by the conventions of the sys-net as mutually combinable within the limit stated above in Section 8.3.3. It is possible to preclude free combination, for example by using the 'if-then' relation indicated by what is referred to as the 'arrow diacritic' below (Section 8.3.1.5). In the absence of that preclusion, the number of selection expressions produced by the concurrent systems of field as they stand will be 2^8, or 256, each describing one particular primary sub-category of FIELD.

Figure 8.5: A schematic network: the union of Figures 8.3 and 8.4

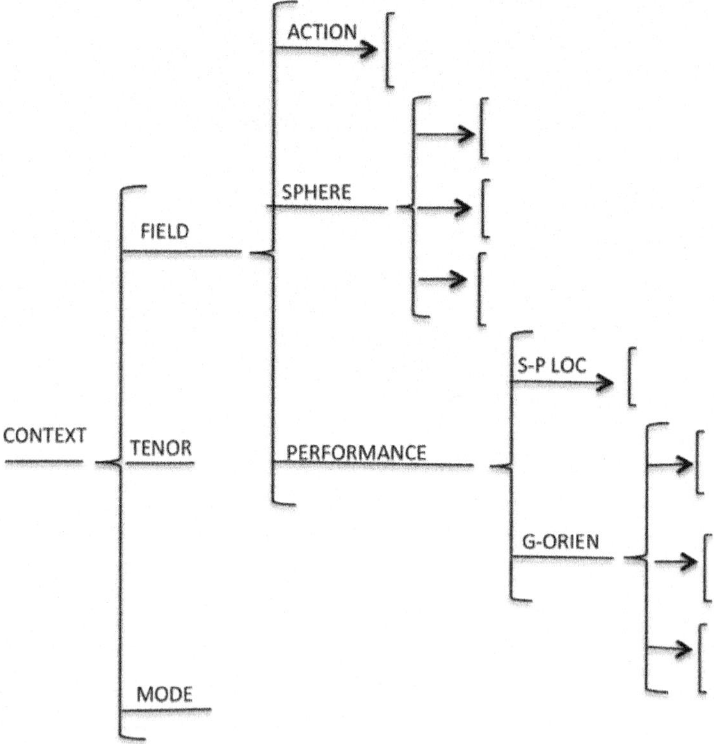

8.3.3.3 *Context as a stratum of linguistics*

Turning now to the third issue: there is no doubt that context of situation is a descriptum in search of description; but can it be viewed as a stratum of linguistics capable of being analysed using a frame of analysis largely designed for linguistic phenomena? Faced with this fundamental question, the issue of whether we can find something corresponding to a *unit* at this stratum pales into insignificance. Nothing close to this has been suggested by sociologists or anthropologists. For linguists to explore this domain might smack of doing 'spontaneous sociology' (a practice Bourdieu 1991: 37–38 criticized while himself presenting a case of 'spontaneous linguistics'). However, it is worth pointing out that the linguists' context is neither the physicists' 'real' world, nor the geographer's material world, nor yet the sociologists' socio-economic structure: it is a different abstraction from that same 'reality'. There exists a valid basis for linguists for making this abstraction, which centres on the notion of SOCIAL PRACTICE. Members of a speech community interact with each other: language participates in a large proportion of this interaction; in fact there is a significant number of social practices that can be performed only by languaging. As argued in Section 8.2, the analysis of the nature of inter-action justifies the recognition three inherent components of human interaction: Action, Relation and Contact; contextual parameters are a specific version of this. The logic behind the contextual parameters and relation of the parameters to the metafunctions is transparent. The metafunctions resonate across the strata of context, meaning, and wording are essential to explaining both why anyone says anything and why the other is able to understand it. It would to be quite illogical for a functional linguist to argue that meanings are metafunctional, but wordings are not.

Halliday (1991a) used the concept of REALIZATION (partly) to model the symbiotic relation between context and language: meaning-wording is realizationally related to the context of culture just as text as parole is, to the context of situation. And just as texts instantiate the system of language so also context of situation in which social practices occur instantiate culture. Nothing new enters a language when a language ceases to be used; no culture changes when its social practices depend on it. An adequate model of language needs to explain the nature of language both as system/*langue*, i.e., as a web of associative bonds, and as language-in-use/ *parole*, i.e., interactive linguistic practices: without this linguistic change and variation will remain a mystery. The perspective adopted in SFL on the text's context has clearly demonstrated that, far from being un-generalizable, *parole* presents a functional and orderly heterogeneity; focus on interactive linguistic practices has strengthened our understanding of the formation of individuals, which occurs always and only in cultural environment by semiotic means, among which language is the most pervasive. The interactants as the producers of the community's texts are persons who have throughout life internalized ways of saying and meaning that are specific to their culture: as Firth reminds us they always carry their culture with them. The strength of SFL's reasoning has its basis in its analysis of language and cultural processes: so, for example, the context metafunction resonance (CMR) hypothesis shows a more robust understanding of the mutual relations of language and reality than are the long established notions of truth, reference and correspondence. Summarizing this argument: the ARC hypothesis (Section 8.2.3.4) strengthens the basis for recognizing the three parameters: if field concerns domain of Action, then it must subsume aspects of forms of doing; on the other hand if the concern in contextual analysis is how it impinges on language, then the primary focus is how doing and saying are enmeshed. The aim of contextual analysis is not to analyse the universe; only those features of it which correlate with language, and focusing on those aspects which correlate with linguistic variation. Halliday's (1973b) realizational hypothesis foregrounds the probabilistic statement: the claim that field is more likely to be realized by the resources of ideational metafunction appears eminently reasonable.

Context of situation as point of origin differs from 'message' or 'clause': but, in general, the unity of context is not subject to doubt, nor is the identity of field, tenor and mode once the CMR hypothesis is accepted. The parameters are not like the units on a rank scale, but, significantly, they share some characteristics of metafunctions. As conceptualized in SFL, the three metafunction are treated as equal, throughout the content plane of language all three are present in the working of every unit at every rank: there is no metafunctions hierarchy. So unlike other models of 'language function' none has a higher status, none is consigned to 'pragmatics', which professes to be about an aspect of language, but somehow falls outside linguistics; none is viewed as that ill-defined phenomenon referred to as 'social meaning'. So the three metafunctions contribute jointly to the description of each linguistic unit, belonging to every rank of every stratum at the plane of content. Viewing the genesis of linguistic metafunctions in nature of human social activities, and seeing each as oriented to a specific parameter helps in conceptualizing the identity of each.

Context of culture and situation are treated as a stratum in linguistic theory, not because it is exactly like language but because its inclusion allows a functional model to explain problems that can otherwise not be explained: it is not 'reality', only that aspect of it that is illuminated by the potential of language to realize it – in other words to present it as encapsulated in language. The aim of linguistics is to describe how language works in the social life of its speakers: the aspects of reality that do not impinge on the working of language are no concern of linguistics.

8.3.4   Complex entry points: conjunction or disjunction

So far in the discussion of sys-net derivation all the entry points have been simple: what this means is that the choice of just one option has acted as the entry point for the next system. Patently every point of origin functions as a simply entry: this step is mandatory; there is no choice. But Figures 8.1 and 8.3 have shown that a point of origin may actually act just like a simple entry point, allowing entry to one primary system, as in Figure 8.1, or to a simultaneous set, as in Figure 8.3. Perhaps the most frequent function of a chosen option is to act as a simple entry point, but sys-nets at each stratum of the content plane also display what is known as 'complex entry point': here not just the choice of one but of two or more options from different systems is needed. There are two types of complex entry points: the 'conjunct' and the 'disjunct'. The former brings more than one option together and is perhaps easier to describe; the latter most probably cannot be understood without understanding what is involved in the creation conjunct entry point. Figure 8.6 happens to present an example of each of these entries: the glossary of its option is presented in Appendix A at the end of this chapter.

Figure 8.6 is a fragment of the paradigmatic description of the MODE OF DISCOURSE (MD) so it could be inserted as the continuing into the system indicated by the third indicator in Figure 8.3; the glossary of terms and options in Figure 8.6 is supplied in Appendix A. MODE, as described in Figure 8.6, is altogether and only concerned with features of *contact*, the two dimensions of which are MATERIAL and SEMANTIC. This concept of MODE reflects a universal characteristic of the semiological unit (the 'sign'), which stands for something other than itself, i.e., 'signified'/meaning: meaning, using Bertrand Russell's term, is not sens-ible; so the only way its presence can be registered is for its shape (the 'signifier') to be material, in other words, made of something that can impinge on the human body, allowing it to be sensed. The sign system of language is one such semiological system, and speakers typically encounter it in the course of 'doing things with words'. Activities of this kind, by definition, depend on the exchange of meaning-wording. This can only occur if meaning wording can be 'transduced' into some sens-ible

Figure 8.6: A tentative fragment of mode: material contact

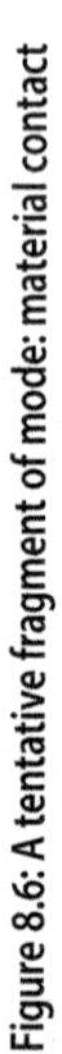

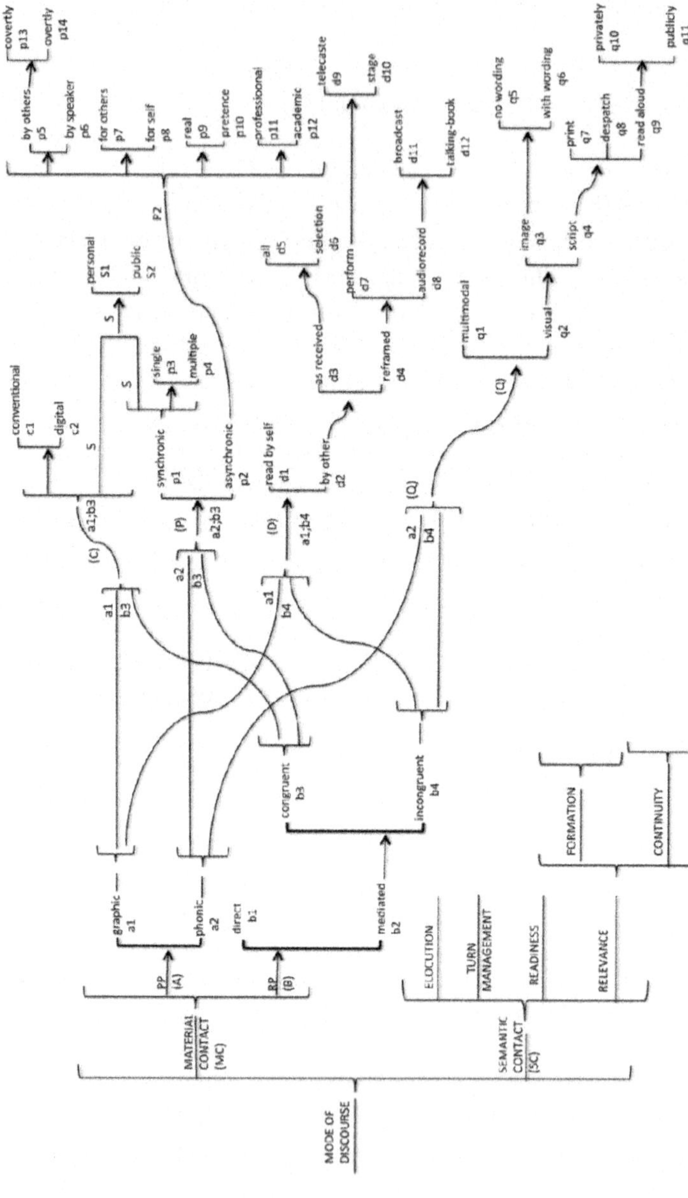

Note: For glossary of options see Appendix A;
For SEs of systems C & S see Appendix B.

matter thereby allowing the body-brain-mind to access those meanings (more discussion of realization in Section 8.3.6.3).

Figure 8.6, MATERIAL CONTACT (MC), is an attempt to describe the possible means of expression that normal human beings can use in producing and receiving meaning-wording in many parts of the world today. The systems of SEMANTIC CONTACT (SC) concern the description of intellig-ible aspects of language, which would primarily facilitate access to those meanings whose choice activates continuity, coherence and textual organization.

As a primary semiological system (Hasan 2014a), by definition, language was an 'embodied' resource, that is to say, meanings were circulated entirely by bodily resources. However, today, graphic relay, i.e., the use of the technology of writing, plays an undeniably prominent part in human life. This has most probably happened by language absorbing writing to such an extent that the words 'written/spoken' no longer refer to just two modes of expression: they actually name two styles of meaning-wording. The written style is typically found in communication that neutralizes material distance while the spoken foregrounds face to face interaction. Although speakers are sensitive to variation in the properties of expression, as is obvious from their evaluative perceptions, such as ACCENT variation (Abercrombie 1965), the 'sing-song' way of speaking, or emphasizing, the linguistic styles, known as spoken/written, cannot be analysed by focusing on ways of expressing alone: these, by way of their realization, mostly depend on the features of meaning-wording, which means the styles in question would be the realization of options described by the systems of SEMANTIC CONTACT. Figure 8.6 does not represent the description of the interconnections between systems of semantic and material contact, which is what makes the figure 'a tentative fragment of MODE': it is highly likely that with the exploration of those aspects, the systems both in MC and in SC might look rather different. Meanwhile it seems that using the words graphic/phonic to refer to MC resources will distinguish between expression and content.

MC opens with a simultaneous set consisting of two primary m-systems, PRODUCTION POINT (PP) and RECEPTION POINT (RP), with two options in each: the PP options [graphic] (a1) or [phonic] (a2) refer to relay, and the RP options [direct] (b1) or [mediated] (b2) to means of access. In [direct] (a1) access no third agency – man or machine – intervenes: so the accessed 'text' reaches the addressee in its original form. The bodily means of access are obviously visual if relay is [graphic] and aural if it is [phonic]. When [phonic] relay is used at production point, the [direct] access at reception point will be more or less synchronic; however, unpredictable degrees of time lag will occur in the case of [graphic; direct] (more on this below). The option [direct] is shown as terminal, i.e., it has not been further developed though this is certainly possible; but the choice of the option [mediated] allows access to a simple system with two options [congruent] (b3) or [incongruent] (b4). Since the PP and RP systems form a simultaneous set the legitimate choice paths for these would be as shown in Table 8.3 (entries 1 and 2).

Table 8.3: Legitimate primary choice paths in material contact

	legitimate primary choice paths in Material Contact	
	options address	option names
1	a1;b1	graphic; direct
2	a2;b1	phonic; direct
3	a1; b2: b3	graphic; mediated: congruent
4	a2; b2: b3	phonic; mediated: congruent
5	a1; b2: b4	graphic; mediated: incongruent
6	a2; b2: b4	phonic; mediated: incongruent

The option [direct] (a1) cannot combine with [phonic] a2: being options of the same system they are in an EITHER/OR relation, not BOTH-AND as in contemporary m-systems. By contrast, options from the other contemporary m-system b, [direct] b1 or [indirect] b2 can freely combine with a1 or a2. Whatever choice path begins with a1 will never combine with any choice path that begins with a2: the principle may be summed up as 'never shall the options of the same system or their inheritor ever meet'. An entry point is conjunct when options from two or more contemporary systems together form the condition for entering a new system, and this principle applies at any stage to any system that enters a choice path: thus, just as b1 and b2 cannot combine so also, the choice path containing b3 cannot ever be part of the same choice path where b4 enters. Choice paths 3–6 conforming to this principle represent feature-relations that are acceptable [see Appendix B for SEs relating to systems C and S].

The signal for indicating a conjunct entry condition is complex. It involves small braces and connecting lines to signal the participating options, as well as the entry point where the options conjoin allowing the entry indicator to point to the next systems. Figure 8.6 clearly displays the formation of the signal. A new address has been given with a capital letter to each indicator of a conjunct entry point; the same address is continued in lower case for the system introduced by each conjunct entry point. The first such entry shown in Figure 8.6 involves options 'a1; b3' and the address of the indicator is the letter C; so the options of its m-system are c1 or c2; a similar arrangement indicates the remaining three conjunct entries. These details are carried by the conjunct entry indicator which is shown as a line IF what ensues is a simultaneous set (as in C), or an arrow IF the ensuing system is an individual (as with P). This shows that the complex conjunct entry point may allow access to either an individual system or to a simultaneous set; and any number of options can be chosen to act together as one conjunct entry point, so long as the principle of system-separation is observed. The most hospitable environment for a conjunct entry condition is a simultaneous set, which naturally allow the legitimate combination of some options from contemporary systems. This of course does not mean that the options of contemporary m-systems always combine: but every time, a new dependence relation enters into a choice path, that choice path must diverge.[21]

The entry C, with the history of choosing the options [graphic; mediated; congruent], gives access to a simultaneous set, the first member of which has two options [conventional] (c1) or [digital] (c2), the second system has the options [personal] (s1) or [public] (s2). Since, for [graphic] relay to be used, typically the addressee is [absent] (see Figure 8.7, especially, TEXTUAL ROLES), some time-lag between relay and reception is inevitable. If relay is [direct], no human or mechanical agency intervenes in the addressee's access, but this is what must happen in [mediated] reception. The options [conventional] or [digital] indicate the nature of the intervening agency: the option [conventional] refers to the use of such older methods as handwriting, typewriting, or print (at PP). The second option [digital] (c2) refers to more recent means (though its reach is growing fast and the difference seems to be being eroded); email is supposedly private; other 'social media' are much less so. But are both these forms of reception used anywhere by anyone as the means of relay is [graphic]? This question is answered *indirectly* by system S in the case of the system of option [conventional] (c1) or [digital] (c2). System S is precisely one system central to a disjunct entry point as will be demonstrated below.

The default expectation is that the speaker has control on the text, i.e., the meaning-wording he produced 'with' his addressee. It is highly likely to protect the privacy of the communication. In mediation, privacy of the original relay is at risk, and never more so than when the original relay was [graphic], which exposes the produced message to displacement. The options of system S are designed to place a grid on the means of mediating as presented in c1/c2. The choice of option [personal] (s1) implies that typically its default realization will be by means most capable of maintaining 'privacy' while the second option [public] (s2) will apply to communication that allows considerably more free access. Because C and S are the m-systems of the same simultaneous set, the possible combinations would be as in Table 8.4, which also shows the most likely realization of this choice path.

Table 8.4: Mediated graphic text: a profile of dissemination

	address	choice path	default realization
1	c1; s1	[conventional; personal]	hand writing, typing
2	c1; s2	[conventional; public]	printed to be publicized
3	c2; s1	[digital; personal]	e-mail
4	c2; s2	[digital; public]	Facebook, Blog, Twitter...

Some five decades ago, situation as presented in Table 8.4 would have been probably completely non-contentious, though it is true that the expression of a linguistic document is closely related to the text type. So further distinctions need to be noted than just [personal] v. [public]. But the arrival of the digital means of relay has substantially changed the situation as described in Table 8.4; typewriters are obsolete; friends are contacted by email; to someone engaged in writing, digital 'writing instruments' are everywhere. The orally produced message is evanescent unless captured by recording; a message in written form comes ready recorded, with a range of implications that the study of communication can hardly ignore. Writing in any case produces a material object; and a materially present message is much more subject to displacement than the spoken words, which typically do not go beyond the intended addressee, vanishing in thin air even as the speech event is occurring. With the advent of the digital means, and their increasing popularity of use, the speaker's text is potentially available to anyone who can lay their hands on the object. The text and the text's receiver do not necessarily match today: text may be in the hands of anyone, irrespective of what addressee the speaker might have had in mind while composing it. What is relevant is the erosion of the speaker's control on the dissemination of messages. An interesting consequence could happen be that the situation might affect common styles of communication. Either everything digitally mediated might be presented with the hidden eavesdropper in mind or one might ignore all differences between the familiar and the not familiar receivers, maintaining as addressee the distinction between 'official'– i.e., someone patently and obviously with a designation in some institution – or 'my group' – someone with fairly close and trusted. These social scenarios appear to provide interesting food for thought, but the more pressing question for this contribution is: where did the system S come from? In answering this question, I enter into a brief account of the complex disjunct entry point.

The above account establishes that the options of m-system S combine systematically with those in m-system C, which might lead to the supposition that system S has been derived in response to a more delicate analysis of the choice path [graphic; mediated: congruent]. It certainly helps in providing such an analysis, but this is not the whole story of system S, which straddles two distinct simultaneous sets, one to which access is allowed by the conjunct entry point called C: this is what was discussed above. But there is another entry point for which system S is accessible: this is by the choice of the option 'synchronic' (p1). The system P is a derivation from the conjunct entry point [phonic; mediated: congruent: synchronic]. Its options are [synchronic] (p1) and [asynchronic] (p2). The choice of option [synchronic] (p1) allows entry to a simultaneous set with two m-systems.

These two choice paths, one of which culminated in C and the other in P, cannot be combined at any point in this sys-net: their choice paths began with the mutually exclusive options [graphic] (a1 in PP) *or* [phonic] (a2 in PP) belonging to the same primary system of PP. But despite this incompatibility, the options of the m-system S are relevant to both. This is the kind of environment where a 'disjunct entry point' comes into action: this type of entry point calls for *at least* three simple systems working together. Thus, in the present case for the disjunct entry to work, both choices from the two systems C and P have to participate in turn: at any one point in the history of MC *either* an option from system C will enter system S combining with one of its options *or* one option of system P will. The elongated left facing square bracket, with one foot in one simultaneous set and the other foot in the other simultaneous set, indicates this 'either/or' requirement. This particular disjunct entry point appear so complex mainly because one by one both options of one m-system each from each simultaneous system need to access both the options one by one from system S. Table 8.4 shows what this looks like with respect to the m-system C; doing the same thing with the m-system P would simply double the number of choice paths. A simpler example of disjunct entry that could have been cited is from the system of MOOD at the stratum of lexicogrammar. It is a well-established fact that the option [declarative] derived from the system of indicative and the option [imperative] make a choice from the system of Tagging: the feature [declarative] may combine with [tagged] or [non-tagged]; similarly the feature [imperative] may combine with [tagged] or [non-tagged]; the history of [declarative] and [imperative] prevents them from ever combining, but either can enter the system in exclusion from the other. Though perhaps less common than the conjunct entry, instances of disjunct entry point are found both in lexicogrammar (c.f., Halliday and Matthiessen 2014, the system of MOOD) and in semantics (c.f., Hasan 2009b, 2013, the system of ROLE EXCHANGE).

System P, like system C, is introduced by the conjunct entry point with the choices path [phonic; mediated: congruent]. With the choice of [phonic] at PP, there will be hardly any time-lag between the 'oral' relay and [direct] 'aural' access. But the possibility of disruption in this normal pattern becomes a significant issue at reception point when the choice path contains the options [mediated: congruent], as it does for P; this is because mediation always allows 'displacement' for the text from its point of production, and in the case of [phonic] relay at PP, this would normally involve the intervention of both man and machine. The two options of the system derived from the conjunct entry are either 'synchronic' (p1) or 'a-synchronic' (p2): this latter is a resource for a number of options (see p5–p14 in Figure 8.6). The option [synchronic] p1 implies no noticeable time-lag; the message is received *as if within earshot*. This option acts as an entry point for a simultaneous set with two member systems. One of these m-system is the continuation of P; its options are [single] (p3) or [multiple] (p4). The option [single] implies one means of relay; while [multiple] refers to the possibility of more than one means of access to the [phonic; mediated; congruent: synchronic] message. At the heart of the options p1: p3 [synchronic: single] there is a mystery: it is [phonic] and [mediated]; nonetheless it is [synchronic]: and uses only one single means for accessing the mediated message; this cannot happen without the help of man and/or machine. The other m-system is none other than the S system that was encountered in the description of C above: the options of m-system S are familiar as either [personal] s1 or [public] s2, and they will combine the options p3 [single] and p3 [multiple]. The choice path produced by the combination 1p: p3; s1 [synchronic: single; personal] offers a clue to the mystery just noted: there does exist one mechanical device whereby the [phonic] relay may be [mediated: congruent: synchronic: single; personal]. The mediation occurs only by use of machine and the machine is the telephone. So the relay is [phonic] but received in [mediated] mode whereby there is no time-lag between message production and reception and only a single means of message access is used. As in the environment of C, the choice of [personal] s1 implies here too, that the speaker has control and chooses who will receive the message. If everything else remaining the same, only instead of [single], the option [multiple] p1 is chosen, this would imply that now more than one means of access is available to the receiver, though who the receiver is remains still under speaker control. It is not hard to recognize that the mediating technology would be some such as Skype; will mediate an oral message synchronically, while using multiple means such as gestures and visual and vocal contact, while also accessing a view of some part of the receiver's material situational setting. The combination of [public] s2 with [single] p3 would refer to a 'live broadcast', as for example with sports commentary, live interview on radio: here the receivers will not be known to the speaker or perhaps even to the interviewer. When [multiple] p4 and [public] s2 combine, then mediation is by audio-visual technology that allows the use of different means of accessing information.

Much of what has been described by the options of the two simultaneous systems in Figure 8.6 implies more than just material contact is at issue; the realizations could often extend to the text's meaning-wording. For example, we know that with the option [a-synchronic], with the aim of retaining aural access at a distant point from relay, the message must be audio-recorded, and that data orally presented and audio-recorded is affected seriously by 'noise' of any kind. This issue has not been raised. The complexities of [phonic] expression reappearing as [phonic] after being 'mediated' clearly go beyond what is indicated above (see the options p5–p14). If some 'real' phonic data is recorded 'by others' 'for others' in carrying out a 'professional' duty, this may often be straight forward, e.g., a person in charge records the proceedings, as often happens on official occasions such as symposia. But suppose the despatch of the message to an addressee is professionally required, and someone records that message on the dictaphone: here the phonically relayed message would be received by that intended addressee in [graphic] not in [phonic] mode. This possibility could be described by some options in Q (dealing with [incongruent] access). What is missing is an intermediate stage: imagine a message is recorded for being mediated to someone in an official capacity, it is obvious that as a recording it would be accessed only by an office staff member, who is clearly not the addressee but the person in the middle who transcribes. The possibilities of what can happen to a recorded message are about as varied as are those of [graphic; mediated: congruent: public], WHETHER [conventional OR digital]. So the description as presented in P (p5–p14), though probably not incorrect, might be in need of some improvement. There appears to be a need for every parameter to recognize the relevance of the others. But is there any sys-net convention to enable this cross referencing?

8.3.5 Cross-referencing diacritics in sys-nets: permeability of parameters

Cross-referencing in the sys-net has been in practice from its early days (e.g., Halliday 1973a: 47; Kress 1976), typically by use of what I am referring to as DIACRITICS here since they consist of signals attached to option(s) or, in some cases, to system entries. Their function in general terms is to signal relations across options or systems, and the signal should be found at each stratum. These are either 'inter-systemic' or 'intra-systemic'. Both may be viewed as a kind of shorthand, since either type can actually be replaced by some more 'wiring' (connecting with lines, brackets, braces, etc.); diacritics are preferred as making less demand on space and energy. Figure 8.7, shows both kinds of diacritics, and would fit into Figure 8.3 in the remaining entry indicator called tenor of discourse, whose description it represents. Here I discuss only those options that will illustrate the important points to be made about the diacritics. The description of the Tenor of discourse is presented from three simultaneous dimensions that together describe INTERACTANT RELATIONS. These are called (1) the AGENTIVE ROLES, (2) the TEXTUAL ROLES, and (3) the SOCIAL ROLES. Figure 8.7, a fragment of the total sys-net, represents only the last two dimensions, and the second is not described with respect to all its features. A glossary of the terms referring to options in this figure is presented as Appendix C, at the end of this chapter.

It is important to add straightaway that the discussion of Figure 8.7 owes much to the research presented in this volume; many comments that might appear cryptic here are most probably elaborated elsewhere. Tenor is conceptualized as purely about interactant relations. Ignoring the dimension of AGENTIVE ROLE, I open the discussion with TEXTUAL ROLES which concerns speaker/addressee relations with reference to the text under production. The features of the TEXTUAL ROLES are described by one simultaneous set and one simple m-system. The concern of the simultaneous set is SPEAKER STANCE, and it opens with two simple independent systems. The first m-system concerns (speaker) ATTITUDE and the second specifies what or who forms the FOCUS of that attitude. The m-system in CONTEXTUAL ROLES is an individual m-system: its concern ADDRESSEE'S MATERIAL PRESENCE. The relations of options in this last m-system appear to be pivotal to register classification, as perhaps indicated by the fact that this system attracts more diacritics than any other. Two distinct kinds of diacritical notation can be seen in this system: the diamond diacritics, each carrying an address, and also paired arrow. The diamond diacritics signal inter-systemic relations, whereas the arrow ones are used to signal the intra-systemic relations.

Figure 8.7: A fragment of tenor: textual and social roles

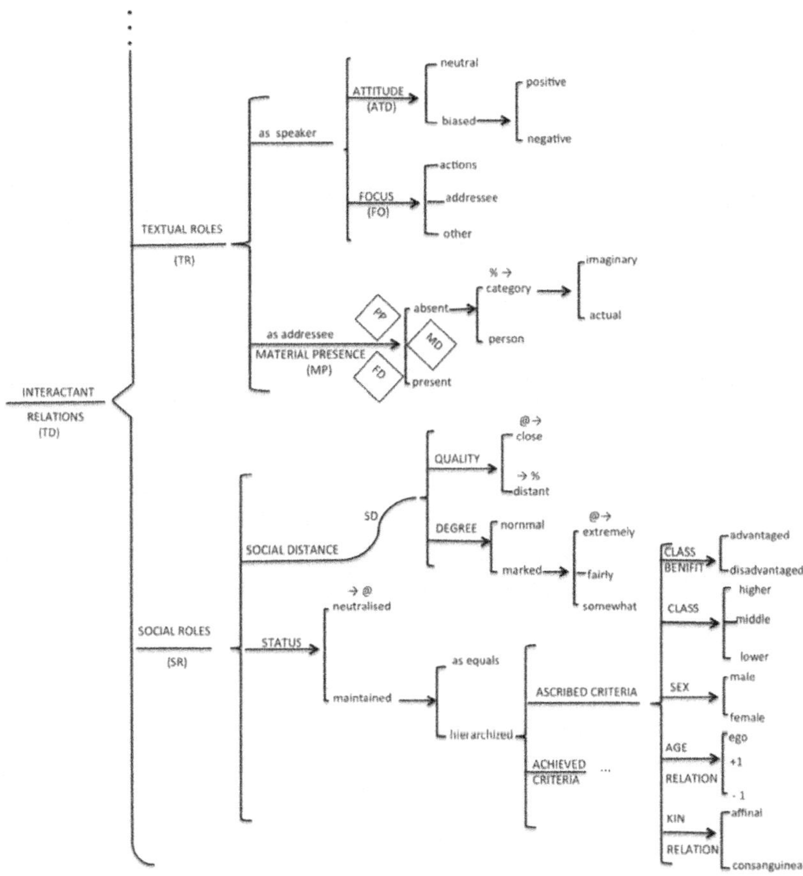

Note: For glossary of options in Figure 8.7, see Appendix C

The early history of the sys-net in SFL shows that the use of the DIA-MOND DIACRITIC signals inter-systemic relation: so, for example, in present-ing 'English system networks' where, most probably, this notation was first used in written form, Kress (1976: 101) says: 'This paper, previously unpublished, was written between May and August 1964 and formed the substance of a course on the description of English given by Halliday in Indiana in the system concerned with University during that time'. Its use has, however, not been much in vogue since the 1970s. I hope to show that the diamond still has its uses. In Figure 8.7, three diamonds jostle for space around the entry indicator for the system ADDRESSEE'S MATERIAL PRESENCE

(MP). Their attachment to this system indicates some relation between the host system here and those systems whose address is shown in the diamonds. Those addresses take one to both the MODE OF DISCOURSE (MD) and the FIELD OF DISCOURSE (FD), as well as indicating by the third diamond that the choice of 'present' in MP is specifically relevant to the choice of options at the PRODUCTION POINT (PP) in MATERIAL CONTACT. The latter were briefly indicated in the previous section (8.3.1.4) by way of discussing the complex entry conditions.

Two interrelated problems are here in this mode of indicating inter-systemic relations. First, the identity of a sys-net – where it begins and ends: it can be simply stipulated that every system that describes any aspect of one particular point of origin belongs to the same sys-net, in other words the 'comprehensive system' (Section 8.3.1.1). But the size of such a sys-net even for just one unit makes it hard to process it in systemic notations, and even if this were practicable, it is not very likely that the kinds of relation pointed out above can then be made to reach across that system to another comprehensive system: this type of inter-systemic relation most often occurs across parts of the same 'comprehensive sys-net'. Second, and related to the previous problem: no matter what rationale is used for dividing the 'comprehensive sys-net' into 'a' series of component sys-nets, this can be of use in indicating inter-systemic relations only if addresses such as MD, FD, PP and so on can be decoded. One way of ensuring this is to 'standardize' terminology as for example with terms such as 'sentence', 'noun', 'word', etc., (although still ill-defined); failing this there has to be some way of clearly indicating the scope of the system under description and those mentioned as addresses in the diamond diacritic, perhaps as legends attached to the sys-net where the diacritics occur. It also seems important to attempt cross-reference in both systems rather than just one: so for example, in Figure 8.6, there should be a cross-reference to ADDRESS-EE'S MATERIAL PRESENCE as relevant to MODE OF DISCOURSE as a whole. But it might be argued that the relation between them is a proof that they belong in 'the system' they are naming; and that raises the questions: rather than face these additional 'fussy bits', why not put all those individual systems together in one and the same system following current suggestions? I briefly return to this issue below in Section 8.4.

Moving now to the 'intra-systemic' cross-referencing, this is signalled by a pair of arrows combined with one symbol. The first clear gloss I find for it is as follows (1973a: 47):

a*→ ....x→* [or any paired symbol] *x* is unmarked with respect to *a* [if *a* then *x*].

As shown above, in fact, the arrow signal has three elements to it. First to occur is some symbol, e.g. %→ attached to *that particular option* to which the relation applies. If the symbol is located *before* the arrow as in %→ then conjunction constitutes the 'if clause' (to be read here as: 'if in MP the option [category] is chosen'); then if the same symbol follows the arrow (e.g., → %) at another point in the system, this would act as the 'then clause' (to be read here as: 'then in the system of QUALITY, only the option [distant] can be chosen'). This clearly shows that the relation indicated by the arrow diacritic is 'pre-emptive': given the specified circumstance, the privilege of free choice is pre-empted from the starting option, which must combine with the option indicated by the second pair part of the diacritic (and whatever other relations that might entail).

The first of these intra-systemic relations occurs in Figure 8.7 where the starting arrow marks the option [category] in the system of MP. (%→), and the second pair part if found on the option [distant] inside the same sys-net. This would be read here as stating 'if addressee is [category], then in the system of Quality, only the choice [distant] is allowed. So according to Figure 8.7 choosing the option 'category' in MP system is equal to choosing 'distant' in the system of QUALITY. This system belongs to SOCIAL DISTANCE (SD) which is a kind of relationship that arises from the interactive biography of speaker-addressee relation. In effect then by using this diacritic what the sys-net has indicated is that IF the speaker is 'talking' to a [category], i.e. if the addressee is not known to the speaker, THEN their social relation arising from their interactive biography can only be [distant]. However entering into that system of QUALITY in SOCIAL DISTANCE entails also choosing from the member system of DEGREE; the choice from here will depend on the nature of the options permitted by [category]. If the category is [imaginary] – i.e., the speaker has personally not encountered any specimens of that category – then the degree of personal relation is likely to be [extremely] [distant]; but if [category] is more delicately described as [actual] – meaning that the speaker has actually met some specimens of that category, e.g., the lecturer in relation to the first year class – then the degree of personal relation might vary accordingly. However, what cannot vary is the fact that relation will be [distant], extremely distant, or fairly distant; but it cannot change over to [close]. This follows from the fact that a realizational statement once made cannot be abrogated.[22]

In this same system of QUALITY there is another signal for a pre-emptive choice relation; it is attached to the option [close] and also to [extremely]; the arrow diacritic that signals it, appears as @→ whose second pair part is the option [neutralized] in the system of STATUS (in SOCIAL ROLE (SR)).

Here there is a complex 'if clause' – if [close] and if [extremely], then in the system of STATUS all choices are pre-empted except [neutralized]. To interpret this in ordinary language: when interactants are in an [extremely] [close] personal relation then the hierarchizing systems that maintain group boundaries do not apply.

The relations indicated by the above diacritics will be found also in sys-nets representing the description of language internal units, though per-haps both kinds of marking seem to occur more densely in the systems of context than elsewhere. That said, without further research, I am not able to say exactly how this actual fact might be interpreted; two explanations come to mind: either less attention has been paid to the facility of diacritics in doing semantics and lexicogrammar, or the contextual systems are truly far more complex than the language internal ones. I am not aware of any full length manual or discussion of what I am calling the representational technology of sys-net; nor am I aware of any courses designed to teach this aspect. So neglect of the facilities seems not an unlikely explanation. At the same time, Halliday has often drawn attention to the fact that language is 'big'; the division of the labour of description has set up different strata, different units at each language internal stratum, and specified relations that bring them together. Culture cannot conceivably be less big than language, but as conceptualized here it is mono-stratal and it has no units. The only organization being imposed on it is that which arises from its resonance with the metafunctions with their foundations in human activity. Seen from that point of view 'The formal properties of any given language event will be those associated with the interaction of field, mode and style [aka tenor, RH]' (Halliday *et al.* 1964: 93): so permeability is logically expected.

Whatever the case, to me the permeability of the parameters has always appealed as a robust feature visible in the shape of 'social practice' (cf., Hasan 1973c), and evident in our community's recognition (e.g., the dis-cussion in this section): it cannot be written off, and I have welcomed the use of both the diacritics to indicate the interactions of field, tenor and mode because any other solution has seemed problematic. Apart from whether the diacritics create an unnecessary complication or if and how they might be relevant to the classification of registers, reflection on them does seem to make contribution to linguistics in general; these should not be ignored: if the diamond relation occurs only at some specific points in the various systems pertaining to contextual parameters, then this might be treated as a validation of the context metafunction resonance hypothesis, which has bearing on other matter. Besides, direct attention to what is in common to those occasions where these relations typically occur is likely to be informative.

8.3.6 The semantics of paradigmatic description

Although the orderly quality of the systemic presentation in the sys-net goes a long way in accurately representing the statements about the descriptum, this by itself does not ensure the accuracy of the represented description itself. The paradigmatic account of language sets itself clear goals: it aims to describe the potential rather than the instance; descriptions in SFL thus seek to characterize the system and its process. But rather than create a barrier between the system and the systemic process of language by examining the patterns of regularity such as can be manifested instantially. This is significant because the regularities of human behaviour form the foundations of a community's social history; and the perspective has the possibility of explaining what motivations might have shaped both *langue* and *parole*.

These goals and aspirations apply not just to meaning-wording but also to the 'handling of speech events' (Firth 1957: 181): the categories for describing context are in principle no different from those of lexicogrammar. So here, too, SFL must seek to characterize the patterns of regularity in con/text while investing also in research on inherent variation in language, which is central to understanding the instance-system relations: this is what makes novelty novel. It follows that the semantics of the paradigmatic description of text-in-context concerns a vast area of enquiry, one face of which is the world that affects speakers living in it and acting on it, and the other, the virtual system of language, the wordings, that allow speakers to externalize their relation to that world. So, no matter what the content of con/text is, it is likely to be, first and foremost, as an area that will be closest to the analyst's own experiences of how things happen in real life. And yet, not ignoring what the tangible reality of situation may seem to be personally to the experiencing subject, it seems that in describing what speaking with reference to context means in linguistics, the primary focus has to be on the typical; it is only this approach that will take the analyst to the relations in the communally recognized potential of the contexts of situation. It is this latter perspective on the 'content of contextual description' that I will discuss below. Ignoring many details, I will limit the discussion to just three issues that appear essential, namely: (1) defining the domain of description; (2) analysing the analytic categories; and (3) using the concept of 'realization' as a means of validating the description offered.

8.3.6.1   Defining the descriptive domain

If it is accepted that the point of origin is the ultimate descriptum, then it might be no more than a truism to claim that the understanding of its nature is the first step in the descriptive enterprise. Nor is it open to question that the process of description will reveal details about the descriptum not suspected before the actual analysis began. In the case of context, the familiarity with the words 'context' and 'situation' has perhaps been rather misleading: the first to raise an alarm against this tendency was of course Firth in his critique of Malinowski (Firth 1968). But, even today it appears necessary to stand back and ask two basic questions: the *first* concerns the relations of culture and situation to language as the object of enquiry in the science of linguistics, and the *second* concerns the positioning of context in systemic functional linguistic theory. I will return to these but first something far less contentious and what follows from it.

In presenting the concept of the point of origin and of the ultimate descriptum, I have tried to show the centrality of these concepts. Thus Section 8.3.1 with its sub-sections leaves no doubt that the description presented in a contextual sys-net is simply an 'un-packing' of some aspect of what these terms mean. This does not happen in one fell swoop, but system by system, SE by SE and option by option; the descriptions represented in the sys-nets build a profile of what contextual parameters stand for. So in the virtual beginning of the descriptum in the linguist's conceptualization of it lies its end as the description represented in a contextual sys-net. All of this suggests one thing: that the conceptualization of the descriptum is the first step; this is where the options come from; this is where the relations of options and systems will be rooted, which is precisely what description consists in. There is no book of rules about this process, but without underplaying the importance of personal experience – though in principle it is not the same as the theoretical concept of instance – the interpretation of terms such as context of situation is best approached theoretically as Firth advised decades ago. That can only mean one thing – to understand how this concept is related to others, and how they act together to achieve the goals of the theory.

From this perspective, the CMR hypothesis (Section 8.2.3.2, and elsewhere) appears attractive. The hypothesis presents the most comprehensive and theoretically based proposition that linguistics has had to offer by way of defining the domain of the three parameters of context. It recommends retaining the integrity of each contextual parameter by treating each as metafunctionally oriented, and, in so doing, it offers general criteria, not just instances, for recognizing the contextual features and their linguistic realization: the correlates are subject to a principle. So far as the metafunctional hypothesis itself is concerned, it has been used successfully in SFL, as is evident from its use in the description of both semantics and lexicogrammar. Register classification becomes a possibility. The paradigmatic mode of description and the technique of its representation as in a sys-net are well suited to testing the probabilistic hypothesis concerning the realizational relations of situational and linguistic features. It is not necessary to repeat that the probabilistic nature of the hypothesis can be handled satisfactorily. If using the full range of representational facilities, the analysis of contextual parameters reveals a significantly higher degree of cross-referencing in and across the sys-nets (such as presented in Section 8.3.1.5) than considered valid in terms of the default metafunctional orientation, then the CMR hypothesis will clearly need to be revisited; it may even have to be jettisoned if a better hypothesis is available, though indications are this would not be the case, c.f., Figure 8.7 where the markings are not at all dense compared to the number of options that will not require cross-reference.

8.3.6.2 *Analysing the categories of analysis*

In SFL description works its way from top down: more specifically, it begins with a category and proceeds by identifying significant properties by reference to which that category may be validly sub-classified; and as the next step, each of the latter properties is further analysed to allow more delicate sub-classification, continuing in this manner right up to the most delicate property. Thus the first step in this process of description is the conceptualization of the top-most category: it is the only un-analysed term in the entire comprehensive sys-net, known as the point of origin, (aka the ultimate descriptum). Following this principle of description, it is the analysis of this term that gives entry to the primary system with at least two options; and following the above mode, the analysis continues what was earlier described as the 'cycle of birth and re-birth' responsible for the derivation of the sys-net. The possibilities of variation in this general process have also been described. Based on the implications of this condensed account of systemic descriptions, some important characteristics of systemic options are presented below.

A system comes into being only when the possibility of choosing options is available; this makes option and choice a central concept in all system-based description. Clearly the options presented in the sys-net are witness to the linguist's conception of the descriptum; it is difficult to say any more on how options find their way into sys-nets, but some general properties of options may be stated. *First,* every option is produced in analysing a given category; this includes the primary system, and each next step adds to the degree of descriptive delicacy. There is no logical end to this process: descriptions are always open to greater delicacy. *Second,* the relation of all the options following the 'entry point' of a system typically stays stable; and through the relations of one option to those along the legitimate systemic paths, all the options are eventually linked to the ultimate descriptum named by the point of origin. *Third,* at any one point in the descriptive process, the properties of each chosen option are described exhaustively by all those options which will constitute the next system; it is assumed that no more can be said at that given degree of delicacy about that previously chosen option. *Fourth,* each option of the system(s) at any given point labels a distinct property of the term whose analysis brings it into being; each further step in delicacy introduces new properties into that analysis. *Fifth,* each system, whether individual or an m-system, has a particular perspective: often, overt labels are not attached to each system in the network so as to avoid crowding the representation, but when a label does appear it is expected to conform with that perspective. In other words, options named in the system will be in 'keeping' with that system's perspective; to give a trite but clear example, no competent linguist would create a simple system that displays the options 'narrate' or [phonic] as contrasting options. *Sixth,* if there are simultaneous sets, this requires a free combination of options across its m-systems; in that case, either all options will be compatible, or in order to prevent internal contradiction, an arrow diacritic will indicate some modification. *Finally,* each system produces some selection expressions (SEs) which, by definition, present the relations of the included options. The legitimacy of the SE cannot even begin to be checked in any real sense unless its options display a coherent picture concerning that which they are describing. Since options are presented and ordered in a sys-net with the purpose of displaying the description of a category, both their compatibility within the SE and their applicability to what is being described are necessary. No matter how huge the sys-net, all its options are mutually related in the manner analogous to that in which the signs in the sign system of language are: it is this interconnectivity that underlies the concept of a comprehensive sys-net.

The above is then a general statement of where the options come from and what they are capable of doing by way of description. Obviously the clearer the ideas about what constitutes the domain of description, the more consistent the description is likely to be. The sys-net itself has no concern with the semantic notions of consistency, compatibility, appliability and so on: so long as it is 'readable', i.e., the signals are as they 'should be', the sys-net presents what has been put into it as the offered description. Validity is a semantic notion; it does not concern the sys-net *per se*: it is the analyst's concern. If it is accepted that the 'cycle of birth and re-birth' of options in systems is what underlies sys-net derivation and that sub-categorization is what underlies the descriptive continuity, then obviously an understanding of what the entry point means will be relevant to the selection of the options and to the relations between them; changing mid-stream the conception of what the system's entry point means is likely to create confusion. For example, if the dimension of FIELD OF DISCOURSE is conceptualized as concerning activity, then the systems introduced by its entry points could cover everything that classifies action, such as types of action ([material] [verbal]), the sphere of action ([local], [institution-alized]), and the status of action ([quotidian] [specialized]). Obviously not anyone can engage in every activity: class, expertise, maturity, sex, and prestige of the doers come readily to mind as some constraining vari-ables. Should these vectors be therefore brought into field? This depends: if the description is purely 'notional' then one might; otherwise tenor is where these properties of interactants would seem more appropriate. The price to pay is a cross-referencing diacritic; while the advantages appear considerable. Apart from the fact that it maintains the CMR predictions thus avoiding regressive consequences, it is very likely that these vectors would be relevant also to choices in the system of STATUS especially in maintaining HIERARCHIZED ROLES. And whether or not this will apply could very much depend on the choice in SOCIAL DISTANCE: if the options [close] and [extremely] apply, then hierarchical constraints might be 'neutralized'.

Inside the system there is no time or space; given the acceptance of greater delicacy as the method for exploring the limits of some potential, the issue is simply what relations need to be selected, what consequences the selection of one option in a system has for another; how the meaning of one influences that of the others. So before and after, previous and follow-ing are used with a meaning that may be quite different from that in which they are applied to material time and space. In the absence of material time and space, what guides the logic of placing a system of options here or there rests on ideas about what would lead to an exhaustive, accurate and explanatory description of that which is described – and that is implicit in the analyst's view of the theory. Thus, having conceptualized mode of discourse as concerned with aspects of contact between the speaker and the addressee, when a simultaneous set of primary systems is presented there (as in Figure 8.6) to describe the nature of the MATERIAL CONTACT, the implication is that all phenomena describable as that part of MODE, i.e., ways of creating *contact between the speaker's message and the addressee* can be exhaustively described by using the options of systems included here. When/if this does not happen, the particular network will be retained, with any necessary modification or will be discarded. If the issues cannot be resolved, it might be thought necessary to go back to the drawing board and create a totally new sys-net.

One quick comment, on context as material phenomena. According to one common saying, seeing is believing: the immediacy of experienced reality is of course undeniable. It seems to me that acknowledging the truth of this axiom does not entail ignoring the fact that reality is refracted through language. Freed from the limits of vision and sensation, the scope of this reality is beyond measure; it is a reality that nurtures and is nurtured by human minds; it is made of meanings that only the semiological system of language can produce, and that can only be 'read' by 'sound' minds familiar with that language. This mind, made by the experience of languaging in the community, knows more about the context of situation than the material situation itself can ever show: and the only way we can establish what that mind views as 'the context' is to be aware of what goes on in language. Register is after all a linguistic category, and the contextual features relevant to its classification are likely to be those realized as some linguistic patterns. Common sense may declare that no action is without a goal; and goal orientation may appear a relevant situational variable to introduce into the description of field. Indeed this is what I had thought when introducing options such as 'visible' or 'invisible' goal orientation, closely related to another kind of goal orientation, i.e., 'short term' or 'long term'.[2] The context for this invention was a debate in socio-semantic variation in mother-child dialogues (Hasan 2009b: 93) from the perspective of the role of every day talk in the formation of consciousness, which was an important issue from the perspective of 'socialization'. Locally, i.e., for that particular set of problems, it had proved helpful. It is true that the semantic style of linguistic action in the long run enacts interpersonal relations: people living together and habitually interacting do tend to develop reciprocal forms of behaviour and attitudes. But in less than a decade I was walking away from the inclusion of these as contextual options; and I did present what seemed fairly careful arguments against my earlier views (Hasan 1999b: 233–237): but unfortunately these concepts have been adopted (sometimes under different names), very often with acknowledgement of those detailed reservations but seldom, if ever, offering any serious reason for ignoring them. It appears to me now that the entire discourse of purpose, goal, and outcome is fraught with problems similar to any discourse of intentionality in relation to any verbal interaction. Had I paid more careful attention to the writings of Wittgenstein, Firth, Whorf, Vygotsky, Halliday or Bernstein, I might have avoided being guilty of introducing these terms. This is not to say that human actions are goal-less: goal inheres in the action. When goals are not 'in' the action, there is no linguistic means of knowing which of the invisible goals is being pursued; and from this perspective, it is worthwhile reflecting on the difference between deception which is successful and deception which gives itself away.

8.3.6.3 *Realization: the renewal of connection with experience*

The centrality of the realizational relation for the semantics of paradigmatic description is quite obvious from the previous pages. A contextual sys-net without an indication of how its options are realized linguistically has serious disadvantages: it is open to misreading; it certainly lacks linguistic validation; and its use in the classification of register is therefore open to doubt. As elsewhere in contextual matters, the discussion is potentially huge. In this section I will limit myself to four issues: (1) the function of realization; (2) realization statements; (3) the selection expression; and (4) the trinocular perspective.

The term 'realization' was introduced in SFL in the second half of the 1960s to model the relations across the strata. Effortless as it seems, language use (aka parole) is a complex activity, and the model postulates different orders of abstraction, each recognized in the theory as a distinct stratum: what realization does is to show how one kind of abstraction, say 'semantic energy', may be 'exchanged' for another, namely 'lexicogrammatical energy', which is itself 'transduced' into yet another order of abstraction, namely 'phonology', and that is 'transformed' into actual sound patterns (the phonic relay) which are what impinge on the addressee's senses. It is usually difficult to produce efficient synonyms, and more so in the case of theoretical terms, which inhabit a virtual universe. I have settled more recently on the term 'transducer' and its derivatives, which had been used in linguistics before as the nearest approximation to what 'realization' does (Lamb 1966). The Macquarie Dictionary defines 'transducer' (1981: 1834) as 'any device which receives energy from one medium or *transmission system*, and supplies *related energy* to another medium or transmission system' [emphasis added, RH]. So the relation of 'realization' acts as a *transducer*, bringing together by a theoretical artifice the different transmission systems which had, in the first place, been separated by an act of analysis. Needless to say, in using metaphors such as 'transmission', 'translation', or 'transduction', there is no implication whatever that in actual language use a distinct transitional point is apprehended by users from one stratum to the next: as I myself have said, the process presents itself as a 'seamless flow', in which for the layman the phonic flow 'becomes' the 'flow of meaning'.

This seemingly simple 'fact' of 'perceiving' the binary nature of the process – sound and meaning – has been recognized since the very beginning of deliberations on language. However, as Saussure himself pointed out this too is, in fact, not a fact, since if meaning and sound stood separate there is neither a signified nor a signifier; in this sense their perception as a beginning and an end is also a fiction. In terms of Saussure, the facts are 'irrational'. Be that as it may, no functional linguist would explain meaning in terms of phones; the solidarity of meaning is on the one hand with context, which acts as the measure of the relevance of speech, and on the other with wording, which is the construer of meaning. Semantic and lexicogrammatical units, i.e., units of meaning-wording, are abstract; they can make no direct connection with the human body; and to be accessed by the intellect there has to exist some bond of association which renders the bodily accessed phonic/graphic pattern 'intellig-ible'. Semantics has been described in SFL as an 'interface'; but its relation to material situation is probably no more direct than that of phonetics to air waves. Modern linguistics has been and still is searching for an explanatory account of how this web of myriad specific associations between the sens-ible and the intellig-ible gains currency so as to allow all the varieties of linguistic interaction, known as registers. The process is immensely complex: and a large number of theoretical concepts and relations spanning two intricate systems, those of culture and those of language, have been conceptualized in the search for a viable solution. The classification of register is a significant issue in this intricate research. And realization features wherever a category occurs.

Different ways of notating realization have been suggested in SFL (for some discussion on kinds of realization statement, see Hasan 1987b). A rather arbitrary demand was to place the realization of a particular option close to where it occurs in the sys-net. This, like the demand to show the name of each simple system in a sys-net, becomes impracticable when, over the years, the description plumbs the depth of complexity in the category, which populates the sys-net thickly with systems and options. The alternative is to tabulate the realizations option by option, as presented here in Appendices A–C, or as a table/note below the sys-net itself, e.g. Figures 8.2 and 8.3 in this paper. Ideally the realization statement should be made in terms of the systemic features representing the categories of the stratum below: so the contextual systemic features are shown to be realized as semantic, the semantic features as lexicogrammatical, the lexicogrammatical features as phonological, and the phonological features as phonetic. In this way the two strata primarily concerned with substance are woven into language, since neither context nor phonetics is a picture of 'what is really out there': context is conditioned by its relation to semantic patterns, and phonetics by its relation to phonological patterns. This way of presenting realization statements has been tried to some extent in systemic functional semantic studies (Cloran 1994, 1995, 1999a; Hasan 2009b, 2013; Williams 1995).

However, much description, especially on the stratum of semantics, remains rather 'patchy': while it is comparatively easy to offer the semantic features relevant to the textual option [present], it is far more difficult to do this for a term such as [imaginary] as located in the choice path [absent: category: imaginary]. So, often, a realizational statement of contextual features is made informally by offering a gloss, as in Hasan (1999b, 2009b or appendices/ tables here) and Butt (2004a, and Figure 8.2 here). The progress in lexicogrammar raises hopes that this problem may be overcome in time (witness, for example, mood sys-net in Cloran 1994 compared with mood in Halliday and Matthiessen 2014). A far more serious point is that the meanings of the terms as options in a particular sys-net are typically specific to it: their meaning is therefore completely conditioned by 'the company they keep'. So 'unifying primary options' from distinct systems is to lose the specific meanings of those options, which were construed originally by their positioning in those sys-nets. This is where the concept of 'selection expression' (SE) comes in as a device that captures that meaning.

The term 'selection expression' was briefly introduced much earlier together with 'choice path'. As a complete statement of all the options and their relations in the traversal of one single systemic path through a sys-net, the SE represents the 'history' of the choices that underlie the properties of one major sub-category of the descriptum. I commented earlier that in a sys-net there is no time or space: the history recorded in an SE is the history of the logical relations among those choices. To guard against contradiction and inconsistency in the description, the 'permanency of realization statements' is an accepted convention. For example, if the primary option [phonic] is glossed as 'relay at PP in speaker's voice', then this meaning cannot be altered at any point in that sys-net (Figure 8.6). I believe this is what Mann (1985) had meant in introducing the concept of REALIZATIONAL INHERITANCE: the appearance of an option in any SE of a particular sys-net will continue to have the significance assigned to it realizationally. Nothing can be altered, deleted, or contradicted (except by increase in delicacy). I would foreground the fact that each option is required to have a unique significance within that sys-net. These principles are clearly necessary to ensure the validity of the description. Continuing with the example of [phonic]: if a choice path represents the relation [phonic; direct: congruent] this, though true, would be redundant, since [phonic] will *always* inherit 'relay at PP in speaker's voice', and its [direct] reception would therefore be aural. Thus the option [congruent] fails to add new information in the absence of any other variant possibility; it would be therefore not a 'good option'. By contrast, [phonic] in conjunction with [mediated: congruent] tells a significantly different story – that despite the intervention of some agency, human or mechanical, the 'natural' pairing of oral-aural is main-tained and the phonic is still original relay in speaker's voice; moreover a credible variant possibility exists that in a 'mediated' environment recep-tion could be [incongruent]. So the placing of the options [congruent] or [incongruent] as in Figure 8.6 is informative: the choice path [phonic; mediated: incongruent] may be glossed as 'original relay in speaker's voice mediated mechanically is accessed by some other modality'. Previously in presenting the analysis in lectures I had adopted the expression 'spoken as if written'. The present version appears preferable as it does not confuse channel and style of wording. Whether the description is 'correct/valid' or not will depend on what Firth called the 'renewal of connection with data': when it comes to language, the only validity condition is this: does the community recognize this convention of presenting content or expression? If the answer is 'yes' then instantiation and realization must meet in the instance of the system. Hence, the claim that the theoretical significance of 'instance' differs from the general conception: the really suitable word for that is the 'actual'. The actual may depart from the 'typical' in unpredict-able ways. With this emphasis on the 'typical', the value of a sys-net may be described as determined by the degree of its validity.

To conclude this discussion of SE, it is not the number of systems or options in a contextual sys-net that make it 'good': what matters is how accurate and insightful it proves to be. Simplifying, this depends on two characteristics: one, the validity of its description – what categories of reg-isters it can identify that would be communally recognized as language varieties, and second, how accurate its statements of the relations of options as represented in the sys-net are. If either is open to doubt, no matter how 'extensive' the set of systemic representations its value is questionable. The SEs of a sys-net present a 'summary' form of the many systemic paths created by the relations of both dependency and simultaneity between the options. Where the path itself proves open to debate, the question of validity cannot be reasonably raised. So if we take Butt's contextual description of the FIELD OF DISCOURSE, this opens with a simultaneous set consisting of four member systems (2004a: 24). This means, unless otherwise indicated, that the options of each of these m-systems are combinable within the limits placed by mutually exclusive options; the computed SEs in this description will be so enormous that their calculation or representation is beyond my means here. But take just one system, that of GOAL ORIENTATION (Butt 2004a: 35), which itself opens with a simultaneous system consisting of three members; and again as before no constraint on the free combination of the options is indicated. But the combinations do appear quite problematic: for example, option 'immediate[1]' when combined with 'unconscious[4]': inaccessible[4.2]' makes little sense. The option 'immediate[1]' is glossed as 'Game-Win or Auction-Buy'; but it is not clear that this could be described as a goal orientation that is 'unconscious: inaccessible'. Similarly, the combination of the three terms referred to Hasan (1999b), namely [independent] or [aligned] or [integrated], with the option [immediate] or with [longitudinal] would be hugely problematic. It is worth pointing out that at present hardly any contextual sys-net is more than tentative: all are at a nascent stage. The danger in taking the 'extensive' sys-nets at face value is that with so many options in the sys-net something from the array of options could be applied to an actual case as being 'the best amongst those available'. In the absence of even a few indicative SEs, it is not easy to know what one is doing and why.

In this situation, to gain some idea of the complexity of the realizational relations, it may be helpful to turn to the concept of 'trinocularity' (Halliday 2009: 79–80). Known as the 'trinocular perspective', it can be adopted in the investigation of any category from three closely related points of view: the perspective can be applied in the environment of other axes, but my concern here is with realization relations, particularly with reference to text-in-context, and I shall focus on the three contiguous strata on the 'content plane' in SFL theory, namely context, semantics, and lexicogrammar, since these are closely relevant to the production of the meaning-wording that, for the most part, constitutes the semantic face of text. Even though the spectrum of the entire verbal interaction will not be described, trinocularity can provide a good insight into the intimate realizational relations from the perspective of these three strata. Stating a general principle, in the middle of the trio is some category that realizes some feature(s) from 'above', and is itself realized by some feature from 'below'; while 'around' the middle category are the resources relevant to the realization of the category above, and to be realized by the ones below.

I begin with a sketchy scenario in order to demonstrate the trinocular perspective in action: suppose that the middle stratum is the semantic one, then the stratum 'above' is context, and the one essential element always present in it is interactants, bearing the 'speaker/addressee roles'. I have argued that the speaker role is always materially present in the situation and semantically present in the text, i.e., in its meaning-wording; as opposed to this the addressee role is always present semantically but may be absent materially. Suppose on this basis, the speaker is an employer; his addressee is his secretary; and the activity is planning a response to a message from a third party. The question on the floor is when this activity should be undertaken; and in response to this query the speaker wishes to use some variant of [demand; service] (Hasan 2009b, 2013).

Now, in terms of contextual features, the kind of field they are concerned with is managing the performance of a category of 'doing', such as despatch, send, write, respond, and a category of related objects, e.g., response, reply, message, letter. This observation presents a profile of field where verbal action has the features [constitutive]; sphere of action is [specialized] (Hasan 1999b: 311). In producing the meaning-wording, i.e., the text, the speaker/addressee will refer to at least the category of actions and objects just noted contextually. The scenario implies that the textual role of addressee is materially [present]; this suggests the relay at point of production will be [phonic]; the exchange between interactants is face to face. Since the addressee is materially present, the textual roles are potentially 'reversible'. Their agentive role is 'quasi permanent'; that is to say, they regularly interact in a specifiable capacity (here postulated as employer-employee). The social distance between them is very likely to be at least [normal] (that is, in keeping with the employer–employee relation) or [somewhat; close]. Whichever the case, it implies that the textual roles are more likely to be 'reversible' than not. This might mean that the feature 'spoken' in the system of ELOCUTION in SEMANTIC CONTACT (SC) will combine with the options [phonic] [direct] in MATERIAL CONTACT. In view of the text's context and the interactant relations stated so far, phoric reference to previously mentioned actions, objects, etc. can be expected by way of CONTINUITY in SC. This is a brief and indicative account of what the interactants are extremely likely to 'know' about their interactive context of situation. There is certainly more to the information provided contextually, but hopefully the above account will suffice in indicating how the contextual features activate the meaning-wording produced by speaker/addressee as the text. Remarkably, as contextual features and the meanings that realize them are discussed, they would appear to support the predictions in the CMR hypothesis.

Turning now to look 'around' at the stratum of semantics: here the question is what resources are around for demanding goods-and-services, i.e., for choosing, as a response to the secretary's question on the floor, some appropriate pattern from the family of messages that consists of 'command-like' messages (Hasan 2009a, 2013). The semantic stratum can present a large set of possibilities each of which will be heard as some kind of demand to undertake an action in a particular way so as to make a difference to the existing scenario (= command), varying in what goods-and-service are being demanded, and what relation the asking will be enacting with the addressee. It is highly probable, in view of the interactants' tenor relations as described above, that the command will NOT have the feature [plea] or such softeners as *if you don't mind, if it is not inconvenient*; and it is even less likely to be [suggestive] e.g., *let's do it straight away, shall we?* But even counting out these categories, the speaker might take an assertive stance as in *I would like it done straight away* or *it better be done straight away*. A more authoritarian near mandatory command might be *you had better/you should/you must do it straight away*. Compare this with *it should/it must be done straight away*. And all of these can be compared with consultative commands 'can, will, could, would, won't, can't you do it …'. As well, there are a large number of exhortative commands such as *do it …, you do it…, better do it…*; and in this context consider the quality of relation enacted by the selection of such additions as … *will you?, … can you?, … would you?, … could you?, … can't you?, … won't you?*. More details about the selectable meanings are not difficult to add; but perhaps this will suffice to indicate the resources 'around' in making demand for service and the 'construal' of context by meaning-wording. In the end, the employer's response to the question does not depend purely on 'what' the action is but more likely on his ATTITUDE and FOCUS with regard to the addressee (see Figures 8.6 and 8.7 for the terms used with reference to mode and tenor).

But there is also the stratum 'below': no language use can come about without the formal resources of the language, and these lie at the lexico-grammatical stratum in immediate relation to 'meaning in context'. In the functional modelling of language, form does not disappear as sometimes implied in setting a binary choice between form and function; nor need it be notional (if notional means intuitive). Rather, the form is seen from the point of view of its own resources as form, and at the same time the question is always raised 'what difference would it make to activate the option declarative as opposed to interrogative or imperative, tagged as opposed to non-tagged, positive, as opposed to negative, and so on. It is a theoretically created 'fiction' that meanings, which is used here as 'meanings *construed linguistically*', can be mentioned, or be known without being said. The speaker's semantic options can only be known by the wording: what process, what participants, what mood, what modality, what phoric relations, what forms of linguistic interaction – all of this is typically 'put in so many words'. Of course the question of errors and deceptions is important, and if space permitted one could discuss these in light of the function of co-text, and of 'reading to make sense' either by direct reference or by implication. What will be seldom found is the surrogate relation of 'correspondence' to some reality out there: the real reality escapes us; the reality with which human communities work is construed largely by language. While revealing the immense complexity of the process of 'meaning making', the concept of the trinocular perspective brings us considerably closer to answering that important question: why does anyone say anything to anyone? In bringing about this outcome, SFL has thrown considerable light not only on how language works, i.e., by what resources, but also on why, i.e., the motivation. The orders of relevance established to answer that beguilingly simple question would most probably need to be taken into account in any credible neurocognitive profile of what it means to speak.

8.4   Concluding remarks: the value of a scientific study of con/text

Section 8.2 of this chapter had concluded that the paramount need in the description of contextual features is precise and orderly statements whose validity can be demonstrated along consistent principles enabled by the theory. I made a case for testing Halliday's context-metafunction resonance (CMR) hypothesis as the approach most likely to meet those needs. Section 8.3 demonstrated that precision and orderliness are built into the paradigmatic method of representation: there has not arisen any need to add or subtract from those conventions; all that is needed is to observe its principles as a language dedicated to presenting a specific kind of information. I have indicated some grounds for concern in the way that the systemic representation of paradigmatic description is being carried out. In my view, unless reconsidered carefully, this neglect of the principles of a precise methodology is likely to delay the achievement of the goal that we have set ourselves. And that goal as I argued in Section 8.2 is to establish reliable ways of classifying registers: this, in turn, requires criteria for recognizing linguistic and contextual correlates. Section 8.3 has attempted to indicate the need for the careful labour necessary in achieving this goal. One is of course entitled to ask if the study of context deserves the attention and care being demanded here. In modern linguistics until quite recently context had been viewed as an optional extra. But to perform their functions in the life of the community, neither context nor language depend on conscious recognition: Hjelmslev (1961) had remarked that the nature of language is to remain invisible; exactly the same is true of context. Context has been relevant not only in ancient theories of rhetoric, but it has also insinuated itself into the categories of grammars such as noun and verb, mood and case, number, person, gender and so on. And some might say this unconscious play of context has worked fine for logicians, philosophers, and supposedly for purely formal grammarians. Why do we need to change this centuries old uneasy relationship now?

My response to this is simple, though it might surprise: a scientific study of language *needs* to include within its fold not only langue, but also parole, i.e., language use. This conviction is central to SFL, a linguistic theory that in my view has followed (most probably not intentionally) in the steps of Ferdinand de Saussure. Elsewhere I have argued (Hasan 2013, 2014a) that Halliday's SFL as it stands today comes nearest to Saussure's dream of the linguistics of langue, but it does so not by following Saussure's disjunction between langue and parole but by showing that Saussure's goals can be achieved (with due respect to Saussure) *only* by ignoring his exclusion of parole. The basis for making this claim is very briefly as follows:

1. Variation inheres in language (Saussure 1966); activated by context, it is realized in parole.
2. Saussure's linguistics of langue recommended the study of langue in isolation from parole by reference to a single synchronic *état de langue*;
3. but as Saussure himself recognized, even a synchronic *état de langue* will have some variation related to age, gender, profession, and social status.
4. A version of langue as representing one synchronic *état de langue* comprehensively is a theoretical fiction, since it is not beyond

possibility that some category of linguistic variation would go beyond parole, extending right into the langue – it might be systemic. That is to say it may infect the associative bonds.

5. Even supposing the above is not the case (which I doubt: consider 'World Englishes'; do they differ only in accent or in semantics and lexicogrammar as well?), a series of successive synchronic *états de langue* will clearly provide evidence of diachronic variation. And on the assumption that diachronic variation does not occur instantaneously as Saussure himself has argued and as historical linguistics has clearly demonstrated, some explanation will be needed for similarities and dissimilarities across the various *états de langue*.

6. Besides being simply a theoretical fiction (cf., 4) a linguistics of *langue sans parole* will be unable to account for these phenomena; the price for a pure linguistics of langue is failure to understand the nature of the semiological system of language.

7. Saussure thought that the foundation of langue is communal; he banished parole claiming that in parole 'Execution is always individual, and the individual is always its master' (Saussure 1966: 13). Even though these statements may be true in bringing about the relay (expression), Saussure himself argued cogently that as a meaningful entity the existence of the sign depends on its social currency. Moreover, parole is not chaotic as he implied; and in any event 'decision making individuals' are produced by the action of parole in society. As Halliday (1991a/2007a) has argued, the separation of langue and parole is based on the mistaken belief that they are two distinct kinds of phenomenon; the same comment might be extended *mutatis mutandis* to community and individual.

8. Without an understanding of parole as active in the evolution of society and in the development of organisms into individuals, Saussurean linguistics of langue would be unable to defend claims about the relations of langue and parole, including a principled study of synchronic and/or diachronic variation. And, most alarmingly, it will have no basis for explaining which associative bonds comprise the grammar of a given langue; for example, what is the evidence for saying that there is a bond between 'enseignement', 'apprintissage' and 'éducation'?

9. A paradigmatic description of con/text as recommended in the previous sections, by implication if not exhortation, is very likely to reveal the orderly nature of parole, thus removing the basis of Saussure's reluctance to include it within linguistics.

10. His item based 'associative bonds' can clearly not be viewed as 'templates' of any kind; and they could never reach the breadth and depth of the paradigmatic description as has been provided by SFL about the internal strata of language (this is not to imply either that SFL descriptions are complete, or that they has been validated at every point).

I am not claiming that SFL set out to be a post-Saussurean model: but as Saussure's work (1966, 2006) suggests the aim of linguistics for him is to make statements about the production of meaning in signs, using an objective, methodical and precise analysis based on templates, not instances. To Saussure, parole was chaotic, unpredictable and consisting of words and vocables used 'wilfully' by individuals as and when they wished. So far as the concept of language as a meaning potential is concerned, the paradigmatic analysis of the internal patterns of language as templates has gone the longest distance in SFL as the 'linguistics of langue'. In addition to this, the theory has shown that parole, i.e., language use, can be scientifically described, so that underlying those descriptions are explicitly stated principles and templates. The methodical study of con/text is not part of the enumeration of what there is out there in the physical world, no matter how clearly demarcated the boundaries of its elements might appear; rather, the theory is concerned with that reality which language is able to construe. This seems to be a justifiable goal to pursue, for in actual fact it is this linguistically construable reality that underlies the majority of human actions and conceptions. The contextual parameters are part of that story: as Firth reminded us, contextual categories are theoretical constructs and they bear no direct relation to items of linguistically non-construable realia. In this respect, contextual categories do not differ from grammatical ones. Their value lies is their 'tool power' (Butt 2005), and that is produced by the artefact of their positioning in the theory.

In this perspective, the relation between theory and description is very much like that between system and instance – instance, not as just any occurrence in time and space, but as one that is a realization of some permissible conjunction of descriptive categories: nothing can be an instance of the language system that is not related realizationally to some categories ultimately specified by that system. The relation between the theory and the possible descriptions allowed by that theory cannot be ignored, particularly when the descriptum at issue is the concept of context as discussed above. As suggested above (8.2.3.4), the foundation of the three contextual parameters lies in the innate human urge for (inter-)action: the conjunction of some range of Action, some kind of Relations and some means of Contact (ARC) is perhaps the first 'intimation of the social world' for the human infant – and it provides the first opportunity for the exercise of that innate faculty which allows the infant to put together the signal and the possibilities that in some way become attached to that signal. These pre-linguistic elements of human interaction have evolved as the basis for the metafunctional nature of language. The CMR hypothesis is not just a hypothesis that makes it easier to identify the linguistic and contextual correlates, important though that is: the resonance is there because the origin of metafunctions as well as of the tri-partite makeup of human social practices is in some way inscribed in the regular patterns of human inter-action. Halliday (1991a/2007a: 274) puts it this way:

> As I wrote myself many years ago, language is as it is because of what it does: which means because of what we do with it, in every aspect of our life. So a theory of language in context is not just a theory of how people *use* language, important though that is. It is a theory about the *nature* and *evolution* of the system, explaining why the system works the way it does.

In a linguistic theory that has borne the title 'systemic functional' for decades, these issues cannot be easily set aside: the way the nature of the con/textual parameters is viewed has a reach that goes beyond local issues to the very foundation of the theory. Whatever the motivation for unifying field and mode, similar patterns of permeability will also be found across field and tenor, and across tenor and mode (Section 8.3.2.5; Figures 8.6 and 8.7). If the unification of the parameters is the answer to this problem, then this would take us back to the pre-paradigmatic description. Yes, without some form of ready material access to the addressee, the speaker would not use the 'phonic relay' – a mode option (Figure 8.6); but when it comes to the system of ROLE REVERSIBILITY (manifested as free turn-taking), this depends not just on material presence or absence: being co-present is one thing, and the constraints on forms of interaction are another; the latter are always sensitive to social relations. Permeability has always been recognized in SFL: in introducing the concept of contextual parameters, Halliday *et al.* had said (1964: 93):

> It is as a product of these three dimensions of classification that we can best define and identify register. The criteria are not absolute or

independent; they are all variable in delicacy, and the more delicate the classification the more the three will overlap.

In some ways the trinocular analysis of con/textual features has not yet begun; and it seems to me the focus is more on what is going on there in the performance of a social practice than on classes of register. If the aim is to achieve reliable register classification, then attention to linguistic realization is necessary: to my mind, *that* is the primary reason for the meticulous care and the demanding labour required in carrying out a valid paradigmatic analysis of the contextual parameters. And I have attempted to show that the conceptualization of the parameters is closely related to some foundational principles of systemic functional linguistics. This leads me to suggest that local solutions of descriptive problems in this domain most probably need to be evaluated in the global context of the SFL theory. This is not to say that the correctness of the theory's architecture is beyond challenge: theories, especially in the domain of human sciences, will change even if only because their object of description must change. So in some sense it may be claimed that flexibility inheres in all good social theories. The question is how deliberately thought out is that enquiry in response to which the change is being un/consciously promoted. Change for the sake of change, change without explicit reason, is typical of trivial fields of enterprise – concerned with appearances without a care for substance.

There is no doubt that the social practices being performed around us in the 'real' world call for much more than language: if I have sometimes argued against the riding tides of multimodality, this is purely because linguistics is the study of the semiological system of language: it is not a theory of everything. Its primary aim is to provide a frame that tests the potential of language for meaning, and I submit that although linguistics is very much more advanced in the description of language than are the disciplines dealing with other semiological systems, there is much more to be said about language, especially from the point of view of semantics, i.e., linguistic meaning. Meaning is the most important aspect of language: it needs to be understood much better in relation to other ways of meaning, and from the perspective of its own power in shaping human communities. There in an ancient, not to say hackneyed, saying: love makes the world go round! I have always felt that it is the meaning potential of language that makes the world go round – though I would not go so far as to say that other ways of meaning do not matter. But then I am a linguist.

Notes

1   This chapter was published by Springer in *Functional Linguistics*, 2014, 2.9. Certain errors will be found in that publication despite long discussions with producers. The main problem is that the Appendices A and B (referred to in *Functional Linguistics* as Additional files 2 and 3_Appendix B and C) are found to contain substantial errors, which means that the Appendices which were supposed to act as guide to the interpretation of Figure 8.6 of the article are out of step with it. I was not allowed to see the penultimate form of the article; after seeing the notification of the publication, and viewing the published article, a request was made for corrections. I have not heard back from any member of the production team. In including the article in this volume, I have corrected these errors; at the same time I have re-organized the arrangement of the section numbered here 8.3.3.3.

2   The version of Systemic Functional Linguistics (SFL) I use here is the one associated with Halliday's name; my concern will not be with the variant versions (e.g., Martin 1992 or Fawcett 2000) since some generalizations I need to make might not be applicable to these variants. I thank Michael Halliday for commenting on an earlier draft of this paper. I alone am responsible for the views/interpretations of the theory as presented here.

3   I refer here specifically to the version associated with Halliday, since the generalization I will make here would most probably not agree with the variant versions

4   As an admirer of Firth, I do not make these remarks lightly but to argue this point paying due respect to his inspiring writings requires another separate paper.

5   Some register families have a strong tendency to suppress idiolectal characteristics; writing a lab report or applying for research funding are two such examples.

6   For more information see the *Collected Works of M. A. K. Halliday*, Volume 3: *On Language and Linguistics*, 2003 and Volume 10: *Language and Society* 2007b. London: Continuum.

7   Hasan (1973c) was first presented at a seminar at London School of Economics in 1969. It criticized the neglect of semantics, and offered reasons for preferring that stratum as the focus for the identification of the linguistic correlates.

8   These relations are evident in the last resort as the interdependence between certain classes of words in a clause. For example, compare the a-normal *I invited him **but** he came* with the normal *I invited him but he didn't come*.

9   Not all departures are necessarily random; in fact they are often 'conditioned' (Hasan 2011c); one might for example consider field and transitivity in connection with the use of grammatical metaphors in scientific domain. Permeability might be another issue.

10   I believe using the expression 'context metafunction hook up hypothesis' is based on an error: it does injustice to Halliday's statements about the

resonance of metafunctions and the contextual parameters, by misapplying the term 'hook up' which had been used by Halliday *only* to refer to the 'unifying' function of grammar as 'a device for hooking up together' into 'one unified structural form' the various elements derived from the metafunctional analysis (e.g. 1973: 42). The issue is not likely to arise with text which is where the linguistic realization of the metafunctional features would be found.

11   The earliest label had been 'general/ized formula' (Hasan 1978); later I also used the term 'generic' meaning 'species'/'type'. And even when Bakhtin's 'speech genre' became popular, they tended to be associated with 'schematic structures'. Unlike the GSP, schematic structures were instantial; they were never explicitly related to features of the CC. I have refrained from using the term 'genre', as the differences between register and genre as in Martin's 'genre theory', became more obvious. The Generalized Formula has meanwhile become Generalized Structure Potential.

12   This is not to say that accidental moves whether material or semantic are 'meaning-less'; however precisely because they are unpredictable, generalizations are hard to establish.

13   I have long felt the need to explore the differences between 'act', 'action' and 'activity': this would bring greater order in understanding field as the parameter concerned with 'doing' of some kind.

14   The nearest (though not identical) to it is Lamb's relational network: this is not surprising. Lamb was inspired by Hjelmslev's theory; Halliday, by Firth's; and both masters, despite reservations, were deeply influenced by Saussure, which is where the idea of the linguistic sign as a relational entity originated. Also Halliday and Lamb began to actively work together from the 1960s, a time when both scholars were deeply interested in the network as a means of explaining the nature of language.

15   The networks were in vogue a good deal up to the mid-1970s; Halliday himself, though he worked closely with Mann and Matthiessen on the Penman project for text generation, seemed not to employ this method in the late 1970s; other colleagues such as Fawcett and Berry were actively involved. My research students and I employed this method of representation in our research (Hasan 1983, 1985d, 1987b; Cloran 1994) consistently; but it has truly come into its own in Matthiessen's work (1995, 2004).

16   I have sometimes recognized MESSAGE COMPONENT as another unit; but on reflection it seems very likely that at SEME COMPLEX could be a better way of handling the relations of SEME. The term RADICAL is best applied to a sub-class of SEME, which may usefully allow the distinction between *walk* and *–ing* as exemplar of RADICAL and DEPENDENT classes of SEME, respectively.

17   I am indebted to Margaret Berry (private conversation) for drawing attention to the distinction between option and choice. I take the responsibility for the extension and interpretation of the terms as presented here.

18   See also Butt (2013) for a revised system network of mode of discourse. By presenting the options in capital letters e.g. 'ANCILLARY' or 'CONSTITUTIVE', Butt

(2004a) kindly indicates that these option names were used in my work on mode, especially in pre-systemic discussions of the three parameters. I have not replicated this practice here: the terms, having been embedded in a largely new systemic environment, no longer mean the same thing, especially when compared with Hasan (1999b).

19   The term 'context of culture and situation' is sometimes abbreviated to just 'context' or just 'situation', neither of which by itself is a satisfactory focus, though it is a great space-saver! I will use the term 'context', except where the discourse requires clarification as for example in showing the difference between the 'context of situation' and 'material situational setting' (Hasan 1999b, 2009a; 2016).

20   Since each simple system represents a particular perspective, in principle, each should be assigned a name but the inclusion of all the system names is problematic for lack of space. It is useful for each simple system to have an address for easy reference; in my work I have tried to identify them by a combination of letters and numbers (Hasan 2009b, 2013); Butt (2004a) employs a decimal numbering system that within limits can be used for tracking delicacy.

21   Very probably there is a mathematical formula that can more elegantly lay down the principles which ordain the continuation or discontinuation of paths.

22   I first called it 'default dependency' (Hasan 1999b: 278). But really what the arrow diacritic placement does is to pre-empt choices, pointing to one as the 'default choice'; in other words it is a form of pre-selection of choice, except that the term 'pre-select' has been dedicated to a form of realization relation.

23   These were not built into a system but described discursively since the readership to which the writing was addressed could be expected to have a working knowledge of sys-nets.

Appendix A: partial Glossary of options in Material Contact (Mode)

SYSTEM ID	SYSTEM/OPTION NAME	GLOSSARY AND COMMENTS
MC	MATERIAL CONTACT	physiological resources for relay. Material, sens-ible
SC	SEMANTIC CONTACT	meaning-wording systems in contact; realised as cohesion and coherence
PP	PRODUCTION POINT	when speaker is relaying at point of language production
RP	RECEPTION POINT	when addressee/receiver is accessing at reception point
a1	graphic	relay is graphological; using orthographic conventions
a2	phonic	oral system operative; relay is oral at PP
b1	direct	addressee receives text as produced at PP; if relay is oral, then accessed aurally without time-lag; if graphic relay, access at RP will be visual, and delayed in varied degrees
b2	mediated	technological and/or human agency other than interactants intervene between receiver and text; text appearance may change
b3	congruent	the pairing of PP and RP systems is 'natural' if relay is oral reception is aural; if graphic then visual
b4	incongruent	pairing of PP and RP systems is not natural; e.g., graphic after mediation accessed phonically; the written is audio-recorded; received aurally
a1;b2:b3 →C	conjunct entry point to C: here allows entry to a simultaneous set	paths of 1a and b2:b3 join= conjunct entry point (for deriving a new system c and another system S which may either combine with options from C or from P
c1	conventional [option in 1st m-system]	conventional mean of graphic relay e.g. handwriting, type script; and/or using public services for access e.g. post office
c2	digital	digital means used for graphic relay e.g. email, face-book ...
S	the second m-system	disjunct system alternates between system c and system p; details in Appendix B
s1	personal	speaker has control on the choice of addressee, who is known to some extent even if materially absent as in telephone talk;
s2	public	access to text is open at RP; digital means may be used
a2;b2:b3 →P	phonic; mediated: congruent = acts as conjunct entry point allows entry to system P and system S	system P is a dependent individual system; S alternates between C and P options

p1	synchronic	no noticeable deal between relay and its reception at a distance by addressee; choice of p1 is the entry point to a simultaneous set with options p3/p4 and access to s1 or s2
p2	asynchronic	asynchronic implies variable amount of time-lag between the relay of phonic at PP and its reception at RP; speaker's voice mediated via recording or digital media; p2 is entry condition for various systems which are not be described here
p3	single	option in system derived from p1, refers to the choice of one single means of relay e.g., just telephone or radio
p4	multiple	option in system derived from p1, refers to the choice of some mediated means which allows more than one means of accessing information, e.g., with Skype, aural, visual, kinesic are available
System C P and S	options of system S can combine alternatively with the options c1 or c2 OR with p3 or p4	Appendix B for the description of c1;s1 c1;s2 c2;s1 c2; s2 p3;s1 p3;s2 p4;s1 p4;s2
a1;b2;b4 →D	graphic; mediated: incongruent = conjunct entry to system D	meaning-wording expressed as graphic at PP will be received in an incongruent mode, e.g., as spoken at RP
d1	option in system derived from conjunct entry D [read by self]	graphic; mediated: incongruent from PP is received at RP as phonic relay by the original producer; e.g. a poem read aloud by the author to addressee
d2	option in system derived from conjunct entry D [read by other]	text produced as above being received at RP in phonic relay by some one other than original speaker; e.g., a literature teacher reads the poem aloud to students
d3	option in system derived from d2 [as received]	e.g., the teacher presents the poem in the original form
d4	option in system derived from d2 [reframed]	e.g., the teacher experiments with the poem changing its original shape
d5	option in system derived from choice of d3 [all]	the whole poem is phonically presented; the only difference is the mode of presentation
d6	option in system derived from the choice of d3 [selection]	or a selection of the poem is presented, by way of example, or comparison etc.
d7	option in system derived from the choice of d4 [perform]	the original text [reframed] in other to be performed on the stage or in some other way; a novel is reframed as a play

d8	option in system derived from the choice of d4 [audio-record]	reframing is needed for presenting the graphic text into speech to record for broadcast
d9	option in system derived from the choice of d7 [telecast]	the reframing for performance might be for television performance as a tv show
d10	option in system derived from the choice of d7 [stage]	or it may be for a play to be staged; this needs a serious amount of 'revamping'; by this point it is no longer a question of relay but of transforming a text type A into text type K
d11	option in system derived from the choice of d8 [broad cast]	many texts dealing with some issue in a specialised field are transformed into a popular presentation;
d12	option in system derived from the choice of d8 [talking book]	strangely turning Jane Austen's Pride and Prejudice into a talking book might not move the original text away so far from its original shape as 'staging' someone's biography!
a2; b2; b4 →Q	phonic; mediated: incongruent = conjunct entry point to system Q	phonic relay at PP mediated to be accessed no longer aurally but as a written document; or a series of paintings, or sketches

Appendix B: disjunct entry points in Figure 6: Mode

Choice paths for systems C & P involving system S disjunctively

System C:

Assume for each SE in system C: (a1;b2: b3) [graphic; mediated: congruent]
This choice path describes a conjunct entry point for entry into system C:
C leads to a simultaneous set with two member systems:
One m-system, an individual has option c1 [conventional] or c2 [digital];
The second m-system S is an individual with option s1 [personal] or s2 [public].
[persona] ↘ speaker has control on dissemination; [public] ↘ access is nearly free.
Being related to pp choices, system C interacts with social distance.

↘

1:      c1; s1   conventional; personal

speaker uses conventional means of text relay such as will allow him to restrict its
dissemination: e.g., handwriting, typewriter. Text types e.g., personal letters, notes to
addressee with close social distance; reminders; circulars to friends/neighbours

2:      c2; s1   digital; personal

Normally implies email relay for personal messages: the message is typically not open to
public gaze; not for category, but for absent addressee known to speaker as a 'person'
(discussion, section 3.4 in text)

3:      c1; s2   conventional; public

The option [public] implies free access to text; typically conventional means of print, either
formal publication or local printed documents for circulation. Text types, personally prepared
documents for circulation; writing to publish book, or magazines etc.

4:      c2; s2   digital; public

The use of Facebook, Blog, Twitter and other such social media.

NOTE: increasingly impossible today to exclude digital mode – a change in progress.

System P:

Assume for each SE in system P has: (a2;b2:b3) [phonic; mediated: congruent];
System P has two options: either p1 [synchronic] ↘ no time-lag between relay and access
or p2 [asynchronic] ↘ indefinite time-lag between relay and reception; message recorded.
Option p1 entry point to a simultaneous set with two m-systems
One individual dependent m-system continuing system p: options [single] p3 or [multiple] p4
[single] p3 ↘ single means of access; [multiple] p4 ↘ more than one means of access
second m-system system S as above: options as above

1:      p1: p3; s1   synchronic: single; personal

p1 implies addressee/receiver will access message without any notable time lag. The choice
option p3 [single] or p4 [multiple] as above; s1 [personal] or s2 [public] as above:
realised as expression of interaction on telephone: telephone mediates speaker's [phonic]
relay, ensures [synchronic] access through single means of expression; personal speaker
control on who the addressee would be.

2:      p1: p3; s2   synchronic: single; public

as above except that now speaker has no control over who the addressee/receiver might be;
access through single means but probably a radio broadcast of some commentary, interview
or discourse. Examples would be radio broadcast of commentary; live interview broadcast
and so on

3:      p1: p4; s1   synchronic: multiple; personal

this choice path varies from choice path 1 only in one respect: the means of receiver's access
of the text is by multiple means; a Skype discussion, or an audio-visual presentation to a
known group would make use of many modes of access while at the same time the identity of
the receiver is established.

4:      p1: p4; s2   synchronic: multiple; public

This choice path differs from both choice path 2 and 3 in respect 1 feature each: it is
altogether like 2 expect that the resources for access are multiple as in live TV, or other online
participation. Perhaps listening to a lecture being broadcast on line where the audience is
unknown to the speaker (except perhaps in some general sense) and receivers are able to not
only listen but see the speaker's gestures, and facial expressions.

Note: the system S can be accessed at anyone given moment either by one of the
options p3 or p 4 or from C1 or C2. Altogether S pivotal system in a complex
disjunct entry,

Appendix C: Glossary of option in TENOR in Figure 7

SYSTEM/OPTIONS	GLOSS AND EXAMPLES
INTERACTANT RELATION	the central concern of tenor
TEXTUAL ROLES	system concerning 'speaker'/'addressee' options; with relations to mode of discourse in both material and semantic contacts
AS SPEAKER	the interactant role is always present in both material situational setting and in relevant context (i.e., as semantic traces in text's meaning-wording)
ATTITUDE & FOCUS	simultaneous set with 2 m-systems: choices apply only to speaker role because only speaker 'translates' them into meaning-wording i.e. typically it is only the speaker's attitude and focus become part of the text.
neutral	neutral attitude = speaker not noticeably biased; no adverse/exuberant comments re task in hand or the 'other' realised
biased	biased attitude = speaker not neutral realised as comments re task in hand or the 'other' (possibly also kinesic behaviour)
positive	if biased: positive = make encouraging/ingratiating comments
negative	if biased: negative = make adverse/discouraging comments
actions	attitude and focus is towards actions that are in process i. e. being done
addressee	attitude and focus targets addressee
other	attitude and focus are directed towards someone else
AS ADDRESSEe	addressee is always semantically present; but has variable relation to material situational setting
MATERIAL PRESENCE (MP)	system locating addressee with respect to material situational setting and relevant context (Hasan, in press a)
PP in diamond	diacritical notation: relevant to choices in production point; discussion on default choice in section 3.2.4
FD in diamond	diacritical notation: MP presence choices related to primary choices in field of discourse
absent	addressee is absent from the material situational setting/ has no material contact with speaker; has the role of 'receiver' of graphic message
category $^{\%\rightarrow}$	'absent' addressee might belong to a 'category'; the diacritical notation indicates that the option so marked imposes a default choice which is indicated by the occurrence of the second pair part. (discussion of this diacritical notation in section 3.5 of this paper).
imaginary	if 'category', is 'imaginary' speaker knows the addressee only as a type that may or may not have been encountered; degree of certainty about reception of meaning-wording may be lower
actual	if 'category' is 'actual', speaker has direct experience of type e.g., 'next year's intake of students' for a university lecturer; speaker has some idea of their patterns of reaction to meaning-wording
present	addressee is either physically 'present' in material situational setting or can have 'direct' access to a variety of phonic channel. Role of listener. The choice of this option (like that of 'absent') is relevant to choices in PP
MD in diamond	the option present has relevance to mode of discourse (MD) in both material (MC) and semantic contact (SC); e.g., dialogue depends on 'co-presence' but 'co-presence' is not sufficient for dialogue to occur: social roles are critical (discussion, Hasan, in press a)
SOCIAL ROLES	relations that correlate with interactant's 'social positioning': simultaneous systems concerning SOCIAL DISTANCE and STATUS.

SOCIAL DISTANCE	simultaneous system of relation based on 'interactive biography', so truly a personal relation arising from previous mutual interactive experience between these specific interactants; the relation are reciprocal; e.g., if speaker is 'close' to addressee, then the addressee must be to speaker;
QUALITY (OF SD)	system specifying what kind of social distance is operating;
close[@→]	the interactants are 'close' to each other; the default choice relation applies if status is 'neutralised' (discussion 3.2.4 in paper)
distant[→%]	interactants are 'distant' from each other; this choice is mandatory if 'addressee: absent: category' and extends to 'imaginary' or 'actual'; it is the second pair part of the same diacritic on option 'category'
DEGREE (OF SD)	system specifying extent of social distance; the second part of the simultaneous system
normal	the option 'normal' indicates the degree of affect that is demanded of the interactants by kind of activity they are co-engaged in achieving;
marked	the option 'marked' indicates a degree of affect that shows lack of interest or strength of commitment that is more than normal;
extremely[@→]	option 'extremely' indicates notably close or distant sort of relation
fairly	option 'fairly' indicates a good deal of affect
slightly	option 'slightly' indicates a low degree of commitment
STATUS	the system(s) that specify options relevant to interactant's standing in culture including how it is maintained and the criteria by which it is established
neutralised[→@]	the significance of option in this system is modified if there is 'close' (SD) between speaker/addressee; second pair part of the diacritic at 'close'
maintained	'maintained' implies SD options will apply as normal to options
as equals	'as equals' is a relation which selectively ignores certain communal distinction, e.g., the majority of ascribed relations are ignored between professional colleagues, degree of expertise is not
hierarchized	criteria by which higher or lower status is communally established
ASCRIBED CRITERIA	simultaneous systems of attributes which result from accident of birth and/or by happenings that are culturally institutionalised; individual options are transparent so not discussed (for brief comments Hasan in press a)
class benefit	what kind of class benefit is available to members: relation 'irrational'
class	selects class of interactant vis a vis other classes: relation 'irrational'
sex	'gender equality' is fashionable, but differences based on gender continue; hierarchisation complementary
age relation	generational relation 'ego' = cohort; +1 = the generation above; -1 the generation below; this relation complementary
kin relation	what kind of family relation; this relation complementary
ACHIEVED CRITERIA	this system of attributes pertain to attributes that can be created supposedly by individual's efforts, unlike the ascribed attributes: include material capital, cultural capital and communal recognition (not developed here; see Hasan, in press a for some details)

References

Abercrombie, D. (1951/1965). R.P. and local accent. In *Studies in Phonetics and Linguistics*. (First presented as 'R.P. and local accent', BBC Broadcast, Third Programme, 29 August 1951.) London: Oxford University Press.

Alatis, J. E. (ed.). (1993). *Language, Communication and Social Meaning: Georgetown University Round Table, 1992*. Washington DC: Georgetown University Press.

Alford, D. K. H. (1980). The demise of the Whorf hypothesis. Mimeo. Berkeley, CA: University of California.

Argyle, M. (1972), *The Psychology of Interpersonal Behaviour*. Harmondsworth: Penguin.

Argyle, M. & Kendon, A. (1967). The experimental analysis of social performance, In J. Laver & S. Hutcheson (eds), *Communication in Face to Face Interaction*. Harmondsworth: Penguin.

Armstrong, E. (1987). Cohesive harmony in aphasic discourse and its significance in listener perception of coherence. In R. H. Brookshire (ed.) *Clinical Aphasiology: Conference Proceedings*. Minneapolis, MN: BRK Publishers.

Armstrong, E. (1992). Clause complex relations in aphasic discourse: A longitudinal study. *Journal of Neurolinguistics, 7* (4), 261–275.

Austin, J. L. (1962/1976). *How to Do Things with Words*. (Second Edition). J. O. Urmson & Marina Sbisa (eds). Oxford: Oxford University Press.

Austin, J. L. (1979). *Philosophical Papers*: (Third Edition). J. O. Urmson & G. J. Warnock (eds). Oxford: Oxford University Press.

Ayer, A. J. (1968). *The Origins of Pragmatism*. London: Macmillan.

Baker, G. P., & P. M. S. Hacker (1980). *Wittgenstein, Meaning and Understanding: Essays on the Philosophical Investigations, Vol.* 1. London: Basil Blackwell.

Bakhtin, M. M. (1981). Discourse in the Novel. In M. Holquist (eds), *The Dialogic Imagination*. Austin: University of Texas Press.

Bakhtin, M. M. (1986). The problem of speech genres. In C. Emerson & M. Holquist (eds), *Speech Genres and Other Late Essays*. Austin: University of Texas Press.

Barnes, B., & Edge, D. (1982). (eds) *Science in Context: Readings in the Sociology of Science*. Milton Keynes: Open University Press.

Bateson, G. (1942). Morale and national character. In G. Watson (ed.), *Civilian Morale. Society for the Psychological Study of Social Issues, Second Yearbook*. New York: Houghton Miflin.

Bateson, G. (1955). A theory of play and fantasy; a report on theoretical aspects of the project for the study of the role of paradoxes of abstraction in communication. *Approaches to the Study of Human Personality*, American Psychiatric Association, Psychiatric Report No. 2.

Bateson, G. (1964). The logical categories of learning and communication. Position paper for the Conference on World-View sponsored by Wenner-Gren, 1968. Reprinted in *Steps to an Ecology of Mind*. New York, Ballantine (1972)

Bateson, G. (1968). Redundancy and coding. In T. A. Sebeok (ed.), *Animal Communication: Techniques of Study and Results of Research*. Bloomington: Indiana University Press.

Bateson, M. C. (1975). Mother-infant exchanges: The Epigenesis of conversational interaction. In D. Aaronson & R. W. Rieber (eds) *Developmental Psycholinguistics and Communication Disorder*. New York: New York Academy of Sciences.

Benson, J. D. & W. S. Greaves (eds) (1985). *Systemic Perspectives on Discourse* Vol. I. Norwood, NJ: Ablex.

Benson, J. D., M. J. Cummings & W. S. Greaves (eds) (1988). *Linguistics in a Systemic Perspective*. Philadelphia: Benjamins.

Berger, P. L., & T. Luckmann. (1967). *The Social Construction of Reality: A Treatise in the Sociology of Knowledge*. New York: Anchor Books.

Berkson, W. (1976). Lakatos one and Lakatos two: An appreciation. In R. S. Cohen, P. K. Feyerabend, & M. W. W. Wartofsky (eds).

Berlin, B. & P. Kay (1969). *Basic Color Terms*. Berkeley, CA: University of California Press.

Bernstein, B. (1971). *Class, Codes and Control, Volume 1: Theoretical Studies Towards a Sociology of Language*. London: Routledge & Kegan Paul.

Bernstein, B. (ed.) (1973). *Class, Codes and Control, Vol 2: Applied Studies Towards a Sociology of Language*. London: Routledge and Kegan Paul.

Bernstein, B. (1975). Classification and framing of educational knowledge. In B. Bernstein, *Class, Codes and Control, Vol. 3: Towards a Theory of Educational Transmission*. London: Routledge & Kegan Paul.

Bernstein, B. (1987). Social class, codes and communication. In V. Ammon, N. Dittmar, & K. J. Matthier (eds), *Sociolinguistics: An International Handbook of the Science of Society* (pp. 563–579). Berlin: Walter de Gruyter.

Bernstein, B. (1990). *The Structuring of Pedagogic Discourse: Class, Codes and Control, Volume 4*. London: Routledge.

Bernstein, B. (1996). *Pedagogy, Symbolic Control and Identity: Theory, Research, Critique*. London: Taylor & Francis.

Bernstein, B. (1999) Vertical and horizontal discourse: An essay. *British Journal of Sociology of Education*, 20 (2), 157–173.

Bernstein, B. (2000). *Pedagogy, Symbolic Control and Identity: Theory, Research, Critique.* (2nd revised edition). Oxford: Rowman & Littlefield.

Berry, M. (1982). Review of Halliday 1978. *Nottingham Linguistic Circular,* 11, 64–94.

Berry, M. (1987). Is teacher an unanalysed concept? In M. A. K. Halliday & R. P. Fawcett (eds), *New Developments in Systemic Linguistics, Vol. I: Theory and Description.* London: Frances Pinter.

Berry, M. (1989). They are all out of steps except our Jonny: A discussion of motivation (or lack of it) in systemic linguistics. In *Occasional Papers in Systemic Linguistics 3,* 5–67. Nottingham: Department of English Studies, University of Nottingham.

Black. M. (1959). Linguistic relativity: The views of B. L. Whorf. *Philosophical Review*, 68 (2): 228–238.

Bloor, D. (1976). *Knowledge and Social Imagery.* London: Routledge & Kegan Paul.

Bloor, D. (1983). *Wittgenstein: A Social Theory of Knowledge.* New York: Columbia University Press.

Bloomfield, L. (1935). *Language.* London: Allen and Unwin.

Bohannan, L. (1971). Shakespeare in the bush. In J. P. Spradley & D. W. McCurdy (eds) *Conformity and Conflict: Readings in Cultural Anthropology.* Boston, MA: Little, Brown & Co.

Bolinger, D. L. (1968). *Aspects of Language.* New York: Harcourt, Brace and Jovanovich.

Bourdieu, P. (1977). *Outline of a Theory of Practice* (translated by R. Nice). Cambridge: Cambridge University Press.

Bourdieu, P. (1981). Men and machines. In K. Knorr-Cetina & A. V. Cicourel (eds), *Advances in Social Theory: Toward an Integration of Micro- and Macro-sociologies.* London: Routledge & Kegan Paul.

Bourdieu, P. (1990). *The Logic of Practice.* (translated by R. Nice). Oxford: Polity.

Bourdieu, P. (1991). *Language and Symbolic Power* (translated by G. Raymond & M. Adamson, edited by J. B. Thompson). Cambridge: Polity Press.

Bowcher, W. L. (2007). Field and multimodal texts. In R. Hasan, C. Matthiessen & J. J. Webster (eds).

Bowcher, W. L. (2014). Issues in developing unified systems for contextual field and mode. *Functions of Language* 12 (2), 176–209.

Brazelton, T. B. (1961). Psychophysiologic reactions in the neonate: I. The value of observations of the neonate. *Journal of Paediatrics*, 58: 508–512.

Brazelton, T. B., B. Koslowski, & M. Main. (1974). The origins of reciprocity: The early mother-infant interaction. In M. Lewis & L. A. Rosenblum (eds).

Brothers, L. (1997). *Friday's Footprint: How Society Shapes the Human Mind.* New York: Oxford University Press.

Brown, R. (1973). *A First Language.* Cambridge, MA: Harvard University Press.

Brown, R. (1976). Reference: In memorial tribute to Eric Lenneberg. *Cognition*, 4 (2), 125–153.

Bruner, J. S. (1972). Nature and the uses of immaturity. *American Psychologist,* 27, (8), 667–708.

Bruner, J L. (1978). Learning how to do things with words. In J. L. Bruner & A. Garton (eds) *Human Growth and Development.* Oxford: Clarendon Press.

Bullowa, M. (1979a). Introduction: Pre-linguistic communication: A field for scientific research. In M. Bullowa (ed.) *Before Speech.* Cambridge: Cambridge University Press.

Bullowa, M. (1979b), Infants as conversational partners. In T. Myers (ed.), *The Development of Conversation and Discourse.* Edinburgh: Edinburgh University Press.

Butler, C. S. (1985a). Discourse systems and structures and their place within an overall systemic model. In J. D. Benson & W. S. Greaves (eds).

Butler, C. S. (1985b). *Systemic Linguistics: Theory and Applications.* London: Batsford Academic.

Butt, D. G. (1989). The object of language. In R. Hasan & J. R. Martin (eds).

Butt, D. G. (1991). Some basic tools in a linguistic approach to personality: A Firthian concept of social process. In Fran Christie (ed.), *Literacy in Social Processes: Papers from the Inaugural Australian Systemic Functional Linguistics Conference,* Deakin University, January 1990, 23–44. Darwin: Centre for Studies of Language in Education, Northern Territory University.

Butt, D. G. (2001). Firth, Halliday and the development of systemic functional theory. In S. Auroux, E. F. K. Koerner, H.-J. Niederehe & K. Versteegh (eds), *History of the Language Sciences.* Berlin: de Gruyter.

Butt, D. G. (2003). *Parameters of Contexts: On establishing Similarities and Dissimilarities between Social Processes.* (Mimeo.). Centre for Language in Social Life, Macquarie University, Sydney.

Butt, D. G. (2004a). Parameters of Context: On Establishing Similarities and Dissimilarities between Social Processes. (Mimeo.) Sydney: Centre for Language in Social Life, Macquarie University.

Butt, D. G. (2004b). How our meanings change: School contexts and semantic evolution. In G. Williams & A. Lukin (eds). *The Development of Language: Functional Perspectives on Species and Individuals.* London: Continuum.

Butt, D. G. (2005). Method and imagination in Halliday's science of linguistics. In R. Hasan, C. Matthiessen & J. J. Webster (eds).

Butt, D. G. (2008). The robustness of realizational systems. In J. J. Webster (ed.).

Butt, D. G. (2013). The medium, the channel and the message: Technologies of mind and matter. A keynote presentation at Third Register and Context Symposium: Mode, Text and Texture. Macquarie University, Department of Linguistics. 13–15 February 2013. Video available at http://Vimeo/com/62212145 (Part 1) and http://Vimeo/com/62212460 (Part 2).

Butt, D. G. & R. K. A. Wegener. (2007). The work of concepts and metafunction in the systemic functional model. In Hasan, Matthiessen & Webster (eds).

Cartwright, A. (1983). *How the Laws of Physics Lie.* Oxford: Clarendon Press.

Cerón, I. M. & U. Canger. (1993). In *Tequil de Morrales: Working with Maguey.* Produced by Bianco Luno, *A/S* Copenhagen. Copenhagen: Denmark.

Chomsky, N. (1965). *Aspects of the Theory of Syntax*, Cambridge, MA: MIT Press.

Christie, F. (1988). The construction of knowledge in junior primary school. In L. Gerot, J. Oldenburg & T. van Leeuwan (eds), *Language and Socialization: Home and School: Proceedings from the Working Conference on Language in Education.* Sydney: Macquarie University.

Christie, F. (1999). (ed.). *Pedagogy and the Shaping of Consciousness.* London: Cassell.

Christie, F. & J. R. Martin. (eds) (1997). *Genre and Institutions: Social Processes in the Workplace and School.* London: Cassell.

Christie, F. & L. Unsworth. (2005). Developing dimensions of an educational linguistics. In R. Hasan, C. Matthiessen & J. J. Webster (eds).

Cicourel, A. V. (1980). Language and social interaction. *Working paper No. 96,* Centro Internatzionale di Semiotica e di Linguistica, Universita di Urbino.

Clark, E. (1973). What's in a word? On the child's acquisition of semantics in his first language. In Moore, T. E. (ed.), *Cognitive Development and the Acquisition of Language.* New York: Academic Press.

Cloran, C. (1981). *Negotiating New Contexts in Conversation.* Unpublished dissertation in requirement of BA Honours, Macquarie University, Sydney, Australia.

Cloran, C. (1982). *The Role of Language in Negotiating New Contexts.* Unpublished B.A. (Hons) Dissertation. Department of Linguistics: Macquarie University.

Cloran, C. (1987). Negotiating new contexts in conversation. *Occasional Papers on Systemic Linguistics,* 14: 85–110.

Cloran, C. (1989). Learning through language: The social construction of gender. In R. Hasan & J. R. Martin (eds).

Cloran, C. (1994). *Rhetorical Units and Decontextualization: An Enquiry into some Relations of Context, Meaning and Grammar.* Monographs in Systemic Functional Linguistics, No. 6. Department of English Studies: Nottingham University.

Cloran, C. (1995). Defining and Relating Text Segments: Subject and Theme in Discourse. In R. Hasan & P. H. Fries, (eds) *On Subject and Theme: A Discourse Functional Perspective.* Amsterdam: John Benjamins.

Cloran, C. (1999a). Context, material situation and text. In M. Ghadessy (ed.).

Cloran, C. (1999b). Contexts for learning. In F. Christie (ed.). London: Cassell.

Cloran, C. (2000). Socio-semantic variation: different wordings, different meanings. In L. Unsworth (ed.), *Researching Language in Schools and Communities: Functional Linguistic Perspectives.* London Cassell.

Cloran, C., D. Butt & G. Williams (1996). (eds) *Ways of Saying, Ways of Meaning: Selected Papers of Ruqaiya Hasan.* London: Cassell.

Cohen, R. S., P. K. Feyerabend, & M. W. W. Wartofsky (eds) (1976). *Essays in Memory of Imre Lakatos.* Dordrecht: Reidel.

Cole. M. & S. Scribner (1974). *Culture and Thought: A Psychological Introduction.* New York: John Wiley & Sons.

Cole, P. & J. L. Morgan (eds) (1975). *Syntax & Semantics, Vol. 3: Speech Acts.* New York: Academic Press.

Cook, G. (1990). Transcribing infinity: Problems of context presentation. *Journal of Pragmatics,* 14 (1): 1–24.

Cranny-Francis, A. & J. R. Martin (1991). Contra-textuality: The poetics of subversion. In F. Christie (ed.), *Literacy and Social Processes: Papers from Inaugural Systemic Congress of Australia.* Darwin: Centre for Studies of Language in Education, NTU.

Cross, M. (1979). *Just Pretend You're the Shopkeeper: The Structure of Children's Cooperative Imaginative Role Play.* Unpublished BA Honours Dissertation. Sydney: Macquaire University, Linguistics Department.

Cross, M. (1991). *Choice in Text: A Systemic Approach to Computer Modelling of Variant Text Production.* Unpublished doctoral dissertation, Macquarie University: Department of Linguistics.

Culler, J. (1976). *Saussure.* Fontana Modern Masters Series. Glasgow, Scotland: Fontana/Collins.

Davies, E. (2014). A retrospective view of systemic functional linguistics, with notes from a parallel Perspective. *Functional Linguistics,* 1 (4).

Davies, M. & L. Ravelli (eds) (1992). *Advances in Systemic Linguistics: Recent Theory and Practice.* London: Pinter.

Dawkins, R. (2006). *The God Delusion.* Bantam Press, UK.

Deacon, T. (1997). *The Symbolic Species: The Co-Evolution of Language and the Human Brain.* London: Penguin.

Dennett, D. C. (1991). *Consciousness Explained.* London: Penguin.

Donaldson, M. (1992). *Human Minds: An Exploration.* London: Penguin.

Dore, J. (1974). A pragmatic description of early language development. *Journal of Psycholinguistic Research,* 3 (4), 343–350.

Dore, J. (1980). Linguistic forms and social frames in interpretation. In *The Sixth LACUS Forum 1979.* Columbia, SC: Hornbeam Press.

Douglas, M. (1966). *Purity and Danger.* London: Routledge & Kegan Paul.

Douglas, M. (1975). Self-evidence. In *Implicit Meanings: Essays in Anthropology.* London: Routledge & Kegan Paul.

Edelman, G. (1987). *Neural Darwinism: The Theory of Neuronal Group Selection.* New York: Basic Books.

Edelman, G. (1992). *Bright Air, Brilliant Fire: On the Matter of the Mind.* New York: Basic Books.

Edelman, G. M. & G. Tononi. (2000). *Consciousness: How Matter becomes Imagination.* London: Penguin.

Eggins, S. & D. Slade. (1997). *Analysing Casual Conversation.* London: Cassell.

Ellis, G. (1966). On contextual meaning. In C. E. Bazell, J. C. Catford, M. A. K. Halliday & R. H. Robins (eds), *In Memory of J. R. Firth.* London: Longmans.

Fawcett, R. P. (1980). *Cognitive Linguistics and Social Interaction: Towards an Integrated Model of a Systemic Functional Grammar and the other Components of a Communicating Mind.* Heidelberg: Julius Groos Verlag.

Fawcett, R. P. (1984). System networks, codes, and knowledge of the universe. In R. P. Fawcett, M. A. K. Halliday, S. M. Lamb, and A. Makkai (eds) (1984).

Fawcett, R. P. (1987). The semantics of clause and verb for relational processes in English. In M. A. K. Halliday & R. P. Fawcett (eds).

Fawcett, R. P. (1999). On the subject of the Subject in English: Two positions on its meaning (and on how to test for it). *Functions of Language* 6(2), 243–273.

Fawcett, R. P. (2000). *A Theory of Syntax for a Systemic Functional Linguistics.* Amsterdam: Benjamins.

Fawcett, R. P., M. A. K. Halliday, S. M. Lamb & A. Makkai. (1984). (eds) *The Semiotics of Culture and Language, Vol 1: Language as Social Semiotic.* London: Pinter.

Feyerabend, P. (1975). *Against Method: Outline of an Anarchistic Theory of Knowledge.* London: Verso.

Feyerabend, P. (1976). On the critique of scientific reason. In R. S. Cohen, P. K. Feyerabend, & M. W. W. Wartofsky (eds), *Essays in memory of Imre Lakatos* (pp. 109–144). Dordrecht: Reidel.

Feyerabend, P. (1978). *Science in a Free Society.* London: New Left Books

Firth, J. R. (1935). The technique of semantics. *Transactions of the Philological Society,* pp. 36–72. Reprinted in Firth, 1957: 7–33.

Firth, J. R. (1948). The semantics of linguistic science. *Lingua,* 1 (4), 393–404. Reprinted in Firth, 1957: 139–147.

Firth, J. R. (1950). Personality and language in society. *The Sociological Review,* 42. Reprinted in Firth 1957: 177–189.

Firth, J. R. (1957). *Papers in Linguistics 1934–1951.* London: Oxford University Press. [All Firth page references to this publication.]

Firth, J. R. (1964). *The Tongues of Men and Speech.* London: Oxford University Press.

Firth, J. R. (1968). *Selected Papers of J. R. Firth,* In F. R. Palmer (ed.). London: Longmans.

Firth, R. (1964). *Man & Culture: An Evaluation of the Work of Bronislaw Malinowski.* Harper Torchbooks. New York: Harper and Row.

Fontaine, L., T. Bartlett & G. O'Grady (eds) (2013). *Systemic Functional Linguistics: Exploring Choice.* Cambridge: Cambridge University Press.

Frake, C. O. (1972). Struck by speech: The Yakan concept of litigation. In J. J. Gumperz & D. Hymes (eds), *Directions in Sociolinguistics: The Ethnography of Communication.* New York: Holt, Rinehart, & Winston.

Fries, P. H. (1981). On the status of theme in English: Arguments from discourse. *Forum Linguisticum,* 6 (1), 1–38. Reprinted in J. S. Petöfi & J. Sözer (eds), *Micro and Macro Connexity of Texts* (pp. 116–152). Hamburg: Helmut Buske Verlag. 1983.

Ghadessy, M. (1999). (ed.) *Text and Context in Functional Linguistics.* Amsterdam: Benjamins.

Giddens, A. (1972). *Emile Durkheim: Selected Writings.* Cambridge: Cambridge University Press.

Gleick, J. (1987). *Chaos: Making a new Science.* London: Penguin Books.

Goffman, E. (1964). The neglected situation. In J. J. Gumperz & D. H. Hymes (eds), *The Ethnography of Communication.* American Anthropologist, 66 (6), Part II: 133–137.

Goffman, E. (1974). *Frame Analysis: An Essay on the Organization of Experience.* London: Harper and Row

Goffman, E. (1975). *Frame Analysis: an Essay on the Organization of Experience.* Harmondsworth: Penguin.

Goffman, E. (1981). *Forms of Talk.* Philadelphia: University of Pennsylvania Press.

Goody, J. (1968). *Literacy in Traditional Society.* Cambridge, England: Cambridge University Press.

Goody, J. (1977). *The Domestication of the Savage Mind.* Cambridge: Cambridge University Press.

Goodwin, C. & A. Duranti. (1992). Rethinking context: An introduction. In A. Duranti & C. Goodwin (eds) *Rethinking Context: Language as an Interactive Phenomenon.* New York: Cambridge University Press.

Greaves, W. S. (2007). Intonation in systemic functional linguistics. In R. Hasan, C. Matthiessen & J. J. Webster (eds).

Greenberg. J. H. (1954). Concerning inferences from linguistics to non-linguistic data. In H. Hoijer (ed.), *Language in Culture: Conference on the Interrelations of Language and Other Aspects of Culture.* Chicago, IL: University of Chicago Press.

Greenfield, P. M. & J. H. Smith. (1976). *Communication and the Beginning of Language: The Development of Semantic Structure in One-word Speech and Beyond.* New York: Academic Press.

Greenfield, S. (1997). *The Human Brain: A Guided Tour.* London: Weidenfeld and Nicholson.

Gregory, M. (1967). Aspects of varieties differentiation. *Journal of Linguistics,* 3, 177–198.

Gregory, M. (1986/1988). Generic situation and register: A functional view of communication. In J. D. Benson, M. Cummings, & W. Greaves (eds).

Gregory, M. (1995). Generic expectancies and discoursal surprises: John Donne's 'The Good Morrow'. In H. Fries & M. Gregory (eds), *Discourse in society: Systemic functional perspectives. Meaning and choice in language: Studies for Michael Halliday.* Norwood, NJ: Ablex.

Gregory, M. & S. Carroll: (1978). Language and Situation. London: Routledge & Kegan Paul.

Grice, H. P. (1975). Logic and conversation. In P. Cole & J. L. Morgan (eds), *Syntax and Semantics, Vol. 3: Speech Acts.* New York: Academic Press.

Gumperz, J. J. & D. Hymes (eds) (1972). *Directions in Sociolinguistics: The Ethnography of Communication.* New York: Holt Rinehart & Winston. Revised edition (with 'corrections and additions'). Oxford: Blackwell. 1986.

Halliday, M. A. K. (1957). Some aspects of systemic description and comparison in grammatical analysis. In *Studies in Linguistic Analysis* (special volume of the Philological Society). Oxford: Blackwell.

Halliday, M. A. K. (1959). *The Language of the Chinese 'Secret History of the Mongols'*. (Publication xvii of the Philological Society). Oxford: Blackwell.

Halliday, M. A. K. (1961). Categories of the theory of grammar. *Language*, 241–292. Reprinted in *Halliday CW1, 2002a.*

Halliday, M A K. (1964). The linguistic study of literary texts. In H. Lunt (ed.), *Proceedings of the Ninth International Congress of Linguists*. The Hague: Mouton. Reprinted in *Halliday, CW2, 2002b.*

Halliday, M A K. (1967a). *Intonation and Grammar in British English*. (Janua Linguarum Series Practica 48). The Hague: Mouton.

Halliday, M. A. K. (1967b). Notes on transitivity and theme in English, Part 1. *Journal of Linguistics* 3 (1): 37–81. Reprinted in *Halliday CW7, 2005b.*

Halliday, M. A. K. (1967c). Notes on transitivity and theme in English, Part 2. *Journal of Linguistics* 3 (2): 199–244. Reprinted in *Halliday CW7, 2005b.*

Halliday, M. A. K. (1968). Notes on transitivity and theme in English, Part 3. *Journal of Linguistics* 4 (2): 179–215. Reprinted in *Halliday CW7, 2005b.*

Halliday, M. A. K. (1969). Options and functions in the English clause. *Brno Studies in English* 8: 81–88. Reprinted in *Halliday CW7, 2005b.*

Halliday, M. A. K. (1970a). Language structure and language function. In J. Lyons (ed.), *New Horizons in Linguistics*. Harmondsworth: Penguin. Reprinted in *Halliday CW1, 2002a.*

Halliday, M. A. K. (1970b). *A Course in Spoken English: Intonation.* London: Oxford University Press.

Halliday, M A K. (1971). Language in a social perspective. *Educational Review*, 23 (3). Reprinted in *Halliday, CW 10, 2007b.*

Halliday, M. A. K. (1973a). *Explorations in the Functions of Language*. London: Edward Arnold.

Halliday, M. A. K. (1973b). Towards a sociological semantics. In Halliday 1973a. (an earlier version reprinted in *Halliday CW3, 2003.*)

Halliday, M A K. (1973c). The functional basis of language. In Halliday 1973a. Reprinted in *Halliday CW3, 2003.*

Halliday, M. A. K. (1974a). *Language and Social Man.* Schools Council Programme in Linguistics and English Teaching, Series II Vol. 3. London: Longmans. Reprinted in *Halliday CW10, 2007b.*

Halliday, M. A. K. (1974b). Language as social semiotic: Towards a general sociolinguistic theory. In A. Makkai & V. B. Makkai, (eds), *The First LACUS Forum*. Columbia, SC: Hornbeam Press.

Halliday, M. A. K. (1975a). *Learning How to Mean: Explorations in the Development of Language*. London: Edward Arnold.

Halliday, M. A. K. (1975b). Sociological aspects of semantic change. In L. Heilmann (ed.), *Proceedings of the Eleventh International Conference of Linguists*. Bologna-Florence, 28 August–2 September 1972. Bologna: Il Mulino.

Halliday, M. A. K. (1976). *System and Function in Language: Selected Papers*. G. Kress (ed.). London: Oxford University Press.

Halliday, M. A. K. (1977a). Text as semantic choice in social contexts. In T. van Dijk, & J. S. Petofi (eds). Reprinted in *Halliday CW2, 2002b*.

Halliday, M. A. K. (1977b). Ideas about language. In *Aims and Perspectives in Linguistics*. Occasional paper no. 1. Publication of ALAA. Reprinted in *Halliday CW3, 2003*.

Halliday, M. A. K. (1977c). Review of Jonathan Culler's Saussure. ABC broadcast.

Halliday, M. A. K. (1978). *Language as Social Semiotic: The Social Interpretation of Language*. London: Edward Arnold.

Halliday, M. A. K. (1979a). One child's proto-language. In M. Bullowa (ed.), *Before Speech: The Beginning of Interpersonal Communication*. Cambridge: Cambridge University Press. Reprinted in *Halliday CW4, 2004*.

Halliday, M. A. K. (1979b). Modes of meaning and modes of expression: types of grammatical structure and their determination by different semantic function. In D. J. Allerton, E. Carney, & D. Holdcroft (eds) *Function and Context in Linguistic Analysis*. Cambridge: Cambridge University Press. Reprinted in *Halliday CW1, 2002a*.

Halliday, M. A. K. (1980). Three aspects of children's language development: learning language, learning through language and learning about language. In Y. M. Goodman, M. M. Haussler & D. M. Strickland (eds), *Oral and Written Language Development: Impact on School*. International Reading Association & National Council of Teachers of English [no place. No date]. Reprinted in *Halliday, CW4, 2004*.

Halliday, M. A. K. (1984a). On the ineffability of grammatical categories. In A. Manning, P. Martin, & K. McCalla (eds), *The Tenth LACUS Forum*. Columbia, SC: Hornbeam Press. Reprinted in J. D. Benson, M. J. Cummings & W. S. Greaves (eds) 1988. Reprinted in *Halliday CW1, 2002a*.

Halliday, M. A. K. (1984b). Language as code and language as behaviour. In R. P. Fawcett, M. A. K. Halliday, S. M. Lamb & A. Makkai (eds). Reprinted in *Halliday CW4, 2004*.

Halliday, M. A. K. (1985a). Dimensions of discourse analysis: Grammar. In T. van Dijk (ed.), *Handbook of Discourse Analysis, Volume 2: Dimensions of Discourse*. London: Academic. Reprinted in *Halliday CW1, 2002a*.

Halliday, M. A. K. (1985b). *Introduction to Functional Grammar*. London: Arnold.

Halliday, M. A. K. (1985c). Context of situation. In M. A. K. Halliday & R. Hasan 1985. Geelong, Vic: Deakin University. Reprinted in *Halliday CW9, 2007a*.

Halliday, M. A. K. (1988). Poetry as scientific discourse: the nuclear sections of Tennyson's 'In Memoriam'. In D. Birch & M. O'Toole (eds), *Functions of Style*. London: Pinter. Reprinted in *Halliday, CW2, 2002b*.

Halliday, M. A. K. (1991a). The notion of 'context' in language education. In T. Lê & M. McCausland (eds), *Language Education: Interaction & Development: Proceedings of the First International Conference*, Vietnam, 1991. Launceston: University of Tasmania. Reprinted in *Halliday CW9, 2007a*.

Halliday, M. A. K. (1991b). Towards probabilistic interpretations. In E. Ventola (ed.), *Functional and Systemic Linguistics: Approaches and Uses*. Berlin: Walter de Gruyter. Reprinted in *Halliday CW6, 2005a*.

Halliday, M. A. K. (1992a). How do you mean? In M. Davies & L. Ravelli (eds). Reprinted in *Halliday CW1, 2002a*.

Halliday, M. A. K. (1992b). Language as system and language as instance: The corpus as a theoretical construct. In J. Svartvik (ed.), *Directions in Corpus Linguistics, Proceedings of Nobel Symposium 82, Stockholm, 4–8 August 1991*. Berlin: Mouton de Gruyter. Reprinted in *Halliday CW6, 2005a*.

Halliday, M. A. K. (1993). The act of meaning. In J. E. Alatis (ed.) Reprinted in Halliday *CW3, 2003*.

Halliday, M. A. K. (1994). 'So you say "pass" thank you three muchly': How conversation 'means': Contexts and functions. In A. D. Grimshaw (ed.), *What's Going on Here? Complementary Studies of Professional Talk (Volume Two of the Multiple Analysis Project). Vol. XLII in Advances in Discourse Processes*, (pp. 173–229). Norwood, NJ: Ablex. Reprinted in *Halliday CW2, 2002b*.

Halliday, M. A. K. (1995a). On language in relation to the evolution of human consciousness. In S. Allén (ed.). *Of Thoughts and Words: The Relation between Language and Mind*, Proceedings of Nobel Symposium 92. London: Imperial College Press. Reprinted in *Halliday CW3, 2003*.

Halliday, M. A. K. (1996). On grammar and grammatics. In R. Hasan, C. Cloran & D. Butt (eds). *Functional Descriptions*. Amsterdam: Benjamins. Reprinted in *Halliday CW1, 2002a*.

Halliday, M. A. K. (1998). Representing the child as a semiotic being. Paper presented at Monash University, (Australia) at the conference 'Representing the Child', 2–3 October, 1998. Reprinted in *Halliday CW 4*, 2004.

Halliday, M. A. K. (1999). The notion of 'context' in language education. In M. Ghadessy (ed.). Reprinted in *Halliday CW9, 2007a*.

Halliday, M. A. K. (2003). *On Language and Linguistics, CW3*. In J. Webster (ed.) London: Continuum.

Halliday, M. A. K. (2005). On matter and meaning: The two realms of human experience. *Linguistics and the Human Sciences, 1 (1)*. 59–82.

Halliday, M. A. K. (2007a). *Language and Education, CW9*. In J. Webster (ed.) London: Continuum.

Halliday, M. A. K. (2007b). *Language and Society, CW10*. In J. Webster (ed.) London: Continuum.

Halliday, M. A. K. (2008). *Complementarities in Language*. Beijing: The Commercial Press.

Halliday, M. A. K. (2009). Methods – techniques – problems. In M. A. K. Halliday & J. J. Webster (eds).

Halliday. M. A. K., A. McIntosh & P. Strevens (1964). *Linguistic Sciences and Language Teaching*. London: Longmans.

Halliday, M. A. K. & R. Hasan (1976). *Cohesion in English*. London: Longmans.

Halliday, M. A. K. & R. Hasan (1985). *Language, Context and Text: Aspects of Language in a Social-Semiotic Perspective.* Geelong, Vic.: Deakin University Press. (A revised version of *Text and Context: Aspects of Language in a Social-Semiotic Perspective.* Sophia Linguistica VI. Tokyo: Sophia University Press. 1980).

Halliday, M. A. K., & R. P. Fawcett (eds). (1987). *New Developments in Systemic Linguistics, Vol.* 1: *Theory and Description.* London: Frances Pinter.

Halliday, M. A. K. & Z. L. James (1993). A quantitative study of polarity and primary tense in the English finite clause. In J. McH. Sinclair, *et al.* (eds) *Techniques of Description: Spoken and Written Discourse.* London: Routledge. Reprinted in *Halliday CW6, 2005a.*

Halliday, M. A. K. and Martin, J. R. (1993). *Writing Science: Literacy and Discursive Power.* London: Falmer.

Halliday, M. A. K. & C. M. I. M. Matthiessen. (1999). *Construing Experience Through Meaning: A Language Based Approach to Cognition.* London: Continuum.

Halliday, M. A. K. & C. M. I. M. Matthiessen. (2004). *Introduction to Functional Grammar.* 3rd edition. London: Hodder.

Halliday, M. A. K. & C. M. I. M. Matthiessen. (2014). Halliday's Introduction to Functional Grammar: Fourth Edition, Revised by C. M. I. M. Matthiessen. London: Routledge.

Halliday, M. A. K. & W. S. Greaves. (2008). *Intonation in the Grammar of English.* London: Equinox.

Halliday, M. A. K. & J. J. Webster. (eds). (2009). *Continuum Companion to Systemic Functional Linguistics.* London: Continuum.

Hammond, J. (1989). The NCELTR literacy project. *Prospect,* 5 (1), 23–30.

Harré, Rom. (1993). *Social Being.* (2nd edition). Oxford: Blackwell.

Harris, Z. S. (1951). *Methods in Structural Linguistics.* Chicago. IL: University of Chicago Press.

Hasan, R. (1964). *A Linguistic Study of Contrasting Features in the Style of Two Contemporary English Prose Writers.* Unpublished Ph.D. thesis. University of Edinburgh.

Hasan, R. (1968). Grammatical Cohesion in Spoken and Written English, Part I: Nuffield Programme in Linguistics and English Teaching, Paper 7. London: Longman.

Hasan, R. (1971a). Syntax and semantics. In J. Morton (ed.), *Social and Biological Factors in Psycholinguistics.* London: Logos.

Hasan, R. (1971b). Rime and reason in literature. In S Chatman (ed.), *Literary Style: A Symposium.* London: Oxford University Press.

Hasan, R. (1973a). Measuring the Length of a Text. Mimeo.

Hasan, R. (1973b). Cohesive Categories. Mimeo.

Hasan, R. (1973c). Code, register and social dialect. In B Bernstein (ed.) 1973. Reprinted in Hasan 2005.

Hasan, R. (1978). Text in the systemic-functional model. In W. U. Dressler (ed.), *Current Trends in Text-linguistics*. Berlin: de Gruyter.

Hasan, R. (1979a). Language in the study of literature. Report on Workshop no. 6 from Working Conference on Language in Education. Sydney University Extension Programme & Department of Linguistics. 19–24 August.

Hasan, R. (1979b). On the notion of text. In J. S. Petofi (ed.), *Text vs. Sentence: Basic Questions of Text-linguistics*. Hamburg: Helmut Buske.

Hasan, R. (1981). What's going on: A dynamic view of context in language. In J. E. Copeland, & P. W. Davies (eds), *The Seventh LACUS Forum*. Columbia. SC: Hornbeam Press.

Hasan, R. (1982). Situation and the definition of conversation. Paper presented at the Multi-Disciplinary Workshop on the Analysis of Naturally Occurring Conversation: The MAP at the Annenburg School of Communications. University of Pennsylvania. 17–20 November. Convener: Allen Grimshaw.

Hasan, R. (1983). *A Semantic Network for the Analysis of Messages in Everyday Talk between Mothers and Their Children*. Department of Linguistics: Macquarie University. Mimeo.

Hasan, R. (1984a). Ways of saying: Ways of meaning. In R. P. Fawcett, M. A. K. Halliday, S. M. Lamb & A. Makkai (eds). Reprinted in C. Cloran, D. Butt & G. Williams (eds). London: Cassell, 1996.

Hasan, R. (1984b). The structure of the nursery tale: An essay in text typology. In L. Coveri (ed.). *Linguistica Testuale*. Rome: Bulzoni.

Hasan, R. (1984c). The nursery tale as a genre. In M. Berry, C. Carter & Stubbs (eds), *Nottingham Linguistic Circular: Special Issue on Systemic Linguistics, Volume 13*. Department of English: University of Nottingham. Edited version reprinted in C. Cloran, D. Butt & G. Williams (eds) *Ways of Saying Ways of Meaning: Selected Papers of Ruqaiya Hasan*. London: Cassell 1996. Full version reprinted in Hasan (2011c).

Hasan, R. (1984d). Coherence and cohesive harmony. In J. Flood (ed.), *Understanding Reading Comprehension: Cognition, Language and the Structure of Prose*. Delaware: International Reading Association.

Hasan, R. (1984e). What kind of resource is language? *Australian Review of Applied Linguistics*, 7 (1): 57–85. Reprinted in C. Cloran, D. Butt & G. Williams (eds): *Ways of Saying, Ways of Meaning: Selected Papers of Ruqaiya Hasan*. London: Cassell, 1996.

Hasan, R. (1985a). The implications of semantic distance for language in education. *Indian Journal of Applied Linguistics*, XI (2): 1–22. Reprinted in R. Hasan (2011c).

Hasan, R. (1985b). On social conditions for semiotic mediation: the genesis of mind in society. In Alan R. Sadovnik (ed.), *Knowledge and Pedagogy: the sociology of Basil Bernstein*, 171–196. Norwood, NJ: Ablex.

Hasan, R. (1985c). The structure of a text, the texture of a text & the identity of a text: Chapters 4, 5 and 6, respectively. In M. A. K. Halliday & R. Hasan (1985).

Hasan, R. (1985d). Meaning, context and text – fifty years after Malinowski. In J. D. Benson & W. S. Greaves (eds). [Chapter 2 in the present volume].

Hasan, R. (1985e). Lending and borrowing: From grammar to lexis. In J. E. Clark (ed.), *The Cultivated Australian: Festschrift in Honour of Arthur Delbridge. Beitrage zur Phonetik und Linguistik, 48.* Hamburg: H. Buske.

Hasan, R. (1986). The ontogenesis of ideology: an interpretation of mother child talk. In T. Threadgold, E. A. Grosz, G. Kress & M. A. K. Halliday (eds).

Hasan, R. (1987a). Directions from structuralism. In N. Fabb, D. Attridge, A. Durant & C. MacCabe (eds), *The Linguistics of Writing: Arguments between Language and Literature.* Manchester: Manchester University Press.

Hasan, R. (l987b). The grammarian's dream: Lexis as most delicate grammar. In M. A. K. Halliday & R. P. Fawcett (eds).

Hasan, R. (1987c). Reading picture reading: Invisible instruction at home and in school. *Proceedings from the 13th Conference of the Australian Reading Association.* Sydney July 1987 [no editor; no publisher indicated]. Revised version reprinted in Hasan 2004 as Reading picture reading: A study in ideology and inference.

Hasan, R. (1988). Language in the processes of socialization: Home and school. In L. Gerot, J. Oldenburg & T. van Leeuwen, (eds), *Language and Socialization: Home and School, Proceedings from the Working Conference on Language in Education, November 1986.* Sydney: Macquarie University. Reprinted in Hasan 2009a.

Hasan, R. (1989). Semantic variation and sociolinguistics. *Australian Journal of Linguistics,* 9 (2): 221–275. Reprinted in Hasan 2009a.

Hasan, R. (1992a). Speech genre, semiotic mediation and the development of higher mental functions. M. A. K. Halliday & F. C. C. Peng (eds). *Current Research in Functional Grammar, Discourse, and Computational Linguistics with Foundation in Systemic Theory: Language Sciences,* 14 (4): Special Issue. Reprinted in Hasan 2005.

Hasan, R. (1992b). Meaning in sociolinguistic theory. In K. Bolton & H. Kwok (eds) *Sociolinguistics Today: International Perspectives.* London: Routledge. Reprinted in Hasan 2009a.

Hasan, R. (1992c). Rationality in everyday talk: from process to system. In J. Svartvik (ed.) *Directions in Corpus Linguistics: Proceedings of Nobel Symposium 82.* Berlin: Mouton de Gruyter. Reprinted in Hasan 2009a.

Hasan, R. (1993). Contexts for meaning. In J. E. Alatis (ed.) Reprinted in Hasan 2009a.

Hasan, R. (1994). Situation and the definition of genre. In A. D. Grimshaw (ed.) *What's Going on Here? Complementary Studies of Professional Talk* (Volume Two of the Multiple Analysis Project). Norwood, NJ: Ablex.

Hasan, R. (1995a). The conception of context in text. In P. H. Fries & M. Gregory (eds), *Discourse in Society: Systemic Functional Perspectives.* Norwood, NJ: Ablex. [Chapter 5 in this volume].

Hasan, R. (1996a). Semantic networks: a tool for the analysis of meaning. In C. Cloran, D. Butt & G. Williams (eds). *Ways of Saying: Ways of Meaning: Selected Papers of Ruqaiya Hasan*. London: Cassell.

Hasan, R. (1996b). On teaching literature across cultural distances. In J. E. James (ed.) *The Language-Culture Connection*. Singapore: SEMEO Regional Language Centre.

Hasan, R. (1996c). Literacy, everyday talk and society. In R. Hasan & G. Williams (eds). Reprinted in Hasan 2011c.

Hasan, R. (1999a). The dis-empowerment game: Bourdieu and language in literacy. *Linguistics and Education*, 10 (1): 25–88. Reprinted in Hasan 2005, under the title 'The dis-empowerment game: Bourdieu on language'.

Hasan, R. (1999b). Speaking with reference to context. In M. Ghadessy (ed.) [Chapter 6 in the present volume].

Hasan, R. (1999c). Society, language and the mind: The meta-dialogism of Basil Bernstein's theory. In F. Christie (ed.). Reprinted in Hasan 2005.

Hasan, R. (2000). The uses of talk. In S. Sarangi & M. Coulthard (eds) *Discourse and Social Life*. Harlow: Pearson Education Limited.

Hasan, R. (2001a). Wherefore context?: The place of context in the system and process of language. In S. Ren, W. Gutherie, & I. W. R. Fong (eds), *Grammar and Discourse: Proceedings of the International Conference on Discourse Analysis*. Macau: University of Macau 1997. [Chapter 4 in the present volume].

Hasan, R. (2001b). The ontogenesis of decontextualized language: Some achievements of classification and framing. In A. Morais, I. Neves, B. Davies & H. Daniels (eds). Reprinted in Hasan 2005.

Hasan, R. (2004a). Reading picture reading: A study in ideology and inference. In J. Foley (ed.). *Language, Education and Discourse*. London: Continuum. Reprinted in Hasan 2005.

Hasan, R. (2004b). The world in words: Semiotic mediation, tenor and ideology. In G. Williams & A. Lukin (eds) *The Development of Language: Functional Perspectives on Species and Individuals*. London: Continuum. Reprinted in Hasan 2009a.

Hasan, R. (2005). *Language, Society and Consciousness: The Collected Works of Ruqaiya Hasan, Volume 1*, edited by J. J. Webster. London: Equinox.

Hasan, R. (2008). Modes of learning, modes of teaching: Semiotic mediation and knowledge. *SPELT Quarterly*, 23 (3): 2–19. Reprinted in Hasan 2011c.

Hasan, R. (2009a). *Semantic Variation: Meaning in Society and in Sociolinguistics: The Collected Works of Ruqaiya Hasan, Volume 2*, edited by J. J. Webster. London: Equinox.

Hasan, R. (2009b). The place of context in a systemic functional model. In Halliday & Webster (eds) [Chapter 7 in the present volume].

Hasan, R. (2009c). Wanted: A theory for integrated sociolinguistics. Chapter 1 in Hasan 2009a.

Hasan, R. (2010). The meaning of 'not' is not in 'not'. In A. Mahboob & N. K. Knight (eds) *Appliable Linguistics*. London: Continuum.

Hasan R. (2011a). *Selected Papers on Applied Linguistics*. Beijing: Foreign Languages Teaching and Research Press.

Hasan, R. (2011b). On the process of teaching: A perspective from functional grammar. In Hasan (2011d).

Hasan, R. (2011c). A timeless journey: On the past and future of present knowledge. In R. Hasan *Selected Works of Ruqaiya Hasan on Applied Linguistics*. Beijing: Foreign Languages Teaching and Research Press.

Hasan, R. (2011d). *Language and Education: Learning and Teaching in Society: The Collected Works of Ruqaiya Hasan, Volume 3*, edited by J. J. Webster. London: Equinox.

Hasan, R. (2012). A view of pragmatics in a social semiotic perspective. *LHS*, 5 (3): 249–279.

Hasan, R. (2013). Choice, system, realization: Describing language as meaning potential. In L. Fontaine, T. Bartlett, & G. O'Grady (eds) *Systemic Functional Linguistics: Exploring Choice*. Cambridge: Cambridge University Press.

Hasan, R. (2014a). Linguistic sign and the science of linguistics: The foundations of appliability. In Y. Fang & J. J. Webster (eds) *Developing Systemic Functional Linguistics*. London: Equinox.

Hasan, R. (2014b). Towards a paradigmatic description of context: Systems, metafunctions, and semantics. *Functional Linguistics*, 2014, 1.9 published by Springer. (Chapter 8 in this volume).

Hasan, R. (2016). In the nature of language: reflections on permeability and hybridity. In D. R. Miller & P. Bailey (eds), *Hybridity in Systemic Functional Linguistics*. London: Equinox.

Hasan, R. (forthcoming). Functionality in language: four European scholars. In *The Collected Works of Ruqaiya Hasan, Volume 5: Describing Language: Theory and practice*, edited by J. J. Webster. London: Equinox.

Hasan, R. & J. R. Martin. (eds). (1989). *Language Development: Learning Language, Learning Culture. Meaning and Choice in Language. Studies for Michael Halliday*. Norwood, NJ: Ablex.

Hasan, R., & C. Cloran. (1990). A sociolinguistic interpretation of everyday talk between mothers and children. In M. A. K. Halliday, J. Gibbons, & H. Nicholas (eds), *Learning, Keeping and Using Language. Selected Papers from the Eighth World Congress of Applied Linguistics, Sydney, 16–21 August* 1987 (Vol. 1, pp. 67–99). Amsterdam: John Benjamins. Reprinted in Hasan 2009a.

Hasan, R. & P. H. Fries (eds) (1995). *On Subject and Theme: A discourse Functional Perspective*. Amsterdam: Bejamins.

Hasan, R., C. Cloran, & D. G. Butt (eds) (1996). *Functional Descriptions: Theory in Practice*. Amsterdam: John Benjamins.

Hasan, R. & G. Williams (eds) (1996). *Literacy in Society*. London: Longman.

Hasan, R. C. Matthiessen & J. J. Webster (eds) (2005). *Continuing Discourse on Language: A Functional Perspective*, Volume 1. London: Equinox.

Hasan, R., C. Matthiessen & J. J. Webster. (eds) (2007) *Continuing Discourse on Language: A Functional Perspective*, Volume 2. London: Equinox.

Hasan, R., C. Cloran, G. Williams & A. Lukin. (2007) Semantic networks: the description of linguistic meaning in SFL. In R. Hasan, C. Matthiessen & J. J. Webster (eds). London: Equinox.

Hasan, R. & D. G. Butt (2011). Forms of discourse, forms of knowledge: reading Bernstein. In R. Hasan (2011c). London: Equinox.

Hjelmslev, L. (1961). *Prolegomena to a Theory of Language*. (Translated and edited by F. J. Whitfield). Madison, WI: University of Wisconsin Press.

Hockett, C. F. (1954). Chinese versus English: an exploration of the Whorfian Theses. In Harry Hoijer (ed.) *Language in Culture: Conference on the Interrelations of Language and Other Aspects of Culture*. Chicago, IL: Chicago University Press.

Huddleston, R. D., R. A. Hudson, E. Winter & A. Henrici. (1968). *Sentence and Clause in Scientific English*. University College London: Communication Research Centre. (mimeo).

Hymes. D. H. (1968). The ethnography of speaking. In J. A. Fishman (ed.), *Readings in the Sociology of Language*. The Hague: Mouton.

Hymes, D. H. (1971). Sociolinguistics and the ethnography of speaking. In E. Ardener (ed.), *Social Anthropology of Linguistics*. Association of Social Anthropology, Monograph 10. London: Tavistock.

Hymes, D. H. (1972). On the communication competence. In J. Pride & J. Holmes, (eds), *Sociolinguistics*. Harmondsworth: Penguin.

Hymes, D. H. (1986). Models of the interaction of language and social life. In J. J. Gumperz & D. H. Hymes (eds) (Revised edition). Oxford: Blackwell.

Jacobson, R. (1966). Concluding statement: Linguistics and Poetics. In T. A. Sebeok (ed.), *Style in Language*. New York: Technology Press & Wiley.

Kappagoda, A. (2005). What people do to know: the construction of knowledge as a social semiotic activity. In R. Hasan, C. Matthiessen & J. J. Webster (eds).

Karmiloff-Smith, A. (1979). *A Functional Approach to Child Language*. Cambridge: Cambridge University Press.

Kitching, G. (1988). *Karl Marx and the Philosophy of Praxis*. London: Routledge.

Knorr-Cetina, K. D. & M. Mulkay (eds). (1983). *Science Observed: Perspectives on the Social Studies of Science*. London: Sage.

Kress, G. R. (1976). English system networks. In G. Kress (ed.). *M. A. K. Halliday: System and Function in Language: Selected Papers*. London: Oxford University Press.

Kress, G. R., & T. Threadgold. (1988). Towards a social theory of genre. *Southern Review,* 21 (3): 215–243.

Kress, G. R., & T. van Leeuwen (1990). *Reading Images*. Geelong: Deakin University Press.

Kress, G. & T. van Leeuwen. (1996). *Reading Images: The Grammar of Visual Design*. London: Routledge.

Labov, W. (1966). *The Social Stratification of English in New York City*. Arlington: Centre of Applied Linguistics.

Labov, W. (1972a). The social motivation of a sound change. In *Sociolinguistic Patterns*. Oxford: Basil Blackwell.

Labov, W. (1972b). The study of language in its social context. In *Patterns of Language*. London: Cambridge University Press.

Labov, W. & D. Fanshel (1977). *Therapeutic Discourse*. New York: Academic Press.

Lakoff, R. (1990). The way we were; or, the real actual truth about generative semantics: A memoir. *Journal of Pragmatics* [Copper Issue], pp. 939–988.

Lamb, S. M. (1966). *Outline of Stratificational Grammar*. (With Appendix by E Newel). Georgetown, DC: Georgetown University Press.

Lamb, S. M. (1998). *Pathways of the Brain: The Neurocognitive Basis of Language*. Amsterdam: Benjamins.

Lamb, S. M. (2004). *Language and Reality*. J. Webster (ed.). London: Continuum.

Latour, B. & S. Woolgar. (1979). *Laboratory Life: The Social Construction of Scientific Facts*. Beverley Hills, CA: Sage.

Leach, E. R. (1957/1964). The epistemological background to Malinowski's pragmatism. In R. Firth (ed.), *Man and Culture: An Evaluation of the Work of Bronislaw Malinowski*. Harper Torchbooks. New York: Harper and Row.

Leckie-Tarry, H. (1995). *Language and Context: A Functional Linguistic Theory of Register.* London: Pinter.

Leech, G. N. (1974). *Semantics.* Harmondsworth: Penguin.

Leech, G N. (1983). *Principles of Pragmatics*. London: Longman.

Leeuwen, T. van. (1991a). The Socio-semiotics of easy-listening Music. *Social Semiotics* 1 (1): 67–80.

Leeuwen, T. van (1991b). Conjunctive structure in documentary film and television. *Continuum: Journal of Media & Cultural Studies*, 5(1), 76–114.

Lemke, J. L. (1984). Towards a model of the functional process. In J. L. Lemke, *Semiotics and Education* (Toronto Semiotic Circle Monographs, pp. 6–22). Toronto: University of Toronto, Victoria College.

Lemke, J. L. (1985). Ideology, inter-textuality, and the notion of register. In J. D. Benson & W. S. Greaves (eds).

Lemke, J. L. (1990). *Talking Science: Language, Learning and Values. Language and Educational Processes, Vol 1*. Norwood, NJ: Ablex.

Lemke, J. L. (1993). Discourse, dynamics and social change. In M. A. K. Halliday (ed.), *Language as Cultural Dynamic, Special Issue of Cultural Dynamics Vol VI*, 1–2. 243–275.

Lenneberg, E. H. (1971). Language and cognition. In *Semantics: An Interdisciplinary Reader in Philosophy, Linguistics and Psychology*. Cambridge: Cambridge University Press.

Levin, S. R. (1976). Concerning what kind of a speech act a poem is. In T. van Dijk (ed.). *Pragmatics of Language and Literature*. Amsterdam: North-Holland.

Levinson, S. (1983). *Pragmatics.* Cambridge: Cambridge University Press.

Levinson, S. (1992). Activity types and language In P. Drew, & J. Heritage (eds), *Talk at Work: Interaction in Institutional Settings*, 66–100. Cambridge: Cambridge University Press.

Lewis, D. K. (1968). *Conventions: A Philosophical Study*. Cambridge, MA: Harvard University Press.

Lewis, M. & L. A. Rosenblum. (1974). *The Effect of the Infant on Its Caregiver*. New York: Wiley.

Lock, A. E. (1978). (ed.) *Action, Gesture and Symbol: The Emergence of Language*. New York: Academic Press.

Luria, A. R. (1976). *Cognitive Development: Its Cultural and Social Foundation*. Cambridge, MA: Harvard University Press.

Lyons, J. (1966). Firth's theory of 'meaning'. In C. E. Bazell, J. C. Catford, M. A. K. Halliday & R. H. Robins (eds) *In Memory of J. R. Firth*. London: Longman.

Lyons, J. (1968). *Introduction to Theoretical Linguistics*. London: Cambridge University Press.

Lyons, J. (ed.) (1970). *New Horizons in Linguistics*. Harmondsworth: Penguin.

Lyons, J. (1977). *Semantics, Volumes 1 and 2*. Cambridge: Cambridge University Press.

Malinowski, B. (1923). The problem of meaning in primitive languages. Supplement I to C. K. Ogden & I. A. Richards, *The Meaning of Meaning*. New York: Harcourt Brace & World.

Malinowski, B. (1935). An ethnographic theory of language, and some corollaries. (Part IV in *Coral Gardens and Their Magic: The Language of Magic and Gardening, Volume Two*.) London: Allen and Unwin.

Mann, W. C. (1985). An introduction to the Nigel text generation grammar. In J. D. Benson & W. S. Greaves (eds).

Mann, W. C., C. M. I. M. Matthiessen & S. A. Thompson (eds) (1992). Rhetorical structure theory and context analysis. In W. C. Mann & S. A. Thompson (eds) *Discourse Descriptions: Diverse Linguistic Analyses of a Fund-Raising Text*. Amsterdam: Benjamins.

Marková, I. (1990). Introduction. In I. Marková & C. Fopper (eds) *The Dynamics of Dialogue*. New York: Harvester.

Marková, I. & C. Fopper. (1991). Conclusion. In I. Marková & C. Fopper (eds) *Asymmetries in Dialogue*. New York: Harvester Wheatsheaf.

Martin, J. R. (1979). Conjunction and the structure of conversation. Sydney: University of Sydney. Mimeo.

Martin, J. R. (1984). Functional components in a grammar: A review of deployable recognition criteria. *Nottingham Linguistic Circular*, 13: 35–70.

Martin, J. R. (1985a). Process and text: two aspects of human semiosis. In J. D. Benson & W. S. Greaves (eds).

Martin, J. R. (1985b). *Factual Writing: Exploring and Challenging Social Reality*. Geelong: Deakin.

Martin, J. R. (1986). Grammaticalizing ecology: the politics of baby seals and kangaroos. In T. Threadgold, E. A. Grosz, G. Kress, & M. A. K. Halliday (eds).

Martin, J. R. (1991). Intrinsic functionality: implications for contextual theory. *Social Semiotics,* 1 (I): 99–162.

Martin, J. R. (1992). *English Text: System and Structure.* Amsterdam: John Benjamins.

Martin, J. R. (1993). Literacy in Science: learning to Handle Text as Technology. In M. A. K. Halliday & J. R. Martin (eds), *Writing Science: Literacy and Discursive Power.* London: Falmer.

Martin, J R. (1996). *Evaluating Disruption: Symbolising Theme in Junior Secondary Narrative.* In R. Hasan & G. Williams (eds).

Martin, J. R. (1997). Analysing genre: functional parameters. In F. Christie & J. R. Martin (eds).

Martin, J. R. (1999). Mentoring semogenesis: 'genre-based' literacy pedagogy. In F. Christie (ed.), *Pedagogy and the Shaping of Consciousness: Linguistic and Social Processes,* 123–155. London: Cassell (Open Linguistics Series).

Martin, J. R. & D. Rose. (2005). Designing literacy pedagogy: scaffolding democracy in the classroom. In R. Hasan, C. Matthiessen & J. J. Webster (eds).

Martinec, R. (2005). Topics in multimodality. In R. Hasan, C. Matthiessen, J. J. Webster (eds).

Matthiessen, C. M. I. M. (1993). Register in the round: diversity in a unified theory of register analysis. In M. Ghadessy (ed.) *Register Analysis: Theory and Practice.* London: Pinter.

Matthiessen, C. M. I. M. (1995). *Lexicogrammatical Cartography: English Systems.* Tokyo: International language Science Publishers.

Matthiessen C. M. I. M. (2004). Descriptive motifs and generalisations. In A. Caffarel, J. R. Martin, C. M. I. M. Matthiessen (eds). *Language Typology: A Functional Perspective.* Amsterdam/Philadelphia: John Benjamins.

Matthiessen, C. M. I. M. (2007). The architecture of language according to systemic functional theory: developments since the 1970s. In R. Hasan, C. Matthiessen, & J. J. Webster (eds).

Matthiessen, C. M. I. M. (2009a) Multisemiotic and context-based register typology: registerial variation in the complementarity of semiotic systems. In Eija Ventola & Jesús Moya Guijarro (eds), *The World Told and the World Shown,* 11–38. Basingstoke: Palgrave Macmillan.

Matthiessen, C. M. I. M. (2009b). Ideas and new directions. In M. A. K. Halliday & J. J. Webster (eds). London: Continuum.

Matthiessen, C. M. I. M. (2015). Halliday on language. In J. J. Webster (ed.) *Companion to M. A. K. Halliday.* London: Bloomsbury.

Matthiessen, C. M. I. M. & C. Nesbitt. (1996). On the idea of theory-neutral descriptions. In R. Hasan, C. Cloran & D. G. Butt, (eds) *Functional Descriptions: Theory in Practice.* Amsterdam: John Benjamins.

Matthiessen, C. M. I. M., A. Lukin, D. Butt, C. Cleirigh & C. Nesbitt (2005). 'A case study in multi-stratal analysis'. *Australian Review of Applied Linguistics,* 19: 123–150.

McTear M. F. (1979). 'Hey! I've got something to tell you' etc. *Journal of Pragmatics*, 3 (3/4).

Mead, G. H. (1934). *Mind, Self and Society: From the Standpoint of a Social Behaviourist*. Chicago: Chicago University Press.

Mehan, H. (1979). *Learning lessons: Social organization in the classroom*. Cambridge, MA: Harvard University Press.

Mitchell, A. G. (1946). *The pronunciation of English in Australia*. Sydney: Angus and Robertson.

Mitchell, T. F. (1975). The language of buying and selling in Cyrenaica. In *Principles of Firthian Linguistics*. London: Longman. (Original work published, 1957).

Moore, E. C. (1961). *American Pragmatism: Peirce. James and Dewey*. New York: Columbia University Press.

Morais, A., I. Neves, B. Davies & H. Daniels (eds) (2001). *Towards a sociology of Pedagogy: The Contribution of Basil Bernstein to Research*. New York: Peter Lang.

Nesbitt, C. & G. Plum (1988). Probabilities in a systemic grammar: Clause complex in English. In R. P. Fawcett & D. J. Young (eds) *New Developments in Systemic Linguistics, Vol 2: Theory and Application*. London: Pinter.

Ochs, E. & B. B. Schieffelin (eds) (1979). *Developmental Pragmatics*. New York: Academic Press.

Oldenburg-Torr, J. (1997). *From Child Tongue to Mother Tongue: A Case Study of Language Development in the First Two and a Half Years*. Monographs in Systemic Linguistics 9. University of Nottingham: Department of English Studies.

Oldroyd, D. (1986). *The Arch of Knowledge: An Introductory Study of the History of the Philosophy and the Methodology of Science*. Sydney: New South Wales University Press.

O'Toole, M. (1990). A systemic-functional semiotics of art. *Semiotica*, 82 (3–4): 185–209.

O'Toole, M. (1994). *The Language of Displayed Art*. Leicester: Leicester University Press.

Painter, C. (1984). *Into the Mother Tongue: A Case Study in Early Language Development*. London: Pinter.

Painter, C. (1989). Language learning: A functional view of language development. In R. Hasan & J. R. Martin (eds).

Painter, C. (1996). The development of language as a resource for thinking: A linguistic view of learning. In R. Hasan & G. Williams (eds).

Painter, C. (1999). *Learning through Language in Early Childhood*. London: Continuum.

Painter, C. (2009). Language development. In M. A. K. Halliday & J. J. Webster (eds) 2009.

Painter, C. & J. R. Martin. (1986). *Writing to Mean: Teaching Genres Across the Curriculum*. Applied Linguistics Association of Australia, Occasional Paper, No. 9.

Painter, C., B. Derewianka & J. Torr. (2005). From micro-function to metaphor: Learning language and learning through language. In R. Hasan, C. M. I. M. Matthiessen, & J. J. Webster (eds).

Palmer, F. R. (1981). *Semantics*. 2nd edn. Cambridge: Cambridge University Press.

Pawley, A. (1985). On speech formulas and linguistic competence. *Linguas Modernas,* 12. Universidad de Chile.

Petofi, J. S. (1978). A formal semiotic text theory as an integrated theory of natural language. In W. U. Dressler (ed.) *Current Trends in Text-Linguistics*. Berlin: de Gruyter.

Pearce, J., G. Thornton, & D. Mackay. (1989). The programme in Linguistics and English teaching, University College London 1964–1971. In R. Hasan & J. R. Martin (eds).

Pêcheux, M. (1983). *Language Semantics and Ideology*. (tr. H. Nagpal). 2nd edition. London: Macmillan.

Pinker, S. (1994). *The Language Instinct*. New York: William Morrow.

Pinker, S. (1995). Language is a human instinct. In J. Brockman (ed.) *The Third Culture*. New York: Simon & Schuster.

Popper, K. R. (1972). *Objective Knowledge: An Evolutionary Approach*. London: Oxford University Press.

Ravelli, L. J. (1995). A dynamic perspective: implications for metafunctional interaction and an understanding of Theme. In R. Hasan and P. H. Fries (eds): 187–235.

Reddy, V., D. Hay, L. Murray & C. Trevarthen. (1997). Communication in infancy: Mutual regulation of communication in infancy. In G. Brenner, A. Slater & G. Butterworth (eds) *Infant Development: Recent Advances*. London: Psychology Press.

Rothery, J. (1989). Learning about language. In R. Hasan & J. R. Martin (eds), *Language Development: Learning Language, Learning Culture, Meaning and Choice in Language: Studies for Michael Halliday* (pp. 199–256). Norwood, NJ: Ablex.

Rorty, R. (1982). Method, social science and social hope. In *Consequences of Pragmatism*. New York: Harvester.

Sadock, J. M. (1974). *Toward a Linguistic Theory of Speech Acts*. New York: Academic Press.

Saussure, F. de (1966). *Course in General Linguistics* (trans. W. Baskin). New York: McGraw-Hill.

Saussure, F. de (2006). Writings in General Linguistics. In S. Bouquet & R. Engler (eds). C. Sanders & M. Pires (trans.). Oxford: Oxford University Press. (digitized copy: 28.4.2008)

Sbisa, M. & P. Fabbri. (1980). Models (?) for a pragmatic analysis. *Working Paper No 91*, Centro Internatzionale di Semiotica e di Linguistica. Urbino: Universita di Urbino.

Schank, R. C. & R. P. Abelson (1977). *Scripts Plans Goals and Understanding: An Inquiry into Human Knowledge Structure*s. New York: John Wiley & Sons.

Searle, J. R. (1969). *Speech Acts: An Essay in the Philosophy of Language*. Cambridge: Cambridge University Press.

Searle, J. R. (1979). Indirect speech acts. In *Expression and Meaning: Studies in the Theory of Speech Acts*. Cambridge: Cambridge University Press.

Sebeok, T. A. (ed.) (1960). *Style in Language*. New York: MIT Technology Press & Wiley.

Shotter, J. (1978). The cultural context of communication studies: Theoretical and methodological issues. In A. E. Lock (ed.).

Sinclair, J. McH. (1990). Trust the text. In M. Davies & L. Ravelli (eds).

Sinclair, J. McH. & M. Coulthard. (1975). *Towards an Analysis of Discourse: The English Used by Teachers and Pupils*. London: Oxford University Press.

Smith, J. E. (1978). *Purpose and Thought: The Meaning of Pragmatism*. London: Hutchinson.

Sperber, D. & D. Wilson. (1986). *Relevance: Communication and Cognition*. London: Blackwell.

Steiner, E. (2005). Halliday and translation theory: Enhancing the options, broadening the range, and keeping the ground. In R. Hasan, C. Matthiessen & J. J. Webster (eds).

Stewart, I. (1989). *Does God Play Dice: The New Mathematics of Chaos*. London: Penguin Books.

Taverniers, M. (2016). *Systemic Functional Grammar and the Legacy of Hjelmslev*. London: Palgrave Macmillan.

Thibault, P. (1989). Genre, social action and pedagogy: Towards a critical social-semiotic account. *Southern Review, 22* (3): 332–368.

Thibault, P. J. (1997). *Re-reading Saussure: The Dynamics of Sign in Social Life*. London: Routledge.

Thibault, P. J. (2004a). *Agency and Consciousness in Discourse: Self-other Dynamics as a Complex System*. London: Continuum.

Thibault, P. J. (2004b). *Brain, Mind and the Signifying Body: An Eco-social Semiotic Theory*. London: Continuum.

Thibault, P. J. (2005). The interpersonal Gateway to the meaning of mind: unifying the inter- and intra-organism perspective on language. In R. Hasan, C. Matthiessen & J. J. Webster (eds).

Threadgold, T., E. A. Grosz, G. Kress, & M. A. K. Halliday (eds) (1986). *Semiotics Ideology Language* (Sydney Studies in Society and Culture 3). Sydney: Sydney Association for Studies in Society and Culture.

Toulmin, S. (1976). History, praxis and the 'third world'. In R. S. Cohen, P. K. Feyerabend, & M. W. W. Wartofsky (eds).

Torr, J. (1997). *From Child Tongue to Mother Tongue*. Monographs in Systemic Functional Linguistics, No. 9. Department of English Studies: Nottingham University.

Trevarthen, C. (1974). Conversations with a two-month old. *New Scientist*, 62, 896: 230–235.

Trevarthen, C. & P. Hubley. (1978). Confidence, confiding and acts of meaning in the first year. In A. E. Lock (ed.).

Turner, G. J. (1973). Social class and children's language of control at age five and age seven. In B. Bernstein (ed.)

Ure, Jean. (1971). Lexical density and register differentiation. In G. Perren & J. L. M. Trim (eds) *Applications of Linguistics: Selected Papers of the 2nd International Congress of Applied Linguistics*. Cambridge: Cambridge University Press.

Ure, J. & G. Ellis. (1977). Register in descriptive linguistics and in linguistic sociology. In O. Uribe-Villas (ed.) *Issues in Sociolinguistics*. The Hague: Mouton.

Vachek, J. (ed.) (1964). *A Prague School Reader in Linguistics*. Bloomington: Indiana University Press.

van Dijk, T. A. (1976). Pragmatics and poetics. In *Pragmatics of Language and Literature*. Amsterdam: North-Holland.

van Dijk, T. A. (1977). Connectives in text grammar and text logic. In T. A. van Dijk, & J. S. Petofi (eds).

van Dijk, T. A. & J. S. Petofi (eds). (1977). *Grammars and Descriptions*. Berlin: de Gruyter.

Ventola, E. (1979). The structure of casual conversations in English. *Journal of Pragmatics*, 3 (3/4): 267–298.

Ventola, E. (1984). The dynamics of genre. *Nottingham Linguistic Circular*, 13, 103–123.

Ventola, E. (1987). *The Structure of Social Interaction: A Systemic Approach to the Semiotics of Service Encounters*. London: Pinter.

Vološinov, V. N. (1973). *Marxism and the Philosophy of Language*. Translated & introduced by L. Matejke & I. R. Titunk. Cambridge, MA: Harvard University Press.

Vygotsky, L. S. (1962). *Thought and Language*. (edited and translated by E. Hanfmann & G. Vakar). Cambridge, MA: MIT Press.

Vygotsky, L. S. (1978). *Mind in Society: The Development of Higher Psychological Processes*. Harvard: Harvard University Press.

Webster, J. J. (ed.) (2008). *Meaning in Context: Implementing Intelligent Applications of Language Studies*. London: Continuum.

Weinreich, U., W. Labov & M. I. Herzog. (1968). Empirical foundations for a theory of language change. In *Directions for Historical Linguistics: A Symposium*. Austin, TX: University of Texas Press.

Wells, G. (1981). *Learning through Interaction*. Cambridge: Cambridge University Press.

Wertsch, J. V. (ed.) (1985a). The concept of internalization in Vygotsky's account of the genesis of higher mental functions. *Culture, Communication, and Cognition: Vygotskian Perspectives.* Cambridge: Cambridge University Press.

Wertsch, J. V. (1985b). *Vygotsky and the Social Formation of Mind.* Cambridge, MA: Harvard University Press.

Whorf, B. L. (1956). *Language, Thought and Reality: Selected Writings of Benjamin Lee Whorf.* Cambridge, MA: MIT Press.

Williams, G. (1990). *Framing Literacy.* Paper presented at the second Australian Systemic Functional Workshop, Brisbane.

Williams, G. (1995). *Joint Book-Reading and Literacy Pedagogy: A Socio-Semantic Interpretation.* Doctoral dissertation. Sydney: Department of Linguistics, Macquarie University.

Williams, G. (1999). The pedagogic device and the production of pedagogic discourse: a case example in early literacy education. In F. Christie (ed.). London: Cassell.

Williams, G. (2001). Literacy pedagogy prior to schooling: relations between social positioning and semantic variation. In A. Morais, I. Neves, B. Davies & H. Daniels (eds) *Towards a Sociology of Pedagogy: The Contribution of Basil Bernstein to Research.* New York: Peter Lang.

Williams, G. (2005). Semantic variation. In J. Webster, C. Matthiessen and R. Hasan (eds), *Continuing Discourse on Language.* Vol. 1, 457–480. London: Equinox.

Williams, G. & A. Lukin (eds) (2004). *The Development of Language: Functional Perspectives on Species and Individuals.* London: Continuum.

Williams, R. E. (ed.) (1956). *A Century of PUNCH.* Melbourne: Heinemann.

Wittgenstein, L. (1953). *Philosophical Investigations* (edited and translated by G. E. M. Anscombe). Oxford: Basil Blackwell.

Index

CPSIA information can be obtained at www.ICGtesting.com
Printed in the USA
BVOW06*2239131016

465016BV00003B/5/P